A Charlton Standard Catalogue

Canadian Coins
Volume Two
Collector and Maple Leaf Issues

FIFTH EDITION

2015

W. K. Cross

The Charlton Press

TORONTO, ONTARIO, CANADA

Library and Archives Canada Cataloguing in Publication

Canadian coins (Charlton Press)
    Canadian coins : a Charlton standard catalogue. volume two: collector
    and maple leaf issues

Annual
Canadian Coins: a Charlton standard catalogue
ISSN 1928-8816
ISBN 978-0-88968-364-8

    1. Coins, Canadian--Catalogs.   2. Coins, Canadian--Prices--Periodicals.
and collecting. I. Title

CJ18610.S82 59- 2005-   737.4971'029   C2005-902187-X

**Printed in Canada
in the Province of Quebec**

EDITORIAL

Editor	W. K. Cross
Editorial Assistant	Jean Dale
Editorial Assistant	Mark Drake
Graphic Technician	Davina Rowan
Photography	Scott Cornwell

SPECIAL MENTION

We would like to thank Alex Reeves of the Royal Canadian Mint for his help providing assistance with the 2013-2014 coin images.

We would also like to thank all past contributors for submitting prices, answering requests or supplying information which assisted in building the many past editions of this catalogue.

CONTRIBUTORS TO THE FIFTH EDITION

We would like to thank the following for their contributions to the 5th edition of *Canadian Coins, Volume Two*: **Randy Ash**, Alberta; **Bill Birney**, British Columbia; **Sandy Campbell**, Nova Scotia; **James Chiu**, British Columbia; **Jamie Flamenbaum**, Ontario; **Michael Joffe**, Quebec; **Roger Kerr**, Ontario; **Ian Laing,** Manitoba; **Christie Paquet**, Senior Engraver, Royal Canadian Mint, Ottawa; **Roger Paulen**, Ontario; **Dennis Pike**, Ontario; **John Polley**, New York; **Todd Sandham**, Ontario; **Ryan Stratton**, British Columbia

The Charlton Press

Editorial Office
P.O. Box 69509
5845 Yonge Street
Toronto, Ontario M2M 4K3
Tel.: (416) 488-1418 Fax: (416) 488-4656
Tel.: (800) 442-6042 Fax.: (800) 442-1542
www.charltonpress.com email: chpress@charltonpress.com

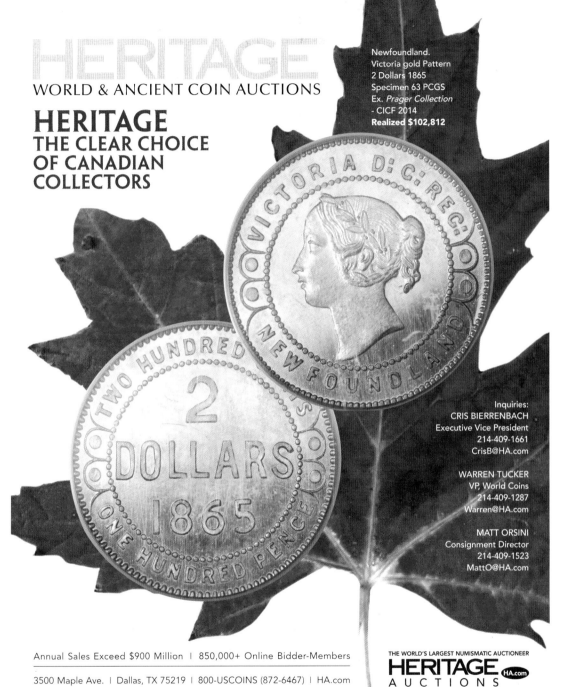

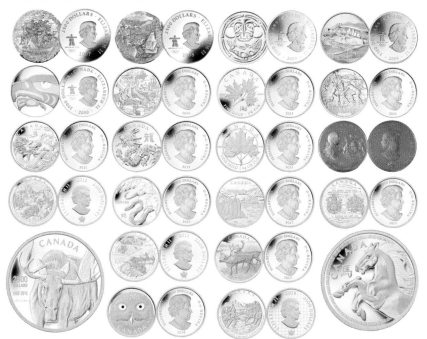

TABLE OF CONTENTS

GOLD COINS

INTRODUCTION

The first non-circulating legal tender coin (NCLT) struck in Canada was a 1908 Edward VII gold sovereign. This coin was struck at the Ottawa Branch Mint in specimen quality along with specimen examples of the other five denominations (one cent, five cents, ten cents, twenty-five cents and fifty cents) that made up the circulating coins of the day. The difference between the five subsidiary coins and the gold sovereign was that the latter, being struck only in specimen quality, had no circulating counterpart. While the 1908 gold sovereign was not a commemorative issue, the current thinking is that it was struck to establish a series. There are still a few questions regarding this NCLT coin that have yet to be answered. One is "How was it distributed?"

Modern Canadian NCLT coinage began with the issue of the 1967 centennial anniversary specimen gold set. This set contained seven coins, the most important being a $20 gold coin. This coin was similar to the 1908 sovereign in that there was no circulating counterpart. This coin set also set the stage for the next forty years. The Royal Canadian Mint sold 334,288 gold sets in 1967, creating a production bottleneck that was not cleared until well into 1968. The sales volume of 1967 collector coins was not lost on the organising officials of the Montreal 1976 Olympics games, for 1972 saw the beginning of the greatest issue of NCLT coins in Canadian history.

Canadian Coins, Volume Two: Collector Issues, 2011, second edition, records and lists over forty years of non-circulating legal tender coins issued by the Royal Canadian Mint in Canada.

COMMEMORATIVE COINS

Commemorative coins are issued to commemorate a particular personage, event, either historic or current, or a place. Such coins have a distinct design with reference to the occasion for which they are issued. Many coins of this category are collector items only, but a great number were issued for circulation to promote a major national event, such as the Vancouver 2010 Olympic Winter Games.

Vast numbers of thematic coins highlighting monuments, sites, historical personalities, endangered species, or just wild species common to a specific area, are now being inserted into this commemorative mix. The line between commemorative and thematic coins is blurred, and probably intentionally so.

Types of Commemoratives

We shall include thematic coins among the commemoratives. Commemorative/thematic coins can be divided into two categories:

1. Commemorative/thematic legal tender circulating issues.

These are the everyday coins used in commerce which bear a design commemorating an event. They are issued at face value, without a premium, within a certain time frame. Usually, the concept is centred on one denomination, but may encompass all denominations for an event of outstanding national significance such as the Centennial of Confederation. This category of commemorative is issued in "business strike" or circulation finish.

2. Non circulating legal tender commemorative/ thematic issues.

NCLT coins are deemed legal tender by a mint, but there is no expectation that they will be released into circulation. In theory, they may be used in commerce to purchase goods and services, but their recognition as a medium of exchange, and their acceptance by the modern day public, is questionable. In this category we will find single coins and sets, depending on how the issuing authorities developed their marketing strategies. The selling price has no relationship either to the face value or the intrinsic value. The selling price, intrinsic value and face value diminish in that order. The issuing authorities generally have no intention ever to redeem commemorative or thematic issues.

The earlier issues may command a substantial market price increase over the original issue price because of the increased intrinsic value of precious metals. Modern commemorative coins usually need time and additional increases in intrinsic value to return a profit.

FINISHES

Sales of modern collector coins are basically driven by the finish on the coins. The Royal Canadian Mint currently uses nine different finishes. See the next page for an outline of the different finishes used. A collector should be well versed in the different finishes as they will, at times, greatly affect the value of the issue.

FRATERNAL AFFILIATION

Over the years, coin clubs have sprung up in many Canadian Communities. In addition, both Canada and the United States have national organisations which hold annual conventions. Coin clubs constitute one of the most attractive features of present-day collecting. They offer beginning collectors the opportunity for good fellowship and the encouragement and knowledge of more experienced collectors. The larger groups maintain lending libraries and publish a journal or newsletter on a regular basis, Memberships and other information can be obtained from:

Royal Canadian Numismatic Association
5694 Highway # 7 East, Suite 432
Markham, Ontario
Canada L3P 1B4
Tel.: (647) 401-4014   Fax: (905) 472-9645
Email: info@rcna.ca

Ontario Numismatic Association
P.O. Box 40033, Waterloo Sq. P.O.
75 King Street South
Waterloo, Ontario
Canada N2J 4V1
www.ontario-numismatic.org/index.html

COLLECTOR COINS

Finishes 1953 to Date

Introduction: A coin finish simply means the surface quality imparted to a blank during the striking process. At the striking stage the main factors influencing the quality of the finish are: (1) the quality of the blanks, (2) the finish of the dies, (3) the speed and pressure of the press, and (4) the number of times the blank is struck.

Circulation Finish: *Brilliant Relief Against a Satin Background*. This is the most common finish found on all business strikes, from the one cent to the two dollar coins. These are production coins struck at the rate of 700 to 800 per minute. They are allowed to tumble into waiting hoppers, then put through counting and wrapping machines before being sent to the banks.

Uncirculated Finish: *Brilliant Relief Against a Satin Background.* This process is very similar to the circulation finish above with common dies being used, but with slower striking speeds and definitely more care in the loading and unloading of the press. There are far less handling marks than the circulation variety, but still marks may be found.

The Uncirculated finish is used by the Numismatic Department of the Mint on singles and sets offered to collectors, or sold into the giftware market.

Proof-Like Finish: *Frosted to Semi-Mirror Relief Against a Semi-Mirror Background*. These coins are produced on a slow moving press with reasonably high pressure. The planchets and dies are polished with each coin being removed from the press individually. Large coins may be struck more than once.

The following die states are found on proof-like coins:

(1) **Ultra Heavy Cameo:** Full frosting across the relief of the coin, both effigy and legend, when viewed from all directions under full lighting conditions.

(2) **Heavy Cameo:** The frosting is neither full nor evenly applied across the relief of the coin. In fact, some areas may appear bright when viewed under full lighting conditions.

(3) **Cameo:** Touches of frosting may appear on the relief of the coin. There will be bright areas when the coin is viewed under full lighting conditions.

(4) **No Cameo**. No frosting, all relief areas will appear bright. There is no difference in contrast between the bright field and a bright relief. The majority of coins are from this die state.

Nickel has a hardness higher than silver making the striking of coins more difficult. In 1968 with the change from silver to nickel coinage came the need for a new finish on numismatic items. That finish is:

Brilliant Uncirculated Finish: *Brilliant Design, Legends and Dates Against a Brilliant Background.* Coins are struck by a slow moving press using high pressure, and polished dies. Blanks are inserted, and coins removed by hand. This finish was used on all packaged singles and sets offered by the Mint from 1968 to 2004. In 2004 production of sets was divided between Uncirculated and Brilliant Uncirculated.

Specimen Finish: From 1968 to 2011 there have been six different modifications used by the Mint on specimen coinage.

1858-1881:	A Brilliant Relief Against a Brilliant Background.
1902-1938:	A Frosted Relief against a Frosted Background.
1937-1967:	A Brilliant Relief Against a Brilliant Background.
1968-1995:	A Brilliant Relief against a Brilliant Background
1996-2009:	A Brilliant Relief, Frosted Legends and Date against a Lined Background
2010-2014:	A Brilliant Relief, Frosted Legends and Date against a Laser Lined Background

Proof Finish: *Frosted Relief Against a Mirror Field.* This is the highest quality finish used by the Royal Canadian Mint on Canadian coinage. By definition, all coins with this finish are designated Ultra Heavy Cameo (UHC). They are identified in the pricing tables by PR.

Reverse Proof Finish: *Mirror Relief Against a Frosted Background.* This type of finish is at times called "satin matte" because of the background texture. All elements of the design that are in relief have a highly reflective finish.

Bullion Finish: *Brilliant Relief Against a Parallel Lined Background.* This finish was first used in 1979 on gold maple leafs for the bullion program. The finish is found on gold, platinum, palladium and silver maples. As this finish is the standard used on the maple leaf issues the grading designation is Mint State (MS).

Bullion-Specimen (Reverse Proof): *Brilliant Relief Against a Satin Background.* A finish not often used, it can be found on special edition bullion singles and sets.

Bullion-Proof: *Frosted Relief Against a Mirror Background.* This finish is the same as that found on all numismatic proof issues.

ONE CENT

ONE CENT, ROUND, ELIZABETH II PROOF, 1997-2012.

From 1997 to 2012 the composition of the one cent coin included in the Standard Proof Set fluctuated between bronze and copper. The one cent coin in the Premium Proof Set for 2012 set was struck on a fine silver planchet.

The last bronze cent issued for circulation was struck in 1996. It was a 12-sided coin and is listed in *Canadian Coins, Volume One*.

| Obverse 1997-2003 | Obverse 2004-2006 Without Mint Logo | Obverse 2007-2012 With Mint Logo | Reverse 1997-2012 |

Designers:
Obv.: 1997-2003: Dora de Pédery-Hunt
2004-2012: Susanna Blunt
Rev.: 1997-2012: G. E. Kruger-Gray

Engravers:
Obv.: 1997-2003: Dora de Pédery-Hunt
2004-2012: Susan Taylor
Rev.: 1997-2012: Thomas Shingles

	Bronze	**Copper**	**Silver**
Composition:	.980 Cu, .005 Tin, .015 Zn	1.00 Cu	99.99% Ag, Selectively gold plated
Silver content:			3.0 g, 0.096 tr oz
Weight:	2.5 g	2.5 g	3.05 g
Diameter:	19.1 mm	19.1 mm	19.05 mm
Thickness:	1.45 mm	1.45 mm	1.3 mm
Edge:	Plain	Plain	Plain
Die Axis:	↑↑	↑↑	
Finish:	Proof	Proof	Proof
Case of Issue:	Included in Proof Sets, see pages 380-381		

DATE	DESCRIPTION	COMP.	QUANTITY SOLD	ISSUE PRICE	FINISH	PR-67	PR-68
1997	Diademed Portrait / Maple Twig	Bronze	113,647	N.I.I.	Proof	25.	35.
1998		Bronze	93,632	N.I.I.	Proof	25.	35.
1999		Bronze	95,113	N.I.I.	Proof	25.	35.
2000		Bronze	90,921	N.I.I.	Proof	25.	35.
2001		Bronze	74,194	N.I.I.	Proof	25.	35.
2002		Bronze	65,315	N.I.I.	Proof	25.	35.
2003		Bronze	62,007	N.I.I.	Proof	25.	35.
2004	Uncrowned Portrait / Maple Twig	Copper	57,614	N.I.I.	Proof	25.	35.
2005		Copper	63,562	N.I.I.	Proof	25.	35.
2006		Bronze	53,822	N.I.I.	Proof	25.	35.
2007	Uncrowned Portrait, Mint Logo / Maple Twig	Copper	37,413	N.I.I.	Proof	25.	35.
2008		Copper	38,630	N.I.I.	Proof	25.	35.
2009		Bronze	27,549	N.I.I.	Proof	25.	35.
2010		Copper	32,342	N.I.I.	Proof	25.	35.
2011		Copper	32,910	N.I.I.	Proof	25.	35.
2012		Copper	27,254	N.I.I.	Proof	25.	35.
2012	Premium Proof Set, Selectively gold plated	Silver	19,789	N.I.I.	Proof	75.	85.

ONE CENT, 90TH ANNIVERSARY OF THE ROYAL CANADIAN MINT, 1908-1998.

To commemorate the opening of the Royal Canadian Mint in 1908 a five-coin set was issued featuring the original reverse designs that appeared on the 1908 coins, except the coins now feature the double date 1908-1998. The set was issued in two finishes, matte and mirror proof. The matte set cent does not carry the country of origin "Canada." This error was corrected on the mirror proof issues.

Matte Proof Issue Without "CANADA" on Obverse **Mirror Proof Issue Reverse** **Mirror Proof Issue With "CANADA" on Obverse**

Designers and Engravers:
Obv.: Dora de Pédery-Hunt
Rev.: Ago Aarand, G. W. DeSaulles
Composition: 92.5% Ag, 7.5% Cu, Copper plate
Silver content: 5.24 g, 0.169 tr oz
Weight: 5.67 g
Diameter: 25.4 mm
Thickness: 1.5 mm   **Die Axis:** ↑↑
Edge: Plain   **Finish:** See below
Case: See Special Issue Proof Sets, page 383

DATE	DESCRIPTION	QUANTITY SOLD	ISSUE PRICE	FINISH	PR-67	PR-68
1998 (1908-)	Matte proof, Without "CANADA"	18,376	N.I.I.	Matte Proof	35.	40.
1998 (1908-)	Mirror proof, With "CANADA"	24,893	N.I.I.	Mirror Proof	25.	30.

ONE CENT, 50TH ANNIVERSARY OF THE CORONATION OF QUEEN ELIZABETH II, 1953-2003.

This one cent coin which carries the double date 1953 2003 is from the Special Edition Proof Set issued in 2003 to commemorate the 50th anniversary of the Coronation of Queen Elizabeth II.

Designers and Engravers:
Obv.: Mary Gillick, Dora de Pédery-Hunt
Rev.: G. E. Kruger-Gray
Composition: Copper
Weight: 2.5 g

Diameter: 19.05 mm
Thickness: 1.25 mm
Edge: Plain
Die Axis: ↑↑
Finish: Proof
Case of Issue: See Special Issue Proof Sets, page 384

DATE	DESCRIPTION	QUANTITY SOLD	ISSUE PRICE	FINISH	PR-67	PR-68
2003 (1953-)	50th Anniv. Coronation Queen Elizabeth II	21,537	N.I.I.	Proof	25.	30.

ONE CENT, ROYAL CANADIAN MINT ANNUAL REPORT, SELECTIVELY GOLD PLATED, 2003.

This one cent coin is the first in a series of six coins, one of which was to be included each year with the Annual Mint Report, leading up to the Royal Canadian Mint's centennial in 2008. However, this series was discontinued with the issue of the 2006 Annual Mint Report. See the One Cent Derivatives listed on page 5.

Designers and Engravers:
Obv.: Dora de Pédery-Hunt, Ago Aarand
Rev.: G. E. Kruger-Gray
Composition: Copper plated zinc, Selectively gold plated
Weight: 2.25 g   **Edge:** Plain
Diameter: 19.05 mm   **Die Axis:** ↑↑
Thickness: 1.45 mm   **Finish:** Proof
Case of Issue: See Derivatives, page 5

DATE	DESCRIPTION	QUANTITY SOLD	ISSUE PRICE	FINISH	PR-67	PR-68
2003	Copper plated zinc, Selectively gold plated	7,746	N.I.I.	Proof	45.	50.

ONE CENT, 75TH ANNIVERSARY OF THE VOYAGEUR DOLLAR PROOF SET, 1935-2010.

This one cent coin is from the Special Limited Edition Proof Set issued in 2010 to commemorate Emanuel Hahn's classic voyageur design which first appeared on the 1935 silver dollar.

Designers and Engravers:
Obv.: Sir. E. B. MacKennal
Rev.: Fred Lewis design
Composition: Copper
Weight: 2.5 g
Case of Issue: See Special Issue Proof Sets, page 385

Diameter: 19.05 mm
Thickness: 1.45 mm
Edge: Plain
Die Axis: ↑↑
Finish: Proof

DATE	DESCRIPTION	QUANTITY SOLD	ISSUE PRICE	FINISH	PR-67	PR-68
2010 (1935-)	75th Anniv. Voyageur Silver Dollar Proof Set	4,996	N.I.I.	Proof	20.	30.

ONE CENT, 100TH ANNIVERSARY OF THE STRIKING OF CANADA'S 1911 SILVER DOLLAR, 1911-2011.

This one cent coin which carries the double date 1911-2011 is from the Special Edition Proof Set issued in 2011 to commemorate the 100th anniversary of the striking of Canada's 1911 silver dollar.

Designers and Engravers:
Obv.: Sir E. B. MacKennal
Rev.: Original design by L. C. Wyon,
Modified by W. H. J. Blakemore
Composition: Copper
Weight: 5.67 g
Diameter: 25.4 mm
Thickness: 1.6 mm   **Die Axis:** ↑↑
Edge: Plain   **Finish:** Proof
Case: See Special Issue Proof Sets, page 385

DATE	DESCRIPTION	QUANTITY SOLD	ISSUE PRICE	FINISH	PR-67	PR-68
2011 (1911-)	100th Anniv. Canada's 1911 Silver Dollar	5,952	N.I.I.	Proof	40.	50.

ONE CENT, FAREWELL TO THE PENNY, SELECTIVELY GOLD PLATED, 2012.

The last one cent coin was struck at the Royal Canadian Mint on May 4th, 2012. This half-ounce silver one cent coin was issued to mark the end of production of Canada's one-cent piece.

Designers and Engravers:
Obv.: Susanna Blunt, Susan Taylor
Rev.: G. E. Kruger-Gray, RCM Staff
Composition: 99.99% Ag, Selectively gold plated
Silver content: 15.87 g, 0.5 tr oz
Weight: 15.87 g
Diameter: 34.0 mm   **Edge:** Reeded
Thickness: 2.2 mm   **Die Axis:** ↑↑
Finish: Proof
Case: Maroon leatherette clam style case, black flocked insert, encapsulated coin, COA, custom box

DATE	DESCRIPTION	QUANTITY SOLD	ISSUE PRICE	FINISH	PR-67	PR-68
2012	Fine silver, (½ oz), Selectively gold plated	29,998	54.95	Proof	75.	85.

ONE CENT, FINE SILVER, 2012.

These coins are from the five-coin "Farewell to the Penny" special limited edition proof set issued in 2012. See also page 386.

Edward VII / Small Leaves Design

George V / Small Leaves Design

George V / Two Maple Leaves Design

| George W. DeSaulles | George W. DeSaulles | Sir E. B. MacKennal | W. H. J. Blakemore | Sir E. B. MacKennal | Fred Lewis |

Elizabeth II / Centennial Design

Elizabeth II / Maple Twig Design

| Arnold Machin | Alex Colville | Susanna Blunt | G. E. Kruger-Gray |

Designers:
  Obv.:   See obverse illustrations
  Rev.:   See reverse illustrations
Composition: 99.99% Ag
Silver content: 14.7 g, 0.473 (per set)
Weight: 2.94 g (per coin); 14.7 (set)
Diameter: 19.1
Thickness: 1.25 mm
Case of Issue: See Special Issue Proof Sets, page 386

Engravers:
  Obv.:   Susan Taylor
  Rev.:   Samantha Strath

Edge: Plain
Die Axis: ↑↑
Finish: Proof

DATE	DESCRIPTION	QUANTITY SOLD	ISSUE PRICE	FINISH	PR-67	PR-68
2012	Edward VII / Small Leaves Design	5,001	N.I.I.	Proof	75.	85.
2012	George V / Small Leaves Design with CANADA	5,001	N.I.I.	Proof	75.	85.
2012	George V / Two Maple Leaves Design	5,001	N.I.I.	Proof	75.	85.
2012	Elizabeth II / Centennial Design	5,001	N.I.I.	Proof	75.	85.
2012	Elizabeth II /Maple Twig Design	5,001	N.I.I.	Proof	75.	85.

ONE CENT, THE PENNY, FIVE OUNCE SILVER COIN, 2012.

This five-ounce silver one cent coin was issued to mark the end of production of Canada's one cent piece.

Designers:
  Obv.:   Susanna Blunt
  Rev.:   G. E. Kruger-Gray
Composition: 99.99% Ag
Silver content: 157.6 g, 5.06 tr oz
Weight: 157.6 g
Diameter: 65.0 mm
Thickness: N/A

Engravers:
  Obv.:   Susan Taylor
  Rev.:   RCM Staff

Edge: Reeded
Die Axis: ↑↑
Finish: Proof

Case of Issue: Maroon leatherette clam style case, black flocked insert, encapsulated coin, COA, custom beauty box

DATE	DESCRIPTION	QUANTITY SOLD	ISSUE PRICE	FINISH	PR-67	PR-68
2012	Fine silver, (5 oz), The Penny	1.499	495.95	Proof	500.	550.

Note: Coin illustrated smaller than actual size.

ONE CENT DERIVATIVES

DATE	DESCRIPTION	QUANTITY SOLD	ISSUE PRICE	ISSUER	FINISH	MARKET VALUE
2003	**2003 Annual Mint Report**, One cent coin, selectively gold plated	7,746	19.95	RCM	PR-67	60.
2003	**Coronation Coin and Stamp Set**, two one cent coins, 1953 and 2003; two fifty cent coins, 2002 Jubilee and 2003 Uncrowned Portrait; two mint and two cancelled stamps of Her Majesty's Jubilee and Coronation; Presentation Case	14,743	22.95	RCM, CP	MS-65	30.

THREE CENTS

THREE CENTS, 150TH ANNIVERSARY OF CANADA'S FIRST POSTAGE STAMP, 2001.

Sir Sandford Fleming's (1851) Three Pence Beaver was Canada's first postage stamp and a symbol of the transfer of postal authority from Britain to Canada.

Designers and Engravers:
Obv.:   Dora de Pédery-Hunt
Rev.:   Sir Sandford Fleming, Cosme Saffioti
Composition: 92.5% Ag, 7.5% Cu,
24-karat gold plate
Silver content: 4.95 g, 0.159 tr oz
Weight: 5.35 g   **Edge:** Plain
Diameter: 21.3 mm   **Die Axis:** ↑↑
Thickness: 1.9 mm   **Finish:** Proof
Case of Issue: See Derivatives below

DATE	DESCRIPTION	QUANTITY SOLD	ISSUE PRICE	FINISH	PR-67	PR-68
2001	Three Cent Beaver	59,573	N.I.I.	Proof	22.	25.

THREE CENT DERIVATIVES

DATE	DESCRIPTION	QUANTITY SOLD	ISSUE PRICE	ISSUER	FINISH	MARKET PRICE
2001	**Three Cents,** Medallion, Stamp set, Maroon leatherette case, COA	59,573	39.95	RCM, CP	PR-67	35.

SPECIAL NOTE ON FINISHES

It is very important to understand the different finishes the Royal Canadian Mint uses on their various issues. These finishes are altered from time-to-time as the Mint develops new products.

For example, the brilliant relief against a parallel lined background finish first used on bullion coins was carried forward in 1996 to be used on the coins contained in the specimen set.

In 2006 this finish was used on giftware coins such as the twenty-five cent coin issued to celebrate the 80th birthday of Queen Elizabeth II.

In 2010 a new specimen finish, brilliant relief against a laser-lined background, was used for the coins contained in the specimen set. There are now two different specimen finishes being utilised on Canadian coinage.

Circulation and Brilliant Uncirculated (proof-like) finishes are another very confusing mixture of finishes, see page xiv for a further explanation.

FIVE CENTS

FIVE CENTS, ELIZABETH II PROOF, 1996-2014.

Starting in 1996 the five-cent coin issued in the proof set, previously struck from cupronickel, was now struck on a sterling silver planchet. The use of sterling silver planchets was discontinued in 2011.

The year 2012 saw the introduction of the Premium Proof Set in which all coins were struck on fine silver planchets.

Standard Proof Sets were issued for 2012 and 2014. The five-cent coin in these sets was struck on a nickel planchet.

| Obverse
1996-2003 | Obverse
2004-2006
Without Mint Logo | Obverse
2007-2014
With Mint Logo | Reverse
1996-2014 |

Designers:
Obv.: 1996-2003: Dora de Pédery-Hunt
2004-2014: Susanna Blunt
Rev.: 1996-2014: G. E. Kruger-Gray

Engravers:
Obv.: 1996-2003: Dora de Pédery-Hunt
2004-2014: Susan Taylor
Rev.: 1996-2014: Thomas Shingles

	Sterling Silver	**Nickel**	**Fine Silver**
Composition:	92.5% Ag, 7.5% Cu	1.00 Ni	99.99% Ag
Silver content:	4.9 g, 0.158 tr oz	—	5.5 g, 0.177 tr oz
Weight:	5.35 g	3.95 g	5.5 g
Diameter:	21.3 mm	21.2 mm	21.0 mm
Thickness:	1.85 mm	1.85 mm	1.85 mm
Edge:	Plain	Plain	Plain
Die Axis:	↑↑	↑↑	↑↑
Finish:	Proof	Proof	Proof

Case of Issue: Included in Proof Sets, see pages 380-382

DATE	DESCRIPTION	COMP.	QUANTITY SOLD	ISSUE PRICE	FINISH	PR-67	PR-68
1996	Diademed Portrait / Beaver	Sterling	112,835	N.I.I.	Proof	15.	20.
1997		Sterling	113,647	N.I.I.	Proof	15.	20.
1998		Sterling	93,632	N.I.I.	Proof	15.	20.
1999		Sterling	95,113	N.I.I.	Proof	15.	25.
2000		Sterling	90,921	N.I.I.	Proof	18.	25.
2001		Sterling	74,194	N.I.I.	Proof	20.	25.
2002		Sterling	65,315	N.I.I.	Proof	20.	25.
2003		Sterling	62,007	N.I.I.	Proof	20.	25.
2004	Uncrowned Portrait / Beaver	Sterling	57,614	N.I.I.	Proof	20.	25.
2005		Sterling	63,562	N.I.I.	Proof	20.	25.
2006		Sterling	53,822	N.I.I.	Proof	20.	25.
2007	Uncrowned Portrait, Mint Logo / Beaver	Sterling	37,413	N.I.I.	Proof	20.	25.
2008		Sterling	38,630	N.I.I.	Proof	20.	25.
2009		Sterling	27,549	N.I.I.	Proof	20.	25.
2010		Sterling	32,342	N.I.I.	Proof	25.	30.
2011		Sterling	32,910	N.I.I.	Proof	25.	30.
2012		Nickel	27,254	N.I.I.	Proof	25.	30.
2012	Premium Proof Set	Fine Silver	19,789	N.I.I.	Proof	25.	30.
2013	Premium Proof Set	Fine Silver	20,182	N.I.I.	Proof	25.	30.
2014		Nickel	30,000	N.I.I.	Proof	25.	30.
2014	Premium Proof Set	Fine Silver	25,000	N.I.I.	Proof	25.	30.

Note: Quantity sold figures are identical to those listed for Proof Sets sold.

FIVE CENTS, 90TH ANNIVERSARY OF THE ROYAL CANADIAN MINT, 1908-1998.

To commemorate the opening of the Royal Canadian Mint in 1908 a five-coin set was issued featuring the original reverse designs that appeared on the 1908 coins, except the coins now feature the double date 1908-1998. The set was issued in two finishes, matte and mirror proof. The matte set cent does not carry the country of origin "Canada." This error was corrected on the mirror proof issues.

Designers and Engravers:
    Obv.: Dora de Pédery-Hunt
    Rev.: Ago Aarand, G. W. DeSaulles
Composition: 92.5% Ag, 7.5% Cu
Silver content: 1.08 g, 0.035 tr oz
Finish: Matte Proof, Mirror Proof
Case of Issue: See Special Issue Proof Sets, page 383

Weight: 1.167 g
Diameter: 15.5 mm
Thickness: 1.0 mm
Edge: Reeded
Die Axis: ↑↑

DATE	DESCRIPTION	QUANTITY SOLD	ISSUE PRICE	FINISH	PR-67	PR-68
1998 (1908-)	90th Anniv. Royal Canadian Mint, Matte Proof	18,376	N.I.I.	Proof	20.	25.
1998 (1908-)	90th Anniv. Royal Canadian Mint, Mirror Proof	24,893	N.I.I.	Proof	20.	25.

FIVE CENTS, LES VOLTIGEURS DE QUEBEC, 2000.

Les Voltigeurs regiment was formed in March 1862, and was headquartered in Quebec. In 1942 it provided an armoured regiment for the Canadian Forces in World War II.

Designers and Engravers:
    Obv.: Dora de Pédery-Hunt
    Rev.: Susan Taylor
Composition: 92.5% Ag, 7.5% Cu
Silver content: 4.9 g, 0.158 tr oz
Finish: Proof
Case of Issue: Black leatherette clam style case; green insert and sleeve; encapsulated coin

Weight: 5.3 g
Diameter: Round: 21.3 mm
Thickness: 1.85 mm
Edge: Reeded
Die Axis: ↑↑

DATE	DESCRIPTION	QUANTITY SOLD	ISSUE PRICE	FINISH	PR-67	PR-68
2000	Les Voltigeurs de Québec	34,024	16.95	Proof	20.	25.

FIVE CENTS, ROYAL MILITARY COLLEGE OF CANADA, 2001.

The Royal Military College was established by an act of Parliament on May 26th, 1874. The college is located in Kingston, Ontario.

Designers and Engravers:
    Obv.: Dora de Pédery-Hunt
    Rev.: G. T. Locklin, Susan Taylor
Composition: 92.5% Ag, 7.5% Cu
Silver content: 4.9 g, 0.158 tr oz
Edge: Plain
Case of Issue: Black leatherette clam style case; green insert, encapsulated coin, multicoloured sleeve

Weight: 5.3 g
Diameter: Round: 21.3 mm
Thickness: 1.85 mm
Finish: Proof
Die Axis: ↑↑

DATE	DESCRIPTION	QUANTITY SOLD	ISSUE PRICE	FINISH	PR-67	PR-68
2001	Royal Military College of Canada	25,834	16.95	Proof	20.	25.

FIVE CENTS, 85TH ANNIVERSARY, BATTLE FOR VIMY RIDGE, 2002.

Vimy Ridge, France was the location of one of the major battles of World War I. It was taken and held by Canadian troops from April 9th to 12th, 1917.

Designers and Engravers:
    Obv.: Dora de Pédery-Hunt
    Rev.: S. A. Allward, Susan Taylor
Composition: 92.5% Ag, 7.5% Cu
Silver content: 4.9 g, 0.158 tr oz
Finish: Proof
Case of Issue: Black leatherette clam style case; maroon insert, encapsulated coin, multicoloured sleeve

Weight: 5.3 g
Diameter: Round: 21.3 mm
Thickness: 1.85 mm
Edge: Plain
Die Axis: ↑↑

DATE	DESCRIPTION	QUANTITY SOLD	ISSUE PRICE	FINISH	PR-67	PR-68
2002	85th Anniv. Battle for Vimy Ridge	22,646	16.95	Proof	25.	30.

FIVE CENTS, 50TH ANNIVERSARY OF THE CORONATION OF QUEEN ELIZABETH II, 1953-2003.

Elizabeth II was crowned Queen on June 2nd, 1953, in Westminster Abbey, London, England.

Designers and Engravers:
Obv.: M. Gillick, D. de Pédery-Hunt
Rev.: G. E. Kruger-Gray, T. Shingles
Composition: 92.5% Ag, 7.5% Cu
Silver content: 4.9 g, 0.158 tr oz
Finish: Proof
Case of Issue: See Special Issue Proof Sets, page 384

Weight: 5.3 g
Diameter: 12-sided: 21.3 mm
Thickness: 1.85 mm
Edge: Plain
Die Axis: ↑↑

DATE	DESCRIPTION	QUANTITY SOLD	ISSUE PRICE	FINISH	PR-67	PR-68
2003 (1953-)	50th Anniv. Coronation Queen Elizabeth II	21,537	N.I.I.	Proof	25.	30.

FIVE CENTS, 60TH ANNIVERSARY, D-DAY LANDING, 1944-2004.

On June 6th, 1944, over 175,000 troops landed on the beaches of Normandy, along a fifty-mile front.

Designers and Engravers:
Obv.: Susanna Blunt, Susan Taylor
Rev.: Thomas Shingles, Christie Paquet
Composition: 92.5% Ag, 7.5% Cu
Silver content: 4.9 g, 0.158 tr oz
Finish: Proof
Case of Issue: See Derivatives, page 10

Weight: 5.3 g
Diameter: 12-sided: 21.3 mm
Thickness: 1.85 mm
Edge: Plain
Die Axis: ↑↑

DATE	DESCRIPTION	QUANTITY SOLD	ISSUE PRICE	FINISH	PR-67	PR-68
2004 (1944-)	60th Anniv. D-Day, 1944-2004	20,019	N.I.I.	Proof	50.	60.

FIVE CENTS, 60TH ANNIVERSARY OF VE-DAY, 1945-2005.

These coins were issued to celebrate the 60th anniversary of the victory over Nazi Germany in Europe. Peace was declared May 8th, 1945. The selectively gold plated Victory five cent coin was issued in conjunction with the 2005 Annual Mint Report. This is the third coin in what was to be an annual series ending in 2008. The series was discontinued with the issue of the 2006 annual report. See the Five Cent Derivatives, page 10.

Common Obverse   **1945-2005 Victory**   **1945-2005 Victory Gold plated**

Designers and Engravers:
Obv.: T. H. Paget, Thomas Shingles
Rev.: Thomas Shingles, Christie Paquet
Composition: 92.5% Ag, 7.5% Cu
Silver content: 4.9 g, 0.158 tr oz
Weight: 5.3 g
Diameter: 12-sided: 21.3 mm
Thickness: 1.85 mm   **Edge:** Plain
Die Axis: ↑↑   **Finish:** Proof
Case of Issue: See Derivatives, page 10

DATE	DESCRIPTION	QUANTITY SOLD	ISSUE PRICE	FINISH	PR-67	PR-68
2005 (1945-)	60th Anniv. VE-Day, 1945-2005	42,792	N.I.I.	Proof	25.	30.
2005 (1945-)	60th Anniv. VE-Day, Selectively gold plated	6,065	N.I.I.	Proof	70.	80.

NOTE TO COLLECTORS

When the initials N.I.I. appear in the pricing table it indicates the coin was part of a set issued by the Royal Canadian Mint, and not issued individually. Coin designs that are found only in sets offered by the Royal Canadian Mint are listed individually by denomination and date in Volume Two.

FIVE CENTS, GEORGE V, STERLING SILVER, PROOF, 1935-2010.

This five-cent coin is from the Special Limited Edition Proof Set issued in 2010 to commemorate Emanuel Hahn's classic voyageur design which first appeared on the 1935 silver dollar.

Designers and Engravers:
    Obv.: Sir. E. B. MacKennal, RCM Staff
    Rev.: W. H. J. Blakemore, RCM Staff
Composition: 92.5% Ag, 7.5% Cu
Silver content: 4.95 g, 0.195 tr oz
Finish: Proof
Case of Issue: See Special Issue Proof Sets, page 385

Weight: 5.35 g
Diameter: 21.2 mm
Thickness: 1.85 mm
Die Axis: ↑↑
Edge: Plain

DATE	DESCRIPTION	QUANTITY SOLD	ISSUE PRICE	FINISH	PR-67	PR-68
2010 (1935-)	George V, Sterling Silver	4,996	N.I.I.	Proof	25.	30.

FIVE CENTS, GEORGE V, STERLING SILVER, PROOF, 1911-2011.

This five-cent coin which carries the double date 1911-2011 is from the Special Edition Proof Set issued in 2011 to commemorate the 100th anniversary of the striking of Canada's 1911 silver dollar.

Designers and Engravers:
    Obv.: Sir. E. B. MacKennal, RCM Staff
    Rev.: Original design by L. C. Wyon,
        Modified by W. H. J. Blakemore
Composition: 92.5% Ag, 7.5% Cu
Silver content: 1.442 g, 0.046 tr oz
Case of Issue: See Special Issue Proof Sets, page 385

Weight: 1.559 g
Diameter: 15.5 mm
Thickness: 1.0 mm
Die Axis: ↑↑
Edge: Reeded
Finish: Proof

DATE	DESCRIPTION	QUANTITY SOLD	ISSUE PRICE	FINISH	PR-67	PR-68
2011 (1911-)	George V (1911), Sterling Silver	5,952	N.I.I.	Proof	25.	30.

FIVE CENT DERIVATIVES

DATE	DESCRIPTION	QUANTITY SOLD	ISSUE PRICE	ISSUER	FINISH	MARKET VALUE
2004 (1944-)	**D-Day Five Cents**, 1944-2004; Bronze medallion, CD, Folder	20,019	29.95	RCM	PR-67	65.
2005 (1945-)	**VE-Day Five Cents**, 1945-2005; Bronze medallion, Booklet	42,792	29.95	RCM	PR-67	40.
2005 (1945-)	**2005 Annual Mint Report**, Five cent coin, selectively gold plated		24.95	RCM	PR-67	
	English	5,213				50.
	French	852				60.

NOTE TO COLLECTORS

When the number appearing in the quantity sold column appears in italic, this signals the maximum number of coins to be issued by the Royal Canadian Mint. The actual number sold will not be known until that year's Mint Report is published.

TEN CENTS

TEN CENTS, ELIZABETH II PROOF, 1996-2014.

Starting in 1996 the ten-cent coin issued in the proof set, previously struck from cupronickel, was now struck on a sterling silver planchet. The use of sterling silver planchets was discontinued in 2011.

The year 2012 saw the introduction of the Premium Proof Set in which all coins were struck on fine silver planchets.

Standard Proof Sets were issued for 2012 and 2014. The ten-cent coin in these sets was struck on a nickel planchet.

Obverse	Obverse	Obverse	Reverse
1996-2003	2004-2006	2007-2014	1996-2014
	Without Mint	With Mint Logo	

Designers:
Obv.: 1996-2003: Dora de Pédery-Hunt
2004-2014: Susanna Blunt
Rev.: Emanuel Hahn

Engravers:
Obv.: 1996-2003: Dora de Pédery-Hunt
2004-2014: Susan Taylor
Rev.: Emanuel Hahn

	Sterling Silver	**Nickel**	**Fine Silver**
Composition:	92.5% Ag, 7.5% Cu	1.00 Ni	99.99% Ag
Silver content:	2.15 g, 0.069 tr oz	—	2.5 g, 0.08 tr oz
Weight:	2.32 g	1.75 g	2.5 g
Diameter:	18.03 mm	18.05 mm	18.0 mm
Thickness:	1.7 mm	1.2 mm	1.2 mm
Edge:	Reeded	Reeded	Reeded
Die Axis:	↑↑	↑↑	↑↑
Finish:	Proof	Proof	Proof

Case of Issue: Included in Proof Sets, see pages 380-382

DATE	DESCRIPTION	COMP.	QUANTITY SOLD	ISSUE PRICE	FINISH	PR-67	PR-68
1996	Diademed Portrait / Bluenose	Sterling	112,835	N.I.I.	Proof	15.	20.
1997		Sterling	113,647	N.I.I.	Proof	15.	20.
1998		Sterling	93,632	N.I.I.	Proof	15.	20.
1999		Sterling	95,113	N.I.I.	Proof	15.	20.
2000		Sterling	90,921	N.I.I.	Proof	15.	20.
2001		Sterling	74,194	N.I.I.	Proof	15.	20.
2002		Sterling	65,315	N.I.I.	Proof	15.	20.
2003		Sterling	62,007	N.I.I.	Proof	15.	20.
2004	Uncrowned Portrait / Bluenose	Sterling	57,614	N.I.I.	Proof	15.	20.
2005		Sterling	63,562	N.I.I.	Proof	15.	20.
2006		Sterling	53,822	N.I.I.	Proof	15.	20.
2007	Uncrowned Portrait, Mint Logo / Bluenose	Sterling	37,413	N.I.I.	Proof	15.	20.
2008		Sterling	38,630	N.I.I.	Proof	15.	20.
2009		Sterling	27,549	N.I.I.	Proof	15.	20.
2010		Sterling	32,342	N.I.I.	Proof	20.	25.
2011		Sterling	32,910	N.I.I.	Proof	20.	25.
2012		Nickel	27,254	N.I.I.	Proof	20.	25.
2012	Premium Proof Set	Fine Silver	19,789	N.I.I.	Proof	20.	25.
2013	Premium Proof Set	Fine Silver	20,182	N.I.I.	Proof	20.	25.
2014		Nickel	30,000	N.I.I.	Proof	20.	25.
2014	Premium Proof Set	Fine Silver	25,000	N.I.I.	Proof	20.	25.

Note: Quantity sold figures are identical to those listed for Proof Sets sold.

TEN CENTS, 500TH ANNIVERSARY OF CABOTO'S FIRST TRANSATLANTIC VOYAGE, 1997.

Giovanni Caboto (c.1450-c.1508) was an Italian navigator and explorer whose 1497 discovery of North America is commonly held to be the first voyage to the continent since those of the Vikings.

Designers and Engravers:
    Obv.: Dora de Pédery-Hunt
    Rev.: Donald H. Curley, Stan Witten
Composition: 92.5% Ag, 7.5% Cu
Silver content: 2.22 g, 0.071 tr oz
Finish: Proof
Case of Issue: Clear plastic case with black insert, white sleeve.
    See Derivatives, page 14

Weight: 2.4 g
Diameter: 18.0 mm
Thickness: 1.2 mm
Edge: Reeded
Die Axis: ↑↑

DATE	DESCRIPTION	QUANTITY SOLD	ISSUE PRICE	FINISH	PR-67	PR-68
1997	500th Anniv. of Caboto's Voyage	49,848	10.95	Proof	20.	30.

TEN CENTS, 90TH ANNIVERSARY OF THE ROYAL CANADIAN MINT, 1908-1998.

First opened on January 2nd, 1908, the Ottawa Branch of the Royal Mint became the Royal Canadian Mint in 1931.

Designers and Engravers:
    Obv.: Dora de Pédery-Hunt
    Rev.: G. W. DeSaulles, RCM Staff
Composition: 92.5% Ag, 7.5% Cu
Silver content: 2.15 g, 0.069 tr oz
Finish: Matte Proof, Mirror Proof
Case of Issue: See Special Issue Proof Sets, page 383

Weight: 2.32 g
Diameter: 18.03 mm
Thickness: 1.7 mm
Edge: Reeded
Die Axis: ↑↑

DATE	DESCRIPTION	QUANTITY SOLD	ISSUE PRICE	FINISH	PR-67	PR-68
1998 (1908-)	Sterling silver, Matte Proof	18,376	N.I.I.	Proof	20.	25.
1998 (1908-)	Sterling silver, Mirror Proof	24,893	N.I.I.	Proof	20.	25.

TEN CENTS, 100TH ANNIVERSARY OF THE BIRTH OF THE CREDIT UNIONS IN NORTH AMERICA, 2000.

The first credit union in North America, The Caisse Populaire de Lévis in Quebec, began operation on January 23rd, 1901, with a ten-cent deposit.

Designers and Engravers:
    Obv.: Dora de Pédery-Hunt
    Rev.: Jean-Guy Lebel, W. Woodruff
Composition: 92.5% Ag, 7.5% Cu
Silver content: 2.22 g, 0.071 tr oz
Finish: Proof
Case of Issue: Green printed card folder with encapsulated coin

Weight: 2.4 g
Diameter: 18.0 mm
Thickness: 1.2 mm
Edge: Reeded
Die Axis: ↑↑

DATE	DESCRIPTION	QUANTITY SOLD	ISSUE PRICE	FINISH	PR-67	PR-68
2000	100th Anniv. Birth of Credit Unions in N.A.	69,791	9.95	Proof	15.	20.

Note: 1. For the ten cent font varieties of 2007 (Curved and Straight 7) see page 349.
      2. For the ten cent Finish variety from the 2010 Special Edition Specimen Set, see page 376.

TEN CENTS, INTERNATIONAL YEAR OF THE VOLUNTEERS, 2001.

The United Nations declaration of International Year of the Volunteers gave cause for celebration for more than 7.5 million Canadian volunteers.

Designers and Engravers:
Obv.: Dora de Pédery-Hunt
Rev.: RCM Design, Stan Witten
Composition: 92.5% Ag, 7.5% Cu
Silver content: 2.22 g, 0.071 tr oz
Finish: Proof
Case of Issue: Multicoloured printed card folder with encapsulated coin

Weight: 2.4 g
Diameter: 18.0 mm
Thickness: 1.2 mm
Edge: Reeded
Die Axis: ↑↑

DATE	DESCRIPTION	QUANTITY SOLD	ISSUE PRICE	FINISH	PR-67	PR-68
2001	International Year of the Volunteers	40,634	14.95	Proof	15.	20.

TEN CENTS, 50TH ANNIVERSARY OF THE CORONATION OF QUEEN ELIZABETH II, 1953-2003.

Elizabeth II was crowned Queen June 2nd, 1953; her 50th anniversary was June 2nd, 2003.

Designers and Engravers:
Obv.: Dora de Pédery-Hunt
Rev.: Emanuel Hahn
Composition: 92.5% Ag, 7.5% Cu
Silver content: 2.15 g, 0.069 tr oz
Finish: Mirror Proof
Case of Issue: See Special Issue Proof Sets, page 384

Weight: 2.32 g
Diameter: 18.0 mm
Thickness: 1.7 mm
Edge: Reeded
Die Axis: ↑↑

DATE	DESCRIPTION	QUANTITY SOLD	ISSUE PRICE	FINISH	PR-67	PR-68
2003 (1953-)	50th Anniv. Coronation Queen Elizabeth II	21,537	N.I.I.	Proof	20.	25.

TEN CENTS, 100TH ANNIVERSARY OF THE CANADIAN OPEN GOLF CHAMPIONSHIP, 2004.

The Canadian Open Golf Tournament was first played on the Royal Montreal Golf Club course in 1904. The tournament was won by the English player, John H. Oke.

Designers and Engravers:
Obv.: Susanna Blunt, Susan Taylor
Rev.: Cosme Saffioti
Composition: Nickel plated steel
Weight: 1.75 g
Case of Issue: See Derivatives, page 14

Diameter: 18.03 mm
Thickness: 1.2 mm
Edge: Reeded
Die Axis: ↑↑
Finish: Circulation

DATE	DESCRIPTION	QUANTITY SOLD	ISSUE PRICE	FINISH	MS-65 NC	MS-66 NC	MS-67 NC
2004	100th Anniv. of Canadian Open Golf Championship	39,486	N.I.I.	Circulation	20.	30.	40.

TEN CENTS, GEORGE V, STERLING SILVER, PROOF, 1935-2010.

This ten-cent coin is from the Special Limited Edition Proof Set issued in 2010 to commemorate Emanuel Hahn's classic voyageur design which first appeared on the 1935 silver dollar.

Designers and Engravers:
Obv.: Sir E. B. MacKennal
Rev.: Original design by L. C. Wyon,
Modified by W. H. J. Blakemore
Composition: 92.5% Ag, 7.5% Cu
Silver content: 2.22 g, 0.071 tr oz
Case of Issue: See Special Issue Proof Sets, page 385

Weight: 2.4 g
Diameter: 18.1 mm
Thickness: 1.1 mm
Edge: Reeded
Die Axis: ↑↑
Finish: Proof

DATE	DESCRIPTION	QUANTITY SOLD	ISSUE PRICE	FINISH	PR-67	PR-68
2010 (1935-)	George V, Sterling Silver	4,996	N.I.I.	Proof	25.	30.

TEN CENTS, GEORGE V, STERLING SILVER, PROOF, 2011.

This ten-cent coin which carries the double date 1911-2011 is from the Special Edition Proof Set issued in 2011 to commemorate the 100th anniversary of the striking of Canada's 1911 silver dollar.

Designers and Engravers:
    Obv.: Sir E. B. MacKennal
    Rev.: Original design by L. C. Wyon,
          Modified by W. H. J. Blakemore
Composition: 92.5% Ag, 7.5% Cu
Silver content: 2.22 g, 0.071 tr oz
Case of Issue: See Special Issue Proof Sets, page 385

Weight: 2.4 g
Diameter: 18.1 mm
Thickness: 1.1 mm
Edge: Reeded
Die Axis: ↑↑
Finish: Proof

DATE	DESCRIPTION	QUANTITY SOLD	ISSUE PRICE	FINISH	PR-67	PR-68
2011 (1911-)	George V, Sterling silver	5,952	N.I.I.	Proof	50.	60.

TEN CENT DERIVATIVES

DATE	DESCRIPTION	QUANTITY SOLD	ISSUE PRICE	ISSUER	FINISH	MARKET VALUE
1997	**John Caboto Ten Cents,** Sterling;. Canada 45¢ stamp; Italy 1300 Lira stamp; Set in multicoloured card folder	15,000	19.95	RCM, CP	PR-67	25.
2000	**Bluenose Ten Cents**, Sterling; Two 46¢ stamps; Blue presentation case	15,000	19.95	RCM, CP	PR-67	20.
2001	**International Year of the Volunteers Ten Cents**, Thank You card and envelope	N/A	N/A	RCM	MS-65	15.
2004	**Ten Cent and Five Dollar Coins,** (100th Anniv. Canadian Open Golf Championship); Framed with two 48¢ circular stamps	18,750	49.95	RCM, CP	MS-65, PR-67	60.
2004	**Canadian Open Championship Ten Cents,** Framed with two circular commemorative stamps, and a divot repair tool	20,736	21.49	RCM, CP	MS-65	25.
2004	**Canadian Open Championship Ten Cents**, Canister also contains four commemorative stamps, a divot repair tool, three golf balls, five golf tees and a T-shirt	N/A	39.95	RCM, CP	MS-65	40.

NOTE TO COLLECTORS

When the initials N.I.I. appear in the pricing table it indicates the coin was part of a set issued by the Royal Canadian Mint, and not issued individually. Coin designs that are found only in sets offered by the Royal Canadian Mint are listed individually by denomination, and date in Volume Two.

TWENTY-FIVE CENTS

TWENTY-FIVE CENTS, ELIZABETH II PROOF, 1996-2014.

Starting in 1996 the twenty-five-cent coin issued in the proof set, previously struck from cupronickel, was now struck on a sterling silver planchet. The use of sterling silver planchets was discontinued in 2011.

The year 2012 saw the introduction of the Premium Proof Set in which all coins were struck on fine silver planchets. Standard Proof Sets were issued for 2012 and 2014. The twenty-five cent coin in these sets was struck on a nickel planchet.

Obverse
1996-2003

Obverse
2004-2006
Without Mint Logo

Obverse
2007-2014
With Mint Logo

Reverse
1996-2014

Designers:
Obv.: 1996-2003: Dora de Pédery-Hunt
2004-2014: Susanna Blunt
Rev.: Emanuel Hahn

Engravers:
Obv.: 1996-2003: Dora de Pédery-Hunt
2004-2014: Susan Taylor
Rev.: Emanuel Hahn

	Sterling Silver	**Nickel**	**Fine Silver**
Composition:	92.5% Ag, 7.5% Cu	1.00%	99.99% Ag
Silver content:	5.458 g, 0.175 tr oz	—	6.0 g, 0.193 tr oz
Weight:	5.9 g	4.4 g	6.0 g
Diameter:	23.9 mm	23.88 mm	23.9 mm
Thickness:	1.6 mm	1.62 mm	1.7 mm
Edge:	Reeded	Reeded	Reeded
Die Axis:	↑↑	↑↑	↑↑
Finish:	Proof	Proof	Proof

Case of Issue: Included in Proof Sets, see pages 380-382

DATE	DESCRIPTION	COMP.	QUANTITY SOLD	ISSUE PRICE	FINISH	PR-67	PR-68
1996	Diademed Portrait / Caribou	Sterling	112,835	N.I.I.	Proof	12.	18.
1997		Sterling	113,647	N.I.I.	Proof	12.	18.
1998		Sterling	93,632	N.I.I.	Proof	15.	20.
1999		Sterling	95,113	N.I.I.	Proof	15.	20.
2000		Sterling	90,921	N.I.I.	Proof	15.	20.
2001		Sterling	74,194	N.I.I.	Proof	15.	20.
2002		Sterling	65,315	N.I.I.	Proof	15.	20.
2003		Sterling	62,007	N.I.I.	Proof	15.	20.
2004	Uncrowned Portrait / Caribou	Sterling	57,614	N.I.I.	Proof	15.	20.
2005		Sterling	63,562	N.I.I.	Proof	15.	20.
2006		Sterling	53,822	N.I.I.	Proof	15.	20.
2007	Uncrowned Portrait, Mint Logo / Caribou	Sterling	37,413	N.I.I.	Proof	15.	20.
2008		Sterling	38,630	N.I.I.	Proof	15.	20.
2009		Sterling	27,549	N.I.I.	Proof	15.	20.
2010		Sterling	32,342	N.I.I.	Proof	20.	25.
2011		Sterling	32,910	N.I.I.	Proof	20.	25.
2012		Nickel	27,254	N.I.I.	Proof	20.	25.
2012	Premium Proof Set	Fine Silver	19,789	N.I.I.	Proof	20.	25.
2013	Premium Proof Set	Fine Silver	20,182	N.I.I.	Proof	20.	25.
2014		Nickel	30,000	N.I.I.	Proof	20.	25.
2014	Premium Proof Set	Fine Silver	25,000	N.I.I.	Proof	20.	25.

Note: Quantity sold figures are identical to those listed for Proof Sets sold.

125TH ANNIVERSARY OF CANADA, SILVER PROOF AND NICKEL UNCIRCULATED SETS, 1992.

Issued by the Royal Canadian Mint, in silver and nickel, the twelve different designs represent a familiar scene from each of the twelve provinces and territories of Canada. This is the first issue of sterling silver twenty-five cent coins since 1919.

Also, a collection of nickel brilliant uncirculated coins mounted in a coloured map of Canada, with each twenty-five-cent coin placed in the province or territory commemorated by its design was released October 7th, 1992. The Canada Day dollar which is the central point of a compass is listed on page 116.

1867-1992
Obverse

Designers and Engravers:
Obv.: Dora de Pédery-Hunt, Ago Aarand
Rev.: See reverse illustrations
Composition: Silver   Nickel
Silver content: 5.458 g   —
0.175 tr oz   —
Weight: 5.9 g   5.05 g
Diameter: 23.8 mm   23.9 mm
Thickness: 1.7 mm   1.6 mm
Edge: Reeded   Reeded
Die Axis: ↑↑   ↑↑
Finish: Proof   Circulation

Issue Price:
Individual proof silver: $9.95
13-coin proof silver set: $129.45
13 coin nickel set, "Map" holder: $17.25
Quantity Total individual silver coins: 651,812
Sold: Total silver sets: 84,397
Nickel sets, "Map" holder: 448,178
Case: (A) Royal blue flocked single coin case
(B) Royal blue flocked case, 13 coins.
Twelve 25¢ coins; one $1.00 coin

New Brunswick	Northwest Territories	Newfoundland	Manitoba	Yukon	Alberta
January 9, 1992	February 6, 1992	March 5, 1992	April 7, 1992	May 7, 1992	June 4, 1992
Ronald Lambert	Beth McEachen	Christopher	Muriel Hope	Libby Dulac	Mel Heath
Sheldon Beveridge		Newhook	Ago Aarand	William Woodruff	William Woodruff

DATE	DESCRIPTION	PROOF STERLING SILVER		UNCIRCULATED NICKEL		
		PR-67	PR-68	MS-65 NC	MS-66 NC	MS-67 NC
1992	New Brunswick	15.	25.	10.	15.	30.
1992	North West Territories	15.	25.	10.	15.	30.
1992	Newfoundland	15.	25.	10.	15.	30.
1992	Manitoba	15.	25.	10.	15.	30.
1992	Yukon	15.	25.	10.	15.	30.
1992	Alberta	15.	25.	10.	15.	30.

125TH ANNIVERSARY OF CANADA, SILVER PROOF AND NICKEL UNCIRCULATED SETS, 1992. (cont.)

| Prince Edward Island July 7, 1992 N. Roe, S. Beveridge | Ontario August 6, 1992 Greg Salmela Susan Taylor | Nova Scotia September 9, 1992 Bruce Wood Terry Smith | Quebec October 1, 1992 R. Bukauskas Stan Witten | Saskatchewan November 5, 1992 Brian Cobb Terry Smith | British Columbia November 9, 1992 Carla Egan Sheldon Beveridge |

DATE	DESCRIPTION	PROOF STERLING SILVER		UNCIRCULATED NICKEL		
		PR-67	PR-68	MS-65 NC	MS-66 NC	MS-67 NC
1992	Prince Edward Island	15.	25.	10.	15.	30.
1992	Ontario	15.	25.	10.	15.	30.
1992	Nova Scotia	15.	25.	10.	15.	30.
1992	Quebec	15.	25.	10.	15.	30.
1992	Saskatchewan	15.	25.	10.	15.	30.
1992	British Columbia	15.	25.	10.	15.	30.
1992	13 Coin Silver Proof Set	100.	—	*	*	*
1992	13 Coin Nickel Set with "Map" Holder	*	*	20.	—	—

TWENTY-FIVE CENTS, 125TH ANNIVERSARY MULE, 1867-1992.

A 1867-1992 obverse is muled with a Caribou reverse. The coin was reportedly issued in a Brilliant Uncirculated set of 1993.

Designers and Engravers:
Obv.: Dora de Pédery-Hunt
Rev.: Emanuel Hahn
Composition: Nickel
Weight: 5.05 g
Diameter: 23.9 mm
Thickness: 1.6 mm   **Edge:** Reeded
Die Axis: ↑↑   **Finish:** Circulation

DATE	DESCRIPTION	MS-65
1992 (1867-)	Mule	Only one known

TWENTY-FIVE CENTS, 90TH ANNIVERSARY OF THE ROYAL CANADIAN MINT, 1908-1998.

Issued to commemorate the opening of the Branch Mint in Ottawa, a five-coin set was struck featuring the same reverse designs as the original 1908 coins, except for the double date 1908-1998. The set was issued in two finishes, matte and mirror proof.

Designers and Engravers:
Obv.: Dora de Pédery-Hunt
Rev.: Ago Aarand, W. H. J. Blakemore
Composition: 92.5% Ag, 7.5% Cu
Silver content: 5.374 g, 0.173 tr oz
Weight: 5.81 g   **Edge:** Reeded
Diameter: 23.6 mm   **Die Axis:** ↑↑
Thickness: 1.7 mm   **Finish:** See below
Case: See Special Issue Proof Sets, page 383

DATE	DESCRIPTION	QUANTITY SOLD	ISSUE PRICE	FINISH	PR-67	PR-68
1998 (1908-)	90th Anniv. R.C. Mint, Matte Proof	18,376	N.I.I.	Matte Proof	25.	35.
1998 (1908-)	90th Anniv. R.C. Mint, Mirror Proof	24,893	N.I.I.	Mirror Proof	25.	35.

MILLENNIUM SILVER PROOF AND NICKEL UNCIRCULATED COMMEMORATIVE SETS, 1999.

The twelve 25-cent nickel coins (circulation finish) of 1999 were issued along with a 1999 millennium medallion, inserted in a replica of a 1785 map of Canada. Two different medallions were issued, one with a maple leaf obverse, the other carried the Nestlé logo; both have the common Royal Mint logo reverse. They were only available in the millennium set. The set of twelve coins was also issued in sterling silver with a proof finish.

1999
Obverse

Designers and Engravers:
Obv.:   Dora de Pédery-Hunt
        Ago Aarand
Rev.:   See reverse illustrations

Composition: Silver   Nickel
Silver content: 5.458 g   —
                    0.175 tr oz —
Weight: 5.9 g   5.05 g
Diameter: 23.88 mm   23.9 mm
Thickness: 1.7 mm   1.6 mm
Edge: Reeded   Reeded
Die Axis: ↑↑   ↑↑
Finish: Proof   Circulation

Issue Price:
Individual proof silver: $14.95
12 coin proof silver set: $149.45
12 coin unc. nickel / RCM set: $24.95
12 coin unc. nickel / Nestlé set: $24.95

Quantity Total individual silver coins: 111,414
Sold: Total silver sets: 60,245
             Total nickel sets: 1,499,973
Case: (A) Gold plastic single hole, oval case,
             royal blue flocked insert
         (B) Gold plastic 12-hole, oval case,
             royal blue flocked insert

January	February	March	April	May	June
P. Ka-Kin Poon	L. Springer	M. Lavoie	Ken Ojnak Ashevac	S. Minenok	G. Ho
Cosme Saffioti	José Osio	Stan Witten	Sheldon Beveridge	William Woodruff	William Woodruff

July	August	September	October	November	December
M. H. Sarkany	A. Botelho	C. Bertrand	J. E. Read	B. R. Bacon	J. L. P. Provencher
Stan Witten	Cosme Saffioti	Stanley Witten	Sheldon Beveridge	Stan Witten	Stan Witten

DATE	DESCRIPTION	PROOF STERLING SILVER		UNCIRCULATED NICKEL		
		PR-67	PR-68	MS-65 NC	MS-66 NC	MS-67 NC
1999	January, A Country Unfolds	18.	25.	10.	15.	30.
1999	February, Etched in Stone	18.	25.	10.	15.	30.
1999	March, The Log Drive	18.	25.	10.	15.	30.
1999	April, Our Northern Heritage	18.	25.	10.	15.	30.
1999	May, The Voyageurs	18.	25.	10.	15.	30.
1999	June, From Coast to Coast	18.	25.	10.	15.	30.
1999	July, A Nation of People	18.	25.	10.	15.	30.
1999	August, The Pioneer Spirit	18.	25.	10.	15.	30.
1999	September, Canada Through a Child's Eye	18.	25.	10.	15.	30.
1999	October, A Tribute to the First Nation	18.	25.	10.	15.	30.
1999	November, The Airplane Opens the North	18.	25.	10.	15.	30.
1999	December, This is Canada	18.	25.	10.	15.	30.
1999	12 Coin Silver Proof Set plus RCM Medallion	100.	—	*	*	*
1999	12 Coin Nickel Set plus RCM Medallion	*	*	15.	—	—
1999	12 Coin Nickel Set plus "Nestlé" Medallion	*	*	15.	—	—

Note: Prices for individual twenty-cent coins are for examples that are certified. The set prices are for raw coins.

TWENTY-FIVE CENT MILLENNIUM MULES OF 1999.

It is in the 1999 millennium nickel set that the "No Denomination" coins of September and November are found. During the Fall of 1999, a Queen Elizabeth II obverse die became paired with the reverse dies of September and November millennium twenty-five cents coins creating two mules. The interesting result of these pairings is that for the first time Canada has a non denominated legal tender coin.

**Queen Elizabeth II
No denomination
Obverse**

**1999 September
Reverse Mule**

**1999 November
Reverse Mule**

DATE	DESCRIPTION	MS-63 NC	MS-64 NC	MS-65 NC	MS-66 NC
1999	September, no denomination, Mule	100.	135.	165.	225.
1999	November, no denomination, Mule	75.	125.	150.	200.

TWENTY-FIVE CENT SOUVENIR MEDALLIONS OF 1999.

Along with the nickel souvenir sets two different medallions were issued: A Royal Canadian Mint medallion and a Nestlé Canada Inc. medallion.

**1999 RCM
Medallion Obv.**

**1999 RCM
Medallion Rev.**

**1999 Nestlé
Medallion Obv.**

**1999 RCM
Medallion Rev.**

DATE	DESCRIPTION	MINTAGE	ISSUE PRICE	FINISH	MS-65 NC	MS-66 NC	MS-67 NC
1999	RCM Medallion	N/A	N.I.I.	Circulation	10.	15.	30.
1999	Nestlé Medallion	N/A	N.I.I.	Circulation	10.	15.	30.

TWENTY-FIVE CENT STERLING SILVER SOUVENIR MEDALLION OF 1999-2000.

The 24-coin sterling silver set which was issued for the Chinese market in Hong Kong contains a 1999-2000 sterling silver medallion.

DATE	DESCRIPTION	MINTAGE	ISSUE PRICE	FINISH	PR-67	PR-68
1999-2000	Stirling Silver Medallion	N/A	N.I.I.	Proof	75.	125.

MILLENNIUM SILVER PROOF AND NICKEL UNCIRCULATED COMMEMORATIVE SETS, 2000.

The 2000 Souvenir set was issued in sterling silver with a proof finish and in nickel with a circulation finish. The nickel set features 12 coins plus the 2000 commemorative medallion which was only issued with the souvenir set. The coins are displayed on an easel featuring an aerial photograph of Canada.

2000 Obverse

Designers and Engravers:
Obv.: Dora de Pédery-Hunt
Ago Aarand
Rev.: See reverse illustrations

Composition:	Silver	Nickel
Silver content:	5.458 g	—
	0.175 tr oz	—
Weight:	5.9 g	5.05 g
Diameter:	23.9 mm	23.9 mm
Thickness:	1.7 mm	1.6 mm
Edge:	Reeded	Reeded
Die Axis:	↑↑	↑↑
Finish:	Proof	Circulation

Case of Issue: **Silver:**
(A) Black plastic single-hole, oval case, royal blue flocked insert
(B) Black plastic 12-hole, oval case, royal blue flocked insert
(C) Red plush presentation case, light brown insert, 24 coins, a 1999 and 2000 medallion. Issued for the Chinese market.

Nickel: (A) 13 hole, Map of Canada. (B) 13 hole, plastic case

Issue Price:
Individual proof silver: $14.95
12 coin proof silver set: $149.45
12 coin unc. nickel/RCM set: $24.95
12 coin unc. nickel set/plastic case: $49.55

Quantity Total silver sets: 37,940
Sold: Total nickel sets: 876,041

January	**February**	**March**	**April**	**May**	**June**
Donald F. Warkentin	John Jaciw	Daryl Dorosz	Annie Wassef	Randy Trantau	Haver Demirer
José Osio	William Woodruff	Stan Witten	Stan Witten	José Osio	José Osio

July	**August**	**September**	**October**	**November**	**December**
Laura Paxton	W. S. Baker	Cezar Serbanescu	Jerik (Kong Tat) Hui	Kathy Vinish	Michelle Thibodeau
Stan Witten	Susan Taylor	Cosme Saffioti	Susan Taylor	William Woodruff	José Osio

DATE	DESCRIPTION	PROOF STERLING SILVER		UNCIRCULATED NICKEL		
		PR-67	PR-68	MS-65 NC	MS-66 NC	MS-67 NC
2000	January, Pride	18.	25.	10.	15.	30.
2000	February, Ingenuity	18.	25.	10.	15.	30.
2000	March, Achievement	18.	25.	10.	15.	30.
2000	April, Health	18.	25.	10.	15.	30.
2000	May, Natural Legacy	18.	25.	10.	15.	30.
2000	June, Harmony	18.	25.	10.	15.	30.
2000	July, Celebration	18.	25.	10.	15.	30.
2000	August, Family	18.	25.	10.	15.	30.
2000	September, Wisdom	18.	25.	10.	15.	30.
2000	October, Creativity	18.	25.	10.	15.	30.
2000	November, Freedom	18.	25.	10.	15.	30.
2000	December, Community	18.	25.	10.	15.	30.
2000	12 Coin Silver Proof Set	100.	—	✳	✳	✳
2000	12 Coin Nickel Set, RCM Medallion	✳	✳	20.	—	—
2000	12 Coin Nickel Set, Nestlé Medallion	✳	✳	20.	—	—

TWENTY-FIVE CENT SOUVENIR MEDALLIONS OF 2000.

Again in 2000 the nickel souvenir sets contained souvenir medallions. Two types were issued: The Royal Canadian Mint and Nestlé Canada Inc.

2000	2000
Royal Canadian Mint Medallion	**Nestle Medallion**

TWENTY-FIVE CENT MEDALLION MULE OF 2000.

In 2000 two dies were mismatched creating a mule. The obverse die of the February twenty-five cents is paired with the obverse die of the 2000 medallion. The mule is found in the February position of the 13-hole, Map of Canada Brilliant Uncirculated Set of 2000.

   Mule

February Reverse	**February Obverse**	**Medallion Obverse**	**Medallion Reverse**

DATE	DESCRIPTION	QUANTITY SOLD	ISSUE PRICE	FINISH	MS-63 NC	MS-64 NC	MS-65 NC	MS-66 NC	MS-67 NC
2000	RCM Medallion	N.I.I.	—	Circulation	—	—	5.	10.	20.
2000	Nestlé Medallion	N.I.I.	—	Circulation	—	—	5.	10.	20.
2000	Coin / Medallion Mule	N.I.I.	—	Circulation	400.	700.	1,000.	2,000.	—

TWENTY-FIVE CENTS, CANADA'S FIRST COLOURISED COIN, 2000.

Issued to celebrate the year 2000, this was the first colourised coin issued by the Royal Canadian Mint.

Designers and Engravers:
Obv.: Dora de Pédery-Hunt
Rev.: Donald F. Warkentin, José Osio
Composition: Nickel
Weight: 5.05 g
Diameter: 23.9 mm   **Edge:** Reeded
Thickness: 1.6 mm   **Die Axis:** ↑↑
Finish: Circulation, Colourised
Case of Issue: Blister packed on information card.

DATE	DESCRIPTION	QUANTITY SOLD	ISSUE PRICE	FINISH	MS-65 NC	MS-66 NC	MS-67 NC
2000	January, Pride, Colourised	49,719	8.95	Circulation	15.	20.	25.

TWENTY-FIVE CENTS, CANADA DAY SERIES, 2000-2008.

The following series of twenty-five cent coins was issued to celebrate the Canada Day celebrations that took place during the last week of June, leading up to July 1st.

In 2004, four thousand six hundred and fifteen "Moose" coins were given to new Canadians during Canada Week Celebrations June 25th to July 1st. Of the initial offering of 27,000, only 16,028 were sold in a "walking bundle" (see page 55).

Years:	2000	2001 to 2008
Composition:	1.00 nickel, Painted	Nickel plated steel, Painted
Weight:	5.05 g	4.4 g
Diameter:	23.9 mm	23.9 mm
Thickness:	1.6 mm	1.6 mm
Edge:	Reeded	Reeded
Die Axis:	↑↑	↑↑
Finish:	Circulation	2001 to 2008: Circulation
		2004: Circulation

Cases of Issue: 2000: Blister packed on information card.
2001: Encapsulated coin fastened to an information card
2002 to 2008: Folder
2004: See Derivatives, page 55

2000

Designers and Engravers:
  Obv.: Dora de Pédery-Hunt
  Rev.: Laura Paxton, Stan Witten

2001

Designers and Engravers:
  Obv.: Dora de Pédery-Hunt
  Rev.: Silke Ware, William Woodruff

2002

Designers and Engravers:
  Obv.: Dora de Pédery-Hunt, Ago Aarand
  Rev.: Judith Chartier, Stan Witten

2003

Designers and Engravers:
  Obv.: Dora de Pédery-Hunt, Ago Aarand
  Rev.: Jade Pearen, Stan Witten

2004

Designers and Engravers:
  Obv.: Susanna Blunt, Susan Taylor
  Rev.: Cosme Saffiotti, Stan Witten

2004

Designers and Engravers:
  Obv.: Susanna Blunt, Susan Taylor
  Rev.: Nick Wooster, William Woodruff

TWENTY-FIVE CENTS, CANADA DAY SERIES, 2000-2008 (cont.).

2005

Designers and Engravers:
  Obv.: Susanna Blunt, Susan Taylor
  Rev.: Stan Witten, Stan Witten

2006

Designers and Engravers:
  Obv.: Susanna Blunt, Susan Taylor
  Rev.: Stan Witten, Stan Witten

2007

Designers and Engravers:
  Obv.: Susanna Blunt, Susan Taylor
  Rev.: José Osio

2008

Designers and Engravers:
  Obv.: Susanna Blunt, Susan Taylor
  Rev.: Stan Witten, Stan Witten

DATE / COMP. MARK	DESCRIPTION	QUANTITY SOLD	ISSUE PRICE	FINISH	MS-65 NC
2000	Canada Day, Colourised	26,106	8.95	Circulation	65.
2001P	Canada Day, Colourised	96,352	9.95	Circulation	15.
2002P (1952-)	Canada Day, Colourised	49,901	9.95	Circulation	15.
2003P	Canada Day, Colourised	63,511	9.95	Circulation	20.
2004P	Canada Day, Colourised	44,752	9.95	Circulation	15.
2004P	Canada Day, Citizenship	16,028	N.I.I.	Circulation	30.
2005P	Canada Day, Colourised	58,370	9.95	Circulation	15.
2006P	Canada Day, Colourised	30,328	9.95	Circulation	20.
2007	Canada Day, Colourised	27,743	9.95	Circulation	20.
2008	Canada Day, Colourised	11,538	9.95	Circulation	20.

TWENTY-FIVE CENTS, CANADA DAY, 2009, (GIFTWARE).
   In 2009 the Royal Canadian Mint discontinued the standard Canada Day colourised twenty-five cent piece, changing it to a crown size coin, with no relation to the standard twenty-five-cent denomination.

Designers and Engravers:
    Obv.: Susanna Blunt, Susan Taylor
    Rev.: RCM Staff
Composition: Nickel plated steel, Painted
Weight: 12.59 g
Diameter: 35.0 mm
Thickness: 2.0 mm
Edge: Plain
Die Axis: ↑↑
Finish: Specimen
Case of Issue: Folder

DATE	DESCRIPTION	QUANTITY SOLD	ISSUE PRICE	FINISH	MS-65 NC
2009	Canada Day, Churchill	11,091	14.95	Specimen	20.

TWENTY-FIVE CENTS, 50TH ANNIVERSARY OF THE CORONATION OF QUEEN ELIZABETH II, 1953-2003.

This twenty-five-cent coin is from the Special Edition Proof Set issued in 2003 to commemorate the 50th anniversary of the Coronation of Queen Elizabeth II.

Designers and Engravers:
Obv.: Mary Gillick, Thomas Shingles
Rev.: Emanuel Hahn, Thomas Shingles
Composition: 92.5% Ag, 7.5% Cu
Silver content: 5.458 g, 0.175 tr oz
Weight: 5.9 g   **Edge:** Reeded
Diameter: 23.9 mm   **Die Axis:** ↑↑
Thickness: 1.6 mm   **Finish:** Proof
Case of Issue: See Special Issue Proof Sets, page 384

DATE	DESCRIPTION	QUANTITY SOLD	ISSUE PRICE	FINISH	PR-67	PR-68
2003 (1953-)	50th Anniv. Coronation Queen Elizabeth II	21,537	N.I.I.	Proof	25.	35.

TWENTY-FIVE CENTS, CHRISTMAS DAY SERIES, COLOURISED, 2004-2010.

The twenty-five cents coloured Christmas Day coins are issued as part of the Holiday Gift Set series, see page 363. The quantity sold figures shown are from the number of Holiday Sets sold for that year. The last colourised twenty-five-cent coin in the Christmas Series was issued in 2010. The Holiday Gift Sets continued in 2011, however, the twenty-five-cent coin was no longer coloured, see pages 30-31.

| Obverse With Mint Mark "P" 2004-2006 | Obverse With RCM Logo 2007-2009 | Obverse Without RCM Logo 2010 | 2004 Santa Claus José Osio | 2005 Christmas Stocking José Osio |

| 2006 Santa in Sleigh and Reindeer M. Hallam, J. Osio | 2007 Christmas Tree RCM Staff | 2008 Santa RCM Staff | 2009 Santa Claus and Maple Leaves RCM Staff | 2010 Santa Claus and Christmas Tree RCM Staff |

Designers and Engravers:
Obv.: Susanna Blunt, Susan Taylor
Rev.: See reverse illustrations
Composition: Nickel plated steel, Decal
Weight: 4.4 g
Finish: Circulation

Diameter: 23.9 mm
Edge: Reeded
Thickness: 1.6 mm
Die Axis: ↑↑
Case of Issue: See Holiday Gift Sets page 363

DATE / COMP. MARK	DESCRIPTION	SOURCE	QUANTITY SOLD	ISSUE PRICE	FINISH	MS-65 NC
2004P	Santa Claus		62,777	N.I.I.	Circulation	35.
2005P	Christmas Stocking	Available	72,831	N.I.I.	Circulation	20.
2006P	Santa in Sleigh and Reindeer	only from	99,258	N.I.I.	Circulation	15.
2007	Christmas Tree	Holiday	66,267	N.I.I.	Circulation	15.
2008	Santa	Gift Sets	42,344	N.I.I.	Circulation	20.
2009	Santa Claus and Maple Leaves		32,967	N.I.I.	Circulation	15.
2010	Santa Claus and Christmas Tree		10,870	N.I.I.	Circulation	15.

TWENTY-FIVE CENTS, SILVER POPPY, ROYAL CANADIAN MINT ANNUAL REPORT, SELECTIVELY GOLD PLATED, 2004.

This coin is the second in the Royal Canadian Mint Annual Report series. This series was cancelled in 2007.

Designers and Engravers:
Obv.: Susanna Blunt, Susan Taylor
Rev.: Cosme Saffioti, Stan Witten
Composition: 92.5% Ag, 7.5% Cu,
Selectively gold plated
Silver content: 5.458 g, 0.175 tr oz
Weight: 5.9 g
Diameter: 23.9 mm   **Edge:** Reeded
Thickness: 1.7 mm   **Die Axis:** ↑↑
Finish: Proof
Case of Issue: See Derivatives, page 55

DATE	DESCRIPTION	QUANTITY SOLD	ISSUE PRICE	FINISH	PR-67	PR-68
2004	Poppy, selectively gold plated	12,677	N.I.I.	Proof	25.	35.

TWENTY-FIVE CENTS, REMEMBRANCE DAY POPPY, COLOURISED, 2005 and 2008, (GIFTWARE).

These twenty-five-cent coins were issued to commemorate Remembrance Day 2005 and 2008. There are encased in plastic bookmarks.

Designers and Engravers:
Obv.: Susanna Blunt, Susan Taylor
Rev.: Cosme Saffioti, Stan Witten
Composition: Nickel plated steel, Colourised
Weight: 4.4 g
Diameter: 23.9 mm   **Edge:** Reeded
Thickness: 1.6 mm   **Die Axis:** ↑↑
Finish: Circulation
Case of Issue: See Derivatives, page 55

DATE / COMP. MARK	DESCRIPTION	SOURCE	QUANTITY SOLD	ISSUE PRICE	FINISH	MS-65 NC
2005P	Remembrance Day Poppy, Colourised	Bookmark	29,975	N.I.I.	Circulation	20.
2008	Remembrance Day Poppy, Colourised	Bookmark	489	12.95	Circulation	10.

Note: A colourised circulation Poppy coin was issued in 2004 to commemorate Remembrance Day 2004. See *Volume One, 66th Edition*, page 165.

TWENTY-FIVE CENTS, 60TH ANNIVERSARY OF THE LIBERATION OF THE NETHERLANDS, 2005.

The Canadian Armed Forces played a leading role in the liberation of the Netherlands that was completed May 5th, 1945. This coin was issued in an eight-coin, Brilliant Uncirculated set, by the Netherlands Mint.

Designers and Engravers:
Obv.: Susanna Blunt, Susan Taylor
Rev.: Peter Mossman, José Osio
Composition: 92.5% Ag, 7.5% Cu
Silver content: 5.458 g, 0.175 tr oz
Weight: 5.9 g
Diameter: 23.9 mm   **Edge:** Reeded
Thickness: 1.7 mm   **Die Axis:** ↑↑
Finish: Specimen
Case of Issue: See Derivatives, page 55

DATE	DESCRIPTION	QUANTITY SOLD	ISSUE PRICE	FINISH	SP-66	SP-67	SP-68
2005	60th Year of Liberation	3,500	N.I.I.	Specimen	75.	100.	200.

TWENTY-FIVE CENTS, QUEBEC WINTER CARNIVAL, 2006 (GIFTWARE).

The Quebec Winter Carnival, the largest in North America, is held each year in Quebec City, Quebec.

Designers and Engravers:
  Obv.: Susanna Blunt, Susan Taylor
  Rev.: RCM Staff, Cecily Mok
Composition: Nickel plated steel, Painted
Weight: 4.4 g
Diameter: 23.9 mm   **Edge:** Reeded
Thickness: 1.6 mm   **Die Axis:** ↑↑
Finish: Circulation
Case: See Miscellaneous Gift Sets, page 370

DATE / COMP. MARK	DESCRIPTION	SOURCE	QUANTITY SOLD	ISSUE PRICE	FINISH	MS-65 NC
2006P	Quebec Winter Carnival, Painted	Promo Gift Set	8,200	N.I.I.	Circulation	20.

TWENTY-FIVE CENTS, BREAST CANCER AWARENESS, 2006 (GIFTWARE).

This coin was issued to promote awareness for breast cancer. It is identical to the circulation issue, except the three outer ribbons and the central ribbon are painted pink. This variety was issued encased in a plastic bookmark. Removal of the coin from the encased plastic is very difficult and may result in the Awareness ribbons being damaged.

Designers and Engravers:
  Obv.: Susanna Blunt, Susan Taylor
  Rev.: C. Saffioti, S. Witten, K. Wachelko
Composition: Nickel plated steel, Painted
Weight: 4.4 g
Diameter: 23.9 mm   **Edge:** Reeded
Thickness: 1.6 mm   **Die Axis:** ↑↑
Finish: Circulation
Case of Issue: See Derivatives, page 55

DATE / COMP. MARK	DESCRIPTION	SOURCE	QUANTITY SOLD	ISSUE PRICE	FINISH	MS-65 NC
2006P	Breast Cancer Awareness, Painted	Bookmark	40,911	N.I.I.	Circulation	20.

TWENTY-FIVE CENTS, QUEEN ELIZABETH II COMMEMORATIVES, 2006-2007 (GIFTWARE).

2006 Obverse	2006 80th Birthday Queen Elizabeth II Designer: Cosme Saffioti Engraver: Cecily Mok	2007 Obverse	207 60th Wedding Anniv. Elizabeth II / Prince Philip Designer: R. R. Carmichael Engraver: Cecily Mok

Designers:
 Obv.: Susanna Blunt
 Rev.: See reverse illustrations
Composition: Nickel plated steel, Decal
Weight: 12.61 g
Diameter: 35.0 mm
Finish: Specimen

Engravers:
 Obv.: Susan Taylor
 Rev.: See reverse illustrations
Thickness: 3.4 mm
Edge: Plain
Die Axis: ↑↑
Case of Issue: Blistered packed on information card

DATE	DESCRIPTION	QUANTITY SOLD	ISSUE PRICE	FINISH	SP-66	SP-67
2006 (1926-)	80th Birthday of Queen Elizabeth II	24,977	19.95	Specimen	20.	25.
2007 (1947-)	60th Wedding Anniversary Elizabeth II and Prince Philip	15,235	21.95	Specimen	25.	30.

TWENTY-FIVE CENTS, NHL HOCKEY SERIES (GIFTWARE), 2006-2007.
  The nine coloured twenty-five cent coins listed below are found in the NHL Team Gift Sets of 2006 and 2007, see page 364.

Designers:
  Obv.: Susanna Blunt
  Rev.: RCM Staff
Composition: Nickel plated steel, Decal
Weight: 4.4 g
Diameter: 23.9 mm
Finish: Circulation
Case of Issue: See NHL Team Gift Sets, page 364

Engravers:
  Obv.: Susan Taylor
  Rev.: RCM Staff
Thickness: 1.6 mm
Edge: Reeded
Die Axis: ↑↑

2006   HOCKEY SEASON, 2005-2006

| Common Obverse | Montreal Canadiens | Ottawa Senators | Toronto Maple Leafs |

DATE / COMP. MARK	DESCRIPTION	SOURCE	QUANTITY SOLD	ISSUE PRICE	FINISH	MS-65 NC
2006P	Montreal Canadiens Logo	NHL Team	11,765	N.I.I.	Circulation	15.
2006P	Ottawa Senators Logo	Gift	Included	N.I.I.	Circulation	15.
2006P	Toronto Maple Leafs Logo	Sets	Included	N.I.I.	Circulation	15.

2007   HOCKEY SEASON, 2006-2007

| Common Obverse | Calgary Flames | Edmonton Oilers | Montreal Canadiens |

| Ottawa Senators | Toronto Maple Leafs | Vancouver Canucks |

DATE / COMP. MARK	DESCRIPTION	SOURCE	QUANTITY SOLD	ISSUE PRICE	FINISH	MS-65 NC
2007	Calgary Flames Logo	Available	1,082	N.I.I.	Circulation	20.
2007	Edmonton Oilers Logo	only from	2,214	N.I.I.	Circulation	20.
2007	Montreal Canadiens Logo	NHL	4,091	N.I.I.	Circulation	20.
2007	Ottawa Senators Logo	Team	2,474	N.I.I.	Circulation	20.
2007	Toronto Maple Leafs Logo	Gift	5,365	N.I.I.	Circulation	20.
2007	Vancouver Canucks Logo	Sets	1,526	N.I.I.	Circulation	20.

OCCASIONS SERIES

TWENTY-FIVE CENTS, OCCASIONS SETS, 2007-2013 (GIFTWARE).

In 2007 the Royal Canadian Mint continued their expansion into the giftware market with an issue of three new Occasion Gift Sets. The sets contain seven circulation finish coins with the Caribou twenty-five cent coin being replaced with a coloured twenty-five-cent coin representing the occasion.

**Common Obverse
2007-2008**

Designers and Engravers:
  Obv.: Susanna Blunt, Susan Taylor
  Rev.: RCM Staff
Composition: Nickel plated steel, Decal
Weight: 4.4 g   **Thickness:** 1.6 mm
Diameter: 23.9 mm   **Die Axis:** ↑↑
Edge: Reeded   **Finish:** Circulation
Case of Issue: See Gift Sets, pages 360-363, 366-369

OCCASIONS - 2007

| Balloons Birthday Set | Bouquet Wedding Set | Fireworks Congratulations Set | Maple Leaf Oh! Canada Set | Rattle Baby Set |

DATE	DESCRIPTION	SOURCE	QUANTITY SOLD	ISSUE PRICE	FINISH	MS-65 NC
2007	Balloons, Birthday Gift Set	Available	24,531	N.I.I.	Circulation	20.
2007	Bouquet, Wedding Gift Set	only from	10,318	N.I.I.	Circulation	20.
2007	Fireworks, Congratulations Gift Set	Occasions	9,671	N.I.I.	Circulation	20.
2007	Maple Leaf, Oh! Canada Gift Set	Gift	24,096	N.I.I.	Circulation	20.
2007	Rattle, Baby Gift Set	Sets	30,090	N.I.I.	Circulation	20.

OCCASIONS - 2008

| Cake Wedding Set | Canadian Flag Oh! Canada Set | Party Hat Birthday Set | Teddy Bear Baby Set | Trophy Congratulations Set |

DATE	DESCRIPTION	SOURCE	QUANTITY SOLD	ISSUE PRICE	FINISH	MS-65 NC
2008	Cake, Wedding Gift Set	Available	7,407	N.I.I.	Circulation	20.
2008	Canadian Flag, Oh! Canada Gift Set	only from	30,567	N.I.I.	Circulation	20.
2008	Party Hat, Birthday Gift Set	Occasions	11,376	N.I.I.	Circulation	20.
2008	Teddy Bear, Baby Gift Set	Gift	29,636	N.I.I.	Circulation	20.
2008	Trophy, Congratulations Gift Set	Sets	6,821	N.I.I.	Circulation	20.

OCCASIONS SERIES (cont.)

TWENTY-FIVE CENTS, OCCASIONS SETS, 2007-2013 (GIFTWARE) [cont.].

In 2009 only the Oh! Canada! and Baby giftware sets were issued. The other twenty-five cent Occasions coins were incorporated into gift cards, see page 32.

Designers:
  Obv.: Susanna Blunt
  Rev.: RCM Staff
Composition: Nickel plated steel, Decal
Weight: 4.4 g
Diameter: 23.9 mm
Finish: Circulation
Case of Issue: See Gift Sets, pages 360-363, 366-369

Engravers:
  Obv.:   Susan Taylor
  Rev.:   RCM Staff
Thickness: 1.6 mm
Edge: Reeded
Die Axis: ↑↑

OCCASIONS - 2009

Common Obv. With RCM Logo	Four Maple Leaves Oh! Canada Set	Teddy Bear Baby Set

DATE	DESCRIPTION	SOURCE	QUANTITY SOLD	ISSUE PRICE	FINISH	MS-65 NC
2009	Four Maple Leaves, Oh! Canada Gift Set	Occasions	14,451	N.I.I.	Circulation	20.
2009	Teddy Bear, Baby Gift Set	Gift Sets	25,182	N.I.I.	Circulation	20.

OCCASIONS - 2010

For 2010, the Wedding Occasion twenty-five cent coin was moved back to the Wedding Gift Set series.

Common Obv. Without RCM Logo	Carriage Baby Set	Heart and Roses Wedding Set	Three Maple Leaves Oh! Canada Set

DATE	DESCRIPTION	SOURCE	QUANTITY SOLD	ISSUE PRICE	FINISH	MS-65 NC
2010	Carriage, Baby Set	Occasions	27,048	N.I.I.	Circulation	25.
2010	Heart and Roses, Wedding Gift Set	Gift	8,194	N.I.I.	Circulation	20.
2010	Maple Leaves, Oh! Canada Gift Set	Sets	19,769	N.I.I.	Circulation	20.

NOTE FOR COLLECTORS

NC – Non-circulating, in the data table signifies the coin was struck as a collectors item and was never meant for circulation.

OCCASIONS SERIES (cont.)

TWENTY-FIVE CENTS, OCCASIONS SETS, 2007-2013 (GIFTWARE) [cont.].

   Beginning in 2011, the reverse designs on the twenty-five-cent coins contained in the Occasions Sets are die struck rather than illustrated with a decal.

Common Obv.
2011-2012

Designers:
   Obv.:   Susanna Blunt
   Rev.:   Gary Taxali
Composition: Nickel plated steel
Weight: 4.4 g
Diameter: 23.6 mm
Finish: Circulation
Case of Issue: See Gift Sets, pages 360-363, 366-369

Engravers:
   Obv.:   Susan Taylor
   Rev.:   See reverse illustrations
Thickness: 1.6 mm
Edge: Reeded
Die Axis: ↑↑

OCCASIONS - 2011

Baby's Feet
Baby Set
Engr.: Matt Bowen

Four Balloons
Birthday Set
Engr.: Stan Witten

Maple Leaf
O Canada Set
Engr.: Cecily Mok

Wedding Rings
Wedding Set
Engr.: Stan Witten

Peace and Joy
Holiday Set
Engr.: C. Paquet

DATE	DESCRIPTION	SOURCE	QUANTITY SOLD	ISSUE PRICE	FINISH	MS-65 NC
2011	Baby's Feet, Baby Gift Set		38,576	N.I.I.	Circulation	15.
2011	Four Balloons, Birthday Gift Set	Occasions	21,173	N.I.I.	Circulation	15.
2011	Maple Leaf, O Canada Gift Set	Gift	22,475	N.I.I.	Circulation	15.
2011	Wedding Rings, Wedding Gift Set	Sets	20,461	N.I.I.	Circulation	15.
2011	Snowflake, Holiday Gift Set		41,666	N.I.I.	Circulation	15.

OCCASIONS - 2012

   The Occasions Sets issued in 2012 contain six coins (1¢, 5¢, 10¢, 25¢, $1 and $2). The use of the fifty-cent coin was discontinued.

Mobiles
Baby Gift Set
Engr.: C. Paquet

Ice Cream Cone
and Balloons
Birthday Gift Set
Engr.: C. Paquet

Stylized Maple
Leaves
O Canada Set
Engr.: C. Paquet

Wedding Rings
and Heart
Wedding Set
Engr.: C. Paquet

Christmas Tree
Ornaments
Holiday Set
Engr.: C. Paquet

DATE	DESCRIPTION	SOURCE	QUANTITY SOLD	ISSUE PRICE	FINISH	MS-65 NC
2012	Mobiles, Baby Gift Set		43,920	N.I.I.	Circulation	15.
2012	Ice Cream Cone and Balloons, Birthday Set	Occasions	24,659	N.I.I.	Circulation	15.
2012	Stylized Maple Leaves, O Canada Gift Set	Gift	31,464	N.I.I.	Circulation	15.
2012	Wedding Rings and Heart, Wedding Gift Set	Sets	24,325	N.I.I.	Circulation	15.
2012	Christmas Tree Ornaments, Holiday Gift Set		26,404	N.I.I.	Circulation	15.

OCCASIONS SERIES (cont.)

TWENTY-FIVE CENTS, OCCASIONS SETS, 2007-2013 (GIFTWARE) [cont.].

The Occasions Sets issued in 2013 contain five coins (5¢, 10¢, 25¢, $1 and $2). The one-cent coin was discontinued in 2012.

Common Obv.

Designers:
    Obv.: Susanna Blunt
    Rev.: Martin Coté
Composition: Nickel plated steel
Weight: 4.4 g
Diameter: 23.9 mm
Finish: Circulation
Case of Issue: See Gift Sets, pages 360-363, 366-369

Engravers:
    Obv.: Susan Taylor
    Rev.: See reverse illustrations
Thickness: 1.6 mm
Edge: Reeded
Die Axis: ↑↑

OCCASIONS - 2013

Baby's Feet	Slice Birthday Cake	Maple Leaf	Wedding Rings	Holly Wreath
Baby Set	Birthday Set	O Canada Set	Wedding Set	Holiday Set
Engr.: Matt Bowen	Engr.: Stan Witten	Engr.: Stan Witten	Engr.: Matt Bowen	Engr.: N/A

DATE	DESCRIPTION	SOURCE	QUANTITY SOLD	ISSUE PRICE	FINISH	MS-65 NC
2013	Baby's Feet, Baby Gift Set		52,762	N.I.I.	Circulation	15.
2013	Slice of Birthday Cake, Birthday Gift Set	Occasions	22,678	N.I.I.	Circulation	15.
2013	Maple Leaf, O Canada Gift Set	Gift	25,901	N.I.I.	Circulation	15.
2013	Intertwined Wedding Rings, Wedding Set	Sets	20,317	N.I.I.	Circulation	15.
2013	Holly Wreath, Holiday Gift Set		N/A	N.I.I.	Circulation	15.

NOTE TO COLLECTORS

When the initials N.I.I. appear in the pricing table it indicates the coin was part of a set issued by the Royal Canadian Mint, and not issued individually. Coin designs that are found only in sets offered by the Royal Canadian Mint are listed individually by denomination, and date in Volume Two.

CARDS WITH COINS (OCCASIONS)

TWENTY-FIVE CENTS, CARDS WITH COINS, 2009-2010 (GIFTWARE).

In 2009 a series of four cards incorporating twenty-five cent Occasions (decal) coins was released into the gift market. The Cards With Coins series was discontinued in 2010.

Designers:
  Obv.: Susanna Blunt
  Rev.: RCM Staff
Composition: Nickel plated steel, Decal
Weight: 4.4 g
Diameter: 23.9 mm
Finish: Circulation
Case of Issue: Folder

Engravers:
  Obv.: Susan Taylor
  Rev.: RCM Staff
Thickness: 1.6 mm
Edge: Reeded
Die Axis: ↑↑

CARDS WITH COINS - 2009

| Common Obv. With RCM Logo | Balloons, Streamers Birthday Card | Doves and Rings Wedding Card | Fireworks Congratulation Card | Stylized Flower Thank You Card |

DATE	DESCRIPTION	QUANTITY SOLD	ISSUE PRICE	FINISH	MS-65 NC
2009	Balloons and Streamers, Birthday Card	9,663	9.95	Circulation	15.
2009	Doves and Rings, Wedding Card	7,571	9.95	Circulation	15.
2009	Fireworks, Congratulations Card	4,126	9.95	Circulation	15.
2009	Stylised Flower, Thank You Card	4,415	9.95	Circulation	15.

CARDS WITH COINS - 2010

| Common Obv. Without RCM Logo | Flowers Thank You Card | Gift Box Birthday Card | Stars Congratulations Card |

DATE	DESCRIPTION	QUANTITY SOLD	ISSUE PRICE	FINISH	MS-65 NC
2010	Flowers, Thank You Card	5,932	9.95	Circulation	10.
2010	Gift Box, Birthday Card	8,751	9.95	Circulation	10.
2010	Stars, Congratulations Card	5,693	9.95	Circulation	10.

TOOTH FAIRY GIFT CARDS

TWENTY-FIVE CENTS, TOOTH FAIRY GIFT CARDS, 2011-2012 (GIFTWARE).
In 2011 a new gift card theme was introduced. The Tooth Fairy Gift Card contains a "ready-to-fill" money envelope to place under a child's pillow to make the trade for the tooth.

Designers:
  Obv.: Susanna Blunt
  Rev.: 2011 RCM Staff
        2012 Gary Taxali
Composition: Nickel plated steel
Weight: 4.4 g
Diameter: 23.9 mm
Finish: Circulation
Case of Issue: Folder

Engravers:
  Obv.: Susan Taylor
  Rev.: 2011 Marcos Hallam
        2012 Christie Paquet
Thickness: 1.6 mm
Edge: Reeded
Die Axis: ↑↑

| Common Obv. | 2011 | 2012 |

DATE		DESCRIPTION	QUANTITY SOLD	ISSUE PRICE	FINISH	MS-65 NC
2011	Fairy		38,200	9.95	Circulation	15.
2012	Stylized Fairy		20,359	9.95	Circulation	15.

ISSUES OF THE VANCOUVER 2010 OLYMPIC WINTER GAMES

TWENTY-FIVE CENTS, VANCOUVER 2010 WINTER OLYMPIC GAMES, 2007-2008.

The painted maple leaf outlined twenty-five cent coins were co-issued with Petro Canada and encased in a collector card format. The coins are listed in issue date order. The Collector Cards though numbered 1 to 15 do not necessarily correspond to the issue date order. The Alpine Skiing painted reverse was issued with a 2007 and 2008 dated obverse.

2007 Obv.
Olympic Games

2010
Olympic
Logo

Designers and Engravers:
Obv.:   Susanna Blunt, Susan Taylor
Rev.:   See reverse illustrations
Composition: Nickel plated steel, Painted
Weight: 4.4 g
Diameter: 23.9 mm
Thickness: 1.6 mm
Edge: Reeded
Die Axis: ↑↑
Finish: Circulation

Curling	Ice Hockey	Biathlon	Alpine Skiing
Des.: Glen Green	Des.: Glen Green	Des.: Glen Green	Des.: Glen Green
Engr.: C. Mok	Engr.: K. Wachelko	Engr.: K. Wachelko	Engr.: RCM Staff

Collector Card No. 4
2007 Alpine Skiing

Ice Hockey
Bookmark and
Lapel Pin

DATE	DESCRIPTION	QUANTITY SOLD	ISSUE PRICE	FINISH	MARKET VALUE
2007	Curling, Sport Card (painted leaf)	90,756	7.95	Circulation	15.
2007	Curling, Bookmark and Lapel Pin	5,332	9.95	Circulation	10.
2007	Ice Hockey, Sport Card (painted leaf)	100,839	7.95	Circulation	15.
2007	Ice Hockey, Bookmark and Lapel Pin	9,062	9.95	Circulation	10.
2007	Biathlon, Sport Card (painted leaf)	30,279	7.95	Circulation	15.
2007	Biathlon, Bookmark and Lapel Pin	Not issued	—	—	—
2007	Alpine Skiing, Sport Card (painted leaf) dated 2007	919	7.95	Circulation	30.
2007	Alpine Skiing, Bookmark and Lapel Pin	6,172	9.95	Circulation	10.
2008	Alpine Skiing, Sport Card (painted leaf) dated 2008	40,470	7.95	Circulation	15.

ISSUES OF THE VANCOUVER 2010 OLYMPIC WINTER GAMES (cont.)

TWENTY-FIVE CENTS, VANCOUVER 2010 WINTER OLYMPIC GAMES, 2008-2009.

2008 Obv.
Olympic Games

Snowboarding
Des.: Glen Green
Engr.: K. Wachelko

2010
Olympic
Logo

Designers and Engravers:
Obv.: Susanna Blunt, Susan Taylor
Rev.: See reverse illustrations
Composition: Nickel plated steel, Painted
Weight: 4.4 g
Diameter: 23.9 mm
Thickness: 1.6 mm
Edge: Reeded
Die Axis: ↑↑
Finish: Circulation

Freestyle Skiing
Des.: Glen Green
Engr.: C. Mok

Figure Skating
Des.: Glen Green
Engr.: C. Mok

Bobsleigh
Des.: Glen Green
Engr.: RCM Staff

Cross Country Skiing
Des.: Glen Green
Engr.: RCM Staff

Speed Skating
Des.: Glen Green
Engr.: K. Wachelko

Collector Card No. 6
Snowboarding

Snowboarding
Bookmark and
Lapel Pin

DATE	DESCRIPTION	QUANTITY SOLD	ISSUE PRICE	FINISH	MARKET VALUE
2008	Snowboarding, Sport Card (painted leaf)	40,771	7.95	Circulation	15.
2008	Snowboarding, Bookmark and Lapel Pin	5,150	9.95	Circulation	10.
2008	Freestyle Skiing, Sport Card (painted leaf)	35,447	7.95	Circulation	15.
2008	Freestyle Skiing, Bookmark and Lapel Pin	Not Issued	—	—	—
2008	Figure Skating, Sport Card (painted leaf)	16,479	7.95	Circulation	15.
2008	Figure Skating, Bookmark and Lapel Pin	6,047	9.95	Circulation	10.
2008	Bobsleigh, Sport Card (painted leaf)	1,383	7.95	Circulation	15.
2008	Bobsleigh, Bookmark and Lapel Pin	Not Issued	—	—	—
2009	Cross Country Skiing, Sport Card (painted leaf)	261	7.95	Circulation	15.
2009	Cross Country Skiing, Bookmark and Lapel Pin	Not Issued	—	—	—
2009	Speed Skating, Sport Card (painted leaf)	309	7.95	Circulation	15.
2009	Speed Skating, Bookmark and Lapel Pin	3,529	9.95	Circulation	10.

ISSUES OF THE VANCOUVER 2010 OLYMPIC WINTER GAMES (cont.)

TWENTY-FIVE CENTS, GOLDEN MOMENTS OLYMPIC COMMEMORATIVES, 2009.

The Golden Moments twenty-five cent coins were issued to commemorate the gold medals won at the Salt Lake City Winter Olympic Games by the Canadian men's and women's hockey teams in 2002, and the gold medal won by Cindy Klassen at the 2006 Turin Winter Olympic Games.

While three different commemorative designs are present, there are also three different major finish varieties within each design, making a total of nine major varieties in this series. Adding to the complication are two minor varieties within the Men's Ice Hockey colourised coins that of a raised and incused 2, making the grand total ten varieties.

Seven varieties are listed in *Canadian Coins, 67th edition, Volume One*, and six are listed here in Volume Two. The overlapping colourised varieties are duplicated in each volume.

The Men's Ice Hockey, colourised, raised 2 variety is NOT found in Petro Canada Sport Cards.

DESIGNS	FINISH VARIETIES	DIE VARIETIES
Men's Ice Hockey	Circulation	Raised 2 (See Volume One)
	Colourised	Incused 2
	Painted	Incused 2
Women's Ice Hockey	Circulation	None
	Colourised	None
	Painted	None
Cindy Klassen	Circulation	None
	Colourised	None
	Painted	None

Collector Card No. 12
Canadian Men's Ice Hockey Team

Collector Card No. 13
Canadian Women's Ice Hockey Team

Collector Card No. 14
Cindy Klassen Speed Skating

ISSUES OF THE VANCOUVER 2010 OLYMPIC WINTER GAMES (cont.)

TWENTY-FIVE CENTS, GOLDEN MOMENTS OLYMPIC COMMEMORATIVES, 2009 (cont.).

**Obverse
2009**

Designers and Engravers:
Obv.:   Susanna Blunt, Susan Taylor
Rev.:   Jason Bouwman, Susan Taylor
Composition: Nickel plated steel
Weight: 4.4 g   **Edge:** Reeded
Diameter: 23.9 mm   **Die Axis:** ↑↑
Thickness: 1.6 mm
Finish: 1. Circulation, Colourised
           2. Brilliant Uncirculated, Painted

**Men's Ice Hockey
Colourised Red**

**Colourised leaf
Incused 2**

**Men's Ice Hockey
Painted Red**

**Painted leaf
Incused 2**

**Women's Ice Hockey
Colourised Red**

Colourised Leaf

**Women's Ice Hockey
Painted Red**

Painted leaf

**Cindy Klassen
Speed Skating
Colourised Red**

Colourised Leaf

**Cindy Klassen
Speed Skating
Painted Red**

Painted leaf

DATE	DESCRIPTION	SOURCE	QUANTITY SOLD	ISSUE PRICE	FINISH	MS-65
2009	Men's Ice Hockey, Incused "2", Colourised	Sport Card	N/A	7.95	Circulation	8.
2009	Men's Ice Hockey Incused "2", Painted	Spec. Ed. Set	8,564	N.I.I.	BU	10.
2009	Women's Ice Hockey, Colourised	Sport Card	N/A	7.95	Circulation	8.
2009	Women's Ice Hockey, Painted	Sp. Ed. Set	8,564	N.I.I.	BU	10.
2009	Cindy Klassen, Speed Skating, Colourised	Sport Card	N/A	7.95	Circulation	8.
2009	Cindy Klassen, Speed Skating, Painted	Spec. Ed. Set	8,564	N.I.I.	BU	10.

ISSUES OF THE VANCOUVER 2010 PARALYMPIC WINTER GAMES

TWENTY-FIVE CENTS, VANCOUVER 2010 PARALYMPIC WINTER GAMES SPORT CARDS, 2007 and 2009.

**2007 Obv.
Paralympic Games**

**2010
Paralympic
Logo**

Designers and Engravers:
Obv.:   Susanna Blunt, Susan Taylor
Rev.:   See reverse illustrations
Composition: Nickel plated steel, Painted
Weight: 4.4 g
Edge: Reeded
Diameter: 23.9 mm
Die Axis: ↑↑
Thickness: 1.6 mm
Finish: Circulation

**Wheelchair Curling
Painted Leaf
Des.: Glen Green
Engr.: C. Mok**

**Ice Sledge Hockey
Painted Leaf
Alpine Skiing
Des.: Glen Green
Engr.: RCM Staff**

25¢ Wheelchair Curling Mule

The Vancouver Olympic obverse was paired with the Paralympic Wheelchair Curling reverse to create a mule. This coin was not issued for circulation, but is found in the Vancouver 2010 Brilliant Uncirculated Sets of 2007, which were assembled in Ottawa. See page 354 for the set listing.

**2007 Obverse with
Olympic Logo**

**2007 Reverse
Wheelchair Curling
Des.: Glen Green
Engr.: C. Mok**

**Collector Card No. 3
Wheelchair Curling**

DATE	DESCRIPTION	QUANTITY SOLD	ISSUE PRICE	FINISH	MARKET VALUE
2007	Wheelchair Curling, Sport Card (painted leaf)	34,956	7.95	Circulation	15.
2007	Wheelchair Curling, Mule	N/A	N.I.I.	BU	600.
2009	Ice Sledge Hockey Sport Card (painted leaf)	N/A	7.95	Circulation	15.

NOTE ON TWENTY-FIVE CENT ISSUES

The Petro Canada sport card twenty-five cent issues of 2007, 2008 and 2009 have a painted outline of a maple leaf supporting a central design. There are twelve different designs. The painted coins were inserted into sport cards and bookmarks which were encased in a plastic film. This film is all but impossible to remove without removing the painted outline from the coin.

ISSUES OF THE VANCOUVER 2010 OLYMPIC AND PARALYMPIC WINTER GAMES

TWENTY-FIVE CENTS, VANCOUVER 2010 OLYMPIC AND PARALYMPIC WINTER GAMES, SILVER PROOF SET, 2007-2009.

The twenty-five cent silver proof coins were issued in a presentation case. The set contains twelve coins and a one ounce sterling silver bar. Single proof coins may only be obtained from a break up of this set.

Designers:
  Obv.: Susanna Blunt
  Rev.: Glen Green

Engravers:
  Obv.: Susan Taylor
  Rev.: RCM Staff

Composition: 92.5% Ag, 7.5 Cu
Silver content: Single Coin: 5.365 g, 0.172 tr oz
                Bar: 28.77 g, 0.925 tr oz
                Set: 93.15 g, 3.0 tr oz
Weight: 5.8 g
Diameter: 23.6 mm
Case of Issue: Black leatherette clam case, 13-hole flocked insert, encapsulated coins, COA

Thickness: 1.7 mm
Edge: Reeded
Die Axis: ↑↑
Finish: Proof

DATE	DESCRIPTION	QUANTITY SOLD	ISSUE PRICE	FINISH	PR-67	PR-68
2007	Curling	N.I.I.	—	Proof	20.	25.
2007	Ice Hockey	N.I.I.	—	Proof	20.	25.
2007	Wheelchair Curling	N.I.I.	—	Proof	20.	25.
2007	Biathlon	N.I.I.	—	Proof	20.	25.
2007	Alpine Skiing,	N.I.I.	—	Proof	20.	25.
2008	Snowboarding	N.I.I.	—	Proof	20.	25.
2008	Free Style Skiing	N.I.I.	—	Proof	20.	25.
2008	Bobsleigh	N.I.I.	—	Proof	20.	25.
2008	Figure Skating	N.I.I.	—	Proof	20.	25.
2009	Cross Country Skiing	N.I.I.	—	Proof	20.	25.
2009	Speed Skating	N.I.I.	—	Proof	20.	25.
2009	Ice Sledge Hockey	N.I.I.	—	Proof	20.	25.
—	Complete Set, 12 coins, 1 one ounce silver bar	3,172	199.95	—	200.	—

TWENTY-FIVE CENT DERIVATIVES OF THE VANCOUVER 2010 OLYMPIC AND PARALYMPIC WINTER GAMES

DATE	DESCRIPTION	QUANTITY SOLD	ISSUE PRICE	FINISH	MARKET VALUE
2007	**Vancouver 2010 Coin Collector Card** (card only)	104,400	4.95	—	5.
2007	**Magnetic lapel pin,** Curling	3,118	9.95	Circulation	10.
2007	**Magnetic lapel pin,** Ice Hockey	3,158	9.95	Circulation	10.
2007	**Magnetic lapel pin,** Alpine Skiing	3,013	9.95	Circulation	10.
2008	**Magnetic lapel pin,** Snowboarding	6,095	9.95	Circulation	10.
2008	**Alpine Skiing**, Twenty-five cents (painted) and lapel pin	3,350	9.95	Circulation	10.
2008	**Snowboarding**, Twenty-five cents (painted) and lapel pin	2,922	9.95	Circulation	10.
2007-2010	**Magnetic Lapel Pin** for interchangeable sport coin	RCM	9.95	Circulation	10.
2007-2010	**Green See Through Tin Can**, Magnetic lapel pin, 5 twenty-five cent coins of various sports	RCM	14.95	Circulation	15.
2007-2010	**Green Tin Can** to hold the 15 Petro Canada Collector Cards	RCM	5.95	—	6.

TWENTY-FIVE CENTS, VANCOUVER 2010 OLYMPIC WINTER GAMES MASCOTS, 2008, (GIFTWARE).

The three mascots, Miga and Quatchi for the Olympic Winter Games, and Sumi for the Paralympic Winter Games, appear on many souvenirs for the Vancouver Winter Games.

Common Obv.   Miga

Quatchi   Sumi

Sumi Introduction Folder
"Meet The Vancouver 2010 Mascots!"

Designers:
 Obv.: Susanna Blunt
 Rev.: Design Team of the Vancouver Organising Committee
   for the 2010 Olympic and Paralympic Games
Composition: Nickel plated steel, Decal
Weight: 4.4 g
Diameter: 23.9 mm
Finish: Circulation
Case of Issue: Introduction Folder "Meet The Vancouver 2010 Mascots!"

Engravers:
 Rev.: Susan Taylor
 Rev.: RCM Staff
Thickness: 1.6 mm
Edge: Reeded
Die Axis: ↑↑

DATE	DESCRIPTION	QUANTITY SOLD	ISSUE PRICE	FINISH	MARKET VALUE
2008	Miga	14,654	10.95	Circulation	15.
2008	Quatchi	15,310	10.95	Circulation	20.
2008	Sumi	15,333	10.95	Circulation	20.

BIRDS OF CANADA SERIES

TWENTY-FIVE CENTS, COLOURISED BIRDS OF CANADA SERIES, 2007-2014 (GIFTWARE).
This series features popular Canadian birds as depicted by artists Arnold Nogy, Trevor Tennant and Tony Bianco..

2007 Common Obv.
With RCM Logo

Ruby-Throated Hummingbird

Red-Breasted Nuthatch

2008 Common Obv.
With RCM Logo

Downy Woodpecker

Northern Cardinal

2010 Common Obv.
Without RCM Logo

Goldfinch

Blue Jay

Designers:
  Obv.: Susanna Blunt
  Rev.: Arnold Nogy
Composition: Nickel plated steel, Decal
Weight: 12.61 to 13.0 g
Diameter: 35.0 mm
Finish: Specimen
Case of Issue: Maroon leatherette clam style case, black flocked insert, encapsulated coin, COA

Engravers:
  Obv.: Susan Taylor
  Rev.: RCM Staff
Thickness: 2.0 mm
Edge: Plain
Die Axis: ↑↑

DATE	DESCRIPTION	QUANTITY SOLD	ISSUE PRICE	FINISH	SP-66	SP-67
2007	Ruby-Throated Hummingbird	17,174	24.95	Specimen	160.	185.
2007	Red-Breasted Nuthatch	11,909	24.95	Specimen	425.	475.
2008	Downy Woodpecker	14,282	24.95	Specimen	225.	250.
2008	Northern Cardinal	11,604	24.95	Specimen	350.	375.
2010	Goldfinch	13,991	24.95	Specimen	200.	225.
2010	Blue Jay	13,965	24.95	Specimen	100.	125.

TWENTY-FIVE CENTS, COLOURISED BIRDS OF CANADA SERIES, 2007-2014 (GIFTWARE) [cont.].

**2011-2014 Common Obv.
Without RCM Logo**

Black-capped Chickadee

Barn Swallow

Rose-Breasted Grosbeak

Evening Grosbeak

American Robin

Barn Owl

Eastern Meadowlark

Designers:
  Obv.: Susanna Blunt
  Rev.: 2011-2012: Arnold Nogy
          2013 Trevor Tennant
          2014 Tony Bianco
Composition: 2011: Nickel plated steel, Decal
                 2012-2014: Cupronickel, Decal
Weight: 12.61 to 13.0 g
Diameter: 35.0 mm
Case of Issue: Maroon leatherette clam style case, black flocked insert, encapsulated coin, COA

Engravers:
  Obv.: Susan Taylor
  Rev.: RCM Staff

Thickness: 2.0 mm
Edge: Plain
Die Axis: ↑↑
Finish: Specimen

DATE	DESCRIPTION	QUANTITY SOLD	ISSUE PRICE	FINISH	SP-66	SP-67
2011	Black-capped Chickadee	13,947	25.95	Specimen	60.	70.
2011	Barn Swallow	14,000	25.95	Specimen	50.	60.
2012	Rose-Breasted Grosbeak	19,897	29.95	Specimen	35.	40.
2012	Evening Grosbeak	19,985	29.95	Specimen	35.	40.
2013	American Robin	17,493	29.95	Specimen	30.	35.
2013	Barn Owl	14,000	29.95	Specimen	30.	35.
2014	Eastern Meadowlark	17,500	29.95	Specimen	30.	35.

TWENTY-FIVE CENTS, 90TH ANNIVERSARY OF THE END OF WORLD WAR I SET, 2008 (GIFTWARE).

These two twenty-five-cent pieces were issued in a 2008 commemorative set to mark the ninetieth anniversary of the end of World War I. The 35 mm crown-size coin depicts the Tomb of the Unknown Soldier at the National War Memorial in Ottawa.

The standard 25-cent colourised Poppy coin was released into circulation during 2008. It was also incorporated into a bookmark that sold in the gift market. A donation of $1.00 per bookmark sold was given to the Legion's Dominion Command Fund.

2008   TOMB OF THE UNKNOWN SOLDIER

Designers and Engravers:
>   Obv.: Susanna Blunt, Susan Taylor
>   Rev.: David Craig, Cecily Mok

Composition: Nickel plated steel
Weight: 12.61 g
Diameter: 35.0 mm
Thickness: 3.4 mm
Edge: Plain
Die Axis: ↑↑
Finish: Specimen

2008   COLOURISED POPPY

Specifications: See 2005 Colourised Poppy, page 25
Cases of Issue:
>   1. Illustrated folder: Two coins, Serialised
>   2. Bookmark: twenty-five cent coin only

DATE	DESCRIPTION	SOURCE	QUANTITY SOLD	ISSUE PRICE	FINISH	SP-66	MS-65 NC
2008	Tomb of the Unknown Soldier and Poppy	Folder	Incl. below	N.I.I.	Specimen	25.	—
2008	Poppy "Remembrance"	Folder	Incl. below	N.I.I.	Circulation	—	5.
2008	Set of Two Coins	Folder	10,167	24.95	—	—	25.
2008	Poppy, Bookmark	Bookmark	489	12.95	Circulation	—	15.

Note: **1.** While the finish on the Tomb of the Unknown Soldier, large size twenty-five cent coin, is listed by the Royal Canadian Mint as specimen, it certainly is not a specimen finish when compared with coins of their specimen set issues of 1996 to 2009.

2. The "quantity sold" figure is understated. The 2008 RCM Report omitted the quantity sold number for that year. That number should been added to the 489 from the RCM Report for 2009.

NOTE ON GIFTWARE

Giftware is produced solely for the souvenir market. In most cases it is packaged in such a way that the coin is never meant to be removed from its package, let alone fill any legal tender status. Even though it is issued as Non Circulating legal tender, it is doubtful that anyone would accept it in exchange for goods or services, for it is not in a form recognisable by the general public as a medium of change.

TWENTY-FIVE CENTS, 100TH ANNIVERSARY OF ANNE OF GREEN GABLES©, 1908-2008 (GIFTWARE).

This coin was issued to commemorate the 100th anniversary *Anne of Green Gables*, which was first published in 1908.

Designers and Engravers:
    Obv.: Susanna Blunt, Susan Taylor
    Rev.: Ben Stahl
Composition: Nickel plated steel, Decal
Weight: 12.61 g
Diameter: 35.0 mm
Thickness: 2.0 mm
Edge: Plain
Die Axis: ↑↑
Finish: Specimen
Case of Issue: Illustrated folder, Serialised

DATE	DESCRIPTION	QUANTITY SOLD	ISSUE PRICE	FINISH	SP-66	SP-67
2008 (1908-)	Anne of Green Gables©	32,795	19.95	Specimen	25.	30.

TWENTY-FIVE CENTS, NOTRE-DAME-DU-SAGUENAY, 2009 (GIFTWARE).

The Lady of the Saguenay Fjord sits high on Cape Trinité in the majestic Saguenay Fjord, three hundred metres above sea level. The solid wooden statue was designed by Louis Jobin in 1881.

Designers and Engravers:
    Obv.: Susanna Blunt, Susan Taylor
    Rev.: Promotion Saguenay, Susan Taylor
Composition: Nickel plated steel, Decal
Weight: 11.7 g
Diameter: 35.0 mm
Thickness: 2.0 mm
Edge: Plain
Die Axis: ↑↑
Finish: Specimen
Case of Issue: Coloured card

DATE	DESCRIPTION	QUANTITY SOLD	ISSUE PRICE	FINISH	SP-66	SP-67
2009	Notre-Dame-Du-Saguenay	16,653	14.95	Specimen	25.	30.

TWENTY-FIVE CENTS, REMEMBRANCE DAY POPPIES, 2010, (GIFTWARE).

This twenty-five-cent coin is included in the Remembrance Day Collector Card. The card also has two die-cut holes to house the 2004 and 2008 "Poppy" coins.

Designers and Engravers:
    Obv.: Susanna Blunt, Susan Taylor
    Rev.: Cosme Saffioti, Stan Witten
Composition: Nickel plated steel, Colourised
Weight: 4.4 g
Diameter: 23.9 mm   **Edge:** Reeded
Thickness: 1.6 mm   **Die Axis:** ↑↑
Finish: Circulation
Case of Issue: See Derivatives, page 55

DATE	DESCRIPTION	QUANTITY SOLD	ISSUE PRICE	FINISH	MS-65	MS-66	MS-67
2010	Remembrance Day Poppies, colourised	21,738	9.95	Circulation	5.	10.	30.

TWENTY-FIVE CENTS, GEORGE V, STERLING SILVER, PROOF, 1935-2010.
This twenty-five-cent coin is from the Special Limited Edition Proof Set issued in 2010 to commemorate Emanuel Hahn's classic voyageur design which first appeared on the 1935 silver dollar.

Designers and Engravers:
Obv.: Sir. E. B. MacKennal
Rev.: L. C. Wyon
Composition: 92.5% Ag, 7.5% Cu
Silver content: 5.458 g, 0.175 tr oz
Weight: 5.9 g   **Edge:** Reeded
Diameter: 23.9 mm   **Die Axis:** ↑↑
Thickness: 1.7 mm   **Finish:** Proof
Case: See Special Issue Proof Sets, page 385

DATE	DESCRIPTION	QUANTITY SOLD	ISSUE PRICE	FINISH	PR-67	PR-68
2010 (1935-)	George V, Sterling Silver	4,996	N.I.I.	Proof	35.	40.

CANADIAN MYTHICAL CREATURES SERIES

TWENTY-FIVE CENTS, CANADIAN MYTHICAL CREATURES SERIES, 2011 (GIFTWARE).
This series features mythical Canadian animals as depicted by artist Emily S. Damstra.

Designers and Engravers:
Obv.: Susanna Blunt, Susan Taylor
Rev.: Emily S. Damstra, RCM Staff
Composition: Nickel plated steel, Decal
Weight: 12.61 to 13.0 g
Diameter: 35.0 mm
Thickness: 2.0 mm
Edge: Plain
Die Axis: ↑↑
Finish: Specimen
Case of Issue: Coloured folder

Common Obv.

Sasquatch

Memphré

Mishepishu

DATE	DESCRIPTION	QUANTITY SOLD	ISSUE PRICE	FINISH	SP-66	SP-67
2011	Sasquatch	12,321	24.95	Specimen	30.	35.
2011	Memphré	5,811	24.95	Specimen	35.	40.
2011	Mishepishu	5,831	24.95	Specimen	30.	35.

CANADA'S FLORA AND FAUNA SERIES

TWENTY-FIVE CENTS, CANADA'S FLORA AND FAUNA SERIES, 2011-2014 (GIFTWARE).
This series of coins is based on the flora and fauna of Canada's natural landscape.

Designers and Engravers:
Obv.: Susanna Blunt, Susan Taylor
Rev.: See reverse illustrations
Composition: 2011: Nickel plated steel, Decal
2012-2014: Cupronickel, Decal
Weight: 12.61 g   **Edge:** Plain
Diameter: 35.0 mm   **Die Axis:** ↑↑
Thickness: 1.9 to 2.0 mm   **Finish:** Specimen
Case of Issue: 2011: Illustrated folder
2012-2013: Maroon leatherette clam style case, black flocked insert, encapsulated coin, COA

Common obverse

Tulip with Ladybug	Aster with Bumble Bee	Purple Coneflower and Eastern Tailed Blue Butterfly	Water-lily and Leopard Frog
Designer: Cosme Saffioti	Designer: Maurice Gervais	Designer: Maurice Gervais	Designer: Maurice Gervais
Engraver: RCM Staff	Engraver: RCM Staff	Engraver: RCM Staff	Engraver: RCM Staff

DATE	DESCRIPTION	QUANTITY SOLD	ISSUE PRICE	FINISH	SP-66	SP-67
2011	Tulip with Ladybug	15,777	24.95	Specimen	45.	50.
2012	Aster with Bumble Bee	16,005	29.95	Specimen	35.	40.
2013	Purple Coneflower and Eastern Tailed Blue Butterfly	13,365	29.95	Specimen	30.	35.
2014	Water-lily and Leopard Frog	17,500	29.95	Specimen	30.	35.

TWENTY-FIVE CENTS, THE WEDDING CELEBRATION, HRH PRINCE WILLIAM and MISS CATHERINE MIDDLETON, 2011 (GIFTWARE).
This coin was issued to commemorate the marriage of HRH Prince William and Miss Catherine Middleton on April 29th, 2011.

Designers and Engravers:
Obv.: Susanna Blunt, Susan Taylor
Rev.: José Osio
Composition: Nickel plated steel, Decal
Weight: 12.61 g
Diameter: 35.0 mm
Thickness: 2.0 mm
Edge: Reeded
Die Axis: ↑↑
Finish: Specimen
Case of Issue: Illustrated folder

DATE	DESCRIPTION	QUANTITY SOLD	ISSUE PRICE	FINISH	SP-66	SP-67
2011	HRH Prince William and Miss Catherine Middleton	59,585	25.95	Specimen	25.	30.

TWENTY-FIVE CENTS, 75TH ANNIVERSARY OF CANADIAN BROADCASTING CORPORATION / RADIO-CANADA, 2011, (GIFTWARE).

Radio Canada's first broadcast was on November 2nd, 1936. The microphone depicted on the reverse of the coin was created by CBC/Radio-Canada for the Royal Tour of King George VI and Queen Elizabeth in 1939. It was designed for outside broadcasts. Its special wind-resisting device represented a major technological advance of the time.

Designers and Engravers:
  Obv.: Susanna Blunt, Susan Taylor
  Rev.: Konrad Wachelko, Nick Martin
Composition: Cupronickel
Weight: 12.61 g
Diameter: 35.0 mm
Thickness: 1.58 mm
Edge: Reeded
Die Axis: ↑↑
Finish: Specimen
Case of Issue: Illustrated folder

DATE	DESCRIPTION	QUANTITY SOLD	ISSUE PRICE	FINISH	SP-66	SP-67
2011	75th Anniversary of CBC/Radio-Canada	7,777	29.95	Specimen	30.	35.

TWENTY-FIVE CENTS, WAYNE GRETZKY, 2011, (GIFTWARE).

Wayne Gretzky "The Great One", whose hockey jersey bore the number 99, is commemorated on this coin.

Designers and Engravers:
  Obv.: Susanna Blunt, Susan Taylor
  Rev.: Glen Green, RCM Staff
Composition: Copper plated steel, Decal
Weight: 12.5 g
Diameter: 35.0 mm
Thickness: 1.9 mm
Edge: Plain
Die Axis: ↑↑
Finish: Specimen
Case of Issue: Illustrated folder

DATE	DESCRIPTION	QUANTITY SOLD	ISSUE PRICE	FINISH	SP-66	SP-67
2011	Wayne Gretzky	13,263	34.99	Specimen	40.	45.

TWENTY FIVE CENTS, GEORGE V, STERLING SILVER, PROOF, 1911-2011.

This twenty-five-cent coin which carries the double date 1911-2011 is from the Special Edition Proof Set issued in 2011 to commemorate the 100th anniversary of the striking of Canada's 1911 silver dollar.

Designers and Engravers:
  Obv.: Sir E. B. MacKennal
  Rev.: Original design by L. C. Wyon,
          Modified by W. H. J. Blakemore
Composition: 92.5% Ag, 7.5% Cu
Silver content: 5.46 g, 0.17 tr oz
Weight: 5.9 g   **Die Axis:** ↑↑
Diameter: 23.9 mm   **Edge:** Reeded
Thickness: 1.7 mm   **Finish:** Proof
Case: See Special Issue Proof Sets, page 385

DATE	DESCRIPTION	QUANTITY SOLD	ISSUE PRICE	FINISH	PR-67	PR-68
2011 (1911-)	George V, Sterling Silver	5,952	N.I.I.	Proof	20.	25.

OUR LEGENDARY NATURE SERIES

TWENTY-FIVE CENTS, OUR LEGENDARY NATURE: CANADIAN CONSERVATION SUCCESSES, 2011.

These coins were issued to commemorate three species brought back from near extinction by Canadian Conversation methods. The Wood Bison, Orca Whale and Peregrine Falcon twenty-five-cent coins were issued as a three-coin set.

Common Obv.

Wood Bison

Orca Whale

Peregrine Falcon

Designers:
  Obv.: Susanna Blunt
  Rev.: RCM Staff
Composition: 92.5% Ag, 7.5% Cu, Painted
Silver content: 5.46 g, 0.17 tr oz
Weight: 5.9 g
Diameter: 23.9 mm
Thickness: 1.5 mm
Case of Issue: Three-hole maroon clam style case, black flocked insert, encapsulated coin, COA

Engravers:
  Obv.: Susan Taylor
  Rev.: Cecily Mok

Edge: Reeded
Die Axis: ↑↑
Finish: Proof

DATE	DESCRIPTION	QUANTITY SOLD	ISSUE PRICE	FINISH	PR-67	PR-68
2011	Wood Bison, Painted	—	N.I.I.	Proof	20.	25.
2011	Orca Whale, Painted	—	N.I.I.	Proof	20.	25.
2011	Peregrine Falcon, Painted	—	N.I.I.	Proof	20.	25.
2011	3-coin set	5,290	49.95	Proof	60.	75.

TWENTY-FIVE CENTS, RMS TITANIC, 1912-2012, (GIFTWARE).

On April 10th, 1912, *RMS Titanic* set sail from England on her maiden voyage to North America. Shortly before midnight on April 14th, 1912, *RMS Titanic* struck an iceberg and sank shortly before dawn on the following morning. This coin was issued to remember the event.

Designers and Engravers:
  Obv.: Susanna Blunt, Susan Taylor
  Rev.: Yves Bérubé, RCM Staff
Composition: Cupronickel, Decal
Weight: 13.8 g
Diameter: 35.0 mm
Thickness: 2.0 mm
Edge: Plain
Die Axis: ↑↑
Finish: Specimen
Case of Issue: Illustrated folder

DATE	DESCRIPTION	QUANTITY SOLD	ISSUE PRICE	FINISH	SP-66	SP-67
2012 (1912-)	RMS Titanic	34,309	25.95	Specimen	30.	35.

PREHISTORIC CREATURES SERIES

TWENTY FIVE CENTS, PREHISTORIC CREATURES SERIES, 2012-2014 (GIFTWARE).
The coins in the Prehistoric Animal Series use a photo-luminescent technology (glow-in-the-dark) on the central image.

Common Obverse

2012
Pachyrhinosaurus Lakustai

Designers and Engravers:
　　Obv.:　Susanna Blunt, Susan Taylor
　　Rev.:　Julius T. Csotonyi, Cecily Mok
Composition: Cupronickel, Photo-luminescent
Weight: 13.8 g　　　　　**Edge:** Plain
Diameter: 35.0 mm　　　**Die Axis:** ↑↑
Thickness: 1.9 to 2.0 mm
Finish: Specimen
Case: Maroon leatherette clam style case, black
　　　　flocked insert, encapsulated coin, COA,
　　　　custom coloured sleeve

2013
Quetzalcoatlus

2013
Tylosaurus Pembinensis

2014
Tiktaalik

DATE	DESCRIPTION	QUANTITY SOLD	ISSUE PRICE	FINISH	SP-66	SP-67
2012	Pachyrhinosaurus Lakustai	24,422	29.95	Specimen	125.	135.
2013	Quetzalcoatlus	29,991	29.95	Specimen	45.	50.
2013	Tylosaurus Pembinensis	29,458	29.95	Specimen	30.	35.
2014	Tiktaalik	30,000	29.95	Specimen	30.	35.

TWENTY-FIVE CENTS, 100TH ANNIVERSARY OF THE CALGARY STAMPEDE, (GIFTWARE) 2012.

This twenty-five-cent coin is part of a coin and stamp set issued to commemorate the 100th anniversary of the Calgary Stampede. A domestic rate, and U.S. rate stamp are included in a colourful illustrated folder.

Designers and Engravers:
Obv.:   Susanna Blunt, Susan Taylor
Rev.:   Tony Bianco, Konrad Wachelko
Composition: Cupronickel, Decal
Weight: 13.9 g
Diameter: 35.0 mm
Thickness: 1.8 mm
Edge: Plain
Die Axis: ↑↑
Finish: Specimen
Case of Issue: See Derivatives, page 55

DATE	DESCRIPTION	QUANTITY SOLD	ISSUE PRICE	FINISH	SP-66	SP-67
2012	100th Anniversary of the Calgary Stampede	16,080	N.I.I.	Specimen	35.	40.

TWENTY-FIVE CENTS, 50TH ANNIVERSARY OF THE CANADIAN COAST GUARD, (GIFTWARE) 2012.

The CCGS *Louis S. St. Laurent* is depicted on this colourful twenty-five-cent coin. During a 1994 science expedition, the ship navigated through 3,700 kilometres of Arctic Ice, visiting the North Pole as it made the first crossing of the Arctic Ocean from the Pacific to the Atlantic. It was a joint Canada-US expedition with the USCGC *Polar Sea*. On August 22nd, 1994, the *Louis S. St. Laurent* was the first Canadian ship to reach the North Pole.

Designers and Engravers:
Obv.:   Susanna Blunt, Susan Taylor
Rev.:   Yves Bérubé, RCM Staff
Composition: Cupronickel, Decal
Weight: 13.8 g
Diameter: 35.0 mm
Thickness: 1.9 mm
Edge: Plain
Die Axis: ↑↑
Finish: Specimen
Case of Issue: Illustrated folder

DATE	DESCRIPTION	QUANTITY SOLD	ISSUE PRICE	FINISH	SP-66	SP-67
2012	50th Anniversary of the Canadian Coast Guard	11,950	24.95	Specimen	25.	30.

CANADIAN FOOTBALL LEAGUE SERIES

TWENTY-FIVE CENTS, CANADIAN FOOTBALL LEAGUE COIN AND STAMP SETS, (GIFTWARE) 2012.

These coin and stamp sets were issued by Canada Post to commemorate the 100th anniversary of the Canadian Football League. Each set honours a CFL team with a twenty-five-cent coin and two commemorative stamps.

Common Obv.

Designers and Engravers:
Obv.: Susanna Blunt, Susan Taylor
Rev.: Filip Mroz of Bensimon Byrne, Marcos Hallam
Composition: Cupronickel, Decal
Weight: 13.8 g
Diameter: 35.0 mm
Thickness: 2.0 mm
Edge: Plain
Die Axis: ↑↑
Finish: Specimen
Case of Issue: See Derivatives, page 56

British Columbia Lions

Calgary Stampeders

Edmonton Eskimos

Hamilton Tiger Cats

Montreal Alouettes

Saskatchewan Rough Riders

Toronto Argonauts

Winnipeg Blue Bombers

DATE	DESCRIPTION	QUANTITY SOLD	ISSUE PRICE	FINISH	SP-66	SP-67
2012	British Columbia Lions	12,097	N.I.I.	Specimen	25.	30.
2012	Calgary Stampeders	12,104	N.I.I.	Specimen	25.	30.
2012	Edmonton Eskimos	12,120	N.I.I.	Specimen	25.	30.
2012	Hamilton Tiger Cats	11,906	N.I.I.	Specimen	25.	30.
2012	Montreal Alouettes	12,227	N.I.I.	Specimen	25.	30.
2012	Saskatchewan Roughriders	15,700	N.I.I.	Specimen	25.	30.
2012	Toronto Argonauts	12,434	N.I.I.	Specimen	25.	30.
2012	Winnipeg Blue Bombers	12,214	N.I.I.	Specimen	25.	30.

DUCKS OF CANADA SERIES

TWENTY-FIVE CENTS, DUCKS OF CANADA SERIES, (GIFTWARE), 2013-2014.

The mallard is one of North America's most well known wild ducks. The male duck has a bright green head and ochre yellow bill, while the female has mottled brown and white plumage.

| Common Obverse | Mallard | Wood Duck | Northern Pintail |

Designers:
  Obv.: Susanna Blunt
  Rev.: Trevor Tennant
Composition: Cupronickel, Decal
Weight: 13.5 g
Diameter: 35.1 mm
Thickness: 1.8 mm
Case of Issue: Maroon leatherette clam style case, black flocked insert, encapsulated coin, COA

Engravers:
  Obv.: Susan Taylor
  Rev.: RCM Staff

Edge: Plain
Die Axis: ↑↑
Finish: Specimen

DATE	DESCRIPTION	QUANTITY SOLD	ISSUE PRICE	FINISH	SP-66	SP-67
2013	Mallard	17,475	29.95	Specimen	30.	35.
2013	Wood Duck	12,211	29.95	Specimen	30.	35.
2014	Northern Pintail	17,500	29.95	Specimen	30.	35.

TWENTY-FIVE CENTS, HER MAJESTY QUEEN ELIZABETH II CORONATION, (GIFTWARE) 2013.

This coin was issued to commemorate the Coronation of Queen Elizabeth II. The reverse image features a detail from Canadian artist Phil Richard's 2012 official portrait of Her Majesty Queen Elizabeth II in celebration of her Diamond Jubilee.

Designers and Engravers:
  Obv.: Susanna Blunt, Susan Taylor
  Rev.: Phil Richards, RCM Staff
Composition: Cupronickel, Decal
Weight: 13.9 g
Diameter: 35.0 mm
Thickness: 1.9 mm
Edge: Plain
Die Axis: ↑↑
Finish: Specimen
Case: Maroon leatherette clam style case, black flocked insert, encapsulated coin, COA

DATE	DESCRIPTION	QUANTITY SOLD	ISSUE PRICE	FINISH	SP-66	SP-67
2013	HM Queen Elizabeth II Coronation	14,956	24.95	Specimen	25.	30.

TWENTY-FIVE CENTS, BIRTH OF THE ROYAL INFANT, (GIFTWARE) 2013.

This coin was issued to commemorate the birth of Prince George of Cambridge, third in the line to the British throne.

Designers and Engravers:
Obv.: Susanna Blunt, Susan Taylor
Rev.: Laurie McGaw, RCM Staff
Composition: Cupronickel
Weight: 13.8 g
Diameter: 35.0 mm
Thickness: 1.9 mm
Edge: Plain
Die Axis: ↑↑
Finish: Specimen
Case: Coloured folder

DATE	DESCRIPTION	QUANTITY SOLD	ISSUE PRICE	FINISH	SP-66	SP-67
2013	Birth of the Royal Infant	14,283	24.95	Specimen	25.	30.

CANADIAN FLOWERS SERIES

TWENTY-FIVE CENTS, THE EASTERN PRICKLY PEAR CACTUS, (GIFTWARE) 2013.

This is the first coin in a new series featuring Canadian flowers.

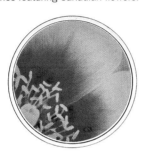

Designers and Engravers:
Obv.: Susanna Blunt, Susan Taylor
Rev.: Claudio D'Angelo, RCM Staff
Composition: Cupronickel, Decal
Weight: 13.7 g
Diameter: 35.0 mm
Thickness: 1.9 mm
Edge: Plain
Die Axis: ↑↑
Finish: Specimen
Case: Custom coloured cardboard box, encapsulated coin, COA

DATE	DESCRIPTION	QUANTITY SOLD	ISSUE PRICE	FINISH	SP-66	SP-67
2013	The Eastern Prickly Pear Cactus	6,840	24.95	Specimen	25.	30.

TWENTY-FIVE CENTS, 2014 FIFA WORLD CUP™, (GIFTWARE) 2014.

In 2014 the FIFA World Cup™ was hosted by Brazil.

Designers and Engravers:
Obv.: Susanna Blunt, Susan Taylor
Rev.: Steve Hepburn, RCM Staff
Composition: Cupronickel, Decal
Weight: 13.7 g
Diameter: 35.0 mm
Thickness: 1.9 mm
Edge: Plain
Die Axis: ↑↑
Finish: Specimen
Case: Black and white clam style case, black flocked insert, encapsulated coin, COA, full colour sleeve

DATE	DESCRIPTION	QUANTITY SOLD	ISSUE PRICE	FINISH	SP-66	SP-67
2014	2014 FIFA World Cup™	20,000	29.95	Specimen	30.	35.

NATIONAL HOCKEY LEAGUE SERIES

TWENTY-FIVE CENTS, NATIONAL HOCKEY LEAGUE COIN AND STAMP SETS, (GIFTWARE) 2014.

These coin and stamp sets were issued by Canada Post. Each set honours a NHL team with a twenty-five-cent coin and two commemorative stamps.

Common Obv.

Calgary Flames

Designers and Engravers:
  Obv.: Susanna Blunt, Susan Taylor
  Rev.: RCM Staff
Composition: Cupronickel, Decal
Weight: 13.8 g
Diameter: 35.0 mm
Thickness: 2.0 mm
Edge: Plain
Die Axis: ↑↑
Finish: Specimen
Case of Issue: See Derivatives, page 56

Edmonton Oilers

Montreal Canadiens

Ottawa Senators

Toronto Maple Leafs

Vancouver Canucks

Winnipeg Jets

DATE	DESCRIPTION	QUANTITY SOLD	ISSUE PRICE	FINISH	SP-66	SP-67
2014	Calgary Flames	5,721	N.I.I.	Specimen	30.	35.
2014	Edmonton Oilers	5,772	N.I.I.	Specimen	30.	35.
2014	Montreal Canadiens	5,953	N.I.I.	Specimen	30.	35.
2014	Ottawa Senators	5,810	N.I.I.	Specimen	30.	35.
2014	Toronto Maple Leafs	5,968	N.I.I.	Specimen	30.	35.
2014	Vancouver Canucks	5,951	N.I.I.	Specimen	30.	35.
2014	Winnipeg Jets	5,925	N.I.I.	Specimen	30.	35.

TWENTY-FIVE CENT DERIVATIVES

DATE	DESCRIPTION	QUANTITY SOLD	ISSUE PRICE	ISSUER	FINISH	MARKET VALUE
1999	**MILLENNIUM SET OF 12 CARDS** each containing a 1999 millennium twenty-five cent coin in a credit card format	N/A	N/A	RCM	MS-65	30.
1999	**JANUARY** "A Country Unfolds"	N/A	N/A	RCM	MS-65	2.
1999	**FEBRUARY** "Etched in Stone"	N/A	N/A	RCM	MS-65	2.
1999	**MARCH** "The Log Drive"	N/A	N/A	RCM	MS-65	2.
1999	**APRIL** "Our Northern Heritage"	N/A	N/A	RCM	MS-65	2.
1999	**MAY** "The Voyageurs"	N/A	N/A	RCM	MS-65	2.
1999	**JUNE** "From Coast to Coast"	N/A	N/A	RCM	MS-65	2.
1999	**JULY** "A Nation of People"	N/A	N/A	RCM	MS-65	2.
1999	**AUGUST** "The Pioneer Spirit"	N/A	N/A	RCM	MS-65	2.
1999	**SEPTEMBER** "Canada Through a Child's Eye"	N/A	N/A	RCM	MS-65	2.
1999	**OCTOBER** "A Tribute to the First Nation"	N/A	N/A	RCM	MS-65	2.
1999	**NOVEMBER** "The Airplane Opens the North"	N/A	N/A	RCM	MS-65	2.
1999	**DECEMBER** "This is Canada"	N/A	N/A	RCM	MS-65	2.
1999/ 2000	**MILLENNIUM SET** 24 silver 25-cent coins, medallion and case	N/A	N/A	RCM	PR-67	250.
2000	**MILLENNIUM SET OF 12 CARDS** each containing a 2000 millennium twenty-five cent coin in a credit card format	N/A	N/A	RCM	MS-65	30.
2000	**JANUARY** - Pride "Tomorrow Today"	N/A	N/A	RCM	MS-65	2.
2000	**FEBRUARY** - Ingenuity "Building for Tomorrow"	N/A	N/A	RCM	MS-65	2.
2000	**MARCH** - Achievement "The Power to Excel"	N/A	N/A	RCM	MS-65	2.
2000	**APRIL** - Health "Quest for a Cure"	N/A	N/A	RCM	MS-65	2.
2000	**MAY** - Natural Legacy "Our Natural Treasures"	N/A	N/A	RCM	MS-65	2.
2000	**JUNE** - Harmony "Hand in Hand"	N/A	N/A	RCM	MS-65	2.
2000	**JULY** - Celebration "Celebrating our Future"	N/A	N/A	RCM	MS-65	2.
2000	**AUGUST** - Family "The Ties That Bind"	N/A	N/A	RCM	MS-65	2.
2000	**SEPTEMBER** - Wisdom "The Legacy"	N/A	N/A	RCM	MS-65	2.
2000	**OCTOBER** - Creativity "Expression For All Time"	N/A	N/A	RCM	MS-65	2.
2000	**NOVEMBER** - Freedom "Strong and Free"	N/A	N/A	RCM	MS-65	2.
2000	**DECEMBER** - Community "Canada in the World"	N/A	N/A	RCM	MS-65	2.
2000	**APRIL**, CIBC "Run For The Cure" Credit Card	N/A	N/A	RCM, CIBC	MS-65	2.
2000	**THE ADVENTURES OF ZAC AND PENNY MONEY** Set of twelve 2000 Millennium twenty five cent coins in a display card; six booklets of stories and games	6,888	N/A	RCM	MS-65	25.
2004P	**WALKING BUNDLE** Twenty-five cent 'Moose' coin, T-shirt, Water bottle, Pouch	11,413	19.95	RCM	MS-65	50.
2004	**2004 ROYAL CANADIAN MINT ANNUAL REPORT** Twenty-five cent "Poppy" coin, sterling silver, selectively gold plated	12,677	24.95	RCM	PR-67	50.
2005P	**BOOKMARK** Twenty-five cent "Poppy" coin; Victory pin	29,951	12.95	RCM	MS-65	20.
2005	**60TH ANNIV. 1945-2005** Liberation Set, Netherlands	3,500	49.95	RCM	SP-66	200.
2006	**BOOKMARK** Twenty-five cent "Breast Cancer" coin; painted; Lapel pin	40,911	13.95	RCM	MS-65	35.
2006	**CANADA DAY 2006**, Twenty-five cents, colourised; Four crayons and a colouring sheet	N/A	9.95	RCM	MS-65	25.
2007	**CANADA DAY**, Twenty-five cents, colourised coin, activity kit	N/A	9.95	RCM	MS-65	20.
2008	**CANADA DAY,** Twenty-five cents, colourised coin, activity kit	N/A	9.95	RCM	MS-65	20.
2009	**CANADA DAY** Twenty-five cents, colourised coin, activity kit	N/A	14.95	RCM	MS-65	20.
2010	**REMEMBRANCE DAY COLLECTOR CARD**, includes 2010 twenty-five cent Remembrance Day coin; two die-cut holes for 2004 and 2008 twenty-five cent Poppy coins; postcard	21,738	9.95	RCM	MS-65	10.
2012	**TITANIC 100**, Twenty-five cent "Titanic" coin, White Star stock certificate, a re-created Titanic cancel, sheet of stamps, three Titanic postcards, leather-bound embossed album	10,000	140.95	RCM/PO	MS-65	125.00
2012	**TITANIC PHILATELIC NUMISMATIC COVER**, Twenty-five cent coin, First Day Cover.	10,000	26.95	RCM/PO	MS-65	30.00
2012	**CALGARY STAMPEDE COIN AND STAMP SET**, Twenty-five cents, colourised coin, A domestic rate and U.S. rate stamp	16,080	25.95	RCM/PO	SP-66	30.00

TWENTY-FIVE CENT DERIVATIVES (cont.)

DATE	DESCRIPTION	QUANTITY SOLD	ISSUE PRICE	ISSUER	FINISH	MARKET VALUE
2012	**CANADIAN FOOTBALL LEAGUE COIN AND STAMP SETS** Twenty-five cent coin, colourised, two commemorative stamps, coloured folder					
	British Columbia Lions	12,097	25.95	RCM/PO	SP-66	30.
	Calgary Stampeders	12,104	25.95	RCM/PO	SP-66	30.
	Edmonton Eskimos	12,120	25.95	RCM/PO	SP-66	30.
	Hamilton Tiger Cats	11,906	25.95	RCM/PO	SP-66	30.
	Montreal Alouettes	12,227	25.95	RCM/PO	SP-66	30.
	Saskatchewan Rough Riders	15,700	25.95	RCM/PO	SP-66	30.
	Toronto Argonauts	12,434	25.95	RCM/PO	SP-66	30.
	Winnipeg Blue Bombers	12,214	25.95	RCM/PO	SP-66	30.
2014	**NATIONAL HOCKEY LEAGUE COIN AND STAMP SETS** Twenty-five cent coin, colourised, two commemorative stamps, coloured folder					
	Calgary Flames	6,000	29.95	RCM/PO	SP-66	35.
	Edmonton Oilers	6,000	29.95	RCM/PO	SP-66	35.
	Montreal Canadiens	6,000	29.95	RCM/PO	SP-66	35.
	Ottawa Senators	6,000	29.95	RCM/PO	SP-66	35.
	Toronto Maple Leafs	6,000	29.95	RCM/PO	SP-66	35.
	Vancouver Canucks	6,000	29.95	RCM/PO	SP-66	35.
	Winnipeg Jets	6,000	29.95	RCM/PO	SP-66	35.

FIFTY CENTS

FIFTY CENTS, ELIABETH II PROOF, 1996-2014.

Starting in 1996 the fifty-cent coin issued in the proof set, previously struck from cupronickel, was now struck on a sterling silver planchet. The use of sterling silver planchets was discontinued in 2011.

The year 2012 saw the introduction of the Premium Proof Set in which all coins were struck on fine silver planchets. Standard Proof Sets were issued for 2012 and 2014. The fifty-cent coin in these sets was struck on a nickel planchet.

Obverse
1996-2003

Obverse
2004-2006
Without RCM Logo

Obverse
2007-2014
With RCM Logo

Reverse
1996-2014

Designers:
Obv.: 1996-2003: Dora de Pédery-Hunt
2004-2014: Susanna Blunt
Rev.: 1996: Thomas Shingles
1997-2014: C. Bursey-Sabourin

Engravers:
Obv.: 1996-2003: Dora de Pédery-Hunt
2004-2014: Susan Taylor
Rev.: 1996: Thomas Shingles
1997-2014: William Woodruff

	Sterling Silver	**Nickel**	**Fine Silver**
Composition:	92.5% Ag, 7.5% Cu	1.00	99.99% Ag
Silver content:	8.603 g, 0.277 tr oz	—	9.4 g, 0.302 tr oz
Weight:	9.3 g	6.9 g	9.4 g
Diameter:	27.1 mm	27.13 mm	27.0 mm
Thickness:	1.9 mm	1.9 mm	2.0 mm
Edge: Reeded	Reeded	Reeded	Reeded
Die Axis:	↑↑	↑↑	↑↑
Finish:	Proof	Proof	Proof

Case of Issue: Included in Proof Sets, pages 380-382

DATE	DESCRIPTION	COMP.	QUANTITY SOLD	ISSUE PRICE	FINISH	PR-67	PR-68
1996	Diademed Portrait / Arms of Canada	Sterling	112,835	N.I.I.	Proof	15.	20.
1997		Sterling	113,647	N.I.I.	Proof	10.	15.
1998		Sterling	93,632	N.I.I.	Proof	10.	15.
1999		Sterling	95,113	N.I.I.	Proof	15.	20.
2000		Sterling	90,921	N.I.I.	Proof	15.	20.
2001		Sterling	74,194	N.I.I.	Proof	15.	20.
2002		Sterling	65,315	N.I.I.	Proof	15.	20.
2003		Sterling	62,007	N.I.I.	Proof	20.	25.
2004	Uncrowned Portrait / Arms of Canada	Sterling	57,614	N.I.I.	Proof	20.	25.
2005		Sterling	63,562	N.I.I.	Proof	15.	20.
2006		Sterling	53,822	N.I.I.	Proof	15.	20.
2007	Uncrowned Portrait, Mint Logo / Arms of Canada	Sterling	37,413	N.I.I.	Proof	15.	20.
2008		Sterling	38,630	N.I.I.	Proof	15.	20.
2009		Sterling	27,549	N.I.I.	Proof	15.	20.
2010		Sterling	32,342	N.I.I.	Proof	20.	25.
2011		Sterling	32,910	N.I.I.	Proof	20.	25.
2012		Nickel	27,254	N.I.I.	Proof	20.	25.
2012	Premium Proof Set	Fine Silver	19,789	N.I.I.	Proof	30.	35.
2013	Premium Proof Set	Fine Silver	20,182	N.I.I.	Proof	30.	35.
2014		Nickel	30,000	N.I.I.	Proof	30.	35.
2014	Premium Proof Set	Fine Silver	25,000	N.I.I.	Proof	30.	35.

Note: Quantity sold figures are identical to those listed for Proof Sets sold.

DISCOVERING NATURE SERIES, 1995-2000

FIFTY CENTS, BIRDS OF CANADA SERIES, 1995.

The first set in the Discovering Nature Series commemorates birds that are native to Canada. This is the first of six sets totalling 24 coins. They are the first sterling silver fifty cents to be issued since 1919.

Designers:
  Obv.: Dora de Pédery-Hunt
  Rev.: Coins 1-4 Jean-Luc Grondin
           Coins 5-8 Dwayne Harty
Composition: 92.5% Ag, 7.5% Cu
Silver content: 8.603 g, 0.277 tr oz
Weight: 9.3 g
Diameter: 27.1 mm
Thickness: 2.1 mm

Engravers:
  Obv.: Dora de Pédery-Hunt
  Rev.: See reverse illustrations

Edge: Reeded
Die Axis: ↑↑
Finish: Proof

Case of Issue: Coins 1 - 4 Encapsulated coin in presentation box with illustrated booklet.
              Coins 5 to 6 (A) Two coin set; encapsulated coins
                             (B) Four coin set; encapsulated coins

Coin No. 1	Coin No. 2	Coin No. 3	Coin No. 4
Atlantic Puffins	Whooping Crane	Gray Jays	White-tailed Ptarmigans
Sheldon Beveridge	Stan Witten	Sheldon Beveridge	Cosme Saffioti

FIFTY CENTS, LITTLE WILD ONES SERIES, 1996.

The second set commemorates the young wildlife of Canada in their natural habitat.

Coin No. 5	Coin No. 6	Coin No. 7	Coin No. 8
Moose Calf	Wood Ducklings	Cougar Kittens	Black Bear Cubs
Ago Aarand	Sheldon Beveridge	Stan Witten	Sheldon Beveridge

DATE	COIN No.	DESCRIPTION	QUANTITY SOLD	ISSUE PRICE	FINISH	PR-67	PR-68
1995	1	Atlantic Puffins	Total	—	Proof	20.	25.
1995	2	Whooping Crane	mintage	29.95	Proof	20.	25.
1995	3	Gray Jays	all coins	—	Proof	20.	25.
1995	4	White-tailed Ptarmigans	172,377	29.95	Proof	20.	25.
1995	—	4 coin set	—	56.95	Proof	70.	—
1996	5	Moose Calf	Total	—	Proof	20.	25.
1996	6	Wood Ducklings	mintage	29.95	Proof	20.	25.
1996	7	Cougar Kittens	all coins	—	Proof	20.	25.
1996	8	Black Bear Cubs	206,552	29.95	Proof	20.	25.
1996	—	4 coin set	—	56.95	Proof	70.	—

Note: Coins 1-2 and 3-4 were issued in 2 coin sets, issue price $29.95.

DISCOVERING NATURE SERIES, 1995-2000 (cont.)

FIFTY CENTS, CANADA'S BEST FRIENDS SERIES, 1997.

The 1997 set honours the friendship and loyalty of four of Canada's favourite canine companions.

Designers:
Obv.: Dora de Pédery-Hunt
Rev.: Coins 9-12 Arnold A. Nogy
Coins 13-16 Pierre Leduc
Composition: 92.5% Ag, 7.5% Cu
Silver content: 8.603 g, 0.277 tr oz
Weight: 9.3 g
Diameter: 27.1 mm
Thickness: 2.1 mm
Case of Issue: Encapsulated coin in presentation box, plus illustrated booklet.

Engravers:
Obv.: Dora de Pédery-Hunt
Rev.: See reverse illustrations

Edge: Reeded
Die Axis: ↑↑
Finish: Proof

Coin No. 9	Coin No. 10	Coin No. 11	Coin No. 12
Newfoundland	Nova Scotia Duck	Labrador Retriever	Canadian Eskimo Dog
William Woodruff	Tolling Retriever	Sheldon Beveridge	Cosme Saffioti
	Stan Witten		

FIFTY CENTS, CANADA'S OCEAN GIANTS SERIES, 1998.

The reverse designs of the 1998 set shows the grace and beauty of the whales that are seen off our coasts.

Coin No. 13	Coin No. 14	Coin No. 15	Coin No. 16
Killer Whale	Humpback Whale	Beluga Whale	Blue Whale
William Woodruff	Sheldon Beveridge	Cosme Saffioti	Stan Witten

DATE	COIN No.	DESCRIPTION	QUANTITY SOLD	ISSUE PRICE	FINISH	PR-67	PR-68
1997	9	Newfoundland	Total	19.95	Proof	25.	35.
1997	10	Nova Scotia Duck Tolling Retriever	mintage	19.95	Proof	25.	35.
1997	11	Labrador Retriever	all coins	19.95	Proof	25.	35.
1997	12	Canadian Eskimo Dog	184,536	19.95	Proof	25.	35.
1997	—	Set of 4 coins	—	59.95	Proof	75.	—
1998	13	Killer Whale	Total	19.95	Proof	25.	35.
1998	14	Humpback Whale	mintage	19.95	Proof	25.	35.
1998	15	Beluga Whale	all coins	19.95	Proof	25.	35.
1998	16	Blue Whale	133,310	19.95	Proof	25.	35.
1998	—	Set of 4 coins	—	59.95	Proof	75.	—

DISCOVERING NATURE SERIES, 1995-2000 (cont.)

FIFTY CENTS, CATS OF CANADA SERIES, 1999.

This set, issued in 1999, honours four species of domestic and wild felines found in Canada, a salute to our rich Canadian wildlife.

Designers:
    Obv.: Dora de Pédery-Hunt
    Rev.: Coins 17-20, John Crosby
            Coin 21, 23, Jean-Luc Grondin
            Coin 22, 24, Pierre Leduc
Composition: 92.5% Ag, 7.5% Cu
Silver content: 8.603 g, 0.277 tr oz
Weight: 9.3 g
Diameter: 27.1 mm
Thickness: 2.1 mm
Case of Issue: Encapsulated coin in presentation box, plus illustrated booklet.

Engravers:
    Obv.: Dora de Pédery-Hunt
    Rev.: See reverse illustrations

Edge: Reeded
Die Axis: ↑↑
Finish: Proof

Coin No. 17
Tonkinese
Susan Taylor

Coin No. 18
Lynx
Susan Taylor

Coin No. 19
Cymric
Susan Taylor

Coin No. 20
Cougar
Susan Taylor

FIFTY CENTS, CANADIAN BIRDS OF PREY, SERIES, 2000.

The sixth and last set of the series features the hunting birds indigenous to Canada.

Coin No. 21
Bald Eagle
William Woodruff

Coin No. 22
Osprey
Susan Taylor

Coin No. 23
Great Horned Owl
Susan Taylor

Coin No. 24
Red-Tailed Hawk
Stan Witten

DATE	COIN No.	DESCRIPTION	QUANTITY SOLD	ISSUE PRICE	FINISH	PR-67	PR-68
1999	17	Tonkinese	Total	19.95	Proof	30.	35.
1999	18	Lynx	mintage	19.95	Proof	30.	35.
1999	19	Cymric	all coins	19.95	Proof	30.	35.
1999	20	Cougar	83,423	19.95	Proof	30.	35.
1999	—	Set of 4 coins	—	59.95	Proof	110.	—
2000	21	Bald Eagle	Total	19.95	Proof	25.	30.
2000	22	Osprey	mintage	19.95	Proof	25.	30.
2000	23	Great Horned Owl	all coins	19.95	Proof	25.	30.
2000	24	Red-Tailed Hawk	123,628	19.95	Proof	25.	30.
2000	—	Set of 4 coins	—	59.95	Proof	90.	—

CANADIAN SPORTS FIRSTS SERIES, 1998-2000

FIFTY CENTS, CANADIAN SPORTS FIRSTS SERIES, 1998.

A new sport series of sterling silver fifty-cent coins began in 1998 with the issue of the following four coins. The series comprises a total of twelve coins. Four issued each of the years 1998, 1999 and 2000.

Designers:
Obv.: Dora de Pédery-Hunt
Rev.: Coins 1 to 4: F. G. Peter
        Coins 5 to 8: D. H. Curley
Composition: 92.5% Ag, 7.5% Cu
Silver content: 8.603 g, 0.277 tr oz
Weight: 9.3 g
Diameter: 27.1 mm
Case of Issue: Singles: Lithographed metal box, black flocked insert, encapsulated coin.
        Set: Twelve coin metal container.

Engravers:
Obv.: Dora de Pédery-Hunt
Rev.: See reverse illustrations

Thickness: 2.1 mm
Edge: Reeded
Die Axis: ↑↑
Finish: Proof

Coin No. 1	Coin No. 2	Coin No. 3	Coin No. 4
First Official Amateur Figure Skating Championships, 1888 Sheldon Beveridge	**First Canadian Ski Running/Ski Jumping Championships, 1898** Ago Aarand	**First Overseas Can. Soccer Tour, 1888** Stan Witten	**Gilles Villeneuve Victory, Grand Prix of Canada for F1 Auto Racing, 1978** Cosme Saffioti

FIFTY CENTS, CANADIAN SPORTS FIRSTS SERIES, 1999.

The 1999 fifty-cent sterling silver coin set commemorates important dates in the history of Canadian sports. The designs reflect both the history of the sport and the growth and development into national pastimes.

Coin No. 5	Coin No. 6	Coin No. 7	Coin No. 8
1904-1999 First Canadian Open Golf Championship, 1904 William Woodruff	**1874-1999 First Int'l Yacht Race Canada vs U.S.A. 1874** Stan Witten	**1909-1999 First Grey Cup in Canadian Football, 1909** Cosme Saffioti	**1891-1999 Invention of Basketball by Canadian James Naismith** Sheldon Beveridge

DATE	COIN No.	DESCRIPTION	QUANTITY SOLD	ISSUE PRICE	FINISH	PR-67	PR-68
1998	1	First Official Amateur Figure Skating Chmpshp, 1888	Total	19.95	Proof	20.	25.
1998	2	First Canadian Ski Running/Ski Jumping Chmpshp, 1898	mintage	19.95	Proof	20.	25.
1998	3	First Overseas Canadian Soccer Tour, 1888	all coins	19.95	Proof	20.	25.
1998	4	Gilles Villeneuve Victory, Grand Prix, F1 Auto Racing, 1978	56,428	19.95	Proof	20.	25.
1998	—	Set of 4 coins	—	59.95	Proof	70.	—
1999	5	First Canadian Open Golf Chmpshp, 1904	Total	19.95	Proof	20.	25.
1999	6	First Int'l Yacht Race between Canada and U.S.A., 1874	mintage	19.95	Proof	20.	25.
1999	7	First Grey Cup in Canadian Football, 1909	all coins	19.95	Proof	20.	25.
1999	8	Invention of Basketball by Canadian James Naismith, 1891	52,115	19.95	Proof	20.	25.
1999	—	Set of 4 coins	—	59.95	Proof	70.	—

CANADIAN SPORTS FIRSTS SERIES, 1998-2000 (cont.)

FIFTY CENTS, CANADIAN SPORTS FIRSTS SERIES, 2000.

The 2000 fifty-cent sterling silver coin set celebrates the first competitions in Hockey, Curling, Steeplechase and Five Pin Bowling held in Canada. This is the last set in the twelve coin series.

Designers:
Obv.: Dora de Pédery-Hunt
Rev.: Brian Hughes
Composition: 92.5% Ag, 7.5% Cu
Silver content: 8.603 g, 0.277 tr oz
Weight: 9.3 g
Diameter: 27.1 mm
Thickness: 2.1 mm
Case of Issue: Singles: Lithographed metal box, black flocked insert, encapsulated coin.
Set: Twelve coin metal case.

Engravers:
Obv.: Dora de Pédery-Hunt
Rev.: See reverse illustrations

Edge: Reeded
Die Axis: ↑↑
Finish: Proof

Coin No. 9	Coin No. 10	Coin No. 11	Coin No. 12
1875-2000 First Recorded Hockey Game Stan Witten	1760-2000 Introduction of Curling to North America Cosme Saffioti	1840-2000 First Steeplechase Race in British North America Susan Taylor	1910-2000 Birth of the First 5-Pin Bowling League William Woodruff

DATE	COIN No.	DESCRIPTION	QUANTITY SOLD	ISSUE PRICE	FINISH	PR-67	PR-68
2000	9	First Recorded Hockey Game, 1875	Total	19.95	Proof	20.	25.
2000	10	Introduction of Curling to North America, 1760	mintage	19.95	Proof	20.	25.
2000	11	First Steeplechase Race in British North America, 1840	all coins	19.95	Proof	20.	25.
2000	12	Birth of the First 5-Pin Bowling League, 1910	50,091	19.95	Proof	20.	25.
2000	—	Set of 4 coins	—	59.95	Proof	75.	—

FIFTY CENT HISTORICAL COMMEMORATIVE SERIES, 1998-2008

FIFTY CENTS, 90TH ANNIVERSARY OF THE ROYAL CANADIAN MINT, 1908-1998.

Issued to commemorate the opening of the Royal Canadian Mint, a five-coin set was struck featuring the same reverse designs as the original 1908 coins, except for the double date 1908-1998. The set was issued in two finishes, matte and mirror proof.

Designers and Engravers:
    Obv.: Dora de Pédery-Hunt
    Rev.: Ago Aarand, W. H. J. Blakemore
Composition: 92.5% Ag, 7.5% Cu
Silver content: 10.749 g, 0.346 tr oz
Weight: 11.62 g   **Edge:** Reeded
Diameter: 29.7 mm   **Die Axis:** ↑↑
Thickness: 2.0 mm   **Finish:** See below
Case of Issue: See Special Issue Proof Sets,
                page 383

DATE	DESCRIPTION	QUANTITY SOLD	ISSUE PRICE	FINISH	PR-67	PR-68
1998 (1908-)	90th Anniv. R.C. Mint, Matte Proof	18,376	N.I.I.	Matte Proof	25.	40.
1998 (1908-)	90th Anniv. R.C. Mint, Mirror Proof	24,893	N.I.I.	Mirror Proof	25.	50.

FIFTY CENTS, 50TH ANNIVERSARY OF THE CORONATION OF QUEEN ELIZABETH II, 1953-2003.

This fifty-cent coin is from the Special Edition Proof Set issued in 2003 to commemorate the 50th anniversary of the Coronation of Queen Elizabeth II.

Designers and Engravers:
    Obv.: Mary Gillick
    Rev.: Thomas Shingles
Composition: 92.5% Ag, 7.5% Cu
Silver content: 10.749 g, 0.346 tr oz
Weight: 11.62 g   **Edge:** Reeded
Diameter: 29.7 mm   **Die Axis:** ↑↑
Thickness: 1.9 mm   **Finish:** Proof
Case of Issue: See Special Issue Proof Sets,
                page 384

DATE	DESCRIPTION	QUANTITY SOLD	ISSUE PRICE	FINISH	PR-67	PR-68
2003 (1953-)	50th Anniv. Coronation Queen Elizabeth II	21,537	N.I.I.	Proof	25.	30.

NOTE TO COLLECTORS

When the initials N.I.I. appear in the pricing table it indicates the coin was part of a set issued by the Royal Canadian Mint, and not issued individually. Coin designs that are found only in sets offered by the Royal Canadian Mint are listed individually by denomination, and date in Volume Two.

FIFTY CENT HISTORICAL COMMEMORATIVE SERIES, 1998-2008 (cont.)

FIFTY CENTS, COAT OF ARMS OF CANADA, 2004.

The Coat of Arms of Canada, which graced the George VI fifty-cent coin in 1937, has evolved over the years. This four-coin set, besides tracing that evolution, records the portrait changes of Elizabeth II.

1953-1964	1953	1965-1989	1954-1958

1990-2003	1959-1996	2003-2004	1997-2004

Obverse Designers: Portraits
1953-1964 Mary Gillick
1965-1989 Arnold Machin
1990-2003 Dora de Pédery-Hunt
2003-2004 Susanna Blunt

Reverse Designers: Arms of Canada
1953   Small date: G. E. Kruger-Gray
           Large date: Thomas Shingles
1954-1958 Thomas Shingles after G. E. Kruger-Gray
1959-1996 Thomas Shingles
1997-2004 C. Bursey-Sabourin

Composition: 92.5% Ag, 7.5% Cu
Silver content: 8.603 g, 0.277 tr oz
Weight: 9.3 g
Diameter: 27.1 mm
Thickness: 2.1 mm
Case of Issue: Maroon leatherette case, black flocked interior, encapsulated coins, COA

Edge: Reeded
Die Axis: ↑↑
Finish: Proof

DATE	DESCRIPTION	QUANTITY SOLD	ISSUE PRICE	FINISH	PR-67	PR-68
2004	Laureate Portrait	—	—	Proof	20.	25.
2004	Tiara Portrait	—	—	Proof	20.	25.
2004	Royal Diademed Portrait	—	—	Proof	20.	25.
2004	Uncrowned Portrait	—	—	Proof	20.	25.
2004	Total coins	12,230	—	Proof	—	—
2004	Total Sets	3,057	79.95	Proof	80.	—

FIFTY CENT HISTORICAL COMMEMORATIVE SERIES, 1998-2008 (cont.)

FIFTY CENTS, ROYAL CANADIAN MINT ANNUAL REPORT, SELECTIVELY GOLD PLATED, 2006.
This sterling silver gold-plated fifty-cent coin dated 2006 was issued in 2007 with the 2006 Royal Canadian Mint Annual Report. This was the last year a coin was combined with the Royal Canadian Mint Report.

Designers and Engravers:
Obv.: Susanna Blunt, Susan Taylor
Rev.: C. Bursey-Sabourin
Composition: 92.5% Ag, 7.5% Cu,
Selectively gold plated
Silver content: 8.603 g, 0.277 tr oz
Weight: 9.3 g
Diameter: 27.1 mm   **Edge:** Reeded
Thickness: 1.9 mm   **Die Axis:** ↑↑
Finish: Proof
Case of Issue: See Derivatives, page 84

DATE	DESCRIPTION	QUANTITY SOLD	ISSUE PRICE	FINISH	PR-67	PR-68
2006	RCM Annual Report	4,162	25.95	Proof	30.	35.

FIFTY CENTS, 100TH ANNIVERSARY OF THE ROYAL CANADIAN MINT, 1908-2008.
This fifty-cent coin is from the Coin and Stamp Set issued in 2008 to commemorate the 100th anniversary of the Royal Canadian Mint. It was also issued with the 2008 Royal Canadian Mint Centennial Book.

Designers and Engravers:
Obv.: Susanna Blunt, Susan Taylor
Rev.: RCM Staff
Composition: 92.5% Ag, 7.5% Cu
Silver content: 10.915 g, 0.351 tr oz
Weight: 11.8 g
Diameter: 29.7 mm   **Edge:** Reeded
Thickness: 2.0 mm   **Die Axis:** ↑↑
Finish: Proof
Case of Issue: See Derivatives, page 84

DATE	DESCRIPTION	QUANTITY SOLD	ISSUE PRICE	FINISH	PR-67	PR-68
2008 (1908-)	100th Anniversary, Royal Canadian Mint	3,248	44.95	Proof	40.	45.

CANADIAN FESTIVALS SERIES, 2001-2003

FIFTY CENTS, CANADIAN FESTIVALS SERIES, 2001-2002.

The Royal Canadian Mint introduced a new series of sterling silver fifty-cent coins in 2001 commemorating Canadian Festivals. Each coin represents a Canadian Province, Territory or Community, celebrating its culture, history and traditions with colourful festivals. The 13-coin set was issued over three years, starting in 2001 and ending 2003. It was available by subscription in 2001 for $249.95 with coins being shipped as they became available.

Designers:
  Obv.: Dora de Pédery-Hunt
  Rev.: See reverse illustrations

Engravers:
  Obv.: Dora de Pédery-Hunt
  Rev.: See reverse illustrations

Composition: 92.5% Ag, 7.5% Cu
Silver content: 8.603 g, 0.277 tr oz
Weight: 9.3 g
Diameter: 27.1 mm
Thickness: 2.1 mm

Edge: Reeded
Die Axis: ↑↑
Finish: Proof

Case of Issue: A: Singles; Multicoloured printed card folder with encapsulated coin.
                   B: Thirteen coin set; Canadian Festivals subscription coffee table book.

ISSUES OF 2001

| Common Obverse | Coin No. 1
Quebec Winter Carnival
(Quebec)
S. Daigneault
S. Witten | Coin No. 2
Toonik Tyme
(Nunavut)
J. Mardon, J. Osio | Coin No. 3
Newfoundland and
Labrador Folk Festival
(Newfoundland)
D. Craig, C. Saffioti | Coin No. 4
Festival of Fathers
(Prince Edward Island)
B. Whiteway,
W. Woodruff |

ISSUES OF 2002

| Coin No. 5
Annapolis Valley
Blossom Festival
(Nova Scotia)
B. Ross, J. Osio | Coin No. 6
Stratford Festival
of Canada
(Ontario)
L. McGaw, S. Taylor | Coin No. 7
Folklorama
(Manitoba)
William Woodruff | Coin No. 8
Calgary Stampede
(Alberta)
M. Grant, S. Witten | Coin No. 9
Squamish Days
Logger Sports
(British Columbia)
José Osio |

DATE	COIN No.	DESCRIPTION	QUANTITY SOLD	ISSUE PRICE	FINISH	PR-67	PR-68
2001	1	Quebec	2001 total	21.95	Proof	20.	35.
2001	2	Nunavut	mintage	21.95	Proof	20.	35.
2001	3	Newfoundland	all coins	21.95	Proof	20.	35.
2001	4	Prince Edward Island	58,123	21.95	Proof	20.	35.
2002	5	Nova Scotia	2002 total	21.95	Proof	20.	35.
2002	6	Ontario	mintage	21.95	Proof	20.	35.
2002	7	Manitoba	all	21.95	Proof	20.	35.
2002	8	Alberta	coins	21.95	Proof	20.	35.
2002	9	British Columbia	61,900	21.95	Proof	20.	35.

FIFTY CENTS, CANADIAN FESTIVALS SERIES, 2003.

This is the third issue in the 13-coin set which commemorates festivals across Canada.

Designers:
Obv.: Dora de Pédery-Hunt
Rev.: See reverse illustrations

Engravers:
Obv.: Dora de Pédery-Hunt
Rev.: See reverse illustrations

Composition: 92.5% Ag, 7.5% Cu
Silver content: 8.603 g, 0.277 tr oz
Weight: 9.3 g
Diameter: 27.1 mm
Thickness: 2.1 mm

Edge: Reeded
Die Axis: ↑↑
Finish: Proof

Case of Issue: A: Singles; Multicoloured printed card folder with encapsulated coin.
B: Thirteen coin set; Canadian Festivals subscription coffee table book.

ISSUES OF 2003

| Common obverse | Coin No. 10 Yukon Festival (Yukon) Ken Anderson José Osio | Coin No. 11 Back to Batoche (Saskatchewan) David Hannan Stan Witten | Coin No. 12 Great Northern Arts Festival (Inuvik) Dawn Oman Susan Taylor | Coin No. 13 Festival Acadien de Caraquet (New Brunswick) Hudson Design Group Susan Taylor |

DATE	COIN No.	DESCRIPTION	QUANTITY SOLD	ISSUE PRICE	FINISH	PR-67	PR-68
2003	10	Yukon	2003 total	21.95	Proof	20.	25.
2003	11	Saskatchewan	mintage	21.95	Proof	20.	25.
2003	12	Inuvik	all coins	21.95	Proof	20.	25.
2003	13	New Brunswick	26,451	21.95	Proof	20.	25.
2001-2003	—	Set of 13 coins	—	249.95	Proof	250.	—

CANADA'S FOLKLORE AND LEGENDS SERIES

FIFTY CENTS, CANADA'S FOLKLORE AND LEGENDS SERIES, 2001-2002.
A new series of fifty-cent sterling silver coins celebrates Canadian Folklore and Legends. The official release date was April 11, 2001.

Designers:
  Obv.: Dora de Pédery-Hunt
  Rev.: See reverse illustrations
Composition: 92.5% Ag, 7.5% Cu
Silver content: 8.603 g, 0.277 tr oz
Weight: 9.3 g
Diameter: 27.1 mm
Thickness: 2.1 mm
Case of Issue: Multicoloured printed card folder with encapsulated coin.

Engravers:
  Obv.: Dora de Pédery-Hunt
  Rev.: See reverse illustrations

Edge: Reeded
Die Axis: ↑↑
Finish: Proof

ISSUES OF 2001

Common Obverse

Coin No. 1
The Sled
Valentina Hotz-Entin
Susan Taylor

Coin No. 2
The Maiden's Cave
Peter Kiss
Susan Taylor

Coin No. 3
Les Petits Sauteux
Miyuki Tanobe
José Osio

DATE	COIN No.	DESCRIPTION	QUANTITY SOLD	ISSUE PRICE	FINISH	PR-67	PR-68
2001	1	The Sled	Mintage	24.95	Proof	20.	25.
2001	2	The Maiden's Cave	2001 coins	24.95	Proof	20.	25.
2001	3	Les Petits Sauteux	28,979	24.95	Proof	20.	25.

ISSUES OF 2002

Common Obverse

Coin No. 4
The Pig That Wouldn't
Get Over the Stile
Laura Jolicoeur
José Osio

Coin No. 5
Shoemaker in Heaven
Francine Gravel
Cosme Saffioti

Coin No. 6
Le Vaisseau Fantome
Colette Boivin
William Woodruff

DATE	COIN No.	DESCRIPTION	QUANTITY SOLD	ISSUE PRICE	FINISH	PR-67	PR-68
2002	4	The Pig That Wouldn't Get Over the Stile	Mintage	24.95	Proof	20.	25.
2002	5	Shoemaker in Heaven	2002 coins	24.95	Proof	20.	25.
2002	6	Le Vaisseau Fantome	19,789	24.95	Proof	20.	25.

CANADA'S GOLDEN FLOWER SERIES

FIFTY CENTS, CANADA'S GOLDEN FLOWER SERIES, 2002-2007.
Beginning in 2002 the Royal Canadian Mint issued a series of sterling silver, selectively gold plated proof fifty cent coins to commemorate different events which had a floral theme.

2002 and 2003
Common obverse

2002
50th Anniversary of the
Canadian Tulip Festival
Anthony Testa
Stan Witten

2003
Golden Daffodil
Symbol of Hope
Christie Paquet
Stan Witten

Designers and Engravers:
    2002-2003
            Obv.: Dora de Pédery-Hunt
            Rev.: See reverse illustrations
    2004-2007
            Obv.: Susanna Blunt
                    Susan Taylor
            Rev.: See reverse illustration
Composition: 92.5% Ag, 7.5% Cu,
    22-karat gold plate on design
Silver content: 8.603 g, 0.277 tr oz
Weight: 9.3 g
Diameter: 27.1 mm
Thickness: 2.2 mm
Edge: Reeded
Die Axis: ↑↑
Finish: Proof

2004 to 2007
Common obverse

2004
Golden Easter Lily
Christie Paquet
Stan Witten

2005
Golden Rose
Christie Paquet

2006
Golden Daisy
Christie Paquet

2007
Golden Forget-Me-Not
Christie Paquet

Cases of Issue: 2002-2004: Folders dated 2002, 2003 and 2004, encapsulated coin
                2005-2006: Maroon plastic display case, black plastic insert, encapsulated coin, COA
                2007: Maroon clam style case, black flocked insert, encapsulated coin, COA

DATE	DESCRIPTION	QUANTITY SOLD	ISSUE PRICE	FINISH	PR-67	PR-68
2002	Canadian Tulip Festival, 50th Anniversary	19,986	24.95	Proof	70.	80.
2003	Golden Daffodil, Symbol of Hope	36,293	34.95	Proof	35.	45.
2004	Golden Easter Lily	24,495	34.95	Proof	45.	50.
2005	Golden Rose	17,418	34.95	Proof	30.	40.
2006	Golden Daisy	18,190	36.95	Proof	45.	55.
2007	Golden Forget-Me-Mot	10,845	38.95	Proof	75.	85.

CANADIAN BUTTERFLY COLLECTION

FIFTY CENTS, CANADIAN BUTTERFLY COLLECTION, 2004-2006.
This series on Canada's butterflies contains the first hologram fifty cent coin.

Common Obverse

Designers:
　Obv.: Susanna Blunt
　Rev.: See reverse illustrations
Composition: 92.5% Ag, 7.5% Cu, Selectively gold plated, Decal, Hologram
Silver content: 8.603 g, 0.277 tr oz
Weight: 9.3 g
Diameter: 27.1 mm
Thickness: 2.1 mm
Finish: Proof

Engravers:
　Obv.: Susan Taylor
　Rev.: See reverse illustrations

Edge: Reeded
Die Axis: ↑↑

Case of Issue:　2004: Red leatherette clam style case, black flocked insert, encapsulated coin, COA
　　　　　　　　2005-2006: Maroon plastic display case, black plastic insert, encapsulated coin, COA

2004
Canadian Tiger
Swallowtail Butterfly
Des.: Jianping Yan
Engr.: RCM Staff

2004
Canadian Clouded
Sulphur Butterfly
Des.: Susan Taylor
Engr.: Susan Taylor

2005
Monarch Butterfly
Des.: Susan Taylor
Engr.: Susan Taylor

2005
Spangled Fritillary
Butterfly
Des.: Jianping Yan
Engr.: Jianping Yan

2006
Short-tailed Swallowtail
Butterfly
Des.: Susan Taylor
Engr.: Susan Taylor

2006
Silvery Blue Butterfly
Des.: Jianping Yan
Engr.: Jianping Yan

DATE	DESCRIPTION	QUANTITY SOLD	ISSUE PRICE	FINISH	PR-67	PR-68
2004	Canadian Tiger Swallowtail Butterfly, Hologram	20,462	39.95	Proof	50.	55.
2004	Canadian Clouded Sulphur Butterfly, Selectively gold plated	15,281	39.95	Proof	50.	55.
2005	Monarch Butterfly, Decal	35,950	39.95	Proof	50.	55.
2005	Spangled Fritillary Butterfly, Hologram	Incl. above	39.95	Proof	50.	55.
2006	Short-tailed Swallowtail Butterfly, Decal	24,568	39.95	Proof	50.	55.
2006	Silvery Blue Butterfly, Hologram	Incl. above	39.95	Proof	50.	55.

SECOND WORLD WAR SERIES

FIFTY CENTS, QUEST FOR PEACE AND FREEDOM DURING THE SECOND WORLD WAR, 2005.
The 60th anniversary of the end of World War II, 1945-2005, and the part Canada played, are commemorated in this six-coin sterling silver set. The coins were issued one per month from May 2005 to October 2005.

Common Obverse

Designers:
Obv.: Susanna Blunt
Rev.: Peter Mossman
Composition: 92.5% Ag, 7.5% Cu
Silver content: 8.603 g, 0.277 tr oz
Weight: 9.3 g
Diameter: 27.1 mm
Thickness: 2.1 mm
Case of Issue: Red leatherette case, black flocked insert, encapsulated coin, COA

Engravers:
Obv.: Susan Taylor
Rev.: See reverse illustrations

Edge: Reeded
Die Axis: ↑↑
Finish: Specimen

Battle of Britain
October 1940
Engr.: Stan Witten

Liberation of the
Netherlands
September 1944
Engr.: José Osio

Conquest of Sicily
August 1943
Engr.: RCM Staff

Battle of the Scheldt
November 1944
Engr.: RCM Staff

Raid on Dieppe
August 1942
Engr.: José Osio

Battle of the Atlantic
1939-1945
Engr.: Christie Paquet

DATE	DESCRIPTION	ISSUE DATE	QUANTITY SOLD	ISSUE PRICE	FINISH	SP-66	SP-67
2005	Battle of Britain	May	20,000	—	Specimen	30.	40.
2005	Liberation of the Netherlands	June	20,000	—	Specimen	30.	40.
2005	Conquest of Sicily	July	20,000	—	Specimen	30.	40.
2005	Battle of the Scheldt	August	20,000	—	Specimen	30.	40.
2005	Raid on Dieppe	September	20,000	—	Specimen	30.	40.
2005	Battle of the Atlantic	October	20,000	—	Specimen	30.	40.
2005	Set of 6 coins and display case	—	20,000	149.95	Specimen	175.	—

NHL HOCKEY SERIES

During the years 2005 to 2010 the Royal Canadian Mint issued many coins, mostly giftware, commemorating the Canadian teams of the National Hockey League.

FIFTY CENTS, NHL HOCKEY LEGENDS, 2005.

Hockey greats are commemorated on this legends series, issued in sets of four coins each: Jean Beliveau, Guy Lafleur, Jacques Plante and Maurice Richard of the Montreal Canadiens, and Johnny Bower, Tim Horton, Darryl Sittler and Dave Keon of the Toronto Maple Leafs.

Common Obverse

Designers:
    Obv.: Susanna Blunt
    Rev.: RCM Staff
Composition: 92.5% Ag, 7.5% Cu, Painted
Silver content: 8.603 g, 0.277 tr oz
Weight: 9.3 g
Diameter: 27.1 mm
Thickness: 2.1 mm
Case of Issue: Maroon plastic display case, black plastic insert, encapsulated coin, COA

Engravers:
    Obv.: Susan Taylor
    Rev.: RCM Staff

Edge: Reeded
Die Axis: ↑↑
Finish: Specimen

2005 MONTREAL CANADIENS

| Jean Beliveau | Guy Lafleur | Jacques Plante | Maurice Richard |

DATE	DESCRIPTION	QUANTITY SOLD	ISSUE PRICE	FINISH	SP-66	SP-67
2005	Jean Beliveau	N/A	N.I.I.	Specimen	30.	35.
2005	Guy Lafleur	N/A	N.I.I.	Specimen	30.	35.
2005	Jacques Plante	N/A	N.I.I.	Specimen	30.	35.
2005	Maurice Richard	N/A	N.I.I.	Specimen	30.	35.
2005	Set of 4 coins (Montreal)	N/A	99.95	Specimen	100.	—

2005 TORONTO MAPLE LEAFS

| Johnny Bower | Tim Horton | Darryl Sittler | Dave Keon |

DATE	DESCRIPTION	QUANTITY SOLD	ISSUE PRICE	FINISH	SP-66	SP-67
2005	Johnny Bower	N/A	N.I.I.	Specimen	30.	35.
2005	Tim Horton	N/A	N.I.I.	Specimen	30.	35.
2005	Darryl Sittler	N/A	N.I.I.	Specimen	30.	35.
2005	Dave Keon	N/A	N.I.I.	Specimen	30.	35.
2005	Set of 4 coins (Toronto)	N/A	99.95	Specimen	110.	—

Note: The Royal Canadian Mint Report of 2005 lists the quantity sold as 11,765 total sets.

NHL HOCKEY SERIES (cont.)

FIFTY CENTS, 2008-2009 NHL SEASON, 2009 (GIFTWARE).
The fifty-cent issues for the 2008-2009 Hockey Season were embedded in an official NHL puck and then blister packed. Each coin has a lenticular (dual images) reverse which by rotating the coin transfers from the old to the new team logo.

2009   HOCKEY PUCKS

Common Obverse

Designers and Engravers:
    Obv.: Susanna Blunt, Susan Taylor
    Rev.: Logos of the NHL
Composition: Nickel plated steel, Lenticular
Weight: 6.9 g
Diameter: 35.0 mm
Thickness: 2.0 mm
Edge: Plain
Die Axis: ↑↑
Finish: Specimen
Case of Issue: Blister packaged

Calgary Flames

Edmonton Oilers

Montreal Canadiens

Ottawa Senators

Toronto Maple Leafs

Vancouver Canucks

DATE	DESCRIPTION	QUANTITY SOLD	ISSUE PRICE	FINISH	SP-66	SP-67
2009	Calgary Flames	270	24.95	Specimen	25.	30.
2009	Edmonton Oilers	248	24.95	Specimen	25.	30.
2009	Montreal Canadiens	1,266	24.95	Specimen	25.	30.
2009	Ottawa Senators	310	24.95	Specimen	25.	30.
2009	Toronto Maple Leafs	606	24.95	Specimen	25.	30.
2009	Vancouver Canucks	318	24.95	Specimen	25.	30.

NHL HOCKEY SERIES (cont.)

FIFTY CENTS, MONTREAL CANADIENS CENTENNIAL COIN SERIES, 1909-2009 (GIFTWARE).
The 100th anniversary of the Montreal Canadiens hockey club was commemorated in 2009 with six giftware fifty-cent coins displaying the hockey jerseys worn by the Montreal players over the last 100 years. Each coin is sealed within a plastic sport card.

2009   MONTREAL CANADIENS CENTENNIAL

Common Obverse

Designers and Engravers:
   Obv.: Susanna Blunt, Susan Taylor
   Rev.: Logos of the NHL
Composition: Nickel plated steel, Decal
Weight: N/A
Diameter: 30.0 mm
Thickness: N/A
Edge: Plain
Die Axis: ↑↑
Finish: Specimen
Case of Issue: Collector Card

Coin No. 1
Montreal Canadiens
Home Jersey

Coin No. 2
1945-1946
Montreal Canadiens
Road Jersey

Coin No. 3
1915-1916
Le Club de
Hockey Canadiens

Coin No. 4
1912-1913
"CAC"

Coin No 5
1910-1911
Club Athletique
Canadien

Coin No 6
1909-1910
Club de Hockey
le Canadien

DATE	DESCRIPTION	QUANTITY SOLD	ISSUE PRICE	FINISH	SP-66	SP-67
2009 (1909-)	Montreal Canadiens Home Jersey	N/A	9.99	Specimen	15.	20.
2009 (1909-)	Montreal Canadiens Road Jersey	N/A	9.99	Specimen	15.	20.
2009 (1909-)	Le Club de Hockey Canadiens	N/A	9.99	Specimen	15.	20.
2009 (1909-)	"CAC"	25,016	9.99	Specimen	15.	20.
2009 (1909-)	Club Athletique Canadien	25,004	9.99	Specimen	15.	20.
2009 (1909-)	Club de Hockey le Canadien	25,004	9.99	Specimen	15.	20.
2009 (1909-)	Complete Set, 6 coins and an album	496	59.95	Specimen	80.	—

Note: 1. Single Collector Cards were issued by Jean Coutu, while the Royal Canadian Mint issued only complete sets.
   2. Quantity sold figures are incomplete due to year-end overruns.

NHL HOCKEY SERIES (cont.)

FIFTY CENTS, 2009-2010 NHL SEASON, 2009-2010 (GIFTWARE).

Common Obverse

Designers and Engravers:
  Obv.: Susanna Blunt, Susan Taylor
  Rev.: RCM Staff
Composition: Nickel plated steel, Decal
Weight: 12.9 g
Diameter: 35.0 mm
Thickness: 2.0 mm
Edge: Plain
Die Axis: ↑↑
Finish: Specimen
Case of Issue: Tent Card

Calgary Flames

Edmonton Oilers

Montreal Canadiens

Ottawa Senators

Toronto Maple Leafs

Vancouver Canucks

DATE	DESCRIPTION	QUANTITY SOLD	ISSUE PRICE	FINISH	SP-66	SP-67
2009-2010	Calgary Flames	3,518	14.95	Specimen	15.	20.
2009-2010	Edmonton Oilers	3,562	14.95	Specimen	15.	20.
2009-2010	Montreal Canadiens	9,865	14.95	Specimen	15.	20.
2009-2010	Ottawa Senators	3,293	14.95	Specimen	15.	20.
2009-2010	Toronto Maple Leafs	5,981	14.95	Specimen	15.	20.
2009-2010	Vancouver Canucks	3,563	14.95	Specimen	15.	20.

HOLIDAY LENTICULAR SERIES

FIFTY CENTS, HOLIDAY LENTICULAR SERIES, 2007-2013 (GIFTWARE).
Beginning in 2007 a large size fifty-cent lenticular coin was issued for the Holiday Season gift market.

Obverse with RCM Logo
2007-2008

Obverse without RCM Logo
2009-2013

Designers and Engravers:
Obv.: Susanna Blunt, Susan Taylor
Rev.: 2007-2011: C. Bursey-Sabourin
2012-2013: Tony Bianco
Composition: 2007-2009: Brass plated steel
2010-2011: Copper plated steel
2012-2013: Cupronickel
Weight: 12.61 to 13.8 g
Diameter: 35.0 mm   **Edge:** Plain
Thickness: 2.0 mm   **Die Axis:** ↑↑
Finish: Specimen, Lenticular
Case of Issue:
2007-2008, 2010-2013: Maroon leatherette
clam style case, black flocked insert,
encapsulated coin, COA
2009: Black leatherette clam style case, black
flocked insert, encapsulated coin, COA

2007
Holiday Ornaments

2008
Holiday Snowman

2009
Holiday Toy Train

2010
Santa Claus and the
Red-nosed Reindeer

2011
Gifts From Santa

2012
Santa's Magical Visit

2013
Snowman

DATE	DESCRIPTION	QUANTITY SOLD	ISSUE PRICE	FINISH	SP-66	SP-67
2007	Holiday Ornaments	16,989	25.95	Specimen	45.	55.
2008	Holiday Snowman	21,679	25.95	Specimen	45.	55.
2009	Holiday Toy Train	19,103	25.95	Specimen	45.	55.
2010	Santa Claus and the Red-Nosed Reindeer	21,394	26.95	Specimen	30.	40.
2011	Gifts from Santa	21,837	26.95	Specimen	30.	35.
2012	Santa's Magical Visit	22,304	29.95	Specimen	30.	35.
2013	Snowman	19,939	29.95	Specimen	30.	35.

TRIANGULAR COIN SERIES

FIFTY CENTS (triangular), MILK DELIVERY, 2008.
From the late 19th century to the middle of the 20th century milk and other dairy products were delivered to the home by a milkman who was paid by a token previously purchased.

Designers and Engravers:
    Obv.: Susanna Blunt, Susan Taylor
    Rev.: RCM Staff, Christie Paquet
Composition: 92.5% Ag, 7.5% Cu,
                Enamel effect on reverse
Silver content: 18.50 g, 0.595 tr oz
Weight: 20.0 g
Size: 36.0 x 34.1 mm
Thickness: 2.7 mm
Edge: Interrupted serrations
Die Axis: ↑↑
Finish: Proof
Case: Maroon leatherette clam style case, black
          flocked insert, encapsulated coin, COA

FIFTY CENTS (triangular), SIX STRING NATION GUITAR, 2009.
Jowi Taylor brought together the rich Canadian Heritage of materials to produce the Six String Nation Guitar. The guitar made its debut on Parliament Hill during the 2006 Canada Day celebrations.

Designers and Engravers:
    Obv.: Susanna Blunt, Susan Taylor
    Rev.: RCM Staff, Christie Paquet
Composition: 75% Cu, 25% Ni,
                Selective hologram on reverse
Weight: 19.1 g
Size: 36.0 x 34.1 mm
Thickness: 2.70 mm
Edge: Interrupted serrations
Die Axis: ↑↑
Finish: Specimen
Case: Folder

DATE	DESCRIPTION	QUANTITY SOLD	ISSUE PRICE	FINISH	SP-66	SP-67	PR-67	PR-68
2008	Milk Delivery	24,448	49.95	Proof	—	—	45.	50.
2009	Six String Nation Guitar	13,602	34.95	Specimen	40.	45.	—	—

SPECIAL NOTE ON FINISHES

It is very important to understand the different finishes the Royal Canadian Mint uses on their various issues. These finishes are altered from time-to-time as the Mint develops new products.

For example, the brilliant relief against a parallel lined background finish first used on bullion coins was carried forward in 1996 to be used on the coins contained in the specimen set.

In 2006 this finish was used on giftware coins such as the twenty-five cent coin issued to celebrate the 80th birthday of Queen Elizabeth II.

In 2010 a new specimen finish, brilliant relief against a laser-lined background, was used for the coins contained in the specimen set. There are now two different specimen finishes being utilised on Canadian coinage.

Circulation and Brilliant Uncirculated (proof-like) finishes are another very confusing mixture of finishes, see page xiv for a further explanation.

VANCOUVER 2010 OLYMPIC AND PARALYMPIC WINTER GAMES

FIFTY CENTS, MASCOT COLLECTOR CARDS, 2010 (GIFTWARE).

Three mascots were adopted for the Vancouver 2010 Winter Games, Miga and Quatchi for the Olympic Games and Sumi for the Paralympic Games.

These crown-size fifty-cent coins are embedded in plastic within a collector card format. As with all embedded Royal Canadian Mint giftware, the coins are very difficult to remove from their packaging without damaging the image on the coin.

Designers:
  Obv.: Susanna Blunt
  Rev.: RCM Staff
Composition: Nickel plated steel, Decal
Weight: 12.61 g
Diameter: 35.0 mm
Finish: Specimen

Engravers:
  Obv.: Susan Taylor
  Rev.: RCM Staff
Thickness: 2.0 mm
Edge: Plain
Die Axis: ↑↑

Case of Issue: Twelve collector cards were issued with the mascots in different sport poses.
               These coins are embedded in plastic.

Common Obverse

Coin No. 1
Miga Ice Hockey

Coin No. 2
Quatchi Ice Hockey

Coin No. 3
Sumi Paralympic
Ice Sledge Hockey

Coin No. 4
Quatchi and Miga
Figure Skating

Coin No. 5
Quatchi and Miga
Bobsleigh

Coin No. 6
Miga Ariels

Coin No. 7
Miga Skeleton

Coin No. 8
Quatchi Snowboard Cross

VANCOUVER 2010 OLYMPIC AND PARALYMPIC WINTER GAMES (cont.)

FIFTY CENTS, MASCOT COLLECTOR CARDS, 2010 (GIFTWARE) [CONT.].

Common Obverse

Coin No. 9
Miga Alpine Skiing

Coin No. 10
Sumi Paralympic
Alpine Skiing

Coin No.11
Quatchi Parallel
Giant Slalom

Coin No. 12
Miga Speed Skating

DATE	CARD No.	DESCRIPTION	QUANTITY SOLD	ISSUE PRICE	FINISH	SP-66	SP-67
2010	1	Miga Ice Hockey	3,096	9.95	Specimen	15.	20.
2010	2	Quatchi Ice Hockey	3,010	9.95	Specimen	15.	20.
2010	3	Sumi Paralympic Ice Sledge Hockey	2,137	9.95	Specimen	15.	20.
2010	4	Quatchi and Miga Figure Skating	2,981	9.95	Specimen	15.	20.
2010	5	Quatchi and Miga Bobsleigh	2,119	9.95	Specimen	15.	20.
2010	6	Miga Ariels	2,114	9.95	Specimen	15.	20.
2010	7	Miga Skeleton	1,672	9.95	Specimen	15.	20.
2010	8	Quatchi Snowboard Cross	2,090	9.95	Specimen	15.	20.
2010	9	Miga Alpine Skiing	2,309	9.95	Specimen	15.	20.
2010	10	Sumi Paralympic Alpine Skiing	1,902	9.95	Specimen	15.	20.
2010	11	Quatchi Parallel Giant Slalom	1,730	9.95	Specimen	15.	20.
2010	12	Miga Speed Skating	1,825	9.95	Specimen	15.	20.
—	—	Collector Card Album	—	12.95	—	15.	20.

VANCOUVER 2010 OLYMPIC AND PARALYMPIC WINTER GAMES (cont.)

FIFTY CENTS, MASCOT HOCKEY PUCKS, 2010.

The Miga, Quatchi, and Sumi ice hockey coins were also issued embedded in NHL official hockey pucks.

<table>
<tr><td align="center">Miga Ice Hockey</td><td align="center">Quatchi Ice Hockey</td><td align="center">Sumi Ice Hockey</td></tr>
</table>

Designers:
Obv.: Susanna Blunt
Rev.: RCM Staff
Composition: Nickel plated steel, Decal
Weight: 12.61 g
Diameter: 35.0 mm
Finish: Specimen

Engravers:
Obv.: Susan Taylor
Rev.: RCM Staff
Thickness: 2.0 mm
Edge: Plain
Die Axis: ↑↑
Cases of Issue: Blister packaged

DATE	CARD No.	DESCRIPTION	QUANTITY SOLD	ISSUE PRICE	FINISH	SP-66	SP-67
2010	1	Miga Ice Hockey	2,179	25.95	Specimen	20.	25.
2010	2	Quatchi Ice Hockey	2,524	25.95	Specimen	20.	25.
2010	3	Sumi Paralympic Ice Sledge Hockey	1,570	25.95	Specimen	20.	25.

FIFTY CENTS, VANCOUVER 2010 LENTICULAR, 2010 (GIFTWARE).

This fifty-cent lenticular coin with images of the Vancouver skyline, and Inukshuk is found in the Vancouver 2010 Gold Collector's Set. It was issued in conjunction with Canada Post (see page 371).

Designers and Engravers:
Obv.: Susanna Blunt, Susan Taylor
Rev.: RCM Staff
Composition: Nickel plated steel, Lenticular
Weight: 13.0 g
Diameter: 35.0 mm
Thickness: 2.0 mm
Edge: Plain
Die Axis: ↑↑
Finish: Specimen
Case of Issue: See Collector Sets, page 371

DATE	DESCRIPTION	QUANTITY SOLD	ISSUE PRICE	FINISH	SP-66	SP-67
2010	Lenticular Images of Vancouver and Inukshuk	11,384	N.I.I.	Specimen	50.	55.

DINOSAUR EXHIBIT SERIES

FIFTY CENTS, DINOSAUR EXHIBIT LENTICULAR SERIES, 2010 (GIFTWARE).
The Royal Canadian Mint in conjunction with various Canadian Museums created this new series of lenticular coins featuring prehistoric dinosaurs found in Canada.

| Common Obverse | Daspletosaurus Torosus | Albertosaurus | Sinosauropteryx |

Designers:
  Obv.: Susanna Blunt
  Rev.: RCM Staff
Composition: Brass-plated steel, Lenticular
Weight: 12.9 g
Diameter: 35.0 mm
Finish: Specimen
Case of Issue: Folded panel containing six collector trading cards

Engravers:
  Obv.: Susan Taylor
  Rev.: RCM Staff
Thickness: 2.0 mm
Edge: Plain
Die Axis: ↑↑

DATE	DESCRIPTION	QUANTITY SOLD	ISSUE PRICE	FINISH	SP-66	SP-67
2010	Daspletosaurus Torosus	11,652	24.95	Specimen	25.	30.
2010	Albertosaurus	14,325	24.95	Specimen	25.	30.
2010	Sinosauropteryx	19,865	24.95	Specimen	25.	30.

FIFTY CENTS, 100TH ANNIVERSARY OF THE STRIKING OF CANADA'S 1911 SILVER DOLLAR, 1911-2011.
This fifty-cent coin which carries the double date 1911-2011 is from the Special Edition Proof Set issued in 2011 to commemorate the 100th anniversary of the striking of Canada's 1911 silver dollar.

Designers and Engravers:
  Obv.: Sir E. B. MacKennal
  Rev.: Original design by L. C. Wyon,
       Modified by W. H. J. Blakemore
Composition: 92.5% Ag, 7.5% Cu
Silver content: 10.76 g, 0.345 tr oz
Weight: 11.629 g   **Die Axis:** ↑↑
Diameter: 29.7 mm   **Edge:** Reeded
Thickness: 2.0 mm   **Finish:** Proof
Case: See Special Issue Proof Sets, page 385

DATE	DESCRIPTION	QUANTITY SOLD	ISSUE PRICE	FINISH	PR-67	PR-68
2011 (1911-)	100th Anniv. Canada's 1911 Silver Dollar	5,952	N.I.I.	Proof	35.	40.

FIFTY CENTS, WINNIPEG JETS, 2011-2012.

Designers and Engravers:
  Obv.:   Susanna Blunt, Susan Taylor
  Rev.:   William Woodruff, RCM Staff
Composition: Nickel plated steel
Weight: 7.0 g
Diameter: 27.1 mm
Thickness: 1.9 mm
Edge: Reeded
Die Axis: ↑↑
Finish: Uncirculated
Case of Issue: Colourised folder

DATE	DESCRIPTION	QUANTITY SOLD	ISSUE PRICE	FINISH	MS-65 NC
2011-2012	Winnipeg Jets	23,712	14.95	Circulation	15.

FIFTY CENTS, ROYAL CYPHER, THE QUEEN'S DIAMOND JUBILEE, 1952-2012 (GIFTWARE).

This coin which carries the double date 1952 2012 celebrates the Queen's Diamond Jubilee. The design is a reproduction of the Diamond Jubilee Emblem for Canada by the Royal Canadian Mint. The reverse design is a garland of maple leaves with the Queen's monogram and St. Edward's crown at the centre.

Designers and Engravers:
  Obv.:   Susanna Blunt, Susan Taylor
  Rev.:   Christie Paquet
Composition: Silver-plated copper, Decal
Weight: 32.82 g
Diameter: 42.0 mm
Thickness: 3.0 mm
Edge: Reeded
Die Axis: ↑↑
Finish: Specimen
Case of Issue: Colourised folder

DATE	DESCRIPTION	QUANTITY SOLD	ISSUE PRICE	FINISH	SP-66	SP-67
2012 (1952-)	Royal Cypher Queen's Diamond Jubilee	30,900	29.95	Specimen	30.	35.

FIFTY CENTS, RMS TITANIC, 2012 (GIFTWARE).

This fifty-cent coin was issued to remember those who perished when *RMS Titanic* sank on April 15th, 1912.

Designers and Engravers:
  Obv.: Susanna Blunt, Susan Taylor
  Rev.: Yves Bérubé, Konrad Wachelko
Composition: Silver-plated copper,
                  Coloured
Weight: 32.82 g
Diameter: 42.0 mm
Thickness: 3.0 mm
Edge: Reeded
Die Axis: ↑↑
Finish: Proof
Case of Issue: Maroon leatherette clam
                   style case, black flocked insert,
                   encapsulated coin, COA

DATE	DESCRIPTION	QUANTITY SOLD	ISSUE PRICE	FINISH	PR-67	PR-68
2012	RMS Titanic	14,997	34.95	Proof	120.	130.

FIFTY CENTS, 75TH ANNIVERSARY OF SUPERMAN™: THEN AND NOW, COIN AND STAMP SET, 2013 (GIFTWARE).
This fifty-cent coin was issued to commemorate the 75th anniversary of Superman™.

Designers and Engravers:
    Obv.: Susanna Blunt, Susan Taylor
    Rev.: DC Comic/Warner Brothers, RCM Staff
Composition: Cupronickel, Lenticular
Weight: 13.7 g
Diameter: 35.0 mm
Thickness: 2.0 mm
Edge: Plain
Die Axis: ↑↑
Finish: Specimen
Case of Issue: See Derivatives

DATE	DESCRIPTION	QUANTITY SOLD	ISSUE PRICE	FINISH	SP-66	SP-67
2013	Superman™: Then and Now	24,896	N.I.I.	Specimen	45.	50.

BUTTERFLIES OF CANADA SERIES

FIFTY CENTS, CANADIAN TIGER SWALLOWTAIL, 2013 (GIFTWARE).
This fifty-cent coin is the first in the new Butterflies of Canada Series.

Designers and Engravers:
    Obv.: Susanna Blunt, Susan Taylor
    Rev.: Celia Godkin, RCM Staff
Composition: Silver-plated copper,
        Painted
Weight: 33.2 g
Diameter: 42.0 mm
Thickness: 3.2 mm
Edge: Reeded
Die Axis: ↑↑
Finish: Proof
Case of Issue: Maroon leatherette clam
        style case, black flocked insert,
        encapsulated coin, COA

DATE	DESCRIPTION	QUANTITY SOLD	ISSUE PRICE	FINISH	PR-67	PR-68
2013	Canadian Tiger Swallowtail	10,757	34.95	Proof	35.	40.

FIFTY CENTS, 100 BLESSINGS OF GOOD FORTUNE, 2014 (GIFTWARE).
This fifty-cent coin was issued as a token of good luck to be given from one collector to another.

Designers and Engravers:
Obv.: Susanna Blunt, Susan Taylor
Rev.: Three Degrees Creative Group,
RCM Staff
Composition: Silver-plated copper,
Coloured
Weight: 32.5 g
Diameter: 42.0 mm
Thickness: 3.0 mm
Edge: Reeded
Die Axis: ↑↑
Finish: Proof
Case of Issue: Silver satin-like clam
style case, black flocked insert,
encapsulated coin, COA, red sleeve

DATE	DESCRIPTION	QUANTITY SOLD	ISSUE PRICE	FINISH	PR-67	PR-68
2014	100 Blessings of Good Fortune	8,988	34.95	Proof	40.	45.

FIFTY CENT DERIVATIVES

DATE	DESCRIPTION	QUANTITY SOLD	ISSUE PRICE	ISSUER	FINISH	MARKET VALUE
2001	**CANADA PROVINCIAL CREST** Credit Card Type	N/A	N/A	RCM	MS-65	5.
2003	**CORONATION COIN AND STAMP SET** Two one cent coins, 1953 and 2003; Two fifty cent coins, 2002 Jubilee, 2003 Uncrowned Portrait; Two mint and two cancelled stamps of Her Majesty's Jubilee and Coronation; Presentation case	14,743	N/A	RCM	MS-65	60.
2008	**100TH ANNIVERSARY COIN AND STAMP SET** Fifty cent coin, double-dated 1908-2008, fifty-two cent postage stamp, wooden presentation case, booklet	16,000	44.95	RCM/PO	PR-67	50.
2008	**ROYAL CANADIAN MINT CENTENNIAL BOOK** Fifty cent coin, double-dated 1908-2008, postage stamp, 200-page book					
	English	136	99.95	RCM	PR-67	50.
	French	46	99.95	RCM	PR-67	50.
2010	**DASPLETOSAURUS TOROSUS** fifty cent coin, six trading cards, folder	N/A	24.95	RCM	MS-65	35.
2010	**ALBERTOSAURUS**. fifty cent coin, six trading cards, folder	N/A	24.95	RCM	MS-65	35.
2010	**SINOSAUROPTERYX**, fifty cent coin, six trading cards, folder	N/A	24.95	RCM	MS-65	35.
2012	**TITANIC 100,** Fifty cent coin, twenty-five cent coin, White Star stock certificate, a re-created *Titanic* cancel, sheet of stamps, three Titanic postcards, leather-bound embossed album	10,000	140.95	RCM/PO	MS-65	150.
2012	**PHILATELIC NUMISMATIC COVER** Royal Cypher fifty cent coin, two dollar Diamond Jubilee stamp	10,000	25.95	RCM/PO	MS-65	35.
2013	**75TH ANNIVERSARY OF SUPERMAN™: THEN AND NOW COIN AND STAMP SET,** Fifty cent coin, collectable stamp	24,896	29.75	RCM/PO	SP-66	45.
2014	**BLESSING COIN AND STAMP COLLECTABLES** Fifty cent coin 100 Blessings of Good Fortune; Chinese stamp 120 fen, "Blossom of Fortune" (issue date Oct. 9, 2008).	N/A	38.88	RCM/PO	PR-67	40.

ONE DOLLAR ISSUES

SILVER DOLLAR ISSUES, 1971-2014

ONE DOLLAR, BRITISH COLUMBIA CENTENNIAL, 1871-1971.

The first non-circulating silver dollar was issued to the public in 1971. It commemorates the entry of British Columbia into Confederation in 1871, with the design based upon the provincial arms. The obverse features a modification of the Machin portrait in which the portrait of the Queen was reduced slightly and her hair extensively redone.

Designers and Engravers:
    Obv.: Arnold Machin, Patrick Brindley
    Rev.: Patrick Brindley
Composition: 50% Ag, 50% Cu
Silver content: 11.65 g, 0.375 tr oz
Weight: 23.3 g   **Thickness:** 2.95 mm
Diameter: 36.07 mm **Die Axis:** ↑↑
Edge: Reeded   **Finish:** Specimen
Case A: Black leatherette clam case, Coat
      of Arms, maroon and black insert
Case B: Black leatherette clam case, Coat of Arms,
      white and black insert

DATE	DESCRIPTION	QUANTITY SOLD	ISSUE PRICE	FINISH	SP-66	SP-67
1971 (1871-)	British Columbia Centennial	585,217	3.00	Specimen	18.	20.

ONE DOLLAR, VOYAGEUR DESIGN, 1972.

The reverse of the 1972 silver dollar is the voyageur design somewhat modified from its last use on the 1966 silver dollar. One of the most noticeable differences is the substitution of beads for denticles at the rim.

Designers and Engravers:
    Obv.: Arnold Machin, Patrick Brindley
    Rev.: Emanuel Hahn, Terry Smith
Composition: 50% Ag, 50% Cu
Silver content: 11.65 g, 0.375 tr oz
Weight: 23.3 g   **Thickness:** 2.95 mm
Diameter: 36.07 mm **Die Axis:** ↑↑
Edge: Reeded   **Finish:** Specimen
Case: Black leatherette clam style case, Coat
      of Arms, maroon and black insert

DATE	DESCRIPTION	QUANTITY SOLD	ISSUE PRICE	FINISH	SP-66	SP-67
1972	Voyageur	341,581	3.00	Specimen	18.	20.

ONE DOLLAR, ROYAL CANADIAN MOUNTED POLICE CENTENNIAL, 1973.

The reverse of the 1973 silver dollar recognizes the founding of the North West Mounted Police which later became the Royal Canadian Mounted Police.

Designers and Engravers:
    Obv.: Arnold Machin, Patrick Brindley
    Rev.: Paul Cedarberg, Patrick Brindley
Composition: 50% Ag, 50% Cu
Silver content: 11.65 g, 0.375 tr oz
Weight: 23.3 g   **Thickness:** 2.95 mm
Diameter: 36.07 mm **Die Axis:** ↑↑
Edge: Reeded   **Finish:** Specimen
Case A: Black leatherette clam style case, Coat
      of Arms, maroon and black insert
Case B: Blue leatherette clam style case, gilt
      RCMP crest, maroon and black insert

DATE	DESCRIPTION	QUANTITY SOLD	ISSUE PRICE	FINISH	SP-66	SP-67
1973 (1873-)	R.C.M.P., Case A	904,723	3.00	Specimen	18.	20.
1973 (1873-)	R.C.M.P., Case B	Included	3.00	Specimen	25.	30.

ONE DOLLAR, WINNIPEG CENTENNIAL, 1974.

The 100th anniversary of the establishment of Winnipeg, Manitoba, as a city is marked by the reverse of the 1974 silver dollar. The design is identical to that of the nickel dollar see page 114.

Designers and Engravers:
Obv.:   Arnold Machin, Patrick Brindley
Rev.:   Paul Pederson, Patrick Brindley
Composition: 50% Ag, 50% Cu
Silver content: 11.65 g, 0.375 tr oz
Weight: 23.3 g   **Thickness:** 2.95 mm
Diameter: 36.07 mm   **Die Axis:** ↑↑
Edge: Reeded   **Finish:** Specimen
Case: Black leatherette clam style case, Coat of Arms, maroon and black plastic insert, encapsulated coin

DATE	DESCRIPTION	QUANTITY SOLD	ISSUE PRICE	FINISH	SP-66	SP-67
1974 (1874-)	Winnipeg Centennial	628,183	3.50	Specimen	18.	20.

ONE DOLLAR, CALGARY CENTENNIAL, 1975.

For the centenary of the founding of Calgary, Alberta, the reverse design of the 1975 silver dollar bears a special reverse showing a cowboy atop a bucking bronco. Oil wells and the modern city skyline appear in the background.

Designers and Engravers:
Obv.:   Arnold Machin, Patrick Brindley
Rev.:   D. D. Paterson, Patrick Brindley
Composition: 50% Ag, 50% Cu
Silver content: 11.65 g, 0.375 tr oz
Weight: 23.3 g   **Thickness:** 2.95 mm
Diameter: 36.07 mm   **Die Axis:** ↑↑, ↑↓
Edge: Reeded   **Finish:** Specimen
Case: Black leatherette clam style case, Coat of Arms maroon and black plastic insert, encapsulated coin

DATE	DESCRIPTION	QUANTITY SOLD	ISSUE PRICE	FINISH	SP-66	SP-67
1975 (1875-)	Calgary Centennial, ↑↑, Medal Axis	833,095	3.50	Specimen	18.	20.
1975 (1875-)	Calgary Centennial, ↑↓, Coinage Axis	Included	3.50	Specimen	Only One	Known

ONE DOLLAR, LIBRARY OF PARLIAMENT, 1976.

The reverse of the 1976 silver dollar commemorates the 100th anniversary of the completion of the Library of Parliament. This attractive building was the only part of the original centre block of the Parliament Buildings that was saved during the disastrous fire of 1916. It is still in use and is a popular tourist attraction in Ottawa.

Designers and Engravers:
Obv.:   Arnold Machin, Patrick Brindley
Rev.:   Walter Ott
Composition: 50% Ag, 50% Cu
Silver content: 11.65 g, 0.375 tr oz
Weight: 23.3 g   **Thickness:** 2.95 mm
Diameter: 36.07 mm   **Die Axis:** ↑↑
Edge: Reeded   **Finish:** Specimen
Case A: Black leatherette clam style case, Coat of Arms, maroon and black insert, encapsulated coin
Case B: Blue leatherette clam style case, Coat of Arms, light blue insert with purple satin cloth printed "Library of Parliament - Bibliothèque du Parlément 1876-1976"

DATE	DESCRIPTION	QUANTITY SOLD	ISSUE PRICE	FINISH	SP-66	SP-67
1976 (1876-)	Library of Parliament, Case A	483,722	4.00	Specimen	18.	20.
1976 (1876-)	Library of Parliament, Case B	Included	4.00	Specimen	20.	25.

ONE DOLLAR, SILVER JUBILEE ELIZABETH II, 1977.

During 1977 Queen Elizabeth II celebrated the 25th anniversary of her accession to the throne. Many countries, including Canada, recognized the event with a special commemorative coin. The design on the reverse depicts the throne of the Senate of Canada, which is used by the Queen or the Governor General for ceremonial occasions. The obverse was specifically designed for this coin and bears a special legend, and the date 1952-1977.

Designers and Engravers:
Obv.: Arnold Machin, RCM Staff
Rev.: Raymond Lee, Ago Aarand
Composition: 50% Ag, 50% Cu
Silver content: 11.65 g, 0.375 tr oz
Weight: 23.3 g   **Thickness:** 2.95 mm
Diameter: 36.07 mm   **Die Axis:** ↑↑
Edge: Reeded   **Finish:** Specimen
Case A: Black leatherette case, Coat of Arms, maroon and black plastic insert, encapsulated coin
Case B: Maroon leatherette case, Coat of Arms, maroon and black plastic insert, encapsulated coin
Case C: Maroon velveteen case, Coat of Arms, maroon velveteen insert, encapsulated coin

DATE	DESCRIPTION	QUANTITY SOLD	ISSUE PRICE	FINISH	SP-66	SP-67
1977 (1952-)	Elizabeth II Silver Jubilee, Case A	744,848	4.25	Specimen	18.	20.
1977 (1952-)	Elizabeth II Silver Jubilee, Case B	Incl. above	—	Specimen	30.	35.
1977 (1952-)	Elizabeth II Silver Jubilee, Case C	Incl. above	—	Specimen	30.	35.

ONE DOLLAR, 11TH COMMONWEALTH GAMES, EDMONTON, 1978.

The 1978 silver dollar commemorates the 11th Commonwealth Games, held in Edmonton, Alberta, August 3-12 of that year. The reverse design features the symbol of the Games in the centre, and the official symbols of the ten sports which comprise the Games along the perimeter. The obverse was modified specifically for this issue.

Designers and Engravers:
Obv.: Arnold Machin, RCM Staff
Rev.: Raymond Taylor, Victor Coté
Composition: 50% Ag, 50% Cu
Silver content: 11.65 g, 0.375 tr oz
Weight: 23.3 g   **Thickness:** 2.95 mm
Diameter: 36.07 mm   **Die Axis:** ↑↑
Edge: Reeded   **Finish:** Specimen
Case: Black leatherette square case, Coat of Arms, maroon and black plastic insert, encapsulated coin, COA

DATE	DESCRIPTION	QUANTITY SOLD	ISSUE PRICE	FINISH	SP-66	SP-67
1978	Commonwealth Games	640,000	4.50	Specimen	18.	20.

ONE DOLLAR, GRIFFON TRICENTENNIAL, 1679-1979.

The 300th anniversary of the first voyage by a commercial ship on the Great Lakes is commemorated on the reverse of the 1979 silver dollar.

Designers and Engravers:
  Obv.: Arnold Machin, Patrick Brindley
  Rev.: Walter Schluep, Terry Smith
Composition: 50% Ag, 50% Cu
Silver content: 11.65 g, 0.375 tr oz
Weight: 23.3 g **Thickness:** 2.95 mm
Diameter: 36.07 mm **Die Axis:** ↑↑
Edge: Reeded **Finish:** Specimen
Case: Black leatherette square case, maroon
    insert, encapsulated coin, COA

DATE	DESCRIPTION	QUANTITY SOLD	ISSUE PRICE	FINISH	SP-66	SP-67
1979 (1679-)	Griffon Tricentennial	688,671	5.50	Specimen	18.	20.

ONE DOLLAR, ARCTIC TERRITORIES CENTENNIAL, 1980.

The 1980 commemorative silver dollar marks the centenary of the transfer of the Arctic islands from the British Government to the Government of the Dominion of Canada.

Designers and Engravers:
  Obv.: Arnold Machin, Patrick Brindley
  Rev.: D. D. Paterson, Walter Ott
Composition: 50% Ag, 50% Cu
Silver content: 11.65 g, 0.375 tr oz
Weight: 23.3 g **Thickness:** 2.95 mm
Diameter: 36.07 mm **Die Axis:** ↑↑
Edge: Reeded **Finish:** Specimen
Case: Black leatherette square case, maroon
    insert, encapsulated coin, COA

DATE	DESCRIPTION	QUANTITY SOLD	ISSUE PRICE	FINISH	SP-66	SP-67
1980	Arctic Territories Centennial	389,564	22.00	Specimen	22.	25.

ONE DOLLAR, TRANS-CANADA RAILWAY CENTENNIAL, 1981.

The 1981 silver dollar commemorates the 100th anniversary of the approval by the Canadian government to build the Trans-Canada Railway. This is the first year of issue by the Mint of two different qualities of silver dollars.

Designers and Engravers:
  Obv.: Arnold Machin, Patrick Brindley
  Rev.: Christopher Gorey, Walter Ott
Composition: 50% Ag, 50% Cu
Silver content: 11.65 g, 0.375 tr oz
Weight: 23.3 g
Diameter: 36.07 mm **Thickness:** 2.95 mm
Edge: Reeded, **Die Axis:** ↑↑
Finish: Proof or Brilliant Uncirculated
Proof: Black leatherette square case, maroon
    insert, encapsulated coin, COA
BU: Clear plastic outer case, black plastic insert,
    silver sleeve, encapsulated coin

DATE	DESCRIPTION	QUANTITY SOLD	ISSUE PRICE	FINISH	65	66	67	68
1981	Trans-Canada Railway Centennial	353,742	18.00	Proof	—	—	22.	24.
1981	Trans-Canada Railway Centennial	148,647	14.00	BU	15.	17.	—	—

ONE DOLLAR, REGINA CENTENNIAL, 1982.

This silver dollar commemorates the centennial of the founding of Regina 1882.

Designers and Engravers:
Obv.: Arnold Machin, RCM Staff
Rev.: Huntley Brown, Walter Ott
Composition: 50% Ag, 50% Cu
Silver content: 11.65 g, 0.375 tr oz
Weight: 23.3 g
Diameter: 36.07 mm   **Thickness:** 2.95 mm
Edge: Reeded   **Die Axis:** ↑↑
Finish: Proof or Brilliant Uncirculated
Proof: Black leatherette square case, maroon insert, encapsulated coin, COA
BU: Clear plastic outer case, black plastic insert, silver sleeve, encapsulated coin

DATE	DESCRIPTION	QUANTITY SOLD	ISSUE PRICE	FINISH	65	66	67	68
1982 (1882-)	Regina Centennial	577,959	15.25	Proof	—	—	18.	20.
1982 (1882-)	Regina Centennial	144,989	10.95	BU	15.	17.	—	—

ONE DOLLAR, WORLD UNIVERSITY GAMES, 1983.

The coin commemorates the World University Games held in Edmonton, Alberta, during July of that year.

Designers and Engravers:
Obv.: Arnold Machin, Patrick Brindley
Rev.: Carola Tietz, Walter Ott
Composition: 50% Ag, 50% Cu
Silver content: 11.65 g, 0.375 tr oz
Weight: 23.3 g
Diameter: 36.07 mm   **Thickness:** 2.95 mm
Edge: Reeded   **Die Axis:** ↑↑
Finish: Proof or Brilliant Uncirculated
Proof: Black leatherette square case, maroon insert, encapsulated coin, COA
BU: Clear plastic outer case, black plastic insert, silver sleeve, encapsulated coin

DATE	DESCRIPTION	QUANTITY SOLD	ISSUE PRICE	FINISH	65	66	67	68
1983	World University Games	340,068	16.15	Proof	—	—	18.	20.
1983	World University Games	159,450	10.95	BU	15.	17.	—	—

ONE DOLLAR, TORONTO SESQUICENTENNIAL, 1984.

The 1984 silver dollar commemorates the 150th anniversary of the incorporation of the City of Toronto in 1834.

Designers and Engravers:
Obv.: Arnold Machin, Patrick Brindley
Rev.: D. J. Craig, Walter Ott
Composition: 50% Ag, 50% Cu
Silver content: 11.65 g, 0.375 tr oz
Weight: 23.3 g
Diameter: 36.07 mm   **Thickness:** 2.95 mm
Edge: Reeded   **Die Axis:** ↑↑
Finish: Proof or Brilliant Uncirculated
Proof: Black leatherette square case, maroon insert, encapsulated coin, COA
BU: Clear plastic outer case, black plastic insert, silver sleeve, encapsulated coin

DATE	DESCRIPTION	QUANTITY SOLD	ISSUE PRICE	FINISH	65	66	67	68
1984 (1834-)	Toronto Sesquicentennial	571,563	17.50	Proof	—	—	18.	20.
1984 (1834-)	Toronto Sesquicentennial	133,563	11.40	BU	15.	17.	—	—

ONE DOLLAR, NATIONAL PARKS CENTENNIAL, 1985.

The 1985 silver dollar commemorates the 100th anniversary of an important part of Canada's heritage, the National Parks.

Designers and Engravers:
Obv.: Arnold Machin, Patrick Brindley
Rev.: Karel Rohlicek, Walter Ott
Composition: 50% Ag, 50% Cu
Silver content: 11.65 g, 0.375 tr oz
Weight: 23.3 g
Diameter: 36.07 mm **Thickness:** 2.95 mm
Edge: Reeded **Die Axis:** ↑↑
Finish: Proof or Brilliant Uncirculated
Proof: Black leatherette square case, maroon insert, encapsulated coin, COA
BU: Clear plastic outer case, black plastic insert, silver sleeve, encapsulated coin

DATE	DESCRIPTION	QUANTITY SOLD	ISSUE PRICE	FINISH	65	66	67	68
1985 (1885-)	National Parks Centennial	537,297	17.50	Proof	—	—	18.	20.
1985 (1885-)	National Parks Centennial	162,873	12.00	BU	15.	17.	—	—

ONE DOLLAR, VANCOUVER CENTENNIAL, 1986.

This coin commemorates the 100th anniversary of the founding of Vancouver and the arrival of the first trans-Canada train in Vancouver. Canadian Pacific Engine No. 371 was the first to arrive, in 1886.

Designers and Engravers:
Obv.: Arnold Machin, Patrick Brindley
Rev.: E. J. Morrison, Victor Coté, Walter Ott
Composition: 50% Ag, 50% Cu
Silver content: 11.65 g, 0.375 tr oz
Weight: 23.3 g
Diameter: 36.07 mm **Thickness:** 2.95 mm
Edge: Reeded **Die Axis:** ↑↑
Finish: Proof or Brilliant Uncirculated
Proof: Black leatherette square case, maroon insert, encapsulated coin, COA
BU: Clear plastic outer case, black plastic insert, silver sleeve, encapsulated coin

DATE	DESCRIPTION	QUANTITY SOLD	ISSUE PRICE	FINISH	65	66	67	68
1986 (1886-)	Vancouver Centennial	496,418	18.00	Proof	—	—	18.	20.
1986 (1886-)	Vancouver Centennial	124,574	12.25	BU	15.	17.	—	—

ONE DOLLAR, JOHN DAVIS, 1987.

This coin commemorates the 400th anniversary of John Davis' historic expedition in search of the North West Passage.

Designers and Engravers:
Obv.: Arnold Machin, Patrick Brindley
Rev.: Christopher Gorey, Victor Coté
Composition: 50% Ag, 50% Cu
Silver content: 11.65 g, 0.375 tr oz
Weight: 23.3 g
Diameter: 36.07 mm **Thickness:** 2.95 mm
Edge: Reeded **Die Axis:** ↑↑
Finish: Proof or Brilliant Uncirculated
Proof: Black leatherette square case, maroon insert, encapsulated coin, COA
BU: Clear plastic outer case, black plastic insert, silver sleeve, encapsulated coin

DATE	DESCRIPTION	QUANTITY SOLD	ISSUE PRICE	FINISH	65	66	67	68
1987 (1587-)	John Davis	405,688	19.00	Proof	—	—	20.	22.
1987 (1587-)	John Davis	118,722	14.00	BU	15.	17.	—	—

ONE DOLLAR, SAINT-MAURICE IRONWORKS, 1988.
This coin commemorates the 250th anniversary of the Saint-Maurice Ironworks, Canada's first heavy industry.

Designers and Engravers:
Obv.: Arnold Machin, Patrick Brindley
Rev.: R. R. Carmichael, Sheldon Beveridge
Composition: 50% Ag, 50% Cu
Silver content: 11.65 g, 0.375 tr oz
Weight: 23.3 g
Diameter: 36.07 mm   **Thickness:** 2.95 mm
Edge: Reeded   **Die Axis:** ↑↑
Finish: Proof or Brilliant Uncirculated
Proof: Black leatherette square case, maroon insert, encapsulated coin, COA
BU: Clear plastic outer case, black plastic insert, silver sleeve, encapsulated coin

DATE	DESCRIPTION	QUANTITY SOLD	ISSUE PRICE	FINISH	65	66	67	68
1988	Saint-Maurice Ironworks	259,230	20.00	Proof	—	—	20.	22.
1988	Saint-Maurice Ironworks	106,702	15.00	BU	15.	17.	—	—

ONE DOLLAR, MACKENZIE RIVER BICENTENNIAL, 1989.
The bicentennial of the first full length voyage of the Mackenzie River by Alexander Mackenzie and his European crew, all the way to the Arctic Ocean, is commemorated on the 1989 silver dollar.

Designers and Engravers:
Obv.: Arnold Machin, Patrick Brindley
Rev.: John Mardon, Sheldon Beveridge
Composition: 50% Ag, 50% Cu
Silver content: 11.65 g, 0.375 tr oz
Weight: 23.3 g
Diameter: 36.07 mm   **Thickness:** 2.95 mm
Edge: Reeded   **Die Axis:** ↑↑
Finish: Proof or Brilliant Uncirculated
Proof: Black leatherette square case, maroon insert, encapsulated coin, COA
BU: Clear plastic outer case, black plastic insert, silver sleeve, encapsulated coin

DATE	DESCRIPTION	QUANTITY SOLD	ISSUE PRICE	FINISH	65	66	67	68
1989	Mackenzie River Bicentennial	272,319	21.75	Proof	—	—	25.	28.
1989	Mackenzie River Bicentennial	110,650	16.25	BU	15.	17.	—	—

ONE DOLLAR, HENRY KELSEY TRICENTENNIAL, 1990.
The 300th anniversary of Henry Kelsey's ventures into the Canadian West is commemorated on the 1990 silver dollar.

Designers and Engravers:
Obv.: Dora de Pédery-Hunt
Rev.: D. J. Craig, Ago Aarand
Composition: 50% Ag, 50% Cu
Silver content: 11.65 g, 0.375 tr oz
Weight: 23.3 g
Diameter: 36.07 mm   **Thickness:** 2.95 mm
Edge: Reeded   **Die Axis:** ↑↑
Finish: Proof or Brilliant Uncirculated
Proof: Black leatherette square case, maroon insert, encapsulated coin, COA
BU: Clear plastic outer case, black plastic insert, silver sleeve, encapsulated coin

DATE	DESCRIPTION	QUANTITY SOLD	ISSUE PRICE	FINISH	65	66	67	68
1990 (1690-)	Henry Kelsey Tricentennial	222,983	22.95	Proof	—	—	25.	28.
1990 (1690-)	Henry Kelsey Tricentennial	85,763	16.75	BU	12.	14.	—	—

ONE DOLLAR, 175TH ANNIVERSARY OF THE FRONTENAC, 1991.

The 1991 silver dollar commemorates the 175th anniversary of the first steamship to sail on the Great Lakes. Built by a partnership of Kingston merchants in 1816, the Frontenac established a regular passenger and freight route between Prescott and Burlington by 1817, thus becoming the first Canadian steamship to operate on Lake Ontario.

Designers and Engravers:
Obv.:   Dora de Pédery-Hunt
Rev.:   D. J. Craig, Sheldon Beveridge
Composition: 50% Ag, 50% Cu
Silver content: 11.65 g, 0.375 tr oz
Weight: 23.3 g
Diameter: 36.07 mm   **Thickness:** 2.95 mm
Edge: Reeded   **Die Axis:** ↑↑
Finish: Proof or Brilliant Uncirculated
Proof: Black leatherette square case, maroon insert, encapsulated coin, COA
BU: Clear plastic outer case, black plastic insert, silver sleeve, encapsulated coin

DATE	DESCRIPTION	QUANTITY SOLD	ISSUE PRICE	FINISH	65	66	67	68
1991 (1816-)	175th Anniversary of the Frontenac	222,892	22.95	Proof	—	—	28.	30.
1991 (1816-)	175th Anniversary of the Frontenac	82,642	16.75	BU	15.	17.	—	—

ONE DOLLAR, KINGSTON TO YORK STAGECOACH, 1992.

The coin commemorates the 175th anniversary of the first stage coach service between Kingston and York in January 1817. Samuel Purdy was only able to maintain regular service during the winter months, hence the sleigh with runners. This is the first issue of a dollar coin in sterling silver since the pattern dollar was struck in London by the Royal Mint in 1911.

Designers and Engravers:
Obv.:   Dora de Pédery-Hunt
Rev.:   Karsten Smith, Susan Taylor
Composition: 92.5 Ag, 7.5% Cu
Silver content: 23.29 g, 0.75 tr oz
Weight: 25.175 g
Diameter: 36.07 mm   **Thickness:** 2.95 mm
Edge: Reeded   **Die Axis:** ↑↑
Finish: Proof or Brilliant Uncirculated
Proof: Black leatherette square case, maroon insert, encapsulated coin, COA
BU: Clear plastic outer case, black plastic insert, silver sleeve, encapsulated coin

DATE	DESCRIPTION	QUANTITY SOLD	ISSUE PRICE	FINISH	65	66	67	68
1992	Kingston to York Stagecoach	187,612	23.95	Proof	—	—	28.	30.
1992	Kingston to York Stagecoach	78,160	17.50	BU	22.	24.	—	—

ONE DOLLAR, 100TH ANNIVERSARY OF THE STANLEY CUP, 1893-1993.

The 1993 silver dollar commemorates the 100th anniversary of the Stanley Cup, first presented during the 1892-1893 season to the Montreal Amateur Athletic Association team by Lord Stanley.

Designers and Engravers:
Obv.: Dora de Pédery-Hunt
Rev.: Stewart Sherwood, Sheldon Beveridge
Composition: 92.5 Ag, 7.5% Cu
Silver content: 23.29 g, 0.75 tr oz
Weight: 25.175 g
Diameter: 36.07 mm **Thickness:** 2.95 mm
Edge: Reeded **Die Axis:** ↑↑
Finish: Proof or Brilliant Uncirculated
Proof: Black leatherette square case, maroon insert, encapsulated coin, COA
BU: Clear plastic outer case, black plastic insert, silver sleeve, encapsulated coin

DATE	DESCRIPTION	QUANTITY SOLD	ISSUE PRICE	FINISH	65	66	67	68
1993 (1893-)	100th Anniv. of the Stanley Cup	294,314	23.95	Proof	—	—	38.	40.
1993 (1893-)	100th Anniv. of the Stanley Cup	88,150	17.50	BU	26.	28.	—	—

ONE DOLLAR, R.C.M.P. NORTHERN DOG TEAM PATROL, 1994.

The 1994 silver dollar commemorates the 25th anniversary of the last RCMP Northern Dog Team Patrol.

Designers and Engravers:
Obv.: Dora de Pédery-Hunt
Rev.: Ian Sparkes, Ago Aarand
Composition: 92.5 Ag, 7.5% Cu
Silver content: 23.29 g, 0.75 tr oz
Weight: 25.175 g
Diameter: 36.07 mm **Thickness:** 2.95 mm
Edge: Reeded **Die Axis:** ↑↑
Finish: Proof or Brilliant Uncirculated
Proof: Black leatherette square case, maroon insert, encapsulated coin, COA
BU: Clear plastic outer case, black plastic insert, silver sleeve, encapsulated coin

DATE	DESCRIPTION	QUANTITY SOLD	ISSUE PRICE	FINISH	65	66	67	68
1994 (1969-)	R.C.M.P. Northern Dog Team Patrol	178,485	24.50	Proof	—	—	38.	40.
1994 (1969-)	R.C.M.P. Northern Dog Team Patrol	65,295	17.95	BU	26.	28.	—	—

ONE DOLLAR, 325TH ANNIVERSARY OF THE HUDSON'S BAY COMPANY, 1995.

From 1670 to the current day the history of the Hudson's Bay Company has been intertwined with that of Canada.

Designers and Engravers:
Obv.: Dora de Pédery-Hunt
Rev.: Vincent McIndoe, Susan Taylor
Composition: 92.5 Ag, 7.5% Cu
Silver content: 23.29 g, 0.75 tr oz
Weight: 25.175 g
Diameter: 36.07 mm **Thickness:** 2.95 mm
Edge: Reeded **Die Axis:** ↑↑
Finish: Proof or Brilliant Uncirculated
Proof: Black leatherette square case, maroon insert, encapsulated coin, COA
BU: Clear plastic outer case, black plastic insert, silver sleeve, encapsulated coin

DATE	DESCRIPTION	QUANTITY SOLD	ISSUE PRICE	FINISH	65	66	67	68
1995	325th Anniv. Hudson's Bay Co.	166,259	24.50	Proof	—	—	34.	36.
1995	325th Anniv. Hudson's Bay Co.	61,819	17.95	BU	26.	28.	—	—

ONE DOLLAR, 200TH ANNIVERSARY JOHN MCINTOSH, 1996.

John McIntosh arrived in Canada in 1796 and settled in Ontario. The 1996 silver dollar pays tribute to the originator of Canada's most important commercial apple.

Designers and Engravers:
Obv.:   Dora de Pédery-Hunt
Rev.:   Roger Hill, Sheldon Beveridge
Composition: 92.5 Ag, 7.5% Cu
Silver content: 23.29 g, 0.75 tr oz
Weight: 25.175 g
Diameter: 36.07 mm   **Thickness:** 2.95 mm
Edge: Reeded   **Die Axis:** ↑↑
Finish: Proof or Brilliant Uncirculated
Proof: Black leatherette square case, maroon insert, encapsulated coin, COA
BU: Clear plastic outer case, black plastic insert, silver sleeve, encapsulated coin

DATE	DESCRIPTION	QUANTITY SOLD	ISSUE PRICE	FINISH	65	66	67	68
1996 (1796-)	200th Anniversary John McIntosh	133,779	29.95	Proof	—	—	38.	40.
1996 (1796-)	200th Anniversary John McIntosh	58,834	19.95	BU	20.	22.	—	—

ONE DOLLAR, 25TH ANNIVERSARY 1972 CANADA/RUSSIA HOCKEY SERIES, 1997.

Paul Henderson's winning goal won the 1972 series for Canada. In 1997 three gift packages were offered: (1) A sterling silver pin/uncirculated dollar, (2) A numbered colour reproduction print/uncirculated dollar, (3) Phone card/stamp set/ uncirculated dollar.

Designers and Engravers:
Obv.:   Dora de Pédery-Hunt
Rev.:   Walter Burden, Stan Witten
Composition: 92.5 Ag, 7.5% Cu
Silver content: 23.29 g, 0.75 tr oz
Weight: 25.175 g
Diameter: 36.07 mm   **Thickness:** 2.95 mm
Edge: Reeded   **Die Axis:** ↑↑
Finish: Proof or Brilliant Uncirculated
Proof: Black leatherette square case, maroon insert, encapsulated coin, COA
BU: Clear plastic outer case, black plastic insert, silver sleeve, encapsulated coin

DATE	DESCRIPTION	QUANTITY SOLD	ISSUE PRICE	FINISH	65	66	67	68
1997 (1972-)	25th Anniv. Canada/Russia Hockey Series	184,965	29.95	Proof	—	—	36.	38.
1997 (1972-)	25th Anniv. Canada/Russia Hockey Series	155,252	19.95	BU	26.	28.	—	—

ONE DOLLAR, 10TH ANNIVERSARY OF THE ONE DOLLAR LOON, 1997.

The sterling silver Flying Loon was issued singly. All were sold by the Numismatic Department of the Royal Canadian Mint as limited editions during 1997.

Designers and Engravers:
Obv.:   Dora de Pédery-Hunt
Rev.:   Jean-Luc Grondin, Sheldon Beveridge
Composition: 92.5 Ag, 7.5% Cu
Silver content: 23.29 g, 0.75 tr oz
Weight: 25.175 g
Diameter: 36.07 mm   **Thickness:** 2.95 mm
Edge: Reeded   **Die Axis:** ↑↑
Finish: Proof
Case: Black leatherette clam case, maroon flocked insert, encapsulated coin, COA

DATE	DESCRIPTION	QUANTITY SOLD	ISSUE PRICE	FINISH	PR-67	PR-68
1997 (1987-)	10th Anniv. of the One Dollar Loon	24,995	49.95	Proof	100.	110.

ONE DOLLAR, 125TH ANNIVERSARY ROYAL CANADIAN MOUNTED POLICE, 1998.

The reverse design for the 1998 silver dollar by Adeline Halvorson features a mounted police officer in a 1900s uniform.

Designers and Engravers:
  Obv.: Dora de Pédery-Hunt
  Rev.: Adeline Halvorson, Sheldon Beveridge
Composition: 92.5 Ag, 7.5% Cu
Silver content: 23.29 g, 0.75 tr oz
Weight: 25.175 g
Diameter: 36.07 mm   **Thickness:** 2.95 mm
Edge: Reeded   **Die Axis:** ↑↑
Finish: Proof or Brilliant Uncirculated
Proof: Dark green clam display case, green
         insert, encapsulated coin, COA
BU: Multicoloured plastic slide case,
         encapsulated coin

DATE	DESCRIPTION	QUANTITY SOLD	ISSUE PRICE	FINISH	65	66	67	68
1998 (1873-)	125th Anniversary R.C.M.P.	130,795	29.95	Proof	—	—	36.	38.
1998 (1873-)	125th Anniversary R.C.M.P.	81,376	19.95	BU	26.	28.	—	—

ONE DOLLAR, 225TH ANNIVERSARY OF THE VOYAGE OF JUAN PEREZ, 1774-1999.

In 1774 Juan Perez led an expedition which made the first documented sighting of the Queen Charlotte Islands. The reverse design of this coin illustrates the 225-ton frigate *The Santiago*, one of the Queen Charlotte Islands, and Haida canoes approaching the ship.

Designers and Engravers:
  Obv.: Dora de Pédery-Hunt
  Rev.: D. J. Craig, Stan Witten
Composition: 92.5 Ag, 7.5% Cu
Silver content: 23.29 g, 0.75 tr oz
Weight: 25.175 g
Diameter: 36.07 mm   **Thickness:** 2.95 mm
Edge: Reeded   **Die Axis:** ↑↑
Finish: Proof or Brilliant Uncirculated
Proof: Dark green clam display case, green
         flocked insert, encapsulated coin, COA
BU: Multicoloured plastic slide case,
         encapsulated coin

DATE	DESCRIPTION	QUANTITY SOLD	ISSUE PRICE	FINISH	65	66	67	68
1999 (1774-)	225th Anniv. Voyage Juan Perez	126,435	29.95	Proof	—	—	38.	40.
1999 (1774-)	225th Anniv. Voyage Juan Perez	67,655	19.95	BU	28.	30.	—	—

ONE DOLLAR, INTERNATIONAL YEAR OF OLDER PERSONS, 1999.

In October 1999 the United Nations declared 1999 the International Year of Older Persons. The 1999 silver dollar supports Canada's concept of "A Society for All Ages."

Designers and Engravers:
  Obv.: Dora de Pédery-Hunt
  Rev.: S. Armstrong-Hodgson, William Woodruff
Composition: 92.5 Ag, 7.5% Cu
Silver content: 23.29 g, 0.75 tr oz
Weight: 25.175 g
Diameter: 36.07 mm   **Thickness:** 2.95 mm
Edge: Reeded   **Die Axis:** ↑↑
Finish: Proof
Case: Multicoloured case, black insert,
         encapsulated coin, COA

DATE	DESCRIPTION	QUANTITY SOLD	ISSUE PRICE	FINISH	PR-67	PR-68
1999	Int'l Year of Older Persons	24, 976	49.95	Proof	50.	52.

ONE DOLLAR, VOYAGE OF DISCOVERY, 2000.

Poised on the launch pad to the next millennium Canada's voyage of discovery promises to be one of energy, ability and achievement.

Designers and Engravers:
Obv.:   Dora de Pédery-Hunt
Rev.:   D. F. Warkentin, Cosme Saffioti
Composition: 92.5 Ag, 7.5% Cu
Silver content: 23.29 g, 0.75 tr oz
Weight: 25.175 g
Diameter: 36.07 mm   **Thickness:** 2.95 mm
Edge: Reeded   **Die Axis:** ↑↑
Finish: Proof or Brilliant Uncirculated
Proof: Dark green clam case, green insert, encapsulated coin, COA
BU: Multicoloured plastic slide case, encapsulated coin

DATE	DESCRIPTION	QUANTITY SOLD	ISSUE PRICE	FINISH	65	66	67	68
2000	Voyage of Discovery	121,575	29.95	Proof	—	—	36.	38.
2000	Voyage of Discovery	62,975	19.95	BU	26.	28.	—	—

ONE DOLLAR, 50TH ANNIVERSARY OF THE NATIONAL BALLET OF CANADA, 1951-2001.

The National Ballet of Canada is Canada's premier dance company, which ranks as one of the world's top international companies. Founded in 1951 by English dancer Celia Franca, the classical company is the only Canadian company to present a full range of traditional full evening ballet classics.

Designers and Engravers:
Obv.:   Dora de Pédery-Hunt
Rev.:   Scott McKowen, Susan Taylor
Composition: 92.5 Ag, 7.5% Cu
Silver content: 23.29 g, 0.75 tr oz
Weight: 25.175 g
Diameter: 36.07 mm   **Thickness:** 2.95 mm
Edge: Reeded   **Die Axis:** ↑↑
Finish: Proof or Brilliant Uncirculated
Proof: Dark green clam case, green insert, encapsulated coin, COA
BU: Multicoloured plastic slide case, encapsulated coin

DATE	DESCRIPTION	QUANTITY SOLD	ISSUE PRICE	FINISH	65	66	67	68
2001 (1951-)	50th Anniv. National Ballet of Canada	89,390	30.95	Proof	—	—	36.	38.
2001 (1951-)	50th Anniv. National Ballet of Canada	53,668	20.95	BU	26.	38.	—	—

ONE DOLLAR, 90TH ANNIVERSARY OF THE STRIKING OF CANADA'S 1911 SILVER DOLLAR, 2001.

The 1911 Canadian silver dollar is the most valuable Canadian coin. Only three examples exist, two sterling silver trial strikes and one lead trial strike. The 2001 dollar commemorates its ninetieth anniversary.

Designers and Engravers:
Obv.:   Dora de Pédery-Hunt
Rev.:   RCM Staff, Cosme Saffioti
Composition: 92.5 Ag, 7.5% Cu
Silver content: 23.29 g, 0.75 tr oz
Weight: 25.175 g
Diameter: 36.07 mm   **Thickness:** 2.95 mm
Edge: Reeded   **Die Axis:** ↑↑
Finish: Proof
Case: Dark green clam case, green insert, encapsulated coin, COA

DATE	DESCRIPTION	QUANTITY SOLD	ISSUE PRICE	FINISH	PR-67	PR-68
2001 (1911-)	90th Anniv. Canada's 1911 Silver Dollar	24,996	49.95	Proof	75.	80.

ONE DOLLAR, 50TH ANNIVERSARY QUEEN ELIZABETH II'S ACCESSION TO THE THRONE, 2002.

For the first time a silver dollar carries a double date (1952-2002) on the obverse.

Designers and Engravers:
Obv.: Dora de Pédery-Hunt
Rev.: RCM Staff, Susan Taylor
Composition: 92.5 Ag, 7.5% Cu
Silver content: 23.29 g, 0.75 tr oz
Weight: 25.175 g
Diameter: 36.07 mm   **Thickness:** 2.95 mm
Edge: Reeded   **Die Axis:** ↑↑
Finish: Proof or Brilliant Uncirculated
Proof: Dark green clam case, green insert, encapsulated coin, COA
BU: Multicoloured plastic slide case, encapsulated coin

DATE	DESCRIPTION	QUANTITY SOLD	ISSUE PRICE	FINISH	65	66	67	68
2002 (1952-)	50th Anniv. Elizabeth II's Accession, Silver	29,688	33.95	Proof	—	—	38.	40.
2002 (1952-)	50th Anniv. Elizabeth II's Accession, Gold-plated	65,315	N.I.I.	Proof	—	—	60.	65.
2002 (1952-)	50th Anniv. Elizabeth II's Accession, Silver	65,410	24.95	BU	26.	28.	—	—

ONE DOLLAR, QUEEN ELIZABETH THE QUEEN MOTHER, 2002.

Available only in proof finish this silver dollar honours the life of Queen Elizabeth, the Queen Mother.

Designers and Engravers:
Obv.: Dora de Pédery-Hunt
Rev.: RCM Staff, Susan Taylor
Composition: 92.5 Ag, 7.5% Cu
Silver content: 23.29 g, 0.75 tr oz
Weight: 25.175 g
Diameter: 36.07 mm   **Thickness:** 2.95 mm
Edge: Reeded   **Die Axis:** ↑↑
Finish: Proof
Case: Dark green clam case, green insert, encapsulated coin, COA

DATE	DESCRIPTION	QUANTITY SOLD	ISSUE PRICE	FINISH	PR-67	PR-68
2002 (1900-)	Queen Elizabeth, the Queen Mother	9,994	49.95	Proof	235.	250.

ONE DOLLAR, 100TH ANNIVERSARY OF THE COBALT DISCOVERY, 1903-2003.

This coin marks 100 years since Fred LaRose, a blacksmith, threw his hammer at a fox, of course missing the fox, but striking a rock revealing a gleaming vein of silver. This is the first issue of a pure silver (.9999 fine) dollar by the Royal Canadian Mint.

Designers and Engravers:
Obv.: Dora de Pédery-Hunt
Rev.: John Mardon, William Woodruff
Composition: 99.99% Ag
Silver content: 25.172 g, 0.809 tr oz
Weight: 25.175 g
Diameter: 36.07 mm   **Thickness:** 3.02 mm
Edge: Reeded   **Die Axis:** ↑↑
Finish: Proof or Brilliant Uncirculated
Proof: Dark green clam case, green insert, encapsulated coin, COA
BU: Multicoloured plastic slide case, encapsulated coin

DATE	DESCRIPTION	QUANTITY SOLD	ISSUE PRICE	FINISH	65	66	67	68
2003 (1903-)	100th Anniv. Cobalt Silver Discovery	88,536	36.95	Proof	—	—	40.	42.
2003 (1903-)	100th Anniv. Cobalt Silver Discovery	51,130	28.95	BU	26.	28.	—	—

GOLD ONE DOLLAR, 50TH ANNIVERSARY QUEEN ELIZABETH II'S ACCESSION TO THE THRONE, 2003.

This undated gold issue is based on the 2002 reverse Accession design, and the new uncrowned obverse design for 2003. This gold dollar was sold on eBay, September 25th, 2003, with 100% of the proceeds being donated to charities.

Designers and Engravers:
Obv.: Dora de Pédery-Hunt
Rev.: RCM Staff, Susan Taylor
Composition: 99.99% Ag
Gold content: 25.172 g, 0.809 tr oz
Weight: 25.175 g
Diameter: 36.07 mm
Thickness: 2.66 mm
Edge: Reeded
Die Axis: ↑↑
Finish: Proof
Case: Not known

DATE	DESCRIPTION	QUANTITY SOLD	ISSUE PRICE	FINISH	65	66	67	68
2003	50th Anniv. Accession/Coronation of Elizabeth II, Gold	One	—	Proof		UNIQUE		

ONE DOLLAR, 50TH ANNIVERSARY OF THE CORONATION OF QUEEN ELIZABETH II, 1953-2003.

This silver dollar is a reissue of the dollar first struck during the coronation year 1953. The design is differentiated by the double dates 1953-2003 on the obverse, as opposed to the single date on the reverse of the 1953 dollar.

Designers and Engravers:
Obv.: Mary Gillick, Thomas Shingles
Rev.: Emanuel Hahn
Composition: 99.99% Ag
Silver content: 25.172 g, 0.809 tr oz
Weight: 25.175 g
Diameter: 36.07 mm
Thickness: 3.02 mm
Edge: Reeded
Die Axis: ↑↑
Finish: Proof
Case: See Special Issue Proof Sets, page 384

DATE	DESCRIPTION	QUANTITY SOLD	ISSUE PRICE	FINISH	PR-67	PR-68
2003 (1953-)	50th Anniv. Coronation Elizabeth II	21,537	N.I.I.	Proof	80.	85.

ONE DOLLAR, UNCROWNED PORTRAIT OF QUEEN ELIZABETH II, 2003.

This was a special edition dollar with the new obverse design for 2003, and the reverse honouring the "Voyageurs" design of Canada's first circulating silver dollar. A fine gold (.9999) example of this design was struck by the Royal Canadian Mint and sold on eBay with the proceeds going to charities.

Designers and Engravers:
Obv.: Susanna Blunt, Susan Taylor
Rev.: Emanuel Hahn, RCM Staff
Composition: Gold: 99.99% Au
Silver: 99.99% Ag
Bullion content: Gold: 25.172 g, 0.801 tr oz
Silver: 25.172 g, 0.801 tr oz
Weight: Gold: 25.175 g, Silver: 25.175 g
Diameter: 36.07 mm
Thickness: Gold: 2.66 mm; Silver: 3.02 mm
Edge: Reeded   **Die Axis:** ↑↑
Finish: Proof

Case: Gold: Unknown
Silver: Black leatherette clam case, maroon insert, encapsulated coin, COA

DATE	DESCRIPTION	QUANTITY SOLD	ISSUE PRICE	FINISH	PR-67	PR-68
2003	Uncrowned Portrait Queen Elizabeth II, Silver	29,586	51.95	Proof	55.	60.
2003	Uncrowned Portrait Queen Elizabeth II, Gold	One	—	Proof		UNIQUE

ONE DOLLAR, 400TH ANNIVERSARY OF THE FIRST FRENCH SETTLEMENT IN NORTH AMERICA, 1604-2004.
In 1604 a tiny island, in what was to be called the St. Croix River, became the first French settlement in North America. A 2004 Ile Sainte-Croix stamp and coin set was issued containing this silver dollar counterstamped with a fleur-de-lis privy mark.

| Proof | BU, Privy Mark Reverse |

Designers:
  Obv.: Susanna Blunt
  Rev.: R. R. Carmichael
Composition: 99.99% Ag
Silver content: 25.172 g, 0.809 tr oz
Weight: 25.175 g
Diameter: 36.07 mm
Edge: Reeded
Finish: Proof or Brilliant Uncirculated

Engravers:
  Obv.: Susan Taylor
  Rev.: Stan Witten

Thickness: 3.02 mm
Die Axis: ↑↑

Case of Issue A: Dark green leatherette clam case, green insert, encapsulated coin, COA
            B: Multicoloured plastic slide case, encapsulated coin
            C: Privy Mark Dollar, see Derivatives, page 132

DATE	DESCRIPTION	QUANTITY SOLD	ISSUE PRICE	FINISH	65	66	67	68
2004 (1604-)	First French Settlement	106,974	36.95	Proof	—	—	40.	42.
2004 (1604-)	First French Settlement	42,582	28.95	BU	25.	27.	—	—
2004 (1604-)	First French Settlement, Privy Mark	8,315	N.I.I.	BU	85.	95.	—	—

ONE DOLLAR, "THE POPPY" ARMISTICE DAY COMMEMORATIVE, 2004.
Throughout the world the poppy has become one of the most powerful symbols that honours the men and women who gave their lives for freedom. For the circulation "Poppy" twenty-five-cent coin, see *Canadian Coins, Volume One, Numismatic Issues*.

Designers and Engravers:
    Obv.:   Susanna Blunt, Susan Taylor
    Rev.:   Cosme Saffioti, Stan Witten
Composition: 99.99% Ag
Silver content: 25.172 g, 0.801 tr oz
Weight: 25.175 g
Diameter: 36.07 mm   **Thickness:** 2.95 mm
Edge: Reeded   **Die Axis:** ↑↑
Finish: Proof
Case: Maroon leatherette clam style case, black
          flock insert, encapsulated coin, COA

DATE	DESCRIPTION	QUANTITY SOLD	ISSUE PRICE	FINISH	PR-67	PR-68
2004	"The Poppy" Armistice Day	24,527	49.95	Proof	60.	65.

ONE DOLLAR, 40TH ANNIVERSARY OF CANADA'S NATIONAL FLAG, 1965-2005.

The Canadian flag, which is composed of the symbolic maple leaf and the national colours first proclaimed in 1921, was raised for the first time February 15th, 1965, on Parliament Hill

The 2005 brilliant uncirculated silver dollar was also issued in a gift set which included and interactive CD Rom (see Derivatives, page 132).

	Proof	Proof, Selectively gold plated	Proof, Red enamel

Designers:
  Obv.: Susanna Blunt
  Rev.: William Woodruff
Composition: 99.99% Ag
Silver content: 25.172 g, 0.801 tr oz
Weight: 25.175 g
Diameter: 36.07 mm
Finish: **1.** Proof
          2. Proof, Selectively gold plated
          3. Proof, Red enamel
          4. Brilliant Uncirculated

Engravers:
  Obv.: Susan Taylor
  Rev.: William Woodruff

Thickness: 3.02 mm
Die Axis: ↑↑
Edge: Reeded

Case of Issue: Maroon plastic slide case, black plastic insert, encapsulated coin, COA

DATE	DESCRIPTION	SOURCE	QUANTITY SOLD	ISSUE PRICE	FINISH	65	66	67	68
2005 (1965-)	Proof	Pr. Single	95,431	34.95	Proof	—	—	45.	50.
2005 (1965-)	Proof, Selectively Gold plated	Pr. Set	63,562	N.I.I.	Proof	—	—	75.	80.
2005 (1965-)	Proof, Red enamel	Pr. Single	4,898	99.95	Proof	—	—	250.	275.
2005 (1965-)	Brilliant Uncirculated	BU Single	50,948	24.95	BU	24.	26.	—	—

ONE DOLLAR, 150TH ANNIVERSARY OF THE VICTORIA CROSS, 2006.

In 1856 Queen Victoria Instituted the Victoria Cross medal. A total of 1,351 Victoria Cross medals have been awarded with 94 being awarded to Canadians.

Proof　　　　　　　　　　Proof, Selectively gold plated

Designers:
　Obv.: Susanna Blunt
　Rev.: RCM Staff
Composition: 99.99% Ag
Silver content: 25.172 g, 0.801 tr oz
Weight: 25.175 g
Diameter: 36.07 mm
Finish: 　**1.** Proof

Engravers:
　Obv.: Susan Taylor
　Rev.: RCM Staff

Thickness: 3.02 mm
Edge: Reeded
Die Axis: ↑↑

Finish: 　**1.** Proof 　　　　**2.** Proof, Selectively gold plated 　　　**3.** Brilliant Uncirculated
Case of Issue: Maroon plastic slide case, black plastic insert, encapsulated coin, COA

DATE	DESCRIPTION	SOURCE	QUANTITY SOLD	ISSUE PRICE	FINISH	65	66	67	68
2006	Victoria Cross, Proof	Pr. Single	55,599	34.95	Proof	—	—	55.	60.
2006	Victoria Cross, Proof, Selectively gold plated	Pr. Set	53,822	N.I.I.	Proof	—	—	100.	110.
2006	Victoria Cross, Brilliant Uncirculated	BU Single	27,254	24.95	BU	40.	42.	—	—

ONE DOLLAR, MEDAL OF BRAVERY, 2006.

The Canadian Medal of Bravery was established in 1972 and is awarded by the Governor General of Canada in recognition of "Acts of Bravery in hazardous circumstances".

Proof　　　　　　　　　　Proof, Red enamel

Designers:
　Obv.: Susanna Blunt
　Rev.: Konrad Wachelko
Composition: 99.99% Ag
Silver content: 25.172 g, 0.801 tr oz
Weight: 25.175 g
Diameter: 36.07 mm
Finish: 　**1.** Proof 　　　　**2.** Proof, Red enamel

Engravers:
　Obv.: Susan Taylor
　Rev.: Konrad Wachelko

Thickness: 3.02 mm
Edge: Reeded
Die Axis: ↑↑

Case of Issue: Maroon plastic slide case, black plastic insert, encapsulated coin, COA

DATE	DESCRIPTION	SOURCE	QUANTITY SOLD	ISSUE PRICE	FINISH	PR-67	PR-68
2006	Medal of Bravery	Pr. Single	8,343	54.95	Proof	75.	80.
2006	Medal of Bravery, Red enamel	Pr. Single	4,999	99.95	Proof	160.	170.

ONE DOLLAR, THAYENDANEGEA, 2007.

Born in 1743, Thayendanegea (Joseph Brant) was a Mohawk Chief who fought along side the British during the American Revolution. Brant died in Canada, November 24th, 1807.

| Proof | Proof, Selectively gold plated | Proof, Enamelled |

Designers:
    Obv.: Susanna Blunt
    Rev.: Laurie McGaw
Composition: 92.5% Ag, 7.5% Cu
Silver content: 23.29 g, 0.749 tr oz
Weight: 25.175 g
Diameter: 36.07 mm
Finish: **1.** Proof
       2. Proof, Selectively gold plated
       3. Proof, Enamelled
       4. Brilliant Uncirculated

Engravers:
    Obv.: Susan Taylor
    Rev.: William Woodruff

Thickness: 3.02 mm
Edge: Reeded
Die Axis: ↑↑

Case of Issue: **1.** Proof, Enamelled: Maroon plastic slide case, black plastic insert, encapsulated coin, COA
               2. Proof / BU: Maroon leatherette clam style case, black flocked insert, encapsulated coin, COA

DATE	DESCRIPTION	SOURCE	QUANTITY SOLD	ISSUE PRICE	FINISH	65	66	67	68
2007	Thayendanegea, Proof	Pr. Single	32,837	42.95	Proof	—	—	50.	55.
2007	Thayendanegea, Proof, Selectively gold plated	Pr. Set	37,413	N.I.I.	Proof	—	—	85.	90.
2007	Thayendanegea, Proof, Enamelled	Pr. Single	5,181	129.95	Proof	—	—	130.	135.
2007	Thayendanegea, Brilliant Uncirculated	BU Single	16,378	34.95	BU	36.	38.	—	—

ONE DOLLAR, CELEBRATION OF THE ARTS, 2007.

This coin was issued to commemorate the 50th anniversary of the founding of the Canada Council of the Arts.

Designers and Engravers:
    Obv.: Susanna Blunt, Susan Taylor
    Rev.: Friedrich Peter, RCM Staff
Composition: 92.5% Ag, 7.5% Cu
Silver content: 23.29 g, 0.749 tr oz
Weight: 25.175 g
Diameter: 36.07 mm   **Thickness:** 2.95 mm
Edge: Reeded   **Die Axis:** ↑↑
Finish: Proof
Case: Maroon plastic slide case, black plastic insert, encapsulated coin, COA

DATE	DESCRIPTION	SOURCE	QUANTITY SOLD	ISSUE PRICE	FINISH	PR-67	PR-68
2007	Celebration of the Arts	Pr. Single	6,704	54.95	Proof	115.	125.

ONE DOLLAR, 400TH ANNIVERSARY OF QUEBEC CITY, 1608-2008.

Founded in 1608 by Samuel de Champlain, Quebec City is one of the oldest cities in North America, and the only one north of Mexico with its ramparts surrounding the Old City still intact.

Proof   Proof, Selectively gold plated

Designers:
Obv.: Susanna Blunt
Rev.: Suzanne Duranceau
Composition: 92.5% Ag, 7.5% Cu
Silver Content: 23.29 g, 0.749 tr oz
Weight: 25.175 g
Diameter: 36.07 mm
Edge: Reeded
Finish: **1.** Proof
2. Proof, Selectively gold plated
3. Brilliant Uncirculated

Engravers:
Obv.: Susan Taylor
Rev.: Susan Taylor, Cecily Mok, Konrad Wachelko

Thickness: 3.02 mm
Die Axis: ↑↑

Case of Issue: Maroon leatherette clam style case, black flocked insert, encapsulated coin, COA

DATE	DESCRIPTION	SOURCE	QUANTITY SOLD	ISSUE PRICE	FINISH	65	66	67	68
2008 (1608-)	Quebec City, Proof	Pr. Single	65,000	42.95	Proof	—	—	45.	47.
2008 (1608-)	Quebec City, Proof, Selectively gold plated	Pr. Set	38,630	N.I.I.	Proof	—	—	100.	110.
2008 (1608-)	Quebec City, Brilliant Uncirculated	BU Single	35,000	34.95	BU	32.	34.	—	—

ONE DOLLAR, CELEBRATING THE ROYAL CANADIAN MINT CENTENNIAL, 1908-2008.

The Ottawa Branch of the Royal Mint, London, struck their first coins on January 2nd, 1908. Control of the Ottawa Mint passed to Canada in 1931 and was renamed the Royal Canadian Mint.

Designers and Engravers:
Obv.: Susanna Blunt, Susan Taylor
Rev.: Jason Bouwman, José Osio
Composition: 92.5% Ag, 7.5% Cu,
Selectively gold plated
Silver content: 23.29 g, 0.749 tr oz
Weight: 25.175 g
Diameter: 36.07 mm   **Thickness:** 3.1 mm
Edge: Reeded   **Die Axis:** ↑↑
Finish: Proof
Case : Maroon leatherette clam style case, black flocked insert, encapsulated coin, COA

DATE	DESCRIPTION	SOURCE	QUANTITY SOLD	ISSUE PRICE	FINISH	PR-67	PR-68
2008 (1908-)	Royal Canadian Mint Centennial	Pr. Single	15,000	59.95	Proof	160.	175.

ONE DOLLAR, "THE POPPY" ARMISTICE, 1918-2008.

A red poppy is worn every November 11th, in memory of our war veterans.

Designers and Engravers:
Obv.:   Susanna Blunt, Susan Taylor
Rev.:   Cosme Saffioti, Stan Witten
Composition: 92.5% Ag, 7.5% Cu
Silver content: 27.75 g, 0.892 tr oz
Weight: 30.0 g
Diameter: 36.2 mm   **Thickness:** 3.3 mm
Edge: Reeded   **Die Axis:** ↑↑
Finish: Proof
Case: Maroon leatherette clam style case, black flocked insert, encapsulated coin, COA

DATE	DESCRIPTION	SOURCE	QUANTITY SOLD	ISSUE PRICE	FINISH	PR-67	PR-68
2008 (1918-)	"The Poppy" Armistice	Pr. Single	4,994	139.95	Proof	150.	160.

Note: There is slight confusion in the Royal Canadian Mint's press release in which the finish on this coin is stated as "proof" in one section and "proof-like" in another. It is listed in this table as proof as that is the finish carried on the certificate of authenticity which accompanies the coins.

ONE DOLLAR, 100TH ANNIVERSARY OF FLIGHT IN CANADA, 1909-2009.

J. A. Douglas McCurdy, a native of Baddeck, flew the Aerial Experiment Association's Silver Dart on February 23rd, 1909 over the frozen Bras d'Or Lakes, in Nova Scotia. This was the first controlled flight in Canada and the British Empire.

Brilliant Uncirculated	**Proof**	**Proof, Selectively gold plated**

Designers:
Obv.:   Susanna Blunt
Rev.:   Jason Bouwman
Composition: 92.5% Ag, 7.5% Cu
Silver content: 23.29 g, 0.749 tr oz
Weight: 25.175 g
Diameter: 36.07 mm
Thickness: 3.1 mm
Finish: 1. Proof
         2. Proof, Selectively gold plated
         3. Brilliant Uncirculated

Engravers:
Obv.: Susan Taylor
Rev.: William Woodruff

Edge: Reeded
Die Axis: ↑↑

Case of Issue: Maroon leatherette clam style case, black flocked insert, encapsulated coin, COA

DATE	DESCRIPTION	SOURCE	QUANTITY SOLD	ISSUE PRICE	FINISH	65	66	67	68
2009 (1909-)	Flight, Proof	Pr. Single	25,000	47.95	Proof	—	—	50.	55.
2009 (1909-)	Flight, Proof, Selectively gold plated	Pr. Set	27,549	N.I.I.	Proof	—	—	90.	100.
2009 (1909-)	Flight, Brilliant Uncirculated	BU Single	13,074	39.95	BU	40.	42.	—	—

ONE DOLLAR, 100TH ANNIVERSARY MONTREAL CANADIENS, 1909-2009.

The Montreal Canadiens, Montreal's hockey team, celebrated their 100th anniversary in 2009.

Designers:
   Obv.: Susanna Blunt
   Rev.: Jason Bouwman

Engravers:
   Obv.: Susan Taylor
   Rev.: RCM Staff, Konrad Wachelko

Composition: 92.5% Ag, 7.5% Cu, Selectively gold plated
Silver content: 23.29 g, 0.749 tr oz
Weight: 25.175 g
Diameter: 36.07 mm
Thickness: 3.1 mm

Edge: Reeded
Die Axis: ↑↑
Finish: Proof

Case of Issue: 1. Black leatherette clam style case, black flocked insert, encapsulated coin, COA
   2. Acrylic stand

DATE	DESCRIPTION	SOURCE	QUANTITY SOLD	ISSUE PRICE	FINISH	PR-67	PR-68
2009 (1909-)	Montreal Canadiens	Pr. Single	10,093	69.95	Proof	175.	185.
2009 (1909-)	Montreal Canadiens	With stand	4,907	74.95	Proof	175.	185.

ONE DOLLAR, VANCOUVER 2010, THE SUN, 2010.

The Sun, representing life, abundance, healing and peace, has been the cornerstone in the cultures of Canada's many First Nation communities.

Designers and Engravers:
   Obv.: Susanna Blunt, Susan Taylor
   Rev.: Xwa lack tun (Ricky Harry), Cecily Mok
Composition: 92.5% Ag, 7.5% Cu
Silver content: 27.75 g, 0.892 tr oz
Weight: 30.0 g
Diameter: 36.2 mm   **Thickness:** 3.3 mm
Edge: Plain   **Die Axis:** ↑↑
Finish: Proof
Case: Black leatherette clam style case, black flocked insert, encapsulated coin, COA, Vancouver 2010 Olympic Winter Games theme sleeve

DATE	DESCRIPTION	SOURCE	QUANTITY SOLD	ISSUE PRICE	FINISH	PR-67	PR-68
2010	The Sun	Pr. Single	5,000	139.95	Proof	235.	260.

ONE DOLLAR, 100TH ANNIVERSARY OF THE ROYAL CANADIAN NAVY, 1910-2010.

Founded in 1910 by the passage of the Naval Service Act, the Royal Canadian Navy served in three wars and many conflicts during the last 100 years. *HMCS Sackville,* one of the original Flower Class Corvettes is portrayed on this commemorative silver dollar.

Designers and Engravers:
  Obv.: Susanna Blunt, Susan Taylor
  Rev.: Yves Bérubé, Stan Witten
Composition: 92.5% Ag, 7.5% Cu,
    Selectively gold plated
Silver content: 23.29 g, 0.749 tr oz
Weight: 25.175 g
Diameter: 36.07 mm **Thickness:** 3.0 mm
Edge: Reeded   **Die Axis:** ↑↑
Finish: Proof
Case: Maroon leatherette clam style case, black flocked insert, encapsulated coin

DATE	DESCRIPTION	SOURCE	QUANTITY SOLD	ISSUE PRICE	FINISH	65	66	67	68
2010 (1910-)	Proof	Pr. Single	29,141	52.95	Proof	—	—	40.	42.
2010 (1910-)	Proof, Selectively gold plated	Pr. Set	32,342	N.I.I.	Proof	—	—	90.	95.
2010 (1910-)	Brilliant Uncirculated	BU	12,946	46.95	BU	40.	42.	—	—

ONE DOLLAR, 75TH ANNIVERSARY OF CANADA'S VOYAGEUR SILVER DOLLAR, 1935-2010.

The first circulating silver dollar was released in 1935. Emanuel Hahn's Voyageur design has become the classic symbol of Canada's silver dollars. This coin was also included in the 75th Anniversary of Canada's First Silver Dollar set, see page 385.

Designers and Engravers:
  Obv.: Emanuel Hahn
  Rev.: Percy Metcalfe
Composition: 92.5% Ag, 7.5% Cu
Silver content: 23.29 g, 0.749 tr oz
Weight: 25.175 g
Diameter: 36.07 mm **Thickness:** 3.0 mm
Edge: Reeded   **Die Axis:** ↑↑
Finish: Proof
Case: Maroon leatherette clam style case, black flocked insert, encapsulated coin

DATE	DESCRIPTION	SOURCE	QUANTITY SOLD	ISSUE PRICE	FINISH	PR-67	PR-68
2010 (1935-)	75th Anniv. First Canadian Silver Dollar	Pr. Single	7,494	69.95	Proof	115.	120.

ONE DOLLAR, ENAMELLED POPPY, 2010.

"*In Flander's Field where poppies grow,*" the poppy has become the flower of remembrance for Allied Service Personnel lost in battle.

Designers and Engravers:
  Obv.: Susanna Blunt, Susan Taylor
  Rev.: Christie Paquet, Christie Paquet
Composition: 92.5% Ag, 7.5% Cu, Red enamel
Silver content: 23.29 g, 0.749 tr oz
Weight: 25.175 g
Diameter: 36.07 mm **Thickness:** 3.1 mm
Edge: Reeded   **Die Axis:** ↑↑
Finish: Proof
Case: Maroon leatherette clam style case, black flocked insert, encapsulated coin, COA

DATE	DESCRIPTION	SOURCE	QUANTITY SOLD	ISSUE PRICE	FINISH	PR-67	PR-68
2010	Poppy, Enamelled	Pr. Single	4,907	139.95	Proof	210.	225.

ONE DOLLAR, 100TH ANNIVERSARY OF PARKS CANADA, 1911-2011.

The Dominion Parks Branch, known today as Parks Canada was founded in 1911. Parks Canada is the world's first system of national parks.

| Brilliant Uncirculated | Proof | Proof, Selectively gold plated |

Designers:
  Obv.: Susanna Blunt
  Rev.: Luc Normandson
Composition: 92.5% Ag, 7.5% Cu
Silver Content: 23.29 g, 0.749 tr oz
Weight: 25.175 g
Diameter: 36.07 mm
Edge: Reeded
Finish: **1.** Proof
       2. Proof, Selectively gold plated
       3. Brilliant Uncirculated

Engravers:
  Obv.: Susan Taylor
  Rev.: Marcos Hallam

Thickness: 3.02 mm
Die Axis: ↑↑

Case of Issue: Maroon leatherette clam style case, black flocked insert, encapsulated coin, COA

DATE	DESCRIPTION	SOURCE	QUANTITY SOLD	ISSUE PRICE	FINISH	65	66	67	68
2011 (1911-)	Parks Canada, Proof	Pr. Single	30,692	55.95	Proof	—	—	60.	65.
2011 (1911-)	Parks Canada, Proof, Selectively gold plated	Pr. Set	32,910	N.I.I.	Proof	—	—	90.	95.
2011 (1911-)	Parks Canada, Brilliant Uncirculated	BU Single	16,394	49.95	BU	50.	55.	—	—

ONE DOLLAR, 100TH ANNIVERSARY OF THE STRIKING OF CANADA'S 1911 SILVER DOLLAR, 1911-2011.

This one dollar coin which carries the double date 1911-2011 is from the Special Edition Proof Set issued in 2011 to commemorate the 100th anniversary of the striking of Canada's 1911 silver dollar.

Designers and Engravers:
  Obv.:   Sir E. B. MacKennal
  Rev.:   W. H. J. Blakemore
Composition: 92.5% Ag, 7.5% Cu
Silver content: 23.29 g, 0.749 tr oz
Weight: 25.175 g
Diameter: 36.07 mm **Thickness:** 3.0 mm
Edge: Reeded **Die Axis:** ↑↑
Finish: Proof
Case: See Special Issue Proof Sets, page 385

DATE	DESCRIPTION	SOURCE	QUANTITY SOLD	ISSUE PRICE	FINISH	PR-67	PR-68
2011 (1911-)	100th Anniv. Canada's 1911 Silver Dollar	Pr. Single	14,569	65.00	Proof	70.	75.

ONE DOLLAR, 200TH ANNIVERSARY OF THE WAR OF 1812, 1812-2012.

The issue of these coins marks the two-hundredth anniversary of the first conflict between the American forces, and the English of Upper Canada, the French of Lower Canada, and the First Nations People who successfully defended against an American invasion. The conflict ran for three years, 1812-1814.

Brilliant Uncirculated	**Proof**	**Proof, Selectively gold plated**

Designers:
    Obv.: Susanna Blunt
    Rev.: Ardell Bourgeois

Engravers:
    Obv.: Susan Taylor
    Rev.: Konrad Wachelko

Composition: 99.99% Ag
Silver Content: 23.17 g, 0.75 tr oz
Weight: 23.17 g
Diameter: 35.9 mm
Edge: Reeded
Finish: **1.** Proof
          2. Proof, Selectively gold plated
          3. Brilliant Uncirculated

Thickness: 2.8 mm
Die Axis: ↑↑

Case of Issue: Maroon leatherette clam style case, black flocked insert, encapsulated coin, COA

DATE	DESCRIPTION	SOURCE	QUANTITY SOLD	ISSUE PRICE	FINISH	65	66	67	68
2012 (1812-)	War of 1812, Proof	Pr. Single	39,569	59.95	Proof	—	—	60.	65.
2012 (1812-)	War of 1812, Proof	Pr. Set	27,254	N.I.I.	Proof	—	—	70.	75.
2012 (1812-)	War of 1812, Proof, Selectively gold plated	Prem. Pr. Set	19,789	N.I.I.	Proof	—	—	110.	120.
2012 (1812-)	War of 1812, Brilliant Uncirculated	BU Single	19,623	54.95	BU	55.	60.	—	—

ONE DOLLAR, TWO LOONS, 2012.
This coin was issued to celebrate the 25th anniversary of the loon coin which replaced the one dollar bill in 1987.

Designers and Engravers:
    Obv.: Susanna Blunt, Susan Taylor
    Rev.: Richard Hunt, Cecily Mok
Composition: 99.99% Ag, Coloured
Silver content: 31.39 g, 1.00 tr oz
Weight: 31.39 g
Diameter: 38.0 mm   **Thickness:** 3.10 mm
Edge: Reeded   **Die Axis:** ↑↑
Finish: Proof
Case: Maroon leatherette clam style case, black
      flocked insert, encapsulated coin, COA,
      custom coloured sleeve

DATE	DESCRIPTION	SOURCE	QUANTITY SOLD	ISSUE PRICE	FINISH	PR-67	PR-68
2012	Two Loons	Pr. Single	9,965	109.95	Proof	150.	160.

ONE DOLLAR, 100 YEARS OF THE CALGARY STAMPEDE, 2012.
First held in 1912, the Calgary Stampede is billed as the greatest outdoor show on earth.

Designers and Engravers:
    Obv.: Susanna Blunt, Susan Taylor
    Rev.: Steve Hepburn, Konrad Wachelko
Composition: 99.99% Ag
Silver content: 23.17 g, 0.75 tr oz
Weight: 23.17 g
Diameter: 36.07 mm   **Thickness:** 2.80 mm
Edge: Reeded   **Die Axis:** ↑↑
Finish: Proof
Case: Maroon leatherette clam style case, black
      flocked insert, encapsulated coin, COA,
      custom coloured sleeve

DATE	DESCRIPTION	SOURCE	QUANTITY SOLD	ISSUE PRICE	FINISH	PR-67	PR-68
2012	100 Years of the Calgary Stampede	Pr. Single	9,996	69.95	Proof	120.	125.

ONE DOLLAR, THE 100TH GREY CUP, 2012.
The first Grey Cup game took place in 1909, with the University of Toronto defeating the Parkdale Canoe Club. There were 3,807 fans in attendance at the game which generated revenues of $2,616.40 for the Canadian Rugby Union.

Designers and Engravers:
    Obv.: Susanna Blunt, Susan Taylor
    Rev.: Filip Mroz of Bensimon Byrne,
        Konrad Wachelko
Composition: 99.99% Ag
Silver content: 23.17 g, 0.75 tr oz
Weight: 23.17 g
Diameter: 36.0 mm   **Thickness:** 2.75 mm
Edge: Reeded   **Die Axis:** ↑↑
Finish: Proof
Case: Maroon leatherette clam style case, black
      flocked insert, encapsulated coin, COA,
      custom box

DATE	DESCRIPTION	SOURCE	QUANTITY SOLD	ISSUE PRICE	FINISH	PR-67	PR-68
2012	The 100th Grey Cup	Pr. Single	9,985	69.95	Proof	80.	85.

ONE DOLLAR, 100TH ANNIVERSARY OF THE CANADIAN ARCTIC EXPEDITION, 1913-2013.

In 1913, Canadian Prime Minister Sir Robert Borden commissioned an expedition, led by Manitoba-born ethnologist Vilhjalmur Stefansson, to explore and map the western Canadian Arctic. Stefansson and zoologist Rudolph Anderson had travelled through the Far North the previous decade. Stefansson planned to continue his earlier journey, but the government of Canada, recognizing the importance of the new sovereign territory, hosted the Expedition and broadened its mission significantly. A Northern Party led by Stefansson would undertake the mapping exercise while the Southern Party led by Anderson would explore the geology, resources, and native inhabitants of the northern mainland.

The year 2013 saw the first fine silver dollar to be included a Specimen Set.

| Brilliant Uncirculated | Specimen | Proof | Proof, Selectively gold plated |

Designers:
   Obv.: Susanna Blunt
   Rev.: Bonnie Ross
Composition: 99.99% Ag
Silver Content: 23.0 g, 0.739 tr oz
Weight: 23.17 g
Diameter: 36.07 mm
Finish: **1.** Proof
      2. Proof, Selectively gold plated

Engravers:
   Obv.: Susan Taylor
   Rev.: RCM Staff, Konrad Wachelko

Thickness: 2.8 mm
Edge: Reeded
Die Axis: ↑↑
3. Specimen
4. Brilliant Uncirculated

Case of Issue: Maroon leatherette clam style case, black flocked insert, encapsulated coin, COA

DATE	DESCRIPTION	SOURCE	QUANTITY SOLD	ISSUE PRICE	FINISH	65	66	67	68
2013 (1913-)	Canadian Arctic Expedition, Proof	Pr. Single	25,244	59.95	Proof	—	—	60.	65.
2013 (1913-)	Canadian Arctic Expedition, Proof, Selectively gold plated	Pr. Set	20,182	N.I.I.	Proof	—	—	100.	110.
2013 (1913-)	Canadian Arctic Expedition, Specimen	Sp. Set	9,247	N.I.I.	Specimen	—	50.	55.	—
2013 (1913-)	Canadian Arctic Expedition, Brilliant Uncirculated	BU Single	13,325	54.95	BU	55.	60.	—	—

ONE DOLLAR, 250TH ANNIVERSARY OF THE END OF THE SEVEN YEARS WAR, 2013.

The Seven Years War (1756-1763) was the world's first global conflict extending far beyond North America to Europe, India and Africa. In North America the war was fought between the English, French, and the First Nations People.

Designers and Engravers:
   Obv.:   Susanna Blunt, Susan Taylor
   Rev.:   Tony Bianco, RCM Staff
Composition: 99.99% Ag
Silver content: 23.17 g, 0.75 tr oz
Weight: 23.17 g
Diameter: 36.0 mm   **Thickness:** 2.75 mm
Edge: Reeded   **Die Axis:** ↑↑
Finish: Proof
Case: Maroon leatherette clam style case, black flocked insert, encapsulated coin, COA, custom design box

DATE	DESCRIPTION	SOURCE	QUANTITY SOLD	ISSUE PRICE	FINISH	PR-67	PR-68
2013	250th Anniv. end of the Seven Years War	Pr. Single	9,994	69.95	Proof	70.	75.

ONE DOLLAR, 60TH ANNIVERSARY OF THE KOREAN ARMISTICE AGREEMENT, 2013.

The reverse design on this coin is a reproduction of the Korean General Service Medal awarded to all troops who participated in the Korean War during 1950-1958.

Designers and Engravers:
    Obv.: Susanna Blunt, Susan Taylor
    Rev.: Edward Carter Preston, RCM Staff
Composition: 99.99% Ag
Silver content: 23.0 g, 0.74 tr oz
Weight: 23.0 g
Diameter: 36.0 mm   **Thickness:** 2.75 mm
Edge: Reeded   **Die Axis:** ↑↑
Finish: Proof
Case: Maroon leatherette clam style case, black flocked insert, encapsulated coin, COA, custom design box

DATE	DESCRIPTION	SOURCE	QUANTITY SOLD	ISSUE PRICE	FINISH	PR-67	PR-68
2013	60th Anniv. Korean Armistice Agreement	Pr. Single	6,858	69.95	Proof	70.	75.

ONE DOLLAR, 100TH ANNIVERSARY OF THE DECLARATION OF THE FIRST WORLD WAR, 2014.

The First World War began in August 1914 and ended November 1918. Thousands of Canadian men and women took part on the battlefields of Europe.

        Brilliant Uncirculated   **Proof**   **Proof, Selectively gold plated**

Designers:
    Obv.: Susanna Blunt
    Rev.: Bonnie Ross
Composition: 99.99% Ag
Silver Content: 22.8 g, 0.73 tr oz
Weight: 22.8 g
Diameter: 36.0 mm
Finish: **1.** Proof
        2. Proof, Selectively gold plated
        3. Brilliant Uncirculated

Engravers:
    Obv.: Susan Taylor
    Rev.: RCM Staff

Thickness: 2.8 mm
Edge: Reeded
Die Axis: ↑↑

Case of Issue: Maroon leatherette clam style case, black flocked insert, encapsulated coin, COA

DATE	DESCRIPTION	SOURCE	QUANTITY SOLD	ISSUE PRICE	FINISH	65	66	67	68
2014	100th Anniv. Declaration WWI, Proof	Pr. Single	40,000	59.95	Proof	—	—	60.	65.
2014	100th Anniv. Declaration WWI, Proof	Pr. Set	30,000	N.I.I.	Proof	—	—	70.	75.
2014	100th Anniv. Declaration WWI, Proof, Selectively gold plated	Prem. Pr. Set	25,000	N.I.I.	Proof	—	—	110.	125.
2014	100th Anniv. Declaration WWI, Brilliant Uncirculated	BU Single	20,000	54.95	BU	55.	60.	—	—

CASED NICKEL DOLLAR ISSUES, 1968-1984

At the start of 1968 the Royal Canadian Mint began the conversion from silver to nickel coinage. The first to participate was the Numismatic Department, which was based in Hull, Quebec. The Hull Mint was opened circa 1965 to carry the increased demand for numismatic products which was overwhelming the Ottawa facilities.

The first full set of nickel coinage, the five, ten and fifty cents, and the one dollar coin are found in the Royal Canadian Mint's uncirculated set of 1968.

Nickel coinage is more difficult to strike than silver coinage, and the Mint needed to adjust their process. One of these adjustments was to reduce the size of the fifty-cent and one dollar coins.

The finish on the coin was also a problem. The proof-like finish of silver was not as easily duplicated on nickel. Thus, the quality of finish varied from 1968 to 1976 when new presses for the Olympic Coin Program were put into use. The Mint did produce proof-like nickel coinage for their uncirculated sets, but not consistently, for at times the standard of finish dropped to circulation. It is best to treat the finish for this period as "brilliant uncirculated" not proof-like, for even the experts have difficulty determining the quality of the finish during this time period.

ONE DOLLAR, VOYAGEUR DESIGN, 1968 and 1969.

A cased 1968 and 1969 nickel dollar was available from the Numismatic Department of the Mint during 1968-69, but the department did not aggressively market this product until 1970. Thus the years 1968 and 1969 saw the development of the "cased dollar" line with the evolution of a "clam" style case.

Designers and Engravers:
  Obv.: Arnold Machin, Patrick Brindley
  Rev.: Raymond Taylor, Walter Ott
Composition: Nickel
Weight: 15.62 g
Diameter: 32.13 mm   **Thickness:** 2.3 mm
Edge: Reeded   **Die Axis:** ↑↑
Finish: Brilliant Uncirculated
Case: Black leatherette, gold side trim, gilt Royal Canadian Mint Building crest, blue interior, black insert, gilt Coat of Arms of Canada

DATE	DESCRIPTION	QUANTITY SOLD	ISSUE PRICE	FINISH	MS-65 NC	MS-66 NC	MS-67 NC
1968	Voyageur	N/A	N/A	BU	5.	10.	40.
1968	Voyageur, Small Island	N/A	N/A	BU	15.	30.	—
1968	Voyageur, No Island	N/A	N/A	BU	10.	25.	—
1969	Voyageur	N/A	N/A	BU	5.	10.	40.

ONE DOLLAR, MANITOBA CENTENNIAL, 1870-1970.

Canada's first commemorative nickel dollar has a special reverse featuring a prairie crocus in recognition of the centenary of Manitoba's entry into Confederation. The finish on the cased dollar is brilliant uncirculated.

Designers and Engravers:
  Obv.: Arnold Machin, Patrick Brindley
  Rev.: Raymond Taylor, Walter Ott
Composition: Nickel
Weight: 15.62 g
Diameter: 32.13 mm   **Thickness:** 2.3 mm
Edge: Reeded   **Die Axis:** ↑↑
Finish: Brilliant Uncirculated

Case of Issue: **A:** Black leatherette square case, gilt RCM crest, blue insert
  B: Maroon leatherette rectangular case, gold stamped crest of Canada, red interior, black insert
  C: Black leatherette rectangular case, gold stamped Japanese characters, Maple Leaf, Canada, red interior, black insert. Card insert. (Sold at the Canada pavilion in Japan, during 1970.)

DATE	DESCRIPTION	QUANTITY SOLD	ISSUE PRICE	FINISH	MS-65 NC	MS-66 NC	MS-67 NC
1970 (1870-)	Manitoba, Case A	349,120	2.00	BU	5.	8.	35.
1970 (1870-)	Manitoba, Case B	Included	N/A	BU	5.	8.	35.
1970 (1870-)	Manitoba, Case C	Included	N/A	BU	5.	8.	35.

ONE DOLLAR, BRITISH COLUMBIA CENTENNIAL, 1871-1971.

The nickel dollar for 1971 commemorates the entry in 1871 of British Columbia into Confederation. Its design is based on the arms of the province, with a shield at the bottom and dogwood blossoms at the top. The design of the brilliant uncirculated nickel dollar is identical to that of the circulating issue.

Designers and Engravers:
　　Obv.:　Arnold Machin, Patrick Brindley
　　Rev.:　Thomas Shingles
Composition: Nickel
Weight: 15.62 g
Diameter: 32.13 mm　　**Thickness:** 2.3 mm
Edge: Reeded　　　　　**Die Axis:** ↑↑
Finish: Brilliant Uncirculated
Case: Blue leatherette clam case, Coat of Arms
　　　　of Canada, blue and black insert

DATE	DESCRIPTION	QUANTITY SOLD	ISSUE PRICE	FINISH	MS-65 NC	MS-66 NC	MS-67 NC
1971 (1871-)	British Columbia Centennial	181,091	2.00	BU	5.	8.	30.

ONE DOLLAR, VOYAGEUR DESIGN, 1972.

The cased brilliant uncirculated nickel dollar issued by the numismatic department of the Royal Canadian Mint has the same design as the circulating dollar with the exception of beads instead of denticles.

Designers and Engravers:
　　Obv.:　Arnold Machin, Patrick Brindley
　　Rev.:　Emanuel Hahn, Terry Smith
Composition: Nickel
Weight: 15.62 g
Diameter: 32.13 mm　　**Thickness:** 2.3 mm
Edge: Reeded　　　　　**Die Axis:** ↑↑
Finish: Brilliant Uncirculated
Case: Blue leatherette clam case, Coat of Arms
　　　　of Canada, blue and black insert

DATE	DESCRIPTION	QUANTITY SOLD	ISSUE PRICE	FINISH	MS-65 NC	MS-66 NC	MS-67 NC
1972	Voyageur	143,392	2.00	BU	5.	8.	30.

ONE DOLLAR, PRINCE EDWARD ISLAND CENTENNIAL, 1873-1973.

The 100th anniversary of the entry of Prince Edward Island into Confederation is commemorated with the reverse design depicting the provincial legislature building in Charlottetown.

Designers and Engravers:
　　Obv.:　Arnold Machin, Patrick Brindley
　　Rev.:　Terry Manning, Walter Ott
Composition: Nickel
Weight: 15.62 g
Diameter: 32.13 mm　　**Thickness:** 2.3 mm
Edge: Reeded　　　　　**Die Axis:** ↑↑
Finish: Brilliant Uncirculated
Case: Blue leatherette clam case, Coat of Arms
　　　　of Canada, blue and black insert

DATE	DESCRIPTION	QUANTITY SOLD	ISSUE PRICE	FINISH	MS-65 NC	MS-66 NC	MS-67 NC
1973 (1873-)	Prince Edward Island Centennial	466,881	2.00	BU	5.	8.	200.

ONE DOLLAR, WINNIPEG CENTENNIAL, 1874-1974.

The 100th anniversary of the establishment of Winnipeg, Manitoba, as a city is marked by the reverse of the 1974 dollar. The 1974 cased specimen silver dollar carries the same design, see page 86.

Designers and Engravers:
Obv.:   Arnold Machin, Patrick Brindley
Rev.:   Paul Pederson, Patrick Brindley
Composition: Nickel
Weight: 15.62 g
Diameter: 32.13 mm   **Thickness:** 2.3 mm
Edge: Reeded   **Die Axis:** ↑↑
Finish: Brilliant Uncirculated
Case: Blue leatherette clam case, Coat of Arms of Canada, blue and black insert

DATE	DESCRIPTION	QUANTITY SOLD	ISSUE PRICE	FINISH	MS-65 NC	MS-66 NC	MS-67 NC
1974 (1874-)	Winnipeg Centennial, Single Yoke	363,786	2.00	BU	5.	15.	60.
1974 (1874-)	Winnipeg Centennial, Double Yoke #1	Included	2.00	BU	1,000.	—	—
1974 (1874-)	Winnipeg Centennial, Double Yoke #3	Included	2.00	BU	1,500.	—	—

ONE DOLLAR, VOYAGEUR DESIGN, 1975-1976.

With falling popularity, the cased nickel dollars were discontinued in 1976.

Designers and Engravers:
Obv.:   Arnold Machin, Patrick Brindley
Rev.:   Emanuel Hahn, Terry Smith
Composition: Nickel
Weight: 15.62 g
Diameter: 32.13 mm   **Thickness:** 2.3 mm
Edge: Reeded   **Die Axis:** ↑↑
Finish: Specimen
Case: Blue leatherette clam case, Coat of Arms of Canada, blue and black insert

DATE	DESCRIPTION	QUANTITY SOLD	ISSUE PRICE	FINISH	MS-65 NC	MS-66 NC	MS-67 NC
1975	Voyageur, Attached Jewel	88,102	2.50	BU	5.	15.	100.
1976	Voyageur	74,209	2.50	BU	5.	15.	125.

NOTES ON NICKEL AND BRONZE DOLLARS

It is important to remember the nickel dollar series 1968 to 1987 was issued, in most instances, for circulation (business strikes), however, they were also issued as collector items either singly or in sets. This section, pages 112 to 115, lists only the single pliofilm pouched or cased nickel dollars for the period 1968 to 1984.

The term "proof-like" which applied to the silver dollars and sets of the period 1953-1967, was not carried forward to the nickel dollar coinage of 1968-1987. Coins of the period 1968 to 1984 have a brilliant uncirculated finish.

Pricing is based on third party, professionally graded coins. It is difficult for the average collector to determine the niceties between MS-65 (NC), MS-66 (NC) and MS-67 (NC). NC is non-circulating.

ONE DOLLAR, CONSTITUTION, 1867-1982

The reverse design of the 1982 nickel dollar commemorates Canada's Constitution. It features a faithful reproduction of the celebrated painting *Fathers of Confederation,* with the inscription 1867 CONFEDERATION above the painting and CONSTITUTION 1982 beneath.

Designers and Engravers:
  Obv.:   Arnold Machin, RCM Staff
  Rev.:   Ago Aarand, RCM Staff
Composition: Nickel
Weight: 15.62 g
Diameter: 32.13 mm   **Thickness:** 2.3 mm
Edge: Reeded   **Die Axis:** ↑↑
Finish: Specimen
Case: Maroon square case with maple leaf logo, maroon insert, encapsulated coin

DATE	DESCRIPTION	QUANTITY SOLD	ISSUE PRICE	FINISH	SP-66	SP-67
1982 (1867-)	Constitution	107,353	9.75	Specimen	15.	20.

ONE DOLLAR, 450TH ANNIVERSARY OF JACQUES CARTIER LANDING, 1534-1984.

The 450th year of Jacques Cartier's landing at Gaspé, Quebec, was honoured on July 24, 1984, by the issuing of a commemorative nickel dollar.

Designers and Engravers:
  Obv.:   Arnold Machin, RCM Staff
  Rev.:   Hector Greville, Victor Coté
Composition: Nickel
Weight: 15.62 g
Diameter: 32.13 mm   **Thickness:** 2.3 mm
Edge: Reeded   **Die Axis:** ↑↑
Finish: Proof
Case: Green velvet square case, green insert, encapsulated coin

DATE	DESCRIPTION	QUANTITY SOLD	ISSUE PRICE	FINISH	PR-67	PR-68
1984 (1534-)	450th Anniv. of Jacques Cartier Landing	87,776	9.75	Proof	10.	15.

NICKEL-BRONZE DOLLAR PROOF ISSUES, 1987-1995

ONE DOLLAR, LOON, 1987.

A proof striking of the loon dollar was issued by the numismatic department of the Royal Canadian Mint in 1987 commemorating the introduction of the nickel-bronze dollar.

Designers and Engravers:
Obv.:   Arnold Machin, Patrick Brindley,
Rev.:   R. R. Carmichael, Terry Smith
Composition: 91.5% Ni, 8.5 Bronze
Weight: 7.0 g   **Thickness:** 1.9 mm
11-sided: 26.5 mm   **Die Axis:** ↑↑
Edge: Plain   **Finish:** Proof
Case: Royal blue velvet square case, blue insert,
           encapsulated coin

ONE DOLLAR, 125TH ANNIVERSARY OF CANADA, 1867-1992.

This coin was part of the "125" coin program by the numismatic department of the Royal Canadian Mint. This proof coin is the companion piece to the circulating issue of the same design.

Designers and Engravers:
Obv.:   Dora de Pédery-Hunt
Rev.:   Rita Swanson, Ago Aarand
Composition: 91.5% Ni, 8.5% Bronze
Weight: 7.0 g   **Thickness:** 1.9 mm
11-sided: 26.5 mm   **Die Axis:** ↑↑
Edge: Plain   **Finish:** Proof
Case: Royal blue velvet square case, blue insert,
           encapsulated coin

ONE DOLLAR, REMEMBRANCE, 1994.

The 1994 nickel Loon dollar depicts the War Memorial, built to commemorate the participation of all Canadians in the First World War. The memorial was rededicated in 1982 to include veterans of the Second World War and the Korean War.

Designers and Engravers:
Obv.:   Dora de Pédery-Hunt
Rev.:   Terry Smith, Ago Aarand
Composition: 91.5% Ni, 8.5% Bronze
Weight: 7.0 g   **Thickness:** 1.9 mm
11-sided: 26.5 mm   **Die Axis:** ↑↑
Edge: Plain   **Finish:** Proof
Case: Royal blue velvet square case, blue insert,
           encapsulated coin, COA

ONE DOLLAR, PEACEKEEPING, 1995.

This coin commemorates Canada's role in the United Nations peacekeeping forces. For the circulating issues see *Canadian Coins, Volume One*.

Designers and Engravers:
Obv.:   Dora de Pédery-Hunt
Rev.:   J.K. Harman, R.G. Henriguez
          C. H. Oberlander, S. Taylor, A. Aarand
Composition: 91.5% Ni, 8.5% Bronze
Weight: 7.0 g   **Thickness:** 1.9 mm
11-sided: 26.5 mm   **Die Axis:** ↑↑
Edge: Plain   **Finish:** Proof
Case: Royal blue velvet square case, blue insert,
           encapsulated coin, COA

DATE	DESCRIPTION	QUANTITY SOLD	ISSUE PRICE	FINISH	PR-67	PR-68
1987	Loon, Nickel-Bronze	178,120	13.50	Proof	12.	18.
1992	125th Anniversary of Canada	24,227	19.95	Proof	15.	20.
1994	Remembrance	54,524	19.95	Proof	15.	20.
1995	Peacekeeping	43,293	17.95	Proof	12.	18.

NICKEL-BRONZE DOLLAR SPECIMEN ISSUES
THE BIRD SERIES, 1997-2014

ONE DOLLAR, 10TH ANNIVERSARY OF THE ONE DOLLAR LOON, 1987-1997.

The Flying Loon one dollar coin was issued only in "Oh! Canada!" and Specimen Sets of 1997 (see pages 366 and 374). Single coins have been removed from sets.

Designers and Engravers:
    Obv.: Dora de Pédery-Hunt
    Rev.: Jean-Luc Grondin, Sheldon Beveridge
Composition: 91.5% Ni, 8.5% Bronze
Weight: 7.0 g
11-sided: 26.5 mm   **Thickness:** 1.9 mm
Edge: Plain   **Die Axis:** ↑↑
Finish: Specimen
Case: See Sets, pages 366 and 374

DATE	DESCRIPTION	QUANTITY SOLD	ISSUE PRICE	FINISH	SP-66	SP-67
1997 (1987-)	Flying Loon	181,719	N.I.I.	Specimen	20.	25.

ONE DOLLAR, 15TH ANNIVERSARY OF THE LOON DOLLAR, 1987-2002.

First struck in 1987, the one dollar coin with the image of a solitary Common Loon soon became Canada's most popular coin, affectionately called the "Loonie." The 2002 commemorative dollar, depicting a loon family, with the male loon doing his "dance" was issued only in special edition specimen sets for 2002. Single coins have been removed from sets.

Designers and Engravers:
    Obv.: Dora de Pédery-Hunt
    Rev.: Cosme Saffioti
Composition: 91.5% Ni, 8.5% Bronze
Weight: 7.0 g
11-sided: 26.5 mm   **Thickness:** 1.9 mm
Edge: Plain   **Die Axis:** ↑↑
Finish: Specimen
Case: See Specimen Sets, page 375

DATE	DESCRIPTION	QUANTITY SOLD	ISSUE PRICE	FINISH	SP-66	SP-67
2002 (1987-)	15th Anniversary of the Loon Dollar	67,672	N.I.I.	Specimen	30.	35.

ONE DOLLAR, CANADA GOOSE, 2004.

This bronze dollar was issued only in the 2004 specimen set as a tribute to Jack Miner, one of the world's most influential conservationists. Miner founded a bird sanctuary near Kingsville, Ontario, in 2004.

Designers and Engravers:
    Obv.: Susanna Blunt, Susan Taylor
    Rev.: Susan Taylor
Composition: 91.5% Ni, 8.5% Bronze
Weight: 7.0 g
11-sided: 26.5 mm   **Thickness:** 1.9 mm
Edge: Plain   **Die Axis:** ↑↑
Finish: Specimen
Case: See Specimen Sets, page 375

DATE	DESCRIPTION	QUANTITY SOLD	ISSUE PRICE	FINISH	SP-66	SP-67
2004	Canada Goose	46,493	N.I.I.	Specimen	40.	45.

ONE DOLLAR, ELUSIVE LOON, 2004.

This dollar coin was issued only as part of the Elusive Loon "$1 Limited Edition Stamp and Coin Set", a joint venture between the Royal Canadian Mint and Canada Post. The Elusive Loon coin which carries a maple leaf privy mark was issued in a wooden presentation case along with mint and cancelled $1.00 Loon stamps.

Designers and Engravers:
Obv.: Susanna Blunt, Susan Taylor
Rev.: Christie Paquet
Composition: 91.5% Ni, 8.5% Bronze
Weight: 7.0 g
11-sided: 26.5 mm   **Thickness:** 1.9 mm
Edge: Plain   **Die Axis:** ↑↑
Finish: Specimen
Case: See Derivatives, page 132

DATE	DESCRIPTION	QUANTITY SOLD	ISSUE PRICE	FINISH	SP-66	SP-67
2004	Elusive Loon	12,550	N.I.I.	Specimen	45.	50.

ONE DOLLAR, TUFTED PUFFIN, 2005.

Issued only in the 2005 specimen set, the limited edition one dollar coin features one of British Columbia's most captivating sea birds. Coins sold singly have been removed from specimen sets. (See page 375).

Designers and Engravers:
Obv.: Susanna Blunt, Susan Taylor
Rev.: Christie Paquet
Composition: 91.5% Ni, 8.5% Bronze
Weight: 7.0 g
11-sided: 26.5 mm   **Thickness:** 1.9 mm
Edge: Plain   **Die Axis:** ↑↑
Finish: Specimen
Case: See Specimen Sets, page 375

DATE	DESCRIPTION	QUANTITY SOLD	ISSUE PRICE	FINISH	SP-66	SP-67
2005	Tufted Puffin	39,818	N.I.I.	Specimen	60.	65.

ONE DOLLAR, SNOWY OWL, 2006.

Issued only in the 2006 Specimen Set, the limited edition one dollar coin features the official bird of Quebec.

Designers and Engravers:
Obv.: Susanna Blunt, Susan Taylor
Rev.: Glen Loates, RCM Staff
Composition: 91.5% Ni, 8.5% Bronze
Weight: 7.0 g
11-sided: 26.5 mm   **Thickness:** 1.9 mm
Edge: Plain   **Die Axis:** ↑↑
Finish: Specimen
Case: See Specimen Sets, page 375

DATE	DESCRIPTION	QUANTITY SOLD	ISSUE PRICE	FINISH	SP-66	SP-67
2006	Snowy Owl	39,935	N.I.I.	Specimen	50.	55.

NOTE TO COLLECTORS

When the initials N.I.I. appear in the pricing table it indicates the coin was part of a set issued by the Royal Canadian Mint, and not issued individually. Coin designs that are found only in sets offered by the Royal Canadian Mint are listed individually by denomination, and date in Volume Two.

ONE DOLLAR, TRUMPETER SWAN, 2007.

This coin was available only in the limited edition Specimen Sets of 2007. The Trumpeter Swan has a wing span of more than two metres.

Designers and Engravers:
Obv.:   Susanna Blunt, Susan Taylor
Rev.:   Kerri Burnett, Christie Paquet
Composition: 91.5% Ni, 8.5% Bronze
Weight: 7.0 g   **Thickness:** 1.9 mm
11-sided: 26.5 mm   **Die Axis:** ↑↑
Edge: Plain   **Finish:** Specimen
Case: See Specimen Sets, page 375

DATE	DESCRIPTION	QUANTITY SOLD	ISSUE PRICE	FINISH	SP-66	SP-67
2007	Trumpeter Swan	27,056	N.I.I.	Specimen	45.	50.

ONE DOLLAR, COMMON EIDER, 2008.

Issued only in the limited edition Specimen Set of 2008 the Common Eider is found along the coast of North America.

Designers and Engravers:
Obv.:   Susanna Blunt, Susan Taylor
Rev.:   M. Dobson, Stan Witten
Composition: 91.5% Ni, 8.5% Bronze
Weight: 7.0 g   **Thickness:** 1.9 mm
11-sided: 26.50 mm   **Die Axis:** ↑↑
Edge: Plain   **Finish:** Specimen
Case: See Specimen Sets, page 375

DATE	DESCRIPTION	QUANTITY SOLD	ISSUE PRICE	FINISH	SP-66	SP-67
2008	Common Eider	21,227	N.I.I.	Specimen	45.	50.

ONE DOLLAR, GREAT BLUE HERON, 2009.

The Great Blue Heron is a large wading bird found near the shores of open water, and in the wet lands of North America.

Designers and Engravers:
Obv.:   Susanna Blunt, Susan Taylor
Rev.:   Chris Jordison, José Osio
Composition: 91.5% Ni, 8.5% Bronze
Weight: 7.0 g   **Thickness:** 1.9 mm
11-sided: 26.5 mm   **Die Axis:** ↑↑
Edge: Plain   **Finish:** Specimen
Case: See Specimen Sets, page 375

DATE	DESCRIPTION	QUANTITY SOLD	ISSUE PRICE	FINISH	SP-66	SP-67
2009	Great Blue Heron	21,677	N.I.I.	Specimen	50.	55.

ONE DOLLAR, NORTHERN HARRIER, 2010.

The Northern Harrier is a bird of prey found throughout the northern hemisphere of Canada.

Designers and Engravers:
Obv.:   Susanna Blunt, Susan Taylor
Rev.:   Arnold Nogy, Susan Taylor
Composition: 91.5% Ni, 8.5% Bronze
Weight: 7.0 g   **Thickness:** 1.9 mm
11-sided: 26.5 mm   **Die Axis:** ↑↑
Edge: Plain   **Finish:** Specimen
Case: See Specimen Sets, page 375

DATE	DESCRIPTION	QUANTITY SOLD	ISSUE PRICE	FINISH	SP-66	SP-67
2010	Northern Harrier	21,111	N.I.I.	Specimen	45.	50.

ONE DOLLAR, GREAT GREY OWL, 2011.

Issued only in the limited edition Specimen Set of 2011 the Great Grey Owl can be found throughout Canada's boreal forests from Quebec to Yukon.

Designers and Engravers:
Obv.: Susanna Blunt, Susan Taylor
Rev.: Arnold Nogy, Christie Paquet
Composition: 91.5% Ni, 8.5% Bronze
Weight: 7.0 g   **Thickness:** 1.9 mm
11-sided: 26.5 mm   **Die Axis:** ↑↑
Edge: Plain   **Finish:** Specimen
Case: See Specimen Sets, page 375

DATE	DESCRIPTION	QUANTITY SOLD	ISSUE PRICE	FINISH	SP-66	SP-67
2011	Great Grey Owl	35,000	N.I.I.	Specimen	45.	50.

ONE DOLLAR, 25TH ANNIVERSARY OF THE LOON DOLLAR, 2012.

This coin depicts a Common Loon swimming on a calm lake. One of her chicks swims behind her the other rides on her back.

Designers and Engravers:
Obv.: Susanna Blunt, Susan Taylor
Rev.: Arnold Nogy, Susan Taylor
Composition: 91.5% Ni, 8.5% Bronze
Weight: 7.0 g   **Thickness:** 1.9 mm
11-sided: 26.5 mm   **Die Axis:** ↑↑
Edge: Plain   **Finish:** Specimen
Case: See Specimen Sets, page 375

DATE	DESCRIPTION	QUANTITY SOLD	ISSUE PRICE	FINISH	SP-66	SP-67
2012	Loon with Chicks	34,939	N.I.I.	Specimen	45.	50.

ONE DOLLAR, BLUE-WINGED TEAL, 2013.

The loon dollar contained in the 2013 Specimen Set has a Blue-Winged Teal as the central image. This set commemorates the 75th anniversary of Ducks Unlimited Canada.

Designers and Engravers:
Obv.: Susanna Blunt, Susan Taylor
Rev.: Glen Loates, Matt Bowen
Composition: 91.5% Ni, 8.5% Bronze
Weight: 7.0 g   **Thickness:** 1.9 mm
11-sided: 26.5 mm   **Die Axis:** ↑↑
Edge: Plain   **Finish:** Specimen
Case: See Specimen Sets, page 375

DATE	DESCRIPTION	QUANTITY SOLD	ISSUE PRICE	FINISH	SP-66	SP-67
2013	Blue-Winged Teal	28,884	N.I.I.	Specimen	45.	50.

ONE DOLLAR, FERRUGINOUS HAWK, 2014.

The loon dollar contained in the 2014 Specimen Set has a Ferrufinous Hawk as the central image.

Designers and Engravers:
Obv.: Susanna Blunt, Susan Taylor
Rev.: Trevor Tennant, RCM Staff
Composition: 91.5% Ni, 8.5% Bronze
Weight: 6.8 g   **Thickness:** 1.9 mm
11-sided: 26.5 mm   **Die Axis:** ↑↑
Edge: Plain   **Finish:** Specimen
Case: See Specimen Sets, page 375

DATE	DESCRIPTION	QUANTITY SOLD	ISSUE PRICE	FINISH	SP-66	SP-67
2014	Ferruginous Hawk	50,000	N.I.I.	Specimen	45.	50.

NICKEL-BRONZE DOLLAR PROOF ISSUES, 2002-2012

ONE DOLLAR, CENTRE ICE LOON, 1987-2002.

A "Centre Ice" 22-karat gold-plated loon dollar coin was issued as part of a souvenir album entitled "Going For Gold." It was jointly offered by the Royal Canadian Mint, Canada Post, and Maclean's Magazine to commemorate the Olympic gold medals for hockey won by the Canadian Mens' and Women's teams in the Salt Lake City Winter Olympic Games in 2002.

Designers and Engravers:
  Obv.: Dora de Pédery-Hunt
  Rev.: R. R. Carmichael, Cosme Saffioti
Composition: 91.5% Ni, 8.5% Bronze, Gold plated
Weight: 7.0 g
11-sided: 26.5 mm   **Thickness:** 1.9 mm
Edge: Plain   **Die Axis:** ↑↑
Finish: Proof
Case: See Derivatives, page 132

DATE	DESCRIPTION	QUANTITY SOLD	ISSUE PRICE	FINISH	PR-67	PR-68
2002 (1987-)	Centre Ice Loon, Gold-plated bronze	25,000	N.I.I.	Proof	50.	55.

ONE DOLLAR, 100TH ANNIVERSARY OF THE MONTREAL CANADIENS, 1909-2009.

Canada Post and the Royal Canadian Mint offered two different sets in 2009 for the 100th anniversary of the Montreal Canadiens:

1. Montreal Canadiens 100th Anniversary Pack which included a lacquered anniversary dollar and a lenticular souvenir sheet
2. Montreal Canadiens 100th Anniversary Set which included three different dollars coins (lacquered, painted Canadiens crest, and gold plated) plus a lenticular souvenir sheet.

| Common obverse | Lacquered | Painted Crest | Gold plated |

Designers:
  Obv.: Susanna Blunt
  Rev.: RCM Staff
Composition: 91.5% Ni, 8.5% Bronze
Weight: 7.0 g
11-sided: 26.5 mm
Finish: 1. Circulation, Lacquered
                    2. Circulation, Painted crest
                    3. Circulation, Gold plated
Case of Issue: See Derivatives, page 132

Engravers:
  Obv.: Susan Taylor
  Rev.: Konrad Wachelko
Thickness: 2.0 mm
Die Axis: ↑↑
Edge: Plain

DATE	DESCRIPTION	SOURCE	QUANTITY SOLD	ISSUE PRICE	FINISH	MS-65 NC	MS-66 NC
2009 (1909-)	Montreal Canadiens, Lacquered	Collector Set / Pack	N/A	N.I.I.	Lacquered	10.	15.
2009 (1909-)	Montreal Canadiens, Painted crest	Collector Set	526	N.I.I.	Painted	30.	35.
2009 (1909-)	Montreal Canadiens, Gold plated	Collector Set	9,500	N.I.I.	Gold plated	35.	40.

ONE DOLLAR, 100TH ANNIVERSARY OF THE CANADIAN NAVY, 1910-2010.

An enlisted seaman of 1910, and a female officer of 2010, in front of *HMCS Halifax* the lead ship in the Navy's current fleet are depicted on this commemorative coin.

Designers and Engravers:
Obv.:   Susanna Blunt, Susan Taylor
Rev.:   Bonnie Ross, Stan Witten
Composition: 1. Nickel bronze
2. Nickel bronze, Gold plated
Weight: 7.0 g
11-sided: 26.5 mm   **Edge:** Plain
Thickness: 1.9 mm   **Die Axis:** ↑↑
Finish: Circulation
Case: See Derivatives, page 132, and
Special Edition Uncirculated Sets, page 356

DATE	DESCRIPTION	QUANTITY SOLD	ISSUE PRICE	FINISH	MS-65 NC	MS-66 NC
2010 (1910-)	Canadian Navy Centennial	N/A	N.I.I.	Circulation	5.	8.
2010 (1910-)	Canadian Navy Centennial, Gold plated	10,085	19.95	Circulation	15.	18.

ONE DOLLAR, 100TH ANNIVERSARY OF THE SASKATCHEWAN ROUGHRIDERS, 1910-2010.

Designers and Engravers:
Obv.:   Susanna Blunt, Susan Taylor
Rev.:   Saskatchewan Roughriders Football
Club, RCM Staff
Composition: 1. Nickel bronze
2. Nickel bronze, Gold plated
Weight: 7.0 g
Diameter: 26.5 mm   **Edge:** Reeded
11-sided: 1.9 mm   **Die Axis:** ↑↑
Finish: Circulation
Case: 1. Uncirculated, See Special Edition
Uncirculated Sets, page 356
2. Gold plated, See Derivatives, page 132

DATE	DESCRIPTION	QUANTITY SOLD	ISSUE PRICE	FINISH	MS-65 NC	MS-66 NC
2010 (1910-)	Saskatchewan Roughriders	N/A	N.I.I.	Circulation	5.	8.
2010 (1910-)	Saskatchewan Roughriders, Gold plated	32,676	19.95	Circulation	12.	15.

ONE DOLLAR, 25TH ANNIVERSARY OF THE LOON DOLLAR, 1987-2012.

This coin was issued to celebrate the 25th anniversary of the loon dollar which was first introduced in 1987.

Designers and Engravers:
Obv.:   Susanna Blunt, Susan Taylor
Rev.:   R. R. Carmichael, RCM Staff
Composition: Silver plated bronze plated steel
Weight: 7.0 g
11-sided: 26.5 mm   **Edge:** Plain
Thickness: 1.9 mm   **Die Axis:** ↑↑
Finish: Circulation
Case: See Derivatives, page 132

DATE	DESCRIPTION	QUANTITY SOLD	ISSUE PRICE	FINISH	MS-65 NC	MS-66 NC
2012 (1987-)	25th Anniversary of the Loon Dollar	8,890	24.95	Circulation	25.	30.

NOTE TO COLLECTORS

The Canadian Navy and Saskatchewan Roughriders uncirculated nickel-bronze dollars are also found in the 2010 Special Edition Uncirculated Set, see page 356.

LOON STYLE NICKEL DOLLAR ISSUES, 2008-2010

ONE DOLLAR, 2007-2008 NHL HOCKEY SEASON, 2008 (GIFTWARE).

ROAD JERSEY CRESTS
This series of dollars is found in the NHL Teams Sets (see page 364).

Common obverse | Calgary Flames | Edmonton Oilers | Montreal Canadiens

Ottawa Senators | Toronto Maple Leafs | Vancouver Canucks

HOME JERSEY CRESTS
This series of dollars is found embedded in official NHL hockey pucks which are blister packaged.

Common Obverse | Calgary Flames | Edmonton Oilers | Montreal Canadiens

Designers and Engravers:
 Obv.: Susanna Blunt, Susan Taylor
 Rev.: RCM Staff
Composition: Nickel, Decal
Weight: 7.0 g
11-sided: 26.5 mm
Thickness: 1.9 mm
Edge: Plain
Die Axis: ↑↑

Ottawa Senators | Toronto Maple Leafs | Vancouver Canucks

Finish: Circulation
Case: Road Jersey Crests: Coloured folder **Home Jersey Crests:** Embedded in an official NHL puck, blister packaged

DATE	DESCRIPTION	SOURCE	QUANTITY SOLD	ISSUE PRICE	FINISH	MS-65 NC	MS-66 NC
2008	Calgary Flames, Road Jersey	NHL Set	N/A	N.I.I.	Circulation	20.	25.
2008	Edmonton Oilers, Road Jersey	NHL Set	1,584	N.I.I.	Circulation	20.	25.
2008	Montreal Canadiens, Road Jersey	NHL Set	2,659	N.I.I.	Circulation	20.	25.
2008	Ottawa Senators, Road Jersey	NHL Set	1,633	N.I.I.	Circulation	20.	25.
2008	Toronto Maple Leafs, Road Jersey	NHL Set	N/A	N.I.I.	Circulation	20.	25.
2008	Vancouver Canucks, Road Jersey	NHL Set	1,302	N.I.I.	Circulation	20.	25.
2008	Calgary Flames, Home Jersey	NHL Puck	1,304	15.95	Circulation	20.	25.
2008	Edmonton Oilers, Home Jersey	NHL Puck	484	15.95	Circulation	20.	25.
2008	Montreal Canadiens. Home Jersey	NHL Puck	62	15.95	Circulation	20.	25.
2008	Ottawa Senators, Home Jersey	NHL Puck	775	15.95	Circulation	20.	25.
2008	Toronto Maple Leafs, Home Jersey	NHL Puck	2,605	15.95	Circulation	20.	25.
2008	Vancouver Canucks, Home Jersey	NHL Puck	1,160	15.95	Circulation	20.	25.

ONE DOLLAR, 2008-2009 NHL HOCKEY SEASON, 2009 (GIFTWARE).

These nickel coloured dollar coins which feature the team logos are each embedded in a mini puck attached to a key chain. The key chain along with a mini hockey stick and an informative insert card are enclosed in a blister pack.

Common obverse

Calgary Flames

Edmonton Oilers

Montreal Canadiens

Ottawa Senators

Toronto Maple Leafs

Vancouver Canucks

Designers:
  Obv.: Susanna Blunt
  Rev.: RCM Staff
Composition: Nickel, Decal
Weight: 6.50 g
11-sided: 26.5 mm
Thickness: 1.7 mm
  Case of Issue: Blister packaged

Engravers:
  Obv.: Susan Taylor
  Rev.: RCM Staff

Edge: Plain
Die Axis: ↑↑
Finish: Circulation

DATE	DESCRIPTION	SOURCE	QUANTITY SOLD	ISSUE PRICE	FINISH	MS-65 NC	MS-66 NC
2009	Calgary Flames, Home Jersey	Mini Puck	73	24.95	Circulation	20.	25.
2009	Edmonton Oilers, Home Jersey	Mini Puck	49	24.95	Circulation	20.	25.
2009	Montreal Canadiens, Home Jersey	Mini Puck	326	24.95	Circulation	20.	25.
2009	Ottawa Senators, Home Jersey	Mini Puck	95	24.95	Circulation	20.	25.
2009	Toronto Maple Leafs, Home Jersey	Mini Puck	199	24.95	Circulation	20.	25.
2009	Vancouver Canucks, Home Jersey	Mini Puck	101	24.95	Circulation	20.	25.

Note: Mintage numbers are from the 2009 Royal Canadian Mint Annual Report. The 2008 and 2010 Annual Reports do not carry mintage numbers for these coins.

ONE DOLLAR, 2008-2009 NHL HOCKEY SEASON, 2009 (GIFTWARE) [cont.].

Road hockey jerseys folded in the shape of a heart are the central device on these nickel dollars. The coloured dollars are included in NHL Team Uncirculated Sets for the 2008-2009 season.

Common Obv.

Calgary Flames

Edmonton Oilers

Montreal Canadiens

Ottawa Senators

Toronto Maple Leafs

Vancouver Canucks

Designers:
  Obv.: Susanna Blunt
  Rev.: RCM Staff
Composition: Nickel, Decal
Weight: 7.0 g
11-sided: 26.5 mm
Thickness: 1.9 mm
Case of Issue: Blister packaged

Engravers:
  Obv.: Susan Taylor
  Rev.: RCM Staff

Edge: Plain
Die Axis: ↑↑
Finish: Circulationl

DATE	DESCRIPTION	SOURCE	QUANTITY SOLD	ISSUE PRICE	FINISH	MS-65 NC	MS-66 NC
2009	Calgary Flames, Road Jersey	NHL Sets	382	24.95	Circulation	20.	25.
2009	Edmonton Oilers, Road Jersey	NHL Sets	472	24.95	Circulation	20.	25.
2009	Montreal Canadiens, Road Jersey	NHL Sets	4,857	24.95	Circulation	20.	25.
2009	Ottawa Senators, Road Jersey	NHL Sets	387	24.95	Circulation	20.	25.
2009	Toronto Maple Leafs, Road Jersey	NHL Sets	1,328	24.95	Circulation	20.	25.
2009	Vancouver Canucks, Road Jersey	NHL Sets	794	24.95	Circulation	20.	25.

ONE DOLLAR, VANCOUVER 2010 LUCKY LOONIE, 2010.

This painted nickel dollar bearing the official emblem of the Vancouver 2010 Olympic Winter Games was used extensively in many giftware products (see derivatives, page 132). An identical variety in sterling silver, and with a proof finish, was issued as a Lucky Loonie, see page 128.

Designers and Engravers:
  Obv.: Susanna Blunt, Susan Taylor
  Rev.: José Osio
Composition: Nickel, Painted
Weight: 6.4 g
11-sided: 26.5 mm   **Edge:** Plain
Thickness: 1.9 mm   **Die Axis:** ↑↑
Finish: Circulation
Case: See Derivatives, page 132

DATE	DESCRIPTION	QUANTITY SOLD	ISSUE PRICE	FINISH	MS-65 NC	MS-66 NC
2010	Inukshuk, Vancouver 2010 Lucky Loonie, Painted	N/A	N.I.I.	Circulation	25.	30.

LOON STYLE STERLING and FINE SILVER DOLLAR PROOF ISSUES, 2004-2014

ONE DOLLAR, STERLING SILVER, LUCKY LOONIE, OLYMPIC LOGO, 2004.

This coin was issued as a Lucky Loonie for the Athens 2004 Olympic Summer Games.

Designers and Engravers:
Obv.:   Susanna Blunt, Susan Taylor
Rev.:   R. R. Carmichael, RCM Staff
Composition: 92.5% Ag, 7.5% Cu, Painted
Silver content: 6.475 g, 0.208 tr oz
Weight: 7.0 g
11-sided: 26.5 mm   **Edge:** Plain
Thickness: 1.9 mm   **Die Axis:** ↑↑
Finish: Proof
Case: Maroon leatherette square case, black flocked insert, encapsulated coin, COA

DATE	DESCRIPTION	SOURCE	QUANTITY SOLD	ISSUE PRICE	FINISH	PR-67	PR-68
2004	"Lucky Loonie"	Pr. Single	19,994	39.95	Proof	75.	80.

ONE DOLLAR, STERLING SILVER, SNOWFLAKE, 2006.

This Snowflake loon style silver dollar was issued in a blue Holiday folder with a Christmas Carol CD, and a picture frame.

Designers and Engravers:
Obv.:   Susanna Blunt, Susan Taylor
Rev.:   Marcos Hallam
Composition: 92.5% Ag, 7.5% Cu, Painted
Silver content: 6.475 g, 0.208 tr oz
Weight: 7.0 g
11-sided: 26.5 mm   **Edge:** Plain
Thickness: 1.9 mm   **Die Axis:** ↑↑
Finish: Proof
Case: Blue Holiday Folder

DATE	DESCRIPTION	SOURCE	QUANTITY SOLD	ISSUE PRICE	FINISH	PR-67	PR-68
2006	Snowflake, Painted	Holiday Set	34,014	34.95	Proof	50.	55.

ONE DOLLAR, STERLING SILVER, LOON SETTLING LUCKY LOONIE, OLYMPIC LOGO, 2006.

This coin was issued as a Lucky Loonie for the Turin 2006 Olympic Winter Games.

Designers and Engravers:
Obv.:   Susanna Blunt, Susan Taylor
Rev.:   RCM Staff, Cecily Mok
Composition: 92.5% Ag, 7.5% Cu, Painted
Silver content: 6.475 g, 0.208 tr oz
Weight: 7.0 g
11-sided: 26.5 mm   **Edge:** Plain
Thickness: 1.7 mm   **Die Axis:** ↑↑
Finish: Proof
Case: Maroon leatherette square case, black flocked insert, encapsulated coin, COA

DATE	DESCRIPTION	SOURCE	QUANTITY SOLD	ISSUE PRICE	FINISH	PR-67	PR-68
2006	Loon Settling, Lucky Loonie	Pr. Single	19,973	39.95	Proof	55.	60.

ONE DOLLAR, STERLING SILVER, LULLABY LOONIE, 2006.

This sterling silver Lullaby Loonie silver dollar was issued in the following packaging: (1) a presentation folder containing a baby's lullabies CD and a sterling silver Lullaby Loonie one dollar coin; (2) a box containing two baby keepsake tins (one for baby's first tooth and the other for a lock of hair) and a sterling silver Lullaby Loonie one dollar coin, and (3) a presentation folder containing a baby's lullabies CD, a sterling silver Lullaby Loonie one dollar coin, and a silver plated picture frame.

Designers and Engravers:
  Obv.:   Susanna Blunt, Susan Taylor
  Rev.:   Susan Taylor
Composition: 92.5% Ag, 7.5% Cu
Silver content: 6.475 g, 0.208 tr oz
Weight: 7.0 g
11-sided: 26.5 mm   **Edge:** Plain
Thickness: 1.9 mm   **Die Axis:** ↑↑
Finish: Proof
Case: See description

DATE	DESCRIPTION	SOURCE	QUANTITY SOLD	ISSUE PRICE	FINISH	PR-67	PR-68
2006	Lullaby Loonie, Sterling silver	Folder and CD	18,225	29.95	Proof	225.	250.
2006	Lullaby Loonie, Sterling silver	Keepsake Box	Included	34.95	Proof	225.	250.
2006	Lullaby Loonie, Sterling silver	CD and Picture Frame	Included	34.95	Proof	225.	250.
2006	Lullaby Loonie, Sterling silver	Premium Baby Gift Set	Included	N.I.I.	Proof	225.	250.

ONE DOLLAR, STERLING SILVER, BABY RATTLE, 2007.

The sterling silver Baby Rattle one dollar coin was issued along with a CD of lullabies in a colourful folder. A gold plated Baby Rattle one dollar coin was included in the Premium Gift Baby Set (see page 384).

Designers and Engravers:
  Obv.:   Susanna Blunt, Susan Taylor
  Rev.:   RCM Staff, Cecily Mok
Composition: 92.5% Ag, 7.5% Cu
Silver content: 6.475 g, 0.208 tr oz
Weight: 7.0 g
11-sided: 26.5 mm   **Edge:** Plain
Thickness: 1.9 mm   **Die Axis:** ↑↑
Finish: 1. Proof
       2. Proof, Gold plated
Case: See description

DATE	DESCRIPTION	SOURCE	QUANTITY SOLD	ISSUE PRICE	FINISH	PR-67	PR-68
2007	Baby Rattle, Silver	Folder and CD	3,207	34.95	Proof	75.	85.
2007	Baby Rattle, Gold plated	Premium Baby Gift Set	1,911	N.I.I.	Proof	75.	85.

ONE DOLLAR, STERLING SILVER, "ABC" BUILDING BLOCKS, 2007.

The "ABC" Building Blocks sterling silver one dollar coin was issued in a "Baby Keepsake Box" which also contained two small tins, one for baby's first tooth and the other for a lock of hair.

Designers and Engravers:
  Obv.:   Susanna Blunt, Susan Taylor
  Rev.:   Susan Taylor
Composition: 92.5% Ag, 7.5% Cu
Silver content: 6.475 g, 0.208 tr oz
Weight: 7.0 g
11-sided: 26.5 mm   **Edge:** Plain
Thickness: 1.9 mm   **Die Axis:** ↑↑
Finish: Proof
Case: See description

DATE	DESCRIPTION	SOURCE	QUANTITY SOLD	ISSUE PRICE	FINISH	PR-67	PR-68
2007	"ABC" Building Blocks	Keepsake Box	3,229	34.95	Proof	375.	400.

ONE DOLLAR, STERLING SILVER LOON, 2007-2008.

The sterling silver one dollar loon was issued in 2007 and 2008 for use in baby and wedding giftware sets. It was incorporated into: For 2007:   Premium sterling silver wedding proof set with medallion, see page 384

For 2008:   1. Premium sterling silver wedding proof set with medallion, see page 384
2. Premium sterling silver baby proof set
3. Baby keepsake tins, sterling silver loon dollar
4. CD and picture frame, sterling silver loon dollar

Designers and Engravers:
Obv.:   Susanna Blunt, Susan Taylor
Rev.:   R. R. Carmichael, Terry Smith
Composition: 92.5% Ag, 7.5% Cu
Silver content: 6.475 g, 0.208 tr oz
Weight: 7.0 g
11-sided: 26.5 mm   **Edge:** Plain
Thickness: 1.9 mm   **Die Axis:** ↑↑
Finish: Proof   **Case:** See above

DATE	DESCRIPTION	SOURCE	QUANTITY SOLD	ISSUE PRICE	FINISH	PR-67	PR-68
2007	Sterling Silver Loon	Premium Wedding Gift Set	849	N.I.I.	Proof	50.	60.
2008	Sterling Silver Loon	Premium Wedding Gift Set	N/A	N.I.I.	Proof	50.	60.
2008	Sterling Silver Loon	Premium Baby Gift Set	N/A	N.I.I.	Proof	50.	60.
2008	Sterling Silver Loon	Keepsake Box	N/A	N.I.I.	Proof	50.	60.
2008	Sterling Silver Loon	CD and Picture Frame Holder	N/A	N.I.I.	Proof	50.	60.

ONE DOLLAR, STERLING SILVER, OLYMPIC LOON DANCE, LUCKY LOONIE, OLYMPIC LOGO, 2008.

This coin was issued as a Lucky Loonie for the Beijing 2008 Olympic Summer Games.

Designers and Engravers:
Obv.:   Susanna Blunt, Susan Taylor
Rev.:   RCM Staff
Composition: 92.5% Ag, 7.5% Cu, Painted
Silver content: 6.475 g, 0.208 tr oz
Weight: 7.0 g   **Edge:** Plain
11-sided: 26.5 mm   **Die Axis:** ↑↑
Thickness: 1.9 mm   **Finish:** Proof
Case: Maroon leatherette clam style case, black flocked insert, encapsulated coin, COA Olympic theme outer sleeve

DATE	DESCRIPTION	SOURCE	QUANTITY SOLD	ISSUE PRICE	FINISH	PR-67	PR-68
2008	Olympic Loon Dance, Lucky Loonie	Pr. Single	52,987	49.95	Proof	40.	50.

ONE DOLLAR, STERLING SILVER, VANCOUVER 2010 LUCKY LOONIE, ANTICIPATING THE GAMES, 2010.

This is the third coin in the Lucky Loonie Inukshuk series issued for the Vancouver 2010 Winter Olympic Games. This coin is a sterling silver painted proof.

Designers and Engravers:
Obv.:   Susanna Blunt, Susan Taylor
Rev.:   José Osio
Composition: 92.5% Ag, 7.5% Cu, Painted
Silver content: 6.475 g, 0.208 tr oz
Weight: 7.0 g   **Edge:** Plain
11-sided: 26.5 mm   **Die Axis:** ↑↑
Thickness: 1.7 mm   **Finish:** Proof
Case: Black leatherette case, black flocked insert, encapsulated coin, COA, Olympic theme sleeve

DATE	DESCRIPTION	SOURCE	QUANTITY SOLD	ISSUE PRICE	FINISH	PR-67	PR-68
2010	Anticipating the Games	Pr. Single	13,285	54.95	Proof	50.	60.

ONE DOLLAR, ELIZABETH II, FINE SILVER, GOLD PLATED, PROOF, 1987-2012.

This double dated one dollar coin is from the Premium Edition Proof Set issued in 2012 to commemorate the 200th anniversary of the War of 1812. The coin is 99.99% silver with 24-karat gold plating.

Designers and Engravers:
Obv.:   Susanna Blunt, Susan Taylor
Rev.:   Ralph-Robert Carmichael, RCM Staff
Composition: 99.99% Ag, Gold plated
Silver content: 8.1 g, 0.26 tr oz
Weight: 8.1 g
11-sided: 26.5 mm   **Die Axis:** ↑↑
Thickness: 1.9 mm   **Edge:** Plain
Finish: Proof
Case: See Premium Proof Sets, page 381

DATE	DESCRIPTION	QUANTITY SOLD	ISSUE PRICE	FINISH	PR-67	PR-68
2012 (1987-)	Fine Silver, Gold Plated	19,789	N.I.I.	Proof	80.	90.

ONE DOLLAR, 25TH ANNIVERSARY OF THE LOONIE, FINE SILVER, 1987-2012.

This coin was issued to commemorate the 25th anniversary of this popular coin. The first loon dollar was struck in 1987 to replace the Bank of Canada one dollar notes.

Designers and Engravers:
Obv.:   Susanna Blunt, Susan Taylor
Rev.:   Robert-Ralph Carmichael, RCM Staff
Composition: 99.99% Ag
Silver content: 7.89 g, 0.254 tr oz
Weight: 7.89 g   **Die Axis:** ↑↑
11-sided: 26.5 mm   **Edge:** Plain
Thickness: 1.8 mm
Finish: Matte Proof
Case: Maroon leatherette clam style case, black flocked insert, encapsulated coin, COA Custom coloured sleeve

DATE	DESCRIPTION	QUANTITY SOLD	ISSUE PRICE	FINISH	PR-67	PR-68
2012 (1987-)	25th Anniversary of the Loonie	15,004	34.95	Proof	40.	45.

ONE DOLLAR, 25TH ANNIVERSARY OF THE LUCKY LOONIE, OLYMPIC LOGO, FINE SILVER, 2012.

This coin was issued as a Lucky Loonie for the London 2012 Olympic Summer Games. It features the Canadian Olympic Team logo on the reverse in support of Canada's athletes.

Designers and Engravers:
Obv.:   Susanna Blunt, Susan Taylor
Rev.:   Emily Damstra, RCM Staff
Composition: 99.99% Ag, Painted
Silver content: 7.89 g, 0.254 tr oz
Weight: 7.89   **Edge:** Plain
11-sided: 26.5 mm   **Die Axis:** ↑↑
Thickness: 1.8 mm   **Finish:** Proof
Case: Maroon leatherette clam style case, black flocked insert, encapsulated coin, COA custom coloured sleeve

DATE	DESCRIPTION	SOURCE	QUANTITY SOLD	ISSUE PRICE	FINISH	PR-67	PR-68
2012	25th Anniversary of the Lucky Loonie	Pr. Single	19,982	39.95	Proof	40.	45.

ONE DOLLAR, ELIZABETH II, FINE SILVER, GOLD PLATED, PROOF, 2013-2014.
These one dollar coins are from Premium Proof Sets. They are 99.99% silver with 24-karat gold plating.

Obverse
"P"
Gold
plated

Designers and Engravers:
　　Obv.:　Susanna Blunt, Susan Taylor
　　Rev.:　RCM Staff
Composition: 99.99% Ag, Gold plated
Silver content: 7.0 g, 0.225 tr oz
Weight: 7.0 g　　　　　**Die Axis:** ↑↑
11-sided: 26.5 mm　　　**Edge:** Plain
Thickness: 1.9 mm
Finish: Proof
Case: See Premium Proof Sets, page 382

DATE	DESCRIPTION	SOURCE	QUANTITY SOLD	ISSUE PRICE	FINISH	PR-67	PR-68
2013	Elizabeth II, Fine Silver, Gold Plated	Pr. Set	20,182	N.I.I.	Proof	35.	40.
2014	Elizabeth II, Fine Silver, Gold Plated	Pr. Set	25,000	N.I.I.	Proof	35.	40.

ONE DOLLAR, LUCKY LOONIE, OLYMPIC LOGO, FINE SILVER, 2014.
This coin was issued as a Lucky Loonie for the Sochi 2014 Olympic Winter Games. It features the Canadian Olympic Team logo on the reverse in support of Canada's athletes.

Designers and Engravers:
　　Obv.:　Susanna Blunt, Susan Taylor
　　Rev.:　Emily Damstra, RCM Staff
Composition: 99.99% Ag, Painted
Silver content: 7.89 g, 0.254 tr oz
Weight: 7.89
11-sided: 26.5 mm　　　**Edge:** Plain
Thickness: 1.8 mm　　　**Die Axis:** ↑↑
Finish: Reverse Proof
Case:　Maroon leatherette clam style case, black
　　　　flocked insert, encapsulated coin, COA

DATE	DESCRIPTION	SOURCE	QUANTITY SOLD	ISSUE PRICE	FINISH	PR-67	PR-68
2014	Olympic Lucky Loonie	Pr. Single	15,000	39.95	Proof	40.	45.

THREE-PLY BRASS-PLATED STEEL DOLLAR ISSUES, 2014

ONE DOLLAR, LOON, OCCASIONS SETS, 2014.
These one dollar coins are from the 2014 Occasions Gift Sets.

| Common Obv. | Stork
Born in 2014 | Gifts and Balloons
Happy Birthday 2014 | Maple Leaf
O Canada 2014 | Two Turtle Doves
Married in 2014 |

Designers:
  Obv.: Susanna Blunt
  Rev.: RCM Staff
Composition: 3-ply brass plated steel
Weight: 6.27 g
11-sided: 26.5 mm
Edge: Plain
Finish: Uncirculated

Engravers:
  Rev.: Susan Taylor
  Rev.: RCM Staff

Thickness: 1.9 mm
Die Axis: ↑↑
Case of Issue: Coloured folder

DATE	DESCRIPTION	QUANTITY SOLD	ISSUE PRICE	FINISH	MS-65
2014	Stork, Born in 2014	N/A	N.I.I.	Circulation	20.
2014	Gifts and Balloons, Happy Birthday 2014	N/A	N.I.I.	Circulation	20.
2014	Maple Leaf, O Canada 2014	N/A	N.I.I.	Circulation	20.
2014	Two Turtle Doves, Married in 2014	N/A	N.I.I.	Circulation	20.

ONE DOLLAR, ELIZABETH II PROOF, 2014.
This coin is from the 2014 Standard Proof Set.

Designers and Engravers:
  Obv.: Susanna Blunt, Susan Taylor
  Rev.: RCM Staff
Composition: 3-ply brass plated steel
Weight: 6.27
11-sided: 26.5 mm   **Edge:** Plain
Thickness: 1.9 mm   **Die Axis:** ↑↑
Finish: Proof
Case of Issue: See Proof Sets, page 382

DATE	DESCRIPTION	SOURCE	QUANTITY SOLD	ISSUE PRICE	FINISH	PR-67	PR-68
2014	Elizabeth II Proof Coin	Pr. Set	30,000	N.I.I.	Proof	25.	30.

ONE DOLLAR DERIVATIVES

DATE	DESCRIPTION	QUANTITY SOLD	ISSUE PRICE	ISSUER	FINISH	MARKET VALUE
1993	**Silver Dollar, 100th Anniversary of the Stanley Cup**, 43¢ Stanley Cup Commemorative Stamp	N/A	28.95	RCM, CP	MS-65	40.
1997	**Silver Dollar, Canada/Russia Hockey;** Two 45¢ mint stamps; $5 phone card; Multicoloured folder	N/A	29.95	RCM, CP	MS-65	50.
1997	**Silver Dollar, Canada/Russia Hockey;** Sterling silver pin	N/A	29.95	RCM	MS-65	40.
1997	**Silver Dollar, Canada/Russia Hockey;** Print	N/A	24.95	RCM	MS-65	40.
1997	**Silver Dollar, Canada/Russia Hockey;** Phone card/stamp set	N/A	N/A	RCM	MS-65	40.
1998	**Loon Dollar;** Mint and cancelled one dollar stamps; Blue presentation case	N/A	17.99	RCM, CP	MS-65	10.
1998	**Silver Dollar, 125th Anniv. R.C.M.P.;** Pin	N/A	29.95	RCM	MS-65	40.
1999	**Silver Dollar, 225th Anniv. Juan Perez;** Journal Gift Set; Multicoloured folder	N/A	N/A	RCM, CP	MS-65	40.
2000	**Loon Dollar**, Mint and cancelled one dollar stamps; Blue presentation case	N/A	17.99	RCM, CP	MS-65	10.
2000	**Loon Dollar**, Encapsulated in a credit card	N/A	N/A	RCM	MS-65	5.
2001	**Loon Dollar**, Encapsulated in a credit card	N/A	N/A	RCM	MS-65	5.
2001	**Loon /Sacagawea Dollars**, Folder	N/A	N/A	RCM, USM	MS-65	10.
2002	**Centre Ice Loon**, 22kt gold-plated bronze; block of four 48¢ stamps, Two Olympic Edition Macleans' magazines (one English, one French); "Going For Gold" Souvenir album, COA	25,000	54.95	RCM, CP, MM	PR-67	60.
2004	**Silver Dollar, 2004 French Settlement with privy mark;** 2004 silver ¼ Euro; Canada 49¢ stamps, mint/cancelled; France .90 Euro stamps, mint/cancelled; Wooden presentation case, blue insert, encapsulated coins, COA	8,273	99.95	RCM, CP	MS-65	100.
2004	**Elusive Loon with Privy Mark**, Mint and cancelled one dollar stamps; Wooden presentation case	12,550	25.22	RCM, CP	PR-67	60.
2005	**Silver Dollar**, 40th Anniversary of Canada's National Flag, CD-Rom; Presentation folder	N/A	34.95	RCM	MS-65	40.
2006	**Lucky Loonie Bookmark** "Celebrate the Legend"	10,095	N/A	RCM	MS-65	15.
2008	**Nickel Bronze Lucky Loonie** embedded in Lucite	N/A	N/A	RCM	MS-65	15.
2009	**Montreal Canadiens 100th Anniversary Pack**, 100th anniv. dollar coin and a lenticular souvenir sheet	15,473	19.95	RCM	MS-65	50.
2009	**Montreal Canadiens 100th Anniversary Collector Set**, three one dollar coins (lacquered, coloured crest, gold plated), a sheet of three stamps, a lenticular souvenir sheet, 15 named retired jersey plaquettes, souvenir booklet	526	149.95	RCM	MS-65	100.
2010	**Vancouver 2010 Colourised Nickel Bronze Lucky Loonie,** encapsulated and embedded in NHL puck; Blister packaged	30,396	19.95	RCM	MS-65	30.
2010	**Sport Bag Tag**, colourised Vancouver 2010 Lucky Loonie dollar and lapel pin, green "See In Tin" container.	N/A	14.95	RCM	MS-65	30.
2010	**Lanyard**, colourised Vancouver 2010 Lucky Loonie dollar	N/A	14.95	RCM	MS-65	35.
2010	**Hockey Player Lapel Pin Set**, colourised 2010 Lucky Loonie dollar and six "hockey player" lapel pins.	N/A	N/A	RCM	MS-65	75.
2010	**100th Anniversary Canadian Navy Coin and Stamp Set**, Gold plated nickel-bronze dollar; souvenir stamp sheet; 40-page booklet; square aluminum tin	20,000	39.95	RCM, CP	MS-65	35.
2010	**100th Anniversary Saskatchewan Roughriders,** Gold plated nickel-bronze dollar; pop-up helmet packaging	N/A	19.95	RCM	MS-65	35.
2012	**25th Anniversary of the Loonie Coin Card**, "Build Your Own" paper toy, Mini-book, Coin card	N/A	24.95	RCM	MS-65	25.
2012	**CFL Ultimate Collector Set,** Grey Cup circulation loon style dollar, a special pane of nine commemorative stamps, a souvenir sheet featuring the eight CFL team logos, 100th Grey Cup 1 oz pure silver wafer, a replica Grey Cup, ten silver-edged collectable pins, souvenir booklet	8,000	199.95	RCM, CP	MS-65	200.

Note: CP = Canada Post; MM = Maclean's Magazine; RCM = Royal Canadian Mint; USM = United States Mint

TWO DOLLARS

TWO DOLLARS, STERLING SILVER PROOF COINS, 1997-2011.

In 1997 the two-dollar coin was added to the proof set. The standard nickel/bronze composition was not used, instead planchets were made from sterling silver with a gold-plated core.

| Obverse
1997-2003 | Obverse
2004-2006
Without Mint Logo | Obverse
2007-2011
With Mint Logo | Reverse
1997-2011 |

Designers:
  Obv.:   1997-2003: Dora de Pédery-Hunt
          2004-2011: Susanna Blunt
  Rev.:   1997-2011: Brent Townsend
Composition: 92.5% Ag, 7.5% Cu
Silver content: 8.17 g, 0.263 tr oz
Weight: 8.83 g
Diameter: 28.1 mm
Thickness: 1.9 mm

Engravers:
  Obv.:   1997-2003: Dora de Pédery-Hunt
          2004-2011: Susan Taylor
  Rev.:   1997-2011: Ago Aarand

Edge: Interrupted serrations
Die Axis: ↑↑
Finish: Proof
Case of Issue: See Proof Sets, page 380

DATE	DESCRIPTION	QUANTITY SOLD	ISSUE PRICE	FINISH	PR-67	PR-68
1997	Diademed Portrait / Polar Bear; Sterling Silver	113,647	N.I.I.	Proof	15.	20.
1998		93,632	N.I.I.	Proof	20.	25.
1999		95,113	N.I.I.	Proof	15.	20.
2000		90,921	N.I.I.	Proof	20.	25.
2001		74,194	N.I.I.	Proof	20.	25.
2002		65,315	N.I.I.	Proof	20.	25.
2003		62,007	N.I.I.	Proof	15.	20.
2004	Uncrowned Portrait / Polar Bear; Sterling Silver	57,614	N.I.I.	Proof	15.	20.
2005		63,562	N.I.I.	Proof	15.	20.
2006		53,822	N.I.I.	Proof	20.	25.
2007	Uncrowned Portrait, Mint Logo / Polar Bear; Sterling Silver	37,413	N.I.I.	Proof	20.	25.
2008		38,630	N.I.I.	Proof	20.	25.
2009		27,549	N.I.I.	Proof	20.	25.
2010		32,342	N.I.I.	Proof	20.	25.
2011		32,910	N.I.I.	Proof	20.	25.

Note: 1. Quantity sold figures are identical to those listed for Proof Sets sold.
  2. Continuation from 2012 forward of the two-dollar proof coins is listed on page 140. The break in the listing is due to a change in composition.

The first Canadian two dollar coin was issued in 1996 to replace the two dollar bank note which was then withdrawn from circulation. To mark this event the Numismatic Department of the Royal Canadian Mint issued four different planchet varieties, in two different finishes. —

TWO DOLLARS, POLAR BEAR, 1996.
The 1996 two dollar Piedfort was not issued singly, but as part of a set. See the Two Dollar Derivatives, page 140.

| Obv.: Nickel / Bronze | Obv.: Nickel / Bronze | Obv.: Gold / Gold | Rev.: Gold / Gold |

Designers:
  Obv.: Dora de Pédery-Hunt
  Rev.: Brent Townsend

Engravers:
  Obv.: Dora de Pédery-Hunt
  Rev.: Ago Aarand

Composition:

	Nickel Ring	Silver Ring	White Gold Ring
	99.0% Ni	92.5% Ag	17.2% Au
		07.5% Cu	77.6% Ag, 5.2% Cu
	Bronze Core	**Silver Gilt Core**	**Yellow Gold Core**
	92.0 % Cu	92.5% Ag	91.7% Au
	6.0% Al, 2.0% Ni	07.5% Cu	04.1% Ag, 4.2% Cu

	Standard	Standard	Piedford	Standard
Weight (g):	Ring 4.84	Ring 5.86	Ring 11.72	Ring 6.31
	Core 2.46	Core 2.97	Core 5.94	Core 5.09
	Total 7.3	Total 8.83	Total 17.66	Total 11.4
Content: Gold	—	—	—	0.185 tr oz
Silver	—	0.263 tr oz	0.525 tr oz	0.164 tr oz
Diameter (mm):	Ring 28.0	Ring 28.1	Ring 28.1	Ring 28.0
	Core 16.8	Core 16.8	Core 16.8	Core 16.8
Thickness (mm):	1.8	1.9	3.6	1.8
Edge:	Interrupted serrations	Interrupted serrations	Interrupted serrations	Interrupted serrations
Die Axis:	↑↑	↑↑	↑↑	↑↑
Finish:	Specimen, Proof	Proof	Proof	Proof

Case of Issue: Nickel / Bronze, Specimen: Blue presentation folder
                 Nickel / Bronze, Proof: Black leatherette case, blue insert, encapsulated coin, COA
                 Silver / Gilt, Proof: Black suede case, blue insert, encapsulated coin, COA
                 Gold / Gold, Proof: Blue suede case, blue insert, encapsulated coin, COA

DATE	DESCRIPTION	QUANTITY SOLD	ISSUE PRICE	FINISH	65	66	67	68
1996	Nickel / Bronze, Blue folder	74,669	10.95	Specimen	—	10.	15.	—
1996	Nickel / Bronze, Black leatherette case	66,843	24.95	Proof	—	—	15.	20.
1996	Silver / Gilt, Black suede case	N/A	N/A	Proof	—	—	20.	25.
1996	Silver / Gilt, Piedfort, See Derivatives	11,526	N.I.I.	Proof	—	—	150.	175.
1996	Gold / Gold, Blue case	5,000	299.95	Proof	—	—	375.	400.

NOTE ON TWO DOLLAR ISSUES
1. The blue presentation folder was printed "uncirculated" but the $2 coin has a specimen finish.
2. Piedfort is a term used to describe a double thickness or essaie coin, usually struck for approval, see Derivatives page 140.

TWO DOLLARS, NUNAVUT, PROOF COMMEMORATIVE, 1999.
   This coin commemorates the formation of Nunavut, Canada's third territory, in 1999. The design honours the native drum dance.

| Obv.: Nickel / Bronze | Rev.: Nickel / Bronze | Obv.: Gold / Gold | Rev.: Gold / Gold |

Designers:
   Obv.: Dora de Pédery-Hunt
   Rev.: G. Arnaktauyok

Engravers:
   Obv.: Dora de Pédery-Hunt
   Rev.: Ago Aarand, José Osio

Composition:

Nickel Ring	Silver Ring	White Gold Ring
99.0% Ni	92.5% Ag	17.2% Au
	07.5% Cu	77.6% Ag, 5.2% Cu
Bronze Core	**Silver Gilt Core**	**Yellow Gold Core**
92.0 % Cu	92.5% Ag	91.7% Au
6.0% Al, 2.0% Ni	07.5% Cu	04.1% Ag, 4.2% Cu

	Standard	**Standard**	**Standard**
Weight (g):	Ring 4.84	Ring 5.86	Ring 6.31
	Core 2.46	Core 2.97	Core 5.09
	Total 7.3	Total 8.83	Total 11.4
Content: Gold	—	—	0.185 tr oz
Silver	—	0.263 tr oz	0.164 tr oz
Diameter (mm):	Ring 28.0	Ring 28.1	Ring 28.0
	Core 16.8	Core 16.8	Core 16.8
Thickness (mm):	1.8	1.9	1.8
Edge:	Interrupted	Interrupted	Interrupted
	serrations	serrations	serrations
Die Axis:	↑↑	↑↑	↑↑
Finish:	Brilliant Uncirculated,	Proof	Proof
	Specimen		

Case of Issue: Nickel / Bronze, Brilliant Uncirculated: Blue presentation folder
   Nickel / Bronze, Specimen: Maple wood case, encapsulated coin, window box
   Silver / Gilt, Proof: Green leatherette case, black insert, encapsulated coin, COA
   Gold / Gold, Proof: Antique case, black insert, encapsulated coin, COA

DATE	DESCRIPTION	SOURCE	QUANTITY SOLD	ISSUE PRICE	FINISH	65	66	67	68
1999	Nickel / Bronze	BU Set	N/A	N/A	BU	10.	15.	—	—
1999	Nickel / Bronze	Specimen Set, Maple wood case	20,000	N/A	Specimen	—	20.	25.	—
1999	Silver / Gilt	Proof Set, Single	39,873	24.95	Proof	—	—	30.	35.
1999	Gold / Gold	Single Case	4,298	299.95	Proof	—	—	375.	400.

VARIETIES OF 1999.

Three different reverse dies were used to produce the three different finishes on the 1999 Nunavut commemorative two dollar coins.

1. Reverse Circulation Die: Raised narrow ring encircling the join between the ring and the core.
2. Reverse Specimen Die: Raised wide ring encircling the join between the ring and the core.
3. Reverse Proof Die: No encircling ring between the ring and the core.

Reverse	Reverse	Reverse:
Narrow Ring	Wide Ring	No Ring
Brilliant Uncirculated	Specimen Dies	Proof Dies
Dies		

Two varieties of brilliant uncirculated sets were produced in 1999. The standard set, where the $2 coin was produced with a pair of brilliant uncirculated dies, and the Mule variety where the $2 coin was produced with an obverse brilliant uncirculated die and a reverse proof die. See page 348 for the listings of the 1999 brilliant uncirculated sets.

Nickel bronze, no ring reverse mule

DATE	DESCRIPTION	QUANTITY SOLD	ISSUE PRICE	FINISH	65	66	67	68
1999	Mule from Brilliant Uncirculated Sets	Unknown	N.I.I.	BU	250.	275.	—	—

TWO DOLLARS, PATH OF KNOWLEDGE COMMEMORATIVE, 2000.

The mother polar bear passes to her cubs the lesson of survival on the Arctic ice floes.

Obverse	**Reverse**	**Obverse**	**Reverse**
Nickel / Bronze	**Nickel / Bronze**	**Gold / Gold**	**Gold / Gold**

Designers:
  Obv.: Dora de Pédery-Hunt
  Rev.: Tony Bianco

Engravers:
  Obv.: Dora de Pédery-Hunt
  Rev.: Cosme Saffioti

Composition:	**Nickel Ring**	**Silver Ring**	**White Gold Ring**
	99.0% Ni	92.5% Ag	17.2% Au
		07.5% Cu	77.6% Ag, 5.2% Cu
	Bronze Core	**Silver Gilt Core**	**Yellow Gold Core**
	92.0 % Cu	92.5% Ag	91.7% Au
	6.0% Al, 2.0% Ni	07.5% Cu	04.1% Ag, 4.2% Cu
	Standard	**Standard**	**Standard**
Weight (g):	Ring 4.84	Ring 5.86	Ring 6.31
	Core 2.46	Core 2.97	Core 5.09
	Total 7.3	Total 8.83	Total 11.4
Content: Gold	—	—	0.185 tr oz
Silver	—	0.263 tr oz	0.164 tr oz
Diameter (mm):	Ring 28.0	Ring 28.1	Ring 28.0
	Core 16.8	Core 16.8	Core 16.8
Thickness (mm):	1.8	1.9	1.8
Edge:	Interrupted	Interrupted	Interrupted
	serrations	serrations	serrations
Die Axis:	↑↑	↑↑	↑↑
Finish:	Brilliant Uncirculated,	Proof	Proof
	Specimen		

Case of Issue: Nickel / Bronze, Specimen: Maple wood case, encapsulated coin, sleeve
                      Silver / Gilt, Proof: Green leatherette case, black insert, encapsulated coin, COA
                      Gold / Gold, Proof: Antique case, black insert, encapsulated coin, COA

DATE	DESCRIPTION	SOURCE	QUANTITY SOLD	ISSUE PRICE	FINISH	65	66	67	68
2000	Nickel / Bronze, wood case	BU Set	186,985	15.95	BU	10.	15.	—	—
2000	Nickel / Bronze	Specimen Single	1,500	N/A	Specimen	—	20.	30.	—
2000	Nickel / Bronze	Specimen Set	N/A	34.95	Specimen	—	20.	30.	—
2000	Silver / Gilt Silver	Proof Single	39,768	24.95	Proof	—	—	25.	30.
2000	Gold / Gold	Proof Single	5,881	299.95	Proof	—	—	375.	400.

TWO DOLLARS, POLAR BEAR, 2000-2001.

Designers and Engravers:
　Obv.:　Dora de Pédery-Hunt
　Rev.:　Brent Townsend, Ago Aarand
Composition:　Bronze
　Ring:　99.0% Nickel
　Core:　92.0% Cu, 6.0% Al, 2.0% Ni
Weight:　Ring: 4.84 g, Core: 2.46 g
　Total weight: 7.3 g
Diameter:　Ring: 28.5 mm, Core: 16.8 mm
Thickness:　1.8 mm
Edge:　Interrupted serrations
Die Axis: ↑↑　　　　　**Finish:**　Specimen
Case:　Maple wood case, encapsulated coin, sleeve

DATE	DESCRIPTION	QUANTITY SOLD	ISSUE PRICE	FINISH	SP-66	SP-67
2000	Nickel / Bronze, wood case	20,000	N/A	Specimen	25.	30.
2001	Nickel / Bronze, wood case	20,000	N/A	Specimen	25.	30.

TWO DOLLARS, PROUD POLAR BEAR, STERLING SILVER, 2004.

Issued jointly by the Royal Canadian Mint and Canada Post, the $2 Proud Polar Bear Stamp and Coin Set contains the first single metal two dollar Canadian coin. The set comprises mint and cancelled $2.00 stamps, along with the $2.00 sterling silver coin. The two dollar coin is unusual in that it carries two maple leaf privy marks.

Designer and Engravers:
　Obv.:　Susanna Blunt, Susan Taylor
　Rev.:　Stan Witten
Composition:　92.5% Ag, 7.5% Cu
Silver content:　8.14 g, 0.262 tr oz
Weight:　8.8 g　　　　　**Edge:**　Reeded
Diameter:　28.0 mm　　**Die Axis:** ↑↑
Thickness:　1.7 mm　　　**Finish:**　Proof
Case:　See Derivatives, page 140

DATE	DESCRIPTION	QUANTITY SOLD	ISSUE PRICE	FINISH	PR-67	PR-68
2004	Proud Polar Bear, Sterling silver	12,607	N.I.I.	Proof	45.	50.

TWO DOLLARS, 10TH ANNIVERSARY, GOLD, 1996-2006.

This gold two dollar coin does not carry the karat marks similar to the previous gold issues of 1996, 1999 and 2000.

Designers and Engravers:
　Obv.:　Susanna Blunt, Susan Taylor
　Rev.:　Brent Townsend, Ago Aarand
Composition:
　Yellow Gold Ring: 91.7% Au, 4.1% Ag, 4.2% Cu
　White Gold Core: 17.5% Au, 77.6 Ag, 5.2% Cu
Gold content:　Gold:　10.352 g, 0.333 tr oz
　　　　　　　　Silver: 3.151 g, 0.101 tr oz
Weight:　Ring: 10.62 g, Core:　3.6 g
　Total:　14.22 g
Diameter:　Ring: 28.0 mm, Core:　16.8 mm
Thickness:　1.8 mm
Edge:　Interrupted serrations
Die Axis: ↑↑　　　　　**Finish:**　Proof
Case:　Maroon clam style case, black insert, encapsulated coin, COA

DATE	DESCRIPTION	QUANTITY SOLD	ISSUE PRICE	FINISH	PR-67	PR-68
2006 (1996-)	Yellow gold ring / White gold core	2,068	399.95	Proof	650.	700.

TWO DOLLARS, CHURCHILL REVERSE, RCM LOGO, 1996-2006.

In 2006 a contest was held to name a new polar bear design to appear of the 10th anniversary two dollar coin. The name "Churchill" was the winner. The 10th anniversary coin has the double dates above the Queen's portrait and the Royal Mint logo below.

Designers and Engravers:
  Obv.: Susanna Blunt, Susan Taylor
  Rev.: Tony Bianco, Stan Witten
Composition:
  Ring: 99.9% Ni
  Core: 92.0% Cu, 6.0% Al, 2.0% Ni
Weight: 7.3 g
Diameter: Ring: 28.0 mm, Core: 16.8 mm
Thickness: 1.8 mm
Edge: Interrupted serrations   **Die Axis:** ↑↑
Finish: Brilliant Uncirculated
Case: See Special Uncirculated Sets, page 353

DATE	DESCRIPTION	QUANTITY SOLD	ISSUE PRICE	FINISH	MS-65 NC	MS-66 NC
2006 (1996-)	"Churchill" Polar Bear	31,636	N.I.I.	BU	15.	20.

YOUNG WILDLIFE SERIES

TWO DOLLARS, YOUNG WILDLIFE SERIES, 2010-2014.

These two dollar coins are from the Special Edition Specimen Sets.

| Common Obverse | 2010 Lynx Kittens | 2011 Elk Calf |

| 2012 Wolf Cubs | 2013 Black Bear Cubs | 2014 Baby Rabbits |

Designers:
  Obv.: Susanna Blunt
  Rev.: 2010-2012: Christie Paquet
         2013: Glen Loates; 2014: Pierre Leduc
Composition:
  Ring: 99.9% Ni
  Core: 92.0% Cu, 6.0% Al, 2.0% Cu
Weight: 7.5 g
Edge: Interrupted serrations
Finish: Specimen; Brilliant portrait, frosted relief lined background
Case of Issue: See Special Edition Specimen Sets, page 376

Engravers:
  Obv.: Susan Taylor
  Rev.: Christie Paquet
Diameter:
  Ring: 28.0 mm
  Core: 16.8 mm
Thickness: 1.9 mm
Die Axis: ↑↑

DATE	DESCRIPTION	QUANTITY SOLD	ISSUE PRICE	FINISH	SP-66	SP-67
2010	Lynx Kittens	14,790	N.I.I.	Specimen	45.	50.
2011	Elk Calf	13,899	N.I.I.	Specimen	65.	70.
2012	Wolf Cubs	14,968	N.I.I.	Specimen	35.	40.
2013	Black Bear Cubs	14,394	N.I.I.	Specimen	35.	40.
2014	Baby Rabbits	17,500	N.I.I.	Specimen	35.	40.

TWO DOLLARS, ELIZABETH II, FINE SILVER, GOLD PLATED INNER CORE, PROOF, 2012-2014.

During 2012 and 2104 the Mint produced two varieties of proof set, a Premium Set in which the planchets used are of fine silver, and a Standard Set, of which the planchets used are of the standard alloys.

| Obv.: 2012 | Obv.: 2013-2014 | Common Reverse |

Designers:
Obv.: Susanna Blunt
Rev.: Tony Bianco

Engravers:
Obv.: Susan Taylor
Rev.: Stan Witten

	Premium - Fine Silver	**Standard - Nickel Brass**
Composition:	Outer ring: Fine silver	Outer ring: Three-ply nickel finish plated steel
	Inner Core: Gold plated, 99.99% Ag,	Inner Core: Brass-plated aluminum bronze
Silver content:	9.0 g, 0.289 tr oz	
Weight:	9.0 (2013) to 9.0 (2012 & 2014) g	6.99 g
Diameter:	Ring: 28.0 mm	Ring: 28.0 mm
	Core: 16.8 mm	Core: 16.8 mm
Thickness:	1.80 mm	1.80 mm
Edge:	Interrupted serrations	Interrupted serrations
Die Axis:	↑↑	↑↑
Finish:	Proof	Proof
Case of Issue:	See Proof and Premium Proof Sets, page 381-382	

DATE	DESCRIPTION	COMPOSITION	QUANTITY SOLD	ISSUE PRICE	FINISH	PR-67	PR-68
2012	Elizabeth II	Nickel brass	26,891	N.I.I.	Proof	40.	45.
2012	Elizabeth II	Fine silver	19,789	N.I.I.	Proof	90.	100.
2013	Elizabeth II	Fine silver	20,182	N.I.I.	Proof	90.	100.
2014	Elizabeth II	Nickel brass	25,000	N.I.I.	Proof	40.	45.
2014	Elizabeth II	Fine silver	25,000	N.I.I.	Proof	90.	100.

TWO DOLLAR DERIVATIVES

The following single coins, coin and note sets, or coin and stamp sets, are based on the numismatic two dollar coins.

DATE	DESCRIPTION	QUANTITY SOLD	ISSUE PRICE	ISSUER	FINISH	MARKET VALUE
1996	**Two Dollar Coin, Specimen;** $2 Regular bank note; Blue folder	91,427	29.95	RCM	SP-66	30.
1996	**Encapsulated Two Dollar Coin, Proof;** Encapsulated $2 BRX Replacement note; Blue presentation case	27,103	79.95	RCM	PR-67	40.
1996	**Encapsulated Two Dollar Coin, Piedfort;** Encapsulated pair of uncut $2 BRX replacement notes; Blue/green presentation case	11,526	179.95	RCM	PR-67	175.
1996	**Two Dollar Coin, Brilliant Uncirculated;** $2 regular issue note; 45¢ mint stamp; Blue/green presentation case	N/A	N/A	RCM, CP	MS-65	30.
1998W	**Two Dollar Coin;** Mint and cancelled $2 stamps; Blue presentation case	N/A	N/A	RCM, CP	MS-65	30.
1999	**Two Dollar Nunavut Coin;** Mint and cancelled 46¢ stamps; Blue presentation case	N/A	17.95	RCM, CP	MS-65	30.
2000W	**Two Dollar Coin;** Mint and cancelled $2 stamps; Blue presentation case	20,000	19.99	RCM, CP	MS-65	20.
2000	**Two Dollar Coin, "Path of Knowledge" (Three Bears);** Credit card-like holder	N/A	N/A	RCM	MS-65	10.
2001	**Two Dollar Coin;** Credit card-like holder	N/A	N/A	RCM	MS-65	10.
2004	**Two Dollar Proud Polar Bear Coin;** Mint and cancelled $2 stamps; Wooden presentation case	12,607	29.95	RCM, CP	PR-67	65.

THREE DOLLARS

THREE DOLLARS, THE BEAVER, SQUARE, 2006.

Designers and Engravers:
 Obv.: Susanna Blunt, Cosme Saffioti
 Rev.: Cosme Saffioti, Cosme Saffioti
Composition: 92.50% Ag, 7.50 %Cu
  plated in 24kt gold
Silver content: 10.84 g, 0.349 tr oz
Weight: 11.72 g
Size: 27.0 x 27.0 mm   **Edge:** Plain
Thickness: 1.80 mm   **Die Axis:** ↑↑
Finish: Specimen
Case: Maroon plastic slide case; black plastic
  insert; encapsulated coin, COA

DATE	DESCRIPTION	QUANTITY SOLD	ISSUE PRICE	FINISH	SP-66	SP-67
2006	The Beaver	20,000	45.95	Specimen	150.	175.

THREE DOLLARS, RETURN OF THE TYEE, 2010.

Salmon has long been the essential food source of the Northwest Coast people. The largest species of Pacific salmon is the Chinook, or black salmon, called the Tyee (King) by the First Nation People. Two tyee are arranged in a circle, representing the "Circle of Life."

Designers and Engravers:
 Obv.: Susanna Blunt, Susan Taylor
 Rev.: Jody Broomfield, Christie Paquet
Composition: 99.99% Ag, Selectively plated in pink
  and yellow gold
Silver content: 7.96 g, 0.256 tr oz
Weight: 7.96 g
Diameter: 27.0 mm   **Edge:** Reeded
Thickness: 1.9 mm   **Die Axis:** ↑↑
Finish: Proof
Case: Maroon leatherette clam style case; black
  flocked insert; encapsulated coin, COA

DATE	DESCRIPTION	QUANTITY SOLD	ISSUE PRICE	FINISH	PR-67	PR-68
2010	Return of the Tyee	8,301	54.95	Proof	65.	75.

ROYAL CANADIAN MINT MARKS ON COINS

"P" is a composition mark for coins struck on multi-ply plated (nickel or copper on steel) planchets

"W" is the mint mark for coins struck at the Winnipeg Mint.

The "Circle M" is the Royal Canadian Mint logo

CANADA'S WILDLIFE CONSERVATION SERIES

THREE DOLLARS, CANADA'S WILDLIFE CONSERVATION SERIES, SQUARE, 2010-2011.

| Common Obverse | Barn Owl
Christie Paquet | Polar Bear
Stan Witten | Orca Whale
José Osio | Black-Footed Ferret
Konrad Wachelko |

Designers:
Obv.: Susanna Blunt
Rev.: Jason Bouwman

Engravers:
Obv.: Susan Taylor
Rev.: See reverse illustrations

Composition: 92.50% Ag; 7.50% Cu, Gold plated
Silver content: 11.1 g, 0.357 tr oz
Weight: 12.0 g
Size: 27.1 x 27.1 mm
Thickness: 2.0 mm

Edge: Plain
Die Axis: ↑↑
Finish: Specimen

Case: Maroon leatherette clam style case; black flocked insert; encapsulated coin, COA

DATE	DESCRIPTION	QUANTITY SOLD	ISSUE PRICE	FINISH	SP-66	SP-67
2010	Barn Owl	10,578	59.95	Specimen	50.	60.
2010	Polar Bear	8,544	59.95	Specimen	50.	60.
2011	Orca Whale	10,698	62.95	Specimen	50.	60.
2011	Black-Footed Ferret	8,237	62.95	Specimen	50.	60.

THREE DOLLARS, FAMILY SCENE, 2011.

Designers and Engravers:
Obv.: Susanna Blunt, Susan Taylor
Rev.: Andrew Qappik, RCM Staff

Composition: 99.99% Ag, Selectively plated in pink and yellow gold
Silver content: 7.96 g, 0.256 tr oz
Weight: 7.96 g
Diameter: 27.0 mm   **Edge:** Reeded
Thickness: 2.0 mm   **Die Axis:** ↑↑
Finish: Proof
Case: Maroon leatherette clam style case; black flocked insert; encapsulated coin, COA

DATE	DESCRIPTION	QUANTITY SOLD	ISSUE PRICE	FINISH	PR-67	PR-68
2011	Family Scene	6,687	64.95	Proof	60.	65.

BIRTH STONE COLLECTION

THREE DOLLARS, BIRTH STONE COLLECTION, 2011 (GIFTWARE).

Common Obv.

Designers and Engravers:
    Obv.: Susanna Blunt, Susan Taylor
    Rev.: Christie Paquet
Composition: 99.99% Ag, Swarovski element
Silver content: 7.96 g, 0.25 tr oz
Weight: 7.96 g
Diameter: 27.0 mm
Thickness: 1.8 mm
Edge: Reeded
Die Axis: ↑↑
Finish: Proof
Case: Maroon leatherette clam style case; black flocked insert; encapsulated coin, COA

January - Garnet

February - Amethyst

March - Aquamarine

April - Diamond

May - Emerald

June - Alexandrite

July - Ruby

August - Peridot

September - Sapphire

October - Tourmaline

November - Topaz

December - Zircon

DATE	DESCRIPTION	QUANTITY SOLD	ISSUE PRICE	FINISH	PR-67	PR-68
2011	January - Garnet	2,534	64.95	Proof	60.	65.
2011	February - Amethyst	2,571	64.95	Proof	60.	65.
2011	March - Aquamarine	2,560	64.95	Proof	60.	65.
2011	April - Diamond	2,528	64.95	Proof	60.	65.
2011	May - Emerald	2,915	64.95	Proof	60.	65.
2011	June - Alexandrite	2,724	64.95	Proof	60.	65.
2011	July - Ruby	3,073	64.95	Proof	60.	65.
2011	August - Peridot	2,673	64.95	Proof	60.	65.
2011	September - Sapphire	2,717	64.95	Proof	60.	65.
2011	October - Tourmaline	2,593	64.95	Proof	60.	65.
2011	November - Topaz	2,870	64.95	Proof	60.	65.
2011	December - Zircon	2,879	64.95	Proof	60.	65.
2011	12-coin set	—	—	Proof	700.	—

BIRTH STONE COLLECTION (cont.)

THREE DOLLARS, BIRTH STONE COLLECTION, 2012 (GIFTWARE).

Common Obv.

Designers and Engravers:
    Obv.: Susanna Blunt, Susan Taylor
    Rev.: Maurice Gervais, Konrad Wachelko
Composition: 99.99% Ag, Swarovski element
Silver content: 7.96 g, 0.25 tr oz
Weight: 7.96 g   **Edge:** Reeded
Diameter: 27.0 mm   **Die Axis:** ↑↑
Thickness: 1.8 mm   **Finish:** Proof
Case: 12-holed black clam style case; black flocked insert; encapsulated coin, COA, grey sleeve

January - Garnet

February - Amethyst

March - Aquamarine

April - Diamond

May - Emerald

June - Alexandrite

July - Ruby

August - Peridot

September - Sapphire

October - Tourmaline

November - Topaz

December - Zircon

DATE	DESCRIPTION	QUANTITY SOLD	ISSUE PRICE	FINISH	PR-67	PR-68
2012	January - Garnet	1,926	64.95	Proof	65.	70.
2012	February - Amethyst	2,017	64.95	Proof	65.	70.
2012	March - Aquamarine	2,229	64.95	Proof	65.	70.
2012	April - Diamond	2,181	64.95	Proof	65.	70.
2012	May - Emerald	2,613	64.95	Proof	65.	70.
2012	June - Alexandrite	2,135	64.95	Proof	65.	70.
2012	July - Ruby	2,464	64.95	Proof	65.	70.
2012	August - Peridot	2,193	64.95	Proof	65.	70.
2012	September - Sapphire	2,334	64.95	Proof	65.	70.
2012	October - Tourmaline	2,094	64.95	Proof	65.	70.
2012	November - Topaz	2,060	64.95	Proof	65.	70.
2012	December - Zircon	2,230	64.95	Proof	65.	70.
2012	12-coin set	200	779.40	Proof	750.	—

THREE DOLLARS, HUMMINGBIRD WITH MORNING GLORY, 2013 (GIFTWARE).

The Ruby-throated Hummingbird depicted on this coin is one of Canada's most common hummingbird species. Measuring 2.75 to 3.5 inches and weighing three to four grams, it is about the size of a large moth.

Designers and Engravers:
Obv.: Susanna Blunt, Susan Taylor
Rev.: Yves Bérubé, RCM Staff
Composition: 99.99% Ag, Siam red Swarovski crystal element
Silver content: 8.06 g, 0.257 tr oz
Weight: 8.0 g
Diameter: 27.0 mm   **Edge:** Reeded
Thickness: 2.0 mm   **Die Axis:** ↑↑
Finish: Reverse Proof
Case: Maroon leatherette clam style case; black flocked insert; encapsulated coin, COA, custom sleeve

DATE	DESCRIPTION	QUANTITY SOLD	ISSUE PRICE	FINISH	PR-67	PR-68
2013	Hummingbird with Morning Glory	7,262	69.95	Proof	70.	75.

CANADA'S ANIMAL ARCHITECTS SERIES

THREE DOLLARS, CANADA'S ANIMAL ARCHITECTS SERIES, 2013-2014 (GIFTWARE).

Common Obv.

Bee and Hive
Des.: Yves Bérubé
Engr.: RCM Staff

Spider and Web
Des.: Yves Bérubé
Engr.: RCM Staff

(Monarch) Caterpillar and Chrysalis
Des.: Trevor Tennant
Engr.: RCM Staff

Designers:
Obv.: Susanna Blunt
Rev.: See reverse illustrations
Composition: 99.99%, Ag, Painted
Silver content: 7.96 g, 0.256 tr oz
Weight: 7.96 g
Diameter: 26.9 mm
Thickness: 1.9 - 2.0 mm
Case of Issue: Maroon leatherette clam style case; black flocked insert; encapsulated coin, COA

Engravers:
Rev.: Susan Taylor
Rev.: See reverse illustrations

Edge: Reeded
Die Axis: ↑↑
Finish: Proof

DATE	DESCRIPTION	QUANTITY SOLD	ISSUE PRICE	FINISH	PR-67	PR-68
2013	Bee and Hive	9,980	69.95	Proof	70.	75.
2013	Spider and Web	4,825	69.95	Proof	70.	75.
2014	Caterpillar and Chrysalis	10,000	69.95	Proof	70.	75.

THREE DOLLARS, FISHING, 2013.

Designers and Engravers:
    Obv.: Susanna Blunt, Susan Taylor
    Rev.: John Mantha, RCM Staff
Composition: 99.99% Ag
Silver content: 7.96 g, 0.256 tr oz
Weight: 7.96 g   **Edge:** Reeded
Diameter: 26.9 mm   **Die Axis:** ↑↑
Thickness: 1.8 mm   **Finish:** Proof
Case: Maroon leatherette clam style case; black
             flocked insert; encapsulated coin, COA

DATE	DESCRIPTION	QUANTITY SOLD	ISSUE PRICE	FINISH	PR-67	PR-68
2013	Fishing	14,985	34.95	Proof	35.	40.

THREE DOLLARS, MISS CANADA: AN ALLEGORY, 2013.

Miss Canada, a visual representation of national value and identity, who first appeared after confederation in 1867.

Designers and Engravers:
    Obv.: Susanna Blunt, Susan Taylor
    Rev.: Laurie McGaw, RCM Staff
Composition: Bronze
Weight: 19.2 g
Diameter: 35.75 mm
Thickness: 2.7 mm
Edge: Plain
Die Axis: ↑↑
Finish: Proof
Case: Maroon leatherette clam style case; black
             flocked insert; encapsulated coin, COA

DATE	DESCRIPTION	QUANTITY SOLD	ISSUE PRICE	FINISH	PR-67	PR-68
2013	Miss Canada: An Allegory	10,810	34.95	Proof	35.	40.

THREE DOLLARS, MARTIN SHORT PRESENTS CANADA, 2013.

Designers and Engravers:
    Obv.: Susanna Blunt, Susan Taylor
    Rev.: Tony Bianco, RCM Staff
Composition: 99.99% Ag
Silver content: 7.96 g, 0.256 tr oz
Weight: 7.96 g   **Edge:** Reeded
Diameter: 26.9 mm   **Die Axis:** ↑↑
Thickness: 1.8 mm   **Finish:** Proof
Case: Maroon leatherette clam style case; black
             flocked insert; encapsulated coin, COA,
             custom case

DATE	DESCRIPTION	QUANTITY SOLD	ISSUE PRICE	FINISH	PR-67	PR-68
2013	Martin Short Presents Canada	5,923	49.95	Proof	50.	55.

THREE DOLLARS, MAPLE LEAF IMPRESSION, 2013.

Designers and Engravers:
   Obv.: Susanna Blunt, Susan Taylor
   Rev.: José Osio, RCM Staff
Composition: 99.99% Ag
Silver content: 7.96 g, 0.256 tr oz
Weight: 7.96 g
Diameter: 27.0 mm   **Edge:** Reeded
Thickness: 1.8 mm   **Die Axis:** ↑↑
Finish: Proof
Case: Maroon leatherette clam style case; black flocked insert; encapsulated coin, COA

DATE	DESCRIPTION	QUANTITY SOLD	ISSUE PRICE	FINISH	PR-67	PR-68
2013	Maple Leaf Impression	9,820	59.95	Proof	60.	65.

THREE DOLLARS, LIFE IN THE NORTH, 2013.

Designers and Engravers:
   Obv.: Susanna Blunt, Susan Taylor
   Rev.: Tim Pitsiulak, RCM Staff
Composition: 99.99% Ag
Silver content: 7.96 g, 0.256 tr oz
Weight: 7.96 g   **Edge:** Reeded
Diameter: 26.85 mm   **Die Axis:** ↑↑
Thickness: 1.8 mm   **Finish:** Proof
Case: Maroon leatherette clam style case; black flocked insert; encapsulated coin, COA

DATE	DESCRIPTION	QUANTITY SOLD	ISSUE PRICE	FINISH	PR-67	PR-68
2013	Life in the North	3,409	34.95	Proof	35.	40.

THREE DOLLARS, JEWEL OF LIFE, 2014.

Designers and Engravers:
   Obv.: Susanna Blunt, Susan Taylor
   Rev.: Caroline Néron, RCM Staff
Composition: 99.99% Ag, Selectively gold plated, Swarovski elements
Silver content: 7.96 g, 0.256 tr oz
Weight: 7.96 g
Diameter: 27.0 mm   **Edge:** Reeded
Thickness: 1.8 mm   **Die Axis:** ↑↑
Finish: Proof
Case: Maroon leatherette clam style case; black flocked insert; encapsulated coin, COA, custom beauty box

DATE	DESCRIPTION	QUANTITY SOLD	ISSUE PRICE	FINISH	PR-67	PR-68
2014	Jewel of Life	15,000	59.95	Proof	60.	65.

FOUR DOLLARS

DINOSAUR COLLECTION

FOUR DOLLARS, DINOSAUR COLLECTION, 2007-2010.

Over 65 million years ago Alberta and Saskatchewan were covered by a great subtropical inland sea, home to more than thirty-five dinosaur species. There are five coins in this series.

**Obverse 2007-2010
With RCM Logo**

Designers:
  Obv.: Susanna Blunt
  Rev.: Kerri Burnett
Composition: 99.99% Ag, Selective aging effect
Silver content: 15.87 g, 0.510 tr oz
Weight: 15.87 g
Diameter: 34.0 mm
Thickness: 2.1 mm

Engravers:
  Obv.: Susan Taylor
  Rev.: See reverse illustrations

Edge: Reeded
Die Axis: ↑↑
Finish: Proof

Case: Maroon leatherette clam style case, black flocked insert, encapsulated coin, COA

**2007
Parasaurolophus
Engraver: Christie Paquet**

**2008
Triceratops
Engraver: Konrad Wachelko**

**2009
Tyrannosaurus Rex
Engraver: Marcos Hallam**

**2010
Dromaeosaurus
Engraver: Cecily Mok**

**Obverse 2010
Without RCM Logo**

**2010
Euoplocephalus Tutus
Engraver: Christie Paquet**

DATE	DESCRIPTION	QUANTITY SOLD	ISSUE PRICE	FINISH	PR-67	PR-68
2007	Parasaurolophus	14,946	39.95	Proof	160.	175.
2008	Triceratops	13,046	39.95	Proof	95.	110.
2009	Tyrannosaurus Rex	13,572	39.95	Proof	65.	75.
2010	Dromaeosaurus	8,982	42.95	Proof	70.	80.
2010	Euoplocephalus Tutus	6,256	49.95	Proof	80.	90.

FOUR DOLLARS, HANGING THE STOCKINGS, 2009.

The link between stockings and Christmas began to emerge with the legend of Saint Nicholas, when he dropped three small bags of gold down the chimney and into the stockings of the three daughters of a poor man, to help with their dowries.

Designers and Engravers:
    Obv.: Susanna Blunt, Susan Taylor
    Rev.: Tony Bianco, RCM Staff
Composition: 99.99% Ag
Silver content: 15.87 oz, .510 tr oz
Weight: 15.87 g
Diameter: 34.0 mm
Thickness: 2.0 mm
Edge: Reeded
Die Axis: ↑↑
Finish: Proof
Case: Maroon leatherette clam style case; black
        flocked insert; encapsulated coin, COA

DATE	DESCRIPTION	QUANTITY SOLD	ISSUE PRICE	FINISH	PR-67	PR-68
2009	Hanging The Stockings	6,011	42.95	Proof	55.	65.

FOUR DOLLARS, WELCOME TO THE WORLD, 2011.

This design is also featured on the twenty-five-cent coins contained in the Baby Gift Sets for 2011 and 2013 (see pages 30-31). It is also featured on the $10 silver issue of 2012-2014 (see page 178).

Designers and Engravers:
    Obv.: Susanna Blunt, Susan Taylor
    Rev.: José Osio, Matt Bowan
Composition: 99.99% Ag
Silver content: 15.87 oz, .510 tr oz
Weight: 15.87 g
Diameter: 34.0 mm
Thickness: 2.2 mm
Edge: Reeded
Die Axis: ↑↑
Finish: Proof
Case: Black leatherette clam style case; black
        flocked insert; encapsulated coin, COA

DATE	DESCRIPTION	QUANTITY SOLD	ISSUE PRICE	FINISH	PR-67	PR-68
2011	Welcome to the World	7,059	59.95	Proof	90.	100.

THE HEROES OF 1812 SERIES

FOUR DOLLARS, THE HEROES OF 1812, 2012-2013.

The War of 1812 was one of the fundamental turning points in Canada's history. It profoundly influenced British North America's (Canada's) sense of identity uniting French and English-speaking inhabitants and Aboriginal communities against an American invasion.

Obverse	**Tecumseh** Engr.: Nick Martin	**Sir Isaac Brock** Engr.: Matt Bowen	**Charles-Michel** **de Salaberry** Engr.: Steven Stewart	**Laura Secord** Engr.: Samantha Strath

Designers:
  Obv.: Susanna Blunt
  Rev.: Bonnie Ross
Composition: 99.99% Ag, Coloured
Silver content: 7.96 g, 0.255 tr oz
Weight: 7.96 g
Diameter: 27.0 mm
Thickness: 1.8 mm

Engravers:
  Obv.: Susan Taylor
  Rev.: See reverse illustrations

Edge: Reeded
Die Axis: ↑↑
Finish: Proof

Case of Issue: Maroon leatherette clam style case, black flocked insert, encapsulated coin, COA, custom coloured box

DATE	DESCRIPTION	QUANTITY SOLD	ISSUE PRICE	FINISH	PR-67	PR-68
2012	Tecumseh	7,521	49.95	Proof	55.	60.
2012	Sir Isaac Brock	6,881	49.95	Proof	55.	60.
2013	Charles-Michel de Salaberry	5,331	49.95	Proof	55.	60.
2013	Laura Secord	5,052	49.95	Proof	55.	60.

Note: These Heroes of 1812 four dollar coins, plus the Battle of Chateuguay kilo silver coin, were issued as a five-coin set. They were issued in a custom wooden maple wood box, limited to an issue of 80 sets.

FIVE DOLLARS

FIVE DOLLARS, NORMAN BETHUNE COMMEMORATIVE, 1998.

In 1998 the Royal Canadian Mint produced a $5 silver coin to commemorate the 60th anniversary of Dr. Norman Bethune's arrival in China. The coin was issued as part of a two-coin set in conjunction with China Gold Coin Incorporation (CGCI).

Designers:
Obv.: Dora de Pédery-Hunt
Rev.: Harry Chan

Engravers:
Obv.: Dora de Pédery-Hunt
Rev.: Ago Aarand, Stan Witten

Case of Issue: Brown plastic two-hole red insert, encapsulated coin, COA, box cover in Chinese brocade

MINT	COMPOSITION	WEIGHT (G)	SILVER CONTENT	DIAMETER	EDGE	THICKNESS
CGCI	99.99% silver	31.10	31.10 g, 1.00 tr oz	40.0	Reeded	3.2 mm
RCM	99.99% silver	31.39	31.39 g, 1.01 tr oz	38.0	Reeded	3.3 mm

DATE	DESCRIPTION	QUANTITY SOLD	ISSUE PRICE	FINISH	PR-67	PR-68
1998	Bethune - CGCI	N.I.I.	—	Proof	50.	55.
1998	Bethune - RCM	N.I.I.	—	Proof	50.	55.
1998	Set of 2 coins	65,831	98.00	Proof	100.	110.

FIVE DOLLARS, THE VIKING SETTLEMENT, 1999.

This coin commemorates the Viking landing at L'Anse-aux-Meadows, Newfoundland, circa 1000 A.D. Norway issued a 20-Kroner coin in 1999 also commemorating the same Viking Landing. These two coins were offered as a set.

| 1999 Obverse Designer and Engraver: Dora de Pédery-Hunt | Canada $5 Designer: D. Curley Engraver: S. Witten | 1999 Obverse Designer and Engraver: Unknown | Norway 20 Kroner Designer and Engraver: Unknown |

Composition: 81.0% Cu, 9.0% Ni, 10.0 Zi
Weight: 9.9 g
Edge: Plain

Thickness: 2.5 mm
Diameter: 27.0 mm
Finish: Proof

Case: Oval imitation resin stone case, two-holes; brown insert, encapsulated coins, printed cardboard outer sleeve.

DATE	DESCRIPTION	QUANTITY SOLD	ISSUE PRICE	FINISH	PR-67	PR-68
1999	Canada $5	—	—	Proof	35.	40.
1999	Norway 20 Kroner	—	—	Proof	35.	40.
1999	Set of 2 coins	28,450	N/A	Proof	60.	65.

FIVE DOLLARS, 100TH ANNIVERSARY OF THE FIRST WIRELESS TRANSMISSION, 2001.

On December 12th, 1901, Gugliemo Marconi (1874-1937) successfully transmitted the first wireless message across the Atlantic from Poldhu in Cornwall, England, to Signal Hill in St. John's, Newfoundland. To commemorate this anniversary, the Royal Canadian Mint in conjunction with the Royal Mint issued this two-coin set.

| 2001 Obverse Designer and Engraver: Dora de Pédery-Hunt | Canada $5 Designer and Engraver: Cosme Saffioti | 2001 Obverse Des.: I. Rank-Bradley Engraver: Robert Evans | British £2 Des.: Royal Mint Staff Engraver: Robert Evans |

Composition: Coin: 92.5% Ag, 7.5% Cu
Cameo: 24-karat gold plate

Coin: 92.5% Ag, 7.5% Cu
Outer circle: Plated 22kt gold
Inner disc: 92.5% Ag, 7.5% Cu

Silver Content: 15.69 g, 0.504 tr oz — 22.2 g, 0.714 tr oz
Weight: 16.96 g — 24.0 g
Diameter: 28.4 mm — 28.4 mm
Thickness: N/A — N/A
Edge: Reeded — Lettering
Die Axis: ↑↑ — ↑↓
Finish: Proof
Case of Issue: Brown resin oval case with a Marconi stamp on upper lid, brown flocked insert, encapsulated coin, COA, brown printed cardboard box.

DATE	DESCRIPTION	QUANTITY SOLD	ISSUE PRICE	FINISH	PR-67	PR-68
2001	Canada $5	—	—	Proof	35.	70.
2001	U.K. £2	—	—	Proof	35.	70.
2001	Set of 2 coins	15,011	99.95	Proof	60.	—

FIVE DOLLARS, 2006 F.I.F.A. WORLD CUP, 2003.

The Canadian Soccer Association, founded in 1912, has been affiliated with the Federation International de Football Association since 1913. The 2006 World Cup championship was held in Germany.

Designers and Engravers:
    Obv.: Susanna Blunt, Susan Taylor
    Rev.: Urszula Walerzak, José Osio
Composition: 99.99% Ag
Silver content: 31.30 g, 1.01 tr oz
Weight: 31.3 g
Diameter: 38.0 mm
Thickness: 3.1 mm
Edge: Reeded
Die Axis: ↑↑
Finish: Proof
Case: Black case, black flocked insert, encapsulated coin, COA, multicoloured sleeve

DATE	DESCRIPTION	QUANTITY SOLD	ISSUE PRICE	FINISH	PR-67	PR-68
2003	2006 F.I.F.A. World Cup	21,542	39.95	Proof	55.	60.

FIVE DOLLARS, 100TH ANNIVERSARY OF THE CANADIAN OPEN CHAMPIONSHIP, 2004

Issued jointly by the Royal Canadian Mint and Canada Post to celebrate the 100th Anniversary of the tournament, this limited edition framed set contains both a five-dollar note and a ten-cent coin. These coins were issued in various combinations.

Designers and Engravers:
    Obv.: Susanna Blunt, Susan Taylor
    Rev.: Cosme Saffioti
Composition: 99.99% Ag
Silver content: 27.90 g, 0.90 tr oz
Weight: 27.9 g
Diameter: 38.0 mm
Thickness: 3.0 mm
Edge: Reeded
Die Axis: ↑↑
Finish: Proof
Case: See Derivatives, page 161

DATE	DESCRIPTION	QUANTITY SOLD	ISSUE PRICE	FINISH	PR-67	PR-68
2004	100th Anniv. Canadian Open Championship	18,750	N.I.I.	Proof	50.	55.

Note: N.I.I. denotes Not Issued Individually.

CANADIAN WILDLIFE SERIES

FIVE DOLLARS, CANADIAN WILDLIFE SERIES, 2004-2006.

These five dollar coins were part of a coin and stamp set series which was issued jointly by the Royal Canadian Mint and Canada Post to pay homage to Canada's diverse wildlife. See Derivatives, page 161.

2004
The Majestic Moose
Obv. Designer: Susanna Blunt
Obv. Engraver: Susan Taylor
Rev. Designer: D. Preston-Smith
Rev. Engraver: Stan Witten

2005 Common Obverse
Designer: Susanna Blunt
Engraver: Susan Taylor

White-tailed Deer and Fawn
Designer: Xerxes Irani
Engraver: José Osio

The Atlantic Walrus and Calf
Designer: Pierre Leduc
Engraver: José Osio

2006 Common Obverse
Designer: Susanna Blunt
Engraver: Susan Taylor

Peregrine Falcon and Nestlings
Designer: Dwayne Harty
Engraver: José Osio

Sable Island Horse and Foal
Designer: N/A
Engraver: Christie Paquet

Composition: 99.99% Ag
Silver content: 28.0 g, 0.9 tr oz
Weight: 28.0 g
Diameter: 38.0 mm
Case of Issue: See Derivatives, page 161

Thickness: 3.0 mm
Edge: Reeded
Die Axis: ↑↑
Finish: Proof

DATE	DESCRIPTION	QUANTITY SOLD	ISSUE PRICE	FINISH	PR-67	PR-68
2004	The Majestic Moose	12,822	N.I.I.	Proof	175.	200.
2005	White-tailed Deer and Fawn	6,439	N.I.I.	Proof	65.	70.
2005	The Atlantic Walrus and Calf	5,519	N.I.I.	Proof	70.	75.
2006	Peregrine Falcon and Nestlings	7,226	N.I.I.	Proof	85.	90.
2006	Sable Island Horse and Foal	10,108	N.I.I.	Proof	80.	85.

FIVE DOLLARS, 60TH ANNIVERSARY OF THE END OF THE SECOND WORLD WAR, 2005.

In the six years of conflict Canada had enlisted more than one million men and women in His Majesty's Armed Forces. Of these, more than 45,000 gave their lives in the cause of peace.

Obverse

Reverse

Reverse with
Maple Leaf Privy Mark

Designers:
  Obv.: Susanna Blunt
  Rev.: Peter Mossman
Composition: 99.99% Ag
Silver content: 31.50 g, 1.01 tr oz
Weight: 31.5 g
Diameter: 38.0 mm
Thickness: 3.2 mm
Case of Issue: Maroon plastic display case, black plastic insert, encapsulated coin, COA

Engravers:
  Obv.: Susan Taylor
  Rev.: Christie Paquet

Edge: Reeded
Die Axis: ↑↑
Finish: See below

DATE	DESCRIPTION	QUANTITY SOLD	ISSUE PRICE	FINISH	66	67	68
2005	60th Anniv. WWII	25,000	39.95	Specimen	55.	60.	—
2005	60th Anniv. WWII with Privy Maple Leaf Mark	10,000	N.I.I.	Proof	—	110.	120.

FIVE DOLLARS, COMMEMORATING THE CENTENNIAL OF THE PROVINCES OF ALBERTA AND SASKATCHEWAN, 2005.

Common obverse
Designer: Susanna Blunt
Engraver: Susan Taylor

Alberta Centennial
Designer: Michelle Grant
Engraver: Stan Witten

Saskatchewan Centennial
Designer: Paulett Sapergia
Engraver: José Osio

Composition: 99.99% Ag
Silver content: 25.20 g, 0.81 tr oz
Weight: 25.2 g
Diameter: 36.0 mm
Thickness: 3.1 mm
Case of Issue: Maroon plastic display case, black plastic insert, encapsulated coin, COA

Edge: Reeded
Die Axis: ↑↑
Finish: Proof

DATE	DESCRIPTION	QUANTITY SOLD	ISSUE PRICE	FINISH	PR-67	PR-68
2005	Alberta Centennial	20,000	49.95	Proof	55.	60.
2005	Saskatchewan Centennial	20,000	49.95	Proof	50.	55.

FIVE DOLLARS, BREAST CANCER AWARENESS, 2006.

Designers and Engravers:
Obv.: Susanna Blunt, Susan Taylor
Rev.: Christie Paquet, Christie Paquet
Composition: 99.99% Ag, Painted
Silver content: 25.17 g, 0.81 tr oz
Weight: 25.175 g
Diameter: 36.1 mm
Thickness: 3.1 mm
Edge: Reeded
Die Axis: ↑↑
Finish: Proof
Case: Maroon plastic display case, black plastic insert, encapsulated coin, COA

DATE	DESCRIPTION	QUANTITY SOLD	ISSUE PRICE	FINISH	PR-67	PR-68
2006	Breast Cancer Awareness, Painted	11,048	59.95	Proof	60.	65.

FIVE DOLLARS, CANADIAN FORCES SNOWBIRDS, 2006.

Designers and Engravers:
Obv.: Susanna Blunt, Susan Taylor
Rev.: Jianping Yan, RCM Staff
Composition: 99.99% Ag, Double hologram
Silver content: 25.17 g, 0.81 tr oz
Weight: 25.175 g
Diameter: 36.1 mm
Thickness: 3.1 mm
Edge: Reeded
Die Axis: ↑↑
Finish: Proof
Case of Issue: See Derivatives, page 161

DATE	DESCRIPTION	QUANTITY SOLD	ISSUE PRICE	FINISH	PR-67	PR-68
2006	Canadian Forces Snowbirds; Double hologram	10,034	N.I.I.	Proof	45.	50.

FIVE DOLLARS, 80TH ANNIVERSARY OF CANADA IN JAPAN, 2009.

The legation of Japan opened in Ottawa in 1928, and in 1929 Canada established its mission in Tokyo. With a mintage of 27,872 worldwide, only 5,000 coins were for sale in Canada.

Designers and Engravers:
Obv.: Susanna Blunt, Susan Taylor
Rev.: José Osio
Composition: 92.5% Ag, 7.5% Cu
Silver content: 23.29 g, 0.75 tr oz
Weight: 25.175 g
Diameter: 36.1 mm
Thickness: 3.1 mm
Edge: Reeded
Die Axis: ↑↑
Finish: Proof
Case: Maroon leatherette clam style case, black flocked insert, encapsulated coin, COA

DATE	DESCRIPTION	QUANTITY SOLD	ISSUE PRICE	FINISH	PR-67	PR-68
2009 (1929-)	80th Anniversary of Canada in Japan	27,872	N/A	Proof	70.	75.

CALENDAR IN THE SKY SERIES

FIVE DOLLARS, CALENDAR IN THE SKY SERIES, 2011-2012.
This series depicts the Full Moons of the Algonquin people. The first coin in the series, Full Buck Moon, is also known as Thunder Moon or Summer Moon. The second coin, Full Wolf's Moon, is also known as Snow Moon or Old Moon. The third coin, Full Hunter's Moon, is also known as Travel Moon or Dying Moon. The April full moon is known as the Pink Moon as a tribute to the pink flowers such as the wild ground phlox depicted on the coin that appears in the springtime.

Common Obverse

Designers and Engravers:
   Obv.: Susanna Blunt, Susan Taylor
   Rev.: John Mantha, Cecily Mok
Composition: Outer ring: 92.50% Ag, 0.75% Cu
   Inner core obverse: 92.50% Ag, 0.75% Cu
   Inner core reverse: Niobium
Silver content: 6.56 g, 0.21 tr oz
Weight: 8.5 g (including 1.4 g Niobium)   **Edge:** Interrupted serrations
Diameter: 28.0 mm   **Die Axis:** ↑↑
Thickness: 1.8 mm   **Finish:** Proof
Case: Maple wood display case; black flocked insert; encapsulated coin, COA

Full Buck Moon

Full Hunter's Moon

Full Wolf Moon

Full Pink Moon

DATE	DESCRIPTION	QUANTITY SOLD	ISSUE PRICE	FINISH	PR-67	PR-68
2011	Full Buck Moon	6,412	119.95	Proof	120.	125.
2011	Full Hunter's Moon	5,446	119.95	Proof	120.	125.
2012	Full Wolf Moon	7,496	121.95	Proof	150.	160.
2012	Full Pink Moon	7,238	121.95	Proof	120.	125.
—	4-coin set	—	487.50	Proof	475.	—

FIVE DOLLARS, 25TH ANNIVERSARY OF THE RICK HANSEN MAN-IN-MOTION TOUR, 2012.
This coin was issued to commemorate the 25th anniversary of Rick Hansen's Man-in-Motion world tour between March 1985 and May 1987. Hansen covered more than 40,000 km through thirty-four countries on four continents during the 26-month trek. He raised $26,000,000. for spinal cord research.

Designers and Engravers:
   Obv.: Susanna Blunt, Susan Taylor
   Rev.: Chris Reid, Rosina Li, Christie Paquet
Composition: 99.99% Ag
Silver content: 23.17 g, 0.75 tr oz
Weight: 23.17 g   **Edge:** Reeded
Diameter: 36.0 mm   **Die Axis:** ↑↑
Thickness: 2.8 mm   **Finish:** Proof
Case: Maroon leatherette clam style case, black flocked insert, encapsulated coin, COA, custom sleeve

DATE	DESCRIPTION	QUANTITY SOLD	ISSUE PRICE	FINISH	PR-67	PR-68
2012 (1987-)	Rick Hansen	3,409	69.95	Proof	70.	75.

FIVE DOLLARS, GEORGINA POPE, 2012.

In 1899 Georgina Pope was one of four volunteer nurses who travelled to South Africa to assist British troops during the South African War. Each nurse was given the rank of lieutenant in the military.

Designers and Engravers:
   Obv.: Susanna Blunt, Susan Taylor
   Rev.: Laurie McGaw, Susan Taylor, Matt Bowen
Composition: 99.99 Ag
Silver content: 23.17 g, 0.75 tr oz
Weight: 23.17 g   **Edge:** Reeded
Diameter: 36.0 mm   **Die Axis:** ↑↑
Thickness: 2.7 mm   **Finish:** Proof
Case: Maroon leatherette clam style case, black flocked insert, encapsulated coin, COA

DATE	DESCRIPTION	QUANTITY SOLD	ISSUE PRICE	FINISH	PR-67	PR-68
2012	Georgina Pope	3,154	69.95	Proof	70.	75.

ABORIGINAL TRADITION OF HUNTING SERIES

FIVE DOLLARS, ABORIGINAL TRADITION OF HUNTING SERIES, 2013-2014.

This series honours the aboriginal tradition of hunting.

Common Obverse	Deer	Bison	Hunting in Harmony

Designers: **Engravers:**
  Obv.: Susanna Blunt   Obv.: Susan Taylor
  Rev.: Darlene Gait   Rev.: Christie Paquet
Composition: 99.99 Ag
Silver content: 22.9 g, 0.736 tr oz
Weight: 22.9 g   **Edge:** Reeded
Diameter: 36.0 mm   **Die Axis:** ↑↑
Thickness: 2.8 mm   **Finish:** Proof
Case of Issue: Maroon leatherette clam style case, black flocked insert, encapsulated coin, COA

DATE	DESCRIPTION	QUANTITY SOLD	ISSUE PRICE	FINISH	PR-67	PR-68
2013	Deer	4,758	69.95	Proof	70.	75.
2013	Bison	1,469	69.95	Proof	70.	75.
2014	Hunting in Harmony	10,000	69.95	Proof	70.	75.

FIVE DOLLARS, DEVIL'S BRIGADE, 2013.
During World War II Canada joined forces with the United States to create the First Special Service Force.

Designers and Engravers:
   Obv.: Susanna Blunt, Susan Taylor
   Rev.: Ardell Bourgeois, RCM Staff
Composition: 99.99 Ag
Silver content: 23.0 g, 0.74 tr oz
Weight: 23.0 g   **Edge:** Reeded
Diameter: 36.00 mm   **Die Axis:** ↑↑
Thickness: 2.8 mm   **Finish:** Proof
Case: Maroon leatherette clam style case, black
            flocked insert, encapsulated coin, COA

DATE	DESCRIPTION	QUANTITY SOLD	ISSUE PRICE	FINISH	PR-67	PR-68
2013	Devil's Brigade	6,879	59.95	Proof	60.	65.

CONTEMPORARY ABORIGINAL ART SERIES

FIVE DOLLARS, CONTEMPORARY ABORIGINAL ART SERIES, 2013.
This series honours contemporary aboriginal art.

Common Obverse	Mother and Baby Ice Fishing	Ice Fishing Father

Designers:
   Obv.: Susanna Blunt
   Rev.: Ulaayu Pilurtuut
Composition: 99.99 Ag, Niobium
Silver content: 8.5 g, 0.273 tr oz
Weight: 8.5 g (including 1.4 g Niobium)
Diameter: 28.0 mm
Thickness: 1.8 mm

Engravers:
   Obv.: Susan Taylor
   Rev.: RCM Staff

Edge: Interrupted serrations
Die Axis: ↑↑
Finish: Proof

Case of Issue: Black leatherette clam style case; black flocked insert; encapsulated coin, COA

DATE	DESCRIPTION	QUANTITY SOLD	ISSUE PRICE	FINISH	PR-67	PR-68
2013	Mother and Baby Ice Fishing	4,791	139.95	Proof	140.	150.
2013	Ice Fishing Father	2,956	139.95	Proof	140.	150.

FIVE DOLLARS, ROYAL INFANT TOYS, 2013.

Designers and Engravers:
    Obv.: Susanna Blunt, Susan Taylor
    Rev.: Laurie McGaw, RCM Staff
Composition: 99.99% Ag, Selectively gold plated
Silver content: 23.17 g, 0.75 tr oz
Weight: 23.17 g   **Edge:** Reeded
Diameter: 36.0 mm   **Die Axis:** ↑↑
Thickness: 2.7 mm
Finish: Proof
Case: Maroon leatherette clam style case, black
        flocked insert, encapsulated coin, COA
        custom beauty box

DATE	DESCRIPTION	QUANTITY SOLD	ISSUE PRICE	FINISH	PR-67	PR-68
2013	Royal Infant Toys	9,701	74.95	Proof	75.	80.

HISTORICAL DESIGNS ON CANADIAN BANK NOTES

FIVE DOLLARS, CANADIAN BANK NOTE SERIES, 2013-2014.
This series depicts the colourful vignettes used on early Canadian bank notes.

Common Obverse	**Canadian Bank of Commerce Bank Note**	**Saint George Slaying the Dragon**

Designers:
   Obv.: Susanna Blunt
   Rev.: RCM Staff
Composition: 99.99% Ag
Silver content: 23.0 g, 0.74 tr oz
Weight: 23.0 g
Diameter: 36.0 mm
Thickness: 2.8 mm

Engravers:
   Obv.: Susan Taylor
   Rev.: RCM Staff

Edge: Reeded
Die Axis: ↑↑
Finish: Proof

Case of Issue: Maroon clam style case; black flocked insert; encapsulated coin, COA, custom beauty box

DATE	DESCRIPTION	QUANTITY SOLD	ISSUE PRICE	FINISH	PR-67	PR-68
2013	Seascape Theme Vignette	7,155	69.95	Proof	70.	75.
2014	Saint George Slaying the Dragon Vignette	6,234	69.95	Proof	70.	75.

FIVE DOLLARS, ALICE MUNRO, 2014.

Canadian author Alice Munro, whose short stories are revered the world over, was the recipient of the 2013 Nobel Prize in Literature.

Designers and Engravers:
    Obv.: Susanna Blunt, Susan Taylor
    Rev.: Laurie McGaw, RCM Staff
Composition: 99.99% Ag
Silver content: 23.17 g, 0.75 tr oz
Weight: 23.17 g   **Edge:** Reeded
Diameter: 36.0 mm   **Die Axis:** ↑↑
Thickness: 2.7 mm   **Finish:** Proof
Case: Maroon leatherette clam style case, black flocked insert, encapsulated coin, COA

DATE	DESCRIPTION	QUANTITY SOLD	ISSUE PRICE	FINISH	PR-67	PR-68
2014	Alice Munro	7,500	69.95	Proof	70.	75.

FIVE DOLLARS, CANADIAN EXPEDITIONARY FORCE, 2014.

This coin was issued to pay tribute to those who served in the regiments, battalions and ancilliary units of the Canadian Expeditionary Force (CEF) during the First World War.

Designers and Engravers:
    Obv.: Susanna Blunt, Susan Taylor
    Rev.: Scott Waters, RCM Staff
Composition: 99.99% Ag
Silver content: 23.17 g, 0.75 tr oz
Weight: 23.17 g   **Edge:** Reeded
Diameter: 36.0 mm   **Die Axis:** ↑↑
Thickness: 2.7 mm   **Finish:** Proof
Case: Maroon leatherette clam style case, black flocked insert, encapsulated coin, COA

DATE	DESCRIPTION	QUANTITY SOLD	ISSUE PRICE	FINISH	PR-67	PR-68
2014	Canadian Expeditionary Force	10,000	64.95	Proof	65.	70.

FIVE DOLLAR DERIVATIVES

DATE	DESCRIPTION	QUANTITY SOLD	ISSUE PRICE	ISSUER	FINISH	MARKET VALUE
2004	**Five Dollar Coin,** Majestic Moose. Two $5 stamps (one mint, one cancelled); COA; Wooden presentation case	12,822	39.95	RCM, CP	PR-67	165.
2004	**Five Dollar and Ten Cent Coins,** Canadian Open Championship.; two commemorative stamps (one mint, one cancelled); two golf tees; RCM medallion; Framed; COA	18,750	49.99	RCM, CP	PR-67	75.
2005	**Allied Forces Silver Proof Set,** six coins: Australia, Canada, Russia, U.S.A. and U.K.	10,000	£245.	RCM, BRM	PR-67	500.
2005	**Five Dollar Coin,** White-tailed Deer and Fawn. Two $1 stamps (one mint, one cancelled); COA; Wooden presentation case.	6,439	49.55	RCM, CP	PR-67	60.
2005	**Five Dollar Coin,** Atlantic Walrus and Calf; Two $1 stamps (one mint, one cancelled); COA; Wooden presentation case.	5,519	49.55	RCM, CP	PR-67	65.
2006	**Five Dollar Coin,** Peregrine Falcon and Nestlings. Two $2 stamps (one mint, one cancelled). COA. Wooded presentation case.	7,226	49.55	RCM, CP	PR-67	75.
2006	**Five Dollar Coin,** Sable Island Horse and Foal. Two $2 stamps (one mint, one cancelled). COA. Wooded presentation case.	10,108	49.55	RCM, CP	PR-67	90.
2006	**Five Dollar Coin,** Snowbirds; Four 51¢ stamps (two mint, two on a "uniquely cancelled" souvenir sheet; Booklet; Numbered plaque; Metallic box	10,034	59.95	RCM, CP	PR-67	60.

FIVE AND TEN DOLLARS

MONTREAL SUMMER OLYMPIC GAMES, SILVER ISSUES, 1973-1976.

In 1976, Montreal, Quebec, hosted the XXI Olympiad. To commemorate and help finance Canada's first Olympics, the federal government agreed to produce a series of twenty-eight silver and two gold coins (see section following for the $100 gold coins). There are seven series of silver coins. Each series has two $5 and two $10 coins, making a total of fourteen coins of each denomination. Each series depicts different Olympic themes on the reverse and has a common design (except for the date) on the obverse. The date on the coins is usually the year of minting. Orders for the Olympic coins were accepted up to the end of December 1976, so a small unit continued to function into 1977 on the Olympic Coin Program. Mintage by series was never recorded, but the annual reports of the Royal Canadian Mint give the following figures by year: 1973 - 537,898 $10, 543,098 $5; 1974 - 3,949,878 $10, 3,981,140 $5; 1975 - 4,952,433 $10, 3,970,000 $5; 1976 - 3,970,514 $10, 3,775,259 $5. These figures do not necessarily coincide with the actual post office sales figures for the coins.

The Olympic coins were offered to the collector in two finishes, brilliant uncirculated and proof. The uncirculated issues were packaged and offered for sale in four different formats: (1) encapsulated (single coins only in styrene crystal capsules); (2) encapsulated one-coin "standard" case (single coins in black case with red interior); (3) encapsulated four-coin "custom" set (two $5 and two $10 coins by series in black case with gold trim and red insert); and (4) encapsulated four-coin "prestige" set (two $5 and two $10 coins by series in matte black leatherette case with blue insert).

The proof coins were only offered in sets, and the "deluxe" case of issue was made of Canadian white birch with a specially tanned steer hide cover with a black insert. All coins in the set are encapsulated.

Because of the fluctuating price of silver during the years of the program (1973 to 1976), the original issue prices varied somewhat from series to series.

SERIES I TO VII

The following information is common to all twenty-eight $5.00 and $10.00 silver coins. Naturally, the date changes with the year of issue.

SPECIFICATIONS

FIVE DOLLARS
Composition: 92.5% Ag, 7.5% Cu
Silver content: 22.48 g, 0.72 tr oz
Weight: 24.30 g
Diameter: 38.0 mm
Thickness: 2.4 mm
Edge: Reeded
Die Axis: ↑↑
Finish: Proof and Circulation
Case of Issue: See above

TEN DOLLARS
Composition: 92.5% Ag, 7.5% Cu
Silver content: 44.95 g, 1.44 tr oz
Weight: 48.60 g
Diameter: 45.0 mm
Thickness: 3.2 mm
Edge: Reeded
Die Axis: ↑↑
Finish: Proof and Circulation
Case of Issue: See above

Original Issue Prices

PACKAGE TYPE	SERIES I	SERIES II	SERIES III-VII
$5 Encapsulated	6.00	7.50	8.00
$10 Encapsulated	12.00	15.00	15.75
Set of 4 Encapsulated	36.00	45.00	47.50
$5 in Standard Case	7.50	9.00	9.00
$10 in Standard Case	14.00	17.00	17.00
Set of 4 in Standard Case	43.00	52.00	52.00
Custom Set	45.00	55.00	55.00
Prestige Set	50.00	60.00	60.00
Deluxe Proof Set	72.50	82.50	82.50

MONTREAL SUMMER OLYMPIC GAMES — SERIES I

1973 $10 Obverse
Designer: Arnold Machin
Engraver: Patrick Brindley

Coin No. 1
Map of the World
Reverse design was
photochemically etched

Coin No. 3
Montreal Skyline
Ago Aarand

1973 $5 Obverse
Designer: Arnold Machin
Engraver: Patrick Brindley

Coin No. 2
Map of North America
Reverse design was
photochemically etched

Coin No. 4
Kingston and Sailboats
Terrence Smith

Theme: Geographic
Official Release Date: December 13, 1973. The Series I issuing period began in late 1973 and was carried over into 1974.
Designer of Reverse: Georges Huel, worked by invitation.
Reverse Engravers: See above
Issue Price: See page 162
Finish: Proof and circulation

DATE	DESCRIPTION	QUANTITY SOLD	FINISH	65	66	67	68
1973	$5 Map of North America	537,898	Circulation	20.	25.	30.	—
1973	$5 Map of North America	Included	Proof	—	—	35.	40.
1973	$5 Kingston and Sailboats	Included	Circulation	20.	25.	30.	—
1973	$5 Kingston and Sailboats	Included	Proof	—	—	35.	40.
1973	$10 Map of the World	543,098	Circulation	40.	50.	60.	—
1973	$10 Map of the World	Included	Proof	—	—	70.	75.
1973	$10 Montreal Skyline	Included	Circulation	40.	50.	60.	—
1973	$10 Montreal Skyline	Included	Proof	—	—	70.	75.

Note: Mintage numbers are simply estimates based on the 1974-1976 Royal Canadian Mint reports.

MONTREAL SUMMER OLYMPIC GAMES —1973-1974 Mule

During the latter half of 1974, a dated obverse die - possibly made in advance for the Series II coins - was paired inadvertently with a Series I reverse die of the Map of the World resulting in the production and release of a Series I-Series II mule dated 1974. The 1973-1974 Mule was found in the 1973 four-coin custom sets, and mostly those with a European release location.

DATE	DESCRIPTION	QUANTITY SOLD	FINISH	MS-65	MS-66	MS-67
1973-74	$10 1974 Obverse - 1973 Map Reverse	Unknown	Circulation	350.	450.	—

NOTE TO COLLECTORS

1. The 1976 Montreal Summer Olympic Games were financed by the sale of five and ten dollar sterling silver coins issued over a four-year period (1973-1976). The volume of coins soon overcame any collector demand. Their value is based on face, or intrinsic value, whichever is greater. Currently, the intrinsic value is the driving force, and this will vary day-to-day with the silver market.
2. A quantity of Series One coins was issued in Styrofoam rolls to the banks for circulation. For these coins see *Canadian Coins, Volume One*. The remainders of Series One coins, and coins from Series Two through Seven were encapsulated. They are assigned a grade of MS-65 or PR-67. To obtain a higher grade the coin must be removed from the capsule and graded by a Canadian grading company.

INTRINSIC VALUE OF MONTREAL OLYMPIC COINS AT VARIOUS SILVER VALUES

PRICE OF SILVER	$5	$10	FOUR COIN SET
$20.00	$14.40	$28.80	$84.40
$25.00	$18.00	$36.00	$108.00
$30.00	$21.60	$43.20	$129.60
$35.00	$25.20	$50.40	$151.10
$40.00	$28.80	$57.60	$172.80
$45.00	$32.40	$64.80	$194.40
$50.00	$36.00	$72.00	$216.00
$55.00	$39.60	$79.20	$237.60
$60.00	$43.20	$86.40	$259.20
$65.00	$46.80	$93.60	$280.80
$70.00	$50.40	$100.80	$302.40
$75.00	$54.00	$108.00	$324.00
$80.00	$57.60	$115.20	$345.60
$85.00	$61.20	$122.40	$367.20
$90.00	$65.80	$131.60	$394.80
$95.00	$69.40	$138.80	$416.40
$100.00	$73.00	$146.00	$438.00

MONTREAL SUMMER OLYMPIC GAMES — SERIES II

1974 $10 Obverse Designer: Arnold Machin Engraver: Patrick Brindley	**Coin No. 5** **Head of Zeus** Patrick Brindley	**Coin No. 7** **Temple of Zeus** Walter Ott

1974 $5 Obverse Designer: Arnold Machin Engraver: Patrick Brindley	**Coin No. 6** **Athlete with Torch** Patrick Brindley	**Coin No. 8** **Olympic Rings** **and Wreath** Walter Ott

Theme: Olympic Motifs
Official Release Date: September 16, 1974
Designer of Reverse: Anthony Mann, winner of an invitational competition.
Reverse Engravers: See above
Issue Price: See page 162
Finish: Proof and circulation

DATE	DESCRIPTION	QUANTITY SOLD	FINISH	65	66	67	68
1974	$5 Athlete with Torch	1,990,570	Circulation	20.	25.	30.	—
1974	$5 Athlete with Torch	Included	Proof	—	—	35.	40.
1974	$5 Olympic Rings and Wreath	Included	Circulation	20.	25.	30.	—
1974	$5 Olympic Rings and Wreath	Included	Proof	—	—	35.	40.
1974	$10 Head of Zeus	1,974,939	Circulation	40.	50.	60.	—
1974	$10 Head of Zeus	Included	Proof	—	—	70.	75.
1974	$10 Temple of Zeus	Included	Circulation	40.	50.	60.	—
1974	$10 Temple of Zeus	Included	Proof	—	—	70.	75.

MONTREAL SUMMER OLYMPIC GAMES — SERIES III

1974 $10 Obverse
Designer: Arnold Machin
Engraver: Patrick Brindley

Coin No. 9
Lacrosse
Walter Ott

Coin No. 11
Cycling
Ago Aarand

1974 $5 Obverse
Designer: Arnold Machin
Engraver: Patrick Brindley

Coin No. 10
Canoeing
Patrick Brindley

Coin No. 12
Rowing
Terrence Smith

Theme: Early Canadian Sports
Official Release Date: April 16, 1975
Designer of Reverse: Ken Danby, winner of an invitational competition.
Engravers: See above
Issue Price: See page 162
Finish: Proof and circulation

DATE	DESCRIPTION	QUANTITY SOLD	FINISH	65	66	67	68
1974	$5 Canoeing	1,990,570	Circulation	20.	25.	30.	—
1974	$5 Canoeing	Included	Proof	—	—	35.	40.
1974	$5 Rowing	Included	Circulation	20.	25.	30.	—
1974	$5 Rowing	Included	Proof	—	—	35.	40.
1974	$10 Lacrosse	1,974,939	Circulation	40.	50.	60.	—
1974	$10 Lacrosse	Included	Proof	—	—	70.	75.
1974	$10 Cycling	Included	Circulation	40.	50.	60.	—
1974	$10 Cycling	Included	Proof	—	—	70.	75.

MONTREAL SUMMER OLYMPIC GAMES — SERIES IV

1975 $10 Obverse
Designer: Arnold Machin
Engraver: Patrick Brindley

Coin No. 13
Men's Hurdles
Patrick Brindley

Coin No. 15
Women's Shot Put
Patrick Brindley

1975 $5 Obverse
Designer: Arnold Machin
Engraver: Patrick Brindley

Coin No. 14
Marathon
Walter Ott

Coin No. 16
Women's Javelin
Walter Ott

Theme: Olympic Track and Field Sports
Official Release Date: August 12, 1975
Designer of Reverse: Leo Yerxa, winner of an invitational competition.
Engravers: See above
Issue Price: See page 162
Finish: Proof and circulation

DATE	DESCRIPTION	QUANTITY SOLD	FINISH	65	66	67	68
1975	$5 Marathon	1,985,000	Circulation	20.	25.	30.	—
1975	$5 Marathon	Included	Proof	—	—	35.	40.
1975	$5 Women's Javelin	Included	Circulation	20.	25.	30.	—
1975	$5 Women's Javelin	Included	Proof	—	—	35.	40.
1975	$10 Men's Hurdles	2,476,217	Circulation	40.	50.	60.	—
1975	$10 Men's Hurdles	Included	Proof	—	—	70.	75.
1975	$10 Women's Shot Put	Included	Circulation	40.	50.	60.	—
1975	$10 Women's Shot Put	Included	Proof	—	—	70.	75.

MONTREAL SUMMER OLYMPIC GAMES — SERIES V

1975 $10 Obverse	Coin No. 17	Coin No. 19
Designer: Arnold Machin	Paddling	Sailing
Engraver: Patrick Brindley	Reverse design was	Reverse design was
	photochemically etched	photochemically etched

1975 $5 Obverse	Coin No. 18	Coin No. 20
Designer: Arnold Machin	Diving	Swimming
Engraver: Patrick Brindley	Reverse design was	Reverse design was
	photochemically etched	photochemically etched

Theme: Olympic Summer Sports
Official Release Date: December 1, 1975
Designer of Reverse: Lynda Cooper, winner of an open national competition.
Engravers: See above
Issue Price: See page 162
Finish: Proof and circulation

DATE	DESCRIPTION	QUANTITY SOLD	FINISH	65	66	67	68
1975	$5 Diving	1,985,000	Circulation	20.	25.	30.	—
1975	$5 Diving	Included	Proof	—	—	35.	40.
1975	$5 Swimming	Included	Circulation	20.	25.	30.	—
1975	$5 Swimming	Included	Proof	—	—	35.	40.
1975	$10 Paddling	2,476,216	Circulation	40.	50.	60.	—
1975	$10 Paddling	Included	Proof	—	—	70.	75.
1975	$10 Sailing	Included	Circulation	40.	50.	60.	—
1975	$10 Sailing	Included	Proof	—	—	70.	75.

MONTREAL SUMMER OLYMPIC GAMES — SERIES VI

1976 $10 Obverse Designer: Arnold Machin Engraver: Patrick Brindley	Coin No. 21 Field Hockey Reverse design was photochemically etched	Coin No. 23 Soccer Reverse design was photochemically etched

1976 $5 Obverse Designer: Arnold Machin Engraver: Patrick Brindley	Coin No. 22 Fencing Reverse design was photochemically etched	Coin No. 24 Boxing Reverse design was photochemically etched

Theme: Olympic Team and Body Contact Sports
Official Release Date: March 1, 1976
Designer of Reverse: Shigeo Fukada, winner of an open international competition.
Engravers: See above
Issue Price: See page 162
Finish: Proof and circulation

DATE	DESCRIPTION	QUANTITY SOLD	FINISH	65	66	67	68
1976	$5 Fencing	1,887,630	Circulation	20.	25.	30.	—
1976	$5 Fencing	Included	Proof	—	—	35.	40.
1976	$5 Boxing	Included	Circulation	20.	25.	30.	—
1976	$5 Boxing	Included	Proof	—	—	35.	40.
1976	$10 Field Hockey	1,985.257	Circulation	40.	50.	60.	—
1976	$10 Field Hockey	Included	Proof	—	—	70.	75.
1976	$10 Soccer	Included	Circulation	40.	50.	60.	—
1976	$10 Soccer	Included	Proof	—	—	70.	75.

MONTREAL SUMMER OLYMPIC GAMES — SERIES VII

1976 $10 Obverse
Designer: Arnold Machin
Engraver: Patrick Brindley

Coin No. 25
Olympic Stadium
Ago Aarand

Coin No. 27
Olympic Velodrome
Terrence Smith

1976 $5 Obverse
Designer: Arnold Machin
Engraver: Patrick Brindley

Coin No. 26
Olympic Village
Sheldon Beveridge

Coin No. 28
Olympic Flame
Walter Ott

Theme: Olympic Games Souvenir Designs
Official Release Date: June 1, 1976
Designer of Reverse: Elliott John Morrison, winner of an invitational competition.
Engravers: See above
Issue Price: See page 162
Finish: Proof and circulation

DATE	DESCRIPTION	QUANTITY SOLD	FINISH	65	66	67	68
1976	$5 Olympic Village	1,887,629	Circulation	20.	25.	30.	—
1976	$5 Olympic Village	Included	Proof	—	—	35.	40.
1976	$5 Olympic Flame	Included	Circulation	20.	25.	30.	—
1976	$5 Olympic Flame	Included	Proof	—	—	35.	40.
1976	$10 Olympic Stadium	1,985,257	Circulation	40.	50.	60.	—
1976	$10 Olympic Stadium	Included	Proof	—	—	70.	75.
1976	$10 Olympic Velodrome	Included	Circulation	40.	50.	60.	—
1976	$10 Olympic Velodrome	Included	Proof	—	—	70.	75.

EIGHT DOLLARS

EIGHT DOLLARS, GREAT GRIZZLY, 2004.

Designers and Engravers:
Obv.: Susanna Blunt, Susan Taylor
Rev.: Unknown, Susan Taylor
Composition: 92.5% Ag, 7.5% Cu
Silver content: 26.64 g, 0.856 tr oz
Weight: 28.8 g
Diameter: 39.0 mm
Thickness: 2.8 mm
Edge: Reeded
Die Axis: ↑↑
Finish: Proof
Case: See Derivatives, page 173

DATE	DESCRIPTION	QUANTITY SOLD	ISSUE PRICE	FINISH	PR-67	PR-68
2004	Great Grizzly	12,942	N.I.I.	Proof	75.	85.

EIGHT DOLLARS, 120TH ANNIVERSARY OF THE CANADIAN PACIFIC RAILWAY, 2005.

A set of two eight-dollar coins was issued in 2005. One honours the Chinese workers in Canada for their enormous contributions; the other commemorates the opening of the Transcontinental Railway in 1885.

Railway Bridge   Chinese Memorial

Designers:
Obv.: Susanna Blunt
Rev.: RCM Staff
Composition: 99.99% Ag with gold plated inner core
Silver content: 32.15 g, 1.03 tr oz
Weight: 32.15 g
Diameter: 40.0 mm
Thickness: 3.0 mm
Case of Issue: Two-hole maroon leatherette clam style case, black flocked insert, encapsulated coin, COA

Engravers:
Obv.: Susan Taylor
Rev.: José Osio

Edge: Reeded
Die Axis: ↑↑
Finish: Proof

DATE	DESCRIPTION	QUANTITY SOLD	ISSUE PRICE	FINISH	PR-67	PR-68
2005	Railway Bridge	—	N.I.I.	Proof	65.	75.
2005	Chinese Memorial	—	N.I.I.	Proof	65.	75.
2005	Set of 2 coins	9,892	120.00	Proof	120.	—

EIGHT DOLLARS, THE SHAPE OF TRADE IN ANCIENT CHINA, 2007.

Designers and Engravers:
Obv.:   Susanna Blunt, Susan Taylor
Rev.:   Harvey Chan, RCM Staff
Composition: 99.99% Ag
Silver content: 25.18 g, 0.81 tr oz
Weight: 25.18 g
Diameter: 36.1 mm
Thickness: 2.9 mm
Edge: Reeded
Die Axis: ↑↑
Finish: Proof
Case: Maroon clam style case, black flock
insert, encapsulated coin, COA

DATE	DESCRIPTION	QUANTITY SOLD	ISSUE PRICE	FINISH	PR-67	PR-68
2007	Ancient China	19,996	49.95	Proof	65.	70.

CHINESE HISTORY AND TRADITIONS SERIES

EIGHT DOLLARS, MAPLE OF LONG LIFE, 2007.

Designers and Engravers:
Obv.:   Susanna Blunt, Susan Taylor
Rev.:   Jianping Yan, RCM Staff
Composition: 99.99% Ag, Hologram
Silver content: 25.18 g, 0.81 tr oz
Weight: 25.18 g
Diameter: 36.1 mm
Thickness: 2.9 mm
Edge: Reeded
Die Axis: ↑↑
Finish: Proof
Case: Maroon clam style case, black flock
insert, encapsulated coin, COA

DATE	DESCRIPTION	QUANTITY SOLD	ISSUE PRICE	FINISH	PR-67	PR-68
2007	Maple of Long Life	12,427	45.95	Proof	55.	65.

EIGHT DOLLARS, MAPLE OF WISDOM, 2009.

Designers and Engravers:
Obv.:   Susanna Blunt, Susan Taylor
Rev.:   Simon Ng, RCM Staff
Composition: 92.5% Ag, 7.5% Cu, Hologram
and crystal
Silver content: 23.40 g, 0.752 tr oz
Weight: 25.3 g
Diameter: 36.1 mm
Thickness: 3.0 mm
Edge: Reeded
Die Axis: ↑↑
Finish: Proof
Case: Maroon clam style case, black flock
insert, encapsulated coin, COA

DATE	DESCRIPTION	QUANTITY SOLD	ISSUE PRICE	FINISH	PR-67	PR-68
2009	Maple of Wisdom	7,273	88.88	Proof	120.	130.

CHINESE HISTORY AND TRADITIONS SERIES (cont.)

EIGHT DOLLARS, MAPLE OF STRENGTH, 2010.

Designers and Engravers:
    Obv.:   Susanna Blunt, Susan Taylor
    Rev.:   Simon Ng, Cecily Mok
Composition: 92.5% Ag, 7.5% Cu, Hologram
Silver content: 23.40 g, 0.752 tr oz
Weight: 25.3 g
Diameter: 36.1 mm
Thickness: 3.0 mm
Edge: Reeded
Die Axis: ↑↑
Finish: Proof
Case: Maroon clam style case, black flock
         insert, encapsulated coin, COA

DATE	DESCRIPTION	QUANTITY SOLD	ISSUE PRICE	FINISH	PR-67	PR-68
2010	Maple of Strength	5,138	88.88	Proof	120.	130.

Note: For other coins in the Chinese History and Traditions Series see page 197.

EIGHT DOLLAR DERIVATIVES

DATE	DESCRIPTION	QUANTITY SOLD	ISSUE PRICE	ISSUER	FINISH	MARKET VALUE
2004	**Eight Dollar Great Grizzly;** Two postage stamps; Wooden presentation case	12,942	48.88	RCM, CP	PR-67	85.

TEN DOLLARS

TEN DOLLARS, YEAR OF THE VETERAN, 2005.

Designers and Engravers:
Obv.: Susanna Blunt, Susan Taylor
Rev.: Elaine Goble, Susan Taylor
Composition: 99.99% Ag
Silver content: 25.175 g, 0.81 tr oz
Weight: 25.175 g
Diameter: 36.1 mm
Thickness: 3.1 mm
Edge: Reeded
Die Axis: ↑↑
Finish: Proof
Case: Maroon plastic case, black plastic insert, encapsulated coin, COA

DATE	DESCRIPTION	QUANTITY SOLD	ISSUE PRICE	FINISH	PR-67	PR-68
2005	Year of the Veteran	6,549	49.95	Proof	55.	60.

TEN DOLLARS, COMMEMORATING THE VISIT OF POPE JOHN PAUL II TO CANADA, 2005.

Designers and Engravers:
Obv.: Susanna Blunt, Susan Taylor
Rev.: Susan Taylor, Susan Taylor
Composition: 99.99% Ag
Silver content: 25.175 g, 0.81 tr oz
Weight: 25.175 g
Diameter: 36.1 mm
Thickness: 3.1 mm
Edge: Reeded
Die Axis: ↑↑
Finish: Proof
Case: Maroon plastic case, black plastic insert, encapsulated coin, COA

DATE	DESCRIPTION	QUANTITY SOLD	ISSUE PRICE	FINISH	PR-67	PR-68
2005	Pope John Paul II	24,716	49.95	Proof	55.	60.

TEN DOLLARS, FORTRESS OF LOUISBOURG, NATIONAL HISTORIC SERIES, 2006.

Designers and Engravers:
Obv.: Susanna Blunt, Susan Taylor
Rev.: Marcos Hallam
Composition: 99.99% Ag
Silver content: 25.175 g, 0.81 tr oz
Weight: 25.175 g
Diameter: 36.1 mm
Thickness: 3.1 mm
Edge: Reeded
Die Axis: ↑↑
Finish: Proof
Case: Maroon plastic case, black plastic insert, encapsulated coin, COA

DATE	DESCRIPTION	QUANTITY SOLD	ISSUE PRICE	FINISH	PR-67	PR-68
2006	Fortress of Louisbourg	5,544	49.95	Proof	55.	65.

TEN DOLLARS, BLUE WHALE, 2010.

This is the last coin and stamp set in the Canadian Wildlife Series which was co-produced by the Royal Canadian Mint and Canada Post.

Designers and Engravers:
  Obv.: Susanna Blunt, Susan Taylor
  Rev.: Pierre Leduc, Stan Witten
Composition: 92.50% Ag, 7.50% Cu
Silver content: 25.70 g, 0.826 tr oz
Weight: 27.78 g
Diameter: 40.0 mm
Thickness: 2.7 mm
Edge: Reeded
Die Axis: ↑↑
Finish: Proof
Case: See Derivatives page 188

DATE	DESCRIPTION	QUANTITY SOLD	ISSUE PRICE	FINISH	PR-67	PR-68
2010	Blue Whale	9,719	N.I.I.	Proof	70.	80.

TEN DOLLARS, 75TH ANNIVERSARY OF THE FIRST BANK NOTES ISSUED BY THE BANK OF CANADA, 2010.

The reverse design on this coin is a reproduction of the allegory that appeared on the original 1935 ten-dollar bank note; a seated woman surrounded by a variety of farm produce to symbolise the harvest.

Designers and Engravers:
  Obv.: Susanna Blunt, Susan Taylor
  Rev.:   Susan Taylor, Susan Taylor
Composition: 99.99% Ag
Silver content: 15.90 g, 0.511 tr oz
Weight: 15.90 g
Diameter: 34.0 mm
Thickness: 2.2 mm   **Edge:** Reeded
Die Axis: ↑↑   **Finish:** Proof
Case: Maroon leatherette clam style case;
        black flock insert, encapsulated coin,
        COA

DATE	DESCRIPTION	QUANTITY SOLD	ISSUE PRICE	FINISH	PR-67	PR-68
2010 (1935-)	75th Anniv. of First Notes Issued by Bank of Canada	6,818	54.95	Proof	55.	65.

TEN DOLLARS, HIGHWAY OF HEROES, 2011.

Designers and Engravers:
  Obv.: Susanna Blunt, Susan Taylor
  Rev.:   Major C. Gauthier/S. Witten, S. Witten
Composition: 99.99% Ag
Silver content: 15.87 g, 0.510 tr oz
Weight: 15.87 g
Diameter: 34.0 mm
Thickness: 2.0 mm   **Edge:** Reeded
Die Axis: ↑↑   **Finish:** Proof
Case: Maroon leatherette clam style case,
        black flocked insert, encapsulated coin,
        COA

DATE	DESCRIPTION	QUANTITY SOLD	ISSUE PRICE	FINISH	PR-67	PR-68
2011	Highway of Heroes	7,732	69.95	Proof	65.	70.

BOREAL FOREST SERIES

TEN DOLLARS, BOREAL FOREST, 2011.

The year 2011 was declared the International Year of Forests by the United Nations, a time to celebrate the important role forests play in our lives.

Common Obv.

Designers:
    Obv.: Susanna Blunt
    Rev.: Corrine Hunt
Composition: 99.99% Ag
Silver content: 15.87 g, 0.510 tr oz
Weight: 15.87 g
Diameter: 34.0 mm
Thickness: 2.0 mm
Case of Issue: Maroon leatherette clam style case, black flocked insert
                  encapsulated coin, COA

Engravers:
    Obv.: Susan Taylor
    Rev.: See reverse illustrations

Edge: Reeded
Die Axis: ↑↑
Finish: Proof

Orca Whale
Engraver: Cecily Mok

Peregrine Falcon
Engraver: Marcos Hallam

Wood Bison
Engraver: Konrad Wachelko

Boreal Forest
Engraver: Marcos Hallam

DATE	DESCRIPTION	QUANTITY SOLD	ISSUE PRICE	FINISH	PR-67	PR-68
2011	Orca Whale	3,131	69.95	Proof	70.	80.
2011	Peregrine Falcon	3,014	69.95	Proof	70.	80.
2011	Wood Bison	3,063	69.95	Proof	70.	80.
2011	Boreal Forest	3,292	69.95	Proof	70.	80.

TEN DOLLARS, WINTER TOWN, 2011.

Designers and Engravers:
    Obv.: Susanna Blunt, Susan Taylor
    Rev.: Virginia Boulay, RCM Staff
Composition: 99.99% Ag, Coloured
Silver content: 15.87 g, 0.510 tr oz
Weight: 15.87 g
Diameter: 34.0 mm   **Edge:** Reeded
Thickness: 2.0 mm   **Die Axis:** ↑↑
Finish: Proof
Case: Maroon leatherette clam style case,
          black flocked insert, encapsulated coin,
          COA

DATE	DESCRIPTION	QUANTITY SOLD	ISSUE PRICE	FINISH	PR-67	PR-68
2011	Winter Town	4,103	69.95	Proof	65.	75.

TEN DOLLARS, LITTLE SKATERS, 2011.

Designers and Engravers:
    Obv.: Susanna Blunt, Susan Taylor
    Rev.: Virginia Boulay, Christie Paquet
Composition: 99.99% Ag, Coloured
Silver content: 15.87 g, 0.510 tr oz
Weight: 15.87 g
Diameter: 34.0 mm   **Edge:** Reeded
Thickness: 2.0 mm   **Die Axis:** ↑↑
Finish: Proof
Case: Maroon leatherette clam style case, black flocked insert, encapsulated coin, COA

DATE	DESCRIPTION	QUANTITY SOLD	ISSUE PRICE	FINISH	PR-67	PR-68
2011	Little Skaters	3,663	69.95	Proof	65.	70.

TEN DOLLARS, YEAR OF THE DRAGON, 2012.

Designers and Engravers:
    Obv.: Susanna Blunt, Susan Taylor
    Rev.: Three Degrees Creative Group Inc., Konrad Wachelko
Composition: 99.99% Ag
Silver content: 15.87 g, 0.510 tr oz
Weight: 15.87 g
Diameter: 33.9 mm   **Edge:** Reeded
Thickness: 2.0 mm   **Die Axis:** ↑↑
Finish: Specimen
Case: Red cardboard pocket, red envelope, encapsulated coin, COA

DATE	DESCRIPTION	QUANTITY SOLD	ISSUE PRICE	FINISH	SP-66	SP-67
2012	Year of the Dragon	51,128	29.95	Specimen	40.	45.

TEN DOLLARS, RMS TITANIC, 2012.
This coin was issued for the 100th anniversary of the sinking of *RMS Titanic* on her maiden voyage.

Designers and Engravers:
    Obv.: Susanna Blunt, Susan Taylor
    Rev.: Yves Bérubé, Konrad Wachelko
Composition: 99.99% Ag
Silver content: 15.87 g, 0.510 tr oz
Weight: 15.87 g
Diameter: 33.9 mm   **Edge:** Reeded
Thickness: 2.0 mm   **Die Axis:** ↑↑
Finish: Proof
Case: Maroon leatherette clam style case, black flocked insert, encapsulated coin, COA

DATE	DESCRIPTION	QUANTITY SOLD	ISSUE PRICE	FINISH	PR-67	PR-68
2012	RMS Titanic	20,000	64.95	Proof	80.	90.

TEN DOLLARS, HMS SHANNON, 2012.

The Leda-class frigate, *HMS Shannon*, was launched from Finsbury, England, in 1806. Captain Philip Broke led his vessel to many victories against the French during the Napoleonic Wars. When tensions rose in the autumn of 1811, *HMS Shanno*n sailed to North American.

Designers and Engravers:
Obv.:   Susanna Blunt, Susan Taylor
Rev.:   Bonnie Ross, Christie Paquet
Composition: 99.99% Ag, Selectively gold plated
Silver content: 15.87 g, 0.510 tr oz
Weight: 15.87 g
Diameter: 34.0 mm   **Edge:** Reeded
Thickness: 2.1 mm   **Die Axis:** ↑↑
Finish: Proof
Case: Black leatherette clam style case, black flocked insert, encapsulated coin, COA, custom coloured box

DATE	DESCRIPTION	QUANTITY SOLD	ISSUE PRICE	FINISH	PR-67	PR-68
2012 (1812-)	HMS Shannon	9,970	64.95	Proof	75.	80.

TEN DOLLARS, PRAYING MANTIS, 2012.

Designers and Engravers:
Obv.:   Susanna Blunt, Susan Taylor
Rev.:   Robert Ganz, Konrad Wachelko
Composition: 99.99% Ag
Silver content: 15.87 g, 0.510 tr oz
Weight: 15.87 g
Diameter: 34.0 mm   **Edge:** Reeded
Thickness: 2.1 mm   **Die Axis:** ↑↑
Finish: Proof
Case: Black leatherette clam style case, black flocked insert, encapsulated coin, COA, custom coloured sleeve

DATE	DESCRIPTION	QUANTITY SOLD	ISSUE PRICE	FINISH	PR-67	PR-68
2012	Praying Mantis	5,727	69.95	Proof	65.	70.

TEN DOLLARS, WELCOME TO THE WORLD, 2012-2014.

This design is also featured on the twenty-five-cent coins contained in the Baby Gift Sets for 2011 and 2013 (see pages 30-31). It is also featured on the $4 silver issue of 2011 (see page 149).

Designers and Engravers:
Obv.:   Susanna Blunt, Susan Taylor
Rev.:   José Osio, Matt Bowan
Composition: 99.99% Ag
Silver content: 15.87 g, 0.510 tr oz
Weight: 15.87 g
Diameter: 34.0 mm   **Edge:** Reeded
Thickness: 2.1 mm   **Die Axis:** ↑↑
Finish: See pricing table
Case: Maroon leatherette clam style case, black flocked insert, encapsulated coin, COA, custom sleeve

DATE	DESCRIPTION	QUANTITY SOLD	ISSUE PRICE	FINISH	PR-67	PR-68
2012	Welcome to the World, Reverse Proof	9,999	59.95	Rev Proof	85.	90.
2013	Welcome to the World, Proof	14,870	59.95	Proof	60.	65.
2014	Welcome to the World, Matte Proof	15,000	59.95	Matte Proof	60.	65.

TEN DOLLARS, YEAR OF THE SNAKE, 2013.

Designers and Engravers:
    Obv.:   Susanna Blunt, Susan Taylor
    Rev.:   Aries Chung, Stan Witten
Composition: 99.99% Ag
Silver content: 15.87 g, 0.510 tr oz
Weight: 15.87 g
Diameter: 34.0 mm   **Edge:** Reeded
Thickness: 2.1 mm   **Die Axis:** ↑↑
Finish: Specimen
Case: Maroon leatherette clam style case,
        black flocked insert, encapsulated coin,
        COA

DATE	DESCRIPTION	QUANTITY SOLD	ISSUE PRICE	FINISH	SP-66	SP-67
2013	Year of the Snake	22,986	39.95	Specimen	40.	45.

TEN DOLLARS, WINTER SCENE, 2013.

Designers and Engravers:
    Obv.:   Susanna Blunt, Susan Taylor
    Rev.:   Rémi Clark, José Osio
Composition: 99.99% Ag, Coloured
Silver content: 15.87 g, 0.510 tr oz
Weight: 15.87 g
Diameter: 34.0 mm   **Edge:** Reeded
Thickness: 2.1 mm   **Die Axis:** ↑↑
Finish: Proof
Case: Maroon leatherette clam style case,
        black flocked insert, encapsulated coin,
        COA

DATE	DESCRIPTION	QUANTITY SOLD	ISSUE PRICE	FINISH	PR-67	PR-68
2013	Winter Scene	8,001	69.95	Proof	70.	80.

TEN DOLLARS, YEAR OF THE SNAKE (CHINESE CHARACTER), 2013.

The Snake personality is graceful and soft-spoken. It has a hypnotic beauty and never gives itself totally away. The mysterious Snake is a strategic planner that has everyone guessing its next move. The Snake is a strong individual and is usually destined for great success. This is a special edition Year of the Snake.

Designers and Engravers:
    Obv.:   Susanna Blunt, Susan Taylor
    Rev.:   Simon Ng, Konrad Wachelko
Composition: 99.99% Ag
Silver content: 15.87 g, 0.510 tr oz
Weight: 15.87 g
Diameter: 34.0 mm   **Edge:** Reeded
Thickness: 2.1 mm   **Die Axis:** ↑↑
Finish: Specimen
Case: Maroon leatherette clam style case,
        black flocked insert, encapsulated coin,
        COA

DATE	DESCRIPTION	QUANTITY SOLD	ISSUE PRICE	FINISH	SP-66	SP-67
2013	Year of the Snake	5,647	43.88	Specimen	45.	55.

O CANADA SERIES ONE

TEN DOLLARS, O CANADA SERIES ONE, 2013.

Common Obverse

Designers and Engravers:
    Obv.: Susanna Blunt, Susan Taylor
    Rev.: See Reverse illustrations
Composition: 99.99% Ag
Silver content: 15.87 g, 0.51 tr oz
Weight: 15.87 g
Diameter: 34.0 mm
Thickness: 2.2 mm
Edge: Reeded
Die Axis: ↑↑
Finish: Matte Proof
Cases of Issue:
    Single: Maroon leatherette clam style case, black flocked insert, encapsulated coin, COA, custom coloured box
    Set: 12-hole wooden case, red flocked top insert, black flocked bottom insert, encapsulated coin, COA, custom box

The Inukshuk
Designer: Tony Bianco
Engraver: Samantha Strath

The Beaver
Designer: Pierre Leduc
Engraver: RCM Staff

**The Royal Canadian
Mounted Police**
Designer: Tony Bianco
En graver: Konrad Wachelko

The Polar Bear
Designer: Pierre Leduc
Engraver: Steven Stewart

Summer Fun
Designer: Claudio D'Angelo
Engraver: Christie Paquet

The Wolf
Designer: Pierre Leduc
Engraver: RCM Staff

Niagara Falls
Designer: Emily Damstra
Engraver: Konrad Wachelko

The Caribou
Designer: Pierre Leduc
Engraver: Stan Witten

Hockey
Designer: Tony Bianco
Engraver: RCM Staff

The Orca
Designer: Pierre Leduc
Engraver: Alex Tirabasso

The Maple Leaf (with colour)
Designer: Emily Damstra
Engraver: RCM Staff

Canadian Holiday Season
Designer: Doug Geldart
Engraver: RCM Staff

TEN DOLLARS, O CANADA SERIES ONE PRICING TABLE.

DATE	DESCRIPTION	QUANTITY SOLD	ISSUE PRICE	FINISH	PR-67	PR-68
2013	The Inukshuk	38,268	39.95	Proof	40.	45.
2013	The Beaver	38,560	39.95	Proof	40.	45.
2013	The Royal Canadian Mounted Police	36,743	39.95	Proof	40.	45.
2013	The Polar Bear	38,555	39.95	Proof	40.	45.
2013	Summer Fun	34,740	39.95	Proof	40.	45.
2013	The Wolf	34,195	39.95	Proof	40.	45.
2013	Niagara Falls	33,522	39.95	Proof	40.	45.
2013	The Caribou	33,168	39.95	Proof	40.	45.
2013	Hockey	32,713	39.95	Proof	40.	45.
2013	The Orca	30,020	39.95	Proof	40.	45.
2013	The Maple Leaf (with colour)	42,551	54.95	Proof	55.	60.
2013	Canadian Holiday Season	29,978	39.95	Proof	40.	45.
2013	12-coin subscription	32,049	479.40	Proof	500.	—

TEN DOLLARS, O CANADA SERIES ONE, SELECTIVELY GOLD PLATED, 2013.

The coins in this set are the same as the O Canada Series issued in 2013, however each coin is framed by a ring of gold plating. Single coins were not available from the Mint, and can only be obtained from the break up of sets.

Common Obverse

Reverse
Maple Leaf

Designers and Engravers: See O Canada Series

Specifications: As O Canada Series except the coins are selectively gold plated

Case of Issue: Wooden case, red flocked insert at top, black flocked insert at bottom, encapsulated coins, COA, custom beauty box

DATE	DESCRIPTION	QUANTITY SOLD	ISSUE PRICE	FINISH	PR-67	PR-68
2013	The Inukshuk, Selectively gold plated	—	N.I.I.	Proof	75.	80.
2013	The Beaver, Selectively gold plated	—	N.I.I.	Proof	75.	80.
2013	The Royal Canadian Mounted Police, Selectively gold plated	—	N.I.I.	Proof	75.	80.
2013	The Polar Bear, Selectively gold plated	—	N.I.I.	Proof	75.	80.
2013	Summer Fun, Selectively gold plated	—	N.I.I.	Proof	75.	80.
2013	The Wolf, Selectively gold plated	—	N.I.I.	Proof	75.	80.
2013	Niagara Falls, Selectively gold plated	—	N.I.I.	Proof	75.	80.
2013	The Caribou, Selectively gold plated	—	N.I.I.	Proof	75.	80.
2013	Hockey, Selectively gold plated	—	N.I.I.	Proof	75.	80.
2013	The Orca, Selectively gold plated	—	N.I.I.	Proof	75.	80.
2013	Maple Leaf (with colour), Selectively gold plated	—	N.I.I.	Proof	75.	80.
2013	Canadian Holiday Season, Selectively gold plated	—	N.I.I.	Proof	75.	80.
2013	Set of 12 coins	637	899.95	Proof	900.	—

Note: For other coins in the O Canada, Series One, see pages 244 and 269.

DUCKS OF CANADA SERIES

TEN DOLLARS, DUCKS OF CANADA SERIES, 2013-2014.

| Common Obverse | Mallard | Wood Duck | Northern Pintail |

Designers:
   Obv.: Susanna Blunt
   Rev.: Trevor Tennant
Composition: 99.99% Ag, Coloured
Silver content: 15.87 g, 0.510 tr oz
Weight: 15.87 g
Diameter: 34.0 mm
Thickness: 2.1 mm

Engravers:
   Obv.: Susan Taylor
   Rev.: RCM Staff

Edge: Reeded
Die Axis: ↑↑
Finish: Proof

Cases of Issue: Single: Maroon leatherette clam style case, black flocked insert, encapsulated coin, COA
   Set: Three-hole wooden case, green flocked insert, encapsulated coin, COA, custom box

DATE	DESCRIPTION	QUANTITY SOLD	ISSUE PRICE	FINISH	PR-67	PR-68
2013	Mallard	8,998	69.95	Proof	70.	75.
2013	Wood Duck	9,675	69.95	Proof	70.	75.
2014	Northern Pintail	10,000	69.95	Proof	70.	75.

DRAGONFLY SERIES

TEN DOLLARS, DRAGONFLY SERIES, 2013-2014.
   These coins were issued to commemorate Canada's dragonfly species and their habitats.

| Common Obverse | Twelve-Spotted Skimmer | Green Darner |

Designers:
   Obv.:   Susanna Blunt
   Rev.:   Celia Godkin
Composition: 99.99% Ag, Hologram with colour
Silver content: 15.87 g, 0.510 tr oz
Weight: 15.87 g
Diameter: 34.0 mm
Thickness: 2.1 mm
Case: Maroon leatherette clam style case, black flocked insert, encapsulated coin, COA

Engravers:
   Obv.: Susan Taylor
   Rev.: Samantha Strath

Edge: Reeded
Die Axis: ↑↑
Finish: Proof

DATE	DESCRIPTION	QUANTITY SOLD	ISSUE PRICE	FINISH	PR-67	PR-68
2013	Twelve-Spotted Skimmer Dragonfly	9,923	79.95	Proof	80.	85.
2014	Green Darner Dragonfly	10,000	79.95	Proof	80.	85.

TEN DOLLARS, DREAMCATCHER, 2013.

Many variations exist across the First Nations cultures, but they all exercise the same tradition of stopping bad dreams, and letting good draw through to the mind of the dreamer.

Designers and Engravers:
  Obv.: Susanna Blunt, Susan Taylor
  Rev.: Darlene Galt, RCM Staff
Composition: 99.99% Ag, Hologram, with colour
Silver content: 15.87 g, 0.510 tr oz
Weight: 15.87 g
Diameter: 34.0 mm   **Edge:** Reeded
Thickness: 2.1 mm   **Die Axis:** ↑↑
Finish: Proof
Case: Maroon leatherette clam style case, black flocked insert, encapsulated coin, COA

DATE	DESCRIPTION	QUANTITY SOLD	ISSUE PRICE	FINISH	PR-67	PR-68
2013	Dreamcatcher	9,864	74.95	Proof	75.	80.

TEN DOLLARS, MAPLE LEAF, 2013.

This coin was issued to commemorate the sugar maples of Canada.

Designers and Engravers:
  Obv.: Susanna Blunt, Susan Taylor
  Rev.: Pierre Leduc, RCM Staff
Silver content: 99.99% Ag
Silver content: 16.1 g, 0.517 tr oz
Weight: 16.1 g
Diameter: 34.0 mm   **Edge:** Reeded
Thickness: 2.1 mm   **Die Axis:** ↑↑
Finish: Specimen
Case: Maroon leatherette clam style case, black flocked insert, encapsulated coin, COA

DATE	DESCRIPTION	QUANTITY SOLD	ISSUE PRICE	FINISH	SP-66	SP-67
2013	Maple Leaf	50,000	39.95	Specimen	40.	45.

TEN DOLLARS, 75TH ANNIVERSARY OF SUPERMAN™: VINTAGE, 2013.

Designers and Engravers:
  Obv.: Susanna Blunt, Susan Taylor
  Rev.: DC Comics/Warner Brothers, RCM Staff
Composition: 99.99% Ag
Silver content: 7.96 g, 0.25 tr oz
Weight: 7.96 g   **Edge:** Reeded
Diameter: 27.0 mm   **Die Axis:** ↑↑
Thickness: 1.8 mm   **Finish:** Proof
Case: Clear plastic cover, black plastic coin display, encapsulated coin, COA, custom beauty box

DATE	DESCRIPTION	QUANTITY SOLD	ISSUE PRICE	FINISH	PR-67	PR-68
2013	75th Anniversary of Superman™: Vintage	14,839	44.75	Proof	55.	60.

TEN DOLLARS, A PARTRIDGE IN A PEAR TREE, 2013.

Designers and Engravers:
Obv.: Susanna Blunt, Susan Taylor
Rev.: Risto Turlinen, RCM Staff
Silver content: 99.99% Ag, Coloured
Silver content: 15.87 g, 0.510 tr oz
Weight: 15.87 g
Diameter: 34.0 mm   **Edge:** Reeded
Thickness: 2.1 mm   **Die Axis:** ↑↑
Finish: Proof
Case: Maroon leatherette clam style case, black flocked insert, encapsulated coin, COA

DATE	DESCRIPTION	QUANTITY SOLD	ISSUE PRICE	FINISH	PR-67	PR-68
2013	A Partridge in a Pear Tree	4,406	64.95	Proof	65.	70.

TEN DOLLARS, HOLIDAY CANDLES, 2013.

Designers and Engravers:
Obv.: Susanna Blunt, Susan Taylor
Rev.: Claudio D'Angelo, RCM Staff
Composition: 99.99% Ag, Coloured
Silver content: 15.87 g, 0.510 tr oz
Weight: 15.87 g
Diameter: 34.0 mm   **Edge:** Reeded
Thickness: 2.0 mm   **Die Axis:** ↑↑
Finish: Proof
Case: Maroon leatherette clam style case, black flocked insert, encapsulated coin, COA

DATE	DESCRIPTION	QUANTITY SOLD	ISSUE PRICE	FINISH	PR-67	PR-68
2013	Holiday Candles	3,039	74.95	Proof	75.	80.

TEN DOLLARS, YEAR OF THE HORSE, 2014.

Designers and Engravers:
Obv.: Susanna Blunt, Susan Taylor
Rev.: Simon Ng, RCM Staff
Composition: 99.99% Ag
Silver content: 15.87 g, 0.510 tr oz
Weight: 15.87 g
Diameter: 34.0 mm   **Edge:** Reeded
Thickness: 2.0 mm   **Die Axis:** ↑↑
Finish: Specimen
Case: Maroon leatherette clam style case, black flocked insert, encapsulated coin, COA

DATE	DESCRIPTION	QUANTITY SOLD	ISSUE PRICE	FINISH	SP-66	SP-67
2014	Year of the Horse	16,509	39.95	Specimen	40.	45.

TEN DOLLARS, 2014 FIFA™ WORLD CUP, 2014.

Designers and Engravers:
    Obv.: Susanna Blunt, Susan Taylor
    Rev.: Greg Banning, RCM Staff
Composition: 99.99% Ag
Silver content: 15.87 g, 0.510 tr oz
Weight: 15.87 g
Diameter: 33.9 mm   **Edge:** Reeded
Thickness: 2.0 mm   **Die Axis:** ↑↑
Finish: Proof
Case: Black and white clam style case, black flocked insert, encapsulated coin, COA, full colour sleeve

DATE	DESCRIPTION	QUANTITY SOLD	ISSUE PRICE	FINISH	PR-67	PR-68
2014	2014 FIFA World Cup™	4,057	54.95	Proof	55.	60.

TEN DOLLARS, SKATING IN CANADA, 2014.

Designers and Engravers:
    Obv.: Susanna Blunt, Susan Taylor
    Rev.: Tony Harris, RCM Staff
Composition: 99.99% Ag, Coloured
Silver content: 15.87 g, 0.510 tr oz
Weight: 15.87 g
Diameter: 34.0 mm   **Edge:** Reeded
Thickness: 2.2 mm   **Die Axis:** ↑↑
Finish: Proof
Case: Maroon clam style case, black flocked insert, encapsulated coin, COA

DATE	DESCRIPTION	QUANTITY SOLD	ISSUE PRICE	FINISH	PR-67	PR-68
2014	Skating in Canada	10,000	64.95	Proof	65.	70.

TEN DOLLARS, THE MOBILISATION OF OUR NATION, 2014.

This coin was issued to commemorate the 100th anniversary of the declaration of World War One.

Designers and Engravers:
    Obv.: Susanna Blunt, Susan Taylor
    Rev.: Maskull Lasserre, RCM Staff
Composition: 99.99% Ag
Silver content: 15.87 g, 0.510 tr oz
Weight: 15.87 g
Diameter: 34.0 mm   **Edge:** Reeded
Thickness: 2.0 mm   **Die Axis:** ↑↑
Finish: Matte proof
Case: Maroon clam style case, black flocked insert, encapsulated coin, COA

DATE	DESCRIPTION	QUANTITY SOLD	ISSUE PRICE	FINISH	PR-67	PR-68
2014	The Mobilisation of our Nation	40,000	44.95	Proof	45.	50.

O CANADA SERIES TWO

TEN DOLLARS, O CANADA SERIES TWO, 2014.

Common Obverse

Designers and Engravers:
Obv.: Susanna Blunt, Susan Taylor
Rev.: See Reverse illustrations
Composition: 99.99% Ag
Silver content: 15.87 g, 0.51 tr oz
Weight: 15.87 g
Diameter: 34.0 mm
Thickness: 2.1 mm
Cases of Issue:

Edge: Reeded
Die Axis: ↑↑
Finish: Matte Proof

Single: Maroon leatherette clam style case, black flocked insert, encapsulated coin, COA, custom coloured box
Set: 10-hole wooden case, red flocked top insert, black flocked bottom insert, encapsulated coin, COA, custom box

The Igloo
Designer: Yves Berube
Engraver: RCM Staff

Grizzly Bear
Designer: Glen Loates
Engraver: RCM Staff

Skiing Canada's Slopes
Designer: Kendra Dixon
En graver: RCM Staff

Moose
Designer: Claudio D'Angelo
Engraver: RCM Staff

Down by the Old Maple Tree
Designer: Claudio D'Angelo
Engraver: RCM Staff

Canada Goose
Des.: Jean Charles Daumas
Engraver: RCM Staff

Canadian Cowboy
Designer: RCM Staff
En graver: RCM Staff

Bison
Designer: Claudio D'Angelo
Engraver: RCM Staff

The Northern Lights
Designer: RCM Staff
Engraver: RCM Staff

Canadian Holiday Scene
Designer: RCM Staff
En graver: RCM Staff

TEM DOLLARS, O CANADA SERIES TWO PRICING.

DATE	DESCRIPTION	QUANTITY SOLD	ISSUE PRICE	FINISH	PR-67	PR-68
2014	The Igloo	40,000	39.95	Proof	40.	50.
2014	Grizzly Bear	40,000	39.95	Proof	40.	50.
2014	Skiing Canada's Slopes	40,000	39.95	Proof	40.	50.
2014	Moose	40,000	39.95	Proof	40.	50.
2014	Down by the Old Maple Tree	40,000	39.95	Proof	40.	50.
2014	Canada Goose	40,000	39.95	Proof	40.	50.
2014	Canadian Cowboy	40,000	39.95	Proof	40.	50.
2014	Bison	40,000	39.95	Proof	40.	50.
2014	The Northern Lights (with colour)	40,000	54.95	Proof	40.	50.
2014	Canadian Holiday Scene	40,000	39.95	Proof	40.	50.
2014	10-coin set	N/A	399.95	Proof	400.	—

TEN DOLLARS, MAPLE LEAF, 2014.

Designers and Engravers:
   Obv.: Susanna Blunt, Susan Taylor
   Rev.: Pierre Leduc, RCM Staff
Composition: 99.99% Ag
Silver content: 15.87 g, 0.510 tr oz
Weight: 15.87 g
Diameter: 34.0 mm   **Edge:** Reeded
Thickness: 2.2 mm   **Die Axis:** ↑↑
Finish: Specimen
Case: Maroon clam style case, black flocked insert, encapsulated coin, COA

DATE	DESCRIPTION	QUANTITY SOLD	ISSUE PRICE	FINISH	SP-66	SP-67
2014	Maple Leaf	50,000	39.95	Specimen	40.	45.

TEN DOLLARS, POPE JOHN PAUL II, 2014.

Designers and Engravers:
   Obv.: Susanna Blunt, Susan Taylor
   Rev.: RCM Staff
Composition: 99.99% Ag
Silver content: 15.87 g, 0.510 tr oz
Weight: 15.87 g
Diameter: 34.0 mm   **Edge:** Reeded
Thickness: 2.0 mm   **Die Axis:** ↑↑
Finish: Matte proof
Case: Maroon clam style case, black flocked insert, encapsulated coin, COA

DATE	DESCRIPTION	QUANTITY SOLD	ISSUE PRICE	FINISH	PR-67	PR-68
2014	Pope John Paul II	8,500	69.95	Proof	70.	75.

TEN DOLLARS, 70TH ANNIVERSARY OF D-DAY, 2014.

Designers and Engravers:
    Obv.: Susanna Blunt, Susan Taylor
    Rev.: Maskull Lasserre, RCM Staff
Composition: 99.99% Ag
Silver content: 15.87 g, 0.510 tr oz
Weight: 15.87 g
Diameter: 34.0 mm   **Edge:** Reeded
Thickness: 2.0 mm   **Die Axis:** ↑↑
Finish: Proof
Case: Maroon clam style case, black flocked insert, encapsulated coin, COA

DATE	DESCRIPTION	QUANTITY SOLD	ISSUE PRICE	FINISH	PR-67	PR-68
2014	70th Anniversary of D-Day	8,000	49.95	Proof	50.	55.

TEN DOLLAR DERIVATIVES

DATE	DESCRIPTION	QUANTITY SOLD	ISSUE PRICE	ISSUER	FINISH	MARKET VALUE
2010	**Ten Dollar Blue Whale;** Souvenir sheet of two $10 Blue Whale postage stamps; Booklet; Maple wood case	9,719	79.95	RCM, CP	PR-67	100.

FIFTEEN DOLLARS

FIFTEEN DOLLARS, 100TH ANNIVERSARY OF THE OLYMPIC MOVEMENT, 1992-1996.

The International Olympic Committee initiated a commemorative coin programme to mark the centennial of the modern Olympic movement in 1996. Five mints, those of Canada, Australia, France, Austria and Greece, participated by each issuing one gold and two silver coins over a five year period. The total collection comprises five gold and ten silver coins.

The Royal Canadian Mint issued the first three coins in 1992. The silver fifteen dollar coins are listed here, the 1992 $175 gold coin on page 297.

The Standard Catalogue lists only the coins issued by Royal Canadian Mint.

Common Obverse
Designer and Engraver:
Dora de Pédery-Hunt

Coin No. 1
Speed Skater,
Pole Vaulter, Gymnast
Designer: David Craig
Engraver: Sheldon Beveridge

Coin No. 2
The Spirit Of the Generations
Designer: Stewart Sherwood
Engraver: Terry Smith

Composition: 92.5% Ag, 7.5% Cu
Silver content: 31.108 g, 1.00 tr oz
Weight: 33.63 g
Diameter: 40.0 mm
Edge: Lettering: Citius, Altius, Fortius
Cases of Issue: Singly: Burgundy leatherette case
                Set: Wooden display case

Thickness: 3.1 mm
Die Axis: ↑↑
Finish: Proof

DATE	DESCRIPTION	QUANTITY SOLD	ISSUE PRICE	FINISH	PR-67	PR-68
1992	Speed Skater, with edge lettering	105,645	46.95	Proof	50.	60.
1992	Speed Skater, without edge lettering	Included	46.95	Proof	400.	500.
1992	Spirit of the Generations, with edge lettering	Included	46.95	Proof	50.	60.
1992	Spirit of the Generations, without edge lettering	Included	46.95	Proof	400.	500.

CHINESE LUNAR CALENDAR SERIES

FIFTEEN DOLLARS, CHINESE LUNAR CALENDAR STERLING SILVER COIN SERIES, 1998-2009.

Common Obverse except for date

Starting in 1998 with the year of the Tiger, the Royal Canadian Mint embarked on a twelve-year series of Chinese Lunar calendar coins which ended in 2009. The twelve sterling silver coins were issued one per year to commemorate the start of each new year of the twelve-year cycle. The coins were available singly or by subscription. The subscription was for a five-year period beginning in 1999 and ending in 2003. The five coins, shipped one per year, were offered at a fixed price of $428.28 including a sterling silver medallion housed in a 13-hole presentation box made of embossed red velvet and gold moiré. The single presentation box is a smaller version of the larger one, red and gold moiré.

Year of the Tiger 1998	Year of the Rabbit 1999	Year of the Dragon 2000	Year of the Snake 2001
Designer: Harvey Chan	Designer: Harvey Chan	Designer: Harvey Chan	Designer: Harvey Chan
Engraver: Stan Witten	Engraver: José Osio	Engraver: José Osio	Engraver: José Osio

Year of the Horse 2002	Year of the Ram 2003	Year of the Monkey 2004	Year of the Rooster 2005
Designer: Harvey Chan	Designer: Harvey Chan	Designer: Harvey Chan	Designer: Harvey Chan
Engraver: José Osio	Engraver: José Osio	Engraver: Stan Witten	Engraver: José Osio

Year of the Dog 2006	Year of the Pig 2007	Year of the Rat 2008	Year of the Ox 2009
Designer: Harvey Chan	Designer: Harvey Chan	Designer: Harvey Chan	Designer: Harvey Chan
Engraver: José Osio	Engraver: José Osio	Engraver: José Osio	Engraver: José Osio

FIFTEEN DOLLARS, CHINESE LUNAR CALENDAR STERLING SILVER COIN SERIES, 1998-2009 (cont.).

Designers:
  Obv.: Dora de Pédery-Hunt
  Rev.: See reverse illustrations
Composition: 92.5% Ag, 7.5% Cu,
          24-karat gold plated cameo
Silver content: 30.71 to 31.45 g, 0.987 to 1.011 tr oz
Weight: 33.2 to 34.0 g
Diameter: 40.0 mm
Thickness: 3.0 to 3.35 mm
Cases of Issue:

Engravers:
  Obv.: Dora de Pédery-Hunt
  Rev.: See reverse illustrations

Edge: Reeded
Die Axis: ↑↑
Finish: Proof

  Set: A thirteen-hole embossed red velvet presentation box with goldmoiré sides. Included is a sterling silver
          medallion carrying the twelve signs of the zodiac.
  Singly: Embossed red velvet presentation box as above, encapsulated, COA

FIFTEEN DOLLARS, CHINESE LUNAR CALENDAR PRICING.

DATE	DESCRIPTION	QUANTITY SOLD	ISSUE PRICE	FINISH	PR-67	PR-68
1998	Empty case to hold 12 sterling silver coins and a sterling silver medallion	—	—	—	200.	—
1998	Year of the Tiger	68,888	68.88	Proof	285.	300.
1999	Year of the Rabbit	77,791	72.88	Proof	85.	95.
2000	Year of the Dragon	88,634	72.88	Proof	125.	140.
2001	Year of the Snake	60,754	94.88	Proof	60.	70.
2002	Year of the Horse	59,395	94.88	Proof	80.	90.
2003	Year of the Ram	53,714	94.88	Proof	75.	80.
2004	Year of the Monkey	46,175	105.88	Proof	125.	140.
2005	Year of the Rooster	44,690	105.88	Proof	95.	100.
2006	Year of the Dog	41,634	112.88	Proof	95.	100.
2007	Year of the Pig	10,752	88.88	Proof	100.	105.
2008	Year of the Rat	9,209	88.88	Proof	100.	105.
2009	Year of the Ox	7,096	88.88	Proof	100.	105.

FIFTEEN DOLLARS, CHINESE LUNAR CALENDAR DERIVATIVES

DATE	DESCRIPTION	QUANTITY SOLD	ISSUE PRICE	ISSUER	FINISH	MARKET VALUE
1998	**Year of the Tiger**, Fifteen dollar coin; Souvenir stamp sheet; Presentation album	8,000	88.88	RCM, CP	PR-67	300.
1999	**Year of the Rabbit,** as 1998	8,000	88.88	RCM, CP	PR-67	100.
2000	**Year of the Dragon,** as 1998	10,000	88.88	RCM, CP	PR-67	150.
2000	**Year of the Dragon**, 18kt gold stamp, Mint stamp, Presentation case	N/A	N/A	RCM, CP	PR-67	650.
2001	**Year of the Snake**, as 1998	8,000	94.88	RCM, CP	PR-67	100.
2002	**Year of the Horse**, as 1998	8,000	98.88	RCM, CP	PR-67	100.
2003	**Year of the Ram**, as 1998	8,000	98.88	RCM, CP	PR-67	100.
2004	**Year of the Monkey**, as 1998	8,000	105.88	RCM, CP	PR-67	150.
2005	**Year of the Rooster**, as 1998	8,000	105.88	RCM, CP	PR-67	125.
2006	**Year of the Dog,** as 1998	8,000	112.88	RCM, CP	PR-67	125.
2007	**Year of the Pig**, as 1998	8,000	112.88	RCM, CP	PR-67	125.
2008	**Year of the Rat**, as 1998	8,000	112.88	RCM, CP	PR-67	125.
2009	**Year of the Ox**, as 1998	8,000	112.88	RCM, CP	PR-67	125.

Note: Coins illustrated smaller than actual size.

VIGNETTES OF ROYALTY SERIES

FIFTEEN DOLLARS, VIGNETTES OF ROYALTY SERIES, 2008-2009.

Common Obverse

Victoria
Designer: Leonard C. Wyon
Engraver: RCM Staff

Edward VII
Designer: G. W. De Saulles
Engraver: RCM Staff

George V
Designer: E. B. MacKennal
Engraver: RCM Staff

George VI
Designer: T. H. Paget
Engraver: RCM Staff

Elizabeth II
Designer: Mary Gillick
Engraver: RCM Staff

Designers:
Obv.: Susanna Blunt
Rev.: See reverse illustrations

Composition: 92.5% Ag, 7.5% Cu
Silver content: 27.75 g, 0.89 tr oz
Weight: 30.0 g
Diameter: 36.2 mm
Thickness: 3.2 mm

Engravers:
Obv.: Susan Taylor
Rev.: See reverse illustrations

Edge: Plain
Die Axis: ↑↑
Finish: Proof-like

Cases of Issue: Singly: Maroon leatherette clam style case, black flocked insert, encapsulated coin, COA
Set: Five-hole maroon clam style case to hold the series of coins.

DATE	DESCRIPTION	ISSUE DATE	QUANTITY SOLD	ISSUE PRICE	FINISH	PL-67	PL-68
2008	Victoria	Oct. 31, 2007	3,442	99.95	Proof-like	115.	125.
2008	Edward VII	July 23, 2008	6,261	99.95	Proof-like	115.	125.
2008	George V	Oct. 1, 2008	—	99.95	Proof-like	115.	125.
2009	George VI	Apr. 15, 2009	10,045	99.95	Proof-like	115.	125.
2009	Elizabeth II	Oct. 1, 2009	2,643	99.95	Proof-like	115.	125.
—	Vignettes of Royalty Set, 5 coins	—	N/A	499.95	Proof-like	500.	—

NOTES FOR COLLECTORS

1. The RCM Report of 2009 does not break down the "quantity sold" figures for the George V and George VI coins, but group all under George VI.
2. It is interesting to note that after 55 years the Royal Canadian Mint recognises a proof-like finish. The vignettes are struck in ultra high relief on a proof-like background.

PLAYING CARD MONEY SERIES

FIFTEEN DOLLARS, PLAYING CARD MONEY SERIES, 2008-2009.

This series was issued to commemorate the issue of playing cards used as money during times of chronic shortages in the 17th- and 18th- centuries in New France.

2008 Obverse

Jack of Hearts

Queen of Spades

2009 Obverse

King of Hearts

Ten of Spades

Designers:
  Obv.: Susanna Blunt
  Rev.: Original artwork by Henry Beau
         Public Archives of Canada

Engravers:
  Obv.: Susan Taylor
  Rev.: José Osio

Composition: 92.5% Ag, 7.5% Cu, Painted; Gold plate on edge
Silver content: 29.193 g, 0.938 tr oz
Weight: 31.56 g
Size: 49.8 x 28.6 mm
Die Axis: ↑↑
Thickness: 2.4 to 2.7 mm
Edge: Plain
Finish: Proof
Cases of Issue: Singly: Maroon leatherette clam style case, black flocked insert, encapsulated coin, COA
            Set: Four-hole maroon clam style case, black flocked insert, encapsulated coins

DATE	DESCRIPTION	ISSUE DATE	QUANTITY SOLD	ISSUE PRICE	FINISH	PR-67	PR-68
2008	Jack of Hearts	July 23, 2008	11,362	89.95	Proof	100.	110.
2008	Queen of Spades	Oct. 1, 2008	8,714	89.95	Proof	100.	110.
2009	King of Hearts	Apr. 15, 2009	5,798	89.95	Proof	100.	110.
2009	Ten of Spades	July 22, 2009	5,921	89.95	Proof	100.	110.
—	Playing Card Money Set	—	278	359.80	Proof	400.	—

LUNAR LOTUS SERIES

FIFTEEN DOLLARS, SILVER LUNAR LOTUS SERIES, 2010-2021.

A new Lunar Calendar series was introduced in 2010. The new series, beginning with the 2010 Year of the Tiger, will run for twelve years. The scalloped coin is reminiscent of a lotus flower.

| 2010 Obverse except for date | Year of the Tiger 2010 Engraver: José Osio | Year of the Rabbit 2011 Engraver: Konrad Wachelko | Year of the Dragon 2012 Engraver: Cecily Wok |

Year of the Snake 2013
Engraver: Christie Paquet

Year of the Horse 2014
Engraver: N/A

Designers:
  Obv.: Susanna Blunt
  Rev.: Three Degrees Creative Group Inc.

Composition: 2010-2012: 92.5% Ag, 7.5% Cu
                   2013-2014: 99.99% Ag

Engravers:
  Obv.: Susan Taylor
  Rev.: See reverse illustrations

Silver content: 2010-2012: 24.327 g, 0.782 tr oz
                      2013-2014: 26.7 g, 0.858 tr oz

Weight: 26.3 to 26.7 g
Diameter (scalloped): 38.0 mm
Thickness: 2.9 mm

Edge: Plain
Die Axis: ↑↑
Finish: Proof

Cases of Issue: Singly: Silver satin-like covered case, black flocked insert, encapsulated coin, COA.
                    Set: Hardwood exterior with high-gloss finish and silk-screened paper. Interior has high-gloss finish in Chinese red with a silver design. Wooden insert accommodates 12 coins.

DATE	DESCRIPTION	QUANTITY SOLD	ISSUE PRICE	FINISH	PR-67	PR-68
2010	Year of the Tiger	10,268	88.88	Proof	145.	160.
2011	Year of the Rabbit	19,888	88.88	Proof	135.	150.
2012	Year of the Dragon	25,216	98.88	Proof	110.	120.
2013	Year of the Snake	21,639	98.88	Proof	110.	120.
2014	Year of the Horse	16,678	98.88	Proof	100.	110.

Note: Coins illustrated smaller than actual size.

CLASSIC CHINESE ZODIAC SERIES

FIFTEEN DOLLARS, CLASSIC CHINESE ZODIAC SERIES, 2010-2021.

A second Lunar Calendar series was introduced in 2010. This new series is distributed by the Asian Business Centre and the Royal Canadian Mint. The proposed quantity was 9,999 units.

Common Obverse

Year of the Tiger 2010
Engraver: Konrad Wachelko

Year of the Rabbit 2011
Engraver: William Woodruff

Year of the Dragon 2012
Engraver: Stan Witten

Year of the Snake 2013
Engraver: Stan Witten

Year of the Horse 2014
Engraver: N/A

Designers:
Obv.: Susanna Blunt
Rev.: Aries Cheung
Composition: 99.99% Ag
Silver content: 31.39 g, 1.01 tr oz
Weight: 31.39 g
Diameter: 38.0 mm
Thickness: 3.2 mm

Engravers:
Obv.: Susan Taylor
Rev.: See reverse illustrations

Edge: Reeded
Die Axis: ↑↑
Finish: Proof

Cases of Issue: Singly: Silver satin-like covered case, black flocked insert, encapsulated coin, COA.
Set: Hardwood exterior with high-gloss finish and silk-screened paper. Interior has high-gloss finish in Chinese red with a silver design. Wooden insert accommodates 12 coins.

DATE	DESCRIPTION	QUANTITY SOLD	ISSUE PRICE	FINISH	PR-67	PR-68
2010	Year of the Tiger	N/A	88.88	Proof	170.	185.
2011	Year of the Rabbit	9,999	98.88	Proof	235.	250.
2012	Year of the Dragon	19,644	98.88	Proof	110.	120.
2013	Year of the Snake	14,210	98.88	Proof	110.	120.
2014	Year of the Horse	12,061	98.88	Proof	100.	115.

CONTINUITY OF THE CROWN SERIES

FIFTEEN DOLLARS, CONTINUITY OF THE CROWN SERIES, 2011.

| Common Obverse | HRH Prince Henry of Wales
Engraver: Stan Witten | HRH Prince William of Wales
Engraver: Konrad Wachelko | The Prince of Wales
Engraver: William Woodruff |

Designers:
 Obv.: Susanna Blunt
 Rev.: Laurie McGaw
Composition: 92.5% Ag, 7.5% Cu
Silver content: 23.29 g, 0.75 tr oz
Weight: 25.175 g
Diameter: 36.2 mm
Thickness: 3.0 mm

Engravers:
 Obv.: Susan Taylor
 Rev.: See reverse illustrations

Edge: Plain
Die Axis: ↑↑
Finish: Proof-like

Cases of Issue: Singly: Maroon clam style case, black flocked insert, encapsulated coin, COA
             Set: Three-hole maroon clam style case to hold the coins.

DATE	DESCRIPTION	QUANTITY SOLD	ISSUE PRICE	FINISH	PR-67	PR-68
2011	HRH Prince Henry of Wales	5,751	109.95	Proof-like	100.	110.
2011	HRH Prince William of Wales	6,217	109.95	Proof-like	100.	110.
2011	The Prince of Wales	4,788	109.95	Proof-like	100.	110.
2011	3-coin Set	—	329.85	Proof-like	275.	—

CHINESE HISTORY AND TRADITIONS SERIES

FIFTEEN DOLLARS, CHINESE HISTORY AND TRADITIONS SERIES, 2011-2013.

Common Obverse	Maple of Happiness Designer: Simon Ng Engraver: Stan Witten	Maple of Good Fortune Designer: Three Degree Creative Group Engraver: Cecily Mok	Maple of Peace Designer: Simon Ng Engraver: N/A

Designers:
  Obv.: Susanna Blunt
  Rev.: See Reverse illustration
Composition: 99.99% Ag, Hologram
Silver content: 31.1 g, 1.0 tr oz
Weight: 31.1 g
Diameter: 38.0 mm
Thickness: 3.1 mm
Case of Issue: Maroon leatherette clam style case, black flocked insert, encapsulated coin, COA.

Engravers:
  Obv.: Susan Taylor
  Rev.: See Reverse illustration

Edge: Reeded
Die Axis: ↑↑
Finish: Proof

DATE	DESCRIPTION	QUANTITY SOLD	ISSUE PRICE	FINISH	PR-67	PR-68
2011	Maple of Happiness	8,209	98.88	Proof	110.	120.
2012	Maple of Good Fortune	8,866	98.88	Proof	110.	120.
2013	Maple of Peace	7,934	98.88	Proof	110.	120.

Note: 1. For the other coins in the Chinese History and Traditions Series see page 173.
1. For the other coins in the Chinese History and Traditions Series see page 173.
  2. Coins illustrated smaller than actual size.

FIFTEEN DOLLARS, 75TH ANNIVERSARY OF SUPERMAN™: MODERN DAY, 2013.

Designers and Engravers:
  Obv.: Susanna Blunt, Susan Taylor
  Rev.: DC Comisc/Warner Brothers, RCM Staff
Composition: 99.99% Ag, Painted
Silver content: 15.87 g, 0.510 tr oz
Weight: 15.87 g
Diameter: 34.0 mm   **Edge:** Reeded
Thickness: 2.1 mm   **Die Axis:** ↑↑
Finish: Matte Proof
Case: Clear plastic cover, black plastic coin
       display, encapsulated coin, COA, custom
       beauty box

DATE	DESCRIPTION	QUANTITY SOLD	ISSUE PRICE	FINISH	PR-67	PR-68
2013	75th Anniv. of Superman™: Modern Day	14,942	69.75	Proof	100.	110.

TWENTY DOLLARS

CALGARY OLYMPIC WINTER GAMES

TWENTY DOLLARS, CALGARY OLYMPIC WINTER GAMES, 1985-1988.

In 1988, Calgary, Alberta, hosted the XV Olympic Winter Games. To commemorate the event, and assist in the financing, the Federal Government, through the Royal Canadian Mint, agreed to produce a series of ten sterling silver coins and one gold coin. The silver coins were issued in sets of two $20.00 coins over the period September 1985 through September 1987. Unlike the 1976 Olympic coins, the Calgary Winter Olympic coins were issued in proof quality only.

The date on the coins (obverse) is the year of minting while the reverse carries the date 1988, the year of the games. Mintage was limited to a total of 5,000,000 coins, resulting if minted in equal numbers, in 500,000 complete sets of the ten coins. The first offering of the coins for sale by the Royal Canadian Mint was based on 350,000 complete sets at $370.00 per set. By the fifth series the complete set was being offered at $420.00.

Edge lettering was used for the first time on Canadian silver coins. "XV OLYMPIC WINTER GAMES - JEUX OLYMPIQUES D'HIVER" appeared on all ten silver coins. There are existing varieties that have missed the edge lettering process.

Designers: See each coin
Composition: 92.5% Ag, 7.5% Cu
Silver content: 31.51 g, 1.01 tr oz
Weight: 34.07 g
Diameter: 40.0 mm
Case: Green velvet, Olympic Logo, one or two coin display.

Engravers: See each coin
Thickness: 3.0 mm
Edge: Lettered
Die Axis: ↑↑
Finish: Proof

SERIES ONE

1985 Reverse
Arnold Machin

Coin No. 1 Downhill Skiing
Ian Stewart, Terrence Smith

Coin No. 2 Speed Skating
Friedrich Peter, Ago Aarand

SERIES TWO

1986 Obverse
Arnold Machin

Coin No. 3 Hockey
Ian Stewart, Victor Coté

Coin No. 4 Biathlon
John Mardon, Sheldon Beveridge

DATE	DESCRIPTION	ISSUE DATE	QUANTITY SOLD	ISSUE PRICE	FINISH	PR-67	PR-68
1985	Downhill Skiing	Sept. 15, 1985	406,360	37.00	Proof	30.	35.
1985	Speed Skating	Sept. 15, 1985	354,222	37.00	Proof	30.	35.
1985	Speed Skating, no edge lettering	Sept. 15, 1985	Included	37.00	Proof	200.	250.
1985	Set of 2 Series One coins	Sept. 15, 1985	Included	74.00	Proof	60.	—
1986	Hockey	Feb. 25, 1986	396,602	37.00	Proof	30.	35.
1986	Hockey, no edge lettering	Feb. 25, 1986	Included	37.00	Proof	200.	250.
1986	Biathlon	Feb. 25, 1986	308,086	37.00	Proof	30.	35.
1986	Biathlon, no edge lettering	Feb. 25, 1986	Included	37.00	Proof	200.	250.
1986	Set of 2 Series Two coins		Included	79.00	Proof	60.	—

CALGARY OLYMPIC WINTER GAMES (cont.)

SERIES THREE

1986 Obverse
Arnold Machin

Coin No. 5 Cross-Country Skiing
Ian Stewart, Terrence Smith

Coin No. 6 Free-Style Skiing
Walter Ott, Walter Ott

SERIES FOUR

1987 Obverse
Arnold Machin

Coin No. 7 Figure Skating
Raymond Taylor, Walter Ott

Coin No. 8 Curling
Walter Ott, Sheldon Beveridge

SERIES FIVE

1987 Obverse
Arnold Machin

Coin No. 9 Ski-Jumping
Raymond Taylor, David Kierans

Coin No. 10 Bobsleigh
John Mardon, Victor Coté

DATE	DESCRIPTION	ISSUE DATE	QUANTITY SOLD	ISSUE PRICE	FINISH	PR-67	PR-68
1986	Cross-Country Skiing	Aug. 18, 1986	303,199	39.50	Proof	30.	35.
1986	Free-Style Skiing	Aug. 18, 1986	294,322	39.50	Proof	30.	35.
1986	Free-Style Skiing, no edge lettering	Aug. 18, 1986	Included	39.50	Proof	200.	250.
1986	Set of 2 Series Three coins	Aug. 18, 1986	Included	79.00	Proof	60.	—
1987	Figure Skating	Mar. 14, 1987	334,875	39.50	Proof	30.	35.
1987	Figure Skating, no edge lettering	Mar. 14, 1987	Included	39.50	Proof	200.	250.
1987	Curling	Mar. 14, 1987	286,457	39.50	Proof	30.	35.
1987	Set of 2 Series Four coins	Mar. 14, 1987	Included	79.00	Proof	60.	—
1987	Ski-Jumping	Aug. 11, 1987	290,954	42.00	Proof	30.	35.
1987	Bobsleigh	Aug. 11, 1987	274,326	42.00	Proof	30.	35.
1987	Set of 2 Series Five coins	Aug. 11, 1987	Included	84.00	Proof	60.	—

AVIATION COMMEMORATIVES

TWENTY DOLLARS, AVIATION COMMEMORATIVES, SERIES ONE, 1990-1994.

Canada's aviation heroes and achievements are commemorated on this series of twenty dollar sterling silver coins. The series consists of ten coins issued two per year over five years. For the first time each coin design contains a 24-karat gold covered oval cameo portrait of the aviation hero commemorated. All coins were issued in proof quality and a maximum of 50,000 of each coin was offered for sale during the program. The issue price of the ten-coin case was $37.00.

Designers:
  Obv. and Rev.: See each coin

Engravers:
  Obv. and Rev.: See each coin

Composition: 92.5% Ag, 7.5% Cu, 24-karat gold-covered cameo
Silver content: 28.77 g, 0.925 tr oz
Weight: 31.103 g
Diameter: 38.0 mm
Thickness: 3.5 mm

Edge: Interrupted serrations
Die Axis: ↑↑
Finish: Proof

Cases of Issue: Aluminum case in the shape of a wing. Single and ten coin display cases made from recycled Canadian airplanes.

1990 Obverse
Designer and Engraver:
Dora de Pédery-Hunt

Coin No. 1
Avro Anson and the North
American Harvard
Robert Leckie
Rev. Designer: Geoff Bennett
Rev. Engraver: S. Beveridge
Portrait Engr.: Terrence Smith

Coin No. 2
Avro Lancaster
J. E. Fauquier
Rev. Designer: R.R. Carmichael
Rev. Engraver: Ago Aarand
Portrait Engr.: S. Beveridge

1991 Obverse
Designer and Engraver:
Dora de Pédery-Hunt

Coin No. 3
A.E.A. Silver Dart
F.W. Baldwin / J.A.D. McCurdy
Rev. Designer: George Velinger
Rev. Engraver: S. Beveridge
Portrait Engr.: Terrence Smith

Coin No. 4
de Havilland Beaver
Phillip C. Garratt
Rev. Designer: Peter Mossman
Rev. Engraver: Ago Aarand
Portrait Engr.: William Woodruff

DATE	DESCRIPTION	SERIES	ISSUE DATE	QUANTITY SOLD	ISSUE PRICE	FINISH	PR-67	PR-68
1990	Avro Anson/N.A. Harvard	One	Sept. 15/90	41,844	55.50	Proof	60.	65.
1990	Avro Lancaster	One	Sept. 15/90	43,596	55.50	Proof	135.	150.
1991	A.E.A. Silver Dart	One	May 16/91	35,202	55.50	Proof	60.	65.
1991	de Havilland Beaver	One	May 16/91	36,197	55.50	Proof	60.	65.

1992 Obverse
Designer and Engraver:
Dora de Pédery-Hunt

Coin No. 5
Curtiss JN-4 (Canuck)
Sir Frank Wilton Baillie
Rev. Designer: George Velinger
Rev. Engr.: Sheldon Beveridge
Portrait Engr.: Terrence Smith

Coin No. 6
de Havilland Gipsy Moth
Murton A. Seymour
Rev. Designer: John Mardon
Rev. Engraver: Ago Aarand
Portrait Engr.: Susan Taylor

1993 Obverse
Designer and Engraver:
Dora de Pédery-Hunt

Coin No. 7
Fairchild 71c
James A. Richardson
Rev. Designer: R. R. Carmichael
Rev. Engraver: Susan Taylor
Portrait Engr.: Susan Taylor

Coin No. 8
Lockheed 14 Super Electra
Zebulon Lewis Leigh
Rev. Designer: R. R. Carmichael
Rev. Engraver: S. Beveridge
Portrait Engr.: S. Beveridge

1994 Obverse
Designer and Engraver:
Dora de Pédery-Hunt

Coin No. 9
Curtiss HS-2L
Stuart Graham
Rev. Designer: John Mardon
Rev. Engraver: S. Beveridge
Portrait Engr.: Susan Taylor

Coin No. 10
Canadian Vickers Vedette
Wilfred T. Reid
Rev. Designer: R. R. Carmichael
Rev. Engraver: S. Beveridge
Portrait Engr.: S. Beveridge

DATE	DESCRIPTION	SERIES	ISSUE DATE	QUANTITY SOLD	ISSUE PRICE	FINISH	PR-67	PR-68
1992	Curtiss JN-4 (Canuck)	One	Aug. 13/92	33,105	55.50	Proof	60.	65.
1992	de Havilland Gipsy Moth	One	Aug. 13/92	32,537	55.50	Proof	60.	65.
1993	Fairchild 71c	One	May 3/93	32,199	55.50	Proof	60.	65.
1993	Lockheed 14 Super Electra	One	May 3/93	32,550	55.50	Proof	60.	65.
1994	Curtiss HS-2L	One	Mar. 24/94	31,242	55.50	Proof	60.	65.
1994	Canadian Vickers Vedette	One	Mar. 24/94	30,880	55.50	Proof	60.	65.
1990-94	Set of 10 Series One coins	One	—	—	—	Proof	550.	—

TWENTY DOLLARS, AVIATION COMMEMORATIVES, SERIES TWO, 1995-1999.

This is the second series of the aviation cameo coins of Canada. The theme of this series is "Powered Flight in Canada — Beyond World War II." The obverses, physical and chemical specifications are the same as the first series.

SERIES TWO

1995 Obverse
Designer and Engraver:
Dora de Pédery-Hunt

Coin No. 1
Fleet 80 Canuck
J. Omer (Bob) Noury
Rev. Designer: Robert Bradford
Rev. Engraver: Cosme Saffioti
Portrait Engr.: Cosme Saffioti

Coin No. 2
DHC-1 Chipmunk
W. C. Russell Bannock
Rev. Designer: Robert Bradford
Rev. Engraver: William Woodruff
Portrait Engr.: Ago Aarand

1996 Obverse
Designer and Engraver:
Dora de Pédery-Hunt

Coin No. 3
Avro Canada CF-100 Canuck
Janus Zurakowski
Rev. Designer: Jim Bruce
Rev. Engraver: Stan Witten
Portrait Engr.: Cosme Saffioti

Coin No. 4
Avro Canada CF-105 Arrow
James A. Chamberlin
Rev. Designer: Jim Bruce
Rev. Engraver: William Woodruff
Portrait Engr.: S. Beveridge

1997 Obverse
Designer and Engraver:
Dora de Pédery-Hunt

Coin No. 5
Canadair F-86 Sabre
Fern Villeneuve
Rev. Designer: Ross Buckland
Rev. Engraver: William Woodruff
Portrait Engr.: Cosme Saffioti

Coin No. 6
Canadair CT-114 Tutor Jet
Edward Higgins
Rev. Designer: Ross Buckland
Rev. Engraver: Stan Witten
Portrait Engr.: Ago Aarand

1998 Obverse
Designer and Engraver:
Dora de Pédery-Hunt

Coin No. 7
Canadair CP-107 Argus
William S. Longhurst
Rev. Designer: Peter Mossman
Rev. Engraver: Sheldon
Beveridge

Coin No. 8
Canadair CL-215 Waterbomber
Paul Gagnon
Rev. Designer: Peter Mossman
Rev. Engraver: Stan Witten
Portrait Engr.: William Woodruff

1999 Obverse
Designer and Engraver:
Dora de Pédery-Hunt

Coin No. 9
de Havilland DHC-6 Twin Otter
George A. Neal
Rev. Designer: Neil Aird
Rev. Engraver: Cosme Saffioti
Portrait Engr.: Cosme Saffioti

Coin No. 10
de Havilland DHC-8 Dash 8
Robert H. (Bob) Fowler
Rev. Designer: Neil Aird
Rev. Engraver: William Woodruff
Portrait Engr.: Cosme Saffioti

DATE	DESCRIPTION	SERIES	ISSUE DATE	ISSUE PRICE	QUANTITY SOLD	FINISH	PR-67	PR-68
1995	Fleet 80 Canuck	Two	Sept. 16/95	57.95	17,438	Proof	65.	70.
1995	DHC-1 Chipmunk	Two	Sept. 16/95	57.95	17,722	Proof	100.	110.
1996	CF-100 Canuck	Two	July 25/96	57.95	18,508	Proof	65.	70.
1996	CF-105 Arrow	Two	July 25/96	57.95	27,163	Proof	150.	175.
1997	F86 Sabre	Two	Aug. 15/97	57.95	16,440	Proof	65.	70.
1997	Tutor Jet	Two	Aug. 15/97	57.95	18,414	Proof	65.	70.
1998	Argus	Two	June 5/98	57.95	14,711	Proof	65.	70.
1998	Waterbomber	Two	June 5/98	57.95	15,237	Proof	65.	70.
1999	Twin Otter	Two	April 15/99	57.95	14,173	Proof	100.	110.
1999	Dash 8	Two	April 15/99	57.95	14,138	Proof	65.	70.
1995-99	Set of 10 Series Two coins	Two	—	—	—	Proof	775.	—

Note: In 1998 a special issue two-coin set (coins 7 and 8) boxed with a cardboard model was offered to collectors. See Derivatives, page 239.

TRANSPORTATION ON LAND, SEA AND RAIL SERIES

TWENTY DOLLARS, TRANSPORTATION ON LAND, SEA AND RAIL, 2000-2003.

Canada's first sterling silver hologram cameo twenty dollar coins were issued in 2000. This series of twelve coins commemorates Canadian achievements in transportation. Each coin bears a holographic cameo of famous Canadian methods of transportation.

Designers:
Obv. and Rev.: See each coin

Engravers:
Obv. and Rev.: See each coin

Composition: 92.5% Ag, 7.5% Cu, Holographic cameo; Selectively gold plated
Silver content: 28.77 g, 0.925 tr oz
Weight: 31.103 g
Diameter: 38.0 mm
Edge: Interrupted serrations
Thickness: 3.5 mm
Die Axis: ↑↑
Finish: Proof
Case of Issue: Charcoal coloured anodized aluminum case with RCM logo, black flocked insert, COA.

TRANSPORTATION ON LAND, SEA AND RAIL, 2000.

2000 Obverse Designer and Engraver Dora de Pédery-Hunt	**Coin No. 1** H.S. Taylor Steam Buggy John Mardon Cosme Saffioti	**Coin No. 2** The Bluenose J. Franklin Wright Stan Witten	**Coin No. 3** The Toronto J. Mardon, Stan Witten Cosme Saffioti

DATE	DESCRIPTION	ISSUE DATE	QUANTITY SOLD	ISSUE PRICE	FINISH	PR-67	PR-68
2000	H.S. Taylor Steam Buggy	Apr.18/2000	Total	59.95	Proof	55.	60.
2000	The Bluenose	Apr.18/2000	mintage	59.95	Proof	175.	200.
2000	The Toronto	Apr.18/2000	all coins	59.95	Proof	60.	65.
2000	Set of 3 coins	—	44,367	179.85	Proof	275.	—

TRANSPORTATION ON LAND, SEA AND RAIL, 2001.

2001 Obverse Designer and Engraver Dora de Pédery-Hunt	**Coin No. 4** The Russell "Light Four" Model L Touring Car John Mardon, José Osio	**Coin No. 5** The Marco Polo J. Franklin Wright Stan Witten	**Coin No. 6** The Scotia Don Curley William Woodruff

DATE	DESCRIPTION	ISSUE DATE	QUANTITY SOLD	ISSUE PRICE	FINISH	PR-67	PR-68
2001	The Russell "Light Four"	Apr.17/2001	Total	59.95	Proof	55.	60.
2001	The Marco Polo	Apr.17/2001	mintage	59.95	Proof	60.	65.
2001	The Scotia	Apr.17/2001	all coins	59.95	Proof	55.	60.
2001	Set of 3 coins	—	41,828	179.85	Proof	150.	—

TRANSPORTATION ON LAND, SEA AND RAIL SERIES (cont.)

TWENTY DOLLARS, TRANSPORTATION ON LAND, SEA AND RAIL, 2002.

2002 Obverse
Designer and Engraver
Dora de Pédery-Hunt

Coin No. 7
The Gray-Dort
John Mardon
Cosme Saffioti

Coin No. 8
The William Lawrence
Bonnie Ross
William Woodruff

Coin No. 9
D-10 Locomotive
Dan Fell
William Woodruff

DATE	DESCRIPTION	ISSUE DATE	QUANTITY SOLD	ISSUE PRICE	FINISH	PR-67	PR-68
2002	The Gray-Dort	Apr.17/2002	Total	59.95	Proof	55.	60.
2002	The William Lawrence	Apr.17/2002	mintage	59.95	Proof	65.	70.
2002	D-10 Locomotive	Apr.17/2002	all coins	59.95	Proof	70.	75.
2002	Set of 3 coins	—	35,944	195.00	Proof	175.	—

TWENTY DOLLARS, TRANSPORTATION ON LAND, SEA AND RAIL, 2003.

2003 Obverse
Designer and Engraver
Dora de Pédery-Hunt

Coin No. 10
HMCS Bras d'Or
Hydrofoil designed by
DeHavilland in 1967
Donald Curley, Stan Witten

Coin No. 11
C.N.R. FA-1 Diesel Electric
Locomotive - No. 9400
John Mardon
William Woodruff

Coin No. 12
Bricklin SV-1 (Land)
designed by Malcolm in 1974
Brian Hughes
José Osio

DATE	DESCRIPTION	ISSUE DATE	QUANTITY SOLD	ISSUE PRICE	FINISH	PR-67	PR-68
2003	HMCS Bras d'Or	Apr.7/2003	Total	59.95	Proof	75.	80.
2003	C.N.R. FA-1 Diesel Electric Locomotive	Apr.7/2003	mintage	59.95	Proof	80.	85.
2003	Bricklin SV-1	Apr.7/2003	all coins	59.95	Proof	75.	80.
2003	Set of 3 coins	—	31,997	195.00	Proof	225.	—

Note: 1. The 2002 Land, Sea and Rail collection was offered with matching COA in a limited edition of 2,500.
2. Coins illustrated smaller than actual size.

NATURAL WONDERS COLLECTION

TWENTY DOLLARS, NATURAL WONDERS COLLECTION, 2003-2005.

The Royal Canadian Mint, in 2003, introduced a new series of twenty dollar commemorative coins. Each coin carries a holographic, decal, or a selectively gold plated image of one of Canada's natural wonders.

Designers and Engravers: See Illustrations
Composition: 99.99% Ag
Silver content: 31.39 g, 1.01 tr oz
Weight: 31.39 g   **Edge:** Reeded
Diameter: 38.0 mm   **Die Axis:** ↑↑
Thickness: 3.5 mm
Finish: Proof
Cases of Issue:
  (A) Veneer, wooden clam style case, light brown flocked interior, encapsulated coin, COA
  (B) Red leatherette clam style case, flocked black insert, encapsulated coin, COA

**2003 Obverse
Designer and Engraver:
Dora de Pédery-Hunt**

**2004-2005 Obv.
Designer: Susanna Blunt
Engraver: Susan Taylor**

**Niagara Falls
Designer and Engraver:
Gary Corcoran**

**Rocky Mountains
Designer and Engraver:
José Osio**

**Icebergs
Designer and Engraver:
RCM Staff**

**Northern Lights
Designer: Gary Corcoran
Engraver: Stan Witten**

**Hopewell Rocks
Designer and Engraver:
Stan Witten**

**Diamonds
Designer and Engraver:
José Osio**

DATE	DESCRIPTION	QUANTITY SOLD	ISSUE PRICE	FINISH	PR-67	PR-68
2003	Niagara Falls, Hologram	29,967	79.95	Proof	85.	90.
2003	Rocky Mountains, Decal	28,793	69.95	Proof	65.	70.
2004	Icebergs, Hologram	24,879	69.95	Proof	65.	70.
2004	Northern Lights, Double Image Hologram	34,135	79.95	Proof	75.	80.
2004	Hopewell Rocks, Selectively gold plated	16,918	69.95	Proof	60.	65.
2005	Diamonds, Double Image Hologram	35,000	69.95	Proof	65.	70.

TALL SHIPS COLLECTION

TWENTY DOLLARS, TALL SHIPS COLLECTION, 2005-2007.

Designers and Engravers:
    Obv.: Susanna Blunt, Susan Taylor
    Rev.: See reverse illustrations
Composition: 99.99% Ag, Hologram
Silver content: 31.39 g, 1.01 tr oz
Weight: 31.39 g
Diameter: 38.0 mm
Thickness: 3.0 mm
Edge: Reeded
Die Axis: ↑↑
Finish: Proof
Case of Issue: Maroon plastic slide case,
    black plastic insert, encapsulated coin,
    COA

2005 Obverse

Three-Masted Ship
Designer: Bonnie Ross
Engraver: William Woodruff

2006 Obverse

Ketch
Designer: John M. Horton
Engraver: Susan Taylor

2007 Obverse

Brigantine
Designer: Bonnie Ross
Engraver: William Woodruff

DATE	DESCRIPTION	QUANTITY SOLD	ISSUE PRICE	FINISH	PR-67	PR-68
2005	Three-Masted Ship, Hologram	18,276	69.95	Proof	75.	80.
2006	Ketch, Hologram	10,299	69.95	Proof	90.	95.
2007	Brigantine, Hologram	7,935	74.95	Proof	95.	100.

NATIONAL PARKS SERIES

TWENTY DOLLARS, NATIONAL PARKS SERIES, 2005-2006.

2005 Obverse
Designer: Susanna Blunt
Engraver: Susan Taylor

**North Pacific Rim National
Park Reserve of Canada (QU)**
Designer: Susanna Blunt
Engraver: Stan Witten

**Mingan Archipelago National
Park Reserve of Canada**
Designer: Pierre Leduc
Engraver: José Osio

2006 Obverse
Designer: Susanna Blunt
Engraver: Susan Taylor

**Georgian Bay Islands
National Park (ON)**
Designer: Tony Bianco
Engraver: William Woodruff

**Nahanni National Park
Reserve of Canada (NWT)**
Designer: Virginia Boulay
Engraver: William Woodruff

**Jasper National Park of
Canada (AL)**
Designer: Michelle Grant
Engraver: William Woodruff

Designers: See obverse illustrations
Composition: 99.99% Ag
Silver content: 31.39 g, 1.01 tr oz
Weight: 31.39 g
Diameter: 38.0 mm
Thickness: 3.0 mm
Case of Issue: Maroon plastic slide case, black plastic insert, encapsulated coin, COA

Engravers: See reverse illustrations

Edge: Reeded
Die Axis: ↑↑
Finish: Proof

DATE	DESCRIPTION	QUANTITY SOLD	ISSUE PRICE	FINISH	PR-67	PR-68
2005	North Pacific Rim National Park Reserve of Canada (QU)	21,695	69.95	Proof	65.	70.
2005	Mingan Archipelago National Park Reserve of Canada	Included	69.95	Proof	70.	75.
2006	Georgian Bay Islands National Park (ON)	20,218	69.95	Proof	70.	75.
2006	Nahanni National Park Reserve of Canada (NWT)	Included	69.95	Proof	85.	90.
2006	Jasper National Park of Canada (AL)	Included	69.95	Proof	85.	90.

Note: 1. National Parks single quantities were not recorded in the RCM Reports of 2005 and 2006 as individual entries, but only as totals sold for those years. There will be a difference between the projected issue as noted on the certificate of authenticity and the actual number sold.

2. Coins illustrated smaller than actual size.

CANADIAN ARCHITECTURAL SERIES

TWENTY DOLLARS, CANADIAN ARCHITECTURAL SERIES, 2006.

**Common
Obverse**

Designers and Engravers:
    Obv.: Susanna Blunt, Susan Taylor
    Rev.: Jianping Yan, RCM Staff
Composition: 99.99% Ag, Photographic hologram
Silver content: 31.1 g, 1.0 tr oz
Weight: 31.1 g
Diameter: 38.0 mm
Thickness: 3.0 mm
Edge: Reeded
Die Axis: ↑↑
Finish: Proof
Case of Issue: Maroon plastic slide case, black
    plastic insert, encapsulated coin, COA

Notre Dame Basilica	**30th Anniversary CN Tower**	**Pengrowth Saddledome**

DATE	DESCRIPTION	QUANTITY SOLD	ISSUE PRICE	FINISH	PR-67	PR-68
2006	Notre Dame Basilica, Photographic Hologram	30,906	69.95	Proof	80.	85.
2006	30th Anniv. CN Tower, Photographic Hologram	Included	69.95	Proof	80.	85.
2006	Pengrowth Saddledome, Photographic Hologram	Included	69.95	Proof	80.	85.

Note: Canadian Architectural Series quantities were not recorded individually in the RCM Report of 2006, but only as the total number of coins sold for the year. While the certificate of authenticity may show a mintage of 15,000 for each coin, it is apparent from the RCM Annual Report that this was not the case.

TWENTY DOLLARS, 125TH ANNIVERSARY OF THE FIRST INTERNATIONAL POLAR YEAR, 2007.

Common Obverse

Silver

Blue Plasma

Designers:
  Obv.: Susanna Blunt
  Rev.: Laurie McGaw
Composition: 92.5% Ag, 7.5% Cu
Silver content: 25.70 g, 0.826 tr oz
Weight: 27.78 g
Diameter: 40.0 mm
Thickness: 2.5 mm

Engravers:
  Obv.: Susan Taylor
  Rev.: Susan Taylor

Edge: Reeded
Die Axis: ↑↑
Finish: Proof and Proof Plasma

Case of Issue: Maroon clam style case, black flocked insert, encapsulated coin, COA

DATE	DESCRIPTION	QUANTITY SOLD	ISSUE PRICE	FINISH	PR-67	PR-68
2007	125th Anniv. First Int'l Polar Year, Silver	9,164	64.95	Proof	40.	45.
2007	125th Anniv. First Int'l Polar Year, Blue Plasma	3,005	249.95	Proof	200.	225.

CRYSTAL SNOWFLAKE SERIES

TWENTY DOLLARS, CRYSTAL SNOWFLAKE, 2007-2013.

Designers:
  Obv.: Susanna Blunt
  Rev.: Konrad Wachelko

Composition: 2007: 92.5% Ag, 7.5% Cu
                   2008-2012: 99.99% Ag,
                   with crystallised Swarovski elements

Weight: 2007: 50.0 g
              2008-2013: 31.0 to 31.39 g

Diameter: 38.0 mm

Thickness: 2007: 4.8 mm
                 2008-2013: 3.0 to 3.2 mm

Engravers:
  Obv.:   Susan Taylor
  Rev.:   Konrad Wachelko

Silver content: 2007: 46.34 g, 1.490 tr oz
                      2008-2011: 31.39 g, 1.01 tr oz
                      2012-13: 31.0 g, 1.0 tr oz

Edge: Reeded
Die Axis: ↑↑
Finish: Proof

Case of Issue: Maroon clam style case, black flocked insert, encapsulated coin, COA

2007-2008
Obverse with RCM Logo

2010-2012
Obverse without RCM Logo

2007 Aquamarine Snowflake

2008 Amethyst Snowflake

2008 Sapphire Snowflake

2009 Blue Snowflake

2009 Rose Snowflake

2010 Blue Snowflake

2010 Tanzanite Snowflake

TWENTY DOLLARS, CRYSTAL SNOWFLAKE SERIES, 2007-2013 (cont.).

2011 Emerald Snowflake

2011 Topaz Snowflake

2011 Hyacinth Snowflake

2011 Montana Snowflake

2012 Holiday Snowstorm

2012 Crystal Snowflake

2013 Winter Snowflake

DATE	DESCRIPTION	QUANTITY SOLD	ISSUE PRICE	FINISH	PR-67	PR-68
2007	Crystal Snowflake, Aquamarine	4,989	94.95	Proof	400.	425.
2007	Crystal Snowflake, Iridescent	4,980	94.95	Proof	500.	525.
2008	Crystal Snowflake, Amethyst	7,172	94.95	Proof	165.	175.
2008	Crystal Snowflake, Sapphire	7,765	94.95	Proof	160.	170.
2009	Crystal Snowflake, Blue	7,477	94.95	Proof	145.	155.
2009	Crystal Snowflake, Rose	7,004	94.95	Proof	145.	155.
2010	Crystal Snowflake, Blue	7,390	94.95	Proof	95.	100.
2010	Crystal Snowflake, Tanzanite	7,241	94.95	Proof	105.	115.
2011	Crystal Snowflake, Emerald	6,586	114.95	Proof	105.	115.
2011	Crystal Snowflake, Topaz	6,041	114.95	Proof	105.	115.
2011	Small Crystal Snowflakes, Hyacinth	5,660	114.95	Proof	105.	115.
2011	Small Crystal Snowflakes, Montana	5,822	114.95	Proof	105.	115.
2012	Holiday Snowstorm	4,886	114.95	Proof	120.	130.
2012	Crystal Snowflake	4,896	114.95	Proof	125.	135.
2013	Winter Snowflake	4,166	114.95	Proof	115.	125.

HOLIDAY SERIES

TWENTY DOLLARS, HOLIDAY SERIES, 2007-2011.

**Obverse 2007-2008
With RCM Logo**

**Obverse 2010-2011
Without RCM Logo**

Designers and Engravers:
Obv.: Susanna Blunt, Susan Taylor
Rev.: See reverse illustrations
Composition: 99.99% Ag
Silver content: 31.39 g, 1.01 tr oz
Weight: 31.39 g
Diameter: 38.0 mm
Thickness: 3.1 to 3.3 mm
Edge: Reeded
Die Axis: ↑↑
Finish: 2007-2008: Proof;
       2010-2011: Proof, with crystallised
        Swarovski elements
Case of Issue: Maroon clam style case, black
flocked insert, encapsulated coin, COA

**2007
Holiday Sleigh Ride
Tony Bianco**

**2008
Holiday Carols
T. Bianco, C. Mok, K. Wachelko**

**2010
Holiday Pine Cones, Moonlight
Susan Taylor**

**2010
Holiday Pine Cones, Ruby
Susan Taylor**

**2011
Christmas Tree
Tony Bianco, José Osio**

DATE	DESCRIPTION	QUANTITY SOLD	ISSUE PRICE	FINISH	PR-67	PR-68
2007	Holiday Sleigh Ride	6,804	69.95	Proof	95.	100.
2008	Holiday Carols	5,224	69.95	Proof	65.	70.
2010	Holiday Pine Cones, Moonlight	4,754	99.95	Proof	105.	110.
2010	Holiday Pine Cones, Ruby	4,907	99.95	Proof	105.	110.
2011	Christmas Tree	7,974	114.95	Proof	110.	120.

CRYSTAL RAINDROP SERIES

TWENTY DOLLARS, CRYSTAL RAINDROP SERIES, 2008-2012.

2008 Obverse
With RCM Logo

2009-2012 Obverse
Without RCM Logo

Designers and Engravers:
Obv.: Susanna Blunt, Susan Taylor
Rev.: See reverse illustrations
Composition: 99.99% Ag, Colourised, Crystallised
Swarovski element
Silver content: 31.39 g, 1.01 tr oz
Weight: 31.39 g
Diameter: 38.0 mm
Thickness: 3.1 mm
Edge: Reeded
Die Axis: ↑↑
Finish: Proof
Case of Issue: Maroon clam style case, black
flocked insert, encapsulated coin, COA

2008	**2009**	**2010**
Crystal Raindrop	Autumn Crystal Raindrop	Maple Leaf with Crystal Raindrop
Designer: Celia Godkin	Designer: Celia Godkin	Designer: Celia Godkin
Engraver: Cecily Mok	Engraver: RCM Staff	Engraver: RCM Staff

2011
Crystal Raindrop and Maple Leaf
Designer: Celia Godkin
Engraver: Cecily Mok

2012
The Sugar Maple
Designer: Celia Godkin
Engraver: RCM Staff

DATE	DESCRIPTION	QUANTITY SOLD	ISSUE PRICE	FINISH	PR-67	PR-68
2008	Crystal Raindrop	13,122	89.95	Proof	165.	175.
2009	Autumn Crystal Raindrop	9,998	94.95	Proof	200.	225.
2010	Maple Leaf with Crystal Raindrop	9,659	104.95	Proof	125.	135.
2011	Crystal Raindrop and Maple Leaf	9,594	109.95	Proof	120.	130.
2012	The Sugar Maple	9,933	119.95	Proof	125.	135.

GREAT CANADIAN LOCOMOTIVES SERIES

TWENTY DOLLARS, GREAT CANADIAN LOCOMOTIVES SERIES, 2008-2011

The Hudson, Locomotive 2850 was chosen to transport King George VI and Queen Elizabeth from Quebec City to Vancouver, during their royal visit of 1939. The royal crest was mounted on the engine and tender, and remained after the visit, thus *The Royal Hudson*.

The Jubilee was introduced in 1936 for the CPR's 50th anniversary of the completion of the Transcontinental Railway in 1886.

Classed as a 2-10-4 engine, *The Selkirk* engines were built by Montreal Locomotive Works for Canadian Pacific Railway to handle the steep grades of the Selkirk Mountains in British Columbia.

The D-10-class ten wheeler type 4-6-0 locomotive was a typical Canadian Pacific Railway steam locomotive. Five hundred and eight locomotives were built between 1905 and 1913 and formed the backbone of CPR's freight locomotive fleet. Most burned coal, but 28 were converted to oil.

2008 Obverse
With RCM Logo

2008
The Royal Hudson
Konrad Wachelko

2009-2011 Obverse
Without RCM Logo

2009
The Jubilee
William Woodruff

2010
The Selkirk
William Woodruff

2011
D-10
Marcos Hallam

Designers:
  Obv.: Susanna Blunt
  Rev.: RCM Engravers (from Canadian
         Canadian Pacific Railway Archives)
Composition: 99.99% Ag
Silver content: 31.39 g, 1.01 tr oz
Weight: 31.39 g
Diameter: 38.0 mm
Thickness: 3.2 mm
Case of Issue: Maroon leatherette clam style case, black flocked insert, encapsulated coin, COA

Engravers:
  Obv.: Susan Taylor
  Rev.: See reverse illustrations

Edge: Plain, edge lettering "ROYAL HUDSON",
          "JUBILEE", "SELKIRK" or "D-10"
Die Axis: ↑↑
Finish: Proof

DATE	DESCRIPTION	QUANTITY SOLD	ISSUE PRICE	FINISH	PR-67	PR-68
2008	The Royal Hudson	8,345	69.95	Proof	95.	100.
2009	The Jubilee	6,036	69.95	Proof	90.	95.
2010	The Selkirk	5,874	79.95	Proof	90.	95.
2011	D-10	8,662	79.95	Proof	85.	90.

Note: Coins illustrated smaller than actual size.

CANADIAN INDUSTRY SERIES

TWENTY DOLLARS, AGRICULTURE TRADE, 2008.

Designers and Engravers:
   Obv.: Susanna Blunt, Susan Taylor
   Rev.: John Mardon, José Osio
Composition: 99.99% Ag
Silver content: 31.39 g, 1.01 tr oz
Weight: 31.39 g
Diameter: 38.0 mm
Thickness: 3.1 mm
Edge: Reeded
Die Axis: ↑↑
Finish: Proof
Case: Maroon clam style case, black flocked insert, encapsulated coin, COA

DATE	DESCRIPTION	QUANTITY SOLD	ISSUE PRICE	FINISH	PR-67	PR-68
2008	Agriculture Trade	5,802	69.95	Proof	70.	75.

TWENTY DOLLARS, COAL MINING TRADE, 2009.

Designers and Engravers:
   Obv.: Susanna Blunt, Susan Taylor
   Rev.: John Mardon, Christie Paquet
Composition: 99.99% Ag
Silver content: 3.39 g, 1.01 tr oz
Weight: 31.39 g
Diameter: 38.0 mm
Thickness: 3.1 mm
Edge: Reeded
Die Axis: ↑↑
Finish: Proof
Case: Maroon clam style case, black flocked insert, encapsulated coin, COA

DATE	DESCRIPTION	QUANTITY SOLD	ISSUE PRICE	FINISH	PR-67	PR-68
2009	Coal Mining Trade	3,349	74.95	Proof	80.	85.

NHL SEASON, 2008-2009

TWENTY DOLLARS, 2008-2009 NHL TEAM GOALIE MASKS, 2009.

The goalie mask, first introduced by all-star Montreal goalie Jacques Plante on November 1st, 1959, has become a necessary part of the goal tender's equipment.

Common Obverse

Designers and Engravers:
    Obv.: Susanna Blunt, Susan Taylor
    Rev.: Marcos Hallam
Composition: 92.5% Ag, 7.5% Cu, Painted
Silver content: 25.70 g, 0.826 tr oz
Weight: 27.78 g
Diameter: 40.0 mm
Thickness: 2.6 mm
Edge: Reeded
Die Axis: ↑↑
Finish: Proof
Case of Issue: Lucite stand, encapsulated coin, COA, cardboard outer box

Calgary Flames

Edmonton Oilers

Montreal Canadiens

Ottawa Senators

Toronto Maple Leafs

Vancouver Canucks

DATE	DESCRIPTION	QUANTITY SOLD	ISSUE PRICE	FINISH	PR-67	PR-68
2009	Calgary Flames	125	74.95	Proof	85.	90.
2009	Edmonton Oilers	147	74.95	Proof	85.	90.
2009	Montreal Canadiens	748	74.95	Proof	85.	90.
2009	Ottawa Senators	95	74.95	Proof	85.	90.
2009	Toronto Maple Leafs	244	74.95	Proof	85.	90.
2009	Vancouver Canucks	129	74.95	Proof	85.	90.

Note: Quantity Sold numbers are those for 2009. The Royal Mint Annual Report for 2010 did not report additional units sold.

TWENTY DOLLARS, SUMMER MOON MASK, 2009.

Designers and Engravers:
Obv.: Susanna Blunt, Susan Taylor
Rev.: Jody Broomfield, Susan Taylor
Composition: 99.99% Ag
Silver content: 31.39 g, 1.01 tr oz
Weight: 31.39 g
Diameter: 38.0 mm
Thickness: 3.2 mm
Edge: Reeded
Die Axis: ↑↑
Finish: Proof
Case: Maroon leatherette clam style case, black flocked insert, encapsulated coin, COA

DATE	DESCRIPTION	QUANTITY SOLD	ISSUE PRICE	FINISH	PR-67	PR-68
2009	Summer Moon Mask	2,834	69.95	Proof	200.	225.

TWENTY DOLLARS, 475TH ANNIVERSARY JACQUES CARTIER'S ARRIVAL AT GASPÉ, 1534-2009.

Designers and Engravers:
Obv.: Susanna Blunt, Susan Taylor
Rev.: John Mardon, Stan Witten
Composition: 99.99% Ag
Silver content: 31.39 g, 1.01 tr oz
Weight: 31.39 g
Diameter: 38.0 mm
Thickness: 3.2 mm
Edge: Reeded
Die Axis: ↑↑
Finish: Proof
Case: Maroon leatherette clam style case, black flocked insert, encapsulated coin, COA

DATE	DESCRIPTION	QUANTITY SOLD	ISSUE PRICE	FINISH	PR-67	PR-68
2009 (1534-)	475th Anniversary of Jacques Cartier's Arrival at Gaspé	1516	169.95	Proof	275.	300.

PAINTED WILDFLOWER SERIES

TWENTY DOLLARS, PAINTED WILDFLOWER SERIES, 2010-2013.

Common Obverse

Designers and Engravers:
Obv.: Susanna Blunt, Susan Taylor
Rev.: See reverse illustrations
Composition: 99.99% Ag, Painted, crystallised Swarovski elements
Silver content: 31.39 g, 1.01 tr oz
Weight: 31.39 g
Diameter: 38.0 mm
Thickness: 3.1 mm
Edge: Reeded
Die Axis: ↑↑
Finish: Proof
Case of Issue: Maroon leatherette clam style case, black flocked insert, encapsulated coin, COA

2010
Water Lily
Designer: Claudio D'Angelo
Engraver: Cecily Mok

2011
Crystal Dewdrop and Wild Rose
Designer: Margaret Dest
Engraver: José Osio

2012
Rhododendron
Designer: Claudio D'Angelo
Engraver: RCM Staff

2013
Blue Flag Iris
Designer: Celia Godkin
Engraver: RCM Staff

DATE	DESCRIPTION	QUANTITY SOLD	ISSUE PRICE	FINISH	PR-67	PR-68
2010	Water Lily	9,990	104.95	Proof	125.	135.
2011	Crystal Dewdrop and Wild Rose	9,989	109.95	Proof	130.	140.
2012	Rhododendron	9,991	119.95	Proof	130.	140.
2013	Blue Flag Iris	9,921	119.95	Proof	130.	140.

TWENTY DOLLARS, 75TH ANNIVERSARY OF THE FIRST BANK NOTES ISSUED BY BANK OF CANADA, 2010.

The reverse design on this coin is a reproduction of the allegory that appeared on the original 1935 $20 bank note; a woman symbolising agriculture admiring fruits of the field presented to her by a kneeling man.

Designers and Engravers:
    Obv.: Susanna Blunt, Susan Taylor
    Rev.: Konrad Wachelko
Composition: 99.99% Ag
Silver content: 31.39 g, 1.01 tr oz
Weight: 31.39 g
Diameter: 38.0 mm
Thickness: 3.2 mm
Edge: Reeded
Die Axis: ↑↑   **Finish:** Proof
Case: Maroon clam style case, black flocked insert, encapsulated coin, COA

DATE	DESCRIPTION	QUANTITY SOLD	ISSUE PRICE	FINISH	PR-67	PR-68
2010 (1935-)	75th Anniversary of First Notes Issued by Bank of Canada	6,720	79.95	Proof	85.	90.

TWENTY DOLLARS, HRH PRINCE WILLIAM OF WALES AND MISS CATHERINE MIDDLETON, 2011.

This coin is embedded with a sapphire colour Swarovski element.

Designers and Engravers:
    Obv.: Susanna Blunt, Susan Taylor
    Rev.: Laurie McGaw, José Osio
Composition: 99.99% Ag, Swarovski element
Silver content: 31.39 g, 1.01 tr oz
Weight: 31.39 g
Diameter: 38.0 mm
Thickness: 3.2 mm
Edge: Plain (laser engraved HRH PRINCE WILLIAM MISS CATHERINE MIDDLETON SAR LE PRINCE WILLIAM ET MLLE CATHERINE MIDDLETON)
Die Axis: ↑↑
Finish: Proof
Case: Maroon clam style case, black flocked insert, encapsulated coin, COA

DATE	DESCRIPTION	QUANTITY SOLD	ISSUE PRICE	FINISH	PR-67	PR-68
2011	HRH Prince William of Wales / Miss Catherine Middleton	24,858	104.95	Proof	100.	110.

TWENTY DOLLARS, WINTER SCENE, 2011.

Designers and Engravers:
    Obv.: Susanna Blunt, Susan Taylor
    Rev.: Rémi Clark, José Osio
Composition: 92.50% Ag, 0.75% Cu
Silver content: 25.70 g, 0.826 tr oz
Weight: 27.78 g
Diameter: 40.0 mm   **Edge:** Reeded
Thickness: 2.5 mm   **Die Axis:** ↑↑
Finish: Proof
Case: Maroon leatherette clam style case, black flocked insert, encapsulated coin, COA

DATE	DESCRIPTION	QUANTITY SOLD	ISSUE PRICE	FINISH	PR-67	PR-68
2011	Winter Scene	5,287	69.95	Proof	95.	100.

CANADIAN GARDEN FLORA AND FAUNA SERIES

TWENTY DOLLARS, CANADIAN GARDEN FLORA AND FAUNA SERIES, 2011-2014.

| **Common Obverse** | **2011**
Tulip with Ladybug
Designer: Cosme Saffioti
Engraver: RCM Staff
Ladybug: Giuliano Donnagio | **2012**
Aster with Bumble Bee
Designer: Cosme Saffioti
Engraver: RCM Staff
Bumble Bee: Giuliano Donnagio |

| **2013**
Purple Coneflower and
Eastern Tailed Blue Butterfly
Designer: Maurice Gervais
Engraver: Cecily Mok
Butterfly: Giuliano Donnagio | **2014**
Water-lily and Leopard Frog
Designer: Maurice Gervais
Engraver: RCM Staff
Leopard Frog: G. Donnagio |

Designers:
Obv.: Susanna Blunt
Rev.: See reverse illustrations

Engravers:
Obv.: Susan Taylor
Rev.: See reverse illustrations

Composition: 99.99% Ag, Coloured, Murano glass insect
Silver content: 31.39 g, 1.01 tr oz
Weight: 31.39 g
Diameter: 38.0 mm
Thickness: 3.1 mm

Edge: Reeded
Die Axis: ↑↑
Finish: Proof

Case of Issue: Maroon clam style case, black flocked insert, encapsulated coin, COA

DATE	DESCRIPTION	QUANTITY SOLD	ISSUE PRICE	FINISH	PR-67	PR-68
2011	Tulip with Ladybug	4,985	139.95	Proof	825.	850.
2012	Aster with Bumble Bee	9,991	139.95	Proof	275.	300.
2013	Purple Coneflower and Eastern Tailed Blue Butterfly	9,992	149.95	Proof	225.	250.
2014	Water-lily and Leopard Frog	12,500	149.95	Proof	150.	175.

THE QUEEN'S DIAMOND JUBILEE SERIES

TWENTY DOLLARS, THE QUEEN'S DIAMOND JUBILEE, 1952-2012.

Designers and Engravers:
Obv.: Susanna Blunt, Susan Taylor
Rev.: Laurie McGaw, Susan Taylor
Composition: 99.99% Ag, Swarovski element
Silver content: 31.39 g, 1.01 tr oz
Weight: 31.39 g
Diameter: 38.0 mm
Thickness: 3.1 mm
Edge: Reeded
Die Axis: ↑↑
Finish: Proof
Case: Maroon clam style case, black flocked insert, encapsulated coin, COA

DATE	DESCRIPTION	QUANTITY SOLD	ISSUE PRICE	FINISH	PR-67	PR-68
2012 (1952-)	The Queen's Diamond Jubilee	10,780	104.95	Proof	115.	125.

TWENTY DOLLARS, QUEEN ELIZABETH II AND PRINCE PHILIP, 1952-2012.

This twenty-dollar silver coin is also found in the Queen's Diamond Jubilee Royal Silver Set.

Designers and Engravers:
Obv.: Susanna Blunt, Susan Taylor
Rev.: Laurie McGaw, Susan Taylor
Composition: 99.99% Ag
Silver content: 31.39 g, 1.01 tr oz
Weight: 31.39 g
Diameter: 38.0 mm
Thickness: 3.1 mm
Edge: Reeded
Die Axis: ↑↑
Finish: Proof
Case: Black clam style case, black flocked insert, encapsulated coin, COA

DATE	DESCRIPTION	QUANTITY SOLD	ISSUE PRICE	FINISH	PR-67	PR-68
2012 (1952-)	Queen Elizabeth II and Prince Philip	5,627	84.95	Proof	85.	90.

TWENTY DOLLARS, ROYAL CYPHER, 60TH JUBILEE, 1952-2012.

Designers and Engravers:
Obv.: Susanna Blunt, Susan Taylor
Rev.: Christie Paquet
Composition: 99.99% Ag
Silver content: 31.39 g, 1.01 tr oz
Weight: 31.39 g
Diameter: 38.0 mm
Thickness: 3.1 mm
Edge: Reeded
Die Axis: ↑↑
Finish: Proof
Case: Maroon clam style case, black flocked insert, encapsulated coin, COA

DATE	DESCRIPTION	QUANTITY SOLD	ISSUE PRICE	FINISH	PR-67	PR-68
2012 (1952-)	Royal Cypher, 60th Jubilee	3,568	84.95	Proof	85.	90.

THE QUEEN'S DIAMOND JUBILEE SERIES (cont.)

TWENTY DOLLARS, THE QUEEN'S PORTRAIT, 2012.

Designers and Engravers:
Obv.: Susanna Blunt, Susan Taylor
Rev.: Laurie McGaw, Christie Paquet
Composition: 99.99% Ag
Silver content: 30.75 g, 0.99 tr oz
Weight: 30.75 g
Diameter: 36.0 mm
Thickness: 3.0 mm
Edge: Plain
Die Axis: ↑↑
Finish: Proof
Case: Maroon clam style case, black flocked insert, encapsulated coin, COA

DATE	DESCRIPTION	QUANTITY SOLD	ISSUE PRICE	FINISH	PR-67	PR-68
2012	The Queen's Portrait	7,473	129.95	Proof	125.	135.

TWENTY DOLLARS, THE QUEEN'S VISIT TO CANADA, 2012.

Queen Elizabeth II has been an Honourary Commissioner of the RCMP since 1953. During a visit to England in 1969 to participate in the Royal Windsor Horse Show, the RCMP presented the Queen with one of their finest horses *Burmese*. The RCMP has presented a further five horses since then, each to commemorate an important milestone.

Designers and Engravers:
Obv.: Susanna Blunt, Susan Taylor
Rev.: Bonnie Ross, Cecily Mok
Composition: 99.99% Ag
Silver content: 31.39 g, 1.01 tr oz
Weight: 31.39 g
Diameter: 38.0 mm
Thickness: 3.1 mm
Edge: Reeded
Die Axis: ↑↑
Finish: Proof
Case: Maroon clam style case, black flocked insert, encapsulated coin, COA

DATE	DESCRIPTION	QUANTITY SOLD	ISSUE PRICE	FINISH	PR-67	PR-68
2012	The Queen's Visit to Canada	11,113	89.95	Proof	85.	90.

TWENTY DOLLARS, WINNIPEG JETS, 2011-2012.

The Winnipeg Jets is a professional (NHL) ice hockey team based in Winnipeg, Manitoba. The team plays its home games at the MTS Centre and takes their name after Winnipeg's original WHA/NHL team.

Designers and Engravers:
   Obv.: Susanna Blunt, Susan Taylor
   Rev.: William Woodruff, RCM Staff
Composition: 99.99% Ag
Silver content: 31.39 g, 1.01 tr oz
Weight: 31.39 g
Diameter: 37.8 mm   **Edge:** Reeded
Thickness: 3.1 mm   **Die Axis:** ↑↑
Finish: Proof
Case: Maroon leatherette clam style case, black flocked insert, encapsulated coin, COA

DATE	DESCRIPTION	QUANTITY SOLD	ISSUE PRICE	FINISH	PR-67	PR-68
2011-2012	Winnipeg Jets	5,536	94.95	Proof	100.	110.

TWENTY DOLLARS, 50 YEARS OF THE CANADIAN COAST GUARD, 1962-2012.

During a 1994 science expedition the CCGS *Louis S. St. Laurent* navigated through 3,700 kilometres of Arctic Ice visiting the North Pole as it made the first crossing of the Arctic Ocean from the Pacific to the Atlantic. It was a joint Canada-US expedition with the USCGC *Polar Sea*. On August 22nd, 1994, the *Louis S. St. Laurent* was the first Canadian ship to reach the North Pole.

Designers and Engravers:
   Obv.: Susanna Blunt, Susan Taylor
   Rev.: Yves Bérube, Stan Witten
Composition: 99.99% Ag
Silver content: 31.39 g, 1.01 tr oz
Weight: 31.39 g
Diameter: 38.0 mm   **Edge:** Reeded
Thickness: 3.0 mm   **Die Axis:** ↑↑
Finish: Proof
Case: Canadian maple wood case, black flocked insert, encapsulated coin, COA

DATE	DESCRIPTION	QUANTITY SOLD	ISSUE PRICE	FINISH	PR-67	PR-68
2012 (1962-)	50 Years of the Canadian Coast Guard	6,696	129.95	Proof	130.	140.

THE GROUP OF SEVEN SERIES

TWENTY DOLLARS, THE GROUP OF SEVEN SERIES, 2012-2013.

The Group of Seven were a group of Canadian landscape artists from the 1920-1933 period, who believed that a distinct Canadian art movement could be developed through direct contact with nature.

Common Obverse

Stormy Weather, Georgian Bay
Designer: F. H. Varley
Engraver: Marcos Hallam

Designers and Engravers:
    Obv.: Susanna Blunt, Susan Taylor
    Rev.: See reverse illustrations
Composition: 99.99% Ag
Silver content: 31.39 g, 1.01 tr oz
Weight: 31.39 g
Diameter: 38.0 mm
Thickness: 3.1 mm
Edge: Reeded
Die Axis: ↑↑
Finish: Proof
Case: Maroon leatherette clam style case, black flocked insert, encapsulated coin, COA

Nova Scotia Fishing Village
Designer: Arthur Lismer
Engraver: Stan Witten

Houses, Cobalt (1931-1932)
Designer: Franklin Carmichael
Engraver: Susan Taylor

Toronto Street Winter Morning (1920)
Designer: Lawren S. Harris
Engraver: Susan Taylor

The Guardian of the Gorge
Designer: Franz Johnston
Engraver: Cecily Mok

Sumacs
Designer: J. E. H. MacDonald
Engraver: N/A

Saint-Tite-des-Caps
Designer: A. Y. Jackson
Engraver: N/A

DATE	DESCRIPTION	QUANTITY SOLD	ISSUE PRICE	FINISH	PR-67	PR-68
2012	Stormy Weather, Georgian Bay, F. H. Varley	6,962	89.95	Proof	150.	160.
2012	Nova Scotia Fishing Village, Arthur Lismer	6,985	89.95	Proof	115.	125.
2012	Houses, Cobalt (1931-1932), Franklin Carmichael	6,946	89.95	Proof	95.	100.
2013	Toronto Street, Winter Morning (1920), Lawren S. Harris	6,694	89.95	Proof	95.	100.
2013	The Guardian of the Gorge, Franz Johnston	6,743	89.95	Proof	95.	100.
2013	Sumacs, J. E. H. MacDonald	6,348	89.95	Proof	95.	100.
2013	Saint-Tite-des-Caps, A. Y. Jackson	6,094	89.95	Proof	95.	100.

TWENTY DOLLARS, THE THREE WISE MEN, 2012.

Designers and Engravers:
    Obv.: Susanna Blunt, Susan Taylor
    Rev.: Jason Bouwman, Stan Witten
Composition: 99.99% Ag, Crystal element
Silver content: 28.1 g, 0.9 tr oz
Weight: 28.1 g
Diameter: 40.0 mm
Thickness: 2.6 mm
Edge: Reeded
Die Axis: ↑↑
Finish: Proof
Case: Maroon clam style case, black flocked insert, encapsulated coin, COA

DATE	DESCRIPTION	QUANTITY SOLD	ISSUE PRICE	FINISH	PR-67	PR-68
2012	The Three Wise Men	3,916	114.95	Proof	120.	130.

TWENTY DOLLARS, BULL MOOSE FROM *THE MOOSE FAMILY*, ROBERT BATEMAN MOOSE COIN SERIES, 2012.

The reverse design on this coin features a bull moose's head and antlers taken from Robert Bateman's painting *The Moose Family*. The coin was issued to commemorate the 50th anniversary of the Canadian Wildlife Federation.

Designers and Engravers:
    Obv.: Susanna Blunt, Susan Taylor
    Rev.: Robert Bateman, Stan Witten
Composition: 99.99% Ag
Silver content: 31.39 g, 1.01 tr oz
Weight: 31.39 g
Diameter: 38.0 mm
Thickness: 3.1 mm
Edge: Reeded
Die Axis: ↑↑
Finish: Proof
Case: Maroon clam style case, black flocked insert, encapsulated coin, COA

DATE	DESCRIPTION	QUANTITY SOLD	ISSUE PRICE	FINISH	PR-67	PR-68
2012 (1962-)	Bull Moose	7,499	94.95	Proof	135.	145.

Note: For other coins in the Robert Bateman Moose Coin Series see pages, 260, 306, and 331.

TWENTY DOLLARS, THE BEAVER, 2013.

Designers and Engravers:
    Obv.: Susanna Blunt, Susan Taylor
    Rev.: Glen Loates, José Osio
Composition: 99.99% Ag
Silver content: 31.39 g, 1.01 tr oz
Weight: 31.39 g
Diameter: 38.0 mm
Thickness: 3.1 mm
Edge: Reeded
Die Axis: ↑↑
Finish: Proof
Case: Maroon clam style case, black flocked insert, encapsulated coin, COA

DATE	DESCRIPTION	QUANTITY SOLD	ISSUE PRICE	FINISH	PR-67	PR-68
2013	The Beaver	8,495	99.95	Proof	105.	115.

WORLD BASEBALL CLASSIC SERIES

TWENTY DOLLARS, WORLD BASEBALL CLASSIC SERIES, 2013.
  These coins were issued to celebrate the World Baseball Classic Tournament held March 2nd to 19th, 2013. For other coins in this series see pages 278 and 296.

Common Obverse

Designers and Engravers:
  Obv.: Susanna Blunt, Susan Taylor
  Rev.: Steve Hepburn, Christie Paquet
Composition: 99.99% Ag
Silver content: 31.1 g, 1.0 tr oz
Weight: 31.1 g
Diameter: 38.0 mm
Thickness: 3.2 mm
Edge: Reeded
Die Axis: ↑↑
Finish: Proof
Case of Issue: Maroon leatherette clam style case, black flocked insert, encapsulated coin, COA, custom sleeve

Fielder

Hitter

Pitcher

Runner

DATE	DESCRIPTION	QUANTITY SOLD	ISSUE PRICE	FINISH	PR-67	PR-68
2013	Fielder	866	114.95	Proof	115.	125.
2013	Hitter	1,405	114.95	Proof	115.	125.
2013	Pitcher	938	114.95	Proof	115.	125.
2013	Runner	864	114.95	Proof	115.	125.

UNTAMED CANADA SERIES

TWENTY DOLLARS, THE ARCTIC FOX, 2013-2014.

This is the first coin in the Untamed Canada Series. The Arctic Fox also known as the white fox, polar fox or snow fox, is a small fox native to the Arctic regions. It has fur on the bottom of its feet to protect it from the cold while digging.

Designers and Engravers:
Obv.: Susanna Blunt, Susan Taylor
Rev.: Tivadar Bote, Steven Stewart
Composition: 99.99% Ag
Silver content: 28.02 g, 0.90 tr oz
Weight: 28.02 g
Diameter: 40.0 mm   **Edge:** Reeded
Thickness: 2.5 mm   **Die Axis:** ↑↑
Finish: Proof
Case: Maroon clam style case, black flocked insert, encapsulated coin, COA

TWENTY DOLLARS, PRONGHORN, 2013.

This is the second coin in the Untamed Canada Series. The Pronghorn is fleet-footed and one of the fastest animals in North America. They can run more than 85 kilometres an hour, outrunning coyotes and bobcats.

Designers and Engravers:
Obv.: Susanna Blunt, Susan Taylor
Rev.: Tivadar Bote, RCM Staff
Composition: 99.99% Ag
Silver content: 31.6 g, 1.01 tr oz
Weight: 31.60 g
Diameter: 40.0 mm   **Edge:** Reeded
Thickness: 2.9 mm   **Die Axis:** ↑↑
Finish: Proof
Case: Maroon clam style case, black flocked insert, encapsulated coin, COA

TWENTY DOLLARS, WOLVERINE, 2014.

This is the third and final coin in the Untamed Canada Series. The wolverine is the largest member of the weasel family and resembles a small bear.

Designers and Engravers:
Obv.: Susanna Blunt, Susan Taylor
Rev.: Tivadar Bote, RCM Staff
Composition: 99.99% Ag
Silver content: 31.6 g, 1.01 tr oz
Weight: 31.60 g
Diameter: 40.0 mm   **Edge:** Reeded
Thickness: 2.9 mm   **Die Axis:** ↑↑
Finish: Proof
Case: Maroon clam style case, black flocked insert, encapsulated coin, COA

DATE	DESCRIPTION	QUANTITY SOLD	ISSUE PRICE	FINISH	PR-67	PR-68
2013	The Arctic Fox	7,538	84.95	Proof	90.	95.
2013	Pronghorn	4,181	89.95	Proof	90.	95.
2014	Wolverine	8,500	89.95	Proof	90.	95.

BUTTERFLIES OF CANADA

TWENTY DOLLARS, CANADIAN TIGER SWALLOWTAIL, 2013.

Designers and Engravers:
  Obv.: Susanna Blunt, Susan Taylor
  Rev.: Celia Godkin, RCM Staff
Composition: 99.99% Ag, Coloured
Silver content: 28.02 g, 0.90 tr oz
Weight: 28.02 g
Diameter: 40.0 mm   **Edge:** Reeded
Thickness: 2.6 mm   **Die Axis:** ↑↑
Finish: Proof
Case: Maroon clam style case, black flocked insert, encapsulated coin, COA, custom beauty box

DATE	DESCRIPTION	QUANTITY SOLD	ISSUE PRICE	FINISH	PR-67	PR-68
2013	Canadian Tiger Swallowtail	8,854	99.95	Proof	105.	115.

CANADIAN MAPLE CANOPY SERIES

TWENTY DOLLARS, CANADIAN MAPLE CANOPY SERIES, 2013-2014.

Common Obverse

Designers and Engravers:
  Obv.: Susanna Blunt, Susan Taylor
  Rev.: See reverse illustrations, RCM Staff
Composition: 99.99% Ag, Coloured
Silver content: 31.2 g, 1.0 tr oz
Weight: 31.2 g   **Edge:** Reeded
Diameter: 38.0 mm   **Die Axis:** ↑↑
Thickness: 3.1 mm   **Finish:** Proof
Case of Issue: Maroon clam style case, black flocked insert, encapsulated coin, COA

Spring
Designer: Emily Damstra

Autumn
Designer: Margaret Best

Spring Splendour
Designer: Margaret Best

DATE	DESCRIPTION	QUANTITY SOLD	ISSUE PRICE	FINISH	PR-67	PR-68
2013	Spring	7,491	99.95	Proof	135.	145.
2013	Autumn	7,426	99.95	Proof	105.	115.
2014	Spring Splendour	7,500	99.95	Proof	100.	110.

THE BALD EAGLE SERIES

TWENTY DOLLARS, THE BALD EAGLE SERIES, 2013.

Common Obverse   **Portrait of Power**

Designers and Engravers:
   Obv.: Susanna Blunt, Susan Taylor
   Rev.: Claudio D'Angelo, RCM Staff
Composition: 99.99% Ag
Silver content: 31.39 g, 1.01 tr oz
Weight: 31.39 g
Diameter: 38.0 mm
Thickness: 3.1 mm
Edge: Plain, Edge lettering "1oz FINE SILVER" "1 oz ARGENT PUR"
Die Axis: ↑↑
Finish: Proof
Case: Maroon clam style case, black flocked insert, encapsulated coin, COA, custom beauty box

Lifelong Mates   **Returning From the Hunt**   **Mother Protecting Her Eaglets**

DATE	DESCRIPTION	QUANTITY SOLD	ISSUE PRICE	FINISH	PR-67	PR-68
2013	Portrait of Power	7,495	99.95	Proof	130.	140.
2013	Portrait of Power, No Edge Lettering	Incl. above	99.95	Proof	200.	225.
2013	Lifelong Mates	7,494	99.95	Proof	115.	125.
2013	Returning From the Hunt	7,468	99.95	Proof	115.	125.
2013	Mother Protecting Her Eaglets	7,443	99.95	Proof	115.	125.

TWENTY DOLLARS, 300TH ANNIVERSARY OF LOUISBOURG, 2013.

Designers and Engravers:
   Obv.: Susanna Blunt, Susan Taylor
   Rev.: John Horton, RCM Staff
Composition: 99.99% Ag
Silver content: 31.6 g, 1.01 tr oz
Weight: 31.6 g
Diameter: 40.0 mm
Thickness: 3.0 mm
Edge: Plain, Edge lettering "LOUISBOURG 300"
Die Axis: ↑↑
Finish: Proof
Case: Maroon clam style case, black flocked insert, encapsulated coin, COA

DATE	DESCRIPTION	QUANTITY SOLD	ISSUE PRICE	FINISH	PR-67	PR-68
2013	300th Anniversary of Louisbourg	4,923	89.95	Proof	95.	100.

DINOSAURS OF CANADA SERIES

TWENTY DOLLARS, DINOSAURS OF CANADA SERIES, 2013-2014.

Common Obverse

Bathygnathus Borealis

Scutellosaurus

Designers:
  Obv.: Susanna Blunt
  Rev.: Julius Csotonyi
Composition: 99.99% Ag
Silver content: 31.39 g, 1.0 tr oz
Weight: 31.39 g
Diameter: 38.0 mm

Engravers:
  Obv.: Susan Taylor
  Rev.: RCM Staff
Thickness: 3.1 mm
Edge: Reeded
Die Axis: ↑↑
Finish: Proof

Case of Issue: Maroon clam style case, black flocked insert, encapsulated coin, COA

DATE	DESCRIPTION	QUANTITY SOLD	ISSUE PRICE	FINISH	PR-67	PR-68
2013	Bathygnathus Borealis	7,973	89.95	Proof	90.	95.
2014	Scutellosaurus	4,113	89.95	Proof	90.	95.

A STORY OF THE NORTHERN LIGHTS

TWENTY DOLLARS, A STORY OF THE NORTHERN LIGHTS, 2013-2014.

Common Obverse

The Great Hare

Howling Wolf

Designers:
  Obv.: Susanna Blunt
  Rev.: Nathalie Bertin
Composition: 99.99% Ag, Hologram
Silver content: 30.4 g, 0.98 tr oz
Weight: 30.4 g
Diameter: 37.8 mm

Engravers:
  Rev.: Susan Taylor
  Rev.: RCM Staff
Thickness: 3.0 mm
Edge: Reeded
Die Axis: ↑↑
Finish: Proof

Case of Issue: Maroon clam style case, black flocked insert, encapsulated coin, COA

DATE	DESCRIPTION	QUANTITY SOLD	ISSUE PRICE	FINISH	PR-67	PR-68
2013	The Great Hare	8,450	109.95	Proof	115.	125.
2014	Howling Wolf	8,500	109.95	Proof	115.	125.

TWENTY DOLLARS, MAPLE LEAF IMPRESSION, 2013.

Designers and Engravers:
Obv.: Susanna Blunt, Susan Taylor
Rev.: José Osio, RCM Staff
Composition: 99.99% Ag, Enamelled
Silver content: 31.39 g, 1.01 tr oz
Weight: 31.39 g
Diameter: 38.0 mm
Thickness: 3.1 mm
Edge: Reeded
Die Axis: ↑↑
Finish: Proof
Case: Maroon clam style case, black flocked insert, encapsulated coin, COA

DATE	DESCRIPTION	QUANTITY SOLD	ISSUE PRICE	FINISH	PR-67	PR-68
2013	Maple Leaf Impression	9,176	114.95	Proof	115.	125.

TWENTY DOLLARS, CANADIAN CONTEMPORARY ART, 2013.

Designers and Engravers:
Obv.: Susanna Blunt, Susan Taylor
Rev.: Claudio D'Angelo, RCM Staff
Composition: 99.99% Ag
Silver content: 31.39 g, 1.01 tr oz
Weight: 31.39 g
Diameter: 38.0 mm
Thickness: 3.1 mm
Edge: Reeded
Die Axis: ↑↑
Finish: Proof
Case: Maroon clam style case, black flocked insert, encapsulated coin, COA

DATE	DESCRIPTION	QUANTITY SOLD	ISSUE PRICE	FINISH	PR-67	PR-68
2013	Canadian Contemporary Art	3,814	89.95	Proof	95.	100.

TWENTY DOLLARS, AUTUMN BLISS, 2013.

Designers and Engravers:
Obv.: Susanna Blunt, Susan Taylor
Rev.: Carlito Dalceggio, Tony Bianco
Composition: 99.99% Ag, Coloured
Silver content: 31.39 g, 1.01 tr oz
Weight: 31.39 g
Diameter: 38.0 mm
Thickness: 3.1 mm
Edge: Reeded
Die Axis: ↑↑
Finish: Proof
Case: Maroon clam style case, black flocked insert, encapsulated coin, COA, custom beauty box

DATE	DESCRIPTION	QUANTITY SOLD	ISSUE PRICE	FINISH	PR-67	PR-68
2013	Autumn Bliss	7,460	99.95	Proof	135.	145.

TWENTY DOLLARS, BIRTH OF THE ROYAL INFANT, 2013.

This three-coin set commemorates the birth of Prince George of Cambridge on July 22nd, 2013.

Common Obverse

Designers and Engravers:
    Obv.: Susanna Blunt, Susan Taylor
    Rev.: Laurie McGaw, RCM Staff
Composition: 99.99% Ag
Silver content: 31.1 g, 1.0 tr oz
Weight: 31.1 to 31.3 g
Diameter: 38.0 mm
Thickness: 3.2 mm
Edge: Reeded
Die Axis: ↑↑
Finish: Proof
Case: Maroon clam style case, 3-hole black flocked insert, encapsulated coin, COA, custom beauty box

Baby Bears

Baby Crib

Hands

DATE	DESCRIPTION	QUANTITY SOLD	ISSUE PRICE	FINISH	PR-67	PR-68
2013	Baby Bears	—	N.I.I.	Proof	85.	90.
2013	Baby Crib	—	N.I.I.	Proof	85.	90.
2013	Hands	—	N.I.I.	Proof	85.	90.
—	Set of 3 coins	5,306	249.95	Proof	250.	—

TWENTY DOLLARS, HOLIDAY WREATH, 2013.

Designers and Engravers:
    Obv.: Susanna Blunt, Susan Taylor
    Rev.: Maurice Gervais, RCM Staff
Composition: 99.99% Ag, Swarovski elements
Silver content: 31.2 g, 1.0 tr oz
Weight: 31.2 g
Diameter: 37.9 mm
Thickness: 3.0 mm
Edge: Reeded
Die Axis: ↑↑
Finish: Proof
Case: Maroon clam style case, black flocked insert, encapsulated coin, COA

DATE	DESCRIPTION	QUANTITY SOLD	ISSUE PRICE	FINISH	PR-67	PR-68
2013	Holiday Wreath	4,534	114.95	Proof	120.	130.

TWENTY DOLLARS, 75TH ANNIVERSARY OF SUPERMAN™, 2013.

Common Obverse

Designers and Engravers:
    Obv.: Susanna Blunt, Susan Taylor
    Rev.: DC Comics/Warner Brothers, RCM Staff
Composition: 99.99% Ag
Silver content: 31.0 g, 1.0 tr oz
Weight: 31.0 to 31.2 g
Diameter: 38.0 mm
Thickness: 3.1 mm
Edge: Reeded
Die Axis: ↑↑
Finish: Proof
Case: Clear plastic cover, black plastic coin display, encapsulated coin, COA, custom beauty box

Man of Steel

Metropolis

The Shield

DATE	DESCRIPTION	QUANTITY SOLD	ISSUE PRICE	FINISH	PR-67	PR-68
2013	Man of Steel™, Painted	9,909	109.75	Proof	175.	185.
2013	Metropolis, Achromatic Hologram	9,932	129.75	Proof	185.	200.
2013	The Shield, Dual Enamel	9,802	119.75	Proof	185.	200.

TWENTY DOLLARS, CANDY CANE, 2013.

Designers and Engravers:
    Obv.: Susanna Blunt, Susan Taylor
    Rev.: Maurice Gervais, RCM Staff
Composition: 99.99% Ag, Coloured Murano glass
Silver content: 31.2 g, 1.0 tr oz
Weight: 31.2 g
Diameter: 37.9 mm
Thickness: 3.0 mm
Edge: Reeded
Die Axis: ↑↑
Finish: Proof
Case: Maroon clam style case, black flocked insert, encapsulated coin, COA

DATE	DESCRIPTION	QUANTITY SOLD	ISSUE PRICE	FINISH	PR-67	PR-68
2013	Candy Cane	9,834	149.95	Proof	155.	165.

TWENTY DOLLARS, POND HOCKEY, 2014.

Designers and Engravers:
  Obv.: Susanna Blunt, Susan Taylor
  Rev.: Richard DeWolfe, RCM Staff
Composition: 99.99% Ag, Coloured
Silver content: 31.2 g, 1.0 tr oz
Weight: 31.2 g
Diameter: 37.9 mm
Thickness: 3.1 mm
Edge: Reeded
Die Axis: ↑↑
Finish: Proof
Case: Maroon clam style case, black flocked insert, encapsulated coin, COA

DATE	DESCRIPTION	QUANTITY SOLD	ISSUE PRICE	FINISH	PR-67	PR-68
2014	Pond Hockey	7,362	99.95	Proof	105.	115.

TWENTY DOLLARS, THE CARIBOU, 2014.

Designers and Engravers:
  Obv.: Susanna Blunt, Susan Taylor
  Rev.: Trevor Tennant, RCM Staff
Composition: 99.99% Ag, Coloured
Silver content: 31.2 g, 1.0 tr oz
Weight: 31.2 g
Diameter: 38.0 mm
Thickness: 3.1 mm
Edge: Reeded
Die Axis: ↑↑
Finish: Proof
Case: Maroon clam style case, black flocked insert, encapsulated coin, COA

DATE	DESCRIPTION	QUANTITY SOLD	ISSUE PRICE	FINISH	PR-67	PR-68
2014	The Caribou	7,641	99.95	Proof	105.	115.

TWENTY DOLLARS, ICONIC POLAR BEAR, 2014.

Designers and Engravers:
  Obv.: Susanna Blunt, Susan Taylor
  Rev.: Glen Loates, RCM Staff
Composition: 99.99% Ag, Coloured
Silver content: 31.2 g, 1.0 tr oz
Weight: 31.2 g
Diameter: 38.0 mm
Thickness: 3.1 mm
Edge: Reeded
Die Axis: ↑↑
Finish: Proof
Case: Maroon clam style case, black flocked insert, encapsulated coin, COA

DATE	DESCRIPTION	QUANTITY SOLD	ISSUE PRICE	FINISH	PR-67	PR-68
2014	Iconic Polar Bear	8,443	99.95	Proof	105.	115.

THE GREAT LAKES SERIES

TWENTY DOLLARS, THE GREAT LAKES, 2014.

Bathymetric maps of the five Great Lakes are detailed by a raised image on these twenty dollar fine silver coins.

Common Obverse

Designers and Engravers:
　　Obv.: Susanna Blunt, Susan Taylor
　　Rev.: RCM Staff
Composition: 99.99% Ag, Enamelled
Silver content: 31.1 g, 1.0 tr oz
Weight: 31.1 g　　　　**Edge:** Reeded
Diameter: 37.9 mm　　**Die Axis:** ↑↑
Thickness: 3.1 mm　**Finish:** Proof
Case:　Single: Maroon clam style case, black
　　　　　flocked insert, encapsulated coin, COA
　　　　　Set: Maple wood display case

Lake Superior

Lake Ontario

Lake Erie

DATE	DESCRIPTION	QUANTITY SOLD	ISSUE PRICE	FINISH	PR-67	PR-68
2014	Lake Superior	7,183	114.95	Proof	115.	125.
2014	Lake Ontario	10,000	114.95	Proof	115.	125.
2014	Lake Erie	10,000	114.95	Proof	115.	125.

TWENTY DOLLARS, 50TH ANNIVERSARY OF CANADIAN PEACEKEEPING IN CYPRUS, 2014.

Designers and Engravers:
　　Obv.: Susanna Blunt, Susan Taylor
　　Rev.: Sylvia Pecota, RCM Staff
Composition: 99.99% Ag, Blue enamel
Silver content: 31.39 g, 1.01 tr oz
Weight: 31.39 g
Diameter: 37.9 mm
Thickness: 3.0 mm
Edge: Reeded
Die Axis: ↑↑
Finish: Proof
Case:　Maroon clam style case, black flocked
　　　　　insert, encapsulated coin, COA

DATE	DESCRIPTION	QUANTITY SOLD	ISSUE PRICE	FINISH	PR-67	PR-68
2014	50th Anniv. of Canadian Peacekeeping in Cyprus	3,507	114.95	Proof	115.	125.

THE WOOD BISON SERIES

TWENTY DOLLARS, THE WOOD BISON, 2014.

Common Obverse

A Portrait
Designer: Doug Comeau

Designers and Engravers:
Obv.: Susanna Blunt, Susan Taylor
Rev.: See reverse illustrations, RCM Staff
Composition: 99.99% Ag
Silver content: 31.39 g, 1.01 tr oz
Weight: 31.39 g
Diameter: 38.0 mm
Thickness: 3.1 mm
Edge: Plain, Edge lettering "1 OZ FINE SILVER 1 OZ ARGENT PUR"
Die Axis: ↑↑
Finish: Proof
Case: Maroon clam style case, black flocked insert, encapsulated coin, COA

The Bull and his Mate
Designer: Doug Comeau

The Fight
Designer: Claudio D'Angelo

A Family at Rest
Designer: Claudio D'Angelo

DATE	DESCRIPTION	QUANTITY SOLD	ISSUE PRICE	FINISH	PR-67	PR-68
2014	A Portrait	7,500	99.95	Proof	100.	110.
2014	The Bull and his Mate	7,500	99.95	Proof	100.	110.
2014	The Fight	7,500	99.95	Proof	100.	110.
2014	A Family at Rest	7,500	99.95	Proof	100.	110.

TWENTY DOLLARS, 100TH ANNIVERSARY OF THE ROYAL ONTARIO MUSEUM, 2014.

Designers and Engravers:
Obv.: Susanna Blunt, Susan Taylor
Rev.: RCM Staff
Composition: 99.99% Ag, Selectively gold plated
Silver content: 31.39 g, 1.01 tr oz
Weight: 31.39 g
Diameter: 38.0 mm
Thickness: 3.0 mm
Edge: Reeded
Die Axis: ↑↑
Finish: Proof
Case: Maroon clam style case, black flocked insert, encapsulated coin, COA

DATE	DESCRIPTION	QUANTITY SOLD	ISSUE PRICE	FINISH	PR-67	PR-68
2014	100th Anniv. of the Royal Ontario Museum	8,500	114.95	Proof	115.	125.

THE LEGEND OF NANABOOZHOO SERIES

TWENTY DOLLARS, THE LEGEND OF NANABOOZHOO, 2014.

Nanaboozhoo is an important cultural character of the Anishinaase. He is a shape-shifting spirit that teaches right from wrong through his adventures.

Common Obverse

Designers and Engravers:
　Obv.: Susanna Blunt, Susan Taylor
　Rev.: Cyril Assiniboine, RCM Staff
Composition: 99.99% Ag
Silver content: 31.39 g, 1.01 tr oz
Weight: 31.39 g
Diameter: 38.0 mm
Thickness: 3.1 mm
Edge: Reeded
Die Axis: ↑↑
Finish: Proof
Case: Maroon clam style case, black flocked insert, encapsulated coin, COA

Nanaboozhoo and the Thunderbird's Nest

Nanaboozhoo and the Thunderbird Selectively gold plated

Legend of Nanaboozhoo Coloured

DATE	DESCRIPTION	QUANTITY SOLD	ISSUE PRICE	FINISH	PR-67	PR-68
2014	Nanaboozhoo and the Thunderbird's Nest	8,500	89.95	Proof	90.	95.
2014	Nanaboozhoo and the Thunderbird, Selectively gold plated	8,500	114.95	Proof	115.	125.
2014	Legend of Nanaboozhoo, Coloured	8,500	99.95	Proof	100.	110.

TWENTY DOLLARS, RIVER RAPIDS, 2014.

The Great Lake, St. Lawrence and Boreal Forest regions meet in central Ontario, creating a special mix if northern and southern ecosystems, the essence of which is captured by Algonquin Provincial Park.

Designers and Engravers:
　Obv.: Susanna Blunt, Susan Taylor
　Rev.: E. Robert Ross, RCM Staff
Composition: 99.99% Ag, Painted, Engraved
Silver content: 31.39 g, 1.0 tr oz
Weight: 31.39 g
Diameter: 38.0 mm
Thickness: 3.1 mm
Edge: Reeded
Die Axis: ↑↑
Finish: Proof
Case: Maroon clam style case, black flocked insert, encapsulated coin, COA

DATE	DESCRIPTION	QUANTITY SOLD	ISSUE PRICE	FINISH	PR-67	PR-68
2014	River Rapids	7,500	99.95	Proof	100.	110.

THE BALD EAGLE SERIES

TWENTY DOLLARS, THE BALD EAGLE, 2014.

Common Obverse

Designers and Engravers:
Obv.: Susanna Blunt, Susan Taylor
Rev.: Claudio D'Angelo, RCM Staff
Composition: 99.99% Ag
Silver content: 31.83 g, 1.0 tr oz
Weight: 31.83 g
Diameter: 38.0 mm
Thickness: 3.1 mm
Edge: Reeded
Die Axis: ↑↑
Finish: Proof
Case: Maroon clam style case, black flocked insert, encapsulated coin, COA

Bald Eagle with Fish

Perched Bald Eagle
Selectively gold plated

Soaring Bald Eagle
Coloured

DATE	DESCRIPTION	QUANTITY SOLD	ISSUE PRICE	FINISH	PR-67	PR-68
2014	Bald Eagle with Fish, Proof	8,500	89.95	Proof	90.	100.
2014	Perched Bald Eagle, Proof, Selectively gold plated	8,500	114.95	Proof	115.	125.
2014	Soaring Bald Eagle, Proof with colour	8,500	99.95	Proof	100.	110.

TWENTY DOLLAR DERIVATIVES

DATE	DESCRIPTION	QUANTITY SOLD	ISSUE PRICE	ISSUER	FINISH	MARKET VALUE
1998	**Twenty Dollars** Argus and Waterbomber boxed with cardboard model	N/A	N/A	RCM	PR-67	275.
2004	**Twenty Dollars** Northern Lights twenty dollar coin mounted in a frame with a large image of the Northern Lights	N/A	399.00	RCM	PR-67	200.
2012	**Twenty Dollars,** The Queen's Diamond Jubilee, The Royal Cypher, Queen Elizabeth II and Prince Philip; 3-coin wooden collector box, within a beauty box with Diamond Jubilee Cypher	1,809	274.95	RCM	PR-67	275.
2012	**Twenty Dollars** Queen Elizabeth II and Prince Philip, Three-coin case holding UK £5, Australian 50¢, Canadian $20,	4,000	399.95	RCM	PR-67	400.

NOTE FOR COLLECTORS

The Bullion Department of the Royal Canadian Mint issued twenty dollar bullion coins in 2004, 2005, 2011- 2014, see pages 432-435.

TWENTY-FIVE DOLLARS

TWENTY FIVE DOLLARS, VANCOUVER 2010 OLYMPIC WINTER GAMES, 2007-2009.

ISSUES OF 2007.

2007 Obverse

Curling
Designer: Steve Hepburn
Engraver: Stan Witten

Ice Hockey
Designer: Steve Hepburn
Engraver: William Woodruff

Athletes' Pride
Designer: Shelagh Armstrong
Engraver: Christie Paquet

Biathlon
Designer: Bonnie Ross
Engraver: Stan Witten

Alpine Skiing
Designer: Brian Hughes
Engraver: Stan Witten

Designers:
Obv.: Susanna Blunt
Rev.: See reverse illustrations
Composition: 92.5% Ag, 7.5% Cu, Selective hologram
Silver content: 25.7 g, 0.826 tr oz
Weight: 27.78 g
Diameter: 40.0 mm
Die Axis: ↑↑

Engravers:
Obv.: Susan Taylor
Rev.: See reverse illustrations

Thickness: 2.5 mm
Edge: Reeded
Finish: Proof

Case of Issue: Singly: Black leatherette clam case; black flocked insert, encapsulated coin, COA, Olympic theme sleeve
                 Set: Black leatherette, 15-hole, square clam style case; two black flocked inserts (one with seven
                     indentations, the other with eight; encapsulated coins; COA for each coin; Olympic theme sleeve

DATE	DESCRIPTION	DATE OF ISSUE	QUANTITY SOLD	ISSUE PRICE	FINISH	PR-67	PR-68
2007	Curling	Feb. 23, 2007	19,531	69.95	Proof	60.	65.
2007	Ice Hockey	April 14, 2007	22,512	69.95	Proof	60.	65.
2007	Athletes' Pride	July 11, 2007	21,886	69.95	Proof	60.	65.
2007	Biathlon	Sept. 12, 2007	16,003	69.95	Proof	60.	65.
2007	Alpine Skiing	Oct. 24, 2007	13,500	69.95	Proof	60.	65.

TWENTY FIVE DOLLARS, VANCOUVER 2010 OLYMPIC WINTER GAMES, 2007-2009 (cont.)

ISSUES OF 2008.

2008 Obverse

Snowboarding
Designer: Steve Hepburn
Engraver: Konrad Wachelko

Freestyle Skiing
Designer: John Mardon
Engraver: Christie Paquet

**Home of the
2010 Olympic Winter Games**
Designer: Shelagh Armstrong
Engraver: Marcos Hallam

Figure Skating
Designer: Steve Hepburn
Engraver: José Osio

Bobsleigh
Designer: Bonnie Ross
Engraver: Stan Witten

Designers:
  Obv.: Susanna Blunt
  Rev.: See reverse illustrations
Composition: 92.5% Ag, 7.5% Cu, Selective hologram
Silver content: 25.7 g, 0.826 tr oz
Weight: 27.78 g
Diameter: 40.0 mm
Die Axis: ↑↑

Engravers:
  Obv.: Susan Taylor
  Rev.: See reverse illustrations

Thickness: 2.5 mm
Edge: Reeded
Finish: Proof

Case of Issue: Singly: Black leatherette clam case; black flocked insert, encapsulated coin, COA, Olympic theme sleeve
  Set: Black leatherette, 15-hole, square clam style case; two black flocked inserts (one with seven
    indentations, the other with eight; encapsulated coins; COA for each coin; Olympic theme sleeve

DATE	DESCRIPTION	DATE OF ISSUE	QUANTITY SOLD	ISSUE PRICE	FINISH	PR-67	PR-68
2008	Snowboarding	Feb. 20, 2008	6,377	71.95	Proof	60.	65.
2008	Freestyle Skiing	April 16, 2008	12,428	71.95	Proof	60.	65.
2008	Home of the 2010 Olympic Winter Games	July 23, 2008	12,606	71.95	Proof	60.	65.
2008	Figure Skating	Sept. 10, 2008	18,930	71.95	Proof	60.	65.
2008	Bobsleigh	Oct. 29, 2008	8,800	71.95	Proof	60.	65.

TWENTY FIVE DOLLARS, VANCOUVER 2010 OLYMPIC WINTER GAMES, 2007-2009 (cont.).

ISSUES OF 2009.

2009 Obverse

Speed Skating
Designer: Tony Bianco
Engraver: William Woodruff

Cross Country Skiing
Designer: Brian Hughes
Engraver: William Woodruff

Olympic Spirit
Designer: Shelagh Armstrong
Engraver: Stan Witten

Skeleton
Designer: Tony Bianco
Engraver: Stan Witten

Ski Jumping
Designer: John Mardon
Engraver: Konrad Wachelko

Designers:
　Obv.: Susanna Blunt
　Rev.: See reverse illustrations
Composition: 92.5% Ag, 7.5% Cu, Selective hologram
Silver content: 25.7 g, 0.826 tr oz
Weight: 27.78 g
Diameter: 40.0 mm
Die Axis: ↑↑

Engravers:
　Obv.: Susan Taylor
　Rev.: See reverse illustrations

Thickness: 2.5 mm
Edge: Reeded
Finish: Proof

Case of Issue:　Singly: Black leatherette clam case; black flocked insert, encapsulated coin, COA, Olympic theme sleeve
　　　　　　Set: Black leatherette, 15-hole, square clam style case; two black flocked inserts (one with seven
　　　　　　indentations, the other with eight; encapsulated coins; COA for each coin; Olympic theme sleeve

DATE	DESCRIPTION	DATE OF ISSUE	QUANTITY SOLD	ISSUE PRICE	FINISH	PR-67	PR-68
2009	Speed Skating	Feb. 18, 2009	27,827	71.95	Proof	60.	65.
2009	Cross Country Skiing	April 15, 2009	14,292	71.95	Proof	60.	65.
2009	Olympic Spirit	June 17, 2009	10,224	71.95	Proof	60.	65.
2009	Skeleton	Aug.. 5, 2009	10,582	71.95	Proof	60.	65.
2009	Ski Jumping	Oct. 7, 2009	11,365	71.95	Proof	60.	65.
2007-2010	Set of 15 coins	—	4,764	—	Proof	800.	—

TWENTY-FIVE DOLLARS, TORONTO CITY MAP, 2011.

The reverse design of this coin depicts the City of Toronto as seen through the visor of an astronaut. These coins were struck in Switzerland.

Designers:
Obv.: Susanna Blunt
Rev.: Google Earth
Composition: 99.99% Ag, Selectively gold plated
Silver content: 62.41 g, 2.01 tr oz
Weight: 62.41 g
Diameter: 60.0 mm
Thickness: 2.5 mm
Case of Issue: Maroon leatherette clam style case, black flocked insert, encapsulated coin, COA

Engravers:
Obv.: Susan Taylor
Rev.: RCM Staff

Edge: Reeded
Die Axis: ↑↑
Finish: Proof

DATE	DESCRIPTION	QUANTITY SOLD	ISSUE PRICE	FINISH	PR-67	PR-68
2011	Toronto City Map	3,948	179.95	Proof	250.	275.

TWENTY-FIVE DOLLARS, WAYNE AND WALTER GRETZKY, 2011.

The reverse design on this coin features Wayne Gretzky (the Great One) in action, with a cameo of his father Walter.

Designers and Engravers:
Obv.: Susanna Blunt, Susan Taylor
Rev.: Glen Green, Konrad Wachelko, José Osio
Composition: 99.99% Ag, (Hologram of jersey number 99)
Silver content: 31.39 g, 1.01 tr oz
Weight: 31.39 g
Diameter: 38.0 mm   **Edge:** Reeded
Thickness: 3.2 mm   **Die Axis:** ↑↑
Finish: Proof
Case: Maroon leatherette clam style case, black flocked insert, encapsulated coin, COA

DATE	DESCRIPTION	QUANTITY SOLD	ISSUE PRICE	FINISH	PR-67	PR-68
2011	Wayne and Walter Gretzky	6,715	99.99	Proof	100.	110.

O CANADA SERIES ONE

TWENTY-FIVE DOLLARS, O CANADA SERIES, 2013.

These coins from the O Canada Series focus on iconic Canadian images as seen through our rich animal history. For other coins in the O Canada Series see pages 180 and 269.

Common Obverse   The Beaver   The Polar Bear

The Wolf   The Caribou   The Orca

Designers:
  Obv.: Susanna Blunt
  Rev.: Pierre Leduc
Composition: 99.99% Ag
Silver content: 31.1 g, 1.00 tr oz
Weight: 31.1 g
Diameter: 38.0 mm
Thickness: 3.0 mm
Case of Issue:

Engravers:
  Obv.: Susan Taylor
  Rev.: RCM Staff

Edge: Reeded
Die Axis: ↑↑
Finish: Proof

Single: Maroon clam style case, black flocked insert, encapsulated coin, COA, custom coloured box
Set: Brown wooden case, 5-hole black flocked insert, encapsulated coin, COA

DATE	DESCRIPTION	QUANTITY SOLD	ISSUE PRICE	FINISH	PR-67	PR-68
2013	The Beaver	8,354	89.95	Proof	90.	95.
2013	The Polar Bear	8,299	89.95	Proof	90.	95.
2013	The Wolf	8,030	89.95	Proof	90.	95.
2013	The Caribou	7,567	89.95	Proof	90.	95.
2013	The Orca	6,019	89.95	Proof	90.	95.

TWENTY-FIVE DOLLARS, GRANDMOTHER MOON MASK, 2013.

The moon is a sacred symbol that appears in countless First Nations traditions.

Designers and Engravers:
Obv.:   Susanna Blunt, Susan Taylor
Rev.:   Richard Cochrane, RCM Staff
Composition: 99.99% Ag
Silver content: 30.5 g, 0.98 tr oz
Weight: 30.5 g   **Edge:** Plain
Diameter: 36.2 mm   **Die Axis:** ↑↑
Thickness: 3.0 mm   **Finish:** Proof
Case: Maroon leatherette clam style case,
black flocked insert, encapsulated coin,
COA

DATE	DESCRIPTION	QUANTITY SOLD	ISSUE PRICE	FINISH	PR-67	PR-68
2013	Grandmother Moon Mask	5,987	149.95	Proof	150.	160.

TWENTY-FIVE DOLLARS, MISS CANADA: AN ALLEGORY, 2013.

"Miss Canada" was first introduced in 1867.

Designers and Engravers:
Obv.:   Susanna Blunt, Susan Taylor
Rev.:   Laurie McGaw, RCM Staff
Composition: 99.99% Ag
Silver content: 31.39 g, 1.01 tr oz
Weight: 31.39 g
Diameter: 38.0 mm   **Edge:** Reeded
Thickness: 3.2 mm   **Die Axis:** ↑↑
Finish: Proof
Case: Maroon leatherette clam style case,
black flocked insert, encapsulated coin,
COA

DATE	DESCRIPTION	QUANTITY SOLD	ISSUE PRICE	FINISH	PR-67	PR-68
2013	Miss Canada: An Allegory	5,503	89.95	Proof	95.	100.

TWENTY-FIVE DOLLARS, MATRIARCH MOON MASK, 2014.

First Nations culture is rich with profound wisdom that eloquently expresses the interconnectedness between humanity and nature.

Designers and Engravers:
Obv.:   Susanna Blunt, Susan Taylor
Rev.:   Carol Young, RCM Staff
Composition: 99.99% Ag
Silver content: 30.76 g, 0.988 tr oz
Weight: 30.76 g
Diameter: 36.15 mm   **Edge:** Reeded
Thickness: 3.2 mm   **Die Axis:** ↑↑
Finish: Proof
Case: Maroon leatherette clam style case,
black flocked insert, encapsulated coin,
COA

DATE	DESCRIPTION	QUANTITY SOLD	ISSUE PRICE	FINISH	PR-67	PR-68
2014	Matriarch Moon Mask	6,000	149.95	Proof	150.	160.

O CANADA SERIES TWO

TWENTY-FIVE DOLLARS, O CANADA SERIES, 2014.

Common Obverse

The Igloo
Designer: Yves Bérube
Engraver: RCM Staff

Scenic Skiing in Canada
Designer: RCM Staff
Engraver: RCM Staff

Under the Maple Tree
Designer: Claudio D'Angelo
Engraver: RCM Staff

Cowboy in the Canadian Rockie
Designer: RCM Staff
Engraver: RCM Staff

**The Arctic Fox and the
Northern Lights**
Designer: RCM Staff
Engraver: RCM Staff

Designers:
  Obv.: Susanna Blunt
  Rev.: Yves Berube
Composition: 99.99% Ag
Silver content: 31.0 g, 1.0 tr oz
Weight: 31.0 g
Diameter: 38.0 mm
Thickness: 3.2 mm
Case of Issue:

Engravers:
  Obv.: Susan Taylor
  Rev.: RCM Staff

Edge: Reeded
Die Axis: ↑↑
Finish: Proof

  Single: Maroon clam style case, black flocked insert, encapsulated coin, COA, custom coloured box
  Set: Walnut display case, 5-hole black flocked insert, encapsulated coins, COA

DATE	DESCRIPTION	QUANTITY SOLD	ISSUE PRICE	FINISH	PR-67	PR-68
2014	The Igloo	8,500	89.95	Proof	90.	95.
2014	Scenic Skiing in Canada	8,500	89.95	Proof	90.	95.
2014	Under the Maple Tree	8,500	89.95	Proof	90.	95.
2014	Cowboy in the Canadian Rockies	8,500	89.95	Proof	90.	95.
2014	The Arctic Fox and the Northern Lights	8,500	89.95	Proof	90.	95.

THIRTY DOLLARS

THIRTY DOLLARS, WELCOME FIGURE (DZUNUK'WA) TOTEM POLE, 2005.

Dzunuk'wa is a giant, hairy, black-bodied, big-breasted, wide-eyed female monster. She is physically strong enough to tear down large trees, spiritually powerful enough to resurrect the dead and possesses magical treasures and great wealth.

Designers and Engravers:
Obv.: Susanna Blunt, Susan Taylor
Rev.: Richard Hunt, Susan Taylor
Composition: 92.5% Ag, 7.5% Cu
Silver content: 29.137 g, 0.937 tr oz
Weight: 31.50 g
Diameter: 40.0 mm
Thickness: 3.0 mm
Edge: Reeded
Die Axis: ↑↑
Finish: Proof
Case of Issue: Maroon plastic slide case, black plastic insert, encapsulated coin, COA

DATE	DESCRIPTION	QUANTITY SOLD	ISSUE PRICE	FINISH	PR-67	PR-68
2005	Welcome Figure Totem Pole	9,904	79.95	Proof	80.	85.

Note: An identical design is utilized on the $300 gold coin for 2005, see page 319.

THIRTY DOLLARS, DOG SLED TEAM, 2006.

Designers and Engravers:
Obv.: Susanna Blunt, Susan Taylor
Rev.: Arnold Nogy, José Osio
Composition: 92.5% Ag, 7.5% Cu, Painted
Silver content: 29.137 g, 0.937 tr oz
Weight: 31.50 g
Diameter: 40.0 mm
Thickness: 3.0 mm
Edge: Reeded
Die Axis: ↑↑
Finish: Proof
Case of Issue: Maroon plastic slide case, black plastic insert, encapsulated coin, COA

DATE	DESCRIPTION	QUANTITY SOLD	ISSUE PRICE	FINISH	PR-67	PR-68
2006	Dog Sled Team	7,384	89.95	Proof	185.	200.

Note: An identical design is utilized on the $250 gold coin for 2006, see page 308.

NATIONAL WAR MEMORIALS SERIES

THIRTY DOLLARS, NATIONAL WAR MEMORIALS SERIES, 2006-2007.

2006 Obverse	2006 National War Memorial	2006 Beaumont-Hamel
Date on Obverse	Designer: Vernon March	Newfoundland Memorial
	Engraver: José Osio	Designer: RCM Staff
		Engraver: Susan Taylor

2007 Obverse
Date on Reverse

2007
Canadian National Vimy Memorial
Designer: RCM Staff
Engraver: José Osio

Designers:
　Obv.: Susanna Blunt
　Rev.: See reverse illustration
Composition: 92.5% Ag, 7.5% Cu
Silver content: 29.137 g, 0.937 tr oz
Weight: 31.50 g
Diameter: 40.0 mm
Thickness: 3.0 mm
Case of Issue: Maroon plastic slide case, black plastic insert, encapsulated coin, COA

Engravers:
　Obv.: Susan Taylor
　Rev.: See reverse illustration

Edge: Reeded
Die Axis: ↑↑
Finish: Proof

DATE	DESCRIPTION	QUANTITY SOLD	ISSUE PRICE	FINISH	PR-67	PR-68
2006	National War Memorial	8,876	79.95	Proof	110.	115.
2006	Beaumont-Hamel Newfoundland Memorial	15,325	79.95	Proof	110.	115.
2007	Canadian National Vimy Memorial	5,335	79.95	Proof	85.	90.

CANADIAN ACHIEVEMENT SERIES

THIRTY DOLLARS, 5TH ANNIVERSARY OF CANADARM, 2006.

Designers and Engravers:
Obv.: Susanna Blunt, Susan Taylor
Rev.: Cecily Mok, Cecily Mok
Composition: 92.5% Ag, 7.5% Cu, Decal
Silver content: 29.137 g, 0.937 tr oz
Weight: 31.50 g
Diameter: 40.0 mm
Thickness: 3.0 mm
Edge: Reeded
Die Axis: ↑↑
Finish: Proof
Case: Maroon plastic slide case, black plastic insert, encapsulated coin, COA

THIRTY DOLLARS, PANORAMIC PHOTOGRAPHY IN CANADA, NIAGARA FALLS, 2007.

Designers and Engravers:
Obv.: Susanna Blunt, Susan Taylor
Rev.: Chris Jordison, RCM Staff
Composition: 92.5% Ag, 7.5% Cu, Hologram
Silver content: 29.137 g, 0.937 tr oz
Weight: 31.50 g
Diameter: 40.0 mm
Thickness: 2.8 mm
Edge: Reeded
Die Axis: ↑↑
Finish: Proof
Case: Maroon leatherette clam style case, black flocked insert, encapsulated coin, COA

THIRTY DOLLARS, IMAX©, 2008.

Designers and Engravers:
Obv.: Susanna Blunt, Susan Taylor
Rev.: IMAX©, RCM Staff
Composition: 92.5% Ag, 7.5% Cu, Hologram
Silver content: 29.137 g, 0.937 tr oz
Weight: 31.50 g
Diameter: 40.0 mm
Thickness: 2.8 mm
Edge: Reeded
Die Axis: ↑↑
Finish: Proof
Case: Maroon leatherette clam style case, black flocked insert, encapsulated coin, COA

DATE	DESCRIPTION	QUANTITY SOLD	ISSUE PRICE	FINISH	PR-67	PR-68
2006	5th Anniversary of Canadarm	9,357	79.95	Proof	90.	95.
2007	Panoramic Photography in Canada, Niagara Falls	5,702	84.95	Proof	95.	100.
2008	IMAX®	3,861	84.95	Proof	90.	95.

Note: For the gold coins in this series see page 321.

THIRTY DOLLARS, INTERNATIONAL YEAR OF ASTRONOMY, 2009.

Designers and Engravers:
    Obv.: Susanna Blunt, Susan Taylor
    Rev.: Colin Mayne, Stan Witten
Composition: 92.5% Ag, 7.5% Cu, Painted
Silver content: 31.22 g, 1.00 tr oz
Weight: 33.75 g
Diameter: 40.0 mm
Thickness: 2.9 mm
Edge: Reeded
Die Axis: ↑↑
Finish: Proof
Case: Maroon leatherette clam style case, black flocked insert, encapsulated coin, COA

DATE	DESCRIPTION	QUANTITY SOLD	ISSUE PRICE	FINISH	PR-67	PR-68
2009	International Year of Astronomy	7,174	89.95	Proof	115.	120.

THIRTY DOLLARS, CANADA THROUGH THE EYES OF TIM BARNARD, 2014.

More than fifty images are found in the reverse design of this coin, all Canadian icons.

Designers:
    Obv.: Susanna Blunt
    Rev.: Tim Barnard
Composition: 99.99% Ag
Silver content: 62.7 g, 2.00 tr oz
Weight: 62.7 g
Diameter: 54.0 mm
Thickness: 3.0 mm

Engravers:
    Obv.: Susan Taylor
    Rev.: RCM Staff

Edge: Reeded
Die Axis: ↑↑
Finish: Proof

Case of Issues: Maroon leatherette clam style case, black flocked insert, encapsulated coin, COA, Custom coloured box

DATE	DESCRIPTION	QUANTITY SOLD	ISSUE PRICE	FINISH	PR-67	PR-68
2014	Canada Through the Eyes of Tim Barnard	5,000	169.95	Proof	175.	185.

FIFTY DOLLARS

FIFTY DOLLARS, THE FOUR SEASONS, 2006.

Designers and Engravers:
Obv.: S. Blunt, S. Taylor
Rev..: T. Bianco, J. Osio
Composition: 99.99% Ag
Silver content:
156.34 g, 5.026 tr oz
Weight: 156.36 g
Diameter: 64.8 mm
Thickness: 5.0
Edge: Reeded
Die Axis: ↑↑
Finish: Proof
Case: Black case, black flocked insert, encapsulated coin, COA

FIFTY DOLLARS, 60TH WEDDING ANNIVERSARY OF QUEEN ELIZABETH AND PRINCE PHILIP, 2007.

Designers and Engravers:
Obv.: S. Blunt, S. Taylor
Rev.: S. Hepburn, S. Taylor
Composition: 99.99% Ag
Silver content:
156.34 g, 5.026 tr oz
Weight: 156.36 g
Diameter: 65.0 mm
Thickness: 5.0
Edge: Reeded
Die Axis: ↑↑
Finish: Proof
Case: Maroon leatherette clam style case, black flocked insert; encapsulated coin, COA

FIFTY DOLLARS, 100TH ANNIVERSARY OF THE ROYAL CANADIAN MINT, 1908-2008.

Designers and Engravers:
Obv.: S. Blunt, S. Taylor
Rev.: Konrad Wachelko
Composition: 99.99% Ag
Silver content:
157.65 g, 5.069 tr oz
Weight: 157.67 g
Diameter: 65.0 mm
Thickness: 5.2 mm
Edge: Reeded
Die Axis: ↑↑
Finish: Proof
Case: Maroon leatherette clam style case, black flocked insert, encapsulated coin, COA

DATE	DESCRIPTION	QUANTITY SOLD	ISSUE PRICE	FINISH	PR-67	PR-68
2006	The Four Seasons	1,999	299.95	Proof	450.	475.
2007	60th Wedding Anniv. Queen Elizabeth / Prince Philip	1,957	299.95	Proof	450.	475.
2008 (1908-)	100th Anniversary of the Royal Canadian Mint	2,078	369.95	Proof	375.	400.

Note: Coins on pages 251-254 illustrated smaller than actual size.

FIFTY DOLLARS, 150TH ANNIVERSARY OF THE START OF THE CONSTRUCTION OF THE PARLIAMENT BUILDINGS, 1859-2009.

Designers and Engravers:
Obv.: S. Blunt, S. Taylor
Rev.: Cecily Mok
Composition: 99.99% Ag
Silver content:
157.65 g, 5.069 tr oz
Weight: 157.67 g
Diameter: 65.0 mm
Thickness: 5.0 mm
Edge: Reeded
Die Axis: ↑↑
Finish: Proof
Case: Maroon leatherette clam style case, black flocked insert, encapsulated coin, COA

FIFTY DOLLARS, 75TH ANNIVERSARY OF THE FIRST BANK NOTES ISSUED BY THE BANK OF CANADA, 2010.

The reverse design on this coin is a reproduction of the allegory that appeared on the original 1935 $50 bank note, a seated woman with elements of radio broadcasting to symbolise modern inventions.

Designers and Engravers:
Obv.: S. Blunt, S. Taylor
Rev.: Cecily Mok
Composition: 99.99% Ag
Silver content:
157.65 g, 5.069 tr oz
Weight: 157.67 g
Diameter: 65.3 mm
Thickness: 5.0 mm
Edge: Reeded
Die Axis: ↑↑
Finish: Proof
Case: Maroon leatherette clam style case, black flocked insert, encapsulated coin, COA

FIFTY DOLLARS, 100TH ANNIVERSARY OF THE CALGARY STAMPEDE, 2012.

In 1912, working cowboy and trick roper Guy Weadick, inspired by the travelling wild-west shows in the early 1900s, convinced four local ranchers to help him produce the first *Frontier Days and Cowboy Championship Contest*, later to be called the Calgary Stampede. One hundred years later Calgary, Alberta remains home to "the greatest outdoor show on earth".

Designers and Engravers:
Obv.: S. Blunt, S. Taylor
Rev.: M. Grant, J. Osio
Composition: 99.99% Ag
Silver content:
157.65 g, 5.069 tr oz
Weight: 157.67 g
Diameter: 65.3 mm
Thickness: 5.0 mm
Edge: Reeded
Die Axis: ↑↑
Finish: Proof
Case: Maroon leatherette clam style case, black flocked insert, encapsulated coin, COA

DATE	DESCRIPTION	QUANTITY SOLD	ISSUE PRICE	FINISH	PR-67	PR-68
2009 (1859-)	150th Anniv. Construction Parliament Buildings	910	459.95	Proof	350.	375.
2010 (1935-)	75th Anniv. Bank of Canada Notes	1,991	389.95	Proof	450.	475.
2012	100th Anniv. of the Calgary Stampede	1,500	495.95	Proof	550.	575.

FIFTY DOLLARS, THE BEAVER, 2013.

The importance of the beaver in the development of Canada through the fur trade led to its official designation as the national animal in 1975.

Designers and Engravers:
  Obv.: S. Blunt, S. Taylor
  Rev.: E. Damstra, C. Mok
Composition: 99.99% Ag
Silver content:
  157.65 g, 5.069 tr oz
Weight: 157.67 g
Diameter: 65.3 mm
Thickness: 5.0 mm
Edge: Reeded
Die Axis: ↑↑
Finish: Proof
Case: Maroon leatherette clam style case, black flocked insert, encapsulated coin, COA

FIFTY DOLLARS, QUEEN'S CORONATION, 2013.

This coin was issued to commemorate the 60th Anniversary of her Majesty Queen Elizabeth II's accession. The reverse image used for this coin is the official coronation photograph taken by Cecil Beaton, June 2nd, 1953, licensed by the Victoria & Albert Museum in London, England.

Designers and Engravers:
  Obv.: Mary Gillick,
      Thomas Shingles
  Rev.: See description
Composition: 99.99% Ag
Silver content:
  157.65 g, 5.069 tr oz
Weight: 157.67 g
Diameter: 65.3 mm
Thickness: 5.0 mm
Edge: Reeded
Die Axis: ↑↑
Finish: Proof, Coloured
Case: Maroon leatherette clam style case, black flocked insert, encapsulated coin, COA

FIFTY DOLLARS, HMS SHANNON and USS CHESAPEAKE, 2013.

Designers and Engravers:
  Obv.: S. Blunt, S. Taylor
  Rev.: J. Horton, RCM Staff
Composition: 99.99% Ag
Silver content:
  157.65 g, 5.069 tr oz
Weight: 157.67 g
Diameter: 65.0 mm
Thickness: 5.0 mm
Edge: Reeded
Die Axis: ↑↑
Finish: Proof
Case: Maroon leatherette clam style case, black flocked insert, encapsulated coin, COA

DATE	DESCRIPTION	QUANTITY SOLD	ISSUE PRICE	FINISH	PR-67	PR-68
2013	The Beaver	1,497	519.95	Proof	525.	550.
2013 (1953-)	Queen's Coronation	1,499	524.95	Proof	600.	625.
2013	HMS Shannon and USS Chesapeake	1,487	499.85	Proof	525.	550.

FIFTY DOLLARS, SWIMMING BEAVER, 2014.

Designers and Engravers:
Obv.: S. Blunt, S. Taylor
Rev.: E. Damstra, RCM Staff
Composition: 99.99% Ag
Silver content:
157.65 g, 5.069 tr oz
Weight: 157.67 g
Diameter: 65.3 mm
Thickness: 5.0 mm
Edge: Reeded
Die Axis: ↑↑
Finish: Proof, Coloured
Case: Maroon leatherette
clam style case, black
flocked insert, encapsulated
coin, COA

DATE	DESCRIPTION	QUANTITY SOLD	ISSUE PRICE	FINISH	PR-67	PR-68
2014	Swimming Beaver	1,116	519.95	Proof	525.	550.

Note: Coins on pages 251-254 illustrated smaller than actual size.

FIFTY DOLLARS, ICONIC POLAR BEAR, 2014.
This is the first coin in the $50 for $50 fine silver coin series.

Designers and Engravers:
Obv.: S. Blunt, S. Taylor
Rev.: E. Damstra, RCM Staff
Composition: 99.99% Ag
Silver content: 15.87 g, .5 tr oz
Weight: 15.87 g
Diameter: 34.0 mm
Thickness: 2.2 mm
Edge: Reeded
Die Axis: ↑↑
Finish: Matte Proof
Case: Clear vinyl pouch, coloured folder

DATE	DESCRIPTION	QUANTITY SOLD	ISSUE PRICE	FINISH	PR-67	PR-68
2014	Iconic Polar Bear	100,000	50.00	Matte Proof	50.	60.

ONE HUNDRED DOLLARS

ONE HUNDRED DOLLARS (one ounce), FINE SILVER COMMEMORATIVE COINS, 2013-2014.
These coins are from the $100 for $100 fine silver coin series.

Common Obv.
2013-2014

Bison Stampede
Des.: Cosme Saffioti
Engr.: N/A

The Grizzly
Des.: Claudio D'Angelo
Engr.: N/A

Majestic Bald Eagle
Des.: Claudio D'Angelo
Engr.: N/A

Rocky Mountain Bighorn Sheep
Des.: Claudio D'Angelo
Engr.: RCM Staff

Designers:
  Obv.: Susanna Blunt
  Rev.: See reverse illustrations
Composition: 99.99% Ag
Silver content: 31.6 g, 1.0 oz
Weight: 31.6 g
Diameter: 40.0 mm
Thickness: 3.0 mm
Case of Issue: **2013 Bison:** Maroon leatherette clam style case, black flocked insert, encapsulated coin, COA
                2013-2014: Customized paper case lined with flock

Engravers:
  Obv.:   Susan Taylor
  Rev.:   See reverse illustrations

Edge: Reeded
Die Axis: ↑↑
Finish: Reverse Proof, Matte Proof

DATE	DESCRIPTION	QUANTITY SOLD	ISSUE PRICE	FINISH	PR-67	PR-68
2013	Bison Stampede, Reverse Proof	49,986	100.00	Proof	120.	125.
2013	The Grizzly, Matte Proof	49,092	100.00	Proof	120.	125.
2014	Majestic Bald Eagle, Matte Proof	50,000	100.00	Proof	120.	125.
2014	Rocky Mountain Bighorn Sheep	50,000	100.00	Proof	120.	125.

ONE HUNDRED TWENTY-FIVE DOLLARS

ONE HUNDRED TWENTY-FIVE DOLLARS, HOWLING WOLF, 2014

The eastern timber wolf resides in the southeastern region of the Great Lakes. This is the first half kilo fine silver coin to be released.

Designers and Engravers:
   Obv.: S. Blunt, S. Taylor
   Rev.: Pierre Leduc,
      RCM Staff
Composition: 99.99% Ag
Silver content:
   500.0 g, 16.07 tr oz
Weight: 500.0 g
Diameter: 85.0 mm
Thickness: N/A
Edge: Reeded
Die Axis: ↑↑
Finish: Proof
Case: Wooden box, black flocked insert, encapsulated coin, COA

DATE	DESCRIPTION	QUANTITY SOLD	ISSUE PRICE	FINISH	PR-67	PR-68
2014	Howling Wolf	*1000*	1,099.95	Proof	1,100.	1,150.

Note: Coin illustrated smaller than actual size.

TWO HUNDRED FIFTY DOLLARS

VANCOUVER 2010 OLYMPIC WINTER GAMES, 2007-2010

These are the first coins produced in pure silver by the Royal Canadian Mint with a guaranteed weight of one kilo.

| **Common Obverse** (Except for date) | **Early Canada** Designer: Stan Witten Engraver: Stan Witten | **Towards Confederation** Designer: Susan Taylor Engraver: Susan Taylor |

The Canada of Today
Designer: Design Team of the Vancouver Organising Committee for the 2010 Olympic and Paralympic Winter Games
Engraver: Konrad Wachelko

Surviving the Flood
Designer: Xwa lac tun (Ricky Harry)

Designers:
  Obv.: Susanna Blunt
  Rev.: See reverse illustrations
Composition: 99.99% Ag
Silver content: 1,000.0 g, 32.151 tr oz
Weight: 1,000.0 g (1 kilo)
Diameter: 101.6 mm
Case of Issue: Black display case, black flocked insert, encapsulated coin, COA; Vancouver 2010 Olympic Winter Games theme sleeve

Engravers:
  Obv.: Susan Taylor
  Rev.: See reverse illustrations
Thickness: 12.5 mm
Edge: Plain
Die Axis: ↑↑
Finish: Proof, Ultra high relief

DATE	DESCRIPTION	DATE OF ISSUE	QUANTITY SOLD	ISSUE PRICE	FINISH	PR-67	PR-68
2007	Early Canada	Feb. 23, 2007	2,500	1,299.95	Proof	2,000.	2,100.
2008	Towards Confederation	Feb. 20, 2008	2,500	1,599.95	Proof	1,800.	1,900.
2009	The Canada of Today	April 15, 2009	905	1,599.95	Proof	1,800.	1,900.
2009	Surviving the Flood	Nov. 17, 2009	815	1,599.95	Proof	1,900.	2,000.

VANCOUVER 2010 OLYMPIC WINTER GAMES, 2007-2010 (cont.)

TWO HUNDRED FIFTY DOLLARS, THE EAGLE, 2010.

The eagle, an important First Nations symbol, represents power, peace and prestige. This is the first time a coin is offered in three different finishes.

Obverse

The Eagle, Proof Enamel

Designers:
  Obv.: Susanna Blunt
  Rev.: Xwa lac tun (Ricky Harry)
Composition: 99.99% Ag
Silver content: 1,000.0 g, 32.151 tr oz
Weight: 1,000.0 g (1 kilo)
Die Axis: ↑↑
Case of Issue: Black display case, black flocked insert, encapsulated coin, COA; Vancouver 2010 Olympic Winter Games theme sleeve

Engravers:
  Obv.: Susan Taylor
  Rev.: Stan Witten
Thickness: 12.5 mm
Edge: Plain
Diameter: 101.6 mm
Finish: Proof

DATE	DESCRIPTION	DATE OF ISSUE	QUANTITY SOLD	ISSUE PRICE	FINISH	PR-67	PR-68
2010	The Eagle, Proof	Nov. 19, 2009	349	1,649.95	Proof	1,700.	1,800.
2010	The Eagle, Proof Enamel	Nov. 19, 2009	74	1,649.95	Enamel	1,750.	1,850.
2010	The Eagle, Proof Antique	Nov. 19, 2009	349	1,649.95	Antique	1,700.	1,800.

Note: 1. Identical designs are utilized on the $2,500 gold coins for 2007, 2008, 2009 and 2010, see page 329.
  2. Coins on pages 257-258 are illustrated smaller than actual size.

TWO HUNDRED FIFTY DOLLARS, 125TH ANNIVERSARY OF BANFF NATIONAL PARK, 2010.

Banff National Park was Canada's first national park, and the world's third, spanning 6,641 square kilometres of valleys, mountains, glaciers, forests, meadows, and rivers.

Designers and Engravers:
Obv.: S. Blunt, S. Taylor
Rev.: T. Bianco, S. Taylor
Composition: 99.99% Ag
Silver content:
1,000.0 g, 32.151 tr oz
Weight: 1,000.0 g (1 kilo)
Diameter: 101.8 mm
Thickness: 12.5 mm
Edge: Plain
Die Axis: ↑↑
Finish: Proof
Case of Issue: Black display case, black flocked insert, encapsulated coin, COA

TWO HUNDRED FIFTY DOLLARS, 375TH ANNIVERSARY OF THE FIRST EUROPEAN OBSERVATION OF LACROSSE, 1636-2011.

First documented by a Jesuit missionary, Jean de Brébeuf in 1636, lacrosse is sport, legend, culture, and history combined. Lacrosse is the national sport of Canada.

Designers and Engravers:
Obv.: S. Blunt, S. Taylor
Rev.: S. Hepburn, C. Paquet
Composition: 99.99% Ag
Silver content:
1,000.0 g, 32.151 tr oz
Weight: 1,000.0 g (1 kilo)
Diameter: 101.8 mm
Thickness: 12.5 mm
Edge: Plain
Die Axis: ↑↑
Finish: Proof
Case of Issue: Black display case, black flocked insert, encapsulated coin, COA

TWO HUNDRED FIFTY DOLLARS, YEAR OF THE (WATER) DRAGON, 2012.

The year 2012 is ruled by the Water Dragon. The Water Dragon occurs every sixty years and personifies creativity at it best.

Designers and Engravers:
Obv.: S. Blunt, S. Taylor
Rev.: Three Degrees Creative Group Inc., Cecily Mok
Composition: 99.99% Ag
Silver content:
1,000.0 g, 32.151 tr oz
Weight: 1,000.0 g (1 kilo)
Diameter: 101.8 mm
Thickness: 12.5 mm
Edge: Plain
Die Axis: ↑↑
Finish: Proof
Case of Issue: Black display case, black flocked insert, encapsulated coin, COA

DATE	DESCRIPTION	QUANTITY SOLD	ISSUE PRICE	FINISH	PR-67	PR-68
2010	100th Anniversary of Banff National Park	525	1,904.95	Proof	2,000.	2,100.
2011 (1636-)	375th Anniv. First European Observation Lacrosse	591	2,195.95	Proof	2,100.	2,200.
2012	Year of the (Water) Dragon	1,616	2,195.95	Proof	2,200.	2,300.

TWO HUNDRED FIFTY DOLLARS, *THE MOOSE FAMILY*, ROBERT BATEMAN MOOSE COIN SERIES, 2012.

The reverse design on this coin features a bull moose's head and antlers taken from Robert Bateman's painting *The Moose Family*. The coin was issued to commemorate the 50th anniversary of the Canadian Wildlife Federation.

Designers and Engravers:
Obv.: S. Blunt, S. Taylor
Rev.: Robert Bateman, RCM Staff
Composition: 99.99% Ag
Silver content:
1,000.0 g, 32.151 tr oz
Weight: 1,000.0 g (1 kilo)
Diameter: 102.1 mm
Thickness: 12.5 mm
Edge: Reeded
Die Axis: ↑↑
Finish: Proof
Case of Issue: Maple wood case, black flocked insert, encapsulated coin, COA

TWO HUNDRED FIFTY DOLLARS, THE BATTLE OF QUEENSTON HEIGHTS, 2012.

This coin was issued to commemorate the first major battle in the War of 1812, which resulted in a Canadian victory.

Designers and Engravers:
Obv.: S. Blunt, S. Taylor
Rev.: John David Kelly, Marcos Hallam
Composition: 99.99% Ag
Silver content:
1,000.0 g, 32.151 tr oz
Weight: 1,000.0 g (1 kilo)
Diameter: 102.1 mm
Thickness: 12.5 mm
Edge: Reeded
Die Axis: ↑↑
Finish: Proof
Case of Issue: Maroon clam style case, black flocked insert, encapsulated coin, COA

TWO HUNDRED FIFTY DOLLARS, CANADA'S ARCTIC LANDSCAPE, 2013.

Designers and Engravers:
Obv.: S. Blunt, S. Taylor
Rev.: W. D. Ward, RCM Staff
Composition: 99.99% Ag
Silver content:
1,000.0 g, 32.151 tr oz
Weight: 1,000.0 g (1 kilo)
Diameter: 101.8 mm
Thickness: 12.5 mm
Edge: Reeded
Die Axis: ↑↑
Finish: Proof
Case of Issue: Maple wood case, black flocked insert, encapsulated coin, COA

DATE	DESCRIPTION	QUANTITY SOLD	ISSUE PRICE	FINISH	PR-67	PR-68
2012 (1962-)	The Moose Family	591	2,249.95	Proof	2,200.	2,300.
2012	The Battle of Queenston Heights	225	2,249.95	Proof	2,250.	2,350.
2013	Canada's Arctic Landscape	319	2,249.95	Proof	2,250.	2,350.

TWO HUNDRED FIFTY DOLLARS, YEAR OF THE SNAKE, 2013.

Designers and Engravers:
  Obv.: S. Blunt, S. Taylor
  Rev.: Three Degrees
      Creative Group Inc.,
      RCM Staff
Composition: 99.99% Ag
Silver content:
  1,000.0 g, 32.151 tr oz
Weight: 1,000.0 g (1 kilo)
Diameter: 102.1 mm
Thickness: 12.5 mm
Edge: Reeded
Die Axis: ↑↑
Finish: Proof
Case of Issue: Silver satin-like
  covered case, black flocked
  insert, encapsulated coin,
  COA

TWO HUNDRED FIFTY DOLLARS, 250TH ANNIVERSARY OF THE END OF THE SEVEN YEARS WAR, 2013.

The Seven Years War (1756-1763) in North America was fought between the English and French over control of the trade in this section of the world.

Designers and Engravers:
  Obv.: S. Blunt, S. Taylor
  Rev.: Luc Normandin,
      RCM Staff
Composition: 99.99% Ag
Silver content:
  1,000.0 g, 32.151 tr oz
Weight: 1,000.0 g (1 kilo)
Diameter: 102.1 mm
Thickness: 12.5 mm
Edge: Reeded
Die Axis: ↑↑
Finish: Proof
Case of Issue: Maple wood
  box, black flocked insert,
  encapsulated coin, COA

TWO HUNDRED FIFTY DOLLARS, BATTLE OF CHATEAUGUAY, WAR OF 1812, 2013.

Designers and Engravers:
  Obv.: S. Blunt, S. Taylor
  Rev.: H. Julien, RCM Staff
Composition: 99.99% Ag
Silver content:
  1,000.0 g, 32.151 tr oz
Weight: 1,000.0 g (1 kilo)
Diameter: 102.1 mm
Thickness: 12.5 mm
Edge: Reeded
Die Axis: ↑↑
Finish: Proof
Case of Issue: Maple wood
  box, black flocked insert,
  encapsulated coin, COA

DATE	DESCRIPTION	QUANTITY SOLD	ISSUE PRICE	FINISH	PR-67	PR-68
2013	Year of the Snake	353	2,249.95	Proof	2,250.	2,350.
2013	250th Anniv., End of the Seven Years War	171	2,249.95	Proof	2,250.	2,350.
2013	Battle of Chateauguay	106	2,249.95	Proof	2,250.	2,350.

TWO HUNDRED FIFTY DOLLARS, THE CARIBOU, 2013.

Designers and Engravers:
Obv.: S. Blunt, S. Taylor
Rev.: Trevor Tennant,
    RCM Staff
Composition: 99.99% Ag
Silver content:
1,000.0 g, 32.151 tr oz
Weight: 1,000.0 g (1 kilo)
Diameter: 102.1 mm
Thickness: 12.5 mm
Edge: Reeded
Die Axis: ↑↑
Finish: Proof
Case of Issue: Maple wood
box, black flocked insert,
encapsulated coin, COA

TWO HUNDRED FIFTY DOLLARS, YEAR OF THE HORSE, 2014.

Designers and Engravers:
Obv.: S. Blunt, S. Taylor
Rev.: Three Degrees
    Creative Group Inc.,
    RCM Staff
Composition: 99.99% Ag
Silver content:
1,000.0 g, 32.151 tr oz
Weight: 1,000.0 g (1 kilo)
Diameter: 102.1 mm
Thickness: 12.5 mm
Edge: Reeded
Die Axis: ↑↑
Finish: Proof
Case of Issue: Silver satin-like
covered case, black flocked
insert, encapsulated coin,
COA

TWO HUNDRED FIFTY DOLLARS, IN THE EYES OF THE SNOWY OWL, 2014.

Designers and Engravers:
Obv.: S. Blunt, S. Taylor
Rev.: A. Nogy, RCM Staff
Composition: 99.99% Ag
Silver content:
1,000.0 g, 32.151 tr oz
Weight: 1,000.0 g (1 kilo)
Diameter: 102.1 mm
Thickness: 12.5 mm
Edge: Reeded
Die Axis: ↑↑
Finish: Proof
Case of Issue: Maple wood
case, black flocked insert,
encapsulated coin, COA

DATE	DESCRIPTION	QUANTITY SOLD	ISSUE PRICE	FINISH	PR-67	PR-68
2013	The Caribou	134	2,249.95	Proof	2,250.	2,350.
2014	Year of the Horse	388	2,249.95	Proof	2,250.	2,350.
2014	In the Eyes of the Snowy Owl	500	2,299.95	Proof	2,300.	2,400.

GOLD COINS

ONE CENT GOLD COIN

ONE CENT, FAREWELL TO THE PENNY, 2012.
This coin was issued in commemoration of the last strike of the Canadian one-cent coin on May 4th, 2011.

Actual Size

Designers and Engravers:
    Obv.:   Susanna Blunt, Susan Taylor
    Rev.:   G. E. Kruger-Gray, RCM Staff
Composition: 99.99% Au
Gold content: 1.27 g, 0.04 tr oz
Weight: 1.27 g
Diameter: 13.9 mm   **Edge:** Plain
Thickness: 0.7 mm   **Die Axis:** ↑↑
Finish: Proof
Case: Maroon leatherette clam style case, black flock insert, encapsulated coin, COA, custom coloured box

DATE	DESCRIPTION	QUANTITY SOLD	ISSUE PRICE	FINISH	PR-67	PR-68
2012	The Penny	11,251	129.95	Proof	150.	160.

TWENTY-FIVE CENT GOLD COINS

LARGE MAMMAL SERIES

TWENTY-FIVE CENTS, LARGE MAMMAL SERIES, 2010-2014.

| Obverse with "P" Mint Mark 2010 | Caribou Des.: E. Hahn Engr.: RCM Staff | Obverse without "P Mint Mark 2011- 2014 | Cougar Des.: E. Damstra Engr.: W. Woodruff | Rocky Mountain Bighorn Sheep Des.: E. Damstra Engr.: RCM Staff | Actual Size |

Designers:
Obv.: Susanna Blunt
Rev.: See reverse illustration
Composition: 99.99% Au
Gold content: 0.5 g, 0.016 tr oz
Weight: 0.5 g
Diameter: 11.0 mm
Case of Issue: Maroon leatherette clam style case, black flock insert, encapsulated coin, COA

Engravers:
Rev.: Susan Taylor
Rev.: See reverse illustration
Thickness: 0.6 mm
Edge: Reeded
Die Axis: ↑↑
Finish: Proof

DATE		DESCRIPTION	QUANTITY SOLD	ISSUE PRICE	FINISH	PR-67	PR-68
2010		Caribou	9,955	74.95	Proof	100.	110.
2011		Cougar	8,627	79.95	Proof	95.	100.
2014		Rocky Mountain Bighorn Sheep	4,693	79.95	Proof	80.	85.

SMALL ANIMAL SERIES

TWENTY-FIVE CENTS, SMALL ANIMAL SERIES, 2013-2014.

| Common Obverse | Hummingbird Des.: C. D'Angelo Engr.: S. Strath | Eastern Chipmunk Des.: Tony Bianco Engr.: RCM Staff | Actual Size |

Designers:
Obv.: Susanna Blunt
Rev.: See reverse illustrations
Composition: 99.99% Au
Gold content: 0.5 g, 0.016 tr oz
Weight: 0.5 g
Diameter: 11.0 mm
Case: Maroon leatherette clam style case, black flock insert, encapsulated coin, COA

Engravers:
Obv.: Susan Taylor
Rev.: See reverse illustrations
Thickness: 0.5 mm
Edge: Reeded
Die Axis: ↑↑
Finish: Proof

DATE		DESCRIPTION	QUANTITY SOLD	ISSUE PRICE	FINISH	PR-67	PR-68
2013		The Hummingbird	9,993	79.95	Proof	90.	95.
2014		Eastern Chipmunk	10,000	79.95	Proof	90.	95.

FIFTY CENT GOLD COINS

FIFTY CENTS, THE BOREAL FOREST, 2011.

The Boreal Forest is a vast woodland that circumvents the globe across the northern hemisphere, and 2011 was declared International Year of the Forest. These are 1/25 ounce coins.

2011   BOREAL FOREST

2011   ORCA WHALE

2011   WOOD BISON

2011   PEREGRINE FALCON

Actual Size

Designers:
  Obv.:   Susanna Blunt
  Rev.:   Corrine Hunt
Composition: 99.99% Au
Gold content: 1.27 g, 0.04 tr oz
Weight: 1.27 g
Diameter: 13.8 to 13.9 mm
Thickness: 0.6 mm
Case of Issue: Maroon leatherette clam style case, black flock insert, encapsulated coin, COA

Engravers:
  Obv.:   Susan Taylor
  Rev.:   Boreal Forest / Peregrine Falcon: Marcos Hallam
          Orca Whale: Cecily Mok,
          Wood Bison: Konrad Wachelko
Edge: Reeded
Die Axis: ↑↑
Finish: Proof

DATE	DESCRIPTION	QUANTITY SOLD	ISSUE PRICE	FINISH	PR-67	PR-68
2011	Boreal Forest	1,859	139.95	Proof	140.	150.
2011	Orca Whale	1,729	139.95	Proof	140.	150.
2011	Wood Bison	1,678	139.95	Proof	140.	150.
2011	Peregrine Falcon	1,686	139.95	Proof	140.	150.

FIFTY CENTS, COMMEMORATIVE GOLD COINS, 2012-2014.

Common Obverse

150th Anniv. of the Caribou Gold Rush
Des.: Tony Bianco
Engr.: C. Paquet

Owl Shaman Holding Goose
Des.: J. Nowkawalk
Engr.: S. Stewart

Bald Eagle
Des.: Trevor Tennant
Engr.: Cecily Mok

300th Anniv. of Louisbourg
Des.: Peter Gough
Engr.: RCM Staff

Actual Size

Starfish
Des.: E. Damstra
Engr.: RCM Staff

Canada's Classic Beaver
Des. G.E. Kruger Gray
Engr.: RCM Staff

Osprey
Des.: RCM Staff
Engr.: RCM Staff

Seahorse
Des.: Emily Damstra
Engr.: RCM Staff

Designers:
Obv.:   Susanna Blunt
Rev.:   See reverse illustrations
Composition: 99.99% Au
Gold content: 1.27 g, 0.04 tr oz
Weight: 1.27 g
Diameter: 13.9 mm
Thickness: 0.5 to 0.7 mm
Case of Issue: Maroon leatherette clam style case, black flock insert, encapsulated coin, COA

Engravers:
Obv.:   Susan Taylor
Rev.:   See reverse illustrations

Edge: Reeded
Die Axis: ↑↑
Finish: Proof

DATE	DESCRIPTION	QUANTITY SOLD	ISSUE PRICE	FINISH	PR-67	PR-68
2012	150th Anniv. of the Caribou Gold Rush	5,988	129.95	Proof	130.	140.
2013	Owl Shaman Holding Goose	5,736	129.95	Proof	130.	140.
2013	Bald Eagle	9,277	129.95	Proof	130.	140.
2013	300th Anniv. of Louisbourg	2,930	129.95	Proof	130.	140.
2013	Starfish	3,877	129.95	Proof	130.	140.
2014	Canada's Classic Beaver	7,500	129.95	Proof	130.	140.
2014	Osprey	7,500	129.95	Proof	130.	140.
2014	Seahorse	7,500	129.95	Proof	130.	140.

ONE DOLLAR GOLD COINS

2006 GOLD LOUIS (1723 LOUIS D'OR MIRLITON)

2007 GOLD LOUIS (1726 LOUIS D'OR AUX LUNETTES)

2008 GOLD LOUIS (1720-1723 LOUIS D'OR AUX DEUX L)

Actual Size

Designers:
Obv.: Susanna Blunt
Rev.: RCM Staff
Composition: 99.99% Au
Gold content: 1.55 g, 0.05 tr oz
Weight: 1.555 g
Diameter: 14.1 mm
Thickness: 0.8 mm
Case of Issue: Maroon plastic slide case, black plastic insert, encapsulated coin, COA

Engravers:
Obv.: Susan Taylor
Rev.: 2006 Konrad Wachelko
2007-2008 Marcos Hallam

Edge: Reeded
Die Axis: ↑↑
Finish: Proof

DATE	DESCRIPTION	QUANTITY SOLD	ISSUE PRICE	FINISH	PR-67	PR-68
2006	1723 Louis d'or Mirliton	5,648	102.95	Proof	125.	135.
2007	1726 Louis d'or Aux Lunettes	4,023	104.95	Proof	165.	175.
2008	1720 to 1723 Louis d'or aux deux L	3,793	124.95	Proof	135.	145.

FIVE DOLLAR GOLD COINS

FIVE DOLLARS, COMMEMORATIVE GOLD COINS, 2011-2014.

Actual Size

| Common Obverse | 2011
Des.: Harvey Chan
Engr.: José Osio | 2012
Des.: RCM Staff
Engr.: C. Paquet | 2014
Des.: Derek Wicks
Engr.: RCM Staff |

Designers:
  Obv.: Susanna Blunt
  Rev.: See reverse illustrations
Composition: 99.99% Au
Gold content: 3.13 g, 0.10 tr oz
Weight: 3.13 g
Diameter: 16.0 mm
Thickness: 1.0 mm

Engravers:
  Obv.: Susan Taylor
  Rev.: See reverse illustrations

Edge: Reeded
Die Axis: ↑↑
Finish: Proof

Case of Issue: 2011, 2014: Maroon leatherette clam style case, black flocked insert, encapsulated coin, COA
2012: Wooden collector case, black flocked insert, encapsulated coin, COA, Beauty box
featuring the official Diamond Jubilee Cypher

DATE	DESCRIPTION	QUANTITY SOLD	ISSUE PRICE	FINISH	PR-67	PR-68
2011	75th Anniversary Dr. Norman Bethune's Invention of the First Mobile Blood Transfusion Vehicle	1,457	319.95	Proof	250.	275.
2012	The Queen's Diamond Jubilee	1,538	259.95	Proof	225.	250.
2014	Bald Eagle	3,000	279.95	Proof	280.	300.

FIVE DOLLARS, CHINESE LUNAR CALENDAR GOLD COINS, 2012-2013.

Actual Size

| Common Obverse | 2012
Des.: Three Degrees
Creative Group Inc.
Engr.: K. Wachelko | 2013
Des.: Aries Cheung
Engr.: Stan Witten |

Designers:
  Obv.: Susanna Blunt
  Rev.: See reverse illustration
Composition: 99.99% Au
Gold content: 3.13 g, 0.10 tr oz
Weight: 3.13 g
Diameter: 16.0 mm
Thickness: 1.0 mm

Engravers:
  Obv.: Susan Taylor
  Rev.: See reverse illustration

Edge: Reeded
Die Axis: ↑↑
Finish: Specimen

Case: Maroon leatherette clam style case, black flocked insert, encapsulated coin, COA

DATE	DESCRIPTION	QUANTITY SOLD	ISSUE PRICE	FINISH	SP-66	SP-67
2012	Year of the Dragon	8,902	229.95	Specimen	250.	275.
2013	Year of the Snake	2,994	229.95	Specimen	250.	275.

O CANADA SERIES 2013-2014

FIVE DOLLARS, O CANADA SERIES, 2013.

The O Canada Series focuses on iconic Canadian animals to celebrate Canadian pride. For other coins in the O Canada Series see pages 180 and 244.

Actual Size

Common Obverse

Designers and Engravers:
Obv.: Susanna Blunt, Susan Taylor
Rev.: Pierre Leduc, Stan Witten
Composition: 99.99% Au
Gold content: 3.13 g, 0.10 tr oz
Weight: 3.13 g   **Edge:** Reeded
Diameter: 16.0 mm   **Die Axis:** ↑↑
Thickness: 1.0 mm   **Finish:** Proof
Case: Maroon leatherette clam style case, black flocked insert, encapsulated coin, COA

Beaver	Polar Bear	Caribou	Wolf	Orca

DATE	DESCRIPTION	QUANTITY SOLD	ISSUE PRICE	FINISH	PR-67	PR-68
2013	Beaver	3,528	279.95	Proof	280.	300.
2013	Polar Bear	3,490	279.95	Proof	280.	300.
2013	Caribou	2,225	279.95	Proof	280.	300.
2013	Wolf	2,462	279.95	Proof	280.	300.
2013	Orca	1,760	279.95	Proof	280.	300.
2013	5-coin set	Incl. above	1,399.95	Proof	1,400.	1,500.

FIVE DOLLARS, O CANADA SERIES, 2014.

Actual Size

Common Obverse

Designers and Engravers:
Obv.: Susanna Blunt, Susan Taylor
Rev.: RCM Staff
Composition: 99.99% Au
Gold content: 3.13 g, 0.10 tr oz
Weight: 3.13 g   **Edge:** Reeded
Diameter: 16.0 mm   **Die Axis:** ↑↑
Thickness: 1.0 mm   **Finish:** Proof
Case: Walnut display case, black flocked insert, encapsulated coin, COA

Grizzly Bear	Moose	Canada Goose	Bison

DATE	DESCRIPTION	QUANTITY SOLD	ISSUE PRICE	FINISH	PR-67	PR-68
2014	Grizzly Bear	4,000	279.95	Proof	280.	300.
2014	Moose	4,000	279.95	Proof	280.	300.
2014	Canada Goose	4,000	279.95	Proof	280.	300.
2014	Bison	4,000	279.95	Proof	280.	300.

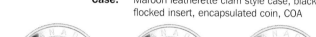

FIVE AND TEN DOLLAR GOLD COMMEMORATIVE COINS

FIVE AND TEN DOLLAR GOLD COMMEMORATIVES 1912-2002.

Issued to mark the 90th anniversary of Canada's first five and ten dollar gold coins in 1912, these double-dated 1912-2002 coins continue a commemorative series which began in 1998, with the issue recalling the first set of coins struck at the Ottawa Mint. Basing the overall design on the 1912 specimen coins from the Bank of Canada collection, the 1912-2002 gold coins differ only in the date and, of course, the obverse effigy.

| $5 Obverse | $5 Reverse | $10 Obverse | $10 Reverse |

Designers:
   Obv.: Dora de Pédery-Hunt
   Rev.: W. H. J. Blakemore

Engravers:
   Obv.: Dora de Pédery-Hunt
   Rev.: Cosme Saffioti

	$5	**$10**
Denominations:		
Composition:	90.0% Au, 10.0 Cu	90.0% Au, 10.0% Cu
Gold content:	7.52 g, 0.242 tr oz	15.05 g, 0.484 tr oz
Weight (grams):	8.36	16.72
Diameter (mm):	21.6	26.9
Thickness (mm):	N/A	N/A
Edge:	Reeded	Reeded
Finish:	Proof	Proof

Case of Issue: Two-coin clam style case

DATE	DESCRIPTION	QUANTITY SOLD	ISSUE PRICE	FINISH	PR-67	PR-68
2002 (1912-)	$5	1,998	N.I.I.	Proof	400.	425.
2002 (1912-)	$10	1,998	N.I.I.	Proof	825.	850.
2002 (1912-)	Set of 2 coins	1,998	749.95	Proof	1,150.	—

TWENTY DOLLAR GOLD COIN

TWENTY DOLLARS, CENTENNIAL OF CONFEDERATION COMMEMORATIVE, 1967.

The highlight of the coins issued in 1967 to mark the centenary of Canadian Confederation was a $20 gold coin. It was issued only as part of a $40.00 specimen set (see page 376 for the set listing), but many were later removed from the sets for separate trading. The reverse design is an adaption of the Canadian coat of arms which appears on the 50-cent piece of 1960-1966. It is the only coin in the Centennial set that bears the single date 1967 instead of 1867-1967.

Designers and Engravers:
Obv.: Arnold Machin, Myron Cook
Rev.: Thomas Shingles, Myron Cook
Composition: 90.0% Au, 10.0% Cu
Gold content: 16.443 g, 0.529 tr oz
Weight: 18.27 g
Diameter: 27.1 mm   **Edge:** Reeded
Thickness: 2.3 mm   **Die Axis:** ↑↑
Finish: Specimen
Case: Black leather case, black flocked insert

DATE	DESCRIPTION	QUANTITY SOLD	ISSUE PRICE	FINISH	SP-66	SP-67
1967	Centennial of Confederation	334,288	N.I.I.	Specimen	800.	825.

TWENTY-FIVE DOLLAR GOLD COINS

TWENTY-FIVE DOLLARS, UNTAMED CANADA SERIES, 2013-2014.

Just slightly larger than the average house cat, the arctic fox is a silent and prolific hunter. The Pronghorn is fleet-footed and one of the fastest animals in North America. The wolverine, which resembles a small bear, is the largest member of the weasel family.

| Common Obverse | Artic Fox | Pronghorn | Wolverine |

Designers and Engravers:
Obv.: Susanna Blunt, Susan Taylor
Rev.: Tividar Bote, Steven Stewart
Composition: 99.99% Au
Gold content: 7.797 g, 0.25 tr oz
Weight: 7.797 g
Diameter: 20.0 mm
Thickness: N/A   **Die Axis:** ↑↑
Edge: Reeded   **Finish:** Proof
Case: Maroon leatherette clam style case, black flocked insert, encapsulated coin, COA

DATE	DESCRIPTION	QUANTITY SOLD	ISSUE PRICE	FINISH	PR-67	PR-68
2013	The Arctic Fox	715	649.95	Proof	650.	675.
2013	Pronghorn	216	649.95	Proof	650.	675.
2014	Wolverine	1,500	649.95	Proof	650.	675.

TWENTY-FIVE DOLLARS, MISS CANADA: AN ALLEGORY 2013.

Designers and Engravers:
Obv.: Susanna Blunt, Susan Taylor
Rev.: Laurie McGaw, RCM Staff
Composition: 99.99% Au
Gold content: 7.797 g, 0.25 tr oz
Weight: 7.797 g   **Edge:** Reeded
Diameter: 20.0 mm   **Die Axis:** ↑↑
Thickness: N/A   **Finish:** Proof
Case: Maroon leatherette clam style case, black flocked insert, encapsulated coin, COA

DATE	DESCRIPTION	QUANTITY SOLD	ISSUE PRICE	FINISH	PR-67	PR-68
2013	Miss Canada: An Allegory	602	649.95	Proof	650.	675.

TWENTY-FIVE DOLLARS, POPE JOHN PAUL II, 2014.

Designers and Engravers:
Obv.: Susanna Blunt, Susan Taylor
Rev.: RCM Staff
Composition: 99.99% Au
Gold content: 7.797 g, 0.25 tr oz
Weight: 7.797 g   **Edge:** Reeded
Diameter: 20.0 mm   **Die Axis:** ↑↑
Thickness: N/A   **Finish:** Proof
Case: Maroon leatherette clam style case, black flocked insert, encapsulated coin, COA

DATE	DESCRIPTION	QUANTITY SOLD	ISSUE PRICE	FINISH	PR-67	PR-68
2014	Pope John Paul II	1,500	649.95	Proof	650.	675.

FIFTY DOLLAR GOLD COINS

FIFTY DOLLARS, 60TH ANNIVERSARY OF THE END OF THE SECOND WORLD WAR, 1945-2005.

World War II was a global conflict which began September 1st, 1939 when Germany invaded Poland. By September 3rd, 1939, Britain and France declared war on Germany.

There are several ending dates: VE (Victory in Europe) Day May 8th, 1945, and VJ Day (Victory in Japan) August 14th, 1945.

Designers and Engravers:
Obv.:   Susanna Blunt, Susan Taylor
Rev.:   Peter Mossman, Christie Paquet
Composition: 58.33% Au, 41.67% Ag
Gold content: 7.00 g, 0.225 tr oz
Silver content: 5.00 g, 0.161 tr oz
Weight: 12.0 g   **Edge:** Reeded
Diameter: 27.0 mm   **Die Axis:** ↑↑
Thickness: 2.0 mm   **Finish:** Specimen
Case: Maroon plastic slide case, black plastic insert, encapsulated coin, COA

DATE	DESCRIPTION	QUANTITY SOLD	ISSUE PRICE	FINISH	SP-66	SP-67
2005 (1945-)	60th Anniv. End of the Second World War	4,000	379.95	Specimen	400.	425.

Note: While this $50 gold coin is listed as proof quality on the certificate of authenticity, the finish on the coins examined is specimen.

FIFTY DOLLARS, THE QUEEN'S DIAMOND JUBILEE, 2012.

This coin was struck for the Queen's Diamond Jubilee in 2012. It is the world's first 99.999% gold coin struck with an ultra high relief.

Designers and Engravers:
Obv.:   Susanna Blunt, Susan Taylor
Rev.:   Laurie McGaw, Christie Paquet
Composition: 99.999% Au
Gold content: 33.17 g, 1.066 tr oz
Weight: 33.17 g   **Edge:** Reeded
Diameter: 30.0 mm   **Die Axis:** ↑↑
Thickness: 2.5 to 4.5 mm   **Finish:** Proof
Case: Maroon leatherette clam style case, black flocked insert, encapsulated coin, COA

DATE	DESCRIPTION	QUANTITY SOLD	ISSUE PRICE	FINISH	PR-67	PR-68
2012	The Queen's Diamond Jubilee	499	2,999.95	Proof	3,000.	3,200.

SEVENTY-FIVE DOLLAR GOLD COINS

SEVENTY-FIVE DOLLARS, COMMEMORATING THE VISIT OF POPE JOHN PAUL II TO CANADA, 2005.

During a 12-day tour in April 2005, Pope John Paul II visited many cities in Canada, drawing more than two million people to the Papal events. This was his third trip to Canada.

Designers and Engravers:
    Obv.: Susanna Blunt, Susan Taylor
    Rev.: Susan Taylor, Susan Taylor
Composition: 41.66% Au, 58.34 Ag
Gold content: 13.1 g, 0.421 tr oz
Silver content: 18.34 g, 0.590 tr oz
Weight: 31.44 g   **Edge:** Reeded
Diameter: 36.1 mm   **Die Axis:** ↑↑
Thickness: 3.0 mm   **Finish:** Proof
Case: Maroon plastic slide case, black plastic
         insert, encapsulated coin, COA

DATE	DESCRIPTION	QUANTITY SOLD	ISSUE PRICE	FINISH	PR-67	PR-68
2005	Commemorating the Visit of Pope John Paul II to Canada	1,870	544.95	Proof	750.	775.

Note: In 2005 a set containing both the $10 (silver) and $75 (gold) coins was issued to commemorate the visit to Canada of Pope John Paul II. This may have been a special presentation set as only nine were issued.

VANCOUVER 2010 OLYMPIC WINTER GAMES

SEVENTY-FIVE DOLLARS, COMMEMORATING THE VANCOUVER 2010 OLYMPIC WINTER GAMES, 2007-2009.
  The Vancouver 2010 Olympic Winter Games $75 gold coins were sold singly, or in three-coin sets. The three different sets offered were Canadian Wildlife, Canadian Icons, and Vancouver 2010 Winter Games.

2007 COMMEMORATIVE ISSUES

Obverse

R.C.M.P.
Des.: Cecily Mok
Engr.: N/A

Athletes' Pride
Des.: Sheila Armstrong
Engr.: Christie Paquet

Canada Geese
Des.: Cecily Mok
Engr.: N/A

2008 COMMEMORATIVE ISSUES

Obverse

Four Host First Nations
Des.: Kerri Burnett
Engr.: Cecily Mok

**Home of the 2010
Olympic Winter Games**
Des.: Sheila Armstrong
Engr.: Marcos Hallam

Inukshuk
Des.: Sheila Armstrong
Engr.: José Osio

2009 COMMEMORATIVE ISSUES

Obverse

Wolf
Des.: Arnold Nogy
Engr.: N/A

Olympic Spirit
Des.: Sheila Armstrong
Engr.: N/A

Moose
Des.: Kerri Burnett
Engr.: José Osio

Designers:
  Obv.: Susanna Blunt
  Rev.: See reverse illustrations
Composition: 58.33% Au, 41.67% Ag, Colour on reverse
Gold content: 7.0 g, 0.225 tr oz
Silver content: 5.0 g, 0.161 tr oz
Weight: 12.0 g
Diameter: 27.0 mm

Engravers:
  Obv.: Susan Taylor
  Rev.: See reverse illustrations

Thickness: 2.0 to 2.2 mm
Edge: Reeded
Die Axis: ↑↑
Finish: Proof

Case of Issue: Singly: Black display case, black flocked insert, encapsulated coin, COA; Vancouver 2010 Olympic Winter Games theme sleeve.
  Sets: See page below.

COMMEMORATING THE VANCOUVER 2010 OLYMPIC WINTER GAMES, 2007-2009, PRICING TABLE.

DATE	DESCRIPTION	DATE OF ISSUE	QUANTITY SOLD	ISSUE PRICE	FINISH	PR-67	PR-68
2007	Royal Canadian Mounted Police	Feb. 23, 2007	6,687	389.95	Proof	500.	525.
2007	Athletes' Pride	July 11, 2007	4,524	389.95	Proof	500.	525.
2007	Canada Geese	Oct. 24, 2007	4,418	409.95	Proof	500.	525.
2008	Four Host First Nations	Feb. 20, 2008	4,897	409.95	Proof	500.	525.
2008	Home of the Winter Games	July 23, 2008	4,581	433.95	Proof	500.	525.
2008	Inukshuk	Oct. 29, 2008	4,907	499.95	Proof	500.	525.
2009	Wolf	Feb. 18, 2009	4,161	499.95	Proof	500.	525.
2009	Olympic Spirit	June 17, 2009	4,479	499.95	Proof	500.	525.
2009	Moose	Sept. 9, 2009	4,075	499.95	Proof	500.	525.

SEVENTY-FIVE DOLLAR VANCOUVER WINTER OLYMPIC GAMES COIN SETS

Sets of the three $75 gold coins were offered for sale in acrylic holders. They were assembled in three themes: Canadian Wildlife, Canadian Icons, and Vancouver 2010 Olympic Winter Games.

DATE	DESCRIPTION	QUANTITY SOLD	ISSUE PRICE	ISSUER	FINISH	MARKET VALUE
2007-2009	**Canadian Wildlife:** 2007 Canada Geese, 2009 Wolf, 2009 Moose; Acrylic holder	25	1,424.95	RCM	PR-67	1,450.
2007-2008	**Canadian Icons:** 2007 R.C.M.P., 2008 Four Host First Nations, 2008 Inukshuk; Acrylic holder	18	1,424.95	RCM	PR-67	1,450.
2007-2009	**Vancouver 2010 Winter Games:** 2007 Athletes' Pride, 2008 Home of the 2010 Olympic Winter Games, 2009 Olympic Spirit; Acrylic holder	32	1,424.95	RCM	PR-67	1,450.

FOUR SEASONS MAPLE LEAVES SERIES

SEVENTY-FIVE DOLLARS, FOUR SEASONS MAPLE LEAVES, 2010.

The four seasons, spring, summer, autumn, and winter bring an ever-changing landscape to Canada. The evolving maple leaves best mirrors this yearly cycle.

Obverse

Designers:
Obv.: Susanna Blunt
Rev.: See reverse illustrations
Composition: 58.33% Au, 41.67% Ag, Painted
Gold content: 7.0 g, 0.225 tr oz
Silver content: 5.0 g, 0.161 tr oz
Weight: 12.0 g
Diameter: 27.0 mm

Engravers:
Obv.: Susan Taylor
Rev.: See reverse illustrations

Thickness: 2.0 mm
Edge: Reeded
Die Axis: ↑↑
Finish: Proof

Case: Singly: Maroon leatherette clam style case, black flock insert, encapsulated coin, COA
Sets: Maple wood display case, 4-hole black flock insert, encapsulated coins, serialised certificate, black sleeve

Spring	Summer	Fall	Winter
Designer: A. Nogy	Designer: M. Grant	Designer: C. D'Angelo	Designer: C. Godkin
Engraver: K. Wachelko	Engraver: S. Taylor	Engraver: M. Hallam	Engraver: K. Wachelko

DATE	DESCRIPTION	QUANTITY SOLD	ISSUE PRICE	FINISH	PR-67	PR-68
2010	Spring Maple Leaves	130	589.95	Proof	600.	625.
2010	Summer Maple Leaves	136	589.95	Proof	600.	625.
2010	Fall Maple Leaves	162	589.95	Proof	600.	625.
2010	Winter Maple Leaves	136	589.95	Proof	600.	625.
2010	Set of Four Coins	587	2,358.95	Proof	2,400.	—

WORLD BASEBALL CLASSIC SERIES

SEVENTY-FIVE DOLLARS, COMMEMORATING THE WORLD BASEBALL CLASSIC, 2013.

These coins were issued to celebrate the World Baseball Classic Tournament held March 2nd to 19th, 2013. For other coins in this series see pages 227 and 296.

Common Obverse

Ball Diamond
Engr.: S. Stewart

Hardball
Engr.: S. Strath

Designers:
  Obv.: Susanna Blunt
  Rev.: Steve Hepburn
Composition: 99.99% Au
Gold content: 7.8 g, 0.25 tr oz
Weight: 7.8 g
Diameter: 20.0 mm
Case of Issue: Maroon leatherette slam style case, black flocked insert, encapsulated coin, COA

Engravers:
  Obv.: Susan Taylor
  Rev.: See reverse illustrations
Thickness: N/A
Edge: Reeded
Die Axis: ↑↑
Finish: Proof

DATE		DESCRIPTION	QUANTITY SOLD	ISSUE PRICE	FINISH	PR-67	PR-68
2013	Ball Diamond		133	899.95	Proof	1,100.	1,150.
2013	Hardball		121	899.95	Proof	1,100.	1,150.

SEVENTY-FIVE DOLLARS, 75TH ANNIVERSARY OF SUPERMAN™: THE EARLY YEARS, 2013.

Designers and Engravers:
  Obv.: Susanna Blunt, Susan Taylor
  Rev.: DC Comics/Warner Brothers, RCM Staff
Composition: 58.33% Au, 41.67% Ag
Gold content: 7.0 g, 0.225 tr oz
Silver content: 5.0 g, 0.161 tr oz
Weight: 12.0 g   **Edge:** Reeded
Diameter: 27.0 mm   **Die Axis:** ↑↑
Thickness: 3.0 mm
Finish: Proof, Painted
Case: Custom case and beauty box

DATE	DESCRIPTION	QUANTITY SOLD	ISSUE PRICE	FINISH	PR-67	PR-68
2013	75th Anniversary of Superman™: The Early Years	1,995	750.00	Proof	2,000.	2,100.

ONE HUNDRED DOLLAR GOLD COINS

ONE HUNDRED DOLLARS, MONTREAL OLYMPIC COMMEMORATIVES, 1976.

As part of the series of collectors' coins struck to commemorate and help finance the XXI Olympiad, two separate $100 gold coins were issued in 1976. The reverse design for each shows an ancient Grecian athlete being crowned with laurel by the goddess Pallas Athena. The uncirculated issue is 14kt gold and has beads around the rim. The proof issue is 22k gold, slightly smaller, and lacks rim beads.

**1976 Obverse
14 kt Gold**

**1976 Reverse
14 kt Gold**

Designers and Engravers:
Obv.: Arnold Machin, Walter Ott
Rev.: Dora de Pédery-Hunt, Walter Ott
Composition: 58.33% Au, 41.67% Ag
Gold content: 7.78 g, 0.25 tr oz
Silver content: 5.56 g, 0.179 tr oz
Weight: 13.338 g   **Edge:** Reeded
Diameter: 27.0 mm   **Die Axis:** ↑↑
Thickness: 2.2 mm   **Finish:** Circulation
Case: Plastic flip in a cardboard sleeve

**1976 Obverse
22kt Gold**

**1976 Reverse
22kt Gold**

Designers and Engravers:
Obv.: Arnold Machin, Walter Ott
Rev.: Dora de Pédery-Hunt, Walter Ott
Composition: 91.67% Au, 8.33% Ag
Gold content: 15.55 g, 0.500 tr oz
Silver content: 1.14 g, 0.045 tr oz
Weight: 16.966 g   **Edge:** Reeded
Diameter: 25.0 mm   **Die Axis:** ↑↑
Thickness: 2.2 mm   **Finish:** Proof
Case: Cowhide and wood case, black suede
insert, COA

DATE	DESCRIPTION	QUANTITY SOLD	ISSUE PRICE	FINISH	65	66	67	68
1976	Montreal Olympics, 14 kt	650,000	105.00	Circulation	400.	425.	—	—
1976	Montreal Olympics, 22 kt	350,000	150.00	Proof	—	—	800.	825.

NOTE FOR COLLECTORS

Beginning with the modern issues, gold coins were offered for sale by the Royal Canadian Mint at a small premium over face value giving investors a call on gold with a limited downside risk. Investors soon realised this and purchased large quantities of coins which resulted in high mintage figures.

Currently, modern gold coins trade close to their intrinsic value. The gold coins listed here are priced at a market value of $1,600. per ounce.

ONE HUNDRED DOLLARS, QUEEN ELIZABETH II SILVER JUBILEE COMMEMORATIVE, 1977.

Following the sales success of the Olympic $100 coins the Royal Canadian Mint decided to embark upon a programme of issuing a $100 coin every year. The 1997 commemorative reverse shows a bouquet of flowers made up of the official flowers of the provinces and territories. All were issued in proof quality, with mirror fields and frosted devices and legends.

Designers and Engravers:
Obv.: Arnold Machin, RCM Staff
Rev.: Raymond Lee, Walter Ott
Composition: 91.67% Au, 8.33% Ag
Gold content: 15.55 g, 0.5 tr oz
Silver content: 1.413 g, 0.045 tr oz
Weight: 16.965 g   **Edge:** Reeded
Diameter: 27.0 mm   **Die Axis:** ↑↑
Thickness: 2.2 mm   **Finish:** Proof
Case: Black leatherette case, maroon insert, plastic coin holder, COA

DATE	DESCRIPTION	QUANTITY SOLD	ISSUE PRICE	FINISH	PR-67	PR-68
1977	Silver Jubilee Elizabeth II	180,396	140.00	Proof	800.	825.

ONE HUNDRED DOLLARS, CANADIAN UNITY COIN, 1978.

The reverse of the proof $100 gold coin for 1978 depicts twelve Canada geese flying in formation. The image represents the ten provinces and two territories, and so promotes Canadian unity.

Designers and Engravers:
Obv.: Arnold Machin, RCM Staff
Rev.: Roger Savage, Ago Aarand
Composition: 91.67% Au, 8.33% Ag
Gold content: 15.55 g, 0.5 tr oz
Silver content: 1.413 g, 0.045 tr oz
Weight: 16.965 g   **Edge:** Reeded
Diameter: 27.0 mm   **Die Axis:** ↑↑
Thickness: 2.2 mm   **Finish:** Proof
Case: Black leatherette case, maroon insert, plastic coin holder, COA

DATE	DESCRIPTION	QUANTITY SOLD	ISSUE PRICE	FINISH	PR-67	PR-68
1978	Canadian Unity	200,000	150.00	Proof	800.	825.

ONE HUNDRED DOLLARS, INTERNATIONAL YEAR OF THE CHILD COMMEMORATIVE, 1979.

Children playing hand in hand beside a globe adorn the reverse of the 1979 $100 gold coin struck in honour of the International Year of the Child.

Designers and Engravers:
Obv.: Arnold Machin, RCM Staff
Rev.: Carola Tietz, Victor Coté
Composition: 91.67% Au, 8.33% Ag
Gold content: 15.55 g, 0.5 tr oz
Silver content: 1.413 g, 0.045 tr oz
Weight: 16.965 g   **Edge:** Reeded
Diameter: 27.0 mm   **Die Axis:** ↑↑
Thickness: 2.2 mm   **Finish:** Proof
Case: Brown leatherette case, brown flocked insert, plastic coin holder, COA

DATE	DESCRIPTION	QUANTITY SOLD	ISSUE PRICE	FINISH	PR-67	PR-68
1979	International Year of the Child	250,000	185.00	Proof	800.	825.

ONE HUNDRED DOLLARS, ARCTIC TERRITORIES COMMEMORATIVE, 1980.

The gold $100 coin for 1980 commemorates the 100th anniversary of the transfer of the Arctic Islands from the British Government to the Government of the Dominion of Canada. Its reverse shows an Inuk paddling a kayak near a small iceberg and has no lettering or date. The obverse features the Machin bust of Queen Elizabeth, with the legend and date.

Designers and Engravers:
Obv.: Arnold Machin, RCM Staff
Rev.: A. Marchetti, Sheldon Beveridge
Composition: 91.67% Au, 8.33% Ag
Gold content: 15.55 g, 0.5 tr oz
Silver content: 1.413 g, 0.045 tr oz
Weight: 16.965 g   **Edge:** Reeded
Diameter: 27.0 mm   **Die Axis:** ↑↑
Thickness: 2.2 mm   **Finish:** Proof
Case: Brown leatherette case, brown flocked
             insert, plastic coin holder, COA

DATE	DESCRIPTION	QUANTITY SOLD	ISSUE PRICE	FINISH	PR-67	PR-68
1980	Arctic Territories	130,000	430.00	Proof	800.	825

ONE HUNDRED DOLLARS, "O CANADA" COMMEMORATIVE, 1981.

The $100 gold coin for 1981 commemorates the decision of the Canadian Parliament on July 1, 1980, to adopt the song "O Canada" as our national anthem.

Designers and Engravers:
Obv.: Arnold Machin, RCM Staff
Rev.: Roger Savage, Walter Ott
Composition: 91.67% Au, 8.33% Ag
Gold content: 15.55 g, 0.5 tr oz
Silver content: 1.413 g, 0.045 tr oz
Weight: 16.965 g   **Edge:** Reeded
Diameter: 27.0 mm   **Die Axis:** ↑↑
Thickness: 2.2 mm   **Finish:** Proof
Case: Brown leatherette case, brown flocked
             insert, plastic coin holder, COA

DATE	DESCRIPTION	QUANTITY SOLD	ISSUE PRICE	FINISH	PR-67	PR-68
1981	"O Canada"	100,950	300.00	Proof	800.	825.

ONE HUNDRED DOLLARS, PATRIATION OF THE CANADIAN CONSTITUTION, 1982.

The $100 gold coin for 1982 commemorates the patriation of the Constitution of Canada. The reverse of the coin portrays this historical event by a page turning in an open book bearing the coat of arms of Canada and a maple leaf. The obverse of this coin, the seventh in the 22 karat $100 series, depicts Arnold Machin's effigy of Her Majesty Elizabeth II and the legend "100 Dollars" and "Elizabeth II."

Designers and Engravers:
Obv.: Arnold Machin, RCM Staff
Rev.: Friedrich Peter, Walter Ott
Composition: 91.67% Au, 8.33% Ag
Gold content: 15.55 g, 0.5 tr oz
Silver content: 1.413 g, 0.045 tr oz
Weight: 16.965 g   **Edge:** Reeded
Diameter: 27.0 mm   **Die Axis:** ↑↑
Thickness: 2.2 mm   **Finish:** Proof
Case: Brown leatherette case, brown flocked
             insert, plastic coin holder, COA

DATE	DESCRIPTION	QUANTITY SOLD	ISSUE PRICE	FINISH	PR-67	PR-68
1982	Patriation of the Canadian Constitution	121,706	290.00	Proof	800.	825.

ONE HUNDRED DOLLARS, SIR HUMPHREY GILBERT'S LANDING IN NEWFOUNDLAND, 1983.

The $100 gold coin for 1983 commemorates Gilbert's landing in Newfoundland, where he proclaimed it England's first overseas colony. The word CANADA appears on the edge for the first time in Canadian coinage.

Designers and Engravers:
    Obv.: Arnold Machin, RCM Staff
    Rev.: John Jaciw, Walter Ott
Composition: 91.67% Au, 8.33% Ag
Gold content: 15.55 g, 0.5 tr oz
Silver content: 1.413 g, 0.045 tr oz
Weight: 16.965 g   **Edge:** Lettered
Diameter: 27.0 mm   **Die Axis:** ↑↑
Thickness: 2.2 mm   **Finish:** Proof
Case: Brown leatherette case, brown flocked
            insert, plastic coin holder, COA

DATE	DESCRIPTION	QUANTITY SOLD	ISSUE PRICE	FINISH	PR-67	PR-68
1983	Gilbert's Landing in Newfoundland	83,128	310.00	Proof	800.	825.

ONE HUNDRED DOLLARS, JACQUES CARTIER'S VOYAGE OF DISCOVERY, 1984.

The $100 gold coin for 1984 commemorates Cartier's landing at Gaspé, Bonaventure in 1534. The reverse portrays a profile of Jacques Cartier and a ship of his era. Arnold Machin's effigy of Her Majesty Queen Elizabeth II is continued. The edge security lettering of 1983 was not continued in 1984.

Designers and Engravers:
    Obv.: Arnold Machin, RCM Staff
    Rev.: Carola Tietz, Walter Ott
Composition: 91.67% Au, 8.33% Ag
Gold content: 15.55 g, 0.5 tr oz
Silver content: 1.413 g, 0.045 tr oz
Weight: 16.965 g   **Edge:** Reeded
Diameter: 27.0 mm   **Die Axis:** ↑↑
Thickness: 2.2 mm   **Finish:** Proof
Case: Brown leatherette case, brown flocked
            insert, plastic coin holder, COA

DATE	DESCRIPTION	QUANTITY SOLD	ISSUE PRICE	FINISH	PR-67	PR-68
1984	Jacques Cartier's Voyage of Discovery	67,662	325.00	Proof	800.	825.

ONE HUNDRED DOLLARS, NATIONAL PARKS CENTENARY, 1985.

The $100 gold coin of 1985 commemorates the centennial of an important part of Canada's heritage, the National Parks. The reverse of the coin portrays a bighorn sheep poised on a cliff in the Canadian Rockies.

Designers and Engravers:
    Obv.: Arnold Machin, RCM Staff
    Rev.: Hector Greville, Walter Ott
Composition: 91.67% Au, 8.33% Ag
Gold content: 15.55 g, 0.5 tr oz
Silver content: 1.413 g, 0.045 tr oz
Weight: 16.965 g   **Edge:** Reeded
Diameter: 27.0 mm   **Die Axis:** ↑↑
Thickness: 2.2 mm   **Finish:** Proof
Case: Brown leatherette book type case with
            maple leaf emblem, beige satin interior,
            encapsulated coin. All enclosed in a brown
            plastic box

DATE	DESCRIPTION	QUANTITY SOLD	ISSUE PRICE	FINISH	PR-67	PR-68
1985	National Parks Centenary	58,520	325.00	Proof	800.	825.

ONE HUNDRED DOLLARS, INTERNATIONAL YEAR OF PEACE, 1986.

The $100 gold coin for 1986 signifies Canada's support for world peace. The reverse depicts a branch of maple leaves intertwined with a branch of olive leaves, symbols of Canada and Peace coming together. The words "Peace-Paix" forming a circle are superimposed on the design.

Designers and Engravers:
Obv.: Arnold Machin, RCM Staff
Rev.: Dora de Pédery-Hunt
Composition: 91.67% Au, 8.33% Ag
Gold content: 15.55 g, 0.5 tr oz
Silver content: 1.413 g, 0.045 tr oz
Weight: 16.965 g   **Edge:** Reeded
Diameter: 27.0 mm   **Die Axis:** ↑↑
Thickness: 2.2 mm   **Finish:** Proof

Case: Brown leatherette book type case with maple leaf emblem, beige satin interior, encapsulated coin. All enclosed in a brown plastic box

DATE	DESCRIPTION	QUANTITY SOLD	ISSUE PRICE	FINISH	PR-67	PR-68
1986	International Year of Peace	76,255	325.00	Proof	800.	825.

ONE HUNDRED DOLLARS, XV OLYMPIC WINTER GAMES, 1987.

The $100 gold coin for 1987 commemorates the XV Olympic Winter Games held in Calgary in 1988. The reverse portrays a hand holding the Olympic Torch with a stylized flame forming an image of the Canadian Rocky Mountains. This is the second $100 gold coin to have a lettered edge. The inscription reads "XV Olympic Winter Games - XVes Jeux Olympiques D'Hiver."

Designers and Engravers:
Obv.: Arnold Machin, RCM Staff
Rev.: Friedrich Peter, Ago Aarand
Composition: 58.33% Au, 41.67% Ag
Gold content: 7.78 g, 0.25 tr oz
Silver content: 5.56 g, 0.179 tr oz
Weight: 13.338 g   **Edge:** Lettered
Diameter: 27.0 mm   **Die Axis:** ↑↑
Thickness: 2.2 mm   **Finish:** Proof

Case: Brown leatherette book type case with maple leaf emblem, beige satin interior, encapsulated coin. All enclosed in a brown plastic box

DATE	DESCRIPTION	QUANTITY SOLD	ISSUE PRICE	FINISH	PR-67	PR-68
1987	XV Olympic Winter Games, With edge lettering	145,175	255.00	Proof	400.	425.
1987	XV Olympic Winter Games, Without edge lettering	Incl. above	255.00	Proof	2,500.	3,000.

ONE HUNDRED DOLLARS, THE BOWHEAD WHALE (BALAENA MYSTICETUS), 1988.

The $100 gold coin for 1988 celebrates a precious national treasure, the Bowhead whale. The reverse of this coin portrays a bowhead whale and her calf enclosed in a circle.

Designers and Engravers:
Obv.: Arnold Machin, RCM Staff
Rev.: Robert R. Carmichael, Ago Aarand
Composition: 58.33% Au, 41.67% Ag
Gold content: 7.78 g, 0.25 tr oz
Silver content: 5.56 g, 0.179 tr oz
Weight: 13.338 g   **Edge:** Lettered
Diameter: 27.0 mm   **Die Axis:** ↑↑
Thickness: 2.2 mm   **Finish:** Proof

Case: Brown leatherette book type case with maple leaf emblem, beige satin interior, encapsulated coin. All enclosed in a brown plastic box

DATE	DESCRIPTION	QUANTITY SOLD	ISSUE PRICE	FINISH	PR-67	PR-68
1988	Bowhead Whale (Balaena Mysticetus)	52,239	255.00	Proof	400.	425.

ONE HUNDRED DOLLARS, SAINTE-MARIE, 1639-1989.

In 1639 the French Jesuits founded a fortified mission village near Midland, Ontario, which they named Sainte-Marie among the Hurons. The year 1989 was the 350th anniversary of this first self-sufficient settlement in Ontario, where one-fifth of the European population of Canada once lived.

Designers and Engravers:
Obv.: Arnold Machin, Patrick Brindley
Rev.: David Craig Ago Aarand
Composition: 58.33% Au, 41.67% Ag
Gold content: 7.78 g, 0.25 tr oz
Silver content: 5.56 g, 0.179 tr oz
Weight: 13.338 g   **Edge:** Lettered
Diameter: 27.0 mm   **Die Axis:** ↑↑
Thickness: 2.2 mm   **Finish:** Proof

Case: Brown leatherette book type case with maple leaf emblem, beige satin interior, encapsulated coin.
All enclosed in a brown plastic box

DATE	DESCRIPTION	QUANTITY SOLD	ISSUE PRICE	FINISH	PR-67	PR-68
1989 (1639-)	Sainte-Marie	63,881	245.00	Proof	400.	425.

ONE HUNDRED DOLLARS, INTERNATIONAL LITERACY YEAR, 1990.

The General Assembly of the United Nations declared 1990 as the International Year of Literacy, setting the stage for the eradication of illiteracy around the world by the year 2000.

Designers and Engravers:
Obv.: Dora de Pédery-Hunt
Rev.: John Mardon, Ago Aarand, Susan Taylor
Composition: 58.33% Au, 41.67% Ag
Gold content: 7.78 g, 0.25 tr oz
Silver content: 5.56 g, 0.179 tr oz
Weight: 13.338 g   **Edge:** Lettered
Diameter: 27.0 mm   **Die Axis:** ↑↑
Thickness: 2.2 mm   **Finish:** Proof

Case: Brown leatherette book type case with maple leaf emblem, beige satin interior, encapsulated coin.
All enclosed in a brown plastic box

DATE	DESCRIPTION	QUANTITY SOLD	ISSUE PRICE	FINISH	PR-67	PR-68
1990	International Literacy Year	49,940	245.00	Proof	400.	425.

ONE HUNDRED DOLLARS, EMPRESS OF INDIA, 1991.

This coin commemorates the 100th anniversary of the *Empress of India*'s first arrival in Vancouver from Yokohama, Japan. The Canadian Pacific's trans-Pacific Empress ships were among the world's first cruise ships.

Designers and Engravers:
Obv.: Dora de Pédery-Hunt
Rev.: Karsten Smith, S. Beveridge
Composition: 58.33% Au, 41.67% Ag
Gold content: 7.78 g, 0.25 tr oz
Silver content: 5.56 g, 0.179 tr oz
Weight: 13.338 g   **Edge:** Lettered
Diameter: 27.0 mm   **Die Axis:** ↑↑
Thickness: 2.2 mm   **Finish:** Proof

Case: Brown leatherette book type case with maple leaf emblem, beige satin interior, encapsulated coin.
All enclosed in a brown plastic box

DATE	DESCRIPTION	QUANTITY SOLD	ISSUE PRICE	FINISH	PR-67	PR-68
1991	Empress of India	33,966	245.00	Proof	400.	425.

ONE HUNDRED DOLLARS, CITY OF MONTREAL, 350TH ANNIVERSARY, 1642-1992.

On May 17, 1642, three vessels arrived from France landing Maisonneuve and his men on an island in the St. Lawrence River. They called the island Ville-Marie which was renamed Montreal in the early 1700s.

Designers and Engravers:
Obv.: Dora de Pédery-Hunt
Rev.: S. Sherwood, A. Aarand, C. Saffioti
Composition: 58.33% Au, 41.67% Ag
Gold content: 7.78 g, 0.25 tr oz
Silver content: 5.56 g, 0.179 tr oz
Weight: 13.338 g   **Edge:** Lettered
Diameter: 27.0 mm   **Die Axis:** ↑↑
Thickness: 2.2 mm   **Finish:** Proof

Case: Brown leatherette book type case with maple leaf emblem, beige satin interior, encapsulated coin. All enclosed in a brown plastic box

DATE	DESCRIPTION	QUANTITY SOLD	ISSUE PRICE	FINISH	PR-67	PR-68
1992 (1642-)	City of Montreal, 350th Anniversary	28,190	239.85	Proof	400.	425.

ONE HUNDRED DOLLARS, 1893 THE ERA OF THE HORSELESS CARRIAGE, 1993.

The five vehicles pictured on the reverse of the 1993 gold coin are, clockwise from the left, the French Panhard-Levassor's Daimler, the American Duryea, the German Benz Victoria, the Simmonds Steam Carriage and, in the centre, the first Canadian built electric car, the Featherstonhaugh.

Designers and Engravers:
Obv.: Dora de Pédery-Hunt
Rev.: John Mardon, Ago Aarand,
William Woodruff
Composition: 58.33% Au, 41.67% Ag
Gold content: 7.78 g, 0.25 tr oz
Weight: 13.338 g   **Edge:** Lettered
Diameter: 27.0 mm   **Die Axis:** ↑↑
Thickness: 2.2 mm   **Finish:** Proof

Case: Brown leatherette book type case with maple leaf emblem, beige satin interior, encapsulated coin. All enclosed in a brown plastic box

DATE	DESCRIPTION	QUANTITY SOLD	ISSUE PRICE	FINISH	PR-67	PR-68
1993	The Horseless Carriage	25,971	239.85	Proof	400.	425.

ONE HUNDRED DOLLARS, THE HOME FRONT, 1994.

The 1994 $100 gold coin is part of the Remembrance and Peace Issue. The design was taken from a 1945 painting by P. Clark, entitled "Maintenance Jobs in the Hangar."

Designers and Engravers:
Obv.: Dora de Pédery-Hunt
Rev.: P. Clark, Susan Taylor, Ago Aarand
Composition: 58.33% Au, 41.67% Ag
Gold content: 7.78 g, 0.25 tr oz
Weight: 13.338 g   **Edge:** Lettered
Diameter: 27.0 mm   **Die Axis:** ↑↑
Thickness: 2.2 mm   **Finish:** Proof

Case: Brown leatherette book type case with maple leaf emblem, beige satin interior, encapsulated coin. All enclosed in a brown plastic box

DATE	DESCRIPTION	QUANTITY SOLD	ISSUE PRICE	FINISH	PR-67	PR-68
1994	The Home Front	17,603	249.95	Proof	400.	425.

ONE HUNDRED DOLLARS, 275TH ANNIVERSARY OF THE FOUNDING OF LOUISBOURG, 1995.

Louisbourg, built in 1720 as a strategic centre for the French military in North America, is commemorated on the $100 gold coin of 1995.

Designers and Engravers:
Obv.: Dora de Pédery-Hunt
Rev.: Lewis Parker, Sheldon Beveridge
Composition: 58.33% Au, 41.67% Ag
Gold content: 7.78 g, 0.25 tr oz
Silver content: 5.56 g, 0.179 tr oz
Weight: 13.338 g   **Edge:** Lettered
Diameter: 27.0 mm   **Die Axis:** ↑↑
Thickness: 2.2 mm   **Finish:** Proof

Case: Brown leatherette book type case with maple leaf emblem, beige satin interior, encapsulated coin.
All enclosed in a brown plastic box

DATE	DESCRIPTION	QUANTITY SOLD	ISSUE PRICE	FINISH	PR-67	PR-68
1995	275th Anniv. Founding of Louisbourg	16,916	249.95	Proof	400.	425.

ONE HUNDRED DOLLARS, 100TH ANNIVERSARY OF THE FIRST MAJOR GOLD DISCOVERY IN THE KLONDIKE, 1996.

In 1896 the Gold Rush began when George and Kate Carmack, Skookum Jim and Dawson Charlie made the Klondike's first major gold find. The year 1996 was the last in which $100 gold coins were packaged in the book-type cases.

Designers and Engravers:
Obv.: Dora de Pédery-Hunt
Rev.: John Mantha, Cosme Saffioti
Composition: 58.33%   Au, 41.67% Ag
Gold content: 7.78 g, 0.25 tr oz
Silver content: 5.56 g, 0.179 tr oz
Weight: 13.338 g   **Edge:** Lettered
Diameter: 27.0 mm   **Die Axis:** ↑↑
Thickness: 2.2 mm   **Finish:** Proof

Case: Brown leatherette book type case with maple leaf emblem, beige satin interior, encapsulated coin.
All enclosed in a brown plastic box

DATE	DESCRIPTION	QUANTITY SOLD	ISSUE PRICE	FINISH	PR-67	PR-68
1996	100th Anniv. Gold Discovery in the Klondike	17,973	259.95	Proof	400.	425.

ONE HUNDRED DOLLARS, 150TH ANNIVERSARY OF ALEXANDER GRAHAM BELL'S BIRTH, 1997.

The $100 gold coin of 1997 honours the creative genius of Alexander Graham Bell. He was born in Scotland in 1847. In 1874, while in Ontario, he carried out the experiments that led to the invention of the telephone. The $100 gold coin was offered for the first time with an optional case.

Designers and Engravers:
Obv.: Dora de Pédery-Hunt
Rev.: D. H. Curley, S. Beveridge
Composition: 58.33% Au, 41.67% Ag
Gold content: 7.78 g, 0.25 tr oz
Silver content: 5.56 g, 0.179 tr oz
Weight: 13.338 g   **Edge:** Lettered
Diameter: 27.0 mm   **Die Axis:** ↑↑
Thickness: 2.2 mm   **Finish:** Proof

Case: Black suede clam type case, black suede interior, encapsulated coin

DATE	DESCRIPTION	QUANTITY SOLD	ISSUE PRICE	FINISH	PR-67	PR-68
1997	150th Anniv. of Alexander Graham Bell's Birth	14,030	254.95	Proof	400.	425.

ONE HUNDRED DOLLARS, 75TH ANNIVERSARY OF THE NOBEL PRIZE FOR THE DISCOVERY OF INSULIN, 1998.

The discovery of insulin by Frederick Banting and John Macleod earned them the Nobel Prize for Physiology and Medicine, in 1923.

Designers and Engravers:
Obv.: Dora de Pédery-Hunt
Rev.: Robert R. Carmichael, Stan Witten
Composition: 58.33% Au, 41.67% Ag
Gold content: 7.78 g, 0.25 tr oz
Silver content: 5.56 g, 0.179 tr oz
Weight: 13.338 g   **Edge:** Lettered
Diameter: 27.0 mm   **Die Axis:** ↑↑
Thickness: 2.2 mm   **Finish:** Proof
Case: Black suede clam type case, black suede interior, encapsulated coin

DATE	DESCRIPTION	QUANTITY SOLD	ISSUE PRICE	FINISH	PR-67	PR-68
1998	75th Anniv. Nobel Prize Discovery Insulin	11,220	254.95	Proof	400.	425.

ONE HUNDRED DOLLARS, 50TH ANNIVERSARY OF NEWFOUNDLAND'S CONFEDERATION WITH CANADA IN 1949, 1999.

The 50th anniversary of Newfoundland's union with Canada on March 31, 1949 is celebrated on the 1999 $100 gold coin.

Designers and Engravers:
Obv.: Dora de Pédery-Hunt
Rev.: J. Gale-Vaillancourt, William Woodruff
Composition: 58.33% Au, 41.67% Ag
Gold content: 7.78 g, 0.25 tr oz
Silver content: 5.56 g, 0.179 tr oz
Weight: 13.338 g   **Edge:** Lettered
Diameter: 27.0 mm   **Die Axis:** ↑↑
Thickness: 2.2 mm   **Finish:** Proof
Case: Black suede clam type case, black suede interior, encapsulated coin

DATE	DESCRIPTION	QUANTITY SOLD	ISSUE PRICE	FINISH	PR-67	PR-68
1999	50th Anniv. Newfoundland's Confederation	10,242	254.95	Proof	400.	425.

ONE HUNDRED DOLLARS, 150TH ANNIVERSARY OF THE SEARCH FOR THE NORTHWEST PASSAGE IN 1850, 2000.

The Franklin Expedition, which was lost on its voyage to discover a Northwest passage to the far East, is commemorated on the gold coin for 2000.

Designers and Engravers:
Obv.: Dora de Pédery-Hunt
Rev.: John Mardon, Stan Witten
Composition: 58.33% Au, 41.67% Ag
Gold content: 7.78 g, 0.25 tr oz
Silver content: 5.56 g, 0.179 tr oz
Weight: 13.338 g   **Edge:** Lettered
Diameter: 27.0 mm   **Die Axis:** ↑↑
Thickness: 2.2 mm   **Finish:** Proof
Case: Metal presentation case, wooden insert, COA

DATE	DESCRIPTION	QUANTITY SOLD	ISSUE PRICE	FINISH	PR-67	PR-68
2000	150th Anniv. Search for NW Passage	10,547	254.95	Proof	400.	425.

ONE HUNDRED DOLLARS, 125TH ANNIVERSARY OF THE LIBRARY OF PARLIAMENT, 2001.

The Library of Parliament is one of the most famous symbols of the Canadian Confederation. "This beautiful building is an architectural marvel, and a treasure for all Canadians to cherish."

Designers and Engravers:
   Obv.: Dora de Pédery-Hunt
   Rev.: R.R. Carmichael, S. Taylor, W. Woodruff
Composition: 58.33% Au, 41.67% Ag
Gold content: 7.78 g, 0.25 tr oz
Silver content: 5.56 g, 0.179 tr oz
Weight: 13.338 g   **Edge:** Lettered
Diameter: 27.0 mm   **Die Axis:** ↑↑
Thickness: 2.2 mm   **Finish:** Proof
Case: Metal presentation case, wooden insert, COA

DATE	DESCRIPTION	QUANTITY SOLD	ISSUE PRICE	FINISH	PR-67	PR-68
2001	125th Anniv. Library of Parliament	8,080	260.95	Proof	400.	425.

ONE HUNDRED DOLLARS, COMMEMORATING CANADA'S OIL INDUSTRY, 2002.

This coin commemorates the major economic importance of oil to the Canadian economy and Canada's place as one of the major oil producers of the world. The sea of 'black gold' at the foot of the oil rig commemorates the major discovery of the Leduc oil field on February 13, 1947.

Designers and Engravers:
   Obv.: Dora de Pédery-Hunt
   Rev.: John Mardon, Stan Witten
Composition: 58.33% Au, 41.67% Ag, Painted
Gold content: 7.78 g, 0.25 tr oz
Silver content: 5.56 g, 0.179 tr oz
Weight: 13.338 g   **Edge:** Lettered
Diameter: 27.0 mm   **Die Axis:** ↑↑
Thickness: 2.2 mm   **Finish:** Proof
Case: Metal presentation case, wooden insert, COA

DATE	DESCRIPTION	QUANTITY SOLD	ISSUE PRICE	FINISH	PR-67	PR-68
2002	Canada's Oil Industry	9,994	260.95	Proof	450.	475.

ONE HUNDRED DOLLARS, 100TH ANNIVERSARY OF DISCOVERY OF MARQUIS WHEAT, 2003.

After 10 years of experiments Dr. William Saunders and his sons Percy and Charles discovered the marquis wheat variety, making Canada forever known as the world's bread basket.

Designers and Engravers:
   Obv.: Dora de Pédery-Hunt
   Rev.: Thom Nelson, Stan Witten
Composition: 58.33% Au, 41.67% Ag, Painted
Gold content: 7.78 g, 0.25 tr oz
Silver content: 5.56 g, 0.179 tr oz
Weight: 13.338 g   **Edge:** Lettered
Diameter: 27.0 mm   **Die Axis:** ↑↑
Thickness: 2.2 mm   **Finish:** Proof
Case: Metal presentation case, wooden insert, COA

DATE	DESCRIPTION	QUANTITY SOLD	ISSUE PRICE	FINISH	PR-67	PR-68
2003	100th Anniv. Discovery Marquis Wheat	9,993	277.95	Proof	400.	425.

ONE HUNDRED DOLLARS, 50TH ANNIVERSARY OF THE COMMENCEMENT OF THE ST. LAWRENCE SEAWAY CONSTRUCTION, 2004.

The $100 gold for 2004 commemorates the commencement of the construction of the St. Lawrence Seaway. On August 10, 1954, a sod turning ceremony signalled the start of a mammoth project by Canada and the United States.

Designers and Engravers:
Obv.: Susanna Blunt, Susan Taylor
Rev.: John Mardon, José Osio
Composition: 58.33% Au, 41.67% Ag
Gold content: 7.0 g, 0.225 tr oz
Silver content: 5.0 g, 0.16 tr oz
Weight: 12.0 g   **Edge:** Reeded
Diameter: 27.0 mm   **Die Axis:** ↑↑
Thickness: 2.2 mm   **Finish:** Proof
Case: Metal presentation case, wooden insert, COA

DATE	DESCRIPTION	QUANTITY SOLD	ISSUE PRICE	FINISH	PR-67	PR-68
2004	50th Anniv., St. Lawrence Seaway	7,454	277.95	Proof	375.	400.

ONE HUNDRED DOLLARS, 130TH ANNIVERSARY OF THE SUPREME COURT OF CANADA, 2005.

On April 8, 1875, Canada's "Court of Last Resort" was founded. It has been an essential component of Canadian justice for 130 years. The 2004 $100 gold coin celebrates the 130th anniversary of the Supreme Court of Canada.

Designers and Engravers:
Obv.: Susanna Blunt, Susan Taylor
Rev.: S. Duranceau, José Osio
Composition: 58.33% Au, 41.67% Ag, Painted
Gold content: 7.0 g, 0.225 tr oz
Silver content: 5.0 g, 0.16 tr oz
Weight: 12.0 g   **Edge:** Reeded
Diameter: 27.0 mm   **Die Axis:** ↑↑
Thickness: 2.2 mm   **Finish:** Proof
Case: Maroon plastic case, black plastic insert, encapsulated coin, COA

DATE	DESCRIPTION	QUANTITY SOLD	ISSUE PRICE	FINISH	PR-67	PR-68
2005	130th Anniv. Supreme Court Canada	5,092	289.95	Proof	375.	400.

ONE HUNDRED DOLLARS, 75TH GAME, WORLD'S LONGEST HOCKEY SERIES, 2006.

The 2006 $100 gold coin celebrates the 75th anniversary of the world's longest running international hockey series between the Royal Military College in Kingston, Ontario and the Military Academy in West Point, New York.

Designers and Engravers:
Obv.: Susanna Blunt, Susan Taylor
Rev.: Tony Bianco, K. Wachelko
Composition: 58.33% Au, 41.67% Ag, Painted
Gold content: 7.0 g, 0.225 tr oz
Silver content: 5.0 g, 0.16 tr oz
Weight: 12.0 g   **Edge:** Reeded
Diameter: 27.0 mm   **Die Axis:** ↑↑
Thickness: 2.2 mm   **Finish:** Proof
Case: Maroon plastic case, black plastic insert, encapsulated coin, COA

DATE	DESCRIPTION	QUANTITY SOLD	ISSUE PRICE	FINISH	PR-67	PR-68
2006	75th Game, World's Longest Hockey Series	5,439	329.95	Proof	375.	400.

ONE HUNDRED DOLLARS, 140TH ANNIVERSARY OF THE DOMINION OF CANADA, 2007.

The 2007 $100 gold coin celebrates the 140th anniversary of the Dominion of Canada.

Designers and Engravers:
Obv.: Susanna Blunt, Susan Taylor
Rev.: Bonnie Ross, Susan Taylor
Composition: 58.33% Au, 41.67% Ag
Gold content: 7.0 g, 0.225 tr oz
Silver content: 5.0 g, 0.16 tr oz
Weight: 12.0 g   **Edge:** Reeded
Diameter: 27.0 mm   **Die Axis:** ↑↑
Thickness: 2.2 mm   **Finish:** Proof
Case: Maroon leatherette clam style case, black flocked insert, encapsulated coin, COA

DATE	DESCRIPTION	QUANTITY SOLD	ISSUE PRICE	FINISH	PR-67	PR-68
2007	140th Anniversary, Dominion of Canada	4,453	369.95	Proof	375.	400.

ONE HUNDRED DOLLARS, 200TH ANNIVERSARY, DESCENDING FRASER RIVER, 2008.

The Fraser River is named for Simon Fraser who on behalf of the North West Company descended the river from a point in the vicinity of Prince Rupert to its mouth at Vancouver. This one hundred dollar gold coin commemorates Fraser's journey in 1808.

Designers and Engravers:
Obv.: Susanna Blunt, Susan Taylor
Rev.: John Mantha, Christie Paquet
Composition: 58.33% Au, 41.67% Ag
Gold content: 7.00 g, 0.225 tr oz
Silver content: 5.00 g, 0.16 tr oz
Weight: 12.0 g   **Edge:** Reeded
Diameter: 27.0 mm   **Die Axis:** ↑↑
Thickness: 2.2 mm   **Finish:** Proof
Case: Maroon leatherette clam style case, black flocked insert, encapsulated coin, COA

DATE	DESCRIPTION	QUANTITY SOLD	ISSUE PRICE	FINISH	PR-67	PR-68
2008	200th Anniversary, Descending Fraser River	3,089	386.95	Proof	400.	425.

ONE HUNDRED DOLLARS, 10TH ANNIVERSARY OF NUNAVUT, 2009.

On April 1st, 1999, Nunavut, Canada's youngest territory, was formed. In 2009 we celebrated the 10th anniversary of its formation.

Designers and Engravers:
Obv.: Susanna Blunt, Susan Taylor
Rev.: Andrew Qappik, Susan Taylor
Composition: 58.33% Au, 41.67% Ag
Gold content: 7.0 g, 0.225 tr oz
Silver content: 5.0 g, 0.16 tr oz
Weight: 12.0 g   **Edge:** Reeded
Diameter: 27.0 mm   **Die Axis:** ↑↑
Thickness: 2.2 mm   **Finish:** Proof
Case: Maroon leatherette clam style case, black flocked insert, encapsulated coin, COA

DATE	DESCRIPTION	QUANTITY SOLD	ISSUE PRICE	FINISH	PR-67	PR-68
2009	10th Anniversary of Nunavut	2,309	509.95	Proof	525.	550.

ONE HUNDRED DOLLARS, 400TH ANNIVERSARY OF THE DISCOVERY OF THE HUDSON'S BAY, 2010.

In 1610 Henry Hudson an English navigator and explorer, on his fourth voyage to discover a passage from Europe to the Far East through the Arctic passage, sailed into the world's second largest bay (Hudson's Bay).

In November 1610, Hudson's ship *Discovery* was locked in ice, and in June 1611, Hudson along with eight other crewmen was set adrift in a small boat by a mutinous crew. Hudson perished. The Hudson's Bay is named after him.

Designers and Engravers:
    Obv.: Susanna Blunt, Susan Taylor
    Rev.: John Mantha, Susan Taylor
Composition: 58.33% Au, 41.67% Ag
Gold content: 7.0 g, 0.225 tr oz
Silver content: 5.0 g, 0.16 tr oz
Weight: 12.0 g   **Edge:** Reeded
Diameter: 27.0 mm   **Die Axis:** ↑↑
Thickness: 2.2 mm   **Finish:** Proof
Case: Maroon leatherette clam style case, black flocked insert, encapsulated coin, COA

DATE	DESCRIPTION	QUANTITY SOLD	ISSUE PRICE	FINISH	PR-67	PR-68
2010	400th Anniversary, Discovery of Hudson's Bay	2,133	589.95	Proof	600.	625.

ONE HUNDRED DOLLARS, 175TH ANNIVERSARY CANADA'S FIRST RAIL ROAD, 2011.

The Champlain and St. Lawrence Rail Road was opened in July 21st, 1836 by Lord Gosford, the Lieutenant-Governor of Lower Canada. The 16-mile line ran between Laprairie and St-Jean in Lower Canada.

Designers and Engravers:
    Obv.: Susanna Blunt, Susan Taylor
    Rev.: Konrad Wachelko based on the painting *Dorchester* by Canadian artist J.D. Kelly courtesy Rogers Communications Inc.
Composition: 58.33% Au, 41.67% Ag, Painted
Gold content: 7.0 g, 0.225 tr oz
Silver content: 5.0 g, 0.16 tr oz
Weight: 12.0 g   **Edge:** Reeded
Diameter: 27.0 mm   **Die Axis:** ↑↑
Thickness: 2.2 mm   **Finish:** Proof
Case: Maroon leatherette clam style case, black flocked insert, encapsulated coin, COA

DATE	DESCRIPTION	QUANTITY SOLD	ISSUE PRICE	FINISH	PR-67	PR-68
2011	175th Anniv. Canada's First Rail Road	2,283	639.95	Proof	650.	675.

ONE HUNDRED DOLLARS, 150TH ANNIVERSARY OF THE CARIBOU GOLD RUSH, 2012.

Beginning in 1858 a gold rush began in British Columbia's Caribou region. Before the rush faded nearly 2.6 million ounces of gold were extracted between 1858 and 1898.

Designers and Engravers:
    Obv.: Susanna Blunt, Susan Taylor
    Rev.: Tony Bianco, RCM Staff
Composition: 58.33% Au, 41.67% Ag, Painted
Gold content: 7.0 g, 0.225 tr oz
Silver content: 5.0 g, 0.16 tr oz
Weight: 12.0 g   **Edge:** Reeded
Diameter: 27.0 mm   **Die Axis:** ↑↑
Thickness: 1.9 mm   **Finish:** Proof
Case: Maroon leatherette clam style case, black flocked insert, encapsulated coin, COA

DATE	DESCRIPTION	QUANTITY SOLD	ISSUE PRICE	FINISH	PR-67	PR-68
2012	150th Anniv. of the Caribou Gold Rush	2,488	599.95	Proof	600.	625.

ONE HUNDRED DOLLARS, 100TH ANNIVERSARY OF THE CANADIAN ARCTIC EXPEDITION, 2013.

In 1913 an international crew of scientists, sailors, guides and crewmen called the Canadian Arctic Expedition sailed on a remarkable five-year voyage of discovery in Canada's high Arctic.

Designers and Engravers:
    Obv.: Susanna Blunt, Susan Taylor
    Rev.: Bonnie Ross, Konrad Wachelko
Composition: 58.33% Au, 41.67% Ag
Gold content: 7.0 g, 0.225 tr oz
Silver content: 5.0 g, 0.16 tr oz
Weight: 12.0 g   **Edge:** Reeded
Diameter: 27.0 mm   **Die Axis:** ↑↑
Thickness: 1.9 mm   **Finish:** Proof
Case: Maroon leatherette clam style case, black flocked insert, encapsulated coin, COA

DATE	DESCRIPTION	QUANTITY SOLD	ISSUE PRICE	FINISH	PR-67	PR-68
2013 (1913-)	100th Anniv. of the Canadian Arctic Expedition	1,937	599.95	Proof	600.	625.

ONE HUNDRED DOLLARS, 150TH ANNIVERSARY OF THE QUEBEC AND CHARLOTTETOWN CONFERENCE, 2014.

The Quebec and Charlottetown Conference was held in 1864 as a prelude to Confederation in 1867.

Designers and Engravers:
    Obv.: Susanna Blunt, Susan Taylor
    Rev.: Luc Normandin, RCM Staff
Composition: 58.33% Au, 41.67% Ag
Gold content: 7.0 g, 0.225 tr oz
Silver content: 5.0 g, 0.16 tr oz
Weight: 12.0 g   **Edge:** Reeded
Diameter: 27.0 mm   **Die Axis:** ↑↑
Thickness: 1.9 mm   **Finish:** Proof
Case: Maroon leatherette clam style case, black flocked insert, encapsulated coin, COA

DATE	DESCRIPTION	QUANTITY SOLD	ISSUE PRICE	FINISH	PR-67	PR-68
2014	150th Anniv. Quebec & Charlottetown Conference	2,500	599.95	Proof	600.	625.

ONE HUNDRED FIFTY DOLLAR GOLD COINS

ONE HUNDRED FIFTY DOLLARS, GOLD HOLOGRAM COINS, 2000-2011.

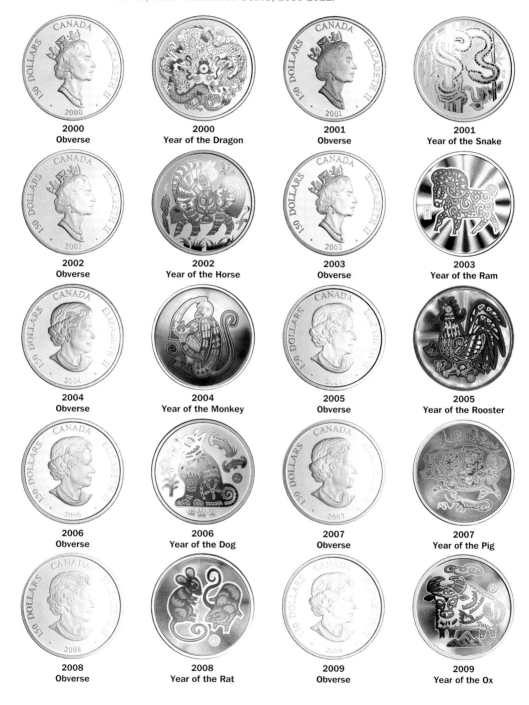

2000 Obverse	**2000** Year of the Dragon	**2001** Obverse	**2001** Year of the Snake
2002 Obverse	**2002** Year of the Horse	**2003** Obverse	**2003** Year of the Ram
2004 Obverse	**2004** Year of the Monkey	**2005** Obverse	**2005** Year of the Rooster
2006 Obverse	**2006** Year of the Dog	**2007** Obverse	**2007** Year of the Pig
2008 Obverse	**2008** Year of the Rat	**2009** Obverse	**2009** Year of the Ox

ONE HUNDRED FIFTY DOLLARS, GOLD HOLOGRAM COINS, 2000-2011 (cont.)

| 2010 Obverse | 2010 Year of the Tiger | 2011 Obverse | 2011 Year of the Rabbit |

Designers:
2000-2003   Obv.: Dora de Pédery-Hunt
2004-2011   Obv.: Susanna Blunt, Susan Taylor

Engravers:
Rev.: Harvey Chan, RCM Staff
Rev.: Harvey Chan, RCM Staff

Composition: 75.0% Au, 25.0% Ag, Hologram
Gold content:
2000-2003   10.20 g, 0.328 tr oz
2004-2011   8.88g, 0.285 tr oz
Weight:
2000-2003   13.61 g
2004-2011   11.84 g
Diameter: 28.0 mm
Thickness: 1.5 to 1.8 mm
Edge: Reeded
Die Axis: ↑↑
Finish: Proof
Case of Issue: Gold satin case, taupe flocked insert, encapsulated coin, COA

Silver Content:
2000-2003   3.40 g, 0.109 tr oz
2004-2011   2.96 g, 0.095 tr oz

DATE	DESCRIPTION	QUANTITY SOLD	ISSUE PRICE	FINISH	PR-67	PR-68
2000	Year of the Dragon, Hologram	8,874	388.88	Proof	850.	900.
2001	Year of the Snake, Hologram	6,571	388.88	Proof	575.	600.
2002	Year of the Horse, Hologram	6,843	388.88	Proof	575.	600.
2003	Year of the Ram, Hologram	3,927	398.88	Proof	575.	600.
2004	Year of the Monkey, Hologram	3,392	398.88	Proof	575.	600.
2005	Year of the Rooster, Hologram	3,731	398.88	Proof	575.	600.
2006	Year of the Dog, Hologram	2,609	448.88	Proof	575.	600.
2007	Year of the Pig, Hologram	826	498.95	Proof	575.	600.
2008	Year of the Rat, Hologram	582	508.95	Proof	600.	625.
2009	Year of the Ox, Hologram	486	638.88	Proof	650.	675.
2010	Year of the Tiger, Hologram	1,507	555.55	Proof	675.	700.
2011	Year of the Rabbit, Hologram	4,888	638.88	Proof	675.	700.

Note: The mintage figures for 2007-2009 appear to be incorrect. There were no mintage figures reported in the 2010 Annual Report.

BLESSINGS SERIES

ONE HUNDRED FIFTY DOLLARS, BLESSINGS SERIES, 2009-2014.

In China blessings of wealth abound in a multitude of ancient symbols and artistic impressions, many of which are represented on these pure gold coins.

| Common Obverse | 2009 Blessings of Wealth Engr.: C. Paquet | 2010 Blessings of Strength Engr.: RCM Staff | 2011 Blessings of Happiness Engr.: C. Mok | 2012 Blessings of Good Fortune Engr.: RCM Staff |

| 2013 Blessings of Peace Engr.: RCM Staff | 2014 Blessings of Longevity Engr.: RCM Staff |

Designers:
Obv.: Susanna Blunt
Rev.: 2009-2011: Harvey Chan
2012: Three Degrees Creative Group Inc.
2013: Aries Cheung
2014: Charles Vinh

Engravers:
Obv.: Susan Taylor
Rev.: See reverse illustrations

Composition: 99.999% Au
Gold content: 10.4 g, 0.334 tr oz
Weight: 10.4 g
Diameter: 22.5 mm
Thickness: 1.8 mm

Edge: Plain
Die Axis: ↑↑
Finish: Proof

Case of Issue: Maroon leatherette clam style case, black flocked insert, encapsulated coin, COA

DATE	DESCRIPTION	QUANTITY SOLD	ISSUE PRICE	FINISH	PR-67	PR-68
2009	Blessings of Wealth	1,273	799.95	Proof	950.	1,000.
2010	Blessings of Strength	765	939.95	Proof	950.	1,000.
2011	Blessings of Happiness	880	988.88	Proof	1,100.	1,150.
2012	Blessings of Good Fortune	889	988.88	Proof	1,100.	1,150.
2013	Blessings of Peace	885	988.88	Proof	1,100.	1,150.
2014	Blessings of Longevity	888	988.88	Proof	1,100.	1,150.

CLASSIC CHINESE LUNAR SERIES

ONE HUNDRED FIFTY DOLLARS, CLASSIC CHINESE LUNAR SERIES. 2010-2021.
Identical designs are utilized on the Classic Chinese Lunar Series $15 silver coins (2010-2021), see page 195.

Common Obverse

Designers and Engravers:
    Obv.: Susanna Blunt, Susan Taylor
    Rev.: Aries Cheung, See reverse illustrations
Composition: 75.0% Au, 25.0% Ag
Gold content: 8.78 g, 0.282 tr oz   **Thickness:** 1.6 mm
Silver content: 2.92 g, 0.094 tr oz   **Edge:** Reeded
Weight: 11.70 g   **Die Axis:** ↑↑
Diameter: 28.0 mm
Finish: Proof
Case of Issue:
    Singly: Gold satin-like covered case, black flocked insert, encapsulated coin, COA.
    Set: Hardwood exterior with high-gloss finish and silk-screened paper. Interior has high-gloss finish in Chinese red with a silver design, wooden insert accommodates 12 coins.

2010	2011	2012	2013	2014
Year of the Tiger	Year of the Rabbit	Year of the Dragon	Year of the Snake	Year of the Horse
Engr.: Konrad Wachelko	Engr.: William Woodruff	Engr.: Stan Witten	Engr.: Stan Witten	Engr.: RCM Staff

DATE	DESCRIPTION	QUANTITY SOLD	ISSUE PRICE	FINISH	PR-67	PR-68
2010	Year of the Tiger	2,500	555.55	Proof	675.	700.
2011	Year of the Rabbit	2,500	638.88	Proof	675.	700.
2012	Year of the Dragon	1,430	688.88	Proof	700.	725.
2013	Year of the Snake	1,392	688.88	Proof	700.	725.
2014	Year of the Horse	1,428	688.88	Proof	700.	725.

WORLD BASEBALL CLASSIC SERIES

ONE HUNDRED FIFTY DOLLARS, CELEBRATE, WORLD BASEBALL CLASSIC SERIES, 2013.
These coins were issued to celebrate the World Baseball Classic Tournament held March 2nd to 19th, 2013. For other coins in this series see pages 227 and 278.

Designers and Engravers:
    Obv.: Susanna Blunt, Susan Taylor
    Rev.: Steve Hepburn, RCM Staff
Composition: 99.99% Au
Gold content: 15.59 g, 0.5 tr oz
Weight: 15.59 g   **Edge:** Reeded
Diameter: 25.0 mm   **Die Axis:** ↑↑
Thickness: 2.0 mm   **Finish:** Proof
Case of Issue: Maroon leatherette clam style case, black flocked insert, encapsulated coin, COA, Custom sleeve

DATE	DESCRIPTION	QUANTITY SOLD	ISSUE PRICE	FINISH	PR-67	PR-68
2013	Celebrate, World Baseball Classic	129	1,549.95	Proof	1,800.	1,850.

ONE HUNDRED SEVENTY-FIVE DOLLAR GOLD COIN

ONE HUNDRED SEVENTY-FIVE DOLLARS, 100TH ANNIVERSARY OF THE OLYMPIC MOVEMENT, 1992-1996.

Commemorating the 100th anniversary of the Olympic movement in 1996, Canada and four other countries, Australia, France, Austria and Greece, issued three-coin sets, consisting of one gold and two silver coins. One set was issued each year beginning with Canada's in 1992. See page 189 for the Royal Canadian Mint silver issues. Only the Royal Canadian Mint issued coins are listed in the Standard Catalogue.

Designers:
  Obv.: Dora de Pédery-Hunt
  Rev.: Stewart Sherwood
Composition: 91.67% Au, 8.33% Cu
Gold content: 15.556 g, 0.5 tr oz
Weight: 16.97 g
Diameter: 28.0 mm
Thickness: 2.0 mm
Case of Issue: Blue clam style case, black insert, encapsulated coin, COA

Engravers:
  Obv.: Dora de Pédery-Hunt
  Rev.: Ago Aarand

Edge: Lettering: Citius, altius, fortius
Die Axis: ↑↑
Finish: Proof

DATE	DESCRIPTION	QUANTITY SOLD	ISSUE PRICE	FINISH	PR-67	PR-68
1992	100th Anniversary of the Olympic Movement	22,092	429.75	Proof	800.	850.

TWO HUNDRED DOLLAR GOLD COINS

TWO HUNDRED DOLLARS, CANADA'S FLAG SILVER JUBILEE, 1990.

The 1990 $200 dollar coin commemorates the 25th anniversary of the proclamation approving Canada's flag.

Designers and Engravers:
Obv.: Dora de Pédery-Hunt
Rev.: Stewart Sherwood, Ago Aarand
Composition: 91.67% Au, 8.33% Ag
Gold content: 15.703 g, 0.505 tr oz
Silver content: 1.427 g, 0.046 tr oz
Weight: 17.13 g   **Edge:** Reeded
Diameter: 29.0 mm   **Die Axis:** ↑↑
Thickness: 2.0 mm   **Finish:** Proof
Case: Woven Jacquard case, black insert, encapsulated coin, COA

DATE	DESCRIPTION	QUANTITY SOLD	ISSUE PRICE	FINISH	PR-67	PR-68
1990	Canada's Flag Silver Jubilee	20,980	395.00	Proof	800.	825.

TWO HUNDRED DOLLARS, A NATIONAL PASSION, 1991.

The 1991 two hundred dollar proof gold coin was issued as a tribute to the spirit and vitality of Canadian youth and the national game of hockey.

Designers and Engravers:
Obv.: Dora de Pédery-Hunt
Rev.: Stewart Sherwood, Susan Taylor
Composition: 91.67% Au, 8.33% Ag
Gold content: 15.703 g, 0.505 tr oz
Silver content: 1.427 g, 0.046 tr oz
Weight: 17.13 g   **Edge:** Reeded
Diameter: 29.0 mm   **Die Axis:** ↑↑
Thickness: 2.0 mm   **Finish:** Proof
Case: Woven Jacquard case, black insert, encapsulated coin, COA

DATE	DESCRIPTION	QUANTITY SOLD	ISSUE PRICE	FINISH	PR-67	PR-68
1991	A National Passion	10,215	425.00	Proof	800.	825.

TWO HUNDRED DOLLARS, NIAGARA FALLS, 1992.

The 1992 two hundred dollar gold coin was issued as a tribute to the beauty and majesty of Niagara Falls. The reverse design features two children playing near the falls.

Designers and Engravers:
Obv.: Dora de Pédery-Hunt
Rev.: John Mardon, Susan Taylor
Composition: 91.67% Au, 8.33% Ag
Gold content: 15.703 g, 0.505 tr oz
Silver content: 1.427 g, 0.046 tr oz
Weight: 17.13 g   **Edge:** Reeded
Diameter: 29.0 mm   **Die Axis:** ↑↑
Thickness: 2.0 mm   **Finish:** Proof
Case: Woven Jacquard case, black insert, encapsulated coin, COA

DATE	DESCRIPTION	QUANTITY SOLD	ISSUE PRICE	FINISH	PR-67	PR-68
1992	Niagara Falls	9,465	389.65	Proof	800.	825.

TWO HUNDRED DOLLARS, ROYAL CANADIAN MOUNTED POLICE, 1993.
The 1993 issue of the two hundred dollar gold coin pays tribute to the unique contribution of the R.C.M.P. to Canadian history.

Designers and Engravers:
Obv.: Dora de Pédery-Hunt
Rev.: Stewart Sherwood, Susan Taylor
Composition: 91.67% Au, 8.33% Ag
Gold content: 15.703 g, 0.505 tr oz
Silver content: 1.427 g, 0.046 tr oz
Weight: 17.13 g **Edge:** Reeded
Diameter: 29.0 mm **Die Axis:** ↑↑
Thickness: 2.0 mm **Finish:** Proof
Case: Woven Jacquard case, black insert, encapsulated coin, COA

DATE	DESCRIPTION	QUANTITY SOLD	ISSUE PRICE	FINISH	PR-67	PR-68
1993	Royal Canadian Mounted Police	10,807	389.65	Proof	800.	825.

TWO HUNDRED DOLLARS, ANNE OF GREEN GABLES©, 1994.
Issued as a tribute to the famous character Anne in the novel by Canadian writer Lucy Maud Montgomery, this is the last coin in the youth and heritage series.

Designers and Engravers:
Obv.: Dora de Pédery-Hunt
Rev.: Phoebe Gilman, Susan Taylor
Composition: 91.67% Au, 8.33% Ag
Gold content: 15.703 g, 0.505 tr oz
Silver content: 1.427 g, 0.046 tr oz
Weight: 17.13 g **Edge:** Reeded
Diameter: 29.0 mm **Die Axis:** ↑↑
Thickness: 2.0 mm **Finish:** Proof
Case: Woven Jacquard case, black insert, encapsulated coin, COA

DATE	DESCRIPTION	QUANTITY SOLD	ISSUE PRICE	FINISH	PR-67	PR-68
1994	Anne of Green Gables	10,655	399.95	Proof	800.	825.

TWO HUNDRED DOLLARS, THE SUGAR BUSH, 1995.
The 1995 $200 coin celebrates the time-honoured rite of spring known in Canada as "sugaring off."

Designers and Engravers:
Obv.: Dora de Pédery-Hunt
Rev.: J. D. Mantha, S. Beveridge, S. Taylor
Composition: 91.67% Au, 8.33% Ag
Gold content: 15.703 g, 0.505 tr oz
Silver content: 1.427 g, 0.046 tr oz
Weight: 17.13 g **Edge:** Reeded
Diameter: 29.0 mm **Die Axis:** ↑↑
Thickness: 2.0 mm **Finish:** Proof
Case: Woven Jacquard case, black insert, encapsulated coin, COA

DATE	DESCRIPTION	QUANTITY SOLD	ISSUE PRICE	FINISH	PR-67	PR-68
1995	The Sugar Bush	9,579	399.95	Proof	800.	825.

TWO HUNDRED DOLLARS, TRANSCONTINENTAL LANDSCAPE, 1996.

The railway, a central symbol of national life, is commemorated on the 1996 $200 gold coin.

Designers and Engravers:
Obv.: Dora de Pédery-Hunt
Rev.: Suzanne Duranceau, Cosme Saffioti
Composition: 91.67% Au, 8.33% Ag
Gold content: 15.703 g, 0.505 tr oz
Silver content: 1.427 g, 0.046 tr oz
Weight: 17.13 g   **Edge:** Reeded
Diameter: 29.0 mm   **Die Axis:** ↑↑
Thickness: 2.0 mm   **Finish:** Proof
Case: Woven Jacquard case, black insert,
            encapsulated coin, COA

DATE	DESCRIPTION	QUANTITY SOLD	ISSUE PRICE	FINISH	PR-67	PR-68
1996	Transcontinental Landscape	8,047	414.95	Proof	800.	825.

TWO HUNDRED DOLLARS, HAIDA "RAVEN BRINGING LIGHT TO THE WORLD," 1997.

This coin was the first issue of a four-year program, celebrating Canadian Native cultures and traditions and was available with or without a case because the mint offered a four-coin case to house the set.

Designers and Engravers:
Obv.: Dora de Pédery-Hunt
Rev.: R. Davidson, Cosme Saffioti, A. Aarand
Composition: 91.67% Au, 8.33% Ag
Gold content: 15.703 g, 0.505 tr oz
Silver content: 1.427 g, 0.046 tr oz
Weight: 17.13 g   **Edge:** Reeded
Diameter: 29.0 mm   **Die Axis:** ↑↑
Thickness: 2.0 mm   **Finish:** Proof
Case: Metal trimmed case, black insert,
            encapsulated coin, COA

DATE	DESCRIPTION	QUANTITY SOLD	ISSUE PRICE	FINISH	PR-67	PR-68
1997	Haida "Raven Bringing Light to the World"	11,610	414.95	Proof	900.	925.

TWO HUNDRED DOLLARS, THE LEGEND OF THE WHITE BUFFALO, 1998.

The is the second coin in the series on Canadian Native cultures and traditions.

Designers and Engravers:
Obv.: Dora de Pédery-Hunt
Rev.: Alex Janvier, Cosme Saffioti
Composition: 91.67% Au, 8.33% Ag
Gold content: 15.703 g, 0.505 tr oz
Silver content: 1.427 g, 0.046 tr oz
Weight: 17.13 g   **Edge:** Reeded
Diameter: 29.0 mm   **Die Axis:** ↑↑
Thickness: 2.0 mm   **Finish:** Proof
Case: Metal trimmed case, black insert,
            encapsulated coin, COA

DATE	DESCRIPTION	QUANTITY SOLD	ISSUE PRICE	FINISH	PR-67	PR-68
1998	Legend of the White Buffalo	7,149	414.95	Proof	800.	825.

TWO HUNDRED DOLLARS, MIKMAQ BUTTERFLY, 1999.

This is the third in the four-coin series celebrating Canadian Native cultures and traditions. The reverse design depicts a butterfly in the traditional Mikmaq double curve, symbolising the balance between the physical and spiritual worlds.

Designers and Engravers:
Obv.: Dora de Pédery-Hunt
Rev.: Alan Syliboy, Cosme Saffioti
Composition: 91.67% Au, 8.33% Ag
Gold content: 15.703 g, 0.505 tr oz
Silver content: 1.427 g, 0.046 tr oz
Weight: 17.13 g   **Edge:** Reeded
Diameter: 29.0 mm   **Die Axis:** ↑↑
Thickness: 2.0 mm   **Finish:** Proof
Case: Woven Jacquard case, black insert, encapsulated coin, COA

DATE	DESCRIPTION	QUANTITY SOLD	ISSUE PRICE	FINISH	PR-67	PR-68
1999	Mikmaq Butterfly	6,510	414.95	Proof	800.	825.

TWO HUNDRED DOLLARS, MOTHER AND CHILD, 2000.

This is the fourth and last coin in the four-coin Native Cultures and Traditions series.

Designers and Engravers:
Obv.: Dora de Pédery-Hunt
Rev.: G. Arnaktauyok, Susan Taylor
Composition: 91.67% Au, 8.33% Ag
Gold content: 15.703 g, 0.505 tr oz
Silver content: 1.427 g, 0.046 tr oz
Weight: 17.13 g   **Edge:** Reeded
Diameter: 29.0 mm   **Die Axis:** ↑↑
Thickness: 2.0 mm   **Finish:** Proof
Case: Metal trimmed case, black insert, encapsulated coin, COA

DATE	DESCRIPTION	QUANTITY SOLD	ISSUE PRICE	FINISH	PR-67	PR-68
2000	Mother and Child	7,410	414.95	Proof	800.	825.

Note: A special collector case designed by Maryanne Barkhouse for the "Canadian Native Cultures and Traditions" series was issued in 1998. The box was made of imitation stone resin, with the Arctic Fox as the central panel, and on each side an animal on which the native aboriginal depended. The four-coin case was available directly from the Mint, priced at $79.95. The complete four-coin set in case was issued at $1,600.00.

TWO HUNDRED DOLLARS, CORNELIUS KRIEGHOFF, 2001.

The 2001 $200 gold coin is the first in a four-coin series featuring Canadian art and artists. Cornelius Krieghoff's famous painting *The Habitant Farm* (1856) is featured on the reverse.

Designers and Engravers:
Obv.: Dora de Pédery-Hunt
Rev.: C. Krieghoff, Susan Taylor
Composition: 91.67% Au, 8.33% Ag
Gold content: 15.703 g, 0.505 tr oz
Silver content: 1.427 g, 0.046 tr oz
Weight: 17.13 g   **Edge:** Reeded
Diameter: 29.0 mm   **Die Axis:** ↑↑
Thickness: 2.0 mm   **Finish:** Proof
Case: Metal trimmed case, black insert, encapsulated coin, COA

DATE	DESCRIPTION	QUANTITY SOLD	ISSUE PRICE	FINISH	PR-67	PR-68
2001	Cornelius Krieghoff, *The Habitant Farm*	5,406	412.95	Proof	800.	825.

TWO HUNDRED DOLLARS, TOM THOMPSON, 2002.

The 2002 $200 gold coin is the second coin of the four-coin series honouring Canada's famous painters. Thompson's (1877-1917) *The Jack Pine*, painted in 1916 in Algonquin Park, is one of Canada's most familiar images.

Designers and Engravers:
Obv.: Dora de Pédery-Hunt
Rev.: Tom Thompson, Susan Taylor
Composition: 91.67% Au, 8.33% Ag
Gold content: 15.703 g, 0.505 tr oz
Silver content: 1.427 g, 0.046 tr oz
Weight: 17.13 g   **Edge:** Reeded
Diameter: 29.0 mm   **Die Axis:** ↑↑
Thickness: 2.0 mm   **Finish:** Proof
Case: Woven Jacquard case, black insert, encapsulated coin, COA

DATE	DESCRIPTION	QUANTITY SOLD	ISSUE PRICE	FINISH	PR-67	PR-68
2002	Tom Thompson, *The Jack Pine*	5,754	412.95	Proof	800.	825.

TWO HUNDRED DOLLARS, LIONEL LEMOINE FITZGERALD, 2003.

The third gold coin in the Canadian Art Series features Fitzgerald's *Houses* painted in 1929. The rural life of the small prairie towns is the theme of this magnificent painting.

Designers and Engravers:
Obv.: Dora de Pédery-Hunt
Rev.: L. L. Fitzgerald, Susan Taylor
Composition: 91.67% Au, 8.33% Ag
Gold content: 15.703 g, 0.505 tr oz
Silver content: 1.427 g, 0.046 tr oz
Weight: 17.13 g   **Edge:** Reeded
Diameter: 29.0 mm   **Die Axis:** ↑↑
Thickness: 2.0 mm   **Finish:** Proof
Case: Metal trimmed case, black insert, encapsulated coin, COA

DATE	DESCRIPTION	QUANTITY SOLD	ISSUE PRICE	FINISH	PR-67	PR-68
2003	Lionel LeMoine Fitzgerald, *Houses*	4,118	412.95	Proof	800.	825.

TWO HUNDRED DOLLARS, ALFRED PELLAN, 2004.

This is the fourth and last gold coin in the Canadian Art Series Alfred Pellan's *Fragments* make him one of the most fascinating figures in Canadian Art.

Designers and Engravers:
Obv.: Susanna Blunt, Susan Taylor
Rev.: Alfred Pellan, Christie Paquet
Composition: 91.67% Au, 8.33% Ag
Gold content: 14.667 g, 0.471 tr oz
Silver content: 1.332 g, 0.043 tr oz
Weight: 16.0 g   **Edge:** Reeded
Diameter: 29.0 mm   **Die Axis:** ↑↑
Thickness: 1.8 mm   **Finish:** Proof
Case: Metal trimmed case, black insert, encapsulated coin, COA

DATE	DESCRIPTION	QUANTITY SOLD	ISSUE PRICE	FINISH	PR-67	PR-68
2004	Alfred Pellan, *Fragments*	3,917	412.95	Proof	750.	775.

TWO HUNDRED DOLLARS, FUR TRADE, 2005.

This is the first issue in the Historical Trade Series. The fur trade in Canada was founded as an adjunct to the fishing trade. In the 16th century European fishermen who dried their catch on the shores of Newfoundland began trade with the Native people.

Designers and Engravers:
Obv.: Susanna Blunt, Susan Taylor
Rev.: John Mardon, José Osio
Composition: 91.67% Au, 8.33% Ag
Gold content: 14.667 g, 0.471 tr oz
Silver content: 1.332 g, 0.043 tr oz
Weight: 16.0 g   **Edge:** Reeded
Diameter: 29.0 mm   **Die Axis:** ↑↑
Thickness: 1.8 mm   **Finish:** Proof
Case: Maroon plastic slide case, black plastic insert, encapsulated coin, COA

DATE	DESCRIPTION	QUANTITY SOLD	ISSUE PRICE	FINISH	PR-67	PR-68
2005	Fur Trade	3,669	489.95	Proof	750.	775.

TWO HUNDRED DOLLARS, TIMBER TRADE, 2006.

The coin which represents the timber trade in Canada is the second issue in the Historical Trade Series. Wood was the great staple of Canadian trade for much of the 19th century, built on European demand for timber which brought investment and immigration to eastern Canada.

Designers and Engravers:
Obv.: Susanna Blunt, Susan Taylor
Rev.: John Mardon, Stan Witten
Composition: 91.67% Au, 8.33% Ag
Gold content: 14.667 g, 0.471 tr oz
Silver content: 1.332 g, 0.043 tr oz
Weight: 16.0 g   **Edge:** Reeded
Diameter: 29.0 mm   **Die Axis:** ↑↑
Thickness: 1.8 mm   **Finish:** Proof
Case: Maroon leatherette clam style case, black flocked insert; encapsulated coin, COA

DATE	DESCRIPTION	QUANTITY SOLD	ISSUE PRICE	FINISH	PR-67	PR-68
2006	Timber Trade	3,218	489.95	Proof	750.	775.

TWO HUNDRED DOLLARS, FISHING TRADE, 2007.

The fishing trade on the Grand Banks began in the 16th century when fishermen from the northwestern section of Europe landed large catches of cod. This is the third coin in the Historical Trade Series.

Designers and Engravers:
Obv.: Susanna Blunt, Susan Taylor
Rev.: John Mardon, Susan Taylor
Composition: 91.67% Au, 8.33% Ag
Gold content: 14.667 g, 0.471 tr oz
Silver content: 1.332 g, 0.043 tr oz
Weight: 16.0 g   **Edge:** Reeded
Diameter: 29.0 mm   **Die Axis:** ↑↑
Thickness: 1.8 mm   **Finish:** Proof
Case: Maroon leatherette clam style case, black flocked insert, encapsulated coin, COA

DATE	DESCRIPTION	QUANTITY SOLD	ISSUE PRICE	FINISH	PR-67	PR-68
2007	Fishing Trade	2,137	579.95	Proof	750.	775.

TWO HUNDRED DOLLARS, AGRICULTURE TRADE, 2008.

The agriculture trade has been one of the staple industries of Canada since the 17th century. Canada is one of the world's major producers of food, particularly cereal grains and dairy products. This coin is the fourth in the Historical Trade Series.

Designers and Engravers:
Obv.: Susanna Blunt, Susan Taylor
Rev.: John Mardon, José Osio
Composition: 91.67% Au, 8.33% Ag
Gold content: 14.667 g, 0.471 tr oz
Silver content: 1.332 g, 0.043 tr oz
Weight: 16.0 g   **Edge:** Reeded
Diameter: 29.0 mm   **Die Axis:** ↑↑
Thickness: 1.8 mm   **Finish:** Proof
Case: Maroon leatherette clam style case, black flocked insert, encapsulated coin, COA

DATE	DESCRIPTION	QUANTITY SOLD	ISSUE PRICE	FINISH	PR-67	PR-68
2008	Agriculture Trade	1,951	619.95	Proof	750.	775.

TWO HUNDRED DOLLARS, COAL MINING TRADE, 2009.

The fifth coin in the Historical Trade Series represents the coal mining industry. Coal was first discovered by the French settlers in the late 1600s along the Nova Scotia coast. It soon became a valuable resource used both by the military and civilians.

Designers and Engravers:
Obv.: Susanna Blunt, Susan Taylor
Rev.: John Mardon, Christie Paquet
Composition: 91.67% Au, 8.33% Ag, Painted
Gold content: 14.667 g, 0.471 tr oz
Silver content: 1.332 g, 0.043 tr oz
Weight: 16.0 g   **Edge:** Reeded
Diameter: 29.0 mm   **Die Axis:** ↑↑
Thickness: 1.8 mm   **Finish:** Proof
Case: Maroon leatherette clam style case, black flocked insert, encapsulated coin, COA

DATE	DESCRIPTION	QUANTITY SOLD	ISSUE PRICE	FINISH	PR-67	PR-68
2009	Coal Mining Trade	2,241	849.95	Proof	750.	775.

TWO HUNDRED DOLLARS, FIRST CANADIAN OLYMPIC GOLD MEDAL ON HOME SOIL, 2010.

This coin was issued to commemorate the first Olympic gold medal to be won by a Canadian in a Canadian hosted Olympic Games. The gold medal was won by Alexandre Bilodeau in the men's mogul event at the Vancouver 2010 Olympic Winter Games.

Designers and Engravers:
Obv.: Susanna Blunt, Susan Taylor
Rev.: Bonnie Ross, Stan Witten
Composition: 91.67% Au, 8.33% Ag
Gold content: 14.667 g, 0.471 tr oz
Silver content: 1.332 g, 0.043 tr oz
Weight: 16.0 g   **Edge:** Reeded
Diameter: 29.0 mm   **Die Axis:** ↑↑
Thickness: 1.8 mm   **Finish:** Proof
Case: Black leatherette display case, black flocked insert, encapsulated coin, COA

DATE	DESCRIPTION	QUANTITY SOLD	ISSUE PRICE	FINISH	PR-67	PR-68
2010	First Canadian Olympic Gold Medal on Home Soil	2,010	989.95	Proof	1,000.	1,050.

TWO HUNDRED DOLLARS, PETROLEUM AND OIL TRADE, 2010.

This is the sixth coin in the Historical Trade Series. The design combines the iconic oil plume with other elements representing turn-of-the-century oil exploration, production, storage, and transportation to create a telling montage of the early days of Canada's oil trade.

Designers and Engravers:
  Obv.: Susanna Blunt, Susan Taylor
  Rev.: John Mardon, RCM Staff
Composition: 91.67% Au, 8.33% Ag, Painted
Gold content: 14.667 g, 0.471 tr oz
Silver content: 1.332 g, 0.043 tr oz
Weight: 16.0 g   **Edge:** Reeded
Diameter: 29.0 mm   **Die Axis:** ↑↑
Thickness: 1.8 mm   **Finish:** Proof
Case: Maroon leatherette clam style case, black flocked insert, encapsulated coin, COA

DATE	DESCRIPTION	QUANTITY SOLD	ISSUE PRICE	FINISH	PR-67	PR-68
2010	Petroleum and Oil Trade	1,732	999.95	Proof	1,000.	1,025.

TWO HUNDRED DOLLARS, S.S. BEAVER, 2011.

This is the seventh and last coin in the historical trade series. The *S.S. Beaver* was commissioned by the Hudson's Bay Company in 1835 as a supply ship.

Designers and Engravers:
  Obv.: Susanna Blunt, Susan Taylor
  Rev.: John Mardon, RCM Staff
Composition: 91.67% Au, 8.33% Ag
Gold content: 14.667 g, 0.471 tr oz
Silver content: 1.332 g, 0.043 tr oz
Weight: 16.0 g   **Edge:** Reeded
Diameter: 29.0 mm   **Die Axis:** ↑↑
Thickness: 1.8 mm   **Finish:** Proof
Case: Maroon leatherette clam style case, black flocked insert, encapsulated coin, COA

DATE	DESCRIPTION	QUANTITY SOLD	ISSUE PRICE	FINISH	PR-67	PR-68
2011	S.S. Beaver	1,392	1,099.95	Proof	1,100.	1,125.

TWO HUNDRED DOLLARS, THE WEDDING CELEBRATION OF THEIR ROYAL HIGHNESSES THE DUKE AND DUCHESS OF CAMBRIDGE, 2011.

Designers and Engravers:
  Obv.: Susanna Blunt, Susan Taylor
  Rev.: Laurie McGaw, José Osio
Composition: 91.67% Au, 8.33% Ag, Blue Swarovski element
Gold content: 14.667 g, 0.471 tr oz
Silver content: 1.332 g, 0.043 tr oz
Weight: 16.0 g   **Edge:** Reeded
Diameter: 29.0 mm   **Die Axis:** ↑↑
Thickness: 1.8 mm
Finish: Proof
Case: Maroon leatherette clam style case, black flocked insert, encapsulated coin, COA

DATE	DESCRIPTION	QUANTITY SOLD	ISSUE PRICE	FINISH	PR-67	PR-68
2011	Duke and Duchess of Cambridge	760	1,199.95	Proof	1,200.	1,225.

TWO HUNDRED DOLLARS, WAYNE AND WALTER GRETZKY, 2011.

Wayne Gretzky along with his father Walter, are well known in the world of ice hockey.

Designers and Engravers:
Obv.: Susanna Blunt, Susan Taylor
Rev.: G. Green, K. Wachelko, J. Osio
Composition: 91.67% Au, 8.33% Ag, Laser
Gold content: 14.667 g, 0.471 tr oz
Silver content: 1.332 g, 0.043 tr oz
Weight: 16.0 g　　**Edge:** Reeded
Diameter: 29.0 mm　**Die Axis:** ↑↑
Thickness: 1.8 mm　**Finish:** Proof
Case:　Maroon leatherette clam style case, black flocked insert, encapsulated coin, COA

DATE	DESCRIPTION	QUANTITY SOLD	ISSUE PRICE	FINISH	PR-67	PR-68
2011	Wayne and Walter Gretzky	471	1,299.99	Proof	1,300.	1,350.

TWO HUNDRED DOLLARS, THE VIKINGS, 2012.

This is the first coin in a new series on the great explorers of Canada. The Vikings established a settlement in L'Anse aux Meadows, which is the most northern point of Newfoundland, in the late tenth century.

Designers and Engravers:
Obv.: Susanna Blunt, Susan Taylor
Rev.: Yves Bérubé, José Osio
Composition: 99.99% Au
Gold content: 15.43 g, 0.5 oz
Weight: 15.43 g　　**Edge:** Reeded
Diameter: 29.0 mm　**Die Axis:** ↑↑
Thickness: 1.6 mm　**Finish:** Proof
Case:　Maroon leatherette clam style case, black flocked insert, encapsulated coin, COA

DATE	DESCRIPTION	QUANTITY SOLD	ISSUE PRICE	FINISH	PR-67	PR-68
2012	The Vikings	1,749	1,199.95	Proof	1,200.	1,250.

TWO HUNDRED DOLLARS, *"THE CHALLENGE"*, ROBERT BATEMAN MOOSE COIN SERIES, 2012.

The reverse design on this coin features the upraised head, neck and multi-pronged antlers taken from Robert Bateman's painting *The Moose Family*. The coin was issued to commemorate the 50th anniversary of the Canadian Wildlife Federation.

Designers and Engravers:
Obv.: Susanna Blunt, Susan Taylor
Rev.: Robert Bateman, RCM Staff
Composition: 99.99% Au
Gold content: 31.1 g. 1.0 tr oz
Weight: 31.1 g　　**Edge:** Reeded
Diameter: 30.0 mm　**Die Axis:** ↑↑
Thickness: N/A　　**Finish:** Proof
Case:　Maroon leatherette clam style case, black flocked insert, encapsulated coin, COA

DATE	DESCRIPTION	QUANTITY SOLD	ISSUE PRICE	FINISH	PR-67	PR-68
2012 (1962-)	The Challenge	359	2,699.95	Proof	2,700.	2,750.

Note: For other coins in the Robert Bateman Moose Coin Series see pages 226, 260, and 331.

TWO HUNDRED DOLLARS, JACQUES CARTIER, 2013.

This is the second of six coins in the Great Explorers Series. Although Cartier was not the first European to visit Eastern Canada, his discovery and exploration of the St. Lawrence laid the groundwork for centuries of trade and settlement.

Designers and Engravers:
    Obv.: Susanna Blunt, Susan Taylor
    Rev.: Laurie McGaw, José Osio
Composition: 99.99% Au
Gold content: 15.43 g. 0.5 tr oz
Weight: 15.43 g   **Edge:** Reeded
Diameter: 29.0 mm   **Die Axis:** ↑↑
Thickness: 1.8 mm   **Finish:** Proof
Case: Maroon leatherette clam style case, black flocked insert, encapsulated coin, COA

DATE	DESCRIPTION	QUANTITY SOLD	ISSUE PRICE	FINISH	PR-67	PR-68
2013	Jacques Cartier	1,474	1,199.95	Proof	1,200.	1,250.

TWO HUNDRED DOLLARS, GRANDMOTHER MOON MASK, 2013.

The moon is a sacred symbol that appears in countless First Nations traditions.

Designers and Engravers:
    Obv.: Susanna Blunt, Susan Taylor
    Rev.: Richard Cochrane, RCM Staff
Composition: 99.99% Au
Gold content: 33.33 g. 1.07 tr oz
Weight: 33.33 g   **Edge:** Reeded
Diameter: 30.0 mm   **Die Axis:** ↑↑
Thickness: N/A   **Finish:** Proof
Case: Maroon leatherette clam style case, black flocked insert, encapsulated coin, COA

DATE	DESCRIPTION	QUANTITY SOLD	ISSUE PRICE	FINISH	PR-67	PR-68
2013	Grandmother Moon Mask	495	2,999.95	Proof	3,000.	3,050.

TWO HUNDRED DOLLARS, SAMUEL DE CHAMPLAIN, 2014.

This is the third coin in the Great Canadian Explorers Series.

Designers and Engravers:
    Obv.: Susanna Blunt, Susan Taylor
    Rev.: Glen Green, RCM Staff
Composition: 99.99% Au
Gold content: 15.43 g. 0.5 tr oz
Weight: 15.43 g   **Edge:** Reeded
Diameter: 29.0 mm   **Die Axis:** ↑↑
Thickness: 1.8 mm   **Finish:** Proof
Case: Maroon leatherette clam style case, black flocked insert, encapsulated coin, COA

DATE	DESCRIPTION	QUANTITY SOLD	ISSUE PRICE	FINISH	PR-67	PR-68
2014	Samuel de Champlain	2,000	1,199.95	Proof	1,200.	1,250.

TWO HUNDRED FIFTY DOLLAR GOLD COINS

TWO HUNDRED FIFTY DOLLARS, DOG SLED TEAM, 2006.

Designers and Engravers:
  Obv.: Susanna Blunt, Susan Taylor
  Rev.: Arnold Nogy, José Osio
Composition: 58.33% Au, 41.67% Ag
Gold content: 26.25 g, 0.844 tr oz
Silver content: 18.75 g, 0.603 tr oz
Weight: 45.0 g
Diameter: 40.0 mm
Thickness: 2.9 mm
Edge: Reeded
Die Axis: ↑↑
Finish: Proof
Case: Maroon leatherette clam style case,
  black flocked insert, encapsulated coin,
  COA

DATE	DESCRIPTION	QUANTITY SOLD	ISSUE PRICE	FINISH	PR-67	PR-68
2006	Dog Sled Team	953	1,089.95	Proof	1,100.	1,200.

Note: An identical design is utilized on the $30 silver coin for 2006, see page 247.

TWO HUNDRED FIFTY DOLLARS, CANADIAN CONTEMPORARY ART, 2014.

Designers and Engravers:
  Obv.: Susanna Blunt, Susan Taylor
  Rev.: Tim Barnard, RCM Staff
Composition: 99.99% Au
Gold content: 62.34 g, 2.0 tr oz
Weight: 62.34 g
Diameter: 42.0 mm
Thickness: N/A
Edge: Reeded
Die Axis: ↑↑
Finish: Proof
Case: Maroon leatherette clam style
  case, black flocked insert,
  encapsulated coin, COA

DATE	DESCRIPTION	QUANTITY SOLD	ISSUE PRICE	FINISH	PR-67	PR-68
2014	Canadian Contemporary Art	300	5,199.95	Proof	5,200.	5,300.

THREE HUNDRED DOLLAR GOLD COINS (Size 50mm)

THREE HUNDRED DOLLARS, TRIPLE CAMEO PORTRAITS OF QUEEN ELIZABETH II, 2002.
This 14-karat gold coin bears triple cameo portraits of Queen Elizabeth II on the obverse: a 1953-1964 portrait by Mary Gillick, a 1965-1989 portrait by Arnold Machin, and a 1990-2003 portrait by Dora de Pédery-Hunt.

Designers:
   Obv.: Dora de Pédery-Hunt
   Rev.: Sheldon Beveridge, Cosme Saffioti
Composition: 58.33% Au, 41.67% Ag
Gold content: 35.00 g, 1.125 tr oz
Silver content: 25.0 g, 0.804 tr oz
Weight: 60.0 g
Diameter: 50.0 mm
Case of Issue: Purple laminated wooden case, cream insert, encapsulated coin, COA, black / gold outer case

Engravers:
   Obv.: Stan Witten
   Rev.: Cosme Saffioti

Thickness: 2.5 mm
Edge: Reeded
Die Axis: ↑↑
Finish: Proof / Bullion

DATE	DESCRIPTION	QUANTITY SOLD	ISSUE PRICE	FINISH	PR-67	PR-68
2002 (1952-)	Triple Cameo Portraits	999	1,095.95	Proof	1,800.	1,850.

Note: Coin illustrated smaller than actual size.

THREE HUNDRED DOLLARS, GREAT SEAL OF CANADA, 2003.

The Royal Seal, or Great Seal of Canada, is the official stamp used to bring the Queen's authority to any documents produced on her behalf.

2003 Obverse

2003 Reverse
Designer: RCM Staff
Engraver: RCM Staff

THREE HUNDRED DOLLARS, QUADRUPLE CAMEO PORTRAITS, 2004.

The four coinage portraits of Queen Elizabeth II are featured on the obverse of the $300 coin for 2004. Each is struck in 24kt gold.

2004 Obverse

2004 Reverse
Designer: Christie Paquet
Engraver: Christie Paquet

Designers:
  Obv.: M Gillick, A. Machin, D. de Pedery-Hunt, S. Blunt
  Rev.: See reverse illustrations
Composition: 58.33% Au, 41.67% Ag
Gold content: 35.00 g, 1.125 tr oz
Silver content: 25.0 g, 0.804 tr oz
Weight: 60.0 g
Diameter: 50.0 mm

Engravers:
  Obv.: Susan Taylor
  Rev.: See reverse illustrations

Thickness: 2.5 mm
Edge: Reeded
Die Axis: ↑↑
Finish: Proof / Bullion

Case of Issue: Black leatherette case, RCM plaque, black flocked insert, encapsulated coin, COA, black and gold outer case

DATE	DESCRIPTION	QUANTITY SOLD	ISSUE PRICE	FINISH	PR-67	PR-68
2003	Great Seal of Canada	998	1,099.95	Proof	1,800.	1,850.
2004	Quadruple Cameo Portraits	998	1,099.95	Proof	1,800.	1,850.

THREE HUNDRED DOLLARS, VIGNETTES OF THE TWENTY-FIVE CENT FRACTIONAL NOTES OF THE DOMINION OF CANADA, 2005-2007.

These coins commemorate the vignettes which appear on the Dominion of Canada twenty-five cent fractional note issues of 1870, 1900 and 1923.

2005-2007
Common Obverse

2005 The 1870 Shinplaster
Vignette of Britannia
Designer: Robert-Ralph Carmichael
Engraver: José Osio

2006 The 1900 Shinplaster
Vignette of Britannia
Designer: Christie Paquet
Engraver: Christie Paquet

2007 The 1923 Shinplaster
Vignette of Britannia
Designer: Robert-Ralph Carmichael
Engraver: Christie Paquet

Designers:
Obv.: Susanna Blunt
Rev.: See reverse illustrations
Composition: 58.33% Au, 41.67% Ag
Gold content: 35.0 g, 1.125 tr oz
Silver content: 25.0 g, 0.804 tr oz
Weight: 60.00 g
Diameter: 50.0 mm
Case of Issue: Black leatherette case, RCM plaque, black flocked insert, encapsulated coin, COA, black and gold outer case

Engravers:
Obv.: Susan Taylor
Rev.: See reverse illustrations

Thickness: 2.5 mm
Edge: Reeded
Die Axis: ↑↑
Finish: Proof / Bullion

DATE	DESCRIPTION	QUANTITY SOLD	ISSUE PRICE	FINISH	PR-67	PR-68
2005	1870 Shinplaster Vignette of Britannia	994	N/A	Proof	1,800.	1,850.
2006	1900 Shinplaster Vignette of Britannia	947	1,295.95	Proof	1,800.	1,850.
2007	1923 Shinplaster Vignette of Britannia	778	1,440.95	Proof	1,800.	1,850.

Note: Coins on pages 310 and 311 illustrated smaller than actual size.

THREE HUNDRED DOLLARS, CRYSTAL SNOWFLAKE SERIES, 2006 and 2010

CRYSTAL SNOWFLAKE, 2006.

CRYSTAL SNOWFLAKE, 2010.

Designers:
   Obv.: Susanna Blunt
   Rev.: Konrad Wachelko
Composition: 58.33% Au, 41.67% Ag,
            Swarovski crystal elements
Gold content: 35.0 g, 1.125 tr oz
Silver content: 25.0 g, 0.804 tr oz
Weight: 60.0 g
Diameter: 50.0 mm

Engravers:
   Obv.: Susan Taylor
   Rev.: Konrad Wachelko

Thickness: 2.5 mm
Edge: Reeded
Die Axis: ↑↑
Finish: Proof

Case of Issue: Maroon leatherette clam style case, black flocked insert, encapsulated coin, COA

DATE	DESCRIPTION	QUANTITY SOLD	ISSUE PRICE	FINISH	PR-67	PR-68
2006	Crystal Snowflake	998	1,520.95	Proof	1,800.	1,850.
2010	Crystal Snowflake	305	2,295.95	Proof	2,300.	2,350.

Note: Coins illustrated smaller than actual size.

THREE HUNDRED DOLLARS, 80TH BIRTHDAY OF QUEEN ELIZABETH II, 2006.

Designers:
  Obv.: Susanna Blunt
  Rev.: Not known
Composition: 58.33% Au, 41.67% Ag, Enamelled
Gold content: 35.0 g, 1.125 tr oz
Silver content: 25.0 g, 0.804 tr oz
Weight: 60.0 g
Diameter: 50.0 mm

Engravers:
  Obv.: Susan Taylor
  Rev.: Cecily Mok

Thickness: 2.5 mm
Edge: Reeded
Die Axis: ↑↑
Finish: Proof

Case of Issue: Maroon leatherette clam style case, black flocked insert, encapsulated coin, COA

DATE	DESCRIPTION	QUANTITY SOLD	ISSUE PRICE	FINISH	PR-67	PR-68
2006 (1926-)	80th Birthday Elizabeth II, Enamelled	1,000	1,520,95	Proof	1,800.	1,850.

Note: Coin illustrated smaller than actual size.

THREE HUNDRED DOLLARS, VANCOUVER 2010 OLYMPIC WINTER GAMES, 2007-2009.

Common Obverse
(except for date)

2007
Olympic Ideals
Engraver: Susan Taylor, José Osio

2008
Competition
Engraver: Susan Taylor, Christie Paquet

2009
Friendship
Engraver: Susan Taylor, José Osio

Designers:
  Obv.: Susanna Blunt
  Rev.: Laurie McGaw, David Craig
Composition: 58.33% Au, 41.67% Ag
Gold content: 35.0 g, 1.125 tr oz
Silver content: 25.0 g, 0.804 tr oz
Weight: 60.0 g
Diameter: 50.0 mm
Case of Issue: Black leatherette case, black flocked insert, encapsulated coin, COA

Engravers:
  Obv.: Susan Taylor
  Rev.: See reverse illustrations

Thickness: 2.5 mm
Edge: Reeded
Die Axis: ↑↑
Finish: Proof

DATE	DESCRIPTION	DATE OF ISSUE	QUANTITY SOLD	ISSUE PRICE	FINISH	PR-67	PR-68
2007	Olympic Ideals	Feb. 23, 2007	953	1,499.95	Proof	1,800.	1,850.
2008	Competition	Feb. 20, 2008	334	1,599.95	Proof	1,800.	1,850.
2009	Friendship	Feb. 18, 2009	880	1,999.95	Proof	2,000.	2,050.

Note: Coins illustrated smaller than actual size.

PROVINCIAL COATS OF ARMS SERIES

THREE HUNDRED DOLLARS, PROVINCIAL COATS OF ARMS SERIES, 2008-2014.

2008-2009
Common Obverse
With RCM Logo

2008
Newfoundland and Labrador
Engraver: Marcos Hallam

2008
Alberta
Engraver: Konrad Wachelko

2009
Yukon Territory
Engraver: Marcos Hallam

Designers:
  Obv.: Susanna Blunt
  Rev.: Reproduction of official Coat of Arms
Composition: 58.33% Au, 41.67% Ag
Gold content: 35.0 g, 1.125 tr oz
Silver content: 25.0 g, 0.804 tr oz
Weight: 60.0 g
Diameter: 50.0 mm

Engravers:
  Obv.: Susan Taylor
  Rev.: See reverse illustrations

Thickness: 2.5 mm
Edge: Reeded
Die Axis: ↑↑
Finish: Proof

Case of Issue: Maroon leatherette clam style case, black flocked insert, encapsulated coin, COA

DATE	DESCRIPTION	QUANTITY SOLD	ISSUE PRICE	FINISH	PR-67	PR-68
2008	Newfoundland and Labrador	472	1,541.95	Proof	2,000.	2,050.
2008	Alberta	344	1,631.95	Proof	2,000.	2,050.
2009	Yukon Territory	325	1,949.95	Proof	2,000.	2,050.

Note: Coins illustrated smaller than actual size.

THREE HUNDRED DOLLARS, PROVINCIAL COATS OF ARMS SERIES, 2008-2014 (cont.).

2009-2014 Common Obverse Without RCM Logo	2009 Prince Edward Island Engraver: Marcos Hallam	2010 British Columbia Engraver: Konrad Wachelko
2010 New Brunswick Engraver: Marcos Hallam	2011 Manitoba Engraver: Cecily Mok	2011 Nova Scotia Engraver: Konrad Wachelko

Designers:
 Obv.: Susanna Blunt
 Rev.: Reproduction of official Coat of Arms
Composition: 58.33% Au, 41.67% Ag
Gold content: 35.0 g, 1.125 tr oz
Silver content: 25.0 g, 0.804 tr oz
Weight: 60.0 g
Diameter: 50.0 mm
Case of Issue: Maroon leatherette clam style case, black flocked insert, encapsulated coin, COA

Engravers:
 Obv.: Susan Taylor
 Rev.: See reverse illustrations

Thickness: 2.5 mm
Edge: Reeded
Die Axis: ↑↑
Finish: Proof

DATE	DESCRIPTION	QUANTITY SOLD	ISSUE PRICE	FINISH	PR-67	PR-68
2009	Prince Edward Island	236	1,949.95	Proof	2,000.	2,050.
2010	British Columbia	421	2,249.95	Proof	2,250.	2,300.
2010	New Brunswick	233	2,249.95	Proof	2,250.	2,300.
2011	Manitoba	472	2,249.95	Proof	2,425.	2,475.
2011	Nova Scotia	238	2,249.95	Proof	2,250.	2,300.

Note: Coins illustrated smaller than actual size.

THREE HUNDRED DOLLARS, PROVINCIAL COATS OF ARMS SERIES, 2008-2014 (cont.).

2012 Quebec Engraver: Nick Martin	**2012** Nunavut Engraver: Christie Paquet	**2013** Ontario Engraver: Steven Stewart
2013 Northwest Territories Engraver: RCM Staff	**2014** Saskatchewan Engraver: RCM Staff	**2014** Canada Engraver: RCM Staff

Designers:
 Obv.: Susanna Blunt
 Rev.: Reproduction of official Coat of Arms
Composition: 58.33% Au, 41.67% Ag
Gold content: 35.0 g, 1.125 tr oz
Silver content: 25.0 g, 0.804 tr oz
Weight: 60.0 g
Diameter: 50.0 mm
Case of Issue: Maroon leatherette clam style case, black flocked insert, encapsulated coin, COA

Engravers:
 Obv.: Susan Taylor
 Rev.: See reverse illustrations

Thickness: 2.5 mm
Edge: Reeded
Die Axis: ↑↑
Finish: Proof

DATE	DESCRIPTION	QUANTITY SOLD	ISSUE PRICE	FINISH	PR-67	PR-68
2012	Quebec	334	2,649.95	Proof	2,650.	2,700.
2012	Nunavut	189	2,649.95	Proof	2,650.	2,700.
2013	Ontario	249	2,649.95	Proof	2,650.	2,700.
2013	Northwest Territories	134	2,649.95	Proof	2,650.	2,700.
2014	Saskatchewan	500	2,649.95	Proof	2,650.	2,700.
2014	Canada	500	2,649.95	Proof	2,650.	2,700.

Note: Coins illustrated smaller than actual size.

MOON MASK SERIES

THREE HUNDRED DOLLARS, FOUR SEASONS MOON MASK, 2008.

THREE HUNDRED DOLLARS, SUMMER MOON MASK, 2009.
Designers: **Engravers:**

Obv.: Susanna Blunt   Obv.: Susan Taylor
Rev.: Jody Broomfield   Rev.: Susan Taylor
Composition: 58.33% Au, 41.67% Ag, Enamelled
Gold content: 35.0 g, 1.125 tr oz   **Thickness:** 2.5 mm
Silver content: 25.0 g, 0.804 tr oz   **Edge:** Reeded
Weight: 60.0 g   **Die Axis:** ↑↑
Diameter: 50.0 mm   **Finish:** Proof
Case of Issue: Maroon leatherette clam style case, black flocked insert, encapsulated coin, COA

DATE	DESCRIPTION	QUANTITY SOLD	ISSUE PRICE	FINISH	PR-67	PR-68
2008	Four Seasons Moon Mask	544	1,559.95	Proof	2,200.	2,250.
2009	Summer Moon Mask	N/A	1,723.95	Proof	2,200.	2,250.

Note: Coins illustrated smaller than actual size.

THREE HUNDRED DOLLAR GOLD COINS (Size 40mm)

THREE HUNDRED DOLLARS, WELCOME FIGURE (DZUNUK'WA) TOTEM POLE, 2005.
   Dzunuk'wa is a giant, hairy, black-bodied, big-breasted, wide-eyed female monster. She is physically strong enough to tear down large trees, spiritually powerful enough to resurrect the dead and possesses magical treasures and great wealth.

Designers and Engravers:
   Obv.: Susanna Blunt, Susan Taylor
   Rev.: Dr. Richard Hunt, Susan Taylor
Composition: 58.33% Au, 41.67% Ag
Gold content: 26.25 g, 0.844 tr oz
Silver content: 18.75 g, 0.603 tr oz
Weight: 45.0 g
Diameter: 40.0 mm
Thickness: 3.0 mm
Edge: Reeded
Die Axis: ↑↑
Finish: Proof
Case: Maroon leatherette clam style case, black flocked insert, encapsulated coin, COA

DATE	DESCRIPTION	QUANTITY SOLD	ISSUE PRICE	FINISH	PR-67	PR-68
2005	Welcome Figure Totem Pole	948	1,199.95	Proof	1,350.	1,400.

Note: An identical design is utilized on the $30 silver coin for 2005, see page 247.

CANADIAN ACHIEVEMENT SERIES

THREE HUNDRED DOLLARS, 120TH ANNIVERSARY OF THE INTERNATIONAL IMPLEMENTATION OF STANDARD TIME, 2005.

In 1885 Sir Sandford Fleming's system of standard time was implemented, dividing the world into 24 time zones. These are the first coins in the Canadian Achievements series.

Designers and Engravers:
    Obv.: Susanna Blunt, Susan Taylor
    Rev.: Bonnie Ross, Stan Witten
Composition: 58.33% Au, 41.67% Ag, Colourised
Gold content: 26.25 g, 0.844 tr oz
Silver content: 18.75 g, 0.603 tr oz
Weight: 45.0 g
Diameter: 40.0 mm   **Edge:** Reeded
Thickness: 3.0 mm   **Die Axis:** ↑↑
Finish: Proof
Case of Issue: Anodized gold-coloured aluminum box with cherry wood stained side panels, encapsulated coin, COA

Pacific Time 4:00

Mountain Time 5:00

Central Time 6:00

Eastern Time 7:00

Atlantic Time 8:00

Newfoundland Time 8:30

DATE	DESCRIPTION	QUANTITY SOLD	ISSUE PRICE	FINISH	PR-67	PR-68
2005	Pacific Time 4:00	200	999.95	Proof	1,525.	1,575.
2005	Mountain Time 5:00	200	999.95	Proof	1,525.	1,575.
2005	Central Time 6:00	200	999.95	Proof	1,525.	1,575.
2005	Eastern Time 7:00	200	999.95	Proof	1,525.	1,575.
2005	Atlantic Time 8:00	200	999.95	Proof	1,525.	1,575.
2005	Newfoundland Time 8:30	200	999.95	Proof	1,525.	1,575.

Note: It is reported in the 2006 Mint Report that a total of 1,199 coins were issued, however, it did not stipulate which coin was short struck.

CANADIAN ACHIEVEMENT SERIES (cont.)

THREE HUNDRED DOLLARS, FIFTH ANNIVERSARY OF CANADARM, 2006.
This is the second coin in the Canadian Achievements series.

Designers and Engravers:
> Obv.: Susanna Blunt, Susan Taylor
> Rev.: Cecily Mok, Cecily Mok

Composition: 58.33% Au, 41.67% Ag
Gold content: 26.25 g, 0.844 tr oz
Silver content: 18.75 g, 0.603 tr oz
Weight: 45.0 g
Diameter: 40.0 mm
Thickness: 3.0 mm
Edge: Reeded
Die Axis: ↑↑
Finish: Proof, Decal
Case: Maroon leatherette clam style case, black flocked insert, encapsulated coin. COA

THREE HUNDRED DOLLARS, PANORAMIC PHOTOGRAPHY IN CANADA, NIAGARA FALLS, 2007.
This is the third coin in the Canadian Achievements series.

Designers and Engravers:
> Obv.: Susanna Blunt, Susan Taylor
> Rev.: Chris Jordison, RCM Staff

Composition: 58.33% Au, 41.67% Ag
Gold content: 26.25 g, 0.844 tr oz
Silver content: 18.75 g, 0.603 tr oz
Weight: 45.0 g
Diameter: 40.0 mm
Thickness: 3.0 mm
Edge: Reeded
Die Axis: ↑↑
Finish: Proof, Hologram
Case: Maroon leatherette clam style case, black flocked insert, encapsulated coin, COA

THREE HUNDRED DOLLARS, IMAX©, 2008.
This fourth and last coin in the Canadian Achievements series.

Designers and Engravers:
> Obv.: Susanna Blunt, Susan Taylor
> Rev.: IMAX©, RCM Staff

Composition: 58.33% Au, 41.67% Ag
Gold content: 26.25 g, 0.844 tr oz
Silver content: 18.75 g, 0.603 tr oz
Weight: 45.0 g
Diameter: 40.0 mm
Thickness: 3.0 mm
Edge: Reeded
Die Axis: ↑↑
Finish: Proof, Hologram
Case: Maroon leatherette clam style case, black flocked insert, encapsulated coin, COA

DATE	DESCRIPTION	QUANTITY SOLD	ISSUE PRICE	FINISH	PR-67	PR-68
2006	5th Anniversary Canadarm, Decal	581	1,089.95	Proof	1,350.	1,400.
2007	Panoramic Photography, Niagara Falls, Hologram	551	1,111.95	Proof	1,350.	1,400.
2008	IMAX©, Hologram	252	1,228.95	Proof	1,350.	1,400.

THREE HUNDRED DOLLAR GOLD COIN (Size 25mm)

THREE HUNDRED DOLLARS, THE QUEEN'S DIAMOND JUBILEE, 1952-2012.

Designers and Engravers:
Obv.:　Susanna Blunt, Susan Taylor
Rev.:　Laurie McGaw, Susan Taylor
Composition: 99.999% Au, Diamond
Gold content: 22.0 g, 0.707 tr oz
Weight: 22.0 g　　　　　**Edge:** Reeded
Diameter: 25.0 mm　　　**Die Axis:** ↑↑
Thickness: N/A　　　　　**Finish:** Proof
Case:　Wooden collector box with the official Diamond Jubilee Cypher

DATE	DESCRIPTION	QUANTITY SOLD	ISSUE PRICE	FINISH	PR-67	PR-68
2012 (1952-)	The Queen's Diamond Jubilee	684	1,999.95	Proof	2,200.	2,250.

Note:　This coin was also issued as part of a three-coin gold commemorative set. The other coins included in the set are a British £5 coin and an Australian fifty-cent piece. There were 375 sets sold to a U.S.A. distributor (APMEX).

THREE HUNDRED FIFTY DOLLAR GOLD COINS

PROVINCIAL FLORAL EMBLEM SERIES
-
THREE HUNDRED FIFTY DOLLARS, PROVINCIAL FLORAL EMBLEM SERIES, 1998-2011.
Begun in 1998 and issued annually, these $350 gold coins bear either a national or provincial flower.

Common Obv.
1998-2003
(except for date)

1998 90th Anniv. Royal
Canadian Mint
Designer: Pierre Leduc
Engraver: Ago Aarand

1999 Golden Slipper
Prince Edward Island
Designer: Henry Purdy
Engraver: José Osio

2000 Pacific Dogwood
British Columbia
Designer: Caren Heine
Engraver: José Osio

2001 Mayflower
Nova Scotia
Designer: Bonnie Ross
Engraver: Susan Taylor

2002 Wild Rose
Alberta
Designer: Dr. A. K. Hellum
Engraver: William Woodruff

2003 White Trillium
Ontario
Designer: Pamela Stagg
Engraver: José Osio

Designers:
  Obv.: Dora de Pédery-Hunt
  Rev.: See reverse illustrations
Composition: 99.999% Au
Gold content: 38.05 g, 1.222 tr oz
Weight: 38.05 g
Diameter: 34.0 mm
Thickness: 3.2 mm

Engravers:
  Obv.: Dora de Pédery-Hunt
  Rev.: See reverse illustrations

Edge: Reeded
Die Axis: ↑↑
Finish: Proof

Cases of Issue: Anodized gold-coloured aluminum box with cherry wood stained side panels, encapsulated coin, COA

DATE	DESCRIPTION	QUANTITY SOLD	ISSUE PRICE	FINISH	PR-67	PR-68
1998	90th Anniversary of the Royal Canadian Min	1,999	999.99	Proof	1,950.	2,000.
1999	Golden Slipper, P.E.I.	1,990	999.99	Proof	1,950.	2,000.
2000	Pacific Dogwood, B.C.	1,971	999.99	Proof	1,950.	2,000.
2001	Mayflower, N.S.	1,988	999.99	Proof	1,950.	2,000.
2002	Wild Rose, Alberta	2,001	1,099.99	Proof	1,950.	2,000.
2003	White Trillium, Ontario	1,865	1,099.99	Proof	1,950.	2,000.

THREE HUNDRED FIFTY DOLLARS, PROVINCIAL FLORAL SERIES, 1998-2011 (cont.).
In 2004 the weight was decreased from 38.05 to 35.0 grams.

**Common Obverse
2004-2011
(except for date)**

Designers and   Engravers:
Obv.: Susanna Blunt, Susan Taylor
Rev.: See reverse illustrations
Composition: 99.999% Au
Gold content: 35.0 g, 1.125 tr oz
Weight: 35.0 g   **Edge:** Reeded
Diameter: 34.0 mm   **Die Axis:** ↑↑
Thickness: 2.8 mm   **Finish:** Proof
Cases of Issue:
2004-2006: Maroon plastic display case, black
plastic insert, encapsulated coin, COA
2007-2011: Maroon leatherette clam style
case, black flocked insert, encapsulated coin,
COA

**2004 Fireweed
Yukon Territory
Des.: Catherine Ann Deer
Eng.: William Woodruff**

**2005 Western Red Lily
Saskatchewan
Designer: Chris Jordison
Engraver: José Osio**

**2006 Iris Versicolor
Quebec
Designer: Susan Taylor
Engraver: Susan Taylor**

**2007 Purple Violet
New Brunswick
Designer: Sue Rose
Engraver: William Woodruff**

**2008 Purple Saxifrage
Nunavut
Designer: Celia Godkin
Engraver: Cecily Mok**

**2009 Pitcher Plant
Newfoundland and Labrador
Designer: Celia Godkin
Engraver: José Osio**

**2010 Prairie Crocus
Manitoba
Designer: Celia Godkin
Engraver: N/A**

**2011 Mountain Avens
Northwest Territories
Designer: Caren Heine
Engraver: Susan Taylor**

DATE	DESCRIPTION	QUANTITY SOLD	ISSUE PRICE	FINISH	PR-67	PR-68
2004	Fireweed, Yukon Territory	1,836	1,099.95	Proof	1,800.	1,850.
2005	Western Red Lily, Saskatchewan	1,634	1,295.99	Proof	1,800.	1,850.
2006	Iris Versicolor, Quebec	1,995	1,295.95	Proof	1,800.	1,850.
2007	Purple Violet, New Brunswick	1,392	1,520.95	Proof	1,800.	1,850.
2008	Purple Saxifrage, Nunavut	1,313	1,675.95	Proof	1,800.	1,850.
2009	Pitcher Plant, Newfoundland and Labrador	1,003	2,149.95	Proof	2,150.	2,200.
2010	Prairie Crocus, Manitoba	775	2,599.95	Proof	2,600.	2,650.
2011	Mountain Avens, Northwest Territories	1,033	2,799.95	Proof	2,800.	2,850.

THREE HUNDRED FIFTY DOLLARS, SIR ISAAC BROCK, THE HERO OF UPPER CANADA, 2012.

Sir Isaac Brock, an English General, was killed at the first major battle of the War of 1812, at Queenston Heights.

Designers and Engravers:
    Obv.: Susanna Blunt, Susan Taylor
    Rev.: RCM Staff
Composition: 99.999% Au
Gold content: 35.0 g, 1.125 tr oz
Weight: 35.0 g   **Edge:** Reeded
Diameter: 34.0 mm   **Die Axis:** ↑↑
Thickness: N/A   **Finish:** Proof
Case: Maroon leatherette clam style case, black
        flocked insert, encapsulated coin, COA

DATE	DESCRIPTION	QUANTITY SOLD	ISSUE PRICE	FINISH	PR-67	PR-68
2012	Sir Isaac Brock, The Hero of Upper Canada	365	2,799.95	Proof	2,800.	2,850.

THREE HUNDRED FIFTY DOLLARS, POLAR BEAR, ICONIC CANADIAN ANIMALS, 2013.

This is the first coin in a new series of Iconic Canadian Animals.

Designers and Engravers:
    Obv.: Susanna Blunt, Susan Taylor
    Rev.: Glen Loates, RCM Staff
Composition: 99.999% Au
Gold content: 35.0 g, 1.125 tr oz
Weight: 35.0 g   **Edge:** Reeded
Diameter: 34.0 mm   **Die Axis:** ↑↑
Thickness: N/A   **Finish:** Proof
Case: Maroon leatherette clam style case, lack
        flocked insert, encapsulated coin, COA

DATE	DESCRIPTION	QUANTITY SOLD	ISSUE PRICE	FINISH	PR-67	PR-68
2013	Polar Bear	593	2,799.95	Proof	2,800.	2,850.

FIVE HUNDRED DOLLAR GOLD COINS

FIVE HUNDRED DOLLARS, 60TH WEDDING ANNIVERSARY OF QUEEN ELIZABETH AND PRINCE PHILIP, 1947-2007.
The coin celebrates the sixtieth wedding anniversary of HM Queen Elizabeth II and HRH Prince Philip, Duke of Edinburgh. The shields are from their respective Coats of Arms, and the mascots on the State vehicles in which they travel.

Designers: and Engravers:
Obv.: S. Blunt, Susan Taylor
Rev.: S. Hepburn, Susan Taylor
Composition: 99.99% Au
Gold content: 155.76 g, 5.01 tr oz
Weight: 155.76 g
Diameter: 60.0 mm
Thickness: N/A
Edge: Reeded
Die Axis: ↑↑
Finish: Proof
Case of Issue: Black clam style case, black insert, encapsulated coin, COA

FIVE HUNDRED DOLLARS, 100TH ANNIVERSARY OF THE ROYAL CANADIAN MINT, 2008.
This coin commemorates the 100th anniversary of the Ottawa Mint (Royal Canadian Mint) which opened January 2nd, 1908.

Designers: and Engravers:
Obv.: S. Blunt, Susan Taylor
Rev.: RCM Staff
Composition: 99.99% Au
Gold content: 155.76 g, 5.01 tr oz
Weight: 155.76 g
Diameter: 60.0 mm
Thickness: N/A
Edge: Reeded
Die Axis: ↑↑
Finish: Proof
Case of Issue: Black clam style case, black insert, encapsulated coin, COA

FIVE HUNDRED DOLLARS, 150TH ANNIVERSARY OF THE START OF CONSTRUCTION OF THE PARLIAMENT BUILDINGS, 2009.
Construction of the Parliament Buildings began in December 1859, and was completed in the summer of 1866.

Designers and Engravers:
Obv.: S. Blunt, Susan Taylor
Rev.: Cecily Mok
Composition: 99.99% Au
Gold content: 156.5 g, 5.03 tr oz
Weight: 156.05 g
Diameter: 60.0 mm
Thickness: N/A
Edge: Reeded
Die Axis: ↑↑
Finish: Proof
Case of Issue: Black clam style case, black insert, encapsulated coin, COA

DATE	DESCRIPTION	QUANTITY SOLD	ISSUE PRICE	FINISH	PR-67	PR-68
2007 (1947-)	60th Wedding Anniversary Queen / Prince Philip	198	5,999.95	Proof	8,000.	8,250.
2008	100th Anniversary of the Royal Canadian Mint	248	8,159.95	Proof	8,000.	8,250.
2009	150th Anniv. Start Construction Parliament Buildings	77	10,199.95	Proof	10,100.	10,350.

FIVE HUNDRED DOLLARS, 75TH ANNIV. OF THE FIRST BANK NOTES ISSUED BY THE BANK OF CANADA, 2010.
  The reverse design on this coin is a reproduction of the central vignette that appears on the $500 bank note of 1935, a seated woman with a sickle, surrounded by the fruits of harvest, symbolising fertility.

Designers and Engravers:
  Obv.: S. Blunt, S. Taylor
  Rev.: S. Hepburn, J. Osio
Composition: 99.99% Au
Gold content: 156.5 g, 5.03 tr oz
Weight: 156.5 g
Diameter: 60.2 mm
Thickness: N/A
Edge: Reeded
Die Axis: ↑↑
Finish: Proof
Case of Issue: Maroon leatherette
  clam style case, black insert,
  encapsulated coin, COA

FIVE HUNDRED DOLLARS, 100TH ANNIVERSARY OF THE FIRST CANADIAN GOLD COINS, 1912-2012.
  The first dollar denomination coins, the five and ten dollar gold coins, were struck at the Ottawa Mint in 1912.

Designers and Engravers:
  Obv.: S. Blunt, S. Taylor
  Rev.: RCM Staff, W. Woodruff
Composition: 99.99% Au
Gold content: 156.5 g, 5.03 tr oz
Weight: 156.5 g
Diameter: 60.2 mm
Thickness: N/A
Edge: Plain
Die Axis: ↑↑
Finish: Proof
Case of Issue: Maroon leatherette
  clam style case, black insert,
  encapsulated coin, COA

FIVE HUNDRED DOLLARS, 100TH ANNIVERSARY OF THE CALGARY STAMPEDE, 2012.

Designers and Engravers:
  Obv.: S. Blunt, S. Taylor
  Rev.: RCM Staff, L. Normandin
Composition: 99.99% Au
Gold content: 156.5 g, 5.03 tr oz
Weight: 156.5 g
Diameter: 60.2 mm
Thickness: N/A
Edge: Reeded
Die Axis: ↑↑
Finish: Proof
Case of Issue: Maroon leatherette
  clam style case, black insert,
  encapsulated coin, COA

DATE	DESCRIPTION	QUANTITY SOLD	ISSUE PRICE	FINISH	PR-67	PR-68
2010	75th Anniversary of the First Bank of Canada Notes	191	9,495.95	Proof	9,500.	9,600.
2012 (1912-)	100th Anniversary of the First Canadian Gold Coins	115	12,274.95	Proof	12,275.	13,000.
2012	100th Anniv. of the Calgary Stampede	96	11,999.95	Proof	12,000.	12,250.

FIVE HUNDRED DOLLARS, MAPLE LEAF FOREVER, 2012.
The reverse design on this coin is also utilized on the $300 platinum coin and the $10 silver maple leaf for 2012, see pages 337 and 431.

Designers and Engravers:
Obv.: S. Blunt, S. Taylor
Rev.: RCM Staff, Michelle Grant
Composition: 99.99% Au
Gold content: 156.5 g, 5.03 tr oz
Weight: 156.5 g
Diameter: 60.2 mm
Thickness: N/A
Edge: Reeded
Die Axis: ↑↑
Finish: Proof
Case of Issue: Maroon leatherette clam style case, black insert, encapsulated coin, COA

FIVE HUNDRED DOLLARS, HMS SHANNON AND USS CHESAPEAKE, 2013.

Designers and Engravers:
Obv.: S. Blunt, S. Taylor
Rev.: J. Horton, RCM Staff
Composition: 99.99% Au
Gold content: 156.5 g, 5.03 tr oz
Weight: 156.5 g
Diameter: 60.2 mm
Thickness: N/A
Edge: Reeded
Die Axis: ↑↑
Finish: Proof
Case of Issue: Maroon leatherette clam style case, black insert, encapsulated coin, COA

FIVE HUNDRED DOLLARS, AN ABORIGINAL STORY, 2013.

Designers and Engravers:
Obv.: S. Blunt, S. Taylor
Rev.: R. Weizlneau, RCM Staff
Composition: 99.99% Au
Gold content: 156.5 g, 5.03 tr oz
Weight: 156.5 g
Diameter: 60.2 mm
Thickness: N/A
Edge: Reeded
Die Axis: ↑↑
Finish: Proof
Case of Issue: Maroon leatherette clam style case, black insert, encapsulated coin, COA

DATE	DESCRIPTION	QUANTITY SOLD	ISSUE PRICE	FINISH	PR-67	PR-68
2012	Maple Leaf Forever	146	11,999.95	Proof	12,000.	12,250.
2013	HMS Shannon and USS Chesapeake	61	11,999.95	Proof	12,000.	12,250.
2013	An Aboriginal Story	34	11,999.95	Proof	12,000.	12,250.

Note: Coins illustrated on pages 326-328 illustrated smaller than actual size.

TWO THOUSAND FIVE HUNDRED DOLLAR GOLD COINS

VANCOUVER 2010 OLYMPIC WINTER GAMES, 2007-2010

Common Obverse
(except for date)

2007 Early Canada
Designer: Stan Witten
Engraver: Stan Witten

2008 Towards Confederation
Designer: Susan Taylor
Engraver: Susan Taylor

2009 The Canada of Today
Designer: Design Team of the Vancouver
Organising Committee for the
2010 Olympic/Paralympic Games
Engraver: Konrad Wachelko

2009 Surviving the Flood
Designer: Design Team of the Vancouver
Organising Committee for the
2010 Olympic/Paralympic Games
Engraver: Christie Paquet

2010 The Eagle
Designer: Xwa lac tun (Ricky Harry)
Engraver: Stan Witten

Designers:
  Obv.: Susanna Blunt
  Rev.: See reverse illustration
Composition: 99.99% Au
Gold content: 1,000.0 g, 32.15 tr oz
Weight: 1,000.0 g (1 kilo)
Diameter: 101.6 mm

Engravers:
  Obv.: Susan Taylor
  Rev.: See reverse illustration
Thickness: N/A
Edge: Plain
Die Axis: ↑↑
Finish: Proof

Case of Issue: Black display case, encapsulated coins, COA, 2010 Olympic Winter Games theme sleeve.

DATE	DESCRIPTION	DATE OF ISSUE	QUANTITY SOLD	ISSUE PRICE	FINISH	PR-67	PR-68
2007	Early Canada	Feb. 23, 2007	20	36,000.	Proof	51,350.	51,700.
2008	Towards Confederation	Feb. 20, 2008	20	49,000.	Proof	51,350.	51,700.
2009	The Canada of Today	Apr. 15, 2009	50	54,000.	Proof	51,350.	51,700.
2009	Surviving the Flood	Nov. 21, 2009	40	49,000.	Proof	51,350.	51,700.
2010	The Eagle	Nov. 19, 2009	20	49,000.	Proof	51,350.	51,700.

Note: Coins illustrated on pages 329- 334 smaller than actual size.

TWO THOUSAND FIVE HUNDRED DOLLARS, 125TH ANNIVERSARY OF BANFF NATIONAL PARK, 2010.

Designers and Engravers:
  Obv.: S. Blunt, Susan Taylor
  Rev.: T. Bianco, S. Taylor
Composition: 99.99% Au
Gold content:
  1000.0 g, 32.15 tr oz
Weight: 1,000.0 g (1 kilo)
Diameter: 101.6 mm
Thickness: N/A
Edge: Plain
Die Axis: ↑↑
Finish: Proof
Case of Issue: Black clam style
  case, black insert, encapsulated
  coin, COA

TWO THOUSAND FIVE HUNDRED DOLLARS, 375TH ANNIVERSARY OF LACROSSE, 2011.

Designers and Engravers:
  Obv.: S. Blunt, Susan Taylor
  Rev.: S. Hepburn, C. Paquet
Composition: 99.99% Au
Gold content:
  1000.0 g, 32.15 tr oz
Weight: 1,000.0 g (1 kilo)
Diameter: 101.6 mm
Thickness: N/A
Edge: Plain
Die Axis: ↑↑
Finish: Proof
Case of Issue: Black clam style
  case, black insert, encapsulated
  coin, COA

TWO THOUSAND FIVE HUNDRED DOLLARS, YEAR OF THE (WATER) DRAGON, 2012.
An identical design is utilized on the $250 silver coin for 2011, see page 259 and on the $15 silver coin from the Lunar Lotus Series, see page 194.

Designers and Engravers:
  Obv.: S. Blunt, Susan Taylor
  Rev.: Three Degrees Creative
    Group Inc., C. Mok
Composition: 99.99% Au
Gold content:
  1000.0 g, 32.15 tr oz
Weight: 1,000.0 g (1 kilo)
Diameter: 101.6 mm
Thickness: N/A
Edge: Plain
Die Axis: ↑↑
Finish: Proof
Case of Issue: Black clam style
  case, black insert, encapsulated
  coin, COA

DATE	DESCRIPTION	QUANTITY SOLD	ISSUE PRICE	FINISH	PR-67	PR-68
2010	125th Anniversary Banff National Park	20	57,000.	Proof	57,875.	58,000.
2011	375th Anniversary of Lacrosse	29	69,000.	Proof	69,000.	69,250.
2012	Year of the (Water) Dragon	37	69,000.	Proof	69,000.	69,250.

TWO THOUSAND FIVE HUNDRED DOLLARS, YEAR OF THE (CLASSIC) DRAGON, 2012.

Designers and Engravers:
  Obv.: S. Blunt, S. Taylor
  Rev.: A. Cheung, S. Witten
Composition: 99.99% Au
Gold content:
  1000.0 g, 32.15 tr oz
Weight: 1,000.0 g (1 kilo)
Diameter: 101.6 mm
Thickness: N/A
Edge: Plain
Die Axis: ↑↑
Finish: Proof
Case of Issue: Black clam style
  case, black insert, encapsulated
  coin, COA

TWO THOUSAND FIVE HUNDRED DOLLARS, *THE CHALLENGE*, ROBERT BATEMAN MOOSE COIN SERIES, 2012.
  The reverse design on this coin features the upraised head, neck and multi-pronged antlers of a moose taken from Robert Bateman's painting *The Moose Family*. The coin was issued to commemorate the 50th anniversary of the Canadian Wildlife Federation. For other coins in the Robert Bateman Moose series, see pages 226, 260 and 306.

Designers and Engravers:
  Obv.: S. Blunt, S. Taylor
  Rev.: R. Bateman, S. Witten
Composition: 99.99% Au
Gold content:
  1000.0 g, 32.15 tr oz
Weight: 1,000.0 g (1 kilo)
Diameter: 101.6 mm
Thickness: N/A
Edge: Plain
Die Axis: ↑↑
Finish: Proof
Case of Issue: Maple wood box
  lacquered in walnut coloured
  finish, black flocked insert,
  encapsulated coin, COA

TWO THOUSAND FIVE HUNDRED DOLLARS, THE BATTLE OF QUEENSTON HEIGHTS, 2012.

Designers and Engravers:
  Obv.: S. Blunt, S. Taylor
  Rev.: John David Kelly,
    Marcus Hallam
Composition: 99.99% Au
Gold content:
  1000.0 g, 32.15 tr oz
Weight: 1000.0 g
Diameter: 102.1 mm
Thickness: N/A
Edge: Reeded
Die Axis: ↑↑
Finish: Proof
Case of Issue: Maroon clam style
  case, black flocked insert,
  encapsulated coin, COA

DATE	DESCRIPTION	QUANTITY SOLD	ISSUE PRICE	FINISH	PR-67	PR-68
2012	Year of the (Classic) Dragon	37	69,000.	Proof	69,000.	69,250.
2012 (1962-)	*The Challenge*, Robert Bateman	12	69,000.	Proof	69,000.	69,250.
2012	Battle of Queenston Heights	19	69,000.	Proof	69,000.	69,250.

TWO THOUSAND FIVE HUNDRED DOLLARS, YEAR OF THE SNAKE, 2013.

Designers and Engravers:
  Obv.: S. Blunt, S. Taylor
  Rev.: Three Degrees Creative
        Group, RCM Staff
Composition: 99.99% Au
Gold content:
  1000.0 g, 32.15 tr oz
Weight: 1000.0 g
Diameter: 102.1 mm
Thickness: N/A
Edge: Reeded
Die Axis: ↑↑
Finish: Proof
Case of Issue: Gold satin-like
  covered case, black flocked insert,
  encapsulated coin, COA

TWO THOUSAND FIVE HUNDRED DOLLARS, 250TH ANNIVERSARY OF THE END OF THE SEVEN YEARS WAR, 2013.

Designers and Engravers:
  Obv.: S. Blunt, S. Taylor
  Rev.: L. Normandin, RCM Staff
Composition: 99.99% Au
Gold content:
  1000.0 g, 32.15 tr oz
Weight: 1000.0 g
Diameter: 102.1 mm
Thickness: N/A
Die Axis: ↑↑
Edge: Reeded
Finish: Proof
Case of Issue: Maple wood case,
  black flocked insert, encapsulated
  coin, COA

TWO THOUSAND FIVE HUNDRED DOLLARS, CANADA'S ARCTIC LANDSCAPE, 2013.

Designers and Engravers:
  Obv.: S. Blunt, S. Taylor
  Rev.: W. David Ward, RCM Staff
Composition: 99.99% Au
Gold content:
  1000.0 g, 32.15 tr oz
Weight: 1000.0 g
Diameter: 102.1 mm
Thickness: N/A
Die Axis: ↑↑
Edge: Reeded
Finish: Proof
Case of Issue: Maple wood case,
  black flocked insert, encapsulated
  coin, COA

DATE	DESCRIPTION	QUANTITY SOLD	ISSUE PRICE	FINISH	PR-67	PR-68
2013	Year of the Snake	37	69,000	Proof	69,000.	69,250.
2013	250th Anniv. of the End of the Seven Years War	11	69,000.	Proof	69,000.	69,250.
2013	Canada's Arctic Landscape	12	69,000.	Proof	69,000.	69,250.

TWO THOUSAND FIVE HUNDRED DOLLARS, 1813 BATTLE OF CRYSLER'S FARM AND BATTLE OF CHATEAUGUAY, 2013.

Designers and Engravers:
  Obv.: S. Blunt, S. Taylor
  Rev.: A. Sherriff-Scott, H. Julie,
       RCM Staff
Composition: 99.99% Au
Gold content:
  1000.0 g, 32.15 tr oz
Weight: 1000.0 g
Diameter: 102.1 mm
Thickness: N/A
Die Axis: ↑↑
Edge: Reeded
Finish: Proof
Case of Issue: Maple wood case,
  black flocked insert, encapsulated
  coin, COA

TWO THOUSAND FIVE HUNDRED DOLLARS, THE CARIBOU, 2013.

Designers and Engravers:
  Obv.: S. Blunt, S. Taylor
  Rev.: Trevor Tennant, RCM Staff
Composition: 99.99% Au
Gold content:
  1000.0 g, 32.15 tr oz
Weight: 1,000.0 g (1 kilo)
Diameter: 101.6 mm
Thickness: N/A
Edge: Reeded
Die Axis: ↑↑
Finish: Proof
Case of Issue: Maple wood case,
  black insert, encapsulated coin,
  COA

TWO THOUSAND FIVE HUNDRED DOLLARS, YEAR OF THE HORSE, 2014

Designers and Engravers:
  Obv.: S. Blunt, S. Taylor
  Rev.: Three Degrees Creative
       Group, RCM Staff
Composition: 99.99% Au
Gold content:
  1000.0 g, 32.15 tr oz
Weight: 1,000.0 g (1 kilo)
Diameter: 101.6 mm
Thickness: N/A
Edge: Reeded
Die Axis: ↑↑
Finish: Proof
Case of Issue: Gold satin-like
  covered case, black flocked insert,
  encapsulated coin, COA

DATE	DESCRIPTION	QUANTITY SOLD	ISSUE PRICE	FINISH	PR-67	PR-68
2013	1813 Battle of Crysler's Farm and Battle of Chateauguay	10	69,000	Proof	69,000.	69,250.
2013	The Caribou	5	69,000.	Proof	69,000.	69,250.
2014	Year of the Horse	10	69,000.	Proof	69,000.	69,250.

TWO THOUSAND FIVE HUNDRED DOLLARS, IN THE EYES OF THE SNOWY OWL, 2014.

Designers and Engravers:
Obv.: S. Blunt, S. Taylor
Rev.: Anold Nogy, RCM Staff
Composition: 99.99% Au
Gold content:
1000.0 g, 32.15 tr oz
Weight: 1,000.0 g (1 kilo)
Diameter: 101.6 mm
Thickness: N/A
Edge: Reeded
Die Axis: ↑↑
Finish: Proof
Case of Issue: Maple wood case, black insert, encapsulated coin, COA

TWO THOUSAND FIVE HUNDRED DOLLARS, BATTLE OF LUNDY'S LANE, 2014.

Designers and Engravers:
Obv.: S. Blunt, S. Taylor
Rev.: Bonnie Ross, RCM Staff
Composition: 99.99% Au
Gold content:
1000.0 g, 32.15 tr oz
Weight: 1,000.0 g (1 kilo)
Diameter: 101.6 mm
Thickness: N/A
Edge: Reeded
Die Axis: ↑↑
Finish: Proof
Case of Issue: Maple wood case, black insert, encapsulated coin, COA

DATE	DESCRIPTION	QUANTITY SOLD	ISSUE PRICE	FINISH	PR-67	PR-68
2014	In the Eyes of the Snowy Owl	10	69,000.	Proof	69,000.	69,250.
2014	Battle of Lundy's Lane	10	69,000.	Proof	69,000.	69,250.

Note: 1. See also page 406 for three $2,500. kilo gold maple leaf coins.
2. Coins illustrated on pages 329- 334 smaller than actual size.

PALLADIUM COINS

FIFTY DOLLAR PALLADIUM COINS

FIFTY DOLLARS, BIG AND LITTLE BEAR CONSTELLATIONS, 2006.
Each coin has been crafted with a special laser effect to illustrate the position of Big Bear and Little Bear constellations above a conceptual Canadian forest, as they would appear when viewed from the nation's capital during each of the four seasons.

Common Obverse

Designers and Engravers:
    Obv.:   Susanna Blunt, Susan Taylor
    Rev.:   Colin Mayne, José Osio
Composition: 99.95% Pl; Laser effect
Palladium content: 31.144 g, 1.0 tr oz
Weight: 31.16 g
Diameter: 34.0 mm
Thickness: 3.5 mm
Edge: Reeded
Die Axis: ↑↑
Finish: Specimen
Case: Maroon clam style case; black flocked
           insert, encapsulated coin, COA

Spring

Summer

Autumn

Winter

DATE	DESCRIPTION	QUANTITY SOLD	ISSUE PRICE	FINISH	SP-66	SP-67
2006	Spring	300	849.95	Specimen	975.	1,000.
2006	Summer	300	849.95	Specimen	975.	1,000.
2006	Autumn	300	849.95	Specimen	975.	1,000.
2006	Winter	300	849.95	Specimen	975.	1,000.

PLATINUM COINS

THREE HUNDRED DOLLAR PLATINUM COINS

PREHISTORIC ANIMAL SERIES

THREE HUNDRED DOLLARS, PREHISTORIC ANIMAL SERIES, 2007-2010.

Obverse 2007-2008
With RCM Logo

Obverse 2009-2012
Without RCM Logo

Designers: and Engravers:
　Obv.:　Susanna Blunt, Susan Taylor
　Rev.:　See reverse illustrations
Composition: 99.95% Pt
Platinum content: 31.14 g, 1.0 tr oz
Weight: 31.16 g
Diameter: 30.0 mm
Thickness: 2.6 mm
Edge: Reeded
Die Axis: ↑↑
Finish: Proof
Case of Issue: Maroon leatherette clam style case, black flocked insert, encapsulated coin, COA

2007 Woolly Mammoth
Des.: RCM Staff
Engr.: José Osio

2008 Scimitar Cat
Des.: RCM Staff
Engr.: Christie Paquet

2009 Steppe Bison
Des. RCM Staff
Engr.: José Osio

2010 Ground Sloth
Des.: Jerri Burnett
Engr.: Stan Witten

DATE	DESCRIPTION	QUANTITY SOLD	ISSUE PRICE	FINISH	PR-67	PR-68
2007	Woolly Mammoth	287	2,999.95	Proof	3,000.	3,100.
2008	Scimitar Cat	200	3,419.95	Proof	3,000.	3,100.
2009	Steppe Bison	197	2,999.95	Proof	3,000.	3,100.
2010	Ground Sloth	189	2,999.95	Proof	3,000.	3,100.

THREE HUNDRED DOLLARS, WILDLIFE SERIES, 2011-2014.

Obverse 2011-2014

2011 Cougar
Des.: William Woodruff
Engr.: RCM Staff

Designers and Engravers:
　Obv.:　Susanna Blunt, Susan Taylor
　Rev.:　See reverse illustrations
Composition: 99.95% Pt
Platinum content: 31.16 g, 1.0 tr oz
Weight: 31.16 g　　　**Edge:** Reeded
Diameter: 30.0 mm　　**Die Axis:** ↑↑
Thickness: 2.6 mm　　**Finish:** Proof
Case: Maroon leatherette clam style case, black flocked insert, encapsulated coin, COA

THREE HUNDRED DOLLARS, WILDLIFE SERIES, 2011-2014 (cont.)

| 2012 The Bull Moose Des.: Robert Bateman Engr.: Cecily Mok | 2013 The Bald Eagle Des.: Claudio D'Angelo Engr.: RCM Staff | 2013 Rocky Mountain Bighorn Sheep Des.: Emily Damstra Engr.: RCM Staff | 2014 Bison Des.: Claudio D'Angelo Engr.: RCM Staff |

DATE	DESCRIPTION	QUANTITY SOLD	ISSUE PRICE	FINISH	PR-67	PR-68
2011	The Cougar	183	2,999.95	Proof	3,000.	3,100.
2012	The Bull Moose	250	2,999.95	Proof	3,000.	3,100.
2013	The Bald Eagle	199	2,999.95	Proof	3,000.	3,100.
2013	Rocky Mountain Bighorn Sheep	152	2,999.95	Proof	3,000.	3,100.
2014	Bison: Challenge For Power	200	2,999,.95	Proof	3,000.	3,100.

THREE HUNDRED DOLLARS, COMMEMORATIVE ISSUES, 2012-2013.

| 2012 Obverse Maple Leaf Forever | 2012 Maple Leaf Forever Des.: Luc Normandin Engr.: RCM Staff | 2013 Obverse HMS Shannon and USS Chesapeake | 2013 HMS Shannon and USS Chesapeake Des.: Luc Normandin Engr.: RCM Staff |

Designers:
  Obv.: Susanna Blunt
  Rev.: See reverse illustration
Composition: 99.95% Pt
Weight: 31.16 g
Diameter: 30.0 mm
Thickness: 2.6 mm

Engravers:
  Obv.: Susan Taylor
  Rev.: See reverse illustration
Platinum content: 31.16 g, 1.0 tr oz
Edge: Reeded
Die Axis: ↑↑
Finish: Proof

Case of Issue: Maroon leatherette clam style case, black flocked insert, encapsulated coin, COA

DATE	DESCRIPTION	QUANTITY SOLD	ISSUE PRICE	FINISH	PR-67	PR-68
2012	Maple Leaf Forever	250	2,999.95	Proof	3,000.	3,100.
2013	HMS Shannon and USS Chesapeake	231	2,999.95	Proof	3,000.	3,100.

COLLECTOR SETS

Note:
1. For some sets the mintage was pre-announced as a maximum number of sets to be issued. In other cases the mintage was open-ended with the issue period a function of time. In the pricing tables for sets the mintage number denotes the number of sets sold. The final number is usually only available after a second year of RCM Reports.

2. Within the set listings are sets with different finishes and compositions. Currently the four main finish categories are Uncirculated, Brilliant Uncirculated, Specimen and Proof. Usually, these sets contain exact design copies of the circulating business strike coins, but there are a few exceptions when commemorative coins are involved.

3. For a complete explanation on finishes, see page xiv in the introduction.

SPECIAL RCM WRAPPED ROLLS OF COINS

Specialty Rolls are generated by the Royal Canadian Mint printing a specially designed wrapper for a standard roll of a denomination.

DATE	DENOMINATION	DESCRIPTION	QUANTITY SOLD	PRICE
2004P	One Cent	Standard, CPS, Roll of 50	N/A	10.00
2004	One Cent	Standard, CPZ, Roll of 50	N/A	12.00
2005	One Cent	Standard, CPZ, Roll of 50	N/A	12.00
2005P	One Cent	Standard, CPS, Roll of 50	N/A	15.00
2012	One Cent	Standard, Mixed CPS and CPZ, Roll of 50	20,000	50.00
2005P	Five Cents	Standard, Roll of 40	N/A	10.00
2005P	Five Cents	V-E Day, Roll of 40	N/A	15.00
2005P	Ten Cents	Standard, Roll of 50	N/A	10.00
2004P	Twenty-five Cents	Poppy, Roll of 40	N/A	20.00
2005P	Twenty-five Cents	Standard, Roll of 40	N/A	25.00
2005P	Twenty-five Cents	Alberta, Roll of 40	N/A	25.00
2005P	Twenty-five Cents	Saskatchewan, Roll of 40	N/A	20.00
2005P	Twenty-five Cents	Veteran, Roll of 40	N/A	20.00
2006P	Twenty-Five Cents	Breast Cancer, Roll of 40	102	25.00
2006P	Twenty-Five Cents	Standard, Roll of 40	N/A	20.00
2006P	Twenty-Five Cents	Bravery, Roll of 40	205	25.00
2007	Twenty-Five Cents	Curling, Roll of 40	10,000	20.00
2007	Twenty-Five Cents	Ice Hockey, Roll of 40	10,000	20.00
2007	Twenty-Five Cents	Biathlon, Roll of 40	10,000	20.00
2007	Twenty-Five Cents	Alpine Skiing, Roll of 40	10,000	20.00
2007	Twenty-Five Cents	Wheelchair Curling, Roll of 40	10,000	20.00
2008	Twenty-Five Cents	Snowboarding, Roll of 40	10,000	20.00
2008	Twenty-Five Cents	Freestyle Skiing, Roll of 40	10,000	20.00
2008	Twenty-Five Cents	Figure Skating, Roll of 40	10,000	20.00
2008	Twenty-Five Cents	Bobsleigh, Roll of 40	10,000	20.00
2009	Twenty-Five Cents	Speedskating, Roll of 40	10,000	20.00
2009	Twenty-Five Cents	Cross Country Skiing, Roll of 40	10,000	20.00
2009	Twenty-Five Cents	Ice Sledge Hockey, Roll of 40	10,000	20.00
2005P	Fifty Cents	Roll of 25	8,000	35.00
2006P	Fifty Cents	Roll of 25	3,920	70.00
2007	Fifty Cents	Roll of 25	4,462	45.00
2008	Fifty Cents	Roll of 25	6,000	30.00
2009	Fifty Cents	Roll of 25	6,000	45.00
2010	Fifty Cents	Roll of 25	6,000	45.00
2011	Fifty Cents	Roll of 25	6,880	45.00
2012	Fifty Cents	Roll of 25	9,960	35.00
2013	Fifty Cents	Roll of 25	15,000	35.00
2014	Fifty Cents	Roll of 25	20,000	25.00
2004	One Dollar	Olympic Flame, Roll of 25	N/A	40.00
2005	One Dollar	Loon, Roll of 25	N/A	40.00
2005	One Dollar	Terry Fox, Roll of 25	N/A	40.00
2008	One Dollar	Loon Dance, Roll of 25	10,000	45.00
2009	One Dollar	Montreal Canadiens, Roll of 25	10,000	45.00
2010	One Dollar	Inukshuk, Roll of 25	10,000	45.00
2005	Two Dollars	Polar Bear, Roll of 25	N/A	80.00
2006	Two Dollars	Double Date, Roll of 25	356	100.00
2006	Two Dollars	Churchill, Roll of 25	N/A	70.00
2008	Two Dollars	Quebec City, Roll of 25	N/A	80.00

FIRST AND LAST DAY OF ISSUE CARDS

DATE	DENOMINATION	DESCRIPTION	QUANTITY SOLD	PRICE
2005P	One Cent	Standard, CPS, First Day	1,919	10.00
2006P / 2006	One Cent	Standard, CPS, Last Day / First Day	750	20.00
2005P	Five Cents	Standard, First Day	1,951	15.00
2006P / 2006	Five Cents	Standard, Last Day / First Day	739	10.00
2006P	Five Cents	Victory, First Day	11,192	8.00
2005P	Ten Cents	Standard, First Day	1,961	8.00
2006P / 2006	Ten Cents	Standard, Last Day / First Day	742	10.00
2004P	Twenty-Five Cents	Poppy, Coloured	N/A	30.00
2005P	Twenty-Five Cents	Standard, First Day	5,000	8.00
2005P	Twenty-Five Cents	Alberta, First Day	9,108	8.00
2005P	Twenty-Five Cents	Saskatchewan, First Day	6,980	8.00
2005P	Twenty-Five Cents	Veteran, First Day	8,361	10.00
2006P / 2006	Twenty-Five Cents	Standard, Last Day / First Day	742	10.00
2006P	Twenty-Five Cents	Breast Cancer, First Day	7,348	10.00
2006	Twenty-Five Cents	Bravery, First Day	4,906	10.00
2007	Twenty-Five Cents	Curling, First Day	10,000	5.00
2007	Twenty-Five Cents	Ice Hockey, First Day	10,000	5.00
2007	Twenty-Five Cents	Biathlon, First Day	10,000	5.00
2007	Twenty-Five Cents	Alpine Skiing, First Day	10,000	5.00
2007	Twenty-Five Cents	Wheelchair Curling, First Day	10,000	5.00
2008	Twenty-Five Cents	Snowboarding, First Day	10,000	5.00
2008	Twenty-Five Cents	Freestyle Skiing, First Day	10,000	5.00
2008	Twenty-Five Cents	Figure Skating, First Day	10,000	5.00
2008	Twenty-Five Cents	Bobsleigh, First Day	10,000	5.00
2009	Twenty-Five Cents	Speed Skating, First Day	10,000	5.00
2009	Twenty-Five Cents	Cross Country Skiing, First Day	10,000	5.00
2009	Twenty-Five Cents	Ice Sledge Hockey, First Day	10,000	5.00
2005P	Fifty Cents	Standard, First Day	2,445	15.00
2006P / 2006	Fifty Cents	Standard, Last Day / First Day	1,065	15.00
2004	One Dollar	Standard, First Day	34,488	5.00
2005	One Dollar	Standard, First Day	2,048	20.00
2005	One Dollar	Terry Fox, First Day	19,933	15.00
2006	One Dollar	Standard, Last Day / First Fay	935	15.00
2006	One Dollar	Loon Settling, First Day	7,481	15.00
2008	One Dollar	Loon Dance, First Day	10,000	15.00
2005	Two Dollars	Standard, First Day	2,501	15.00
2006	Two Dollars	Standard, Last Day /First Day	1,971	20.00
2006	Two Dollars	10th Anniversary, First Day	1,971	20.00

BOOKMARKS

DATE	DENOMINATION	DESCRIPTION	QUANTITY SOLD	PRICE
2004P	Twenty-Five Cents	Poppy, Coloured	29,951	30.00
2005P	Twenty-Five Cents	Poppy, Coloured	N/A	25.00
2006P	Twenty-Five Cents	Breast Cancer	40,911	15.00
2007	Twenty-Five Cents	Curling	N/A	15.00
2007	Twenty-Five Cents	Ice Hockey	N/A	5.00
2007	Twenty-Five Cents	Biathlon	N/A	5.00
2007	Twenty-Five Cents	Alpine Skiing,	N/A	5.00
2007	Twenty-Five Cents	Wheelchair Curling	N/A	5.00
2008	Twenty-Five Cents	Snowboarding	N/A	5.00
2008	Twenty-Five Cents	Freestyle Skiing,	N/A	5.00
2008	Twenty-Five Cents	Figure Skating	N/A	5.00
2008	Twenty-Five Cents	Bobsleigh	N/A	5.00
2008	Twenty-Five Cents	Armistice	N/A	15.00
2009	Twenty-Five Cents	Speed Skating	N/A	5.00
2009	Twenty-Five Cents	Cross Country Skiing	N/A	5.00
2009	Twenty-Five Cents	Ice Sledge Hockey	N/A	5.00

COLLECTOR CARDS FOR CIRCULATION COINAGE, 2004-2013

2004 "Lest We Forget" The Poppy Coin Collector Card

DATE	DESCRIPTION	QUANTITY SOLD	ISSUE PRICE	FINISH	MS-65
2004	**Lucky Loonie Coin Collector Card** to hold Standard 5 coins, Lucky Loonie $1	N/A	Free	—	5.
2004	**"Lest We Forget" Poppy Coin Collector Card** to hold Standard 5 coins, Poppy 25¢	21,738	Free	—	5.
2004	**400th Anniversary First French Settlement Collector Card** to hold Standard 5 coins, Île Sainte-Croix 25¢	N/A	Free	—	5.
2005	**Alberta Centennial Collector Card** to hold Standard 5 coins, Alberta 25¢	N/A	Free	—	5.
2005	**Saskatchewan Centennial Collector Card** to hold Standard 5 coins, Saskatchewan 25¢	N/A	Free	—	5.
2005	**"Canada Celebrates Peace" Victory Anniversary Collector Card** to hold Standard 5 coins, 1945-2005 Victory 5¢	N/A	Free	—	5.
2005	**Year of the Veteran Collector Card** to hold Standard 5 coins, Veteran 25¢	N/A	Free	—	5.
2005	**Terry Fox Coin Collector Card** to hold Standard 5 coins, Terry Fox $1	N/A	Free	—	5.
2005	**Creating a Future Without Breast Cancer 25-Cent Collector Card** to hold Standard 5 coins, Breast Cancer 25¢	N/A	Free	—	5.

COLLECTOR CARDS FOR CIRCULATION COINAGE, 2004-2013 (cont.)

2007-2010 Inukshuk Coin Collector Card

CANADA

2010 Polar Bear Coin Collection Card

DATE	DESCRIPTION	QUANTITY SOLD	ISSUE PRICE	FINISH	MS-65
2006	**Lucky Loonie Collector Card** to hold Standard 5 coins, 2006 Lucky Loonie $1	N/A	Free	—	5.
2006	**10th Anniversary Toonie Collector Card** to hold Standard 5 coins, Churchill $2	N/A	Free	—	5.
2006	**Medal of Bravery Collector Card** to hold Standard 5 coins, Medal of Bravery 25¢	N/A	Free	—	5.
2006	**Creating a Future without Breast Cancer Coin Collector Card** to hold Standard 5 coins, Breast Cancer 25¢	N/A	Free	—	5.
2007-2010	**Vancouver Landscape** display card holding 10 Olympic and 2 Paralympic 25¢ coins; $1 Loon Dance, $1 Inukshuk	48,198	29.95	Circulation	15.
2007-2010	**Vancouver City** display card holding 10 Olympic and 2 Paralympic 25¢ coins; $1 Loon Dance, $1 Inukshuk	47,691	29.95	Circulation	15.
2007-2010	**Vancouver Skier** display card holding 10 Olympic and 2 Paralympic 25¢ coins; $1 Loon Dance, $1 Lucky Loonie	46,361	29.95	Circulation	15.
2007-2010	**Inukshuk** display card holding 10 Olympic and 2 Paralympic 25¢ coins; $1 Loon Dance, $1 Inukshuk	111,283	29.95	Circulation	15.
2010	**Canoe Coin Collector Card** holds Standard six coins (1¢–$2)	1,466	19.95	Circulation	15.
2010	**Maple Leaves Coin Collector Card** holds Standard six coins (1¢–$2)	2,734	19.95	Circulation	15.
2010	**Polar Bear Coin Collector Card** holds Standard six coins (1¢–$2)	2,127	19.95	Circulation	15.
2010	**RCMP Coin Collector Card** holds Standard six coins (1¢ – $2)	13,036	19.95	Circulation	15.
2010	**11-sided Red Maple Vancouver 2010 Olympic Winter Games Display Card** to hold 10 Olympic and 2 Paralympic 25¢ coins; 2008 Loon Dance $1; and 2010 Inukshuk $1	104,400	4.95	—	5.
2010	**11-sided Red Maple Vancouver 2010 Olympic Winter Games Display Card** holding 10 Olympic and 2 Paralympic 25¢; 2008 Loon Dance $1; 2010 Inukshuk $1	164,295	29.95	Circulation	20.
2010	**Vancouver 2010 Olympic Winter Games Collector Card**, to hold 10 Olympic/2 Paralympic 25¢; 2008 Loon Dance $1; 2010 Inukshuk $1	N/A	Free	—	5.
2010	**Remembrance Day Collector Card** contains the 2010 25¢ Remembrance Day coin, two die-cut holes to hold the 2004 and 2008 25¢ Poppy coins; Postage paid postcard	21,738	9.95	Circulation	10.
2011	**Our Legendary Nature Collector Card** to hold 8 coins, 2011 $2 Boreal Forest, $1 Parks Canada, 2011 25¢ coloured and plain Peregrine Falcon, Orca Whale and Wood Bison	N/A	Free	—	5.
2011	**CN Tower Coin Collector Card** holds Standard six coins (1¢–$2)	6,064	19.95	Circulation	15.
2011	**Vancouver Coin Collector Card** holds Standard six coins (1¢–$2)	3,784	19.95	Circulation	15.
2012	**The War of 1812 Collector Card** to hold 9 coins, 2012 $1 HMS Shannon, 2012 25¢ coloured and plain Brock, Tecumseh, de Salaberry and Secord	N/A	Free	—	5.
2013	**Heart of the Arctic Collector Card** to hold four 25¢ coins, two Canadian Arctic Expedition Centennial and two Arctic Symbols	N/A	Free	—	5.

PROOF-LIKE SETS 1954-1967

SIX COIN SILVER PROOF-LIKE SETS, 1954-1960

The year 1953 saw the first use of the white cardboard six-coin holder that in 1954 became the package for public sale of sets. The holder with the coins included was wrapped in cellophane. The finish on the coins offered acquired the name proof-like.

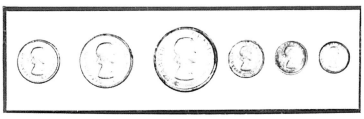

1954-1959

In 1960 the white cardboard holders appeared with a Royal Canadian Mint domicile. Three varieties of stamps exist. A sealed wooden box containing 250 proof-like sets was available directly from the Mint in 1960.

ROYAL CANADIAN MINT
320 SUSSEX DRIVE
OTTAWA 2, ONTARIO.

Stamp One

ROYAL CANADIAN MINT
OTTAWA   CANADA

Stamp Two

ROYAL CANADIAN MINT
OTTAWA   CANADA

Stamp Three

DATE	QUANTITY SOLD	ISSUE PRICE	FINISH	PL-65
1954 NSF	3,000	2.50	Proof-like	2,500.
1954 SF	Included	2.50	Proof-like	750.
1955	6,300	2.50	Proof-like	500.
1955 ARN	Included	2.50	Proof-like	600.
1956	6,500	2.50	Proof-like	300.
1957	11,862	2.50	Proof-like	200.
1957 1WL	Included	2.50	Proof-like	225.
1958	18,259	2.50	Proof-like	150.
1959	31,577	3.00	Proof-like	85.
1960	64,097	3.00	Proof-like	70.

NOTES ON 1954 TO 1960 PROOF-LIKE SETS

1. The 1954 No Shoulder Fold designation applies only to the one cent coin; the balance of the coins (5) are of the Shoulder Fold variety.
2. Proof-like-65 prices are for sets in their original packaging.
3. The single denomination proof-like coins have now been incorporated into the pricing tables in the circulating coinage section of Volume One.

SIX COIN SILVER PROOF-LIKE SETS, 1961-1967

In 1961 a new system of packaging sets was introduced. The six coins were heat sealed between two layers of pliofilm which was embossed with the words ROYAL CANADIAN MINT. The set was then inserted in an envelope along with an explanatory card.

1961-1967

DATE	QUANTITY SOLD	ISSUE PRICE	FINISH	PL- 65
1961	98,373	3.00	Proof-like (PL)	65.
1962	200,950	3.00	Proof-like (PL)	50.
1963	673,006	3.00	Proof-like (PL)	30.
1964	1,653,162	3.00	Proof-like (PL)	30.
1965 Type 1	2,904,352	4.00	Proof-like (PL)	30.
1965 Type 2	Included	4.00	Proof-like (PL)	30.
1966 LB	672,514	4.00	Proof-like (PL)	35.
1967 5¢ ↑↑	963,714	4.00	Proof-like (PL)	40.
1967 5¢ ↑↓	Included	4.00	Proof-like (PL)	500.

NOTES ON 1961 TO 1967 PROOF-LIKE SETS

1. The 1961 set, which of course was the first set packaged in the pliofilm, did not come without problems. The one cent coin was prone to discolouring, making a brilliant, red PL-65 cent a scarcity.
2. Only Types One, Small Bead, Pointed 5 and Type 2, Small Bead, Blunt 5, 1965 silver dollars were used in the assembly of proof-like sets for that year.
3. The following variety combinations will be found in the 1965 proof-like sets.
    A. Type 1 dollar with Type 1 cent
    B. Type 1 dollar with Type 3 cent
    C. Type 2 dollar with Type 1 cent
    D. Type 2 dollar with Type 3 cent
4. Since they were not officially released, no 1966 small bead dollars were issued in proof-like sets.
5. A very limited number of 1967 Proof-like sets contain a striking variety: a coinage (↑↓) five cent coin.

BRILLIANT UNCIRCULATED and UNCIRCULATED SETS, 1968-2014

SIX COIN NICKEL BRILLIANT UNCIRCULATED SETS, 1968-1987

This is a continuation of the silver proof-like sets previously offered, except that the 10 cents through one-dollar coins were now nickel in composition. Naturally, the one cent and five cents remained the same, and the pliofilm packaging continued. The outer envelope was white with blue printing. The finish on the coins in the sets is brilliant uncirculated (MS-65-NC): brilliant relief on brilliant background.

The qualities of the coins in the sets were mixed but by 1977 the quality began to improve, probably as a result of the purchase of numismatic presses in 1972 to produce Canada's first officially recognised proof coins for the Montreal Olympic sets. The finish on the coins in the sets was now advertised by the Royal Canadian Mint as brilliant relief against a brilliant background. In 1980 the Mint's marketing department began a restructuring of the selection of sets and coins offered to collectors with the result the Mint Set was officially called "The Brilliant Uncirculated Set.". This set featured one coin of each denomination issued for circulation in Canada. The quality improvement which began in 1977 continued with the 1981 introduction of a confirmed finish on the pliofilm set of "brilliant relief on brilliant background."

In 1985 the Mint experimented with a clear hard plastic package to replace the soft pliofilm package used in previous years. As it did not prove to be practical, the experimental package was not adopted. The last year the nickel voyageur dollar was used in the brilliant uncirculated sets was 1987.

Pliofilm packaging, 1968-1987

1973 TWENTY-FIVE CENT VARIETIES IN SETS

1973 Large Bust
Beads near rim

1973 Small Bust
Beads far from rim

1974 NICKEL DOLLAR VARIETIES IN SETS

1974 Double Yoke
Doubled Die, Variety 1

1974 Double Yoke
Doubled Die, Variety 3

1968 NICKEL DOLLAR VARIETIES IN SETS

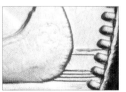

Normal Island

Small Island (S Is)

No Island (N Is)

1968 Double Waterlines
Doubled Die (DD)

DATE	QUANTITY SOLD	ISSUE PRICE	FINISH	MS-65 NC
1968	521,641	4.00	BU	5.
1968 S. Is.	Included	4.00	BU	50.
1968 No Is.	Included	4.00	BU	20.
1968 DD	Included	4.00	BU	60.
1969	326,203	4.00	BU	7.
1970	349,120	4.00	BU	7.
1971	253,311	4.00	BU	7.
1972	224,275	4.00	BU	7.
1973 L.B.	243,695	4.00	BU	300.
1973 S.B.	Included	4.00	BU	8.
1974	213,589	5.00	BU	7.
1974 Var. 1	Included	5.00	BU	1,000.
1974 Var. 3	Included	5.00	BU	1,500.

1975 NICKEL DOLLAR VARIETIES IN SETS

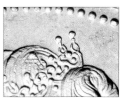
1975 Attached Jewels (AJ)

1975 Detached Jewels (DJ)

1978 FIFTY CENT VARIETIES IN SETS

**1978 Reverse
Square Jewels (SJ)**

**1978 Reverse
Round Jewels (RJ)**

1976 NICKEL DOLLAR VARIETIES IN SETS

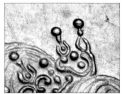
1976 Attached Jewels (AJ)

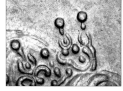
1976 Detached Jewels (DJ)

1977 NICKEL DOLLAR VARIETIES IN SETS

1977 Attached Jewels (AJ)

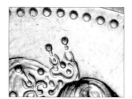
1977 Detached Jewels (DJ)

1977 Full Water Lines

1977 Short Water Lines

DATE	QUANTITY SOLD	ISSUE PRICE	FINISH	MS-65 NC
1975 AJ, FWL	197,372	5.00	BU	10.
1975 DJ, FWL	Included	5.00	BU	10.
1976 AJ, FWL	171,737	5.15	BU	40.
1976 DJ, FWL	Included	5.15	BU	8.
1977 AJ, SWL	225,307	5.15	BU	15.
1977 DJ, FWL	Included	5.15	BU	7.
1977 DJ, SWL	Included	5.15	BU	15.
1978 SJ	260,000	5.25	BU	7.
1978 RJ	Included	5.25	BU	25.
1979	187,624	6.25	BU	8.
1980	169,390	8.00	BU	7.
1981	186,250	5.00	BU	8.
1982	203,287	5.00	BU	7.
1983	190,838	5.00	BU	9.
1984	181,415	5.00	BU	9.
1985 Pliofilm	173,924	6.95	BU	10.
1985 Plastic	Included	N/A	BU	40.
1986	167,338	6.95	BU	10.
1987	212,136	6.95	BU	10.

Note: Currently no examples of the 1977 Attached Jewel obverse and Full Water Line reverse nickel dollar have been found.

SIX COIN NICKEL BRILLIANT UNCIRCULATED SETS, 1988-1996

In 1987 the nickel Voyageur dollar was retired and in 1988 the bronze Loon dollar was introduced into the Brilliant Uncirculated Set. The finish on the coins in these sets was brilliant relief on a brilliant background.

In 1989 the pliofilm heat-sealing dies were modified. The embossed words ROYAL CANADIAN MINT were removed from the dies and replaced with the Circle M logo.

In 1996 the finish on the coins was changed to brilliant relief against a parallel lined background. This finish was first developed for the bullion maple leaf program, and used in 1981 on the Specimen sets issued by the Mint for that year.

DATE	QUANTITY SOLD	ISSUE PRICE	FINISH	MS-65 NC
1988	182,048	6.95	BU	10.
1989	158,636	7.70	BU	15.
1990	170,791	7.70	BU	15.
1990 CNA	Included	7.70	BU	30.
1991	147,814	8.50	BU	35.
1992	217,597	9.50	BU	15.
1993	171,680	9.50	BU	8.
1993 CNA	Included	9.50	BU	40.
1994	141,676	9.75	BU	13.
1995	143,892	9.75	BU	13.
1996	120,217	11.95	Specimen	40.

NOTES FOR COLLECTORS

1. The 1990 and 1993 CNA sets are packaged in commemorative envelopes.
2. The 1996 Brilliant Uncirculated set contains the 5¢ Near Six 6 variety, see *Canadian Coins, Volume One*, for details.

SEVEN COIN NICKEL BRILLIANT UNCIRCULATED SETS WITH SPECIMEN FINISH, 1997

In 1997 the two-dollar Polar Bear coin was added to the set. In mid-1997 the Royal Canadian Mint transferred production of the Brilliant Uncirculated Sets to the Winnipeg mint. The Ottawa and Winnipeg issues of 1997 can be distinguished by the method of packaging, and by the finish on the two dollar coins. Those produced in Ottawa have a brilliant, or shiny, polar bear, whereas on coins produced at Winnipeg, the bear has a frosted appearance. They coins are indicated by (O) for Ottawa and (W) for Winnipeg in the listings. No mint marks appear on 1997-dated coins. The finishes on both sets (1997) are technically equal, being Brilliant Relief on Parallel Lined background.

1997 Ottawa Brilliant Uncirculated Set with Specimen Finish
The $1.00 Loon is at top right with the $2.00 (shiny) Polar Bear at top centre

1997 Winnipeg Brilliant Uncirculated Set with Specimen Finish
The $1.00 Loon is at top left with the $2.00 (frosted) Polar Bear at top centre

DATE	DESCRIPTION	QUANTITY SOLD	ISSUE PRICE	FINISH	SP-65
1997 (O)	Loon/Polar Bear	174,692	13.95	Specimen	30.
1997 (W)	Loon/Polar Bear	Included	13.95	Specimen	15.

SEVEN COIN NICKEL BRILLIANT UNCIRCULATED SETS, 1998-2000

In 1998 the finish on the coins returned to a brilliant relief with a brilliant background, and this was continued until 2000. To distinguish the sets produced at the Winnipeg mint in 1998, a "W" was added to all coins from the one cent through to the two-dollar coin. This is the first time the Canadian mint placed a mint mark on Canadian coins. When the set production was moved back to Ottawa, in mid-1998, the coins were struck without a mint mark. In 2000, the mint mark appeared again as set production was moved back to the Winnipeg mint. The packaging of the sets in transparent plastic film was continued, and 2000 was the last year of issue for sets containing pure nickel coinage. The Winnipeg mint mark 'W' is found on the obverse, to the lower left of the portrait.

"W" Mint Mark

DATE	DESCRIPTION	QUANTITY SOLD	ISSUE PRICE	FINISH	MS-65 NC
1998	Loon/Polar Bear	145,439	13.95	BU	30.
1998 W	Loon/Polar Bear	Included	13.95	BU	30.
1999	Loon/Polar Bear	117,318	13.95	BU	16.
1999	Loon/Nunavut	74,821	13.95	BU	18.
1999	Loon/Nun. Mule	Included	13.95	BU	325.
2000	Loon/Knowledge	186,985	15.95	BU	20.
2000 W	Loon/Polar Bear	Included	15.95	BU	20.

Note: See page 136 for the listing and explanation of the 1999 Nunavut Mule.

FIVE COIN MULTI-PLY PLATED STEEL TEST SET FOR 1999

This set is a Royal Canadian Mint test token set (TTS-3); see *Canadian Coins, Volume One* for a complete listing.

SEVEN COIN MULTI-PLY PLATED STEEL BRILLIANT UNCIRCULATED SETS, "P" COMPOSITION MARK, 2001-2006

The first issue of the new multi-ply plated steel Brilliant Uncirculated Sets was in 2001. Five coins, one cent through fifty cents, carried the new composition mark "P". The $1.00 and $2.00 coins did not; they were struck on the standard planchets for those denominations. The finish on the multi-ply plated steel coins is brilliant relief on a brilliant background, continuing from the 2000 nickel sets.

In 2002, to commemorate the Golden Jubilee of Queen Elizabeth II, the Mint issued double dated (1952-2002) plated steel coinage for circulation. These coins were used in the collectors' sets, and are identical to those of the previous year except for the double dates. Special Edition Jubilee Sets are found on page 384.

Mid year 2003 the tiara portrait of Elizabeth II, which had been used since 1990, was replaced with the new uncrowned portrait by Susanna Blunt. The first set with this portrait was issued in 2004.

DATE	DESCRIPTION	QUANTITY SOLD	ISSUE PRICE	FINISH	MS-65 NC
2001P	Loon/Polar Bear	115,897	15.95	BU	25.
2002P (1952-)	Loon/Polar Bear	100,467	15.95	BU	18.
2003P	Loon/Polar Bear	94,126	15.95	BU	35.
2004P	Loon/Polar Bear	96,847	15.95	BU	30.
2005P	Loon/Polar Bear	114,650	15.95	BU	20.
2006P (1996-)	Loon/Polar Bear	93,361	15.95	BU	25.

Note: The 2006 Brilliant Uncirculated set contains the 10th anniversary two dollar coin, double dated 1996-2006.

SEVEN COIN MULTI-PLY PLATED STEEL BRILLIANT UNCIRCULATED SETS, MAPLE LEAF LOGO, 2007-2010

Two thousand and seven saw the first coins to carrying the new Royal Canadian Mint logo (Circle M) in brilliant uncirculated sets. The composition mark "P" was now removed.

Also, in 2007 two different pairs of dies were used to strike the ten cent pieces. One pair has an obverse die carrying a small, far logo, with the reverse die having a curved 7. The other pair has an obverse die carrying a large, near logo, with the reverse die having a straight 7.

In 2009 brilliant uncirculated sets were assembled in two locations, the Mint in Ottawa, and an outside contractor. The sets assembled at the Mint have the Circle M logo embossed into the pliofilm packaging, while those assembled by the contractor do not.

**Ten Cents 2007
Obverse:
Small, Far
RCM Logo**

**Ten Cents 2007
Reverse:
Curved 7**

**Ten Cents 2007
Obverse:
Large, Near
RCM Logo**

**Ten Cents 2007
Reverse:
Straight 7**

DATE	DESCRIPTION	QUANTITY SOLD	ISSUE PRICE	FINISH	MS-65 NC
2007	Standard 7 coins, 10 Cents Small RCM Logo / Curved 7	45,733	21.95	BU	30.
2007	Standard 7 coins, 10 Cents Large RCM Logo / Straight 7	Incl. above	21.95	BU	150.
2008	Standard 7 coins	42,833	21.95	BU	25.
2009	Standard 7 coins, with RCM logo embossed into pliofilm	37,980	22.95	BU	25.
2009	Standard 7 coins, without RCM logo embossed into pliofilm	Incl. above	22.95	BU	30.
2009	Standard 7 coins, without RCM logo; World Money Fair, Berlin, Germany	1,000	50.00	BU	75.
2010	Standard 7 coins	43,074	23.95	BU	50.

SEVEN COIN MULTI-PLY PLATED STEEL UNCIRCULATED SETS, MAPLE LEAF LOGO, 2011-2012

Beginning in 2011, the finish on the coins was lowered to circulation. The brilliant uncirculated (MS-65-NC) finish found on the coins in sets since 1968 was discontinued.

DATE	DESCRIPTION	QUANTITY SOLD	ISSUE PRICE	FINISH	MS-65 C
2011	Standard 7 coins	37,881	23.95	Circulation	30.
2012	Standard 7 coins	75,083	23.95	Circulation	50.

SIX COIN MULTI-PLY PLATED STEEL UNCIRCULATED SETS, MAPLE LEAF LOGO, 2013-2014

With production of the penny ending May 4th, 2012, the uncirculated sets for 2013 do not contain a one cent coin. The six coins contained in the set are: 5¢, 10¢, 25¢, 50¢, $1 and $2.

DATE	DESCRIPTION	QUANTITY SOLD	ISSUE PRICE	FINISH	MS-65 C
2013	Standard 6 coins	60,863	24.95	Circulation	25.
2014	Standard 6 coins	75,000	24.95	Circulation	25.

NOTES FOR COLLECTORS

1. In the description column of the pricing table the use of the word "standard" refers to the everyday denominations in use for daily transactions.
2. While the 2007 ten-cent coin with the Large, Near RCM Logo obverse and the Straight 7 Reverse is a relatively common coin, the rarity factor changes when it is struck with a Brilliant Uncirculated finish, and is packaged in a Brilliant Uncirculated set.
3. The 2009 Brilliant Uncirculated sets sold at the World Money Fair in Berlin, Germany, included a certificate of authenticity for the Fair. The set was issued in a limited edition of 1,000.

SEVEN COIN NICKEL CUSTOM SETS, 1971-1975

The custom set contains one coin of each denomination, with an extra cent to show the obverse. The finish of the coins is identical to the corresponding year of brilliant uncirculated, brilliant relief on a brilliant background.

Cases: **1971:**   Coins in black vinyl-covered case with Canada's coat of arms and the word "CANADA" stamped in gold on the top.

1972-1973:   As 1971, except the outer case is red.

1974-1975:   As 1971, except the outer case is maroon.

1973 Custom Set

1973 Large Bust

1973 Large Bust

1973 Small Bust

1973 Small Bust

DATE	DESCRIPTION	QUANTITY SOLD	ISSUE PRICE	FINISH	MS-65 NC
1971		33,517	6.50	BU	10.
1972		38,198	6.50	BU	12.
1973	Large Bust 25¢	49,376	6.50	BU	375.
1973	Small Bust 25¢	Included	6.50	BU	10.
1974		44,296	8.00	BU	10.
1975		36,581	8.00	BU	10.

SPECIAL EDITION BRILLIANT UNCIRCULATED SETS, 2002-2010

QUEEN ELIZABETH II, DIADEM PORTRAIT, GOLDEN JUBILEE, 1952-2002

The Special Edition Brilliant Uncirculated Set of 1952-2002 contains the Golden Jubilee 50-cent piece, and the 1952-2002 Canada Day 25-cent coin. The remaining coins in the set are the regular double-dated Jubilee 1952-2002P issue.

Golden Jubilee, 1952-2002

DATE	DESCRIPTION	QUANTITY SOLD	ISSUE PRICE	FINISH	MS-65 NC
2002P (1952-)	Diadem Portrait Obverse	49,869	15.95	BU	18.

QUEEN ELIZABETH II, MATURE PORTRAIT, 2003

In mid-year 2003, the "Diadem Portrait" of Queen Elizabeth, by Dora de Pédery-Hunt, was replaced by a more mature portrait by Susanna Blunt. The Special Edition Brilliant Uncirculated Set of 2003 contains the seven circulating denominations, with the new effigy of Queen Elizabeth II. This set was struck at the Winnipeg Mint, and naturally carries the mint mark W (WP). The lower denominations, one cent to fifty cents, also carry the composition mark "P."

Mature Portrait Obverses

Mint and Composition Mark

DATE	DESCRIPTION	QUANTITY SOLD	ISSUE PRICE	FINISH	MS-65 NC
2003WP	Mature Portrait Obverse	71,142	15.95	BU	28.

CENTENARIES OF ALBERTA AND SASKATCHEWAN, 2005

This Special Edition Brilliant Uncirculated Set was issued to commemorate the centenaries of both Alberta and Saskatchewan. The set contains two commemorative twenty-five-cent coins, one depicting an oil derrick (Alberta), the other the Western Meadowlark (Saskatchewan). The remaining coins in the set are the regular 2005P issue.

**Alberta Centenary
25¢ Coin**

**Saskatchewan
Centenary
25¢ Coin**

Alberta and Saskatchewan 100th Anniversary Set

DATE	DESCRIPTION	QUANTITY SOLD	ISSUE PRICE	FINISH	MS-65 NC
2005P	Centenaries of Alberta and Saskatchewan	N/A	15.95	BU	20.

10TH ANNIVERSARY OF THE TWO DOLLAR COIN, RCM LOGO, 2006

This 2006 Special Edition Brilliant Uncirculated Set contains the "Churchill" two dollar coin. The unique Royal Canadian Mint logo that was introduced to Canadian circulating coins in 2006 is featured on the obverse of all coins in this set.

10th Anniversary of the Two Dollar Coin

**Churchill
Two Dollar Coin**

DATE	DESCRIPTION	QUANTITY SOLD	ISSUE PRICE	FINISH	MS-65 NC
2006	10th Anniversary; Churchill two dollar coin	31,636	19.95	BU	30.

VANCOUVER 2010 WINTER OLYMPIC GAMES, 2007-2008

Over the four years, 2007-2010, all Vancouver 2010 twenty-five cent coins, and the two bronze one dollar coins, were incorporated into Special Edition Brilliant Uncirculated Sets.

2007 Vancouver 2010 Olympic Winter Games

| 2007 Obverse | 2007 Reverse |
| Paralympic Logo | Wheelchair Curling |

Standard 25¢ Wheelchair Curling

| 2007 Obverse | 2007 Reverse |
| Vancouver Logo | Wheelchair Curling |

25¢ Wheelchair Curling Mule

The Vancouver Olympic obverse was paired with the Paralympic Wheelchair Curling reverse to form a mule which is found only in the 2007 Vancouver Olympic Winter Games Special Edition Set.

2008 Vancouver 2010 Olympic Winter Games

Note For Collectors

The 2007 Special Edition Brilliant Uncirculated Set contains the 10-cent variety: Small, Far Logo Obverse / Curved 7 Reverse

DATE	DESCRIPTION	QUANTITY SOLD	ISSUE PRICE	FINISH	MS-65 NC
2007	Standard 5 coins 1¢, 5¢, 10¢, 50¢ and $2; 5 x 25¢ Alpine Skiing, Biathlon, Curling, Ice Hockey, Wheelchair Curling, $1 Loon Dance; (11 coins)	28,852	23.95	BU	30.
2007	As above, but with the Mule 25¢ Vancouver Logo Obverse paired with the Wheelchair Curling Reverse	Included	23.95	BU	550.
2008	Standard 5 coins 1¢, 5¢, 10¢, 50¢ and $2; 4 x 25¢ Bobsleigh, Figure Skating, Freestyle Skiing, Snow Boarding;, $1 Loon Dance; (10 coins)	16,471	23.95	BU	25.

VANCOUVER 2010 OLYMPIC WINTER GAMES, 2009-2010

The Golden Moments Set commemorates the Olympic gold medals won by the Men's and Women's Hockey Teams in 2002, and Cindy Klassen's gold medal of 2006. These quarters have the partial maple leaf painted red.

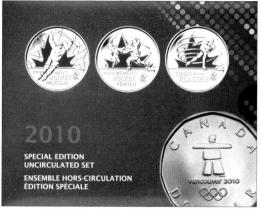

2009 Vancouver 2010 Olympic Winter Games   **2010 Golden Moments Special Edition Set**

DATE	DESCRIPTION	QUANTITY SOLD	ISSUE PRICE	FINISH	MS-65 NC
2009	Standard 5 coins 1¢, 5¢, 10¢, 50¢ and $2; 3 x 25¢ Cross Country Skiing, Ice Sledge Hockey, Speed Skating, $1 Loon Dance; (9 coins)	11,313	23.95	BU	25.
2010	Standard 5 coins 1¢, 5¢, 10¢, 50¢ and $2; 3 x 25¢ Painted Men's Ice Hockey 2002, Painted Women's Ice Hockey 2002, Painted Speed Skating, Cindy Klassen; $1 Inukshuk; (9 coins)	21,432	27.95	BU	45.

SPECIAL EDITION UNCIRCULATED SETS, 2010-2013

SPECIAL EDITION UNCIRCULATED SET, 2010

This 8-coin set features the standard 1¢, 5¢, 10¢, 50¢ and $2 coins, but also includes the 2010 25¢ Remembrance Day Poppy coin, and two one-dollar coins which commemorate the 100th Anniversary of the Royal Canadian Navy, and the Saskatchewan Roughriders Centennial. The finish on all coins is circulation. The set is shrink wrapped in clear plastic.

25¢ Remembrance Day Poppies

$1 Royal Canadian Navy

$1 Saskatchewan Roughriders

DATE	DESCRIPTION	QUANTITY SOLD	ISSUE PRICE	FINISH	MS-65 C
2010	8-coin set, $2 with 16 serrations	19,233	25.95	Circulation	30.
2010	8-coin set, $2 with 14 serrations	Incl above	25.95	Circulation	75.

SPECIAL EDITION UNCIRCULATED SET, 2011

This 8-coin set features the following coins: $2 Boreal Forest, $1 Parks Canada, 25¢ Wood Bison, coloured and uncoloured; 25¢ Orca Whale, coloured and uncoloured; 25¢ Peregrine Falcon, coloured and uncoloured. It was issued in a keepsake envelope with a serial certificate of authorization. The finish on all coins is circulation.

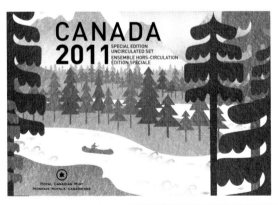

$1 Parks Canada

$2 Boreal Forest

DATE	DESCRIPTION	QUANTITY SOLD	ISSUE PRICE	FINISH	MS-65 C
2011	Special Edition Uncirculated Set (8 coins)	19,233	23.95	Circulation	40.

SPECIAL EDITION UNCIRCULATED SET, 2012

$1 Grey Cup

$1 Lucky Loonie

DATE	DESCRIPTION	QUANTITY SOLD	ISSUE PRICE	FINISH	MS-65 C
2012	Special Edition Uncirculated Set (4 coins)	14,987	19.95	Circulation	25.

SPECIAL EDITION UNCIRCULATED SET, 2013
THE WAR OF 1812

DATE	DESCRIPTION	QUANTITY SOLD	ISSUE PRICE	FINISH	MS-65 C
2013	The War of 1812 (9 coins)	14,927	26.95	Circulation	30.

COMMEMORATIVE GIFT SET, 2013
THE WAR OF 1812

HMS Shannon

HMS Shannon
Security Device

25¢ Laura Secord

25¢ Charles-Michel
de Salaberry

DATE	DESCRIPTION	QUANTITY SOLD	ISSUE PRICE	FINISH	MS-65 C
2013	The War of 1812 (5 coins)	11,368	19.95	Circulation	30.

BABY GIFT SETS, 1995-2014

BUNDLE OF JOY / TINY TREASURES

NICKEL BRILLIANT UNCIRCULATED SETS, 1995-2000.

First issued in 1995, the brilliant uncirculated set of coins was specially packaged for the gift market using the six coins from the brilliant uncirculated set of that year. In 1997 this set was expanded to include the two-dollar polar bear coin.

In 1998 the name changed from Bundle of Joy to Tiny Treasures Brilliant Uncirculated Sets. In that same year the packaging of the sets of Tiny Treasures changed from card displays to clear plastic display units. The movement of set production to Winnipeg and back to Ottawa that occurred in 1998 also affected the Oh! Canada! and Tiny Treasures sets.

In 2000, production of the sets occurred in both the Ottawa and Winnipeg mints.

The finish on the coins in these sets (1995-2005) is brilliant relief on brilliant background, brilliant uncirculated (MS-65-NC). The finish was downgraded in 2006 to uncirculated. See page xiv for an outline on finishes.

1997 Bundle of Joy Set

DATE	DESCRIPTION	QUANTITY SOLD	ISSUE PRICE	FINISH	MS-65 NC
1995	Standard 6 coins; Folder	36,443	19.95	BU	25.
1996	Standard 6 coins; Folder	56,618	19.95	BU	20.
1997	Standard 7 coins; Folder	55,199	21.95	BU	25.
1998	Standard 7 coins; Display case	46,139	21.95	BU	24.
1998W	Winnipeg Mint, 7 coins; Display case	12,625	21.95	BU	24.
1999	Standard 7 coins; Display case	67,694	21.95	BU	25.
2000	Standard 7 coins; Display case	82,964	21.95	BU	25.
2000W	Winnipeg Mint, 7 coins; Display case	Included	21.95	BU	25.

TINY TREASURES

MULTI-PLY PLATED STEEL BRILLIANT UNCIRCULATED SETS, 2001-2003.

As with the Brilliant Uncirculated sets of 2001, the nickel coinage of the previous year was replaced with the new patented multi-ply plated steel coins. In the 2002 set all coins bear the double dates 1952-2002 to commemorate the 50th anniversary of Her Majesty Queen Elizabeth II's accession to the throne. Two thousand and three was the last year of issue for the Tiny Treasures sets. The finish on the coins in these sets is brilliant uncirculated (MS-65-NC).

2002 Tiny Treasures Set

DATE	DESCRIPTION	QUANTITY SOLD	ISSUE PRICE	FINISH	MS-65 NC
2001P	Standard 7 coins; Display case	52,085	22.95	BU	25.
2002P (1952-)	Standard 7 coins; Display case	51,491	22.95	BU	24.
2003P	Standard 7 coins; Display case	43,197	22.95	BU	25.

BABY GIFT SETS

MULTI-PLY PLATED STEEL BRILLIANT UNCIRCULATED SETS, 2004-2005.

With the revamping of the Gift Sets in 2004, a name change took place, Tiny Treasures became Baby Gift Sets. The finish on the coins remained the same as the previous sets.

DATE	DESCRIPTION	QUANTITY SOLD	ISSUE PRICE	FINISH	MS-65 NC
2004P	Standard 7 coins; Folder	53,726	19.95	BU	45.
2005P	Standard 7 coins; Folder	42,245	19.95	BU	47.

BABY GIFT SETS (cont.)

MULTI-PLY PLATED STEEL UNCIRCULATED SETS, 2006-2010.

Beginning in 2006, the finish on the coins in these sets was changed to circulation. The uncirculated sets were struck and assembled at the Winnipeg Mint, however, they do not carry the "W" mint mark.

In 2007 the Caribou design on the twenty-five-cent coin was replaced with a coloured design. The ten cent coins contained in the 2007 Birthday Gift Sets are the Large, Near Logo obverse / Straight 7 reverse variety.

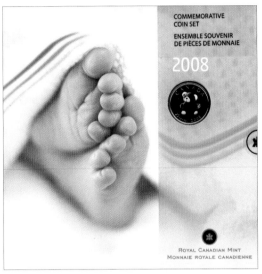

2008 Commemorative Coin Set	2009 Baby Gift Set

DATE	DESCRIPTION	QUANTITY SOLD	ISSUE PRICE	FINISH	MS-65 C
2006P	Standard 7 coins; Folder	33,786	19.95	Circulation	30.
2007	Standard 6 coins; plus coloured 25¢ Rattle; Folder	30,090	19.95	Circulation	25.
2008	Standard 6 coins; plus coloured 25¢ Teddy Bear; Folder	29,819	19.95	Circulation	25.
2009	Standard 6 coins; plus coloured 25¢ Teddy Bear and Blanket; Folder	25,182	19.95	Circulation	25.
2010	Standard 6 coins; plus coloured 25¢ Baby Carriage; Folder	27,048	19.95	Circulation	30.

MULTI-PLY PLATED STEEL UNCIRCULATED SETS, 2011-2014.

In 2011 the coloured designs used on the reverse of the twenty-five cent pieces were discontinued. The twenty-five-cent coin now carries a new yearly struck design.

Coins contained in set:

2011 - 7 coins in set: 1¢, 5¢, 10¢, 25¢, 50¢, $1, $2
2012 - 6 coins in set: 1¢, 5¢, 10¢, 25¢, $1, $2
2013-2014 - 5 coins in set: 5¢, 10¢, 25¢, $1, $2

DATE	DESCRIPTION	QUANTITY SOLD	ISSUE PRICE	FINISH	MS-65 C
2011	Standard 6 coins, plus 25¢ Baby's Feet, Folder	38,576	19.95	Circulation	125.
2012	Standard 5 coins; plus 25¢ Mobiles, Folder	43,920	19.95	Circulation	25.
2013	Standard 4 coins, plus 25¢ Baby's Feet, Folder	52,762	19.95	Circulation	20.
2014	Standard 4 coins, plus $1 Stock, Folder	N/A	19.95	Circulation	20

Note: For the designs of the twenty-five cent coins contained in the sets of 2007-2013 see pages 28-31.
For the design of the one dollar coin contained in the 2014 set see page 131.

BIRTHDAY GIFT SETS, 2004-2014

MULTI-PLY PLATED STEEL BRILLIANT UNCIRCULATED SETS, 2004-2005.

The Baby Gift Set was first introduced in 2004. The finish on these seven-coin sets is brilliant uncirculated.

| 2006 Birthday Gift Set | 2008 Commemorative Coin Set |

DATE	DESCRIPTION	QUANTITY SOLD	ISSUE PRICE	FINISH	MS-65
2004P	Standard 7 coins; Folder	N/A	19.95	BU	20.
2005P	Standard 7 coins; Folder	20,227	19.95	BU	20.

MULTI-PLY PLATED STEEL UNCIRCULATED SETS, 2006-2008.

Beginning in 2006, the finish on the coins contained in the Baby Gift Sets was circulation. The uncirculated sets were struck and assembled at the Winnipeg Mint, however, they do not carry the "W" mint mark.

In 2007 the Caribou design on the twenty-five-cent coin was replaced with a coloured design. The ten cent coins contained in the 2007 Birthday Gift Sets are the Large, Near Logo obverse / Straight 7 reverse variety.

For 2008 the set carried the name "Commemorative Coin Set."

The Birthday Gift Set was discontinued in 2009 and replaced by the Cards With Coins series, see page 32.

DATE	DESCRIPTION	QUANTITY SOLD	ISSUE PRICE	FINISH	MS-65
2006P	Standard 7 coins; Folder	11,984	19.95	Circulation	20.
2007	Standard 6 coins; plus coloured 25¢ Balloons; Folder	12,547	19.95	Circulation	24.
2008	Standard 6 coins; plus coloured 25¢ Party Hat; Folder	11,366	19.95	Circulation	25.

MULTI-PLY PLATED STEEL UNCIRCULATED SETS, 2011-2014.

The Birthday Gift Set was reintroduced in 2011. Coins contained in the sets are:

2011 - 7 coins in set: 1¢, 5¢, 10¢, 25¢, 50¢, $1, $2   2013-2014 - 5 coins in set: 5¢, 10¢, 25¢, $1, $2
2012 - 6 coins in set: 1¢, 5¢, 10¢, 25¢, $1, $2

DATE	DESCRIPTION	QUANTITY SOLD	ISSUE PRICE	FINISH	MS-65
2011	Standard 6 coins, plus 25¢ Four Balloons, Folder	21,173	19.95	Circulation	20.
2012	Standard 5 coins; plus 25¢ Ice Cream Cone, Folder	24,659	19.95	Circulation	20.
2013	Standard 4 coins, plus 25¢ Slice of Birthday Cake, Folder	22,678	19.95	Circulation	20.
2014	Standard 4 coins, plus $1 Gift Box and Balloons, Folder	N/A	19.95	Circulation	20.

Note: For the designs of the twenty-five cent coins contained in the sets of 2007-2013 see pages 28-31.
For the design of the one dollar coin contained in the 2014 set see page 131.

CONGRATULATIONS / GRADUATION GIFT SETS, 2004-2008

MULTI-PLY PLATED STEEL BRILLIANT UNCIRCULATED SETS, 2004-2005.

The gift set in 2004 was directed at the school or college graduation market. By 2006 the scope was broadened to a Congratulations Gift Set. The Graduation Sets have a brilliant uncirculated finish, while the Congratulations Gift Sets have a circulation finish.

2005 Graduation Gift Set

2008 Congratulations Gift Set

DATE	DESCRIPTION	QUANTITY SOLD	ISSUE PRICE	FINISH	MS-65 NC
2004P	Graduation Set, Standard 7 coins; Folder	22,094	19.95	BU	15.
2005P	Graduation Set, Standard 7 coins; Folder	12,411	19.95	BU	20.

MULTI-PLY PLATED STEEL UNCIRCULATED SETS, 2006-2008.

Beginning in 2006, the finish on the coins in these sets was changed to circulation. The circulation sets were struck and assembled at the Winnipeg Mint, however, they do not carry the "W" mint mark.

The ten cent coins contained in the 2007 Congratulations Gift Sets are the Large, Near Logo obverse / Straight 7 reverse variety.

These sets were discontinued in 2009 and replaced by the Cards With Coins Series, see page 32.

DATE	DESCRIPTION	QUANTITY SOLD	ISSUE PRICE	FINISH	MS-65 C
2006P	Congratulations Set, Standard 7 coins; Folder	9,428	19.95	Circulation	20.
2007	Congratulations Set, Standard 6 coins; plus coloured 25¢ Fireworks; Folder	9,571	19.95	Circulation	24.
2008	Congratulations Set, Standard 6 coins; plus coloured 25¢ Trophy; Folder	6,821	19.95	Circulation	25.

Note: For the coloured designs of the twenty-five cent coins contained in the sets of 2007-2008, see page 28.

HOLIDAY GIFT SETS, 2004-2013

MULTI-PLY PLATED STEEL, BRILLIANT UNCIRCULATED SETS, 2004-2005.
  In 2004 the Royal Canadian Mint introduced a new Holiday Gift Set to their product line. This set was issued in a colourful Season's Greetings folder and included a coloured twenty-five-cent coin in place of the standard Caribou design. The finish on all coins is Brilliant Uncirculated.

2005 Holiday Gift Set

2008 Holiday Gift Set

DATE	DESCRIPTION	QUANTITY SOLD	ISSUE PRICE	FINISH	MS-65 NC
2004P	Standard 6 coins; plus coloured 25¢ Santa Claus; Folder	22,094	19.95	BU	40.
2005P	Standard 6 coins; plus coloured 25¢ Christmas Stocking; Folder	72,831	19.95	BU	20.

MULTI-PLY PLATED STEEL, UNCIRCULATED SETS 2006-2010.
  In 2006 the finish on all coins contained in these sets was downgraded to circulation.
  The ten cent coin contained in the 2007 Holiday Gift Set is the Large, Near Logo obverse / Straight 7 reverse variety.

DATE	DESCRIPTION	QUANTITY SOLD	ISSUE PRICE	FINISH	MS-65 C
2006P	Standard 6 coins; plus coloured 25¢ Santa in Sleigh .Reindeer; Folder	99,258	19.95	Circulation	20.
2007	Standard 6 coins; plus coloured 25¢ Christmas Tree; Folder	66,267	19.95	Circulation	20.
2008	Standard 6 coins; plus coloured 25¢ Santa, Folder	42,344	19.95	Circulation	25.
2009	Standard 6 coins; plus coloured 25¢ Santa, 3 Maple Leaves; Folder	32,967	19.95	Circulation	20.
2010	Standard 6 coins; plus coloured 25¢ Santa, Christmas Tree; Folder	10,870	19.95	Circulation	20.

MULTI-PLY PLATED STEEL UNCIRCULATED SETS, 2011-2013.
  Coins contained in set:
  2011 - 7 coins in set: 1¢, 5¢, 10¢, 25¢, 50¢, $1, $2   2013 - 5 coins in set: 5¢, 10¢, 25¢, $1, $2
  2012 - 6 coins in set: 1¢, 5¢, 10¢, 25¢, $1, $2

DATE	DESCRIPTION	QUANTITY SOLD	ISSUE PRICE	FINISH	MS-65 C
2011	Standard 6 coins; plus 25¢ Snowflake, Folder	41,666	19.95	Circulation	20.
2012	Standard 5 coins; plus 25¢ Christmas Tree Ornaments, Folder	26,404	19.95	Circulation	20.
2013	Standard 4 coins; plus 25¢ Wreath, Folder	N/A	19.95	Circulation	20.

Note: For the designs of the twenty-five cent coins contained in the sets of 2004-2012 see pages 24, and 30-31.

NHL TEAM GIFT SETS, UNCIRCULATED, 2006-2009

MULTI-PLY PLATED STEEL, UNCIRCULATED SETS, 2006-2009.

These sets were introduced for the 2005-2006 hockey season with only three Canadian NHL teams being represented: Montreal Canadiens, Ottawa Senators and the Toronto Maple Leafs. Each set contained the standard six coins, 1¢, 5¢, 10¢, 50¢, $1 and $2, with the twenty-five-cent Caribou design being replaced by a coloured NHL team logo. For the 2006-2007 Season, all six Canadian NHL teams were represented.

In the Fall of 2008 the sets issued for the 2008-2009 season had the twenty-five-cent Caribou design as one of the standard six coins, but the loon design on the one dollar coin was replaced by a coloured team jersey logo.

The finish on all sets is circulation.

2005-2006 Season
Toronto Maple Leafs

2006-2007 Season
Toronto Maple Leafs

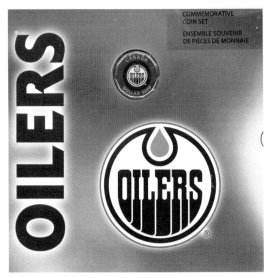

2007-2008 Season
Edmonton Oilers

2008-2009 Season
Calgary Flames

MULTI-PLY PLATED STEEL, UNCIRCULATED SETS, 2006-2009, PRICING TABLE.

DATE	DESCRIPTION	QUANTITY SOLD	ISSUE PRICE	FINISH	MS-65 C
2006P	Montreal Canadiens, Standard 6 coin set; Coloured 25¢	11,765	24.95	Circulation	20.
2006P	Ottawa Senators; Standard 6 coin set; Coloured 25¢	Included	24.95	Circulation	18.
2006P	Toronto Maple Leafs; Standard 6 coin set; Coloured 25¢	Included	24.95	Circulation	15.
2007	Calgary Flames; Standard 6 coins; Coloured 25¢	1.082	24.95	Circulation	25.
2007	Edmonton Oilers; Standard 6 coins; Coloured 25¢	2,214	24.95	Circulation	25.
2007	Montreal Canadiens; Standard 6 coins; Coloured 25¢	4,091	24.95	Circulation	25.
2007	Ottawa Senators; Standard 6 coin set; Coloured 25¢	2,474	24.95	Circulation	25.
2007	Toronto Maple Leafs; Standard 6 coin set; Coloured 25¢	5,365	24.95	Circulation	25.
2007	Vancouver Canucks; Standard 6 coin set; Coloured 25¢	1,526	24.95	Circulation	25.
2008	Calgary Flames; Standard 6 coins; Coloured $1	N/A	24.95	Circulation	20.
2008	Edmonton Oilers; Standard 6 coins; Coloured $1	1,584	24.95	Circulation	20.
2008	Montreal Canadiens; Standard 6 coins; Coloured $1	2,659	24.95	Circulation	20.
2008	Ottawa Senators; Standard 6 coin set; Coloured $1	1,633	24.95	Circulation	20.
2008	Toronto Maple Leafs; Standard 6 coin set; Coloured $1	1,302	24.95	Circulation	20.
2008	Vancouver Canucks; Standard 6 coin set; Coloured $1	N/A	24.95	Circulation	20.
2009	Calgary Flames; Standard 6 coins; Coloured $1	382	24.95	Circulation	25.
2009	Edmonton Oilers; Standard 6 coins; Coloured $1	472	24.95	Circulation	25.
2009	Montreal Canadiens; Standard 6 coins; Coloured $1	4,857	24.95	Circulation	28.
2009	Ottawa Senators; Standard 6 coin set; Coloured $1	387	24.95	Circulation	25.
2009	Toronto Maple Leafs; Standard 6 coin set; Coloured $1	1,328	24.95	Circulation	30.
2009	Vancouver Canucks; Standard 6 coin set; Coloured $1	794	24.95	Circulation	25.

NOTES

1. For the coloured designs of the twenty-five cent coins used in the NHL Team Gift Sets see page 27.
2. For the coloured designs of the one dollar coins used in the NHL Team Gift Sets see pages 123-125.
3. The "Quantity Sold" numbers may or may not be reported in a single year, but may carry over to the following year. The collector must wait a year or two before the final numbers are known.
4. No "Quantity Sold" number was listed in the 2008 Royal Canadian Mint Report for the 2008 issue of NHL Team Gift Sets. There is a partial listing in 2009.
5. The 2007 NHL Team Gift Sets contain the Large, Near Logo obverse / Straight 7 reverse variety ten cent coin.

OH! CANADA! GIFT SETS, 1994-2014

BRILLIANT UNCIRCULATED SETS, 1994-2000

First issued in 1994, this set included the bronze dollar plus the other five denominations for that year. In 1997 this set was expanded to include the two-dollar polar bear coin. In 1998 the packaging of the Oh! Canada! Gift Sets changed from card displays to clear plastic display units. The coins in the Oh! Canada! set are identical in finish to those of the corresponding year of the Brilliant Uncirculated Set.

1997 Oh! Canada! Gift Set with Flying Loon Dollar

DATE	DESCRIPTION	QUANTITY SOLD	ISSUE PRICE	FINISH	MS-65 NC
1994	Standard 6 coins	18,794	16.95	BU	15.
1995	Standard 5 coins, Peacekeeping dollar	50,927	16.95	BU	15.
1996	Standard 6 coins	31,083	16.95	BU	25.
1997	Standard 6 coins, Flying Loon dollar	84,124	21.95	Specimen	50.
1998	Standard 7 coins	42,710	21.95	BU	25.
1998W	Winnipeg Mint, 7 coins	24,792	21.95	BU	20.
1999	Standard 7 coins	82,754	21.95	BU	18.
2000	Standard 7 coins	107,884	21.95	BU	15.
2000W	Standard 7 coins	Included	21.95	BU	20.

Note: The Oh! Canada Gift Set was struck at both the Ottawa and Winnipeg (W) branches of the Royal Canadian Mint.

MULTI-PLY PLATED STEEL BRILLIANT UNCIRCULATED SETS, 2001-2005.

In 2001, the five subsidiary coins in the Oh! Canada! Set were replaced by the five multi-ply plated steel coins.

In the 2002 set all coins bear the double dates 1952-2002 to commemorate the 50th anniversary of Her Majesty Queen Elizabeth II's accession to the throne.

Beginning in 2004 the coins carried the new Susanna Blunt effigy of Queen Elizabeth II. The coins in the "Oh Canada!" set were identical in finish to coins of the Brilliant Uncirculated Set of that year.

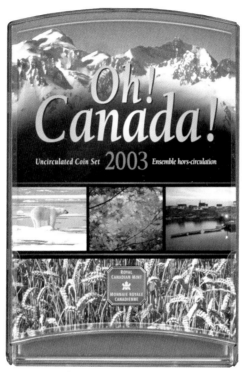

2003 Oh! Canada! Gift Set

DATE	DESCRIPTION	QUANTITY SOLD	ISSUE PRICE	FINISH	MS-65 NC
2001P	Standard 7 coins	66,726	22.95	BU	20.
2002P (1952-)	Standard 7 coins, Double Date	61,484	22.95	BU	18.
2003P	Standard 7 coins	51,146	23.95	BU	25.
2004P	Standard 7 coins	53,111	23.95	BU	28.
2005P	Standard 7 coins	40,890	19.95	BU	15.

MULTI-PLY PLATED STEEL UNCIRCULATED SET, 2006.

In 2006 the finish on all coins contained in these sets was changed to circulation. This was also the last year the composition mark "P" would be seen on coins in the sets.

DATE	DESCRIPTION	QUANTITY SOLD	ISSUE PRICE	FINISH	MS-65 C
2006P	Standard 7 coins	28,213	19.95	Circulation	20.

MULTI-PLY PLATED STEEL UNCIRCULATED SETS, 2007-2010.

Starting in 2007 several changes were made to the Oh! Canada! Set. All coins now carried the Royal Canadian Mint logo on the obverse, and the Caribou design on the twenty-five-cent coin was replaced by a coloured design. For the coloured designs of the twenty-five cent coins of 2007-2010, see pages 28 and 29.

2008 Oh! Canada! Gift Set   **2009 Oh! Canada! Gift Set**

DATE	DESCRIPTION	QUANTITY SOLD	ISSUE PRICE	FINISH	MS-65 C
2007	Standard 6 coins, plus coloured 25¢ Maple Leaf; Folder	24,096	19.95	Circulation	30.
2008	Standard 6 coins, plus coloured 25¢ Canadian Flag; Folder	30,567	19.95	Circulation	25.
2009	Standard 6 coins, plus coloured 25¢ Four Maple Leaves; Folder	14,451	19.95	Circulation	25.
2010	Standard 6 coins, plus coloured 25¢ Three Maple Leaves; Folder	19,769	19.95	Circulation	23.

Note: The ten-cent coins contained in the 2007 Oh! Canada! sets are the Large, Near Logo obverse / Straight 7 reverse variety.

MULTI-PLY PLATED STEEL UNCIRCULATED SETS, 2011-2014.

The 2011 Oh! Canada! Set saw the return of the struck twenty-five cent piece. The reverse design is a single maple leaf.

The Oh! Canada! Gift Set for 2012 contains the standard coins, 1¢, 5¢, 10¢, $1, $2, and a 25¢ coin with a struck multiple maple leaf design. The fifty-cent coin is not included in the set.

Coins contained in set:

2011 - 7 coins in set: 1¢, 5¢, 10¢, 25¢, 50¢, $1, $2   2013-2104 - 5 coins in set: 5¢, 10¢, 25¢, $1, $2

2012 - 6 coins in set: 1¢, 5¢, 10¢, 25¢, $1, $2

DATE	DESCRIPTION	QUANTITY SOLD	ISSUE PRICE	FINISH	MS-65 C
2011	Standard 6 coins, plus 25¢ Single maple leaf design, Folder	22,475	19.95	Circulation	20.
2012	Standard 5 coins; plus 25¢ Multiple maple leaf design, Folder	34,201	19.95	Circulation	20.
2013	Standard 4 coins, plus 25¢ Maple Leaf, Folder	25,901	19.95	Circulation	20.
2014	Standard 4 coins; plus $1 Maple Leaf, Folder	N/A	19.95	Circulation	20.

Note: For the designs of the twenty-five cent coins contained in the sets of 2007-2013 see pages 28-31.
For the design of the one dollar coin contained in the 2014 set see page 131.

WEDDING GIFT SETS, 2004-2014

MULTI-PLY PLATED STEEL UNCIRCULATED SETS, 2004-2006.

The Gift Set line was expanded in 2004 to include a Wedding set, which included the seven standard circulating denominations housed in a colourful wedding folder. The finish on these sets is circulation.

2004 Wedding Gift Set

2008 Wedding Gift Set

DATE	DESCRIPTION	QUANTITY SOLD	ISSUE PRICE	FINISH	MS-65 C
2004P	Standard 7 coin set; Folder	18,660	19.95	Circulation	15.
2005P	Standard 7 coin set; Folder	11,597	19.95	Circulation	20.
2006P	Standard 7 coin set; Folder	8,012	19.95	Circulation	20.

MULTI-PLY PLATED STEEL UNCIRCULATED SETS, 2007-2010.

In 2007 the standard twenty-five-cent Caribou design was replaced with a coloured design which changed each year. The finish on this set is uncirculated. The ten-cent coin contained in the 2007 Wedding Gift Set is the Large, Near Logo obverse / Straight 7 reverse variety.

The Wedding Gift Set was not issued in 2009, it was replaced by the Cards With Coins series (see page 32), however it was reintroduced in 2010.

DATE	DESCRIPTION	QUANTITY SOLD	ISSUE PRICE	FINISH	MS-65 C
2007	Standard 6 coins; plus coloured 25¢ Bouquet; Folder	10,687	19.95	Circulation	25.
2008	Standard 6 coins; plus coloured 25¢ Wedding Cake; Folder	7,404	19.95	Circulation	25.
2010	Standard 6 coins; plus coloured 25¢ Heart and Roses; Folder	8,194	19.95	Circulation	25.

MULTI-PLY PLATED STEEL UNCIRCULATED SETS, 2011-2014.

Coins contained in set:
2011 - 7 coins in set: 1¢, 5¢, 10¢, 25¢, 50¢, $1, $2   2013-2014 - 5 coins in set: 5¢, 10¢, 25¢, $1, $2
2012 - 6 coins in set: 1¢, 5¢, 10¢, 25¢, $1, $2

DATE	DESCRIPTION	QUANTITY SOLD	ISSUE PRICE	FINISH	MS-65 C
2011	Standard 6 coins, plus 25¢ Wedding Rings, Folder	20,461	19.95	Circulation	20.
2012	Standard 5 coins; plus 25¢ Wedding Rings/Heart Folder	24,325	19.95	Circulation	20.
2013	Standard 4 coins; plus 25¢ Wedding Rings, Folder	20,317	19.95	Circulation	20.
2014	Standard 4 coins; plus $1 Two Turtle Doves, Folder	N/A	19.95	Circulation	20.

Note: For the designs of the twenty-five cent coins contained in the sets of 2007-2013 see pages 28-31.
For the design on the one dollar coin contained in the 2014 set see page 131.

MISCELLANEOUS GIFT SETS, 1983-2007

The miscellaneous gift sets issued between 1983 and 2001 have a brilliant uncirculated finish, while sets from 2006 forward have a circulation finish.

2006 Québec Winter Carnival Gift Set

DATE	DESCRIPTION	QUANTITY SOLD	ISSUE PRICE	ISSUER	FINISH	MARKET VALUE
1983	British Royal Mint, Standard 6 coins	N/A	N/A	RCM,BRM	BU	100.
1998	Canadian Imperial Bank of Commerce,"Oh! Canada!" Set; Standard 7 coins	N/A	21.95	RCM	BU	15.
2001P	Canada 2001 Set, Standard 7 coins; Medallion	N/A	N/A	RCM	BU	15.
2001P	"OH! CANADA!", Banff, Standard 7 coins	500	22.95	RCM	BU	15.
2001P	"OH! CANADA!", Calgary, Standard 7 coins	500	22.95	RCM	BU	15.
2001P	"OH! CANADA!", Halifax, Standard 7 coins	500	22.95	RCM	BU	15.
2001P	"OH! CANADA!", Montreal, Standard 7 coins	500	22.95	RCM	BU	15.
2001P	"OH! CANADA!", Niagara Falls, Standard 7 coins	500	22.95	RCM	BU	15.
2001P	"OH! CANADA!", Quebec City, Standard 7 coins	500	22.95	RCM	BU	15.
2001P	"OH! CANADA!", R.C.M., Standard 7 coins	500	22.95	RCM	BU	15.
2001P	"OH! CANADA!", St. John's, Standard 7 coins	500	22.95	RCM	BU	15.
2001P	"OH! CANADA!", Vancouver, Standard 7 coins	500	22.95	RCM	BU	15.
2001P	"OH! CANADA!", Whistler, Standard 7 coins	500	22.95	RCM	BU	15.
2006P	QUEBEC WINTER CARNIVAL; Standard 6 coins; Colourised 25¢ "Bonhomme"; Festive folder	8,200	19.95	RCM	Circulation	25.
2007	Calendar Coin Set, Standard 7 coins	5,264	29.95	RCM	Circulation	30.

Note: 1. For the coloured design of the Quebec Winter Carnival twenty-five cent coin, see page 26.
2. The 2007 Calendar Coin Set contains the Large, Near Logo obverse / Straight 7 reverse.

VANCOUVER 2010 WINTER OLYMPIC AND PARALYMPIC GAMES COIN AND STAMP SETS, 2010

These sets were issued in conjunction with Canada Post in three versions: gold, silver and bronze.

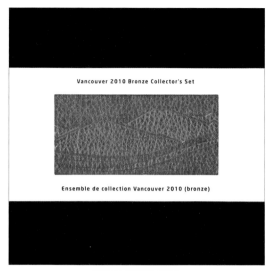

Bronze Collector Set

Silver Collector Set

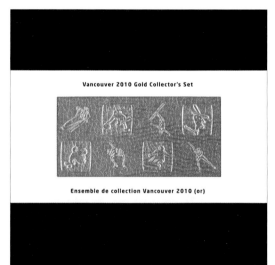

Gold Collector Set

DATE	DESCRIPTION	QUANTITY SOLD	ISSUE PRICE	FINISH	MS-65 C
2010	**Vancouver 2010 Emblems and Mascots Set, Bronze Collector Set**, Three 50¢ Mascot coins, Vancouver 2010 Souvenir Sheet of five Mascot theme stamps, 2 bronze lapel pins	*16,000*	49.95	Uncirculated	75.
2010	**Vancouver 2010 Winter Games Sports Set, Silver Collector Set**, Five painted 25¢ coins, Bobsleigh, Curling, Free Style Skiing, Ice Sledge Hockey, Snowboarding; Vancouver 2010 Souvenir Sheet of five Olympic theme stamps; 2 silver lapel pins	*16,000*	49.95	Uncirculated	75.
2010	**Vancouver 2010 Logo Set, Gold Collector Set**, Bronze Inukshuk dollar, Nickel painted Inukshuk dollar, 50¢ Inukshuk lenticular coin; Vancouver 2010 Souvenir Sheet of two stamps (Whistler and Vancouver)2 gold plated pins.	11,991	49.95	Uncirculated	175.

COMMEMORATIVE CANADIAN COIN, TOKEN, OR MEDAL SETS, 2010-2013

COMMEMORATIVE CANADIAN COIN AND TOKEN SETS, 2010-2011.

These sets contain six coins: 1¢, 10¢, 25¢, 50¢, $1.00, $2.00, plus a copper token commemorating the Fair or Exposition where the set was introduced.

DATE	DESCRIPTION	QUANTITY SOLD	ISSUE PRICE	FINISH	MS-65 C
2010	Beijing International Coin Exposition	500	N/A	BU	75.
2011	World's Money Fair Berlin	500	N/A	BU	50.

COMMEMORATIVE CANADIAN COIN AND MEDAL SETS, 2011.

These sets contain six coins: 1¢, 10¢, 25¢, 50¢, $1.00 $2.00, plus a copper medallion.

DATE	DESCRIPTION	QUANTITY SOLD	ISSUE PRICE	FINISH	MS-65 C
2011	Royal Canadian Numismatic Association Convention	500	N/A	Circulation	50.
2011	American Numismatic Association	500	N/A	Circulation	50.
2011	Beijing International Coin Exposition	500	N/A	Circulation	60.

COMMEMORATIVE CANADIAN COIN AND TOKEN SET, 2012.

This set contains six coins: 1¢, 5¢, 10¢, 25¢, $1.00, $2.00 plus a nickel token commemorating the World Money Fair, Berlin, Germany.

DATE	DESCRIPTION	QUANTITY SOLD	ISSUE PRICE	FINISH	MS-65 C
2012	World Money Fair, Berlin, Germany	500	N/A	Circulation	50.

COMMEMORATIVE CANADIAN COIN AND MEDAL SETS, 2012.

These sets contains six coins: 1¢, 5¢, 10¢, 25¢, $1.00 and $2.00 (coins with security devices), plus a nickel medallion commemorating each venue.

DATE	DESCRIPTION	QUANTITY SOLD	ISSUE PRICE	FINISH	MS-65 C
2012	Royal Canadian Numismatic Association, Calgary	217	N/A	Circulation	50.
2012	American Numismatic Association, Philadelphia	97	N/A	Circulation	50.
2012	Beijing International Stamp and Coin Exposition, Beijing, China	500	N/A	Circulation	50.

COMMEMORATIVE COIN AND MEDAL SETS, 2013.

These set contains five coins: 5¢, 10¢, 25¢, $1.00 and $2.00 (the $1 and $2 coins have security devices) plus a nickel medallion commemorating each venue.

DATE	DESCRIPTION	QUANTITY SOLD	ISSUE PRICE	FINISH	MS-65 C
2013	World Money Fair, Berlin, Germany	492	N/A	Circulation	50.
2013	Royal Canadian Numismatic Association, Winnipeg	667	19.95	Circulation	50.
2013	American Numismatic Association, Chicago	500	19.95	Circulation	50.
2013	Beijing International Stamp and Coin Exposition, Beijing, China	492	19.95	Circulation	50.

SPECIMEN SETS, 1970-2014

SIX COIN NICKEL SPECIMEN SET, 1970

In 1968 the Royal Canadian Mint began to study the feasibility of offering for sale six-coin specimen sets to the public. The 1967 specimen set was extremely successful and opened the way for expanded offerings. Trial cases were prepared and a small number of specimen nickel and bronze coins of the years 1968 and 1969 were struck. These coins were not made available to the public.

In 1970 the Royal Canadian Mint provided special specimen sets to Prime Minister Pierre Trudeau for presentation purposes during his trip to China that year. A quantity of specimen sets in narrow cases were made up. After Trudeau's trip, some of these sets were sold to the public for $13 each. The total quantity of 1970 specimen sets issued in Canada is believed to be fewer than 1,000 and the only way 1970 specimen coins were available was in these sets. When the Mint made specimen sets available to the public starting in 1971, they were housed in larger, seven-coin cases. These sets are listed under prestige sets 1971-1980 on page 377.

In the early 1970's empty narrow specimen cases became available. The coins that could be housed in them were taken from prestige sets of the year.

Finish: Specimen, Brilliant relief on brilliant background

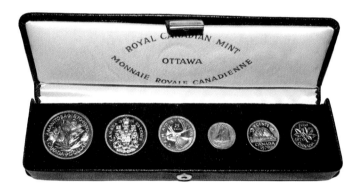

DATE	DESCRIPTION	FINISH	SP-65
1970	Specimen set in black case	Specimen	650.

SEVEN COIN NICKEL CUSTOM SPECIMEN SETS, 1976-1980

With the end of the 1976 Montreal Olympic Coin program, and with a new numismatic production facility now in place, the Mint staff turned their attention to improving the quality of their numismatic product line. The quality of the custom sets was upgraded to specimen. The packaging remained constant except for the modifications listed below.

Finish: Specimen, Brilliant relief on a parallel lined background
Cases: **1976-1978:** Coins in maroon vinyl-covered case with Canada's coat of arms and the word "CANADA" stamped in gold on the top.
1979-1980: As 1977, except a gold maple leaf replaces the coat of arms and "CANADA"

DATE	DESCRIPTION	QUANTITY SOLD	ISSUE PRICE	FINISH	SP-66
1976 DJ	Voyageur	28,162	8.15	Specimen	20.
1977 AJ, SWL	Voyageur	44,198	8.15	Specimen	20.
1977 DJ, FWL	Voyageur	Included	8.15	Specimen	45.
1977 DJ, SWL	Voyageur	Included	8.15	Specimen	20.
1978 SJ 50¢	Voyageur	41,000	8.75	Specimen	20.
1978 RJ 50¢	Voyageur	Included	8.75	Specimen	25.
1979	Voyageur	31,174	10.75	Specimen	23.
1980	Voyageur	41,447	12.50	Specimen	23.

SIX COIN NICKEL SPECIMEN SETS, 1981-1996

1981 saw the first officially stated issue of specimen coinage. The package was redesigned, and the coins were marketed as being of specimen quality. The number of coins in the set was reduced to six. The finish on the coins from 1981 to 1995 was brilliant relief on a brilliant background, and in 1996 was changed to brilliant relief against parallel lined background.

Finish: **1981-1995:**   Specimen, Brilliant relief on a brilliant background
              1996:   Specimen, Brilliant relief on a parallel lined background
Cases: **1981-1987:**   Blue leatherette, booklet type (103 mm x 141 mm), inside a hinged blue plastic frame housing, six encapsulated coins. All enclosed in a silver box.
              1988-1996:   Blue leatherette, wallet type, (96 mm x 153 mm) silver stamped mint crest, inside clear plastic frame with blue plastic insert. All enclosed in a silver sleeve.

DATE	DESCRIPTION	QUANTITY SOLD	ISSUE PRICE	FINISH	SP-66
1981	Voyageur	71,300	10.00	Specimen	12.
1982	Voyageur	62,298	11.50	Specimen	12.
1983	Voyageur	60,329	12.75	Specimen	12.
1984	Voyageur	60,030	12.95	Specimen	12.
1985	Voyageur	61,533	12.95	Specimen	12.
1986	Voyageur	67,152	12.95	Specimen	12.
1987	Voyageur	74,441	14.00	Specimen	12.
1988	Loon	70,205	14.00	Specimen	15.
1989	Loon	66,855	16.95	Specimen	20.
1990	Loon	76,611	17.95	Specimen	20.
1991	Loon	68,552	17.95	Specimen	35.
1992 (1967-)	Loon	78,328	18.95	Specimen	25.
1993	Loon	77,351	18.95	Specimen	18.
1994	Loon	75,973	19.25	Specimen	18.
1995	Loon	77,326	19.25	Specimen	15.
1996	Loon	62,125	19.25	Specimen	30.

SEVEN COIN NICKEL SPECIMEN SETS, 1997-2000

In 1997 the two dollar coin was added to the set, raising the number of coins to seven. The set continued as specimen quality with the packaging being revised in 1998.

Finish: **1997-2000:**   Specimen, Brilliant relief on a parallel lined background
Cases: **1997:**   Blue leatherette, wallet type, (96 mm x 153 mm) silver stamped mint crest, inside clear plastic frame with blue plastic insert. All enclosed in a silver sleeve.
              1998-2000:   Green leatherette outer cover with RCM logo. All enclosed in a multicoloured box.

DATE	DESCRIPTION	QUANTITY SOLD	ISSUE PRICE	FINISH	SP-66
1997	Flying Loon/Bear	97,595	26.95	Specimen	34.
1998	Loon/Bear	67,697	26.95	Specimen	25.
1999	Loon/Bear	46,786	26.95	Specimen	25.
1999	Loon/Nunavut	45,104	26.95	Specimen	25.
2000	Loon/Bear	87,965	34.95	Specimen	25.
2000	Loon/Bears	Included	34.95	Specimen	25.

SIX OR SEVEN COIN MULTI-PLY PLATED STEEL SPECIMEN SETS, 2001-2014

The 2002 specimen set is a double anniversary set issued to commemorate the Golden Jubilee of Queen Elizabeth II, and the 15th anniversary of the Loon dollar coin which was introduced in 1987. This is the only set which contains the "Family of Loons" one dollar coin.

The 2004 issue carries the new uncrowned effigy of Queen Elizabeth II, by Susanna Blunt. In 2006 only the $2 coin carried the double date (1996-2006) which commemorated the tenth anniversary of the "Toonie."

From 2007 to 2009 all coins that comprise the specimen set carried the Royal Canadian Mint logo, but in 2010 the logo was discontinued.

In 2010 the finish used on specimen coinage was changed. The earlier finish, in use since 1996, was a variety of that used by the Bullion Department on their maple leaf coinage. However, this finish was surfacing on giftware coinage, so it is thought the time had arrived to again make specimen set coinage a distinct finish, brilliant relief on the obverse portrait and reverse design, with a frosted relief of the legends and date, all on a lined matte background.

The one dollar "Bird Series" that began in 1997 with the Flying Loon was continued to 2014 with the Ferruginous Hawk. For design illustrations of these coins see pages 117-120.

In 2012 production of the one cent coin was discontinued, bringing the number of coins in the specimen set to six.

Finish: **2001-2009:** Specimen, Brilliant relief on a raised lined background.

2010-2014: Specimen, Brilliant relief on obverse portrait and reverse design, frosted relief on legends and date, all on a laser lined background

Cases: Maroon leatherette display case, RCM Logo, black insert encased in clear plastic black shipping box.

DATE	DESCRIPTION	No. of Coins	QUANTITY SOLD	ISSUE PRICE	FINISH	SP-66
2001P	Loon	7	54,613	39.95	Specimen	20.
2002P (1952-)	Loon Family	7	67,672	39.95	Specimen	35.
2003P	Loon	7	41,640	39.95	Specimen	25.
2004P	Canada Goose	7	46,493	44.95	Specimen	50.
2005P	Tufted Puffin	7	39,818	39.95	Specimen	70.
2006P	Snowy Owl	7	39,935	44.95	Specimen	65.
2007	Trumpeter Swan	7	27,056	45.95	Specimen	60.
2008	Common Eider	7	21,227	45.95	Specimen	50.
2009	Great Blue Heron	7	21,677	47.95	Specimen	60.
2010	Northern Harrier	7	21,111	49.95	Specimen	50.
2011	Great Grey Owl	7	25,665	49.95	Specimen	65.
2012 (1987)	Loon with Chicks	7	34,975	49.95	Specimen	55.
2013	Blue-Winged Teal	6	28,884	49.95	Specimen	50.
2014	Ferruginous Hawk	6	50,000	49.95	Specimen	50.

Note: 1. The Loon Family design of 2002 commemorates the fifteenth anniversary of the $1.00 loon coin.

2. The ten cent coins contained in the 2007 specimen sets are the Small, Far Logo obverse / Curved 7 reverse variety.

3. The Loon Mother and Chicks design of 2012 commemorates the 25th anniversary of the $1.00 loon coin.

SPECIAL NOTE ON FINISHES

It is very important to understand the different finishes the Royal Canadian Mint uses on their various issues. These finishes are altered from time-to-time as the Mint develops new products.

For example, the brilliant relief against a parallel lined background finish first used on bullion coins was carried forward in 1996 to be used on the coins contained in the specimen set.

In 2006 this finish was used on giftware coins such as the twenty-five cent coin issued to celebrate the 80th birthday of Queen Elizabeth II.

In 2010 a new specimen finish, brilliant relief against a laser-lined background, was used for the coins contained in the specimen set. There are now two different specimen finishes being utilised on Canadian coinage.

Circulation and Brilliant Uncirculated (proof-like) finishes are another very confusing mixture of finishes, see page xiv for a further explanation.

SPECIAL EDITION SPECIMEN SETS, 1967 and 2010-2014

100TH ANNIVERSARY OF CONFEDERATION, 1867-1967

In 1967 the Royal Canadian Mint produced two special cased coin sets to mark the 100th anniversary of Confederation. The silver medallion set in the red leather-covered case contained one each of the 1¢ to $1 (proof-like finish) and a sterling silver medallion designed and modelled by Thomas Shingles. The gold presentation set contained a $20 gold coin and one each of the 1¢ to $1, all of specimen finish. This set was housed in a black leather presentation case.

DATE	DESCRIPTION	QUANTITY SOLD	ISSUE PRICE	FINISH	GRADE	PRICE
1967	Medallion	72,463	12.00	Proof-like	PL-65	70.
1967	Gold	337,687	40.00	Specimen	SP-66	875.

SPECIAL EDITION "YOUNG WILDLIFE" SPECIMEN SETS, 2010-2014

The two-dollar "Young Wildlife Series" that began in 2010 with Two Lynx Kittens was continued to 2014 with the Baby Rabbits. For design illustrations of these coins see page 139.

A "finish" ten cent mule is found in the 2010 Lynx Specimen Set. The coin has an obverse with a brilliant relief on a raised lined background (2009 finish), and a reverse with a brilliant relief on the legend and date, with a lined matte finish background (2010 finish).

TEN CENT "FINISH" MULE

10¢ Obverse with
2009 Specimen Finish

10¢ Reverse with
2010 Specimen Finish

10¢ Finish Mule
Actual Size

Finish: Specimen, Brilliant relief on obverse portrait and revere design, frosted relief on legends and date, all on a laser lined background

Case: Maroon leatherette clam style case, RCM logo, 6- or 7-hole .black insert in clear plastic, multicoloured box.

DATE	DESCRIPTION	No. of Coins	QUANTITY SOLD	ISSUE PRICE	FINISH	SP-66	SP-67
2010	$2 Two Lynx Kittens	7	14,790	49.95	Specimen	65.	—
2010	'Finish' Mule ten cent coin	7	Included	49.95	Specimen	450.	550.
2011	$2 Elk Calf	7	13,899	49.95	Specimen	65.	—
2012	$2 Wolf Cubs	7	14,968	49.95	Specimen	65.	—
2013	$2 Black Bear Cubs	6	14,394	49.95	Specimen	50.	—
2014	$2 Baby Rabbits	6	17,500	49.95	Specimen	50.	—

SPECIAL EDITION "CANADIAN ARCTIC EXPEDITION" SPECIMEN SET, 2013

This set contains a specimen silver dollar commemorating the 100th anniversary of the Canadian Arctic Expedition.

DATE	DESCRIPTION	No. of Coins	QUANTITY SOLD	ISSUE PRICE	FINISH	SP-66	SP-67
2013	Specimen Silver Dollar	7	9,247	99.95	Specimen	100.	—

PRESTIGE SETS, 1971-1980

SEVEN COIN PRESTIGE SETS, 1971-1980

When it was first introduced in 1971, the prestige set (double dollar set) contained two nickel dollars, with the second nickel dollar being used to display the obverse. This was also true for the 1972 set; however, from 1973 on the second nickel dollar was replaced with a silver dollar. The coins in the prestige sets were of specimen quality until 1980, and proof quality thereafter.

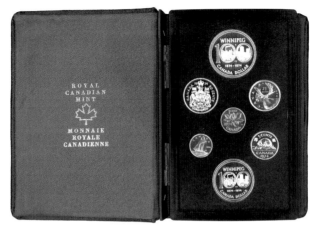

1974 Prestige Set

Finish: **1971-1980:** Specimen, Brilliant relief on a brilliant background

Cases: **1971-1973:** Crest of Canada; black leather, book type with clasp. Red satin inside red flocked 7-hole stationary display - coloured flocked jackets.

  1974-1978: Crest of Canada; black leather, book type with clasp. Red satin inside, hinged black plastic 7-hole display, encapsulated coins - coloured flocked jackets.

  1979-1980: Maple Leaf; black cardboard box, book type with clasp. Red satin inside, hinged black plastic 7-hole display, encapsulated coins - coloured flocked jackets.

DATE	DESCRIPTION	QUANTITY SOLD	ISSUE PRICE	FINISH	SP-66
1971	B.C./B.C.	66,860	12.00	Specimen	20.
1972	Voyageur/Voyageur	36,349	12.00	Specimen	45.
1973 LB 25¢	P.E.I./R.C.M.P.	119,891	12.00	Specimen	350.
1973 SB 25¢	P.E.I./R.C.M.P.	Included	12.00	Specimen	25.
1974	Winnipeg/Winnipeg	85,230	15.00	Specimen	25.
1974 DYT3	Winnipeg/Winnipeg	Included	15.00	Specimen	1,200.
1975	Voyageur/Calgary	97,263	15.00	Specimen	20.
1976	Voyageur/Parliament	87,744	16.00	Specimen	20.
1977	Voyageur/Jubilee	142,577	16.00	Specimen	20.
1977 SWL	Voyageur/Jubilee	Included	16.00	Specimen	25.
1978 SJ	Voyageur/Edmonton	147,000	16.50	Specimen	20.
1978 RJ	Voyageur/Edmonton	Included	16.50	Specimen	35.
1979	Voyageur/Griffon	155,698	18.50	Specimen	25.
1980	Voyageur/Polar Bear	162,875	36.00	Specimen	25.

Note: For images of the large bust (LB) and small bust (SB) twenty-five cent varieties of 1973, see page 351
For an image of the 1974 nickel dollar, double yoke type 3 variety, see page 344.
For an image of the 1977 nickel dollar, short water line (SWL) variety, see page 345.
For and image of the 1978 fifty cent, square jewels (SJ) and round jewels (RJ) varieties, see page 345.

PROOF SETS, 1981-2014

PROOF SETS, 1981-1995.
SEVEN STANDARD COINS

With the product reorganization in 1981, the standard coins of the Prestige Set were converted to Proof finish.

Finish: **1981-1995:** Proof, Frosted relief against a mirror background

Cases: **1981-1985:** Maple Leaf; black cardboard box, book type with clasp. Red satin inside, hinged black plastic 7-hole display, coloured flocked jackets.
1986-1995: Maple leaf; black plastic box, wallet type. Red satin inside, hinged black plastic 7-hole display, encapsulated coins

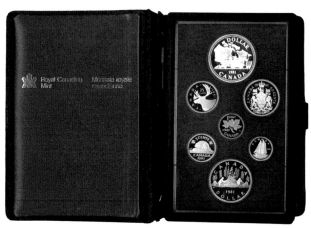

1981 Proof Set

DATE	DESCRIPTION	QUANTITY SOLD	ISSUE PRICE	FINISH	PR-67
1981	Voyageur/Train	199,000	36.00	Proof	25.
1982	Voyageur/Skull	180,908	36.00	Proof	25.
1983	Voyageur/Games	166,779	36.00	Proof	25.
1984	Voyageur/Toronto	161,602	40.00	Proof	25.
1985	Voyageur/Parks	153,950	40.00	Proof	25.
1986	Voyageur/Vancouver	176,224	40.00	Proof	25.
1987	Voyageur/Davis Strait	175,686	43.00	Proof	25.
1988	Loon/Ironworks	175,259	43.00	Proof	25.
1989	Loon/MacKenzie	154,693	46.95	Proof	25.
1990	Loon/Kelsey	158,068	48.00	Proof	28.
1991	Loon/Frontenac	131,888	48.00	Proof	55.
1992	Loon/Stagecoach	147,061	49.75	Proof	35.
1993	Loon/Hockey	143,065	49.75	Proof	35.
1994	Loon/Dogsled Team	104,485	50.75	Proof	35.
1995	Loon/Hudson's Bay	101,560	50.75	Proof	40.

PROOF SET, 1996.
SEVEN COIN SET WITH FOUR STERLING SILVER COINS

Beginning in 1996, the five, ten, twenty-five and fifty cent coins were struck on sterling silver planchets (92.5% Ag and 7.5% Cu). The one cent, and both the nickel and silver dollars were of standard specifications.

Finish: Proof, Frosted relief against a mirror background
Case: Maple Leaf logo; black leatherette wallet type case. Red satin inside, hinged black plastic 7-hole display, encapsulated coins

DATE	DESCRIPTION	QUANTITY SOLD	ISSUE PRICE	FINISH	PR-67
1996	Loon/McIntosh	112,835	66.25	Proof	60.

PROOF SETS, 1997-2011
EIGHT COIN SET WITH FIVE STERLING SILVER COINS

In 1997 the two dollar coin was added to the set, raising the total to eight coins. The two dollar coin, following the practice established in 1996, was made of sterling silver with a gold-plated centre. The one cent coin up to and including 2003, was not of the multi-ply plated steel, but of bronze composition.

Mid-year 2003 the tiara portrait of Elizabeth II, which had been in use since 1990, was replaced with the new uncrowned portrait by Susanna Blunt. The first proof set with the new portrait was dated 2004.

The 2005 proof set was the first set to feature a commemorative dollar selectively gold plated on the reverse and rim.

1997 Proof Set

Finish:	**1997:**	Proof, frosted relief against a mirror background
Case:	**1997:**	Maple Leaf logo; black leather wallet type case. Red satin inside, hinged black plastic 7-hole display, encapsulated coins

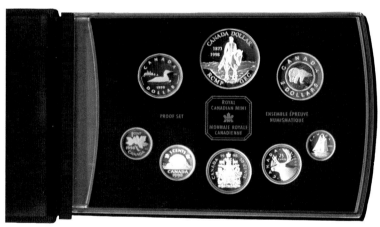

1998 Proof Set

Finish:	**1998-2003:**	Proof, frosted relief against a mirror background
Cases:	**1998-2003:**	Mint logo; dark green leather wallet style case, black plastic 8-hole insert, encapsulated coins, green flocked interior; four-colour outer box

2005 Proof Set

Finish: **2004-2011:**   Proof, frosted relief against a mirror background
Cases: **2004-2011:**   Mint logo; maroon leather wallet style case, black plastic 8-hole insert, encapsulated coins,
black flocked interior; black outer box

DATE	DESCRIPTION	QUANTITY SOLD	ISSUE PRICE	FINISH	PR-67
1997	Loon/Hockey/Polar Bear	113,647	79.95	Proof	70.
1997	CNA Edition signed Cournoyer / Ferguson	N/A	N/A	Proof	110.
1997	ANA Edition, signed Gilbert / Park	N/A	N/A	Proof	100.
1998	Loon/R.C.M.P./Polar Bear	93,632	79.95	Proof	80.
1999	Loon/Juan Perez/Polar Bear	95,113	79.95	Proof	80.
2000	Loon/Discovery/Polar Bear	90,921	79.95	Proof	65.
2001	Loon/Ballet/Polar Bear	74,194	81.95	Proof	80.
2001	ANA Edition	750	69.95	Proof	175.
2001	CNA Edition	N/A	89.95	Proof	90.
2002 (1952-)	Loon/Queen Elizabeth II/Polar Bear	65,315	81.95	Proof	70.
2002 (1952-)	ANA Edition	500	69.95	Proof	80.
2003	Loon/Cobalt/Polar Bear	62,007	81.95	Proof	80.
2003	ANA Edition	500	74.95	Proof	100.
2004	Loon/French Settlement/Polar Bear	57,614	83.92	Proof	75.
2004	ANA Edition	500	74.95	Proof	100.
2004	CNA Edition	250	74.95	Proof	100.
2005	Loon/Flag (gold plated) /Polar Bear	63,562	81.95	Proof	95.
2005	CNA Edition	197	74.95	Proof	120.
2006 (1996-)	Loon/Victoria Cross (gold plated) /Polar Bear	53,822	84.95	Proof	120.
2006	CNA Edition	200	84.95	Proof	130.
2007	Loon/Thayendanegea (gold plated)/Polar Bear	37,413	89.95	Proof	95.
2008	Loon/Quebec City (gold plated)/Polar Bear	38,630	89.95	Proof	100.
2009	Loon/First Flight (gold plated)/Polar Bear	27,549	99.95	Proof	110.
2009	RCNA Edition	200	99.95	Proof	110.
2010	Loon/Corvette (gold plated)/Polar Bear	32,342	109.95	Proof	120.
2011 (1911-)	Loon/Parks Canada/Bear	32,910	114.95	Proof	115.

Note: The ten cent coins contained in the 2007 proof sets are the Small, Far Logo obverse / Curved 7 reverse variety.

PROOF SET, 2012
EIGHT STANDARD COINS

For the first time two variations of the proof set were issued in 2012: a standard proof set where all coins are struck in their standard circulation alloys, and a premium fine silver proof set where all coins are struck in 99.99% pure silver.

Finish: Proof, frosted relief against a mirror background
Case: Mint logo; maroon leatherette case with black plastic 8-hole insert, encapsulated coins, black interior, black outer box

DATE	DESCRIPTION	QUANTITY SOLD	ISSUE PRICE	FINISH	PR-67
2012 (1812-)	Loon/War of 1812/Polar Bear	27,254	99.95	Proof	100.

PREMIUM PROOF SET, 2012
EIGHT COIN SET, FINE SILVER

2012 Premium Proof Set

Finish: Proof, frosted relief against a mirror background
Cases: Mint logo; black genuine leather case with black plastic 8-hole insert, encapsulated coins, black flocked interior, black outer box

DATE	DESCRIPTION	QUANTITY SOLD	ISSUE PRICE	FINISH	PR-67
2012 (1812-)	Loon/War of 1812 (gold plated)/Polar Bear	19,789	224.95	Proof	225.

PREMIUM PROOF SETS, 2013-2014
SEVEN COIN SET, FINE SILVER

With the one cent coin being phased out in 2012, the number of coins contained in the premium proof sets is now reduced to seven. Each coin contained in these sets is struck on a fine silver planchet.

2013 Premium Proof Set

h: Proof, frosted relief against a mirror background
:   Mint logo; black genuine leather case with black plastic 7-hole insert, encapsulated coins, black flocked interior, black outer box

ATE	DESCRIPTION	QUANTITY SOLD	ISSUE PRICE	FINISH	PR-67
.3	Loon/100th Anniv. Canadian Arctic Expedition	20,182	229.95	Proof	230.
.3	Loon/100th Anniv. Canadian Arctic Expedition, RCNA Edition	229	229.95	Proof	250.
L4	Loon/100th Anniv. of the Start of World War I	25,000	229.95	Proof	230.

PROOF SET, 2014
SEVEN STANDARD COINS

Again, in 2014 two varieties of proof sets were issued. This set contains seven proof coins struck on the standard alloys.

nish: Proof, frosted relief against a mirror background
ase: Mint logo; maroon leatherette case with black plastic 7-hole insert, encapsulated coins, black interior, black outer box

DATE	DESCRIPTION	QUANTITY SOLD	ISSUE PRICE	FINISH	PR-67
014	Loon/100th Anniv. Declaration of First World War	30,000	99.95	Proof	100.

SPECIAL ISSUE PROOF SETS, 1994-2012

SPECIAL LIMITED EDITION PROOF SETS, 1994-1995

First issued in 1994, these proof sets were limited to 50,000. They contained the silver commemorative dollar, along with the bronze/nickel commemorative of the year. The other five coins are the same as contained in the proof set of that year.

Finish: Proof, frosted relief against a mirror background
Case: Burgundy display case, wallet type, dated on spine with year of issue. Interior: White satin with brown plastic display frame - burgundy plastic box.

DATE	DESCRIPTION	QUANTITY SOLD	ISSUE PRICE	FINISH	PR-67	PR-68
1994	Remembrance/Dog Team Patrol	49,222	59.50	Proof	45.	—
1995	Peacekeeping/Hudson's Bay	49,802	66.95	Proof	40.	—

90th ANNIVERSARY OF THE ROYAL CANADIAN MINT, 1908-1998

Issued to commemorate the 90th Anniversary of the Royal Canadian Mint, this five-coin set features the same reverse designs as the original 1908 coins, except for the double date 1908-1998. The set was issued in two finishes, matte and mirror proof. The matte one cent coin does not carry the country of origin, "Canada." This error was corrected on the mirror proof cent.

1¢ Matte Issue Without CANADA

1¢ Mirror Issue With CANADA

Designers:
Obv.: Dora de Pédery-Hunt
Rev.: Ago Aarand

Engravers:
Obv.: Dora de Pédery-Hunt
Rev.: 1¢ – G. W. DeSaulles
       5¢, 10¢, 25¢, 50¢ –
       W. H. J. Blakemore

1¢ Mirror Issue

5¢ Mirror Issue

10¢ Mirror Issue

25¢ Mirror Issue

50¢ Mirror Issue

Finish: Proof, matte or mirror
Case of Issue: Burgundy leather clam style case, RCM Mint logo, white lining, five-hole plastic insert, COA
Matte set with bronze logo on case. Mirror set with nickel logo on the case

COIN	COMPOSITION	WEIGHT	DIAMETER	EDGE	DIE AXIS
1¢	92.5% Ag, 7.5% Cu, copper plated	5.90	25.30	Plain	↑↑
5¢	92.5% Ag, 7.5% Cu	1.30	15.25	Reeded	↑↑
10¢	92.5% Ag, 7.5% Cu	2.50	17.90	Reeded	↑↑
25¢	92.5% Ag, 7.5% Cu	5.80	23.50	Reeded	↑↑
50¢	92.5% Ag, 7.5% Cu	11.80	29.60	Reeded	↑↑

DATE	DESCRIPTION	QUANTITY SOLD	ISSUE PRICE	FINISH	PR-67	PR-68
1998 (1908-)	Without "CANADA" on 1¢	24,893	99.00	Matte proof	70.	—
1998 (1908-)	With "CANADA" on 1¢	18,376	99.00	Mirror proof	65.	—

SPECIAL LIMITED EDITION PROOF SETS, 2002-2003

The Special Edition Proof Set for 1952-2002 contains the 2002 commemorative dollar (22kt gold plated), the two-dollar coin with a 24kt gold plated inner core, and the 2002 fifty-cent commemorative coin. The remaining coins in the set are as the regular issue.

The coins in the Special Edition Proof Set for 1953-2003, carry the laureate portrait of Queen Elizabeth II which was first issued in 1953. This set commemorates Queen Elizabeth II's Coronation in 1953, and her Jubilee in 2003, with the double date 1953-2003.

Finish: Proof, frosted relief against a mirror background

DATE	DESCRIPTION	QUANTITY SOLD	ISSUE PRICE	FINISH	PR-67	PR-68
2002 (1952-)	Accession	33,490	99.95	Proof	100.	—
2003 (1953-)	Coronation	21,537	99.95	Proof	100.	—

PREMIUM GIFT BABY AND WEDDING, STERLING SILVER PROOF SETS, 2006-2008

This set contains a commemorative sterling silver loon dollar and a commemorative medallion; the remaining coins are the regular proof set issue.

2006 Premium Gift Baby Proof Set

2006 Premium Gift Baby Proof Set

Finish: Proof, frosted relief, against mirror background　　**Case of Issue:** Leatherette folder

DATE	DESCRIPTION	QUANTITY SOLD	ISSUE PRICE	FINISH	PR-67	PR-68
2006	Sterling Silver Loon, Lullaby Loonie, Teddy Bear Medallion	3,863	79.95	Proof	250.	—
2007	Sterling Silver "Gold Plated Rattle", Baby Medallion	1,911	89.95	Proof	900.	—
2007	Sterling Silver Loon, Wedding Medallion	849	89.95	Proof	900.	—
2008	Sterling Silver Loon, Baby Medallion	1,168	99.95	Proof	250.	—
2008	Sterling Silver Loon, Wedding Medallion	508	99.95	Proof	750.	—

SPECIAL LIMITED EDITION PROOF SET, 2010

Canada's first circulating silver dollar was introduced in 1935 featuring Emanuel Hahn's classic Voyageur design. This special edition proof set, with four other coins carrying the 1935 design commemorates the 75th anniversary of our famous dollar.

Finish: Proof
Case of Issue: Maple wood display case

DATE	DESCRIPTION	QUANTITY SOLD	ISSUE PRICE	FINISH	PR-67	PR-68
2010 (1935-)	75th Anniv. of the Voyageur Dollar	4,996	159.95	Proof	250.	—

SPECIAL LIMITED EDITION PROOF SET, 1911-2011

This set was Issued to commemorate the 100th Anniversary of the striking of the 1911 silver dollars.

1¢ Obverse   **1¢ Reverse**

Designers and Engravers:
Obv.: Sir E. B. MacKennal
Rev.: 1¢, 5¢, 10¢, 25¢, 50¢ –
Original design by L. C. Wyon,
Modified by W. H. J. Blakemore

Finish: Proof
Case of Issue: Cherry wood box

5¢   **10¢**   **25¢**   **50¢**   **One Dollar**

DATE	DESCRIPTION	QUANTITY SOLD	ISSUE PRICE	FINISH	PR-67	PR-68
2011 (1911-)	100th Anniv. of the 1911 Silver Dollar	5,952	179.95	Proof	300.	—

SPECIAL LIMITED EDITION PROOF SET, 2012

FAREWELL TO THE PENNY, 2012
This set was issued to commemorate the withdrawal of the one cent coin from circulation.

OBVERSE DESIGNS

| George W. DeSaulles 1908-1910 | Sir E. B. MacKennal 1911-1920 | Sir E. B. MacKennal 1920-1936 | Arnold Machin 1967 | Susanna Blunt 2003-2012 |

REVERSE DESIGNS

| George W. DeSaulles 1908-1910 | W. H. J. Blakemore 1911-1920 | Fred Lewis 1920-1936 | Alex Colville 1967 | G. E. Kruger-Gray 1937-2012 |

Designers:
Obv.:   See obverse illustrations
Rev.:   See reverse illustrations

Engravers:
Obv.:   Susan Taylor
Rev.:   Samantha Strath

Composition: 99.99% au
Silver content: 14.7 g, 0.473 (per set)
Weight: 2.94 g (per coin); 14.7 (set)
Diameter: 19.1
Thickness: N/A
Edge: Plain
Die Axis: ↑↑
Finish: Proof
Case of Issue: RCM branded wooden case, Black flocked insert, encapsulated coins, COA, custom box

DATE	DESCRIPTION	QUANTITY SOLD	ISSUE PRICE	FINISH	PR-67	PR-68
2012	Farewell to the Penny	5,001	149.95	Proof	425.	—

PROOF GOLD SET

YEAR OF THE DRAGON, 2012.

The reverse design on these coins features a mythical water dragon surrounded by lotus flowers and clouds of good fortune, the Chinese lunar symbol for the year 2012.

Obverse

Physical and chemical specifications:

Denomination:	$50	$20	$10	$5
Weight (oz);	1.0	½	¼	1/10
Diameter (mm):	30.0	25.0	20.0	16.0
Thickness (mm):	N/A	N/A	N/A	N/A

Composition: 99.99% Au
Gold content:

	$50	$20	$10	$5
Grams	31.15	15.59	7.8	3.13
Troy ounces	1.00	0.50	0.25	0.10

Edge: Reeded
Die Axis: ↑↑
Finish: Proof
Case of Issue: Gold silk-covered case, black suede four-hole insert, encapsulated, COA

$50

$20

$10

$5

Designers:
Obv.: Susanna Blunt
Rev.: Susan Taylor
Engravers:
Rev.: Three Degrees Creative Group
Rev.: Cecily Mok

DATE	DESCRIPTION	QUANTITY SOLD	ISSUE PRICE	FINISH	PR-67	PR-68
2012	Year of the Dragon	357	5,499.95	Proof	5,500.	—

PROOF PLATINUM SETS

In 1990 the Royal Canadian Mint entered the luxury market for high quality collector coins. While the proof platinum sets are scarce their value is linked to the market price of platinum. The value of these sets is based on a Canadian market price of $1,540. for platinum as of April 23rd, 2014.

CANADIAN WILDLIFE SERIES, 1990-1994.

Physical and chemical specifications:

Denomination:	$300	$150	$75	$30
Weight (oz);	1.0	0.5	0.25	0.1
Diameter (mm):	30.0	25.0	20.0	16.0
Thickness (mm):	2.6	2.12	1.65	1.08

Composition: 99.95% Pt

Platinum content:

	$300	$150	$75	$30
Grams	31.1	15.55	7.75	3.1
Troy ounces	1.0	0.5	0.25	0.1

Edge: Reeded

Die Axis: ↑↑

Finish: Proof

Case of Issue: 1992-1994: Walnut case, black suede four hole insert, encapsulated, COA.

1990-1994 Obverse

POLAR BEARS PLATINUM SET 1990.

Canada's "Monarch of the North" has been transferred by Robert Bateman from the sparkling Arctic environment to the gleaming surfaces of pure platinum coins.

$300 $150 $75 $30

Designers:
Obv.:   Dora de Pédery-Hunt
Rev.:   Robert Bateman

Engravers:
Obv.:   Dora de Pédery-Hunt
Rev.: $300 - Terry Smith
$150 - William Woodruff
$ 75 - Ago Aarand
$ 30 - Sheldon Beveridge

DATE	DESCRIPTION	QUANTITY SOLD	ISSUE PRICE	FINISH	PR-67	PR-68
1990	Polar Bears, 4-coin set	2,629	1,990.00	Proof	3,150.	—

SNOWY OWLS PLATINUM SET 1991.

This is the second set in the series of proof platinum coins dedicated to Canadian wildlife.

$300 $150 $75 $30

Designers:
Obv.:   Dora de Pédery-Hunt
Rev.:   Glen Loates

Engravers:
Obv.:   Dora de Pédery-Hunt
Rev.: $300 - Sheldon Beveridge
$150 - Ago Aarand
$ 75 - Terry Smith
$ 30 - William Woodruff

DATE	DESCRIPTION	QUANTITY SOLD	ISSUE PRICE	FINISH	PR-67	PR-68
1991	Snowy Owls, 4-coin set	1,164	1,990.00	Proof	3,150.	—

COUGARS PLATINUM SET 1992.
This is the third set in the series of proof platinum coins dedicated to Canadian wildlife.

| $300 | $150 | $75 | $30 |

Designers:
Obv.: Dora de Pédery-Hunt
Rev.: George McLean
Engravers:
Obv.: Dora de Pédery-Hunt
Rev.: $300 - Ago Aarand,
                Cosme Saffioti
        $150 - Susan Taylor
        $ 75 - Sheldon Beveridge
        $ 30 - Ago Aarand

DATE	DESCRIPTION	QUANTITY SOLD	ISSUE PRICE	FINISH	PR-67	PR-68
1992	Cougars, 4-coin set	1,081	1,955.00	Proof	3,150.	—

ARCTIC FOXES PLATINUM SET 1993.
This is the fourth set in the series of proof platinum coins dedicated to Canadian wildlife.

| $300 | $150 | $75 | $30 |

Designers:
Obv.: Dora de Pédery-Hunt
Rev.: Claudio D'Angelo
Engravers:
Obv.: Dora de Pédery-Hunt
Rev.: $300 - Susan Taylor
        $150 - Sheldon Beveridge
        $ 75 - Ago Aarand
        $ 30 - Ago Aarand

DATE	DESCRIPTION	QUANTITY SOLD	ISSUE PRICE	FINISH	PR-67	PR-68
1993	Arctic Foxes, 4-coin set	1,033	1,955.00	Proof	3,150.	—

SEA OTTERS PLATINUM SET 1994.
This is the fifth and last set in the series of proof platinum coins dedicated to Canadian wildlife.

| $300 | $150 | $75 | $30 |

Designers:
Obv.: Dora de Pédery-Hunt
Rev.: Ron S. Parker
Engravers:
Obv.: Dora de Pédery-Hunt
Rev.: $300 - Sheldon Beveridge
        $150 - William Woodruff
        $ 75 - Terry Smith
        $ 30 - Susan Taylor

DATE	DESCRIPTION	QUANTITY SOLD	ISSUE PRICE	FINISH	PR-67	PR-68
1994	Sea Otters, 4-coin set	766	1,995.00	Proof	3,150.	—

ENDANGERED WILDLIFE SERIES, 1995-2004

1995-2004 Obverse

Specifications: See page 388
Case of Issue:
1/10 oz coin: Leather display case, encapsulated coin
½ oz coin: Mahogany case, encapsulated coin
Set, 4 coins: Mahogany case, inside green satin, coins individually
encapsulated

CANADA LYNX PLATINUM SET, 1995.
This is the first set in the series of proof platinum coins commemorating Canada's endangered wildlife.

$300 $150 $75 $30

Designers:
Obv.: Dora de Pédery-Hunt
Rev.: Michael Dumas
Engravers:
Obv.: Dora de Pédery-Hunt
Rev.: $300 - Susan Taylor
$150 - Cosme Saffioti
$ 75 - Stan Witten
$ 30 - Ago Aarand

DATE	DESCRIPTION	QUANTITY SOLD	ISSUE PRICE	FINISH	PR-67	PR-68
1995	30 Dollars	620	179.95	Proof	175.	200.
1995	150 Dollars	226	599.95	Proof	800.	850.
1995	Canada Lynx, 4-coin set	682	1,950.00	Proof	3,150.	—

PEREGRINE FALCON PLATINUM SET 1996.
This is the second set in the series of proof platinum coins commemorating Canada's endangered wildlife.

$300 $150 $75 $30

Designers:
Obv.: Dora de Pédery-Hunt
Rev.: Dwayne Harty
Engravers:
Obv.: Dora de Pédery-Hunt
Rev.: $300 - Sheldon Beveridge
$150 - Stan Witten
$ 75 - Cosme Saffioti
$ 30 - Ago Aarand

DATE	DESCRIPTION	QUANTITY SOLD	ISSUE PRICE	FINISH	PR-67	PR-68
1996	30 Dollars	910	179.95	Proof	175.	200.
1996	150 Dollars	196	599.95	Proof	800.	850.
1996	Peregrine Falcon, 4-coin set	675	2,095.95	Proof	3,150.	—

WOOD BISON PLATINUM SET, 1997.
This is the third set in the series of proof platinum coins commemorating Canada's endangered wildlife.

$300 $150 $75 $30

Designers:
Obv.:   Dora de Pédery-Hunt
Rev.:   Chris Bacon
Engravers:
Obv.:   Dora de Pédery-Hunt
Rev.: $300 - Sheldon Beveridge
        $150 - William Woodruff
        $ 75 - Stan Witten
        $ 30 - Ago Aarand

DATE	DESCRIPTION	QUANTITY SOLD	ISSUE PRICE	FINISH	PR-67	PR-68
1997	30 Dollars	469	179.95	Proof	175.	200.
1997	150 Dollars	116	599.95	Proof	800.	850.
1997	Wood Bison, 4-coin set	413	1,950.00	Proof	3,150.	—

GREY WOLF PLATINUM SET, 1998.
This is the fourth set in the series of proof platinum coins commemorating Canada's endangered wildlife.

$300 $150 $75 $30

Designers:
Obv.:   Dora de Pédery-Hunt
Rev.:   Kerri Burnett
Engravers:
Obv.:   Dora de Pédery-Hunt
Rev.: $300 - Sheldon Beveridge
        $150 - Cosme Saffioti
        $ 75 - William Woodruff
        $ 30 - A. Aarand, J. Osio

DATE	DESCRIPTION	QUANTITY SOLD	ISSUE PRICE	FINISH	PR-67	PR-68
1998	30 Dollars	664	179.95	Proof	175.	200.
1998	150 Dollars	194	599.95	Proof	800.	850.
1998	Grey Wolf, 4-coin set	661	2,095.00	Proof	3,150.	—

MUSKOX PLATINUM SET, 1999.
This is the fifth set in the series of proof platinum coins commemorating Canada's endangered wildlife.

$300 $150 $75 $30

Designers:
Obv.:   Dora de Pédery-Hunt
Rev.:   Mark Hobson
Engravers:
Obv.:   Dora de Pédery-Hunt
Rev.: $300 -William Woodruff
        $150 - Stan Witten
        $ 75 - Cosme Saffioti
        $ 30 - Sheldon Beveridge

DATE	DESCRIPTION	QUANTITY SOLD	ISSUE PRICE	FINISH	PR-67	PR-6
1999	30 Dollars	999	179.95	Proof	175.	200.
1999	Muskox, 4-coin set	495	2,095.95	Proof	3,150.	—

PRONGHORN PLATINUM SET, 2000.
This is the sixth set in the series of proof platinum coins commemorating Canada's endangered wildlife.

$300 $150 $75 $30

Designers:
Obv.: Dora de Pédery-Hunt
Rev.: Mark Hobson
Engravers:
Obv.: Dora de Pédery-Hunt
Rev.: $300 - José Osio
$150 - Susan Taylor
$ 75 - Stan Witten
$ 30 - William Woodruff

DATE	DESCRIPTION	QUANTITY SOLD	ISSUE PRICE	FINISH	PR-67	PR-68
2000	Pronghorn, 4-coin set	599	2,095.95	Proof	3,150.	—

HARLEQUIN DUCK PLATINUM SET 2001.
This is the seventh set in the series of proof platinum coins commemorating Canada's endangered wildlife.

$300 $150 $75 $30

Designers:
Obv.: Dora de Pédery-Hunt
Rev.: C. Saffioti, S. Taylor
S. Witten
Engravers:
Obv.: Dora de Pédery-Hunt
Rev.: $300 - Stan Witten
$150 - Susan Taylor
$ 75 - Cosme Saffioti
$ 30 - Susan Taylor

DATE	DESCRIPTION	QUANTITY SOLD	ISSUE PRICE	FINISH	PR-67	PR-68
2001	Harlequin Duck, 4-coin set	448	2,395.95	Proof	3,150.	—

GREAT BLUE HERON PLATINUM SET 2002.
This is the eighth set in the series of proof platinum coins commemorating Canada's endangered wildlife.

$300 $150 $75 $30

Designers:
Obv.: Dora de Pédery-Hunt
Rev.: John-Luc Grondin
Engravers:
Obv.: Dora de Pédery-Hunt
Rev.: $300 - Stan Witten
$150 - Susan Taylor
$ 75 - Stan Witten
$ 30 - José Osio

DATE	DESCRIPTION	QUANTITY SOLD	ISSUE PRICE	FINISH	PR-67	PR-68
2002	Great Blue Heron, 4-coin set	344	2,495.95	Proof	3,150.	—

ATLANTIC WALRUS PLATINUM SET 2003.
This is the ninth set in the series of proof platinum coins commemorating Canada's endangered wildlife.

$300	$150	$75	$30

Designers:
Obv.:   Dora de Pédery-Hunt
Rev.:   Pierre Leduc
Engravers:
Obv.:   Dora de Pédery-Hunt
Rev.: $300 - Susan Taylor
$150 - José Osio
$ 75 - Stan Witten
$ 30 - Stan Witten

DATE	DESCRIPTION	QUANTITY SOLD	ISSUE PRICE	FINISH	PR-67	PR-68
2003	Atlantic Walrus, 4-coin set	365	2,995.95	Proof	3,150.	—

GRIZZLY BEAR PLATINUM SET 2004.
This is the tenth and final set in the Endangered Wildlife proof platinum series, and it commemorates Canada's Great Grizzly bears.

$300	$150	$75	$30

Designers:
Obv.:   Susanna Blunt
Rev.:   Kerri Burnett
Engravers:
Obv.:   Susan Taylor
Rev.: $300 - José Osio
$150 - José Osio
$ 75 - José Osio
$ 30 - José Osio

DATE	DESCRIPTION	QUANTITY SOLD	ISSUE PRICE	FINISH	PR-67	PR-68
2004	Grizzly Bear, 4-coin set	380	2,995.95	Proof	3,150.	—

MAPLE LEAF BULLION COINS

GUIDE AND INDEX TO MAPLE LEAF BULLION COINS

The following categories were generated to divide the maple leaf bullion coins into a frame work for listing. These coins needed a logical listing order due to the many special effects that are used with them. It appears that special effects are first tested on maple leaf bullion coins before they are used on general collector coins.

The only criteria for a coin to be listed in this section are that the reverse must carry the bullion designation of weight or fineness.

GOLD MAPLE LEAFS

INTRODUCTION

In 1979 the Canadian Government introduced a gold bullion coin to compete with similar coins issued by other countries (such as the Krugerrand of South Africa). From 1979 to 1981 only the 50-dollar coin (Maple Leaf) in the one troy ounce size was produced. The Maple Leaf during this period was issued with a gold fineness of .999. During November 1982 the range of the gold Maple Leaf bullion coins being offered was expanded to three sizes. Now included in the offering were the five dollar or 1/10 maple and the ten dollar or ¼ maple. With the addition of the two fractional Maple Leafs all sizes were upgraded in gold content to .9999 fine. July of 1986 saw the offering range expanded once again to include the 20 dollar or ½ maple. All four coins are produced from .9999 fine gold and are legal tender coinage of Canada. In 1988 the Royal Canadian Mint, again expanding their bullion program, introduced five new coins; four platinum (1/10, ¼, ½ and one maple) and one silver (one maple). In 1990 the reverse hub of the one ounce gold Maple Leaf was re-engraved, enhancing veins in the maple leaf design. Other changes included a more slender stem on the maple leaf and wider spacing of the letters in the legend "Fine Gold 1 oz Or Pur." In 1993 the Royal Canadian Mint added to the series of bullion coin by issuing a 1/20 of an ounce ($1.00) size in gold and platinum. Again in 1994 the $2.00 denomination was added to the bullion coin series (1/15 of an ounce) in both platinum and gold. The $2.00 - 1/15 Maple denomination was discontinued in 1995.

The original finish developed by the Mint in 1979 for the Maple Leaf Gold Program was "The Bullion Finish," a brilliant relief on a parallel lined background.

FINISHES USED ON MAPLE LEAF COINS

Bullion: 1979-2013 Brilliant relief against a parallel lined background
2014 Satin relief against a radial lined background
      Coloured
      Hologram

Specimen: Brilliant relief on a satin background (Reverse proof)
      Coloured
      Hologram

Proof: Frosted relief against a mirror background
      Coloured
      Hologram

PRIVY AND SECURITY MARKS ON BULLION COINS

The year 1999 marked the 20th anniversary of the Maple Leaf program. To commemorate this event a privy mark was incorporated into the reverse design of all regular issue Maple Leafs.

A special issue of maple leafs was produced for January 1st, 2000. These were given a double date, 1999-2000, and a Fireworks privy mark.

To celebrate the millennium year the privy mark added to all maple leaf denominations was "Fireworks" above the numerals 2000.

Beginning in 2013, a new security mark was added to the design of the one ounce gold maple leaf. The security mark consists of a textured maple leaf micro-engraved with a laser on a small area on the reverse of the coin. In the centre of this mark is another maple leaf containing a lasered two-digit number. The two-digit number indicates the year of issue and will change annually.

1999
20 YEARS ANS

1999-2000
Fireworks

2000
Fireworks 2000

2013-2014
Security Mark

GOLD MAPLE LEAF SPECIFICATIONS

CHARACTERISTICS	.50¢ = 1/25 oz	$1 =1/20 oz	$2 = 1/15 oz	$5 = 1/10 oz	$10. = ¼ oz	$20 = ½ oz	$50 = 1 oz
Fineness (1979-1982)	—	—	—	—	—	—	99.90%
Fineness (1982 to date)	99.99%	99.99%	99.99%	99.99%	99.99%	99.99%	99.99%
Weight (grams)	1.244	1.555	2.074	3.110	7.776	15.552	31.1035
Diameter (mm)	13.92	14.1	15.0	16.0	20.0	25.0	30.0
Thickness (mm)	0.63	0.92	0.98	1.22	1.70	2.23	2.93
Edge	Reeded	Reeded	Reeded	Reeded	Reeded	Reeded	Reeded
Die Axis	↑↑	↑↑	↑↑	↑↑	↑↑	↑↑	↑↑
Finish	Bullion	Bullion	Bullion	Bullion	Bullion	Bullion	Bullion

GOLD MAPLE LEAF OBVERSES

Tiara Portrait
1979-1989

Royal Diadem Portrait
1990-2003

Uncrowned Portrait
2004-2014

GOLD MAPLE LEAF REVERSES

.999 Fine
1979-1982

.9999 Fine
1983-1989

.9999 Fine
Re-engraved Leaf
1990-2012

.9999 Fine
Security Mark
2013-2014

		Designers	**Engravers:**
Obv.:	1979-1989	Arnold Machin	Walter Ott
	1990-2003	Dora de Pédery-Hunt	Dora de Pédery-Hunt
	2004-2013	Susanna Blunt	Susan Taylor
Rev.:	1979-1982	Walter Ott	RCM Staff
	1983-1989	Walter Ott	RCM Staff
	1990-2012	Walter Ott	RCM Staff
	2013-2014	Walter Ott	RCM Staff

GOLD MAPLE LEAFS

BULLION ISSUES

FINISH: 1979-2013 – Brilliant relief against a parallel lined background
2014 – Satin relief against a radial lined background

MINTAGES: The production (quantity minted) of regular issue gold maple leaf bullion coins is on a demand basis. As coins are ordered by the distributors, they are struck and shipped by the Mint.

PRICING: Buying and selling prices are based on the interday spot price of bullion plus a small percentage premium for the striking and handling. The smaller the unit the larger the percentage premium charged on buying; however, in later selling the premium could very well disappear.

	QUANTITIES SOLD				
DATE	**$1 = 1/20 oz**	**$5 = 1/10oz**	**$10 = 1/4oz**	**$20 = 1/2oz**	**$50 = 1oz**
1979	N/I	N/I	N/I	N/I	1,000,000
1980	N/I	N/I	N/I	N/I	1,215,000
1981	N/I	N/I	N/I	N/I	863,000
1982	N/I	184,000	246,000	N/I	883,000
1983	N/I	224,000	130,000	N/I	695,000
1984	N/I	226,000	355,200	N/I	1,098,000
1985	N/I	476,000	607,200	N/I	1,747,500
1986	N/I	483,000	879,200	386,400	1,093,500
1987	N/I	459,000	376,800	332,800	978,000
1988	N/I	412,000	380,000	521,600	800,500
1989	N/I	539,000	328,800	259,200	856,000
1990	N/I	476,000	253,600	174,400	815,000
1991	N/I	322,000	166,400	96,200	290,000
1992	N/I	384,000	179,600	116,000	368,900
1993	37,080	248,630	158,452	99,492	321,413
1994	78,860	313,150	148,792	104,766	180,357
1995	85,920	294,890	127,596	103,162	208,729
1996	56,520	179,220	89,148	66,246	143,682
1997	59,720	188,540	98,104	63,354	478,211
1998	44,260	301,940	85,472	65,366	593,704
1999	62,820	709,920	98,928	64,760	627,067
1999-2000	Included	Included	Included	Included	Included
2000	31,280	52,970	31,688	24,404	86,375
2001	20,720	63,470	35,168	26,556	138,878
2002	17,140	45,020	42,940	28,706	344,883
2003	3,890	26,940	23,228	23,470	194,631
2004	9,880	33,480	18,296	13,160	253,978
2005	10,220	30,380	25,748	20,052	281,647
2006	19,340	40,960	25,964	21,138	209,937
2007	17,900	21,300	17,004	13,476	189,462
2008	15,740	38,510	34,368	28,782	710,718
2009	39,020	227,670	71,268	54,506	1,011,235
2010	9,000	111,160	41,628	34,302	1,036,832
2011	19,320	81,280	36,164	31,536	1,107,974
2012	12,400	95,700	129,156	28,594	712,193
2013	12,940	64,700	173,084	43,706	1,050,564
2014	N/A	N/A	N/A	N/A	N/A

Note: N/I denotes Not Issued.

GOLD MAPLE LEAF SPECIAL ISSUES

SPECIAL ISSUE SINGLES

FIFTY CENTS

FIFTY CENT (1/25 ounce) ISSUES, 2004-2012.
The 1/25 oz gold coin is the smallest ever produced by the Royal Canadian Mint.

Designers:
  Obv.: Susanna Blunt
  Rev.: See reverse illustrations
Composition: 99.99% Au
Gold content: 1.27 g, 0.041 tr oz
Weight: 1.27 g
Diameter: 13.9 mm
Thickness: 0.6 mm

Engravers:
  Obv.: Susan Taylor
  Rev.: See reverse illustrations

Edge: Reeded
Die Axis: ↑↑
Finish: Proof

Actual Size

Case of Issue: 2004: Maroon leatherette case, black flocked insert, encapsulated coin, COA
                 2005-2006: Maroon plastic slide case, black plastic insert, encapsulated coin, COA
                 2007-2012: Maroon leatherette clam style case, black flocked insert, encapsulated coin, COA

Common Obverse

2004
Majestic Moose
Des. and Engr.:
José Osio

2005
Voyageur
Des.: E. Hahn
Engr.: Stan Witten

2006
Cowboy
Des.: M. Grant
Engr.: Stan Witten

2007
Wolf
Des. and Engr.:
William Woodruff

2008
De Havilland
Beaver
Des.: P. Mossman
Engr.: K. Wachelko

2009
Red Maple Leaves
Des. and Engr.:
Christie Paquet

2010
R.C.M.P.
Des.: J. Griffin-Scott
Engr.: K. Wachelko

2011
Canada Geese
Des.: E. Damstra
Engr.: K. Wachelko

2012
The Bluenose
Des.: From the late
Nova Scotia artist
P. MacCready's
watercolour
painting
Engr.: S. Witten

DATE	DESCRIPTION	QUANTITY SOLD	ISSUE PRICE	FINISH	PR-67	PR-68
2004	Majestic Moose, 25th Anniv. Gold Maple Leafs	24,992	69.95	Proof	175.	185.
2005	70th Anniversary of Voyageur Design	13,933	69.95	Proof	125.	135.
2006	Cowboy	13,524	69.95	Proof	125.	135.
2007	Wolf	12,514	81.95	Proof	185.	195.
2008	de Havilland Beaver	13,526	85.95	Proof	135.	145.
2009	Red Maple Leaves	11,854	99.95	Proof	125.	135.
2010	Royal Canadian Mounted Police	9,594	109.95	Proof	125.	135.
2011	Canada Geese	7,498	109.95	Proof	135.	145.
2012	The Bluenose	13,524	129.95	Proof	135.	145.

TWO DOLLAR COIN

TWO DOLLAR (1/15 ounce) BULLION ISSUE, 1994.

Issued 1994 as a new addition to the line of bullion coins offered by the Royal Canadian Mint, the two dollar (1/15 troy ounce) coin was not a success and was discontinued in 1995. It is a one-year type, and for this reason popular.

Actual Size

Designers and Engravers:
Obv.: Dora de Pédery-Hunt
Rev.: Walter Ott, RCM Staff
Composition: 99.99% Au
Gold content: 1.244 g, 0.04 tr oz
Weight: 1.244 g
Diameter: 13.9 mm   **Edge:** Reeded
Thickness: 0.6 mm   **Die Axis:** ↑↑
Finish: Bullion
Case: Mylar pouch

DATE	DESCRIPTION	QUANTITY SOLD	ISSUE PRICE	FINISH	MS-65	MS-66
1994	$2 (1/15 oz), Bullion Issue	3,540	BV	Bullion	400.	425.

FIVE DOLLAR COINS

FIVE DOLLARS, MAPLE LEAF FOREVER, 2012.

The maple leaf has been a national symbol of Canada for almost 300 years. The sugar maple is an important member of the northeastern Canadian boreal forest. Its sap produces some of the world's purest and finest maple syrup.

Actual Size

Designers and Engravers:
Obv.: Susanna Blunt, Susan Taylor
Rev.: Luc Normandin, Steven Stewart
Composition: 99.99% Au
Gold content: 3.13 g, 0.1 tr oz
Weight: 3.13 g
Diameter: 16.0 mm   **Edge:** Reeded
Thickness: 1.0 mm   **Die Axis:** ↑↑
Finish: Proof
Case: Maroon leatherette clam style case, black flock insert, encapsulated coin(s), COA

DATE	DESCRIPTION	QUANTITY SOLD	ISSUE PRICE	FINISH	PR-67	PR-68
2012	$5 (1/10 oz), Maple Leaf Forever	4,373	229.95	Proof	210.	225.

FIVE DOLLARS, DEVIL'S BRIGADE, 2013.

Canada joined forces with the United States in World War II to create the First Special Service Force.

Actual Size

Designers and Engravers:
Obv.: Susanna Blunt, Susan Taylor
Rev.: Ardell Bourgeois, RCM Staff
Composition: 99.99% Au
Gold content: 7.8 g, 0.25 tr oz
Weight: 7.8 g
Diameter: 20.0 mm   **Edge:** Reeded
Thickness: 1.7 mm   **Die Axis:** ↑↑
Finish: Proof
Case: Maroon leatherette clam style case, black flock insert, encapsulated coin(s), COA

DATE	DESCRIPTION	QUANTITY SOLD	ISSUE PRICE	FINISH	PR-67	PR-68
2013	$5 (¼ oz), Devil's Brigade	494	649.95	Proof	650.	675.

TEN DOLLAR COINS

TEN DOLLARS, PIEDFORT MAPLE LEAF, 2010.

This ten-dollar gold maple leaf was issued in a set of two coins (see page 410), the second coin being a five-dollar silver maple (see page 426).

Actual
Size

Designers and Engravers:
Obv.: Susanna Blunt, Susan Taylor
Rev.: RCM Staff
Composition: 99.999% Au
Gold content: 6.25 g, 0.2 tr oz
Weight: 6.25 g
Diameter: 15.9 mm   **Edge:** Reeded
Thickness: 1.9 mm   **Die Axis:** ↑↑
Finish: Bullion
Case: Maroon leatherette clam style case, black flock insert, encapsulated coin(s), COA

DATE	DESCRIPTION	QUANTITY SOLD	ISSUE PRICE	FINISH	MS-65	MS-66
2010	$10 Gold Piedfort Maple Leaf	1,264	N.I.I.	Bullion	500.	510.

TEN DOLLARS, THE WAR OF 1812, 1812-2012.

The reverse of this coin features a heraldic design commemorating the 250th anniversary of the war between the United Stated and England over the control of Canadian territories.

Actual Size

Designers and Engravers:
Obv.: Susanna Blunt, Susan Taylor
Rev.: Cathy Bursey-Sabourin, Konrad Wachelko
Composition: 99.99% Au
Gold content: 7.80 g, 0.25 tr oz
Weight: 7.80 g
Diameter: 20.0 mm   **Edge:** Reeded
Thickness: 1.7 mm   **Die Axis:** ↑↑
Finish: Proof
Case: Maroon leatherette clam style case, black flock insert, encapsulated coin(s), COA

DATE	DESCRIPTION	QUANTITY SOLD	ISSUE PRICE	FINISH	PR-67	PR-68
2012 (1812-)	$10 gold (¼ oz) The War of 1812	1,997	569.95	Proof	650.	675.

TEN DOLLARS, POLAR BEAR, 2013.

This ten-dollar gold maple leaf was issued in a set of two coins (see page 410), the second coin being an eight-dollar silver maple, see page 430.

Actual Size

Designers and Engravers:
Obv.: Susanna Blunt, Susan Taylor
Rev.: Germaine Arnaktauyak, RCM Staff
Composition: 99.99% Au
Gold content: 7.87 g, 0.25 tr oz
Weight: 7.8 g
Diameter: 20.0 mm   **Edge:** Reeded
Thickness: 1.7 mm   **Die Axis:** ↑↑
Finish: Proof
Case: See page 410

DATE	DESCRIPTION	QUANTITY SOLD	ISSUE PRICE	FINISH	PR-67	PR-68
2013	$10 Gold (¼ oz) Polar Bear	4,229	N.I.I.	Proof	500.	525.

FIFTY DOLLAR COINS

FIFTY DOLLARS (1 ounce), 10TH ANNIVERSARY OF THE MAPLE LEAF BULLION COINS, 1989.

To commemorate the 10th anniversary of the maple leaf bullion coin program in 1989 the Royal Canadian Mint issued a series of proof quality silver, gold and platinum coins individually and in sets. The single coins and sets were packaged in solid maple wood presentation cases with brown velvet liners.

Designers and Engravers:
Obv.: Arnold Machin, Walter Ott
Rev.: Walter Ott, RCM Staff
Composition: 99.99% Au
Gold content: 31.10 g, 1.0 tr oz
Weight: 31.1035 g, 1oz
Diameter: 30.0 mm   **Edge:** Reeded
Thickness: 2.9 mm   **Die Axis:** ↑↑
Finish: Proof
Case of Issue: Maple wood case, black flocked insert, encapsulated coin, COA

DATE	DESCRIPTION	QUANTITY SOLD	ISSUE PRICE	FINISH	PR-67	PR-68
1989	$50 (1 oz) 10th Anniv. of Maple Leaf Coins	6,817	BV	Proof	1,700.	1,725.

FIFTY DOLLARS (1 ounce), 125TH ANNIVERSARY OF THE R.C.M.P. 1997.

In 1997 the Royal Canadian Mint issued a $50.00 gold (1 oz .9999 fine) coin with a guaranteed value of U.S. $310.00 in effect until January 1st, 2000. Since that date the coin has traded at the market price of gold bullion.

Designer: Ago Aarand
Engraver: Stan Witten
Composition: 99.99% Au
Gold content: 31.10 g, 1.0 tr oz
Weight: 31.1035 g, 1 oz
Diameter: 30.0 mm   **Edge:** Plain, 10-sided
Thickness: 3.3 mm   **Die Axis:** ↑↑
Finish: Bullion
Case of Issue: Black card folder

DATE	DESCRIPTION	QUANTITY SOLD	ISSUE PRICE	FINISH	MS-65	MS-66
1997	$50 (1 oz) 125th Anniv. R.C.M.P.	12,913	310. USF	Bullion	1,700.	1,725.

FIFTY DOLLARS (1 ounce), 25TH ANNIVERSARY OF THE GOLD MAPLE LEAF COIN, 2004.

In 2004 a special commemorative design for the one ounce maple celebrating Canada's 25 years as a world leader in bullion coin production was issued at the A.N.A. World's Fair of Money.

Designers and Engravers:
Obv.: Susanna Blunt, Susan Taylor
Rev.: Cosme Saffioti, Christie Paquet
Composition: 99.99% Au
Gold content: 31.10 g, 1.0 tr oz
Weight: 31.1035 g, 1 oz
Diameter: 30.0 mm   **Edge:** Reeded
Thickness: 2.9 mm   **Die Axis:** ↑↑
Finish: Bullion
Case of Issue: Mylar pouch

DATE	DESCRIPTION	QUANTITY SOLD	ISSUE PRICE	FINISH	MS-65	MS-66
2004	$50 (1 oz) 25th Anniv. Gold Maple Leaf	10,000	BV	Bullion	1,700.	1,725.

FIFTY DOLLARS (1 ounce), TEST MAPLE LEAF, FIVE 9'S GOLD, 2005.

This was a production test for "five 9's" fineness of the one ounce maple leaf. Of the six hundred pieces which were produced, two hundred were melted, and four hundred were released sealed in Mylar pouches.

Designers and Engravers:
    Obv.: Susanna Blunt, Susan Taylor
    Rev.: Walter Ott, RCM Staff
Composition: 99.999% Au
Gold content: 31.10 g, 1.0 tr oz
Weight: 31.1035 g, 1 oz
Diameter: 30.0 mm   **Edge:** Reeded
Thickness: 2.9 mm   **Die Axis:** ↑↑
Finish: Bullion
Case: Mylar pouch

DATE	DESCRIPTION	QUANTITY SOLD	ISSUE PRICE	FINISH	MS-65	MS-66
2005	$50 (1 oz) .99999, Pattern	400	BV	Bullion	3,000.	3,250.

FIFTY DOLLARS (1 ounce), MAPLE LEAF, 2012.

This coin was issued to commemorate the 5th anniversary of the striking of the one million dollar maple leaf coin in 2007.

Designers and Engravers:
    Obv.: Susanna Blunt, Susan Taylor
    Rev.: Walter Ott, RCM Staff
Composition: 99.999% Au
Gold content: 31.16 g, 1.0 tr oz
Weight: 31.16 g, 1 oz
Diameter: 30.0 mm   **Edge:** Reeded
Thickness: 2.9 mm   **Die Axis:** ↑↑
Finish: Reverse Proof
Case: Maroon leatherette clam style case, black flock insert, encapsulated coin, COA

DATE	DESCRIPTION	QUANTITY SOLD	ISSUE PRICE	FINISH	MS-65	MS-66
2012	$50 (1 oz) 99.999% gold	543	BV	Bullion	2,000.	2,100.

FIFTY DOLLARS (1 ounce), BULLION REPLICA MAPLE LEAF, 2014.

This is a premium-struck one ounce gold maple leaf issued to celebrate the success of the gold maple leaf which was introduced in 1979.

Designers and Engravers:
    Obv.: Susanna Blunt, Susan Taylor
    Rev.: Walter Ott, RCM Staff
Composition: 99.99% Au
Gold content: 31.16 g, 1.0 tr oz
Weight: 31.16 g, 1 oz
Diameter: 30.0 mm   **Edge:** Reeded
Thickness: 2.9 mm   **Die Axis:** ↑↑
Finish: Reverse Proof
Case: Maroon leatherette clam style case, black flock insert, encapsulated coin, COA

DATE	DESCRIPTION	QUANTITY SOLD	ISSUE PRICE	FINISH	PR-67|	PR-68
2014	$50 (1 oz) Bullion Replica Maple Leaf	2,000	2,699.95	Proof	2,700.	2,800.

VANCOUVER 2010 OLYMPIC WINTER GAMES

FIFTY DOLLARS (1 ounce), VANCOUVER 2010 WINTER OLYMPIC GAMES, 2008-2010

2008   MAPLE LEAF AND VANCOUVER 2010 OLYMPIC LOGO

2009   THUNDERBIRD

2010   HOCKEY PLAYER

Designers:
Obv.:   Susanna Blunt
Rev.:   2008 and 2010: RCM Staff
       2009: Xwa lac tun (Ricky Harry)
Composition: 99.99% Au
Gold content: 31.1 g, 1.0 tr oz
Weight: 31.1035 g, 1 oz
Diameter: 30.0 mm
Cases: Singly: Mylar pouch
       Coloured Set: Maple wood box, black flocked insert, encapsulated coins, COA

Engravers:
Rev.:   Susan Taylor
Rev.:   2008 and 2010: Stan Witten
       2009: Marcos Hallam
Thickness: 2.9 mm
Edge: Reeded
Die Axis: ↑↑
Finish: Bullion; Bullion, Painted

DATE	DESCRIPTION	QUANTITY SOLD	ISSUE PRICE	FINISH	MS-65	MS-66
2008	$50 (1oz) Maple Leaf and 2010 Logo	49,802	BV	Bullion	1,750.	1,775.
2008	$50 (1oz) Maple Leaf and 2010 Logo, Painted	200	2,000.	Bullion	2,250.	2,275.
2009	$50 (1oz) Thunderbird	49,802	BV	Bullion	1,750.	1,775.
2009	$50 (1oz) Thunderbird, Painted	200	2,000.	Bullion	2,250.	2,275.
2010	$50 (1oz) Hockey Player	49,802	BV	Bullion	2,000.	2,050.
2010	$50 (1oz) Hockey Player, Painted	200	2,000.	Bullion	2,250.	2,275.
—	3 coin set, 2008, 2009, 2010, Painted	200	5,999.95	Bullion	6,750.	—

Note: The RCM Annual Reports list the Olympic gold maple leafs struck as 2008 - 75,876 oz, 2009 - 74,214 oz, and 2010 - 6 oz, totalling 150,006 units truck. Using 200 reported painted sets as struck there are 149,406 coins to be divided among the three years (49,802 per year).

TWO HUNDRED DOLLAR COINS

TWO HUNDRED DOLLARS (1 ounce), MAPLE LEAF, FIVE 9'S GOLD, 2007-2012.

Testing was continued of the five 9's gold concept first started in 2005. However, the test coins were now offered to the numismatic market. The issue of 2007 was offered with and without a privy mark.

| 2007 Obverse | 2007 Reverse Des./Engr.: Stan Witten | 2007 Obverse | 2007 Reverse, Privy Mark Des./Engr.: Stan Witten |

| 2008 Obverse | 2008 Reverse Des.: G. E. Kruger-Gray Engr.: RCM Staff | 2009 Obverse | 2009 Reverse Des.: Walter Ott Engr.: RCM Staff |

| 2011 Obverse | 2011 Reverse Des.: Stan Witten Engr.: Stan Witten | 2012 Obverse | 2012 Reverse Des./Engr.: S. Witten |

Designers:
Obv.: Susanna Blunt
Rev.: See reverse illustrations
Composition: 99.999% Au
Gold content: 31.1 g, 1.0 tr oz
Weight: 31.1035 g, 1 oz
Diameter: 30.0 mm
Thickness: 2.8 mm
Case of Issue: 1. Maroon clam style case, black flocked insert, encapsulated maple leaf, COA
2. Card capsule

Engravers:
Obv.: Susan Taylor
Rev.: See reverse illustrations

Edge: 2007: Plain
2008-2012: Interrupted serrations
Die Axis: ↑↑
Finish: Bullion

DATE	DESCRIPTION	QUANTITY SOLD	ISSUE PRICE	FINISH	MS-65	MS-66
2007	$200 (1 oz) 99.999% gold	30,848	BV	Bullion	2,000.	2,050.
2007	$200 (1 oz) 99.999% gold, with Privy Mark	595	1,899.95	Bullion	2,750.	3,000.
2008	$200 (1 oz) 99.999% gold	27,476	BV	Bullion	2,000.	2,050.
2009	$200 (1 oz) 99.999% gold	13,765	BV	Bullion	2,000.	2,050.
2011	$200 (1 oz) 99.999% gold	N/A	BV	Bullion	2,000.	2,050.
2012	$200 (1 oz) 99.999% gold	N/A	BV	Bullion	2,000.	2,050.

TWO HUNDRED DOLLARS (1 ounce), HOWLING WOLF, FIVE 9'S GOLD, 2014.

Designers and Engravers:
　Obv.: Susanna Blunt, Susan Taylor
　Rev.: Pierre Leduc, RCM Staff
Composition: 99.999% Au
Gold content: 31.1 g, 1.0 tr oz
Weight: 31.1035 g, 1 oz
Diameter: 30.0 mm　　**Die Axis:** ↑↑
Thickness: 2.8 mm　　**Finish:** See below
Edge: Interrupted serrations
Case:
　Proof: Maroon leatherette clam style case,
　　　　black flock insert, encapsulated coin,
　　　　COA
　Buillion: Card capsule

DATE	DESCRIPTION	QUANTITY SOLD	ISSUE PRICE	FINISH	MS-65	MS-66
2014	$200 (1 oz) 99.999% gold, Howling Wolf	2,000	2,799.95	Proof	2,800.	2,900.
2014	$200 (1 oz) 99.999% gold, Howling Wolf	N/A	BV	Bullion	1,550.	1,575.

TWO HUNDRED DOLLARS (1 ounce), CANADA'S WILDLIFE SERIES, 2014.

| 2013 Reverse | Bald Eagle Protecting Her Nest | The Bison at Home on the Plains |

Designers:
　Obv.: Susanna Blunt
　Rev.: Claudio D'Angelo
Composition: 99.99% Au
Gold content: 31.16 g, 1.0 tr oz
Weight: 31.16 g, 1oz
Diameter: 30.0 mm
Thickness: 2.8 mm
Case of Issue:　Maroon leatherette clam style case, black flock insert, encapsulated coin, COA

Engravers:
　Obv.: Susan Taylor
　Rev.: RCM Staff

Edge:　**Bald Eagle** and **Bison**: Reeded
　　　　Howling Wolf: Interrupted serrations
Die Axis: ↑↑
Finish: Proof

DATE	DESCRIPTION	QUANTITY SOLD	ISSUE PRICE	FINISH	PR-67	PR-68
2014	$200 (1 oz) Bald Eagle Protecting Her Nest	346	2,699.95	Proof	3,000.	3,100.
2014	$200 (1 oz) The Bison at Home on the Plains	350	2,699.95	Proof	3,000.	3,100.

TWO THOUSAND FIVE HUNDRED DOLLAR COINS

MAPLE LEAF FOREVER, 2011 and 2012.

| **Common Obverse** (except for date) | **2011** Designer: Debbie Adams Engraver: Konrad Wachelko | **2012** Designer: Luc Normandin Engraver: RCM Staff |

KING GEORGE III PEACE MEDAL, THE WAR OF 1812, 2012.

Obverse

Des.: RCM engravers' representation of the King George III Peace Medal
Engr.: Konrad Wachelko, Matt Bowen Samantha Strath, Steven Stewart

Designers:
  Obv.: Susanna Blunt
  Rev.: See reverse illustrations
Composition: 99.99% Au
Gold content: 1000.0 g, 32.15 tr oz
Weight: 1,000.0 g (1 kilo)
Diameter: 101.6 mm
Thickness: N/A

Engravers:
  Obv.: Susan Taylor
  Rev.: See reverse illustrations

Edge: Plain
Die Axis: ↑↑
Finish: Proof

Case of Issue: 2011: Black clam style case, black insert, encapsulated coin, COA
    2012: Maple wood case, black flocked insert, encapsulated coin, COA
    2012: Maroon leatherette clam style case, black flocked insert, encapsulated coin, COA

DATE	DESCRIPTION	QUANTITY SOLD	ISSUE PRICE	FINISH	PR-67	PR-68
2011	Maple Leaf Forever	35	69,000	Proof	69,000.	69,000.
2012	Maple Leaf Forever	20	69,000	Proof	69,000.	69,000.
2012	King George III Peace Medal	20	69,000.	Proof	69,000.	69,000.

Note: See also pages 329-334 for other $2,500 gold coins. Coins illustrated smaller than actual size.

ONE HUNDRED THOUSAND DOLLAR GOLD COIN

THE SPIRIT OF HAIDA GWAII, 2011

The Spirit of Haida Gwaii is the world's first 10,000 kilogram gold coin of 99.999% purity. The design features Bill Ried's monumental sculpture which was commissioned for the courtyard of the new Canadian Embassy which was being built in Washington. *The Spirit of Haida Gwaii* was completed and installed in 1992, subtitled *The Black Canoe*. The bronze casting was given a glossy black patina to give the appearance of argillite. The sculpture is 6.05 m long, 3.9 m high, 3.35 m wide and weighs 4.9 kg. A duplicate sculpture was commissioned by the Vancouver International Airport, with a green patina, in recognition of the dark green jade found in British Columbia. *The Jade Canoe* was completed in 1994.

Designers:
  Obv.: Susanna Blunt
  Rev.: Bill Reid
Composition: 99.999% Au
Gold content: 10,000.0 g, 321.50 tr oz
Weight: 10,000.0 g (10 kilos)
Diameter: 180.0 mm
Thickness: N/A
Case of Issue: Walnut case

Engravers:
  Obv.: Susan Taylor
  Rev.: Cosme Saffioti

Edge: Reeded
Die Axis: ↑↑
Finish: Proof

DATE	DESCRIPTION	QUANTITY SOLD	ISSUE PRICE	FINISH	PR-67	PR-68
2011	The Spirit of Haida Gwaii	2	BV	Proof	Market	Value

Note: 1. An identical design is utilized on the $500 silver coin for 2011, see page 440.
      2. Coin illustrated smaller than actual size.
      3. Price is subject to the price of gold plus a premium on the day of purchase or sale.

ONE MILLION DOLLAR GOLD COIN

This coin was issued May 3, 2007, as a promotional item for a new line of five 9's (99.999% fine gold) maple leaf gold coins. The million-dollar gold coin, being the largest and heaviest minted, attracted buyers from all over the world. The Canadian Mint received orders for five coins. The 3,215 troy ounce coin is produced by casting, engraving and hand polishing. The reverse design of the million-dollar maple leaf coin is very similar to the five dollar (2006) coloured silver maple, see page 447.

Designers:
  Obv.: Susanna Blunt
  Rev.: Stan Witten
Composition: 99.999% Au
Gold content: 100 kilos, 3,215 tr oz
Weight: 100 kilos
Diameter: 53.0 cm
Thickness: N/A

Engravers:
  Obv.: Stan Witten
  Rev.: Stan Witten

Edge: Plain
Die Axis: ↑↑
Finish: Bullion

DATE	DESCRIPTION	QUANTITY SOLD	ISSUE PRICE	FINISH	PR-67	PR-68
2007	One Million Dollar Coin, 3,215 tr oz	4	BV	Bullion	—	—

Note: 1. The last recorded sale of this coin was $4,300,250. at auction on June 25th, 2010. It was auctioned by Dorotheum of Vienna, Austria, at their headquarters.
     2. Coin illustrated smaller than actual size.

GOLD MAPLE LEAF SPECIAL ISSUES

SPECIAL ISSUE SETS

10TH ANNIVERSARY OF THE GOLD MAPLE LEAF COIN, 1979-1989.
The three sets detailed below were issued for the tenth anniversary of the maple leaf bullion program.

THREE-COIN SET (1 oz gold, silver and platinum maple leafs)

1 oz Gold Maple Leaf

1 oz Silver Maple Leaf

1 oz Platinum Maple Leaf

THREE-COIN SET (1oz silver, 1/10 oz gold and platinum maple leafs)

1 oz Silver Maple Leaf

1/10 oz Gold Maple Leaf

1/10 oz Platinum Leaf

Designers:
Obv.: Arnold Machin
Rev.: Walter Ott

Engravers:
Obv.: Walter Ott
Rev.: RCM Staff

Specifications: Gold: See page 396
Platinum: See page 417
Silver: See page 421

Finish: Proof

Case of Issue: Maple wood presentation box, black flocked insert, encapsulated coin, COA

DATE	DESCRIPTION	QUANTITY SOLD	ISSUE PRICE	FINISH	PR-67	PR-68
1989	3-coin set: 1oz gold, 1oz silver, 1oz platinum	3,966	1,795.00	Proof	3,450.	—
1989	3-coin set: 1/10 oz gold, 1/10 oz platinum, 1 oz silver	10,000	195.00	Proof	400.	—

TEN DOLLAR GOLD AND FIVE DOLLAR SILVER PIEDFORT MAPLE LEAF SET, 2010.

Ten
Dollars
Gold

Five
Dollars
Silver

Designers:
  Obv.: Susanna Blunt
  Rev.: RCM Staff
$10 Gold
Composition: 99.999% Au
Gold content: 6.25 g, 0.20 tr oz
Weight: 6.25 g
Diameter: 15.9 mm
Thickness: 1.9 mm
Edge: Reeded
Die Axis: ↑↑
Finish: Bullion

Engravers:
  Rev.: Susan Taylor
  Rev.: RCM Staff
$5 Silver
Composition: 99.99% Ag
Silver content: 31.39 g, 1.01 tr oz
Weight: 31.39 g
Diameter: 34.0 mm
Thickness: 4.0 mm
Edge: Reeded
Die Axis: ↑↑
Finish: Bullion

Case of Issue: Maroon leatherette clam style case, black flock insert, encapsulated coin(s), COA

DATE	DESCRIPTION	QUANTITY SOLD	ISSUE PRICE	FINISH	MS-65	MS-66
2010	Piedfort Set, $10 Gold and $5 Silver	1,264	679.95	Bullion	675.	—

TEN DOLLAR GOLD AND EIGHT DOLLAR SILVER POLAR BEAR SET, 2013.

Ten
Dollars
Gold

Eight
Dollars
Silver

Designers:
  Obv.: Susanna Blunt
  Rev.: Germaine Arnaktauyok
$10 Gold
Composition: 99.99% Au
Gold content: 7.97 g, 0.25 tr oz
Weight: 7.97 g
Diameter: 20.0 mm
Thickness: 1.7 mm
Edge: Reeded
Die Axis: ↑↑
Finish: Proof

Engravers:
  Rev.: Susan Taylor
  Rev.: RCM Staff
$8 Silver
Composition: 99.99% Ag
Silver content: 46.65 g, 1.5 tr oz
Weight: 46.65 g
Diameter: 38.0 mm
Thickness: 4.5 mm
Edge: Reeded
Die Axis: ↑↑
Finish: Proof

Case of Issue: Maple wood box, black flock insert, encapsulated coins, COA

DATE	DESCRIPTION	QUANTITY SOLD	ISSUE PRICE	FINISH	PR-67	PR-689
2013	$10 and $8 Polar Bear Set	4,229	774.95	Proof	750.	—

GOLD FRACTIONAL SETS

2012   **5TH ANNIVERSARY OF THE ROYAL CANADIAN MINT MILLION DOLLAR COIN**

2012 Obverse

Des.: Susanna Blunt
Engr.: Susan Taylor

2012 Reverse

Des.: Stan Witten
Engr.: Stan Witten

2013   **25TH ANNIVERSARY OF THE FRACTIONAL SET**

2013 Obverse

Des.: Susanna Blunt
Engr.: Susan Taylor

2013 Reverse

Des.: Claudio D'Angelo
Engr.: RCM Staff

2014   **INCUSED FRACTIONAL SET**

2014 Obverse

Des.: Susanna Blunt
Engr.: Susan Taylor

2014 Reverse

Des.: Pierre Leduc
Engr.: RCM Staff

SPECIFICATIONS

Specifications: See below
Finish: Specimen
Case of Issue: 2012 Canadian maple wood case, black flocked insert, encapsulated coins, COA, black sleeve
                     2013 Canadian maple wood case, black flocked insert, encapsulated coins, COA, black sleeve
                     2014 Canadian maple wood case, black flocked insert, encapsulated coins, COA, black sleeve

CHARACTERISTICS	.50¢ = 1/25oz	$1 = 1/20oz	$5 = 1/10oz	$10 =1/4oz	$20 = 1/2oz	$50 = 1oz
Composition: Au	99.99%	99.99%	99.99%	99.99%	99.99%	99.999%
Weight (grams)	1.27	1.581	3.131	7.797	15.552	31.15
Diameter (mm)	13.9	14.1	16.0	20.0	25.0	30.0
Thickness (mm)	0.7	0.7	1.1	1.7	2.23	2.7
Edge:	Reeded	Reeded	Reeded	Reeded	Reeded	Interrupted serrations/ Reeded
Die Axis	↑↑	↑↑	↑↑	↑↑	↑↑	↑↑

DATE	DESCRIPTION	QUANTITY SOLD	ISSUE PRICE	FINISH	PR-67	PR-68
2012	5 coin set (1, 1/2, 1/4, 1/10, 1/20, 1/25 oz)	543	3,999.95	Proof	4,000.	—
2013	4 coin set (1, 1/4, 1/10, 1/20 oz)	730	3,899.95	Proof	4,000.	—
2014	4 coin set (1, 1/4, 1/20, 1/20 oz)	299	3,999.95	Proof	4,000.	—

GOLD FRACTIONAL SETS WITH PRIVY MARKS

GOLD MAPLE LEAF PRIVY MARK SET, 2001.

Each of the five coins in this set carries the bow of a Viking ship as a privy mark. The maples in this set are: 1 oz, ½ oz, ¼ oz, 1/10 oz, and 1/20 oz.

**2001 Viking
Privy Mark**

100TH ANNIVERSARY OF THE ROYAL CANADIAN MINT REFINERY, 1911-2011.

Each of the four coins in this set carries the 100 YEARS/ANS privy mark. The maples in this set are: 1 oz, ¼ oz, 1/10 oz and 1/20 oz. This set includes a bronze medallion commemorating The Mint refinery.

**100 Years/ans
Privy Mark**

Designers:
 Obv.: Dora de Pédery-Hunt
 Rev.: Walter Ott

Engravers:
 Obv.: Dora de Pédery-Hunt
 Rev.: RCM Staff

Specifications: See page 396
Finish: Specimen (reverse proof)
Case of Issue: Red mahogany wooden case, black insert, encapsulated coins, green velour with metal trim box.

DATE	DESCRIPTION	PRIVY MARK	QUANTITY SOLD	ISSUE PRICE	FINISH	SP-66	SP-67
2001	5 coin set (1, 1/2, 1/4, 1/10, 1/20 oz)	Viking	850	N/A	Specimen	3,250.	—
2011	4 coin set (1, 1/4, 1/10, 1/20 oz)	100 Years/ans	479	N/A	Specimen	2,450.	—

COLOURED FRACTIONAL SET WITH PRIVY MARK

20TH ANNIVERSARY OF THE MAPLE LEAF PROGRAM, 1979-1999.
   This limited edition five-coin set, (1 oz, ½ oz, ¼ oz, 1/10 oz and 1/20 oz) struck by the Royal Canadian Mint and coloured in Balerna, Switzerland, was issued with a mintage of 500. They are the first coloured Canadian coins.

**1979-1999
Privy Mark**

Designers:
   Obv.   Dora de Pédery-Hunt
   Rev.:   Walter Ott
Specifications: See page 396
Case of Issue: Wooden maple display case, black leatherette sleeve, black flocked insert, encapsulated coins, COA, red and gold outer box.

Engravers:
   Obv.:   Dora de Pédery-Hunt
   Rev.:   RCM Staff
Finish: Bullion, Coloured

DATE	DESCRIPTION	PRIVY MARK	QUANTITY SOLD	ISSUE PRICE	FINISH	MS-65	MS-66
1999	5 coin set (1, 1/2, 1/4, 1/10, 1/20 oz)	20 Years / ans	500	N/A	Bullion	3,350.	—

Note: For the Vancouver 2010 Winter Olympic Coloured Set see page 403.

BIMETALLIC FRACTIONAL SET WITH PRIVY MARK

25TH ANNIVERSARY OF THE GOLD MAPLE LEAF, 1979-2004.
 To celebrate 25 years as an international standard in bullion coins, a new bimetallic maple leaf set was issued. The six-coin set is the first to include the 1/25 oz maple leaf denomination. Each coin is double-dated 1979-2004, and the 1 ounce coin features a 25-year commemorative privy mark.

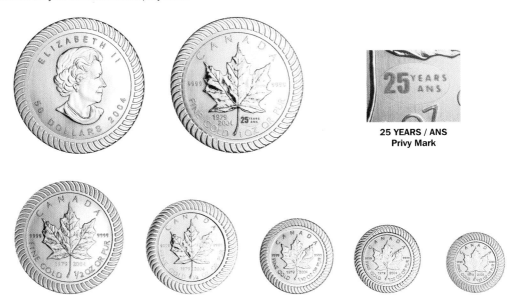

**25 YEARS / ANS
Privy Mark**

Designers and Engravers: RCM Staff
Finish: Bullion
Case: Black leather presentation case, black velour insert, encapsulated coins, COA

CHARACTERISTICS	.50¢ = 1/25oz	$1 = 1/20oz	$5 = 1/10oz	$10 =1/4oz	$20 = 1/2oz	$50 = 1oz
Composition						
Ring - fine silver	99.99%	99.99%	99.99%	99.99%	99.99%	99.99%
Core - fine gold	99.99%	99.99%	99.99%	99.99%	99.99%	99.99%
Weight (grams)	1.27	1.581	3.136	7.802	15.589	31.65
Diameter (mm)	16.0	18.03	20.0	25.0	30.0	36.07
Thickness (mm)	N/A	N/A	N/A	N/A	N/A	N/A
Edge:	Plain	Plain	Plain	Plain	Plain	Plain
Die Axis	↑↑	↑↑	↑↑	↑↑	↑↑	↑↑

DATE	DESCRIPTION	PRIVY MARK	QUANTITY SOLD	ISSUE PRICE	FINISH	MS-65	MS-66
2004 (1979-)	6 coin set	25 Years / ans	801	2,495.95	Bullion	3,350.	—

GOLD MAPLE LEAFS HOLOGRAM ISSUES

HOLOGRAM SINGLES AND SETS

TEN DOLLARS (¼ ounce), **GOLD MAPLE LEAF HOLOGRAM, 2001.**
 A distinctive maple leaf design appears as a high resolution dot matrix hologram, which is struck directly into the coin.

Designers and Engravers:
  Obv.: Susanna Blunt, Susan Taylor
  Rev.: Walter Ott, RCM Staff
Composition: 99.99% Au
Gold content: 7.775 g, 0.25 tr oz
Weight: 7.776 g
Diameter: 20.0 mm   **Edge:** Reeded
Thickness: 1.7 mm   **Die Axis:** ↑↑
Finish: Specimen (reverse proof), Hologram
Case of Issue: Wooden presentation case

DATE	DESCRIPTION	QUANTITY SOLD	ISSUE PRICE	FINISH	SP-66	SP-67
2001	$10 (¼ oz)	14,614	195.00	Specimen	450.	475.

GOLD MAPLE LEAF HOLOGRAM SETS 1999, 2001 and 2009.
 The Hologram gold maple leaf set of 1999 was the first official issue of hologram coins in Canada. The five coins in this set are: 1oz, ½oz, ¼oz, 1/10 oz and 1/20 oz. All coins carry identical designs.
 The 2009 thirtieth anniversary hologram set was issued with four coins: 1 oz, ¼ oz, 1/10 oz and 1/20 oz maples.

Designers and Engravers:
  Obv.: Dora de Pédery-Hunt
  Rev.: Walter Ott, RCM Staff
Specifications: See page 396
Finish: Bullion, Hologram
Case of Issue: Presentation case

Obv. $50 (1 oz)   **Rev. $50 (1 oz)**

DATE	DESCRIPTION	QUANTITY SOLD	ISSUE PRICE	FINISH	MS-65	MS-66
1999	20th Anniversary, 5 coin set (1, ½, ¼, 1/10, 1.20 oz)	500	1,995.00	Bullion	3,350.	—
2001	5 coin set	600	1,995.00	Bullion	3,350.	—
2009	30th Anniversary, 4 coin set	739	N/A	Bullion	2,500.	—

GOLD MAPLE LEAFS WITH PRIVY MARKS

PRIVY MARK SINGLES

GOLD MAPLE LEAF PRIVY MARKS.
In 1997, the Royal Canadian Mint began adding privy marks to specific gold maple leaf denominations to commemorate special events. These privy mark maples were commissioned by different organizations and struck by the Royal Canadian Mint.

$5 — 1/10 oz Maple Leaf Privy Marks

1997 $5	1998
Family	Eagles $5

$10 — ¼ oz Maple Leaf Privy Marks

2000 $10	2001 $10	2005 $10	2005-2006 $10
Expo Hannover	Basle Coin Fair	Liberation Royal Dutch Mint	M7 Privy Mark

DATE	DENOMINATION	CASE OF ISSUE	QUANTITY SOLD	ISSUE PRICE	FINISH	SP-66	SP-67
1997	$5, Family (1/10 oz)	Plastic case	100,730	N/A	Specimen	200.	210.
1998	$5, Eagles (1/10 oz)	Plastic case	51,440	N/A	Specimen	200.	210.
2000	$10, Expo (¼ oz)	N/A	1,000	N/A	Specimen	575.	600.
2001	$10, Basle (¼ oz)	N/A	750	N/A	Specimen	750.	750.
2005	$10, Liberation (¼ oz)	N/A	500	€299	Specimen	400.	425.
2005	$10, M7 (¼ oz)	Wooden display case	600	N/A	Specimen	400.	425.
2006	$10, M7 (¼ oz)	Mylar pouch	1,093	N/A	Specimen	400.	425.

PLATINUM MAPLE LEAFS

BULLION ISSUES

Obverse
1988-1989

Obverse
1990-1999

Obverse
2009-2012

Platinum Maple
Leaf Reverse

Designers: See page 396
Finish: Bullion

Engravers: See page 396
Case of Issue: Mylar pouch

PLATINUM MAPLE LEAF SPECIFICATIONS

CHARACTERISTICS	$1 = 1/20oz	$2 = 1/15oz	$5 = 1/10oz	$10 = 1/4oz	$20 = 1/2oz	$50 = 1oz
Fineness	99.95%	99.95%	99.95%	99.95%	99.95%	99.95%
Weight (grams)	1.555	2.074	3.110	7.776	15.552	31.1035
Diameter (mm)	14.1	15.0	16.0	20.0	25.0	30.0
Thickness (mm)	0.92	0.94	1.01	1.5	2.02	2.52
Edge	Reeded	Reeded	Reeded	Reeded	Reeded	Reeded
Die Axis	↑↑	↑↑	↑↑	↑↑	↑↑	↑↑

MINTAGES

The production of platinum maple leafs was on an order basis, unlike the production of coinage for circulation where the Mint will anticipate the number of coins required to fulfill the needs of the economy. Maple leafs are not struck unless ordered.

	QUANTITIES SOLD				
DATE	$1 = 1/20oz	$5 = 1/10oz	$10 = 1/4oz	$20 = 1/2oz	$50 - 1oz
1988	N/I	46,000	87,200	23,600	26,000
1989	N/I	18,000	3,200	4,800	10,000
1990	N/I	9,000	1,600	2,600	31,900
1991	N/I	13,000	7,200	5,600	31,900
1992	N/I	16,000	11,600	12,800	40,500
1993	2,120	14,020	8,048	6,022	17,666
1994	4,260	19,190	9,456	6,710	36,245
1995	460	8,940	6,524	6,308	25,829
1996	1,640	8,820	6,160	5,490	62,273
1997	1,340	7,050	4,552	3,990	25,480
1998	2,000	5,710	3,816	5,486	10,403
1999	4,000	4,080	2,092	788	3,248
2009	N/I	N/I	N/I	N/I	33,000
2011	N/I	N/I	N/I	N/I	5,000
2012	N/I	N/I	N/I	N/I	34,600
2013	N/I	N/I	N/I	N/I	19,349
2014	N/I	N/I	N/I	N/I	N/A

PRICING

Buying and selling prices are based on the interday spot price of platinum plus a small percentage premium for striking and handling. The smaller the unit the larger the percentage premium charged on buying; however, in later selling the premium could very well disappear.

Note: 1. No platinum bullion coins were produced from 2000 to 2008, or in 2010.
2. N/I indicates Not Issued.

ONE AND TWO DOLLAR PLATINUM COINS

TWO DOLLAR (1/15 ounce) BULLION ISSUE, 1994, and ONE DOLLAR (1/20 OUNCE), 1995.

Issued 1994 as a new addition to the line of bullion coins offered by the Royal Canadian Mint, the two dollar (1/15 troy ounce) coin was not a success and was discontinued in 1995. It is a one-year type and for this reason is popular.

The 1995 one dollar (1/20 ounce) has an extremely small mintage of 460 coins. Even so, the slightest demand will affect the price without regard for the market price of platinum.

1994 Obv.   **1994 Rev.**   **1995 Obv.**   **1995 Rev.**
$2 (1/15 oz) $2 (1/15 oz) $1 (1/20 oz) $1 (1/20 oz)

Designers and Engravers:
See page 396
Specifications: See page 417
Finish: Bullion
Case: Mylar pouch

DATE	DESCRIPTION	QUANTITY SOLD	ISSUE PRICE	FINISH	MS-65	MS-66
1994	$2 (1/15 oz), Bullion Issue	600	BV	Bullion	1,000.	1,200.
1995	$1 (1/20 oz), Bullion Issue	460	BV	Bullion	1,250.	1,350.

THREE HUNDRED DOLLAR PLATINUM COIN

THREE HUNDRED DOLLARS, 25TH ANNIVERSARY OF THE PLATINUM MAPLE LEAF, 2013.

This coin celebrates the 25th anniversary of the first platinum maple leaf which was struck in 1988.

Designers and Engravers:
Obv.:   Susanna Blunt, Susan Taylor
Rev.:   Jean-Louis Sirois, RCM Staff
Composition: 99.95% Pl, Selectively gold plated
Platinum content: 31.16 g, 1.00 tr oz
Weight: 31.16 g
Diameter: 30.0 mm   **Die Axis:** ↑↑
Thickness: 2.5 mm   **Edge:** Reeded
Finish: Proof
Case of Issue: Maroon leatherette clam style case, black flocked insert, encapsulated coin, COA

DATE	DESCRIPTION	QUANTITY SOLD	ISSUE PRICE	FINISH	PR-67	PR-68
2013	25th Anniv. of the Platinum Maple Leaf	250	2,999.95	Proof	3,000.	3,100.

THREE HUNDRED DOLLARS, MAPLE LEAF FOREVER, 2014.

Designers and Engravers:
Obv.:   Susanna Blunt, Susan Taylor
Rev.:   Lilyane Coulombe, RCM Staff
Composition: 99.95% Pl
Platinum content: 31.16 g, 1.00 tr oz
Weight: 31.16 g
Diameter: 30.0 mm   **Die Axis:** ↑↑
Thickness: 2.5 mm   **Edge:** Reeded
Finish: Proof, selectively gold plated
Case of Issue: Red wood lacquered case, black flocked insert, encapsulated coin, COA

DATE	DESCRIPTION	QUANTITY SOLD	ISSUE PRICE	FINISH	PR-67	PR-68
2014	Maple Leaf Forever	250	2,999.95	Proof	3,000.	3,100.

PLATINUM MAPLE LEAF SPECIAL ISSUES
FRACTIONAL SETS

10TH ANNIVERSARY OF MAPLE LEAF BULLION COINS, 1989.
This four-coin proof platinum set was issued to commemorate the 10th anniversary of the first maple leaf coins issued in 1979.

Designers and Engravers:
  Obv.: Arnold Machin, Walter Ott
  Rev.: Walter Ott
Case of Issue: Wooden maple presentation case, black flocked insert, encapsulated coin, COA

Specifications: See page 417
Finish: Proof

DATE	DESCRIPTION	QUANTITY SOLD	ISSUE PRICE	FINISH	PR-67	PR-68
1989	Set of 4 coins (1 oz, ½ oz, ¼ oz, 1/10 oz)	1,999	1,995.	Proof	3,250.	—

POLAR BEAR ISSUE, 1999.
In 1999 the Royal Canadian Mint issued a special set of platinum Maple Leafs at the request of a distributor, MTB Bank. They are legal tender coins issued in five denominations with the same specifications as the bullion issues but with a polar bear reverse design. The reverse design is a modification of the two-dollar polar bear reverse by Brent Townsend.

 **$20 (½ oz)**

Designers and Engravers:
  Obv.: Dora de Pédery-Hunt
  Rev.: Brent Townsend, Ago Aarand
Specifications: See page 417
Finish: Bullion, Brilliant relief against a parallel lined background
Case of Issue: N/A

DATE	DESCRIPTION	QUANTITY SOLD	ISSUE PRICE	FINISH	MS-65	MS-66
1999	Set of 5 coins (1, ½, ¼, 1/10, 1/20 oz)	500	N/A	Bullion	3,250.	—

HOLOGRAM SET

PLATINUM MAPLE LEAF PROOF HOLOGRAM FIVE-COIN SET, 2002.
In this set the distinctive maple leaf appears as a high-resolution dot matrix hologram which has been struck directly onto regular issues of each of the five coins. The five coins are struck with the same specifications and denominations as the regular issues of 1988-1999.

Designers and Engravers:
  Obv.: Dora de Pédery-Hunt
  Rev.: RCM Staff
Specifications: See page 417
Finish: Specimen (reverse proof), Brilliant relief on a satin background, Hologram
Case: Red mahogany wooden case, black insert, encapsulated coins, green velour with metal trim box.

DATE	DESCRIPTION	QUANTITY SOLD	ISSUE PRICE	FINISH	MS-65	MS-66
2002	Set of 5 coins (1, ½, ¼, 1/10, 1/20 oz)	500	2,895.95	Specimen	3,250.	—

PALLADIUM MAPLE LEAFS

BULLION ISSUES

FIFTY DOLLARS (1 ounce), PALLADIUM MAPLE LEAF, 2005-2010.

Designers and Engravers:
- Obv.: Susanna Blunt, Susan Taylor
- Rev.: Walter Ott, RCM Staff

Composition: 99.95% Pl
Platinum content: 31.1 g, 1.0 tr oz
Weight: 31.1035 g
Diameter: 30.0 mm   **Edge:** Reeded
Thickness: 2.9 mm   **Die Axis:** ↑↑
Finish: Bullion
Case of Issue: Mylar pouch

DATE	DESCRIPTION	QUANTITY SOLD	ISSUE PRICE	FINISH	MS-65	MS-66
2005	$50 (1 oz) 99.99%	62,919	BV	Bullion	850.	875.
2006	$50 (1 oz)	68,707	BV	Bullion	850.	875.
2007	$50 (1 oz)	15,415	BV	Bullion	850.	875.
2008	$50 (1 oz)	9,694	BV	Bullion	850.	875.
2009	$50 (1 oz)	40,000	BV	Bullion	850.	875.
2010	$50 (1 oz)	25,000	BV	Bullion	850.	875.

Note: No palladium maple leafs were produced between 2011 and 2014.

SPECIAL ISSUES

EXPERIMENTAL FINISH TEST PALLADIUM MAPLES, 2005.

In 2005 the Royal Canadian Mint conducted tests on palladium planchets. Planchets with the Royal Canadian Mint logo A were finished outside mint facilities, and planchets with the Royal Canadian Mint logo B were finished inside the Mint. Test results showed little variation in the manufacture, resulting in the internal planchets being used in the production of palladium maple leafs.

Reverse
Privy Mark "A"   **Privy Mark "A"**

Reverse
Privy Mark "B"   **Privy Mark "B"**

Designers:
- Obv.: Susanna Blunt
- Rev.: Walter Ott

Engravers:
- Obv.: Susan Taylor
- Rev.: RCM Staff

Composition: 99.95% Pl
Platinum content: 31.1 g, 1.0 tr oz
Weight: 31.1035 g
Diameter: 30.0 mm
Finish: Bullion, Brilliant relief against a parallel lined background

Thickness: 2.9 mm
Edge: Reeded
Die Axis: ↑↑

DATE	DESCRIPTION	QUANTITY SOLD	ISSUE PRICE	FINISH	MS-65	MS-66
2005	Royal Mint Privy Mark "A"	146	1,300.00	Bullion	2,500.	2,750.
2005	Royal Mint Privy Mark "B"	144	1,300.00	Bullion	2,500.	2,750.

SILVER MAPLE LEAFS

BULLION ISSUES

The first silver one ounce maple leaf was issued in 1988. The design is a continuation of that first conceived for the gold maples in 1979. The 1999-2000, and the 2000-dated silver maple leaf $5.00 coins carry the fireworks privy mark for 1999-2000, and the millennium privy mark for 2000.

Midway through 2013 a security mark (privy) was added to the reverse of the maple leaf. This security mark is a laser etched maple leaf, and within that leaf another smaller leaf which contains two digits representing the year of striking.

The finish used on the silver maple leaf was changed in 2014. The new finish is a series of radial lines originating at the centre and flowing out to the rim. This complex feature is part of the advanced visual security.

SILVER MAPLE LEAF SPECIFICATIONS

CHARACTERISTICS	$1 = 1/20 oz	$2 = 1/10 oz	$3 = ¼ oz	$4 = ½ oz	$5 = 1 oz
Fineness	99.99%	99.99%	99.99%	99.99%	99.99%
Weight (grams)	1.555	3.11	7.776	15.552	31.1035
Diameter (mm)	16.0	20.0	27.0	34.0	38.0
Thickness (mm)	1.1	1.3	1.8	2.1	3.15
Edge	Reeded	Reeded	Reeded	Reeded	Reeded
Die Axis	↑↑	↑↑	↑↑	↑↑	↑↑

FIVE DOLLAR or ONE OUNCE MAPLES

OBVERSES

Tiara Portrait
1988-1989

Royal Diadem Portrait
1990-2003

Uncrowned Portrait
2004-2014

REVERSES

1988-2014

All maple leafs dated
1999-2000
"Fireworks"

All maple leafs dated
2000
"Fireworks 2000"

Security Mark
Partial 2013 to date

Designers and Engravers:
  1988-1989: Obv.: Arnold Machin, Walter Ott   Rev.: Walter Ott, R.C.M. Staff
  1989-2003: Obv.: Dora de Pédery Hunt   Rev.: Walter Ott, R.C.M. Staff
  2004-2014: Obv.: Susanna Blunt, Susan Taylor   Rev.: Walter Ott, R.C.M. Staff

FINISH: 1988-2012: Bullion, Brilliant relief against a parallel lined background
       2014: Brilliant relief against a radial lined background

CASE OF ISSUE: 1988-1998: (A) Single coin sealed in clear Mylar pouch
                        (B) Plastic tubes of 20 coins
              1999-2014: (A) Sealed singly in clear Mylar pouches, in strips of 10 coins
                        (B) Plastic tubes of 25 coin

PRICING: Please remember that silver maple leaf prices are linked to the price of silver and may be priced higher, or lower, than prices shown depending on market conditions. Unlike gold and platinum maple leafs, silver leafs do experience a collector demand which will result in price differentials between dates. The price is affected by the total mintage and the pattern of distribution during year of issue.

SILVER MAPLE LEAF SPECIFICATIONS

DATE	PRIVY MARKS	QUANTITY SOLD	ISSUE PRICE	FINISH	MS-65	MS-66	MS-67
1988		1,062,000	BV	Bullion	35.	45.	60.
1989		3,332,200	BV	Bullion	35.	45.	60.
1990		1,708,800	BV	Bullion	35.	45.	60.
1991		644,300	BV	Bullion	35.	45.	60.
1992		343,800	BV	Bullion	35.	45.	60.
1993		889,946	BV	Bullion	35.	45.	60.
1994		1,133,900	BV	Bullion	35.	45.	60.
1995		326,244	BV	Bullion	40.	50.	60.
1996		250,445	BV	Bullion	70.	80.	100.
1997		100,970	BV	Bullion	60.	70.	100.
1998		591,359	BV	Bullion	35.	45.	75.
1999		1,229,442	BV	Bullion	35.	45.	75.
1999-2000	Fireworks	Included	BV	Bullion	35.	50.	75.
2000	Fireworks 2000	403,652	BV	Bullion	35.	50.	75.
2001		398,563	BV	Bullion	35.	50.	75.
2002		576,196	BV	Bullion	35.	50.	75.
2003		684,750	BV	Bullion	35.	45.	60.
2004		680,925	BV	Bullion	35.	45.	60.
2005		955,694	BV	Bullion	35.	45.	60.
2006		2,464,727	BV	Bullion	35.	45.	60.
2007		3,526,052	BV	Bullion	35.	45.	60.
2008		7,909,161	BV	Bullion	35.	45.	60.
2009		9,727,592	BV	Bullion	35.	45.	60.
2010		17,799,992	BV	Bullion	35.	45.	60.
2011		23,129,966	BV	Bullion	35.	45.	60.
2012		18,132,297	BV	Bullion	35.	45.	60.
2013		28,222,061	BV	Bullion	30.	35.	60.
2013	Security	Included	BV	Bullion	30.	35.	60.
2014	Security	N/A	BV	Bullion	30.	35.	60.

NOTES FOR COLLECTORS

1 Silver maple leafs are priced based on the world market price for silver, plus a small premium on the day the transaction takes place. Premiums will vary depending on the size of the transaction.

2. The packaging of silver maple leafs changed in 2009 from single coins in mylar pouches to twenty-five coin packaged in plastic tubes. In 2010 the silver maple leafs were available again in mylar pouches or plastic tubes of twenty-five.

3. The silver maple leafs listed in the table above are priced at a silver market value of $23.75 an ounce as at March 14th, 2014. Market changes, up or down, from $23.75 will necessitate a price revision.

4. The strong demand for one ounce silver rounds during the last year has resulted in an increase in premium over metal value.

SILVER MAPLE LEAF SPECIAL ISSUES

SINGLES

ONE DOLLAR (half ounce), SILVER WOLF, 2006.

Designers and Engravers:
Obv.: Susanna Blunt, Susan Taylor
Rev.: William Woodruff, William Woodruff
Composition: 99.99% Ag
Weight: 15.552 g, ½ oz
Diameter: 34.0 mm   **Edge:** Reeded
Thickness: 2.1 mm   **Die Axis:** ↑↑
Finish: Bullion
Case of Issue: Mylar Pouch

DATE	DESCRIPTION	QUANTITY SOLD	ISSUE PRICE	FINISH	MS-65	MS-66	MS-67
2006	$1 (½ oz), Silver Wolf	106,800	BV	Bullion	40.	45.	75.

ONE DOLLAR (¾ ounce), THE WAR OF 1812, 1812-2012.

Designers and Engravers:
Obv.: Susanna Blunt, Susan Taylor
Rev.: Cathy Bursey-Sabourin, K. Wachelko
Composition: 99.99% Ag
Weight: 23.33 g, ¾ oz
Diameter: 38.0 mm
Thickness: 2.4 mm
Edge: Reeded
Die Axis: ↑↑
Finish: Bullion
Case of Issue: Tubes of 30

DATE	DESCRIPTION	QUANTITY SOLD	ISSUE PRICE	FINISH	MS-65	MS-66	MS-67
2012	$1 (¾ oz), The War of 1812	N/A	BV	Bullion	35.	40.	75.

TWO DOLLARS (¾ ounce), DEVIL'S BRIGADE, 2013.

Designers and Engravers:
Obv.: Susanna Blunt, Susan Taylor
Rev.: Ardell Bourgeois, RCM Staff
Composition: 99.99% Ag
Weight: 23.33 g, ¾ oz
Diameter: 38.07 mm
Thickness: 2.4 mm
Edge: Reeded
Die Axis: ↑↑
Finish: Bullion
Case of Issue: Tubes of 30

DATE	DESCRIPTION	QUANTITY SOLD	ISSUE PRICE	FINISH	MS-65	MS-66	MS-67
2013	$2 (¾ oz), Devil's Brigade	N/A	BV	Bullion	50.	55.	75.

FIVE DOLLARS (1 ounce), 10TH ANNIVERSARY OF MAPLE LEAF BULLION COINS, 1989.
Issued in 1989 in proof finish to commemorate the 10th anniversary of the introduction of the maple leaf in 1979.

Designers and Engravers:
  Obv.: Arnold Machin
  Rev.: Walter Ott, RCM Staff
Composition: 99.99% Ag
Weight: 31.1035 g, 1 oz
Diameter: 38.0 mm
Thickness: 3.2 mm
Edge: Reeded
Die Axis: ↑↑
Finish: Proof
Case of issue: Maple wood presentation box, black flocked insert, encapsulated coins, COA, outer maple leaf printed box.

DATE	DESCRIPTION	QUANTITY SOLD	ISSUE PRICE	FINISH	PR-67	PR-68
1989	$5 (1 oz), 10th Anniv. Maple Leaf coins	29,999	39.00	Proof	60.	75.

FIVE DOLLARS (1 ounce), 20TH ANNIVERSARY OF THE SILVER MAPLE LEAF, 1988-2008.
This bullion coin was issued to commemorate the 20th anniversary of the silver maple leaf which was introduced in 1988.

Designers and Engravers:
  Obv.: Arnold Machin
  Rev.: RCM Staff
Composition: 99.99% Ag, Selectively gold plated
Weight: 31.3035 g, 1 oz
Diameter: 38.0 mm
Thickness: 3.2 mm
Edge: Reeded
Die Axis: ↑↑
Finish: Bullion
Case: Maroon leatherette clam style case, black flocked insert, encapsulated coin, COA

DATE	DESCRIPTION	QUANTITY SOLD	ISSUE PRICE	FINISH	MS-65	MS-66	MS-67
2008	$5 (1 oz), 20th Anniv. of the Silver Maple Leaf	9,998	74.95	Bullion	100.	110.	150.

FIVE DOLLARS (1 ounce), VANCOUVER 2010 WINTER OLYMPIC GAMES, 2008-2010.

2008   MAPLE LEAF AND VANCOUVER 2010 OLYMPIC LOGO

2009   THUNDERBIRD

2010   HOCKEY PLAYER

Designers:
  Obv.:   Susanna Blunt
  Rev.:   2008, 2010 RCM Staff;
          2009 Xwa lac tun (Ricky Harry)
Composition: 99.99% Ag
Weight: 31.1035 g, 1 oz
Diameter: 38.0 mm
Thickness: 3.2 mm
Finish: 1. Bullion
          2. Bullion, Selectively gold plated
          3. Bullion, Gilt
Cases: Singly: Mylar pouch
          Coloured Set: Maple wood box, black flocked insert, encapsulated coins, COA

Engravers:
  Obv.:   Susan Taylor
  Rev.:   2008 and 2010: Stan Witten
          2009: Marcos Hallam

Edge: Reeded
Die Axis: ↑↑

DATE	DESCRIPTION	QUANTITY SOLD	ISSUE PRICE	FINISH	MS-65	MS-66	MS-67
2008	$5 (1oz) 2010 Logo	937,839	BV	Bullion	45.	50.	60.
2008	$5 (1oz) 2010 Logo, Selectively gold plated	N/A	N.I.I.	Bullion	100.	110.	—
2009	$5 (1oz) Thunderbird	569,048	BV	Bullion	45.	50.	60.
2009	$5 (1oz) Thunderbird, Selectively gold plated	N/A	N.I.I.	Bullion	100.	110.	—
2010	$5 (1oz) Hockey Player	79,278	BV	Bullion	45.	50.	60.
2010	$5 (1oz) Hockey Player, Selectively gold plated	N/A	N.I.I.	Bullion	100.	110.	—
2010	$5 (1oz) Hockey Player, Gold plated	N/A	71.95	Bullion	85.	100.	150.
—	3-Coin Set, Selectively gold plated	4,000	199.95	Bullion	295.	—	—

Note: 1. Images illustrated smaller than actual size.

2. The mintages reported are for the total number of pieces struck that year. There is no breakdown by design reported. Total mintage for the three designs 1,586,165.

FIVE DOLLARS (1 ounce), PIEDFORT MAPLE LEAF, 2010.

This five-dollar silver Piedfort maple leaf was issued singly, or as part of the Piedfort Maple Leaf Set. The set, which consists of a ten-dollar gold and a five-dollar coin, is listed on page 410.

Designers and Engravers:
Obv.: Susanna Blunt, Susan Taylor
Rev.: RCM Staff
Composition: 99.99% Ag
Weight: 31.39 g, 1.01 tr oz
Diameter: 34.0 mm   **Edge:** Reeded
Thickness: 4.0 mm   **Die Axis:** ↑↑
Finish: Bullion
Case: Maroon leatherette clam style case, black flock insert, encapsulated coin, COA

DATE	DESCRIPTION	QUANTITY SOLD	ISSUE PRICE	FINISH	MS-65	MS-66
2010	$5 (1 oz), Silver Piedfort Maple Leaf	6,843	79.95	Bullion	65.	70.

FIVE DOLLARS (1 ounce), **CANADIAN WILDLIFE SERIES (BULLION ISSUES), 2011-2014.**
This six-coin Canadian Wildlife Series was issued over a three-year period beginning in 2011. The Timber Wolf first appeared as the reverse design on the 2006 half-ounce silver maple and, then again in 2007 on the gold fifty-cent issue.

Common Obverse
except for date

2011 Timber Wolf
Designer and Engraver:

Designers and Engravers:
Obv.: Susanna Blunt, Susan Taylor
Rev.: See reverse illustrations
Composition: 99.99% Ag
Weight: 31.11 g, 1.00 tr oz
Diameter: 38.0 mm
Thickness: 3.0 mm
Edge: Reeded
Die Axis: ↑↑
Finish: Bullion
Case: Mylar pouch

2011 Grizzly
Designer and Engraver:
William Woodruff

2012 Moose
Designer and Engraver:
William Woodruff

2012 Cougar
Designer and Engraver:
José Osio

2013 Pronghorn Antelope
Designer and Engraver:
Emily Damstra

2013 Wood Bison
Designer and Engraver:
Emily Damstra

2014 Peregrine Falcon
Des.: Emily Damstra
Engr.: RCM Staff

DATE	DESCRIPTION	QUANTITY SOLD	ISSUE PRICE	FINISH	MS-65	MS-66
2011	Timber Wolf	N/A	BV	Bullion	40.	45.
2011	Grizzly	N/A	BV	Bullion	40.	45.
2012	Moose	N/A	BV	Bullion	40.	45.
2012	Cougar	N/A	BV	Bullion	40.	45.
2013	Pronghorn	1,000,000	BV	Bullion	40.	45.
2013	Wood Bison	N/A	BV	Bullion	40.	45.
2014	Peregrine Falcon	1,000,000	BV	Bullion	40.	45.

FIVE DOLLARS (1 ounce), 25TH ANNIVERSARY OF THE SILVER MAPLE LEAF, 2013.

This selectively gold plated silver maple leaf was issued to celebrate 25 years of the Royal Canadian Mint's silver maple leaf.

Designers and Engravers:
Obv.: Susanna Blunt, Susan Taylor
Rev.: Jean-Louis Sirois, Cecily Mok
Composition: 99.99% Ag, Selectively gold plated
Weight: 31.10 g, 1.00 tr oz
Diameter: 38.0 mm   **Edge:** Reeded
Thickness: 3.0 mm   **Die Axis:** ↑↑
Finish: Proof
Case: Maroon leatherette clam style case, black flock insert, encapsulated coin, COA

DATE	DESCRIPTION	QUANTITY SOLD	ISSUE PRICE	FINISH	PR-67	PR-68
2013	$5 (1 oz), 25th Anniv. of the Silver Maple Leaf	9,960	109.95	Proof	110.	120.

FIVE DOLLARS (1 ounce), PIEDFORT, 25TH ANNIVERSARY OF THE SILVER MAPLE LEAF, 2013.

This Piedfort silver maple leaf was issued to celebrate 25 years of the Royal Canadian Mint's silver maple leaf.

Designers and Engravers:
Obv.: Susanna Blunt, Susan Taylor
Rev.: Jean-Louis Sirois, RCM Staff
Composition: 99.99% Ag
Weight: 31.39 g, 1.01 tr oz
Diameter: 34.0 mm   **Edge:** Reeded
Thickness: 3.8 mm   **Die Axis:** ↑↑
Finish: Proof
Case: Maroon leatherette clam style case, black flock insert, encapsulated coin, COA

DATE	DESCRIPTION	QUANTITY SOLD	ISSUE PRICE	FINISH	PR-67	PR-68
2013	$5 (1 oz), Piedfort 25th Anniv. of Silver Maple Leaf	9,981	99.95	Proof	110.	120.

FIVE DOLLARS (1 ounce), 25TH ANNIVERSARY OF THE SILVER MAPLE LEAF, 2013.

This silver maple leaf was issued to celebrate 25 years of the Royal Canadian Mint's silver maple leaf program.

Designers and Engravers:
Obv.: Susanna Blunt, Susan Taylor
Rev.: RCM Staff
Composition: 99.99% Ag
Weight: 31.2 g, 1.0 tr oz
Diameter: 38.0 mm   **Edge:** Reeded
Thickness: 3.25 mm   **Die Axis:** ↑↑
Finish: Bullion
Case: Tubes of 25, or sealed thermotron film

DATE	DESCRIPTION	QUANTITY SOLD	ISSUE PRICE	FINISH	MS-65	MS-66
2013	$5 (1 oz), 25th Anniv. of Silver Maple Leaf	N/A	BV	Bullion	30.	40.

FIVE DOLLARS (1 ounce), CANADIAN WILDLIFE SERIES (PREMIUM ISSUES), 2014.

In 2014 a premium quality issue of the Canadian Wildlife Series was introduced. These silver maple leaf coins are struck with a proof finish and in 99.99% pure silver.

Common Obverse

2014 Peregrine Falcon
Des.: Emily Damstra
Engr.: RCM Staff

2014 Arctic Fox
Des.: Maurice Gervais
Engr.: RCM Staff

Designers:
Obv.: Susanna Blunt
Rev.: See reverse illustrations
Composition: 99.99% Ag
Weight: 31.39 g, 1.01 tr oz
Diameter: 38.0 mm
Thickness: 3.2 mm
Case: Maroon leatherette clam style case, black flock insert, encapsulated coin, COA

Engravers:
Obv.: Susan Taylor
Rev.: See reverse illustrations

Edge: Reeded
Die Axis: ↑↑
Finish: Proof

DATE	DESCRIPTION	QUANTITY SOLD	ISSUE PRICE	FINISH	PR-67	PR-68
2014	$5 (1 oz), Peregrine Falcon	20,000	89.95	Proof	90.	95.
2014	$5 (1 oz), Arctic Fox	7,500	89.95	Proof	90.	95.

FIVE DOLLARS (1 ounce), BULLION REPLICA SILVER MAPLE LEAF, 2014.

Common Obverse

Replica Silver Maple Leaf

**Replica Silver Maple Leaf
with Privy Mark**

Designers:
Obv.: Susanna Blunt
Rev.: RCM Staff
Composition: 99.99% Ag
Weight: 31.1 g, 1.0 tr oz
Diameter: 38.0 mm
Thickness: 3.3 mm
Case: Maroon leatherette clam style case, black flock insert, encapsulated coin, COA

Engravers:
Obv.: Susan Taylor
Rev.: RCM Staff

Edge: Reeded
Die Axis: ↑↑
Finish: Reverse Proof

Privy Mark

DATE	DESCRIPTION	QUANTITY SOLD	ISSUE PRICE	FINISH	PR-67	PR-68
2014	$5 (1 oz), Replica Silver ML	20,000	79.95	Rev. Proof	80.	90.
2014	$5 (1 oz), Replica Silver ML with privy mark	7,500	79.95	Rev. Proof	80.	90.

EIGHT DOLLARS (1½ ounce), SILVER MAPLE LEAF, 2013-2014.

Common Obverse

2013 Polar Bear
Des.: A. Germain
Engr.: S. Stewart

2014 Arctic Fox
Des.: Maurice Gervais
Engr.: RCM Staff

Designers:
  Obv.: Susanna Blunt
  Rev.: See reverse illustrations
Composition: 99.99% Ag
Weight: 46.65 g, 1.5 tr oz
Diameter: 38.1 mm
Thickness: 4.5 mm
Case of Issue: Bullion: None

Engravers:
  Obv.: Susan Taylor
  Rev.: See reverse illustrations

Edge: Reeded
Die Axis: ↑↑
Finish: See pricing table

          Proof: Maroon leatherette clam style case, black flocked insert, encapsulated coin, COA

DATE	DESCRIPTION	QUANTITY SOLD	ISSUE PRICE	FINISH	MS-65	MS-66	PR-67	PR-68
2013	$8 (1½ oz) Polar Bear, Bullon	N/A	BV	Bullion	50.	55.	—	—
2013	$8 (1½ oz) Polar Bear, Proof	8,168	124.95	Proof	—	—	150.	165.
2014	$8 (1½ oz) Arctic Fox, Bullion	N/A	BV	Bullion	50.	55.	—	—
2014	$8 (1½ oz) Arctic Fox, Proof	7,500	124.95	Proof			150.	165.

TEN DOLLARS (½ ounce), MAPLE LEAF FOREVER, 2011.

The design on the reverse of this maple leaf coin commemorates the three maple leaf design that has graced Canada's one cent coin since 1937.

Designers, and Engravers:
Obv.:   Susanna Blunt, Susan Taylor
Rev.:   Debbie Adams, Konrad Wachelko
Composition: 99.99% Ag
Weight: 15.87 g, 0.5 oz
Diameter: 34.0 mm
Thickness: 2.0 mm
Edge: Reeded
Die Axis: ↑↑
Finish: Specimen
Case of Issue: Maroon leatherette clam style case, black insert, encapsulated coin, COA

DATE	DESCRIPTION	QUANTITY SOLD	ISSUE PRICE	FINISH	SP-66	SP-67
2011	$10 (½ oz) Maple Leaf Forever	41,712	34.95	Specimen	40.	50.

TEN DOLLARS (½ ounce), MAPLE LEAF FOREVER, 2012.

Designers, and Engravers:
Obv.:   Susanna Blunt, Susan Taylor
Rev.:   Luc Normandin
Composition: 99.99% Ag
Weight: 15.87 g, 0.5 oz
Diameter: 34.0 mm
Thickness: 2.1 mm
Edge: Reeded
Die Axis: ↑↑
Finish: Specimen
Case of Issue: Black card envelope with green maple leaf design, black card coin holder, encapsulated coin, COA

DATE	DESCRIPTION	QUANTITY SOLD	ISSUE PRICE	FINISH	SP-66	SP-67
2012	$10 (½ oz) Maple Leaf Forever	29,173	34.95	Specimen	40.	45.

Note: Identical designs are utilized on the $500 gold coin (page 328) and the $300 platinum maple leaf (page 337) for 2012.

TWENTY DOLLARS (1 ounce), SAMBRO ISLAND LIGHTHOUSE, 2004.

This silver maple was issued to commemorate the oldest working lighthouse in North America. Sambro Lighthouse has guided ships in and out of Halifax Harbour for more than 200 years.

Designers, and Engravers:
  Obv.: Susanna Blunt, Susan Taylor
  Rev.: Hedley Doty. William Woodruff
Composition: 99.99% Ag
Weight: 31.1035 g, 1 oz
Diameter: 38.0 mm
Thickness: 3.2 mm
Edge: Reeded
Die Axis: ↑↑
Finish: Proof, Frosted relief against a
  mirror background
Case of Issue: Maroon leatherette clam style
  case, black insert, encapsulated coin, COA

DATE	DESCRIPTION	QUANTITY SOLD	ISSUE PRICE	FINISH	PR-67	PR-68
2004	$20 Sambro Island Lighthouse	18,476	69.95	Proof	35.	40.

Note: See page 449 for Sambro Island Lighthouse derivative.

TWENTY DOLLARS (1 ounce), TORONTO ISLAND LIGHTHOUSE, 2005.

The Toronto Island Lighthouse built in 1809 on Gibraltar Point, on what is now Toronto Island, guided ships into the Port of York (Toronto). It is the oldest existing lighthouse on the Great Lakes.

Designers and Engravers:
  Obv.: Susanna Blunt, Susan Taylor
  Rev.: Brian Hughes, William Woodruff
Composition: 99.99% Ag
Weight: 31.1035 g, 1 oz
Diameter: 38.0 mm
Thickness: 3.2 mm
Edge: Reeded
Die Axis: ↑↑
Finish: Proof, Frosted relief against a mirror
  background
Case of Issue: Maroon plastic display case,
  black plastic insert, encapsulated coin,
  COA

DATE	DESCRIPTION	QUANTITY SOLD	ISSUE PRICE	FINISH	PR-67	PR-68
2005	$20 Toronto Island Lighthouse	14,006	69.95	Proof	60.	70.

TWENTY DOLLARS (quarter ounce), FINE SILVER COMMEMORATIVE COINS, 2011-2014.
This quarter ounce (0.25 tr oz) series was issued at face value to attract collectors to the Royal Canadian Mint.

Common Obv.
2011-2014

2011
Five Maple Leaves
Des.: Cosme Saffioti
Engr.: RCM Staff

2011
Canoe
Des.: Jason Bouwman
Engr.: William Woodruff

2012
Polar Bear
Des.: Emily Damsta
Engr.: Stan Witten

2012
Farewell to the Penny
Des.: Jesse Koreck
Engr.: José Osio

2012
Magical Reindeer
Des.: Virginia Boulay
Engr.: José Osio

2013
Hockey
Des.: Greg Banning
Engr.: José Osio

2013
Wolf
Des.: Glen Loates
Engr.: Eric Boyer

2012
Obverse: Queen's
Diamond Jubilee
Des.: Mary Gilllick
Engr.: RCM Staff

2012
Reverse: Queen's
Diamond Jubilee
Des.: Laurie McGaw
Engr.: RCM Staff

Designers:
   Obv.: Susanna Blunt
   Rev.: See reverse illustrations
Composition: 99.99% Ag
Weight: 7.96 g, 0.25 tr oz
Diameter: 27.0 mm
Thickness: 1.8 mm
Case of Issue: **2011 Five Maple leaves:** Vinyl pouch
      2011-2013: Vinyl pouch, encapsulated coin, coloured folder

Engravers:
   Obv.: Susan Taylor
   Rev.: See reverse illustrations

Edge: Reeded
Die Axis: ↑↑
Finish: Specimen

DATE	DESCRIPTION	QUANTITY SOLD	ISSUE PRICE	FINISH	SP-66	SP-67
2011	$20, Five Maple Leaves	198,000	20.00	Specimen	25.	30.
2011	$20, Canoe	244,000	20.00	Specimen	25.	30.
2012	$20, Polar Bear	174,474	20.00	Specimen	25.	30.
2012 (1952-)	$20, Queen's Diamond Jubilee	180,020	20.00	Specimen	25.	30.
2012	$20, Farewell to the Penny	192,010	20.00	Specimen	25.	30.
2012	$20, Magical Reindeer	162,620	20.00	Specimen	25.	30.
2013	$20, Hockey	245,325	20.00	Specimen	25.	30.
2013	$20, Wolf	248,779	20.00	Specimen	25.	30.

TWENTY DOLLARS (quarter ounce), FINE SILVER COMMEMORATIVE COINS, 2011-2014 (cont.).

This quarter ounce (0.25 tr oz) series was issued at face value to attract collectors to the Royal Canadian Mint.

| Common Obv. 2011-2014 | 2013 Iceberg Des.: Emily Damstra Engr.: RCM Staff | 2013 Santa Des.: Jesse Koreck Engr.: RCM Staff | 2014 Canada Goose Des.: Trevor Tennant Engr.: RCM Staff |

| 2014 Bobcat Des.: Ken Ryan Engr.: RCM Staff | 2014 Summertime Des.: RCM Staff Engr.: RCM Staff | 2014 Snowman Des.: RCM Staff Engr.: RCM Staff |

Designers:
Obv.: Susanna Blunt
Rev.: See reverse illustrations
Composition: 99.99% Ag
Weight: 7.96 g, 0.25 tr oz
Diameter: 26.9 mm
Thickness: 1.8 mm
Case of Issue: Vinyl pouch, encapsulated coin, coloured folder

Engravers:
Obv.: Susan Taylor
Rev.: See reverse illustrations

Edge: Reeded
Die Axis: ↑↑
Finish: Specimen

DATE	DESCRIPTION	QUANTITY SOLD	ISSUE PRICE	FINISH	SP-66	SP-67
2013	$20, Iceberg	207,699	20.00	Specimen	25.	30.
2013	$20, Santa	221,922	20.00	Specimen	25.	30.
2014	$20, Canada Goose	225,000	20.00	Specimen	25.	30.
2014	$20, Bobcat	225,000	20.00	Specimen	25.	30.
2014	$20, Summertime	225,000	20.00	Specimen	25.	30.
2014	$20, Snowman	225,000	20.00	Specimen	25.	30.

TWENTY DOLLARS (quarter ounce), YEAR OF THE SNAKE, 2013.

Designers and Engravers:
Obv.:   Susanna Blunt, Susan Taylor
Rev.:   Christie Paquet
Composition: 99.99% Ag
Silver content: 8.0 g, 0.257 tr oz
Weight: 8.0 g   **Edge:** Reeded
Diameter: 27.0 mm   **Die Axis:** ↑↑
Thickness: 1.8 mm   **Finish:** Specimen
Case of Issue: Maroon leatherette clam style
case, black flocked insert,
encapsulated coin, COA

DATE	DESCRIPTION	QUANTITY SOLD	ISSUE PRICE	FINISH	SP-66	SP-67
2013	Year of the Snake (¼ oz)	33,002	31.95	Specimen	35.	40.

THE SEVEN SACRED TEACHINGS

TWENTY DOLLARS, THE SEVEN SACRED TEACHINGS, 2014.
  "Love" is the first coin in a series on the seven sacred teachings. Other coins in this series will represent respect, courage, honesty, wisdom, humility and truth.

Common Obverse

Designers and Engravers:
Obv.: Susanna Blunt, Susan Taylor
Rev.: Nathalie Bertin, RCM Staff
Composition: 99.99% Ag, Selectively gold
plated
Silver content: 31.83 g, 1.0 tr oz
Weight: 31.83 g
Diameter: 40.0 mm
Thickness: 2.9 mm
Edge: Reeded
Die Axis: ↑↑
Finish: Proof
Case: Maroon clam style case, black flocked
insert, encapsulated coin, COA

Love   **Respect**   **Courage**

DATE	DESCRIPTION	QUANTITY SOLD	ISSUE PRICE	FINISH	PR-67	PR-68
2014	Love	7,000	109.95	Proof	110.	120.
2014	Respect	7,000	109.95	Proof	110.	120.
2014	Courage	7,000	109.95	Proof	110.	120.

FIFTY DOLLARS (10 ounces), 10TH ANNIVERSARY OF THE SILVER MAPLE LEAF, 1998.

In 1998 the Royal Canadian Mint issued the 10-ounce silver maple leaf in celebration of the 10th anniversary of the silver maple leaf bullion coin. The coin is accompanied by a sterling silver plaque of authenticity. The coin is shown smaller than its actual size.

Designers:
    Obv.: Dora de Pédery-Hunt
    Rev.: RCM Staff
Composition: 99.99% Ag
Silver content: 311.0 g, 10.0 tr oz
Weight: 311.04 g, 10.0 tr oz
Diameter: 65.0 mm
Thickness: 11.0 mm

Engravers:
    Obv.: Dora de Pédery-Hunt
    Rev.: RCM Staff
Edge: Lettered, 10th Anniversary 10e Anniversaire
Die Axis: ↑↑
Finish: Reverse proof
Nominal Value: $50.00

Case of Issue: Black leather case with silver "Royal Canadian Mint" plaque, black flock lining, encapsulated coin, Sterling silver certificate of authenticity

DATE	DESCRIPTION	QUANTITY SOLD	ISSUE PRICE	FINISH	MS-65	MS-66
1998	$50 (10 oz), 10th Anniv. Silver Maple Leaf	13,533	200.00	Proof	700.	750.

Note: Coin illustrated smaller than actual size.

FIFTY DOLLARS (5 ounces), 25TH ANNIVERSARY OF THE SILVER MAPLE LEAF, 2013.
These coins were issued to commemorate the striking of the first silver maple leaf in 1988.

Common Obverse

Designers and Engravers:
    Obv.: Susanna Blunt, Susan Taylor
    Rev.: See reverse illustrations
Composition: 99.99% Ag
Silver content: 157.6 g, 5.0 tr oz
Weight: 157.6 g, 5.0 tr oz
Diameter: 65.0 mm
Thickness: N/A
Edge: Reeded
Die Axis: ↑↑
Finish: See reverse illustrations
Nominal Value: $50.00
Case: **1.** Lacquered red wooden case, black
        lining, encapsulated coin, COA
        2. Maroon leatherette clam style case
        black flocked insert, encapsulated coin,
        COA, custom beauty box

2013
25th Anniv. of the Silver Maple Leaf
Reverse Proof
Designer: Arnold Nogy
Engraver: RCM Staff

2013
25th Anniv. of the Silver Maple Leaf
Matte Proof, Selectively Gold Plated
Designer: Jean Louis Sirois
Engraver: RCM Staff

DATE	DESCRIPTION	QUANTITY SOLD	ISSUE PRICE	FINISH	MS-65	MS-66
2013 (1988-)	$50 (5 oz), 25th Anniv. Silver Maple Leaf	2,297	499.95	Rev. Proof	600.	625.
2013 (1988)	$50 (5 oz) 25th Anniv. Silver Maple Leaf, Selectively gold plated	1,900	549.95	Matte Proof	625.	650.

Note: Coins illustrated smaller than actual size.

TWO HUNDRED FIFTY DOLLARS (kilogram), MAPLE LEAF FOREVER, 2011-2012.
The reverse design used on the one cent coin since 1937 is used on the 2011 silver kilogram denomination.

2011 Obverse

2011 Maple Leaf Forever
Des.: Debbie Adams
Engr.: Konrad Wachelko

2012 Obverse

2012 Maple Leaf Forever
Des.: Luc Normandin
Engr.: RCM Staff

Designers:
  Obv.: Susanna Blunt
  Rev.: See reverse illustrations
Composition: 99.99% Ag
Silver content: 1,000.0 g, 32.151 tr oz
Weight: 1,000.0 g (1 kilo)
Diameter: 101.8 mm

Engravers:
  Obv.: Susan Taylor
  Rev.: See reverse illustrations
Thickness: 13.2 mm
Edge: 2011: Plain 2012: Reeded
Die Axis: ↑↑
Finish: Proof

Case of Issue: 2011: Black display case, black flocked insert, encapsulated coin, COA
            2012: Canadian maple wood box, black flocked insert, encapsulated coin, COA, custom sleeve

DATE	DESCRIPTION	QUANTITY SOLD	ISSUE PRICE	FINISH	PR-67	PR-68
2011	Maple Leaf Forever	997	2,195.95	Proof	2,200.	2,250.
2012	Maple Leaf Forever	934	2,249.95	Proof	2,250.	2,300.

Note: 1. Identical designs are utilized on the $2,500 gold (maple leaf) coins for 2011 and 2012, see page 406.
    2. Coins illustrated smaller than actual size.

TWO HUNDRED FIFTY DOLLARS (kilogram), GEORGE III PEACE MEDAL, 2012.

The presentation of Indian Chief Medals to the First Nations Chiefs in Canada was begun by King Louis XIV of France. This practice was continued by the Kings and Queens of England as a symbol of maintaining peaceful relations with the Indian Nations. See page 406 for the gold version of this medal.

2012 Obverse

Des.: RCM Staff's representation of the King George III Peace Medal
Engravers: K. Wachelko, M. Bowen
S. Strath, S. Stewart

TWO HUNDRED FIFTY DOLLARS (kilogram), MAPLE LEAF FOREVER, 2013.

2013 Obverse

Des.: Emily Damstra
Engr.: RCM Staff

Designers:
Obv.: Susanna Blunt
Rev.: See reverse illustration
Composition: 99.99% Ag
Silver content: 1,000.0 g, 32.151 tr oz
Weight: 1,000.0 g (1 kilo)
Diameter: 102.1 mm

Engravers:
Obv.: Susan Taylor
Rev.: See reverse illustration
Thickness: 12.5 mm
Edge: Reeded
Die Axis: ↑↑
Finish: 2012 Proof, 2013 Proof, Selectively gold plated

Case of Issue: 2012 Maroon leatherette clam style case, black flocked insert, encapsulated coin, COA
2013 Maple wood box, black flocked insert, encapsulated coin, COA

DATE	DESCRIPTION	QUANTITY SOLD	ISSUE PRICE	FINISH	PR-67	PR-68
2012	George III Peace Medal	590	2,249.95	Proof	2,250.	2,300.
2013	Maple Leaf Forever, Selectively gold plated	596	2,249.95	Proof	2,250.	2,300.

Note: Coins illustrated smaller than actual size.

FIVE HUNDRED DOLLARS

GREAT CANADIAN ARTISTS SERIES

FIVE HUNDRED DOLLARS, THE SPIRIT OF HAIDA GWAII, 2012.
This is the first coin in the series: *The Spirit of Haida Gwaii* by Bill Reid.

Designers and Engravers:
   Obv.: S. Blunt, S. Taylor
   Rev.: Bill Reid, C. Saffioti
Composition: 99.99% Ag
Silver content:
   5.000.0 g, 160.75 tr oz
Weight: 5,000.0 g
Diameter: 180.0 mm
Thickness: N/A
Edge: Reeded
Die Axis: ↑↑
Finish: Proof
Case: Canadian walnut wood
   case, black velvet insert,
   encapsulated coin, COA

DATE	DESCRIPTION	QUANTITY SOLD	ISSUE PRICE	FINISH	PR-67	PR-68
2012	The Spirit of Haida Gwaii	95	9,999.95	Proof	10,000.	10,000.

Note: An identical design is utilized on the $100,00 gold coin for 2011, see page 407.

FIVE HUNDRED DOLLARS, TSATSISNUKOMI, BC, 2013.
The second coin in the series: *Tsatsisnukomi* by Emily Carr.

Designers and Engravers:
   Obv.: S. Blunt, S. Taylor
   Rev.: Emily Carr,
         C. Paquet, S. Witten
Composition: 99.99% Ag
Silver content:
   5,000.0 g, 32.160.7 tr oz
Weight: 5,000.0 g (5 kilos)
Diameter: 180.0 mm
Thickness: N/A
Edge: Reeded
Die Axis: ↑↑
Finish: Proof
Case: Canadian walnut wood
   case, acrylic holder,
   serialised certificate in
   booklet format

DATE	DESCRIPTION	QUANTITY SOLD	ISSUE PRICE	FINISH	PR-67	PR-68
2013	Tsatsisnukomi, BC, 1912	99	10,500.	Proof	10,500.	10,500.

Note: Coins illustrated smaller than actual size.

SILVER MAPLE LEAF SPECIAL ISSUES

SETS

ARCTIC FOX FINE SILVER COIN SET, 2004.
The first fractional fine silver coins feature wildlife designs that were originally created for platinum proof coins. The Arctic Fox first appeared on the Platinum proof coins of 1993.

Designers and Engravers:
Obv.: S. Blunt, S. Taylor
Rev.: Claude D'Angelo
Rev.: $5 – Susan Taylor
$4 – Sheldon Beveridge
$3 – Ago Aarand
$2 – Ago Aarand
Specifications: See page 421
Finish: Proof, Frosted relief against a mirror background
Case of Issue: Black case, multicoloured outer sleeve

DATE	DESCRIPTION	QUANTITY SOLD	ISSUE PRICE	FINISH	PR-67	PR-68
2004	Arctic Fox, 4-coin set	14,566	89.95	Proof	175.	—

CANADA LYNX FINE SILVER COIN SET, 2005.
The Canada Lynx first appeared on the platinum proof coins of 1995.

Designers and Engravers:
Obv.: S. Blunt, S. Taylor
Rev.: Michael Dumas
Rev.: $5 – Susan Taylor
$4 – Cosme Saffioti
$3 – Stan Witten
$2 – Ago Aarand
Specifications: See page 421
Finish: Proof, Frosted relief against a mirror background
Case of Issue: N/A

DATE	DESCRIPTION	QUANTITY SOLD	ISSUE PRICE	FINISH	PR-67	PR-68
2005	Canada Lynx, 4-coin set	7,942	89.95	Proof	200.	—

Note: Arctic Fox and Canadian Lynx coins are illustrated smaller than actual size.

SILVER MAPLE LEAFS WITH PRIVY MARKS

SINGLES

FIVE DOLLARS (1 ounce), SILVER MAPLE LEAFS WITH PRIVY MARKS, 1998-2014.
  Beginning in 1998 the Royal Canadian Mint started a special issue of the $5.00 - 1 oz silver Maple Leafs. Privy marks were added to the reverses, commemorating special events for each year. For Designers, Engravers see page 396 and for Specifications see page 421.

1998 Titanic
Dillon - Gage

1998 Tiger
MTB Bank

1998 R.C.M.P.
Post Office

1908-1998 Anniv.
R.C.M.

1999 Rabbit
MTB Bank

2000 Dragon
MTB Bank

2000 Expo Hanover
R.C.M.

2001 Snake
R.C.M.

2002 Horse
R.C.M.

2003 Sheep
R.C.M.

2004 Monkey
R.C.M.

2004 D-Day
R.C.M.

2004 Desjardins
R.C.M.

2005 Rooster
R.C.M.

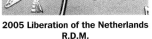

2005 Liberation of the Netherlands
R.D.M.

2005 VE Day
R.C.M.

2005 VJ Day
R.C.M.

2006
Year of Dog
R.C.M.

2007
Year of the Pig
R.C.M.

2007, 2008, 2009
Fabulous 12

2008
Year of the Rat
R.C.M.

2008
Brandenburg Gate

2009
Year of the Ox
R.C.M.

2009
Tower Bridge

2012
Tower of Pisa

2010-2013
Fabulous 15

2012
Titanic 100th Anniv.

2012
Year of the Dragon
R.C.M.

FIVE DOLLARS (1 ounce), SILVER MAPLE LEAFS WITH PRIVY MARKS, 1998-2014, PRICING TABLE.

2013
Year of the Snake
R.C.M.

2014
Year of the Horse
R.C.M.

DATE	DESCRIPTION	CASE OF ISSUE	QUANTITY SOLD	ISSUE PRICE	FINISH	66	67
1998	Titanic	Mylar pouch	26,000	N/A	Specimen	75.	85.
1998	Tiger	Mylar pouch	25,000	N/A	Specimen	65.	75.
1998	R.C.M.P.	Mylar pouch	25,000	N/A	Specimen	80.	90.
1998	90th Anniv.	Mylar pouch	13,025	N/A	Specimen	60.	70.
1999	Rabbit	Mylar pouch	25,000	N/A	Specimen	65.	75.
2000	Dragon	Mylar pouch	25,000	N/A	Specimen	75.	85.
2000	Expo	Mylar pouch	15,000	N/A	Specimen	100.	110.
2001	Snake	Mylar pouch	25,000	N/A	Specimen	65.	75.
2002	Horse	Mylar pouch	25,000	N/A	Specimen	60.	70.
2003	Sheep	Mylar pouch	25,000	N/A	Specimen	60.	70.
2004	Monkey	Mylar pouch	25,000	N/A	Specimen	60.	70.
2004	D-Day	Red display	11,698	39.95	Specimen	95.	105.
2004	Desjardins	Red display	15,000	39.95	Bullion	75.	85.
2005	Rooster	Mylar pouch	15,000	24.95	Specimen	60.	70.
2005	Liberation	Mylar pouch	3,500	E45.95	Specimen	150.	160.
2005	VE Day	Mylar pouch	6,998	49.95	Specimen	85.	95.
2005	VJ Day	Mylar pouch	6,998	49.95	Specimen	85.	95.
2006	Year of the Dog	Mylar pouch	10,000	24.95	Specimen	60.	70.
2007	Year of the Pig	Mylar pouch	8,000	29.95	Specimen	60.	70.
2007	Fabulous 12	Mylar pouch	5,000	39.95	Specimen	110.	120.
2008	Fabulous 12	Mylar pouch	5,000	N/A	Specimen	250.	275.
2008	Year of the Rat	Mylar pouch	8,000	24.95	Specimen	60.	65.
2008	Brandenburg Gate	Mylar pouch	50,000	39.95	Bullion	75.	80.
2009	Year of the Ox	Mylar pouch	8,000	23.95	Specimen	70.	80.
2009	Tower Bridge	Mylar pouch	75,000	34.95	Bullion	75.	80.
2009	Fabulous 12	Mylar pouch	5,000	N/A	Specimen	165.	175.
2010	Fabulous 15	Plastic case	5,000	44.95	Specimen	150.	175.
2011	Fabulous 15	Plastic case	5,000	44.95	Specimen	350.	375.
2012	Leaning Tower of Pisa	Mylar pouch	50,000	N/A	Bullion	50.	55.
2012	Fabulous 15	Mylar pouch	10,000	N/A	Bullion	135.	150.
2012	Titanic 100th Anniversary	Mylar pouch	25,000	N/A	Specimen	65.	70.
2012	Year of the Dragon	Mylar pouch	25,000	N/A	Specimen	50.	55.
2013	Fabulous 15	Mylar pouch	10,000	55.95	Bullion	100.	110.
2013	Year of the Snake	Display box	N/A	N/A	Specimen	45.	50.
2014	Year of the Horse	Mylar pouch	N/A	32.75	Specimen	35.	40.

SPECIAL PRIVY MARK SET

FIVE DOLLARS (1 ounce), SILVER MAPLE LEAFS, ZODIAC PRIVY MARK SET, 2004.
This twelve-coin set was struck by the Royal Canadian Mint, and issued by Universal Coins of Ottawa. Each coin carries one of the twelve signs of the zodiac as a privy mark.

| Aries | Taurus | Gemini | Cancer | Leo | Virgo |

| Libra | Scorpio | Sagittarius | Capricorn | Aquarius | Pisces |

Designers:
  Obv.: Susanna Blunt
  Rev.: RCM Staff
Composition: 99.99% Ag
Weight: 31.1035 g, 1 oz
Diameter: 38.0 mm
Finish: Specimen (reverse proof)
Case of Issue: Singly: Mylar pouch
              Set: Red 12-hole case

Engravers:
  Obv.: Susan Taylor
  Rev.: José Osio
Thickness: 3.2 mm
Edge: Reeded
Die Axis: ↑↑

DATE	DESCRIPTION	QUANTITY SOLD	ISSUE PRICE	FINISH	SP-66	SP-67
2004	Set of 12 coins	5,000	368.88	Specimen	700.	—
2004	Single coin	Included	39.95	Specimen	60.	70.

NOTES

1. A specimen finish on a bullion coin is also known as a reverse proof — a brilliant relief on a matte or satin background.
2. The method of packaging may vary from the normal mylar pouch to red or black flocked clam style cases, depending on the distributor.
3. The maple leaf coins which carry either an "F12" or "F15" privy mark commemorate the winning coin design at the Berlin Money Fair for the year which they are dated.
4. The Brandenburg Gate, The Tower Bridge, and the Leaning Tower of Pisa form part of a series.

SILVER MAPLE LEAF FRACTIONAL SETS

CHARACTERISTICS	$1 = 1/20 oz	$2 = 1/10 oz	$3 = ¼ oz	$4 = ½ oz	$5 = 1 oz
Fineness	99.99%	99.99%	99.99%	99.99%	99.99%
Weight (grams)	1.555	3.11	7.776	15.552	31.1035
Diameter (mm)	16.0	20.0	27.0	34.0	38.0
Thickness (mm)	1.1	1.3	1.8	2.1	3.15
Edge	Reeded	Reeded	Reeded	Reeded	Reeded
Die Axis	↑↑	↑↑	↑↑	↑↑	↑↑

15TH ANNIVERSARY OF THE SILVER MAPLE (HOLOGRAM SET), 2003.

These maple leaf coins were struck to commemorate the 15th anniversary of the silver maple leaf, 1988-2003. This five-coin set contains two new denominations for Canadian coinage, a $3 and a $4 coin. All coins are struck with a maple leaf hologram.

Designers and Engravers:
Obv.: Dora de Pédery-Hunt
Rev.: RCM Staff
Specifications: See page 421
Finish: Bullion, Hologram
Case of Issue: Red wooden case, black flocked insert, encapsulated coin, COA, silver outer box

DATE	DESCRIPTION	QUANTITY SOLD	ISSUE PRICE	FINISH	MS-65	MS-66	MS-67
2003	5 coin set (1, ½, ¼, 1/10, 1/20 oz)	28,947	149.95	Bullion	175.	—	—

ROYAL CANADIAN MINT LOGO SET, 2004.

Each coin in this set carries the Royal Canadian Mint logo on each coin.

Designers and Engravers:
Obv.: Susanna Blunt, Susan Taylor
Rev.: RCM Staff
Specifications: See page 421
Finish: Specimen (reverse proof)
Case of Issue: Dark blue leatherette clam style case, black insert, encapsulated coin, COA, silver sleeve

DATE	DESCRIPTION	QUANTITY SOLD	ISSUE PRICE	FINISH	SP-66	SP-67
2004	5 coin set (1, ½, ¼, 1/20, 1/20 oz)	13,859	99.95	Specimen	130.	—

SILVER MAPLE LEAF FRACTIONAL SETS

CHARACTERISTICS	$1 = 1/20 oz	$2 = 1/10 oz	$3 = ¼ oz	$4 =1/2 oz	$5 = 1 oz
Composition: Ag	99.99%	99.99%	99.99%	99.99%	99.99%
Weight (grams)	1.63	3.23	7.96	15.87	31.39
Diameter (mm)	16.0	20.0	27.0	34.0	38.0
Thickness (mm)	1.0	1.25	1.75	2.1	3.1
Edge:	Reeded	Reeded	Reeded	Reeded	Reeded
Die Axis	↑↑	↑↑	↑↑	↑↑	↑↑

SILVER MAPLE LEAF 25TH ANNIVERSARY FRACTIONAL SET, 2013.

This set was issued to commemorate the twenty-fifth anniversary of the Silver Maple Leaf bullion coin first issued in 1988.

Designers and Engravers:
  Obv.: Susanna Blunt, Matt Bowen
  Rev.: Arnold Nogy, Steven Stewart
Specifications: See above
Finish: Reverse Proof
Case of Issue: Maroon leatherette clam style case, black flocked insert, encapsulated coins, COA

DATE	DESCRIPTION	QUANTITY SOLD	ISSUE PRICE	FINISH	PR-67	PR-68
2013 (1988-)	5 coin set (1, ½, ¼, 1/10, 1/20 (oz)	9,993	199.95	Proof	250.	—

SILVER MAPLE LEAF FRACTIONAL SET, 2014.

Designers and Engravers:
  Obv.: Susanna Blunt, Matt Bowen
  Rev.: Arnold Nogy, RCM Staff
Specifications: See above
Finish: Reverse Proof, Selectively gold plated
Case of Issue: Maroon leatherette clam style case, black flocked insert, encapsulated coins, COA

DATE	DESCRIPTION	QUANTITY SOLD	ISSUE PRICE	FINISH	PR-67	PR-68
2014	5 coin set (1, ½, ¼, 1/10, 1/20 oz)	8,912	249.95	Proof	250.	—

COLOURED SILVER MAPLES

SINGLE COINS

FIVE DOLLARS (1 ounce), SILVER MAPLE LEAFS, COLOURED COIN SERIES, 2001-2007.

2001-2003 Obverse
Designer and Engraver:
Dora de Pédery-Hunt

2001 Autumn
Designer: Debbie Adams
Engraver: W. Woodruff

2002 Spring
Designer and Engraver:
William Woodruff

2003 Summer
Designer and Engraver:
Stan Witten

2004-2007 Obverse
Designer: Susanna Blunt
Engraver: Susan Taylor

2004 Winter
Designer and Engraver:
Stan Witten

2005 Bigleaf Maple
Designer and Engraver:
Stan Witten

2006 Silver Maple
Designer and Engraver:
Stan Witten

2007 Sugar Maple
Designer and Engraver:
Stan Witten

Designers and Engravers: See obverse and reverse illustrations
Specifications: See page 421
Finish: Bullion, colourised
Case of Issue: 2001-2004: Dark green clam case, black flocked insert, encapsulated coin, COA
                    2005-2007: Maroon plastic slide case, black plastic insert, encapsulated coin, COA

DATE	DESCRIPTION	QUANTITY SOLD	ISSUE PRICE	FINISH	MS-65	MS-66	MS-67
2001	Autumn	49,709	34.95	Bullion	65.	70.	75.
2002	Spring	29,509	34.95	Bullion	65.	75.	80.
2003	Summer	29,416	34.95	Bullion	65.	70.	75.
2004	Winter	26,763	34.95	Bullion	75.	90.	100.
2005	Bigleaf Maple	21,233	39.95	Bullion	90.	100.	110.
2006	Silver Maple	14,157	45.95	Bullion	115.	125.	150.
2007	Sugar Maple	11,495	49.95	Bullion	160.	170.	180.

Note: Coins illustrated smaller than actual size.

SILVER MAPLE LEAFS WITH HOLOGRAMS

SINGLE COINS

FIVE DOLLARS (1 ounce), "MAPLE OF GOOD FORTUNE" HOLOGRAM, 2001, 2003 and 2005.

First issued in 2001, the $5 Maple Leaf coin carries a privy mark of Chinese characters, meaning Maple of Good Fortune, or Hope, as part of the hologram.

2001 Obverse

2001 Reverse

Privy Mark 2001

2003 Obverse

2003 Reverse

Privy Mark 2003

2005 Obverse

2005 Reverse

Privy Mark 2005

Designers:
2001, 2003:   Obv.: Dora de Pédery-Hunt
                  Rev.: RCM Staff
2005:   Obv.: Susanna Blunt
                  Rev.: RCM Staff
Specifications: See page 421
Finish: Specimen (reverse proof), hologram
Case of Issue: Red clam oval case, taupe flocked insert, encapsulated coin, COA

Engravers:
  Obv.: Dora de Pédery-Hunt
  Rev.: RCM Staff
  Obv.: Susan Taylor
  Rev.: RCM Staff
Case of Issue: Mylar pouch

DATE	DESCRIPTION	QUANTITY SOLD	ISSUE PRICE	FINISH	SP-66	SP-67
2001	Good Fortune	29,817	59.99	Specimen	80.	85.
2003	Good Fortune	29,731	39.99	Specimen	70.	75.
2005	Good Fortune	19,888	39.95	Specimen	60.	65.

SILVER MAPLE LEAFS WITH HOLOGRAMS

SINGLE COINS

FIVE DOLLARS (1 ounce), 15TH ANNIVERSARY OF THE ONE DOLLAR LOON, 2002.

These maple leaf coins were struck to commemorate the 15th anniversary of the one dollar loon coin issued in 1987. The reverse design on this coin depicts a male loon flapping its wings in the "Loon Dance" protecting its nest from intruders.

Designers and Engravers:
Obv.: Dora de Pédery-Hunt
Rev.: RCM Staff
Composition: 99.99% Ag
Weight: 31.1035 g, 1 oz
Diameter: 38.0 mm   **Edge:** Reeded
Thickness: 3.2 mm   **Die Axis:** ↑↑
Finish: Specimen (reverse proof), Hologram
Case of Issue: Black leatherette clam case, hunter green interior, encapsulated coin, COA

DATE	DESCRIPTION	QUANTITY SOLD	ISSUE PRICE	FINISH	SP-66	SP-67
2002	$5 (1 oz) 15th Anniv. of One Dollar Loon	29,970	39.95	Specimen	75.	85.

SILVER MAPLE LEAF SETS

$5 SILVER MAPLE LEAF WITH PROOF SETS, 2001.

Three varieties of silver maples (colourised, hologram and regular) were combined with seven proof coins, 1¢ to $2, of the 2001 Proof Set to form the following Premium Proof sets:

DATE	DESCRIPTION	QUANTITY SOLD	ISSUE PRICE	ISSUER	FINISH	MARKET VALUE
2001	**Proof Set 2001.** Seven proof coins. Reverse proof hologram, silver maple leaf	3,000	150.00	RCM	PR-67, SP-66	175.
2001	**Proof Set 2001.** Seven proof coins. Reverse proof privy snake, silver maple leaf	Included	100.00	RCM	PR-67, MS-65	150.
2001	**Proof Set 2001.** Seven proof coins and a colourised 2001 silver maple leaf	Included	75.00	RCM	PR-67, MS-65	100.

SILVER MAPLE LEAF DERIVATIVES

DATE	DESCRIPTION	QUANTITY SOLD	ISSUE PRICE	ISSUER	FINISH	MARKET VALUE
1998	**125th Anniv. of R.C.M.P.**, Silver maple with R.C.M.P. privy mark. Souvenir sheet. Dark blue presentation case. COA. Booklet	25,000	47.95	RCM, CP	SP-66	75.
2004	**Sambro Island.** Framed image and twenty dollar coin	N/A	249.00	RCM	PR-67	100.

Application for **RCNA** Membership / Demande d'adhésion à l' **ARNC**

Application for membership in **The Royal Canadian Numismatic Association** may be made by any reputable party upon payment of the required dues.

Les demandes d'adhésion à **l'Association royale de numismatique du Canada** peuvent être faites par une partie de bonne réputation sur paiement des frais exigés.

❏ Mr. / M.　　　　　❏ Mrs. / Mme　　　　　❏ Ms. / Mlle

❏ Renewal / Renouvèlement　　❏ Reinstatement / Réintégration *previous #_____*

_____

Full Name / Nom　　　*for family membership include name of spouse / pour une adhésion familiale, inclure le nom du conjoint*

_____

Mailing Address / Adresse postale complète

_____

City / Ville　　　　　　　Province / State / État　Country / Pays　Postal Code/Zip

_____

Phone / N^o de téléphone　　　Email / Courriel

W.K. Cross & Randy Ash

_____

Signature of Applicant / Signature du demandeur　　Sponsored By / Commandité par

Junior applicants (under age 18), state birth date / pour une adhésion junior (moins de 18 ans), inclure la date de naissance: _____

My numismatic speciality / spécialité numismatique *(optional/optionnel)*: _____

❏ *I would like to be contacted by a mentor who also has my speciality.*
J'aimerais être mis en contact avec un mentor qui partage mes intérêt numismatiques.

Membership Types: *Check only one* **Types d'adhésion**: *cochez une seule option*	Standard		Digital*	
	1 year	**2 year**	**1 year**	**2 year**
Regular: Canada and USA residents, age 18+ **Régulier:** adresses **Canadiennes et aux États-unis** (18 ans et plus)	❏ $42.00	❏ $82.00	❏ $32.00	❏ $62.00
Regular: Foreign (non-USA) **Régulier:** étranger (autre que les États-unis)	❏ $78.00	❏ $154.00	❏ $32.00	❏ $62.00
Junior: Applicants under age 18 *must be sponsored by a parent or guardian* *Les membres de moins de 18 ans doivent être commandités par un parent ou un gardien*	❏ $25.50	❏ $49.00	❏ $18.50	❏ $35.00
Family: Canada and USA residents. Member, spouse & children under age 18, (one printed and mailed *CN Journal* only) **Familial**: membre, époux (se) et enfants de moins de 18 ans. Un seul Journal	❏ $44.00	❏ $92.00	❏ $32.00	❏ $62.00
Corporate / Entreprises: Clubs, Societies / Sociétés, Libraries / Librairies & non-profit organizations / et autres organisations sans but lucratif	❏ $42.00	❏ $82.00	N.A.	N.A.
Life Membership / Adhésion à Vie:**	❏ $1,195.00		❏ $895.00	
Life Membership Senior: (65+) **Adhésion à Vie Aîné:**** (65 ans et plus)	❏ $895.00		❏ $695.00	
Life Membership Foreign: **Adhésion à Vie Etranger:**	❏ $2,195.00		❏ $895.00	

Dues shown below are in Canadian$ to Canadian addresses and US$ to all other addresses and are exempt from Canadian sales taxes.

* (A Digital Membership includes all of the benefits of membership except a printed copy of *The CN Journal*.)

** (After one year of regular membership. Details of payment plan available on request.) Mail completed application with dues to:

Les cotisations sont indiquées en dollars canadiens à des adresses canadiennes, ou en dollars américains à toutes les autres adresses. Les cotisations sont exonérées de taxes sur les ventes domestiques.

* (Adhésions numériques comprennent tous les avantages de l'adhésion, sauf une copie imprimée de *Le Journal canadien de numismatique*.)

** (Après un an comme membre régulier. Détails du plan de paiement disponibles sur demande.) Envoyez la demande d'adhésion dûment complétée et le paiement à :

The Royal Canadian Numismatic Association
l'Association royale de numismatique du Canada
5694 Highway #7 East, Suite 432, Markham ON Canada L3P 1B4
Phone / Tel: 647–401–4014 Fax / Télécopie: 905–472–9645 Email / Courriel: *info@rcna.ca*
*Apply online at: **www.rcna.ca/paydues.php***